HUMOR IN
AMERICAN LITERATURE

GARLAND REFERENCE LIBRARY
OF THE HUMANITIES
(VOL. 1049)

HUMOR IN AMERICAN LITERATURE
A Selected
Annotated Bibliography

Don L.F. Nilsen

GARLAND PUBLISHING, INC. • NEW YORK & LONDON
1992

Library of Congress Cataloging-in-Publication Data

Nilsen, Don Lee Fred.
    Humor in American literature : a selected annotated bibliography /
Don L.F. Nilsen.
        p. cm. — (Garland reference library of the humanities ;
vol. 1049)
    Includes index.
    ISBN 0-8240-8395-4 (alk. paper)
    1. American wit and humor—History and criticism—Bibliography.
2. American literature—History and criticism—Bibliography.
I. Title. II. Series.
Z1231.W8N55 1992
[PS430]
016.817009—dc20   91-42821
                                                                          CIP

Printed on acid-free, 250-year-life paper
Manufactured in the United States of America

Dedicated to the people the author is most dedicated to:

Alleen, Kelvin and Lorrain, Sean and Kath, Jeff and Nicolette, Taryn, Britton, Kami Lynne, and two tadpoles, David Sean and James Loren

Contents

Preface

The reader may notice that some major authors are slighted and some minor authors are given considerable space in this book. This is not done arbitrarily. Inclusion was not determined by the significance of the author or the significance of the author's writing, but rather by the significance of the author's writing to the field of humor studies. Therefore the only items included here were those edited books, critical articles, or reviews that were written specifically about the author's humor. Another principle of selection was recentness. Most literary criticism concerning humorous works has been written in the past two decades; furthermore, much pre-1970 criticism was simply not available to the author.

Although longer annotations could have been written about many of the critical pieces, space limitations required a maximum of 250 words per annotation. This allows the annotation only to suggest the major contributions of the critical pieces and to provide enough information for the reader to find and read the original pieces in their entirety.

Introduction

"Humor can be dissected, as a frog can, but the thing dies in the process and the innards are discouraging to any but the pure scientific mind," wrote E. B. and Katharine White in their 1941 preface to A Subtreasury of American Humor. They went on to say that humor "won't stand much blowing up, and it won't stand much poking. It has a certain fragility, and evasiveness, which one had best respect. Essentially it is a complete mystery." In one of the Essays of E. B. White published in 1977, White reiterated this idea by writing, "To interpret humor is as futile as explaining a spider's web in terms of geometry." When he made these statements, White was either preaching to himself or perhaps expressing a sense of frustration because both statements appeared in essays where he was doing the very thing that he said couldn't be done. He was examining the nature of humor and making philosophical observations about it.

The present book is a compilation and condensation of the work of hundreds of people who, like E. B. White, respect humor and out of that respect are drawn into examining, interpreting, explaining, poking, blowing up, and dissecting the humorous writings of American authors. But I hope that contrary to what E. B. White said, this book is living proof that humor doesn't have to die in the process of being examined.

One of the values of collecting such a quantity of writing about American humor is to study how various humorous works and movements influenced later writing. Hence, the basic organization of this collection is chronological, with the first four sections focusing on the works of individual authors arranged by date of birth. However, more valuable writing about humor is not limited to the work of a single author or to writings that appeared in one particular time period, and so the following thematic sections were included: "Black/Gallows Humor," "Children's and Adolescent Literature," "Ethnic Literature," "Humor through American Eyes," "Humor through Foreign Eyes," "Geography," "History," "Oral Literature," "Parody," "Poetry," "Politics," "Satire," "Sex Roles," and "Theory." The regional humor in the "Geography" section was subdivided into humor from Midwestern, New England, Southern, Southwestern and Western literature. "Humor in History" was subdivided into writings about "Pre-Colonial," "16th Century," "17th Century," "18th Century," "19th Century," and "20th Century" humor.

This collection focuses on humorous writings so that it excludes criticism of non-humorous works by authors generally regarded as humorous, while including analyses of humor in the writings of authors not generally considered to be funny. For example, in an article entitled "Anything Goes: Comic Aspects in 'The Cask of Amontillado'" John Clendenning showed how Poe could harmonize the arabesque with the grotesque to produce an ironic blend of two countervailing features. Poe was fascinated by the

3

interrelationships between the crude and the fantastic, the comic and the serious. Francis Gillen pointed out similar contrasts in Joseph Heller's Catch 22, except that here readers expect to laugh and they do, only to be horrified a page or two later when they discover what they are laughing at.

In doing the research for this volume, I enjoyed finding support for notions I had already formulated and collecting evidence to refine and revise these formulations. But even more I enjoyed making unexpected discoveries. For example, before writing this volume, I had thought that Black Humor was a contemporary phenomenon beginning basically with Richard Friedman's anthology on the subject published in 1965. I was therefore surprised to find how many features of the Black-Humor genre were to be found in Mark Twain's The Mysterious Stranger. I was also surprised at the similarities of the causes between the absurd and Black Humor of The Mysterious Stranger and contemporary absurd and Black Humor. Another interesting connection was seeing the influence of sixteenth-century Spanish author Miguel de Cervantes Saavedra on Tabitha Tenney's Female Quixotism and Washington Irving's The Legend of Sleepy Hollow, both published in the mid-1800s.

From preparing this anthology of criticism, I learned that the basic difference between drama and tragedy, on the one hand, and humor or comedy, on the other, is displacement. We view tragedy from the standpoint of a participant, while we view comedy from the standpoint of a spectator. A piece cannot be tragic if the reader is a spectator, nor can it be comic if the reader is a participant, which relates to the relationship between pleasure and pain. In an interview with Edythe McGovern, Neil Simon said that he writes about situations, and that he's funniest when the situations are at their worst. He indicated that he used to look for funny situations, but that now he looks for sad situations and figures out how to tell them humorously.

David Russell suggests that the comic spirit is the denial of limitations. Whereas tragedy involves a confrontation with the world as it is, comedy seeks a way to make the world better than it is. This comic vision gives children their relentless spirit and their optimism. Russell illustrated his point by telling an anecdote about his daughter. She drew a picture of a man with a top hat, a beard, and a long black coat and then later described the picture to her father. She had started out to draw a picture of a Christmas Tree, but it wasn't turning out right, so she drew a picture of President Lincoln instead. This story explains both children's and adults' senses of humor for the basic difference between tragedy and comedy is that tragedy is represented by chaos while comedy is represented by order--and for many adults, just as for many children, it is order at any cost.

Ronald Wallace points out the difference between romance and comedy. A romance should be read in terms of established cultural values expressed as antithetical propositions--the self versus the society, the human versus the mechanical, the emotional versus the reasonable, the primitive versus the civilized, freedom versus control, in sum, heart versus mind. In Wallace's view, a comedy employs reversal of expectations and inversion of values. Wallace feels that Ken Kesey's One Flew Over the Cuckoo's Nest was intended to be read as a comedy, not a romance. People who have criticized the novel as sexist because of the unflattering portrayal of Big Nurse should understand that what makes Big Nurse so despicable is that she exhibits "male" features in her manipulating, controlling, and domineering manner.

Of special interest in a study of American humor is how soon the first settlers began enjoying published humor. Thomas Morton, was forty years old when he arrived in Plymouth, Massachusetts, from England in 1624, only four years after the first settlers. He established a style of living that many considered scandalous and when he was exiled back to England he wrote The New English Canaan-- part diary and part satire. It was published in 1637 and read on both sides of the Atlantic. Perhaps the most surprising fact from the Colonial period is that three of the first seven humorous authors were women: Anne Dudley Bradstreet (c1612-1672), Sarah Kemble Knight (1666-1727), and Mercy Otis Warren (1728-1814). Knight is thought to have been one of Benjamin Franklin's teachers.

Knowing about these early women humorists made me more ready to accept the writings of contemporary critics who argue against the stereotype that women lack a sense of humor. They point out that men are the ones who have promoted such a belief, not because women don't enjoy humor, but because their humor is different from men's humor. The stereotype is strongest for feminists, yet Flo Kennedy and Gloria Steinem have both made the point that a revolution without humor is as senseless as is a revolution without music.

Learning American history through its humor is fun, especially in the eighteenth century with such notable authors as Benjamin Franklin (1706-1790), Mercy Otis Warren (1728-1814), and Francis Hopkinson (1737-1791). The writing of American humor gained momentum so that by the nineteenth century it was a viable topic for scholarly analyses and the kinds of observations made by Del Kehl. For example, he shows how the frontier Southwestern region of the United States has made an indelible impression on the American psyche and on the genre of humorous literature on two different occasions. He shows how the dominance of the Old Southwest (Georgia, the Carolinas, Alabama, Tennessee, Arkansas, and Louisiana) lasted only about twenty-six years (1835-1861), yet the humor of the Old Southwest is the most consistent and sustained humor genre in America. Likewise, the cattle-drive drama and the cowboy-Indian confrontations of the New Southwest (Texas, New Mexico, Arizona, Nevada and Southern California) lasted only a relatively brief period but nevertheless had an exaggerated influence on the American imagination in the Western novels, pulp magazines, movies, and television programs it stimulated. Furthermore, Kehl notes that over half of the twenty subjects and themes that Henig Cohen and William Dillingham listed as characteristics of Old Southwestern humor can also be found in New Southwestern humor but with some variation. "Games, horse races, and other contests" become "the rodeo"; "the hunt" becomes the "cattle drive"; and "the riverboat" becomes "the horse" or "the pickup truck."

In the 1800s, the work of Mark Twain stands head and shoulders above that of any other humorist. He set the stage for the sophisticated humor of the twentieth century written by such authors as H. L. Mencken (1880-1956), Max Eastman (1883-1969), Robert Benchley (1889-1945), Dorothy Parker (1893-1967), James Thurber (1894-1961), and E. B. White (1899-1985).

This whole volume is a testament to the way that literary humor reflects the culture in which it develops. The chronological sections trace American humor from Revolutionary War mentality to frontier mentality to Civil War mentality to urbanization mentality to New Yorker mentality. Throughout these stages, we see that although the literary mind may be grounded in reality, it is also capable of wild speculation and fantasy. Over the centuries, American humor has become more subtle and sophisticated, and the characters have changed from Alazon (characters who claim to be more than they are) to Eiron (characters who claim to be less than they are). Until the most recent period, American comic heroes tended to be bigger than life, but today they are more likely to be smaller than life, overwhelmed by technology, social and business constraints, and the threat of annihilation.

The result of the atomic bomb was a general feeling of malaise and despair that resulted in absurdist and Black Humor--a humor of chaos. To this, Thomas Pynchon added Werner Heisenberg's "uncertainty principle" and the second law of thermodynamics which stated that machines and individuals and social systems and galaxies are all gradually losing their energy. In reviewing Pynchon's work Charles Harris points out that there are accidents and natural disasters and wars, crises and riots. There are dehumanizing processes where a mechanized society transforms man into an animal or into a machine as illustrated by the title of Pynchon's prototypical short story, "Entropy."

Fortunately not all of today's humor is that of despair. If there's one lesson to be learned from this collection of criticism, it is the variety of humor that exists at any one time. An inherent requisite for humor is surprise, and if all humor writers, and all critics of humor, fit into predictable molds there would be no surprise and no fun.

In conclusion, I wish to thank Arizona State University for its support of this work through a sabbatical leave and also to thank my wife, Alleen Pace Nilsen, who each evening enthusiastically read aloud what I had written during the day.

Don L. F. Nilsen
Tempe, Arizona

Chapter 1
Seventeenth Century

(1575-1647) TO (1691-1752)

Thomas Morton (c1575-1647)

1. Butler, Michael D. "Thomas Morton" Encyclopedia of American
   Humorists. Ed. Steven H. Gale. New York: Garland, 1988, 329-
   333.

   Demonstrates the irony of the fact that Thomas Morton saw in
the pilgrims and puritans exactly what they saw in him--chaos.
According to Butler, Morton saw the Pilgrims and Puritans not as
monsters or demons but as buffoons, dullards, and humorously obvious
hypocrites as can be seen in such names as "Captain Shrimp,"
"Ananais Increase," "Captain Littleworth," and "Master Bubble."
Morton's most important work was entitled The New English Canaan,
and in it Morton showed how much he liked New England by comparing
it to Canaan in Israel, with its mild temperatures, wonderful
natives, and laughing streams. Morton had a playful style, and his
book is filled with learned words, ornate phrases, allusions, and
witty, often cryptic puns.

2. Holliday, Carl. "Thomas Morton." The Wit and Humor of Colonial
   Days. Williamstown, Massachusetts, 1975, 29-33.

   Portrays Morton as a Whitmanesque Puritan. He erected an
eighty-foot May-pole at Merry Mount, brewed some excellent beer, and
celebrated with his friends in the shouting of such Bacchanalian
verses as "Drink and be merry, merry, merry, boys,/ Let all your
delight be in Hymen's joys, / Io to Hymen now the day is come, /
About the Merry May-pole take a roame.". Morton also wrote a
humorous book about Merry Mount entitled New English Canaan in which
he makes a number of quaint observations.

Nathaniel Ward (c1578-1652)

3. Holliday, Carl. "Nathaniel Ward." The Wit and Humor of Colonial
   Days. Williamstown, Massachusetts: Corner House, 1975, 17-28.

   Places Ward as the first important American satirist and The
Simple Cobler of Aggawam as the first American book of humor. The
Cobler is a very sarcastic protagonist who explains how out of joint
the world is both theologically and socially. The Cobler
foreshadows Franklin's Poor Richard in its bluntness and common
sense tone. The real significance of the book, however, is to
illustrate that the stern Pilgrim fathers did after all have a sense

7

of humor--even if it was a bit grim and didactic. The early Puritan did smile and indeed smiled often, though it is true that most of what he smiled at was human faults and weaknesses. The Cobler looked upon himself as the "divinely appointed scolder plenipontentiary to the world at large."

4. O'Bryan, Daniel. "Nathaniel Ward." Encyclopedia of American Humorists. Ed. Steven H. Gale. New York: Garland, 1988, 456-57.

Suggests that Nathaniel Ward's The Simple Cobler of Aggawam is the first sustained prose satire to appear in New England. This book employs elaborate tropes, classical allusions, and theological subtleties to comment satirically on various religious sects, English politics, and women's fashions. "Puns, extended analogies, parallelism, classical and Biblical quotation mixed heterogeneously, doggerel verse, and recondite allusion blend into each other and almost achieve a life of their own apart from the original issues."

5. Zall, Paul M. ed. "Introduction." The Simple Cobler of Aggawam in America, Auth. Nathaniel Ward. Lincoln: Univ of Nebraska Press, 1969, xviii + 81 pp.

Explains that Ward's The Simple Cobler of Aggawam is generally recognized as "the first American satire" or "the first humorous book written in America." However, there is no edition of this book which explains the obscure terms and allusions that were clear only in the book's historical setting. It is therefore, "one of those select classics that everyone has heard about but very few have read." Ward assumes the role of an eccentric frontier cobler by the name of Theodore de la Guard. This is "a transparent pseudonym, since "Theodore" is the Greek equivalent of "Nathaniel," and "de la Guard" the French of "Ward." In contrast to the formal books and pamphlets of the day, this book is narrated in the vernacular and both the images and the language are quite exaggerated. Zall feels that the book should be read aloud for full effect because of the numerous analogies, puns, parallelisms, and antithetical statements. Epigrams are juxtaposed with biblical citations, and classical quotations allude to philosophy, plays, and poems, but pornography as well. There are so many theatrical asides that they become digressions; indeed the entire book could be viewed as a single long digression, with only the Cobler's personality holding it together.

Anne Dudley Bradstreet (c1612-1672)

6. McElrath, Joseph R., Jr., and Allan P. Robb, eds. "Introduction." The Complete Works of Anne Bradstreet. Boston: Twain, 1981, xlii + 536 pp.

Credits Anne Bradstreet as one of America's best early poets. Women during Bradstreet's time were not generally well educated; nevertheless, Bradstreet became well known by displaying traits that were then thought to be exclusively masculine--political savvy, an inclination to be critical, a familiarity with Renaissance art, and an excellent feel for poetry--an avocation then considered to be exclusively in the domain of men. Bradstreet is important in the feminist movement because she scoffs at the slow progress that was being made in the acceptance of women's wit.   McElrath and Robb point out that even though Bradstreet is very strong in her criticism of puritan values in general and masculine values in particular, there is no evidence that she was "censured, disciplined, or in any way ostracized for her art." On the basis of such evidence as this, they suggest that colonial New England may have been "less repressive in its attitude toward women than we imagine."

7. Walker, Nancy, and Zita Dresner. "Anne Bradstreet." Redressing the Balance: American Women's Literary Humor from Colonial Times to the 1980s. Jackson: University Press of Mississippi, 1988, 3-4.

Considers Bradstreet to have been not only America's first published poet but also America's first witty woman.   Bradstreet published a collection of poems entitled The Tenth Muse in 1650. She entitled the preface to this book "The Author to Her Book," and in this preface she denounces the fact that the book was published in London without her knowledge or permission before the author felt the book was ready for publication.   She refers to the book as a poorly-dressed child, snatched from her before she had been able to clothe it properly.   In this metaphor, Bradstreet was gently poking fun at those who would misunderstand or disapprove of her writing, and at the same time she was gently chiding her publishers for their presumptuousness.   Bradstreet's poetry expresses her love for her husband, her grief at the death of one of her grandchildren, and the incongruity of being a poet and a thinking woman during Colonial times in America.

George Alsop (1638-1666)

8. Holliday, Carl. "George Alsop." The Wit and Humor of Colonial Days. Williamstown, Massachusetts: Corner House, 1975, 33-38.

Considers Alsop to have been a witty man with a snappy tongue and an originality of view.   Alsop's wit exhibits a conscious effort.   He is glib in his wish to glitter--his wish to present his thoughts through eye-catching phrases.   Holliday feels that only one writer of seventeenth-century America surpassed Alsop in comic ability, Nathaniel Ward.   Like Ward, Alsop's writing was mirthful, grotesque, and had a kind of slashing energy.   There is a bit of sarcasm and piquancy in the vigorous figures of speech of his Maryland humor.   In a tradition already long established by humorous authors, Alsop liked to construct elaborate and dignified prose to talk about very simple and mundane matters.

Cotton Mather (1663-1728)

9. Safer, Elaine B. "Twentieth-Century Comic Epic Novels and Cotton Mather's Magnalia." The Contemporary American Comic Epic: The Novels of Barth, Pynchon, Gaddis, and Kesey. Detroit, MI: Wayne State University Press, 1988, 25-38.

Gives three reasons why a study of Mather's Magnalia Christi Americana (1702) is important in understanding the American epic

novels of John Barth, Thomas Pynchon, William Gaddis, and Ken Kesey.
Mather's Magnalia contains themes that are mocked in the
contemporary American comic epic novel. It considers America to be
a new Garden of Eden, a new Canaan, the high point of advancement in
culture and the arts which are again mocked in the later novels.
And it employs genres that are parodied in twentieth-century novels
such as the chronicle, the recounting of saints' lives, and the
jeremiad sermon that asks men to repent and preach God's
forgiveness. Mather's Magnalia is the prototype of the novel that
twentieth century American authors parody in their farcical
allusions. Barth burlesques the John Smith-Pocahontas legend in The
Sot-Weed Factor. Pynchon makes humorous allusions to his ancestor,
William Pynchon. In The Recognitions, Gaddis' protagonist, Wyatt
Gwyon longs to rediscover his New England ancestors by making a
pilgrimage back to England. In Sometimes a Great Notion, Kesey
observes that early members of the Stamper family had travelled
westward across frontier America, not as pioneers doing the Lord's
work in a heathen land but rather as a clan of aimless wanderers.
Contemporary American comic epic novels cannot be properly
understood without understanding the novels and the belief systems
they are satirizing and the disparity that exists between the
Colonial American dream and 20th-century ironic treatment of this
dream.

Sarah Kemble Knight (1666-1727)

10. Stewart, E. Kate. "Sarah Kemble Knight." Encyclopedia of
    American Humorists. Ed. Steven H. Gale. New York: Garland,
    1988, 258-59.

    Says that Sarah Kemble Knight, who was born in Boston
Massachusetts in 1666, Sarah Kemble Knight was the teacher of
Benjamin Franklin. Her most important work, The Journal of Mme.
Knight, is an account of her unchaperoned 200-mile journey from
Boston to New Haven, Connecticut, and on to New York, and then back
to Boston. As a trained paralegal, she made the journey in order to
settle the estate of a family member. From beginning to end, the
journal entertains readers with Madame Knight's wry spontaneous wit.
The journal is a revealing history for present-day readers because
it provides a fresh wit in which Knight looks with amusement upon
the rough roads, the river crossings, the manners and speech of the
inland rustics, and the intolerable inns in her travels between
Boston and New York. Although the journal does not radically depart
from the religious orthodoxy of the day, Knight's unique brand of
earthy humor and practical wisdom, blended with sophisticated wit,
captivated her nineteenth-century audience and continues to amuse
contemporary readers.

11. Walker, Nancy, and Zita Dresner. "Sarah Kemble Knight."
    Redressing the Balance: American Women's Literary Humor from
    Colonial Times to the 1980s. Jackson: University Press of
    Mississippi, 1988, 5-10.

    Consider Knight to have been a typical woman writer of
Colonial times in that she was more concerned with her immediate
surroundings than with political or religious issues of the time.
Her journal focuses on the lack of manners, the dialects, the dress,

and the modes of life she observed during a journey from Boston to New York and back. Knight noted, for example, that the purple color of a dish of pork and cabbage suggested to her that it might have been boiled in a cook's dye kettle. Knight found amusement in the behavior of her unsophisticated frontier neighbors, friends, and acquaintances. She wrote with wit and candor.

William Byrd (1674-1744)

12. Holliday, Carl. "William Byrd." The Wit and Humor of Colonial Days. Williamstown, Massachusetts: Corner House, 1975, 45-52.

Considers Byrd to have been a witty Virginian and "the most brilliant colonist before the days of Jefferson." Byrd collected the largest and most impressive library in the American colonies and wrote "some of the most sprightly and entertaining prose in early American literature." Just as Artemus Ward had the Mormons as his favorite topic, Byrd loved to tease the North Carolinians. One of his most sarcastic pieces concerns the surveying of the boundary line between Virginia and North Carolina. This highly sarcastic work is entitled History of the Dividing Line. Byrd's Journey to the Land of Eden is also about North Carolina, and is also highly sarcastic. The Westover Manuscripts, and The Byrd Manuscripts are filled with the individuality, frothy wit, and fun that can come only from actual experiences. These light sketches were written mainly for self-enjoyment, but the sophistication of the style is unequalled by any other colonial writers except for Franklin and Jefferson. Byrd had an ability to express things in a laughably novel way. He was one of our earliest American humorists, but his sparkle, quick wit, and mature style make him comparable with our latest American humorists.

William Douglass (1691-1752)

13. Holliday, Carl. "William Douglass." The Wit and Humor of Colonial Days. Williamstown, Massachusetts: Corner House, 1975, 65-66.

Feels that Douglass had a merciless wit and caustic sarcasm that he used on any man or movement which he felt to be hypocritical. Douglass delighted in the resulting quarrels with governors, citizens, and quacks of all kinds.

(1706-1788) TO (1748-1816)

Mather Byles (1706-1788)

14. Holliday, Carl. "Mather Byles." <u>The Wit and Humor of
     Colonial Days</u>. Williamstown, Massachusetts, 1975, 53-58.

Considers Mather Byles and Joseph Green to have been two
eighteenth century witty rhymesters who caused more merriment in the
sober town of Boston than all other townspeople combined. They were
both brilliant speakers and profound scholars, and on Sunday, they
were stern-faced Christians as well. Byles was educated at Harvard
and became the pastor of the Hollis Street Church. For forty-three
years he preached sermons designed to thrill the stolid souls and
cracked jokes calculated to upset the long-faced Puritans in his
congregation. Byles had a witty observation for every situation.

Benjamin Franklin (1706-1790)

15. Bell, Robert H. "Benjamin Franklin's 'Perfect Character.'"
     <u>Eighteenth-Century Life</u> 5.2 (Winter 1978): 13-25.

Describes Franklin's <u>Autobiography</u> as a great moral fable, the
secular equivalent of Bunyan's <u>Pilgrim's Progress</u>. The tone is
light and often humorous, as when Franklin describes his arrival in
Philadelphia. He had had a hard trip. He was tired, dirty, dingy,
and hungry, and he had only a Dutch dollar and a shilling in his
pocket. So he bought some rolls and wandered around the city
becoming familiar with the new sights, smells, and sounds. Walking
up Market Street, he came to Fourth Street and read a sign above Mr.
Read's store. The girl in the doorway thought that Franklin
presented "a most awkward ridiculous appearance." Franklin later
married this girl. Throughout his <u>Autobiography</u>, Franklin smiles
with an ironic wink at his youthful folly, realizing that he was to
become a pillar of Philadelphia (and American) society. In 1728
Franklin authored his epitaph (which never appeared on his
tombstone), comparing his life to a tattered and torn book but
suggesting that the book would appear once more "In a new and More
perfect Edition/ Corrected and amended/ by the Author." Franklin's
<u>Autobiography</u>, like the epitaph, is a fitting monument to the
importance of his own life but is balanced by his candor and comedy.
He was secure enough that he didn't have to resort to self-
aggrandizement.

16. Blair, Walter, and Hamlin Hill, eds. "Franklin: Muddied Giant." America's Humor: From Poor Richard to Doonesbury. New York: Oxford University Press, 1978, 53-62.

Considers Franklin to have been full of ironies. Although he was unschooled he learned to get along rather well in five languages and mastered natural science, political science, and social science as well as diplomacy and economics. He started out poor but became rich as a printer, shopkeeper, publisher, and businessman and was able to "retire" at the young age of forty-two to devote the rest of his life to the study of science and philosophy and his activities in public service. He founded not only the American Philosophical Society but a university as well, and he invented the Philadelphia municipal government system. Throughout his life he was witty at will, and his humor was pleasant, delicate, and delightful. His satire was caustic, but good natured, and he had a talent for irony, allegory, and fable. In his writing, Franklin was one of the earliest developers of the homespun, unlettered but shrewd man of common sense, and he also pioneered in the development of the tall tale. Franklin was as different from his writings as he was from his earlier life. The real-life Franklin was rich; his protagonist, Richard, was poor. The real Franklin lived in the city; Richard lived in the country. The real Franklin's speech was quite sophisticated and erudite; Richard's speech was homely.

17. Glowka, Wayne. "Franklin's Perfumed Proposer." Studies in American Humor NS 4.4 (Winter 1985-86): 229-41.

Maintains that Franklin was being intentionally ambiguous when he entitled his essay "To the Royal Academy." In one sense, "the Royal Academy" referred to gatherings of famous and learned men in the home of Mme. Helvetius. Her home had been nicknamed "the Academy" because of the large number of intellectuals who frequently met there. Franklin had written his piece primarily for this audience and had published it privately on his press at Passy. But "the Academy" also referred to the Belgian Royal Academy, which had the more complete title of "Academie Royale des Sciences des Lettres et des Beaux-Arts de Belgique." Glowka compares Franklin's "To the Royal Academy" to Part III of Jonathan Swift's Gulliver's Travels. Both Franklin and Swift were using strong and scatalogical language to attack the impractical research that was being conducted by scientists of the day. Franklin's bagatelle was printed and circulated primarily among his French audience, but it had probably been written especially for two of his intimate lady companions, Mme. d'Hardancourt Brillon de Jouy and Mme. Ligniville de Helvetius. Mme. Brillon was much younger than Franklin, and he called her "Daughter," while she called him "Papa." In "To the Royal Academy" he was primarily dispensing some of his fatherly wisdom about the world of academe.

18. Holliday, Carl. "Benjamin Franklin." The Wit and Humor of Colonial Days. Williamstown, Massachusetts: Corner House, 1975, 70-90.

Considers Franklin to have been a genial humorist, philosopher, scientist, statesman, editor, and man of common sense. His jokes and shrewd sayings would fill a very large tome, and he was in fact the central figure playing in a "lengthy myth or comic

epic." His writing style was simple, direct, and mature. Poor
Richard's Almanac began publication in 1732 and was issued
consecutively for twenty-five years at the rate of ten thousand
copies per year. Very few families in all of New England and the
neighboring colonies escaped its influence. It was filled with
shrewd sayings, proverbs, and statements so full of common sense as
to border on the ridiculous. All of Franklin's humor teaches a
lesson. Even Franklin's practical jokes had a message.

19. Leary, Lewis. "Benjamin Franklin." The Comic Imagination in
    American Literature. Ed. Louis D. Rubin, Jr. New Brunswick,
    New Jersey: Rutgers Univ. Press, 1983, 33-48.

Suggests that one of the factors contributing to Franklin's
fame was that he was a pioneer. He started libraries, civic clubs,
volunteer fire departments, good street lighting, and he was the
first to use "humor as a practical device." Because he was a
pioneer and because he was not shy about telling people about his
pioneering accomplishments, "Franklin may sometimes be credited with
more than he deserves." Franklin was like Whitman, Twain, and
Hemingway in creating an attractive public image. It was mainly
because of Franklin's influence that dialect humor became so closely
associated with "the plain American, simple and wise, sly and
forthright."

20. Skaggs, Merrill Maguire. "Review of Ben Franklin Laughing."
    Studies in American Humor. NS 1.3 (February 1983): 202-
    04.

States that Ben Franklin is a cross between a national enigma
and a chameleon, as he "...has obligingly taken on the shape and
color each generation needed most to see, and has metamorphosed, as
each required, from plucky inventor to ingenious politician, to
stunningly effective diplomat, to successful lover, to salacious
wit." The anecdotes which are about Franklin make smoother reading,
but they are more predictable and soon become bland compared to
those by Franklin. Skaggs reminds us that Franklin assiduously
cultivated his sexual image even in "...his 70s, when he was
severely incapacitated by gout, kidney stones, and prostatitis, and
often almost totally immobilized." That he was successful in this
image building is evidenced by A. S. W. Rosenbach's 1932 book, All-
Embracing Doctor Franklin, "a book which punningly declares its
subject to be 'America's upstanding genius.'"

21. Zall, Paul M. Ben Franklin Laughing: Anecdotes from Original
    Sources by and about Ben Franklin. Berkeley: Univ. of
    California Press, 1980, 104 pp.

Presents anecdotes which Franklin told (sixty-six of them,
including fables, jokes, and experiences) in the first of its two
parts and anecdotes told about Franklin in the second part. The
book makes the point that anecdotes are much like folk tales in that
they are reshaped on each telling to convey not only the event but
the meaning of that event for the particular teller. They also
inculcate folk wisdom as well as specific information. The topics
covered include Advice, Aging, America, Animals, Aristocrats,
Artisans, Blacks, Books and Bookselling, Children, Congress,
Diplomacy, Doctors, Education, Extravagance, Fashion, Foibles,

France, Frugality, Games, Hoaxers, Idleness, Indians, Inventions,
Kings, Lawyers, Love, Philosophers, Politicians, Preachers,
Printing, Religion, Revolution, Sailors, Sects, Servants, Speakers,
Visitors, Women, and Writers.

Joseph Green (1706-1780)

22. Holliday, Carl. "Joseph Green." The Wit and Humor of Colonial
    Days." Williamstown, Massachusetts: Corner House, 1975, 58-64.

    Considers Joseph Green to have been the only wit in
eighteenth-century Boston equal to Mather Byles. Green and Byles
joked with tireless enthusiasm furnishing laughter for any occasion
and with no prior notice. Green wrote amusing and popular poems,
one of which was Entertainment for a Winter's Evening, a boisterous
and sarcastic account of a Masonic meeting held in a church. It was
frequently read by New Englanders for fireside entertainment.
Another successful Green poem was Mournful Lamentation over the
Death of Mr. Old Tenor. Mr. Old Tenor was not a musician, but was
rather a kind of currency which the government had withdrawn from
circulation. Green's greatest writing was his parody of Byles' Hymn
Written during a Voyage. This competition of wits between Green and
Byles provided Boston with ample entertainment in early colonial
days.

Nathaniel Ames (1708-1764)

23. Holliday, Carl. "Nathaniel Ames." The Wit and Humor of
    Colonial Days. Williamstown, Massachusetts: Corner House,
    1975, 67-69.

    Points out that like William Douglass, Nathaniel Ames was a
shrewd, self-confident, and witty Massachusetts physician. Ames was
also an inn keeper, and much of his wit is based on human
experiences. His Astronomical Diary and Almanac was published eight
years before anyone had heard of Poor Richard, and in fact paved the
way both in American and in Europe for Franklin's almanac. It was
filled with shrewd and tactful wisdom about men in the world, and
was extremely popular in New England while Ames was alive. He gave
homely advice to "fops, broilers, flirts, and scamps," and also made
absurd prophecies. In eighteenth century America, Nathaniel Ames
and Benjamin Franklin's almanacs could be found in many homes where
the only other book was the Bible. These almanacs had a steadying
effect on the common folk.

Mercy Otis Warren (1728-1814)

24. Franklin, Benjamin V, ed. "Introduction." The Plays and Poems
    of Mercy Otis Warren. Delmar, New York: Scholars' Facsimiles,
    1980, xxx + 252 pp.

    Considers Mercy Otis Warren to be one of the most important
American women of her time. The Adulateur satirizes Governor
Hutchinson and other Loyalists. The Group, Warren's "third and best

play," was so popular that at least three separate editions were published. Published after Governor Hutchinson's removal to England, it satirizes the unreasonable laws that Parliament imposed upon Massachusetts in 1774. In 1775 John Burgoyne published The Blockade of Boston, a play which satirizes Americans. In response to Burgoyne's play, Warren published The Blockheads: or, the Affrighted Officers in 1776. Since The Blockheads contains sexual and scatalogical language, some critics have argued that it could not have been written by Warren. Franklin argues that Warren did indeed write The Blockheads. "Its theme--American virtue and British incompetence--is similar to that of her first three plays." It also includes three characters from earlier plays. Warren had difficulty ending The Blockheads and finally wrote three separate endings. "The play's multiple endings are politically, not artistically, appropriate." All of Warren's plays satirize "social climbing women" and all demonstrate the tensions "between American and British values."

25. Walker, Nancy, and Zita Dresner. "Mercy Otis Warren." Redressing the Balance: American Women's Literary Humor from Colonial Times to the 1980s. Jackson: University Press of Mississippi, 1988, 11-17.

Indicates that Warren is the only woman satirist typically cited in treatments of the Revolutionary-War period. Mercy Otis Warren had access to much of the political thought of her day because she was the sister of James Otis, an anti-British activist, and the wife of James Warren, a political leader in Massachusetts. Many of the leaders of the American Revolution were in constant communication with Warren attempting to convince her to write materials that would help their patriotic causes. Warren wrote mainly about politics, philosophy, and religion, topics which during her day were considered to be men's topics, and she frequently satirized men's positions on these issues as well as their positions on women's roles. As the first recognized female political satirist in America, Warren was laying the groundwork for later women who used humor and satire to effect political change.

Francis Hopkinson (1737-1791)

26. Holliday, Carl. "Francis Hopkinson." The Wit and Humor of Colonial Days. Williamstown, Massachusetts: Corner House, 1975, 146-69.

Feels that it is ironic that Hopkinson was not a Tory after all the favors he had received from England. But Hopkinson loved America more than he loved position. He wrote a large number of sharp letters, sarcastic essays, and satirical poems. His most famous piece is entitled The Battle of the Kegs; it was the most popular ballad written in Revolutionary days. It was copied in every colony, and was recited at many social functions. When public speakers wished to have a laugh on the British, they would quote stanzas from it. The story goes that a bunch of kegs were filled with gun powder by American patriots and then floated down the river to destroy the British fleet at anchor near Philadelphia. The British soldiers had to spend the day "bravely" shooting the kegs. As with all of Hopkinson's humor, The Battle of the Kegs demonstrated more amusement than anger. "He simply had a good-humored laugh over the follies of his opponents." Another example of Hopkinson's gentle humor was <u>Pretty Story</u>. This piece was a lively allegory telling the story of the disturbance between England and the colonies up to the year 1774.

27. Zall, Paul M. ed. <u>Comical Spirit of Seventy-Six: The Humor of Francis Hopkinson</u>. San Marino, California: The Huntington Library, 1976, 207 pp.

Describes Hopkinson's style as "an effervescent mixture of tomfoolery and common sense" that set the stage for such later national jesters as Will Rogers and Art Buchwald. Hopkinson's humor "appealed alike to radicals, conservatives, and the vast undecided majority in between whose support proved decisive in the end." He was kept out of the Revolutionary War by his tiny size (John Adams described his head as no bigger than a large apple), so he supported the war effort with his satires. He was especially skilled at parody and "could imitate Addison and Steele for the genteel, Swift or Sterne for the middle class, Franklin for apprentices and farmers--or any other popular model who could be turned to purposes of propaganda." He would sometimes promote an argument in one article and then, under a different pseudonym, demolish it in the next edition of the same paper. The primary target of Hopkinson's political satires was the American Tories, because he saw them as a subversive threat to the new government. His secondary target was the British forces, "whose presence was awesome until Hopkinson pilloried their leaders with parodies of their own proclamations." For Hopkinson, the humor resided in "the live interplay of words, images, feelings, and ideas."

Joseph Stansbury (1740-1809)

28. Holliday, Carl. "Joseph Stansbury." <u>The Wit and Humor of Colonial Days</u>. Williamstown, Massachusetts: Corner House, 1975, 137-44.

Describes Stansbury as a "gentle Loyalist," but Stansbury nevertheless received harsh treatment from the patriots. Stansbury's wit was mild and with little animosity. His humor was more of smiles than of sneers. Up till 1776 he wrote hardly any satire about the patriots because he hoped that the war could be averted. After 1776, Stansbury was frequently called upon to write Loyalist songs for various gatherings. Unfortunately for scholarship, after the surrender, he burnt a great mass of his papers. Fortunately for scholarship, enough of his papers remain that we can assume that he must have caused a roar of laughter in the old days of Tory festivity.

Hugh Henry Brackenridge (1748-1816)

29. Holliday, Carl. "Hugh Brackenridge." The Wit and Humor of Colonial Days. Williamstown, Massachusetts: Corner House, 1975, 272-88.

Portrays Brackenridge as a "furious Democrat" and one of the most notable and worthy opponents of the Hartford Wits. He was a prolific satirist, yet very little of his material has survived to the present time. His son indicates that his father was extremely careless about his manuscripts, considering them worthless as soon as they had been distributed. His fame as a brilliant political wit, therefore, rests mainly on tradition. Brackenridge's masterpiece, Modern Chivalry, or the Adventures of Captain Farrago and Teague O'Regan, His Servant, is one of the best political satires ever written. Some of the most laughable portions deal with matters of excise and rebellion. The book became a household classic in the Western territories. One time, when Brackenridge stopped at an inn after a long day's travel, he asked the landlord if he had anything to read. The Inn Keeper quickly produced Modern Chivalry and told Brackenridge that this was a book which would surely make him laugh, "and the man that wrote it was no fool neither." Modern Chivalry is rough in tone and often indelicate in expression but is always positive and manly in its sentiments. Captain Farrago, the protagonist, is a keen practical man with a great sense of humor.

30. Pribek, Thomas. "Hugh Henry Brackenridge." Encyclopedia of American Humorists. Ed. Steven H. Gale. New York: Garland, 1988, 59-62.

Indicates that Brackenridge was born is Scotland and settled in a Scots-Irish town in Pennsylvania. He was a "colorful" judge, who "heard court cases in work boots, feet on his table, shirt open, face unshaven, and hair unbrushed. As an attorney, he chased clients from his office who brought frivolous cases." His only novel, Modern Chivalry, uses absurdity to dramatize national issues and local controversies. Modern Chivalry's use of coarse language, commonplace detail, and exaggerated physical action is a preview of frontier humor. The novel also anticipates frontier humor with the use of comic epithets instead of actual names--Traddle (treadle) the weaver, Drug the doctor, Grab the lawyer, and Harum-Scarum the gamecock. Most of the tall tales in Modern Chivalry feature Teague, a character people could relate to because he is "uncorrupted by education." Another of Brackenridge's picaresque novels is Father Bombo's Pilgrimage, which is about the travels of Father Bombo, who extricates himself from trouble by using his wit to fool whatever ignorant and low types he falls among, changing his dialect at will, and misleading people with sham erudition. The prevailing tone that is seen throughout Brackenridge's work is that of Democritus, the "laughing philosopher."

31. Schultz, Lucille M. "Hugh Henry Brackenridge." Dictionary of Literary Biography: Volume 11: American Humorists, 1800-1950. Ed. Stanley Trachtenberg. Detroit, MI: Gale, 1982, 49-55.

Reports that Brackenridge achieved wide literary fame from Modern Chivalry, a picaresque novel that follows the adventures of

Captain John Farrago and Teague O'Regan, in their Pennsylvania travels. "Teague is a caricature of the illiterate servant, often described in terms of animal metaphors. Farrago, his 'master' and 'trainer,' explains that Teague had been captured on the bogs and tamed, and that Farrago himself is attempting to refine the bog trotter." Teague fails at one position after another; however, he "never hesitates to seek an office for which he is not qualified, and the people never hesitate to support his ambition." The reader may laugh at the antics of Teague, but at the same time be aware of Brackenridge's serious message, that there is evil in "men seeking office for which they are not qualified." Critics have mainly focused on Brackenridge's role as a satirist and as a political activist. Writers celebrate his humorous characterizations, language, imagery, and episodes. Schultz suggests more investigation of the link between Brackenridge's humor and the "philosophical underpinnings of Brackenridge's thought." She suggests ways that his humor can be linked to Brackenridge's favorite philosopher, John Witherspoon.

Lemuel Hopkins (1750-1801)

32. Holliday, Carl. "Lemuel Hopkins." <u>The Wit and Humor of Colonial Days</u>. Williamstown, Massachusetts: Corner House, 1975, 267-71.

Depicts Hopkins as an eccentric, long-legged, staring physician who was skilled as a doctor and strikingly intelligent. He very much disliked the quacks and the lax medical laws of his day, and some of his bitterest poetry was written against such targets. An example is <u>Victim of the Cancer Quack</u>. It begins, "Here lies a fool flat on his back, / The victim of a cancer quack.... / The case was this--A pimple rose / South-east a little of his nose." The poem continues, showing that too much drinking made the pimple grow bigger, and the town gossips blew the pimple all out of proportion. The fearful patient went to a quack doctor whose treatment killed him. Lemuel Hopkins was one of the major contributors to <u>The Anarchiad</u>, <u>The Echo</u>, <u>The Political Green House</u>, and other publications of the Connecticut Wits. Whatever this group produced was wildly applauded by their friends and dreaded by their enemies.

John Trumbull (1750-1831)

33. Holliday, Carl. "John Trumbull." <u>The Wit and Humor of Colonial Days</u>. Williamstown, Massachusetts, 1975, 199-226.

Retells the tradition of the name of Trumbull. One of the kings of England is said to have attracted the attention of a bull while walking through an open field. The vicious bull is said to have been bellowing and rushing to gore the royalty when John Trumbull's ancestors bravely diverted the bull and rescued the king from certain death. The grateful king proclaimed that the rescuer's name should henceforth be "Turnbull," and that a pension of one hundred marks and a coat of arms copiously decorated with bulls' heads be given to the gallant lad. Legend has it that centuries later the name was changed to "Trunbull" to avoid the wrath of the owners and customers of a particular scornful butcher shop. Trumbull was very precocious. By five he had read the Bible and was composing verses of his own. By six he had learned Latin and Greek. By seven he had passed the entrance exams for Yale. His father, however, did not allow him to attend college until the age of thirteen. Trumbull was considered to be one of the most learned men of Colonial America, and one of the keenest wits of his day. He wrote a column for the <u>Boston Chronicle</u> appropriately named <u>The Meddler</u>. He wrote a burlesque (<u>Connecticut Courant</u>), and a mock-epic masterpiece (<u>McFingal</u>).

34. Lacky, Kris. "John Trumbull." <u>Encyclopedia of American Humorists</u>. Ed. Steven H. Gale. New York: Garland, 1988, 453-56.

Comments on Trumbull's style in <u>The Progress of Dulness</u> by saying that his stylistic strengths "are to be found not so much in

21

his use of the Hudabrastic multiple rhyme or in an Alexander Pope-
like cleverness and density of expression (though he has been justly
praised for these elements of his style), but in an unassuming
fluency of statement, a flair for droll anticlimax, and a generally
sustained high quality of verse." Trumbull's most famous work, An
Elegy on the Times, is a stern but not inflammatory condemnation of
the British. In it he said, "in defense of British conduct" that
their numerous retreats were "sincere efforts to prevent civil war."
Although An Elegy is generally anti-Tory in tone, the poem also
satirizes Whig excesses. Because of his devastating attacks of the
British, Trumbull's satires were often used to promote revolutionary
causes, but Trumbull was never fully committed to the cause of the
revolution, and late in his life he joined the Tory cause and with
three other members of the Connecticut Wits he wrote The Anarchiad,
a satire attacking democratic liberalism. Trumbull's adoption of
the genre of the mock epic allowed him to "attack all brands of
fanaticism, while it provided him a means of displaying his
considerable learning and his talent for satire."

Judith Sargent Murray (1751-1820)

35. Walker, Nancy, and Zita Dresner. "Judith Sargent Murray."
    Redressing the Balance: American Women's Literary Humor from
    Colonial Times to the 1980s. Jackson: University Press of
    Mississippi, 1988, 18-23.

    Considers Murray's wit and satire to have targeted both
private and public vices and deceptions that led to corruption and
disharmony both on the personal level and on the civic level. She
wrote two comedies of manners, The Medium; or Virtue Triumphant, and
The Traveller Returned. These novels concentrated on the importance
of women's independence and self-sufficiency and criticized
flirtatiousness and frivolity in young women, saying that instead of
these qualities they should nurture virtue and intellectualism.
Murray felt that marriages should be based on mutual respect,
encouraging the interests and values of both the husband and the
wife.

Timothy Dwight (1752-1817)

36. Cuningham, Charles E. Timothy Dwight--1752-1817--A
    Biography. New York: Macmillan, 1942, viii + 403 pp.

    Asserts that Dwight was one of the Connecticut Wits. Dwight
showed precocious brilliance by entering Yale at the age of
thirteen, later becoming a Yale tutor, and still later the president
of the university. His heroic couplet satire, as can be seen in
"The Triumph of Infidelity," uses a light, thrusting caricature
prose style.

37. Holliday, Carl. "Timothy Dwight." The Wit and Humor of
    Colonial Days. Williamstown, Massachusetts: Corner House,
    1975, 246-47.

    Feels that Timothy Dwight has little claim to be included in
any book of humor because his humorous verse was meager, and he was

not a very humorous person. He was, however, one of the Hartford
Wits, and in his younger days he wrote lines against Harvard
sinfulness. He later became president of Yale.

Philip Freneau (1752-1832)

38. Holliday, Carl. "Philip Freneau." The Wit and Humor of
    Colonial Days. Williamstown, Massachusetts: 1975, 170-98.

    Considers Freneau poet of hatred rather than of love. He
wrote vitriolic satires and was perhaps the most vehement, the most
earnest, and the most powerful of the Revolutionary satirists.
There were times when he was playful but only in the same way that
a tiger is playful. Underneath were the cruel claws and the
merciless heart. 1775 marked Freneau's "first ferocious outburst of
patriotic ire." During this year he wrote such bitter satires as
"On the Conquest of America Shut Up in Boston," "General Gage's
Soliloquy," "The Midnight Consultations," "Libera Nos," "Domine,"
and "Mac Swiggen." These were all venomous pieces--especially to
the Tories.

David Humphreys (1753-1818)

39. Holliday, Carl. "David Humphreys." The Wit and Humor of
    Colonial Days. Williamstown, Massachusetts: Corner House,
    1975, 247-51.

    Portrays Humphreys as having lived his life to the brim.
Humprheys was a soldier, a diplomat, a wit, and a genial gentleman.
When he graduated from Yale he entered the Revolutionary Army as a
captain and became an aide-de-camp to General Washington. He
developed a close tie with Washington and during his frequent visits
to Mount Vernon he and Washington acted like brothers. When the War
of 1812 broke out, he re-enlisted as a brigadier-general at the age
of sixty. Humphreys was not a strikingly original author, but he
could polish a line or add a sharp word or two to improve his own
work or that of his colleagues. His most famous poem is "The
Monkey." It concerns a monkey in a barber shop who tries to shave
himself and his friends but ends up by cutting a customer's throat.
The moral to the poem is that people should not handle sharp tools
unless they have genuine skill, and by sharp tools, the author is
referring not only to razors but to pens as well.

Joel Barlow (1754-1812)

40. Holliday, Carl. "Joel Barlow." The Wit and Humor of
    Colonial Days. Williamstown, Massachusetts: Corner House,
    1975, 252-61.

    Considers John Trumbull and Joel Barlow to be the most well
known of the Hartford Wits today. Barlow wrote "Hasty Pudding" in
Paris in 1793. It begins as follows: "I sing the sweets I know, the
charms I feel, / My morning incense and my evening meal, / The
sweets of Hasty Pudding." Holliday comments that any poet who could
present such a mundane subject of "mush" in so poetic a way was a

poet indeed. When dealing with more poetic subjects, Barlow waxed
even more poetic. Barlow's sarcastic pieces about the Englishmen and
the Tories were undoubtedly an aid to the American cause.

Royall Tyler (1757-1826)

41. Lang, William. "The Yankee Specialists." WHIMSY 5 (April 1,
    1987): 39-41.

    Traces the origin of the "Yankee" character in American drama
to Jonathan Ploughboy, the Yankee waiter of Royall Tyler's The
Contrast (1787). Jonathan was originally conceived to display the
admirable qualities of the true American--the Yankee--as contrasted
with various other stereotypes. David Humpreys stated in the
preface to his 1815 edition of The Yankee in England that the Yankee
is made up of contraries: simple but cunning, inquisitive but
inexperienced, docile when managed rightly but otherwise obstinate
and bull headed, able to parry or repel an attack of raillery not by
original and refined humor, but rather by rustic wit and sarcasm.
Even today, there are vestiges of the Yankee in such characters as
Gomer Pyle and Will Stockdale in No Time for Sergeants. A case may
even be made that such characters as Radar O'Reilly on M*A*S*H and
other "innocents" of situation comedy come out of this same
tradition, originally started by Royall Tyler in the 1700s.

Mason Locke Weems (1759-1825)

42. Downs, Robert B. "Mason Locke Weems." Memorable Americans:
    1750-1950. Littleton, Colorado: Libraries Unlimited, 1983,
    338-44.

    Depicts Weems as an aggressive book seller who was "not
satisfied merely to sell other men's books." On his travels Parson
Weems would preach, play the violin, make book sales, or write books
of his own. His biography of George Washington "has been issued in
at least eight-four editions, including French and German
translations." Weems' books were popular mainly because they were
"aimed at the young and uncultured, the relatively unlettered
farmers, pioneers, and backwoodsmen of the new country." The books
were easy, exciting reading, and cheap, and they "appealed to the
people's patriotic instincts." The insertion of Weems' story about
George Washington chopping down the cherry tree into the McGuffey
readers "increased its circulation by tens of millions of copies."
To demonstrate that Washington led a charmed life, Weems told a
story about an Indian warrior who "was often heard to swear, that
'Washington was not born to be killed by a bullet! For' continued
he, 'I had seventeen fair fires at him with my rifle, and after all
could not bring him to the ground.'" Robert Downs suggests that
American history would be thinner without Weem's creative historical
anecdotes.

43. Hall, Dean G. "Mason Locke Weems." American Writers before
    1800: A Biographical and Critical Dictionary. Westport,
    Connecticut: Greenwood Press, 1983, 1543-46.

Explains that Weems wrote anecdotal histories "that have
become mainstays of American folklore about its early leaders."
Weems wrote a very successful anecdotal history of George Washington
that told the story of Washington chopping down the cherry tree and
confessing that he had done it, and about Washington's father
planting cabbages in such a way that "the sprouts spelled George's
name." Weems is personally responsible for these and other
Washington anecdotes. Weems started by writing a pamphlet about
Washington, but he thought that the pamphlet was too stuffy, so he
started adding made-up anecdotes. "To his 5th edition (1806), he
added the lively anecdotes to become so popular, and to the 6th
(1808), he added even more "personal" although fictitious material,
resulting in a volume well over 200 pages." Weems later wrote other
biographies in the same vein. "He began with the skeletal facts of
a person's life and hung upon them anecdotes, associates'
impressions, and laudatory gossip to create one-sided, unsullied
characterizations." It was Weems' purpose to "make a new nation
proud of its founders." Although Weems' anecdotes were debunked by
later historians, "they are sources for that mythic America that by
now has become cultural fact by virtue of repetition."

Richard Alsop (1761-1815)

44. Holliday, Carl. "Richard Alsop." The Wit and Humor of
    Colonial Days. Williamstown, Massachusetts: Corner House,
    1975, 262-66.

Considers Richard Alsop to have been the most enthusiastic of
the Hartford Wits. He would have preferred to have written
witticisms without touching anyone's tender spots, for he enjoyed
creating humor for its own sake and liked to write humor that both
friend and foe could enjoy. Although his style is sarcastic, it is
not written with the offensive tone that was so common in his day.
It must be remembered that Richard Alsop's gentler satire was by
choice; he had the ability to fence with a sharper blade if he had
so desired.

Tabitha Gilman Tenney (1762-1837)

45. Hoople, Sally C. "Tabitha Gilman Tenney." Encyclopedia of
    American Humorists. Ed. Steven H. Gale. New York: Garland,
    1988, 430-34.

Indicates that Tabatha Tenney's Female Quixotism is a parody
of Miguel de Cervantes' Don Quixote but written from the female
point of view. Tenney's primary purpose (like that of Cervantes)
was to use satire to expose the dangers of reading sentimental
fiction. Female Quixotism was probably the first American spoof of
the Gothic novel. Here Tenney uses "dialogue ranging from elaborate
protestations of love to obscene vituperation" as she attempts to
startle and even shock the reader into attention. She also uses
cacography, as when Betty, the maid, in the role of Dorcasina's

lover, disappoints and irritates her mistress with the incoherence of her low-class speech. Female Quixotism emerges as a novel which "in spite of its exaggerated ridiculousness, deserves the attention of today's reader and scholar because of its great popularity in the first half of nineteenth-century America, its significance as a satiric and nationalistic response to late eighteenth-century imported sentimental fiction, the vivid exposure of human foibles, and its enduring powers of description and humor."

46. Hoople, Sally C. "Tabitha Tenney: Humorist of the New Republic." WHIMSY 6   (April 1, 1988): 300-01.

Shows Tabitha Tenney's Female Quixotism to be a rollicking, sometimes racy, satire, ridiculing the maudlin romances that provided popular reading entertainment for the New England ladies at the end of the eighteenth century. At the time Tenney wrote the novel, many colonists believed the Scottish sentiment that the reading of fiction would corrupt and subvert the reality of the external world. The fear was even more intense in regard to sentimental novels, because it was felt that the readers would either plunge into an impetuous love affair with disastrous results or else become so disillusioned with the local suitors, who simply could not compare with the dashing heroes of the novels, that they would wait forever and die miserable old maids. Tenney's novel is Cervantes' novel from the female point of view. Dorcas Sheldon becomes the heroine of the novel with the mellifluous name of Dorcasina, very reminiscent of the Cervantes heroine. Like Dulcinea, Dorcasina is plain, and like Dulcinea, Dorcasina becomes ravishingly beautiful through the process of fantasy. Dorcasina is convinced that every man who sees her is hopelessly in love with her, so she rejects the more prosaic types of men who could offer a solid and satisfying marriage to take up with a series of silver tongued male gold-diggers. In fact, Female Quixotism is a hyperbolic and satiric sentimental novel, written to show the dangers of sentimental novels.

47. Walker, Nancy, and Zita Dressner. "Tabitha Gilman Tenney." Redressing the Balance: American Women's Literary Humor from Colonial Times to the 1980s. Jackson: University Press of Mississippi, 1988, 27-38.

Considers Tenney's Female Quixotism, Exhibited in the Romantic Opinions and Extravagant Adventures of Dorcasina Sheldon (1801) to have started the tradition of satiric advice literature by women for women. The tradition went on to include Fanny Fern's Fern Leaves (1853) and Josephine Daskam's Fables for the Fair (1901). The novel attempts to caution women against believing in the romantic notions of men that were so popular during the nineteenth century. Ironically, the novel also supports the nineteenth century belief that the reading of romantic novels would cause women to be foolish and sentimental. Dorcasina Sheldon, the protagonist of Tenney's novel is very similar to Betsey Bobbet, Marietta's Holley's protagonist much later in the century. Both protagonists were susceptible to flattery and to romantic visions of themselves. Tenney's ability to make fun of the sentimental novel suggests that she was an avid reader. One antecedent of Tenney's novel is Cervantes' Don Quixote. A more immediate antecedent, however, is The Female Quixote; or, The Adventures of Arabella by British author

Charlotte Lennox (1752). _Female Quixotism_ was both the peak and the conclusion of Tenney's writing. Following the death of her husband in 1816, Tenney moved back to her native New Hampshire where she died in 1837.

Wallace Admah Irwin (1766-1821)

48. Masson, Thomas L. "Wallace Irwin." _Our American Humorists_. Freeport, New York: Books for Libraries, 1931, 164-81.

Indicates that Mark Twain felt that Irwin's "Togo Letters" were the best thing he had read in American humorous literature. Irwin got a job writing a poem a day for a New York evening paper. In return, Irwin got $25.00 a week and a very wide readership. His writing attracted the attention of Lincoln Steffens, who had a reputation for helping other people. One day Steffens dropped in on Irwin, told him that he was an excellent writer, and asked him why he didn't write for other papers. Irwin replied that he didn't dare give up his present job, that it was a steady job, and it made him feel secure. At that point, Steffens talked to the proprietor of the paper and got him to fire Irwin, saying "He'll never get anywhere unless you fire him." So it was Lincoln Steffens who forced Wallace Irwin into prominence as a writer.

Joseph Dennie (1768-1812)

49. Sloane, David E. E. "Joseph Dennie." _Encyclopedia of American Humorists_. Ed. Steven H. Gale. New York: Garland, 1988, 117-19.

Demonstrates that Joseph Dennie, one of the first professional writers in America, was capable of both the elevated humor of Richard Addison and Oliver Goldsmith and sarcastic burlesques of political and social events and issues. As editor of _The Tablet_, Dennie wrote articles attacking Harvard University, lampooning the social bon vivant, and applying the gentle humor of Goldsmith and Lawrence Sterne to recollections of his earlier life and family relations. Dennie was also the editor of _The Port Folio_, where he took on the pen name of Oliver Oldschool, Esq. Here and elsewhere, he teamed up with Royall Tyler to write what were called "Colon and Spondee" sketches. The whimsy, burlesque, and satire that were characteristic of Dennie both as editor and as writer influenced Washington Irving and perhaps even H. L. Mencken. Dennie was the leader of a group of conservative Federalist writers, and in 1804, his spirited attacks of democracy, including sarcastic poetry about Jefferson's alleged affair with a slave woman and other racy topics, made _The Port Folio_ spicy reading for its period, but it also caused Dennie to be indicted for sedition.

Mike Fink (c1770-c1823)

50. Blair, Walter, and Hamlin Hill, eds. "Mike Fink." America's
    Humor: From Poor Richard to Doonesbury. New York: Oxford
    University Press, 1978, 113-21.

       Indicate that Mike Fink was a keelboatman on the Ohio and
    Mississippi Rivers at the end of the eighteenth century. For
    recreation he whomped all challengers, and this allowed him to
    continue wearing the red feather in his hatband that showed him to
    be the champion of all the boatmen. The Mike Fink stories were
    written by many different writers with many different backgrounds,
    aims, and talents, and these stories were written in many different
    genres--"a couple of plays, a ladies' gift book, a pamphlet on
    navigating the Ohio and Mississippi Rivers, government reports,
    local histories, humorous books, books of sketches, travel books,
    anthologies, several almanacs, many magazines, and innumerable
    newspapers."

51. Blair, Walter, and Franklin J. Mein. Half Horse Half Alligator:
    The Growth of the Mike Fink Legend. Lincoln: Univ of Nebraska
    Press, 1957, ix + 289 pp.

       Born to Scotch-Irish parents, Mike Fink was an important
    character on the American frontier. The humorous Mike Fink stories
    contrasted with the romances of the day, emphasizing the incongruity
    between the rustic characters of the Southwestern frontier and the
    pretentious and ornate style of the characters in the romances.
    Although the exaggeration in the Mike Fink tales gives them the
    appearance of being non-realistic, this vulgar and cacophonous
    humorous literature was the first realistic depiction of American
    life that entered American fiction. It was plain men with plain
    speech who tamed the frontier. Their major defect was their
    recklessness, but this "defect" made the frontier habitable for law-
    abiding but less enterprising citizens. Recklessness was not only
    useful but essential in taming the wilderness to allow the
    civilization to exist. As a frontier hero, Mike Fink shouted
    boasts, and writer after writer attributed their most imaginative
    boasts to Mike Fink. Like David Crockett, sixteen years his junior,
    Mike Fink is a strange combination of "history and legend, of humor
    and fiction" that can "teach the reader a great deal about our
    American past."

James Kirke Paulding (1778-1860)

52. Aderman, Ralph M. "James Kirke Paulding." Antebellum Writers in
    New York and the South. Detroit, Michigan: Gale, 1979, 246-49.

       Indicates that Paulding's John Bull in America (1825) is a
    satire proposing that the British in America so often slandered the
    United States because they refused to look at the scenes around them
    and instead read the biased Quarterly Review for their attitudes.
    After the second war with Great Britain, Paulding parodied English
    literary styles and patterns as a defense against the
    misrepresentational view the British had of the Americans. Paulding
    continued his satires through the 1820s, when he changed to the
    genre of the tall tale or short story. His The Merry Tales of the
    Three Wise Men of Gotham (1826) ridiculed Robert Dale Owen's version

of a social utopia. His <u>Tales of the Good Woman</u> (1829) was a collection of stories depicting human failings and foibles. And his <u>Chronicles of the City of Gotham</u> (1830), contained humorous characterizations of the bluestocking and the politician. The hyperbolic tale was Paulding's most successful vehicle not only for instruction but for entertainment and escapism as well. Although he wrote hastily and excessively, he always displayed vigor and enthusiasm. He received widespread attention both for his social criticism and for his satiric attacks on the British.

53. Blair, Walter, and Raven I. McDavid, Jr., eds. "James Kirke Paulding." <u>The Mirth of a Nation: America's Great Dialect Humor</u>. Minneapolis: Univ of Minnesota Press, 1983, 37-41.

Describes a play-writing contest in 1830 that Paulding entered. But before entering, Paulding wrote to his friend John Wesley Jarvis, a widely traveled and superb story teller, asking him for a few incidents involving Kentucky or Tennessee manners and for some phrases peculiar to that area. Jarvis supplied Paulding with such expressions as "lion of the west," "tetotaciously," "exclunctified," "catawampus," and "catfish." This last term, "catfish" was used in the West to describe lawyers because they were "all head, and their head's all mouth." With Jarvis' help, Paulding won the contest with his play entitled "The Lion of the West." In this play he introduced Nimrod Wildfire (played by James H. Hackett). The play did very well both in the United States and in England, where it was doctored by the British dramatist, William Bayle Bernard. Ironically, it is only Bernard's revision of the play that has survived.

54. Cohen, Hennig, and William B. Dillingham, eds. "James Kirke Paulding." <u>Humor of the Old Southwest</u>. 2nd ed. Athens: Univ of Georgia Press, 1975, 8-14.

Considers Paulding to have been among the first American authors to use extensively the half-horse, half-alligator type of frontier humor. Originally, Paulding was closely associated with Washington Irving and other members of the Knickerbocker group in New York City and wrote tales about the Dutch pioneers such as <u>The Dutchman's Fireside</u>. But he also had a lifelong fascination with the South and the West and wrote <u>Letters from the South</u>, an account of his travels in Virginia, and <u>Westward Ho!</u>, a melodramatic novel in which a Virginia cavalier learns to cherish Western values. <u>The Lion of the West</u> brought into prominence Paulding's most famous protagonist, Nimrod Wildfire. At the time it was written, there were many stories being circulated about the exploits of Congressman David Crockett, even though the Crockett biographies and Crockett almanacs had not yet been published. When newspapers confronted Paulding with the suggestion that Wildfire was a caricature of Crockett, Paulding denied the charge. Nevertheless, when <u>The Lion of the West</u> opened in Washington, Crockett was sitting in the front row of the audience. James H. Hackett, playing Nimrod Wildfire in the play, bowed ostentatiously to Crockett, and Crockett arose from his seat and bowed in return. These acknowledgements were greeted with wild applause from the crowd.

55. Fisher, Benjamin F. IV. "James Kirke Paulding." Encyclopedia
    of American Humorists. Ed. Steven H. Gale. New York: Garland,
    1988, 349-53.

Asserts that Paulding will be remembered as a writer who
"mined the same Dutch Materials as those used by Washington Irving
and other Knickerbockers, and as a forerunner of Southwestern
humor." Paulding used Neoclassical irony and satire but he also
wrote rough frontier humor and barrages of anti-Gothic sentiments.
Paulding's Salmagundi (not to be confused with the Salmagundi
Paulding co-authored with Washington and Peter Irving) contains
topical satire on the follies in Paulding's native New York. Like
most of Paulding's work, this novel depicts eccentric characters and
emphasizes realistic colloquial language. Paulding lambasts ghosts,
spiritualism, devils, saints, crosses, crescents, magic, witchery,
spiritualism, infernalism, hobgoblinism, and bug-a-booism to show
his lack of respect for the Gothic adventures, but he nevertheless
"incorporated such paraphernalia into his own imaginative writings."
Paulding's Letters from the South anticipates the tradition of the
"ring-tailed roarer" that flourished in the 1860s. The Lion of the
West continues this frontier tradition with its lead character
Colonel Nimrod Wildfire, Kentucky frontiersman and self-proclaimed
"half horse and half alligator," whom many critics feel is patterned
on the life of David Crockett.

John Wesley Jarvis (1780-1840)

56. Blair, Walter, and Hamlin Hill, eds. "John Wesley Jarvis,
    Storyteller." America's Humor: From Poor Richard to
    Doonesbury. New York: Oxford University Press, 1978, 92-111.

Believes that Jarvis stories and anecdotes set off a chain
reaction that exploded American dialect comedy. These stories and
anecdotes were presented in a number of different genres--a
burlesque travel book, many sketches, and at least six plays. Blair
and Hill conclude that the contributions of John Wesley Jarvis to
the development of French, Yankee, and frontier dialect humor were
"prodigious."

Washington Irving (1783-1859)

57. Blair, Walter, and Hamlin Hill, eds. "Ichabod and Rip."
    America's Humor: From Poor Richard to Doonesbury. New York:
    Oxford University Press, 1978, 165-71.

Feels that Irving had a good eye for stereotypes. In History
of New York, Irving developed six stereotypes--the pedant (Diedrich
Knickerbocker), the Dutchman, the Yankee, the settler, the ring-
tailed roarer, and the backwoods squatter. Ichabod Crane in "The
Legend of Sleepy Hollow" continues the stereotype of the pedant, but
this time a pedant out of his element. Ichabod was a Connecticut
school teacher, a Yankee in the tradition of Brother Jonathan, who
goes West to teach in a closed and comfortable community. Crane is
shrewd in his way as he plots to woo the Van Tassel daughter with an
eye toward the Van Tassel wealth. As soon as they are married,

Crane plans to sell off the Van Tassel farm and invest the money in immense tracts of wild land and build palaces in the wilderness. But Ichabod is from Puritan New England and believes in the supernatural world. He truly believes in and fears the things that go bump in the night, while the community he has invaded treats such things with good-natured indulgence, so he is an easy target for Brom Bones. Rip Van Winkle is not so ambitious as Ichabod Crane. He himself is a story teller rather than the target of a story teller. Rip tries to escape the bonds of society. He mismanages his estate, his marriage, and his labor.

58. Clark, William Bedford. "Washington Irving." Dictionary of Literary Biography, Vol 11: American Humorists, 1800-1950. Ed. Stanley Trachtenberg. Detroit, Michigan: Gale, 1982, 224-37.

Declares that Irving's detractors "are generally united in their disparagement of what they see as his lack of earnestness, his tacit refusal to consider the weighty philosophical and political controversies of his day, and his evasive flights of fanciful whimsy." But Irving also had a lot of important supporters. Irving's wit presented a "surprising range of fictive voices and [was] nearly always controlled by a stylistic mastery few of his contemporaries could match." Irving's caricature "won the enthusiasm of later masters of that mode such as Thackeray and Dickens." His detractors and supporters would agree that "from first to last, the vision of human experience articulated in Irving's writing is profoundly comic." "The influence of Irving on American humor...would be difficult to overestimate." Throughout the history of American comic writing, Irving's contribution may at times have been elusive "but is nonetheless subtly ubiquitous."

59. Leary, Lewis. "Washington Irving." The Comic Imagination in American Literature. Ed. Louis D. Rubin, Jr. New Brunswick, New Jersey: Rutgers Univ Press, 1983, 63-76.

Believes that the reason Irving has been called the father of American humor by many critics is not because he was first but because he was more widely read and therefore more influential than those who preceded him--Ebenezer Cook, Benjamin Franklin, William Byrd, John Trumbull, Philip Freneau, and others. He started as a a humorous writer at the age of nineteen when he contributed a number of letters to a newspaper his older brother edited. His penname, Jonathan Oldstyle Gent, was very appropriate. Jonathan was a respected Yankee name. Oldstyle clued the reader that this character was "conservative and retrospective, suspicious of what was new," and Gent signalled that he was a member of the gentry--a gentleman. Leary feels that Irving is a typical nineteenth century comic figure and compares Irving to J. Alfred Prufrock, "who ventures only tentatively, then draws back, content to polish and to please."

60. Myers, Andrew B. "Washington Irving." Antebellum Writers in New York and the South. Ed. Joel Myerson. Detroit, MI: Gale, 1979, 166-87.

Depicts Salmagundi as a mixed dish, a potpourri of prose and poetry, designed to "instruct the young, reform the old, correct the town, and castigate the age." Salmagundi was written by Washington

Irving, his older brother, William, and William's brother-in-law, James Kirke Paulding. Washington Irving's A History of New York is also fun to read. It is a look at the fast-fading New Amsterdam era of seventeenth-century New York. The reader becomes aware of the informal comic tone of the history as soon as he or she finds the epigram in Low Dutch on the title page. History is a satire and a parody of the guidebooks of the day. It's a half-serious joke with humorous descriptions and outrageously comic events in the lives of Manhattan's early Dutch settlers, their wily Yankee neighbors to the North (Connecticut), and their Scandinavian competitors to the South. History concentrates on the rule of three Dutch governors, Wouter Van Twiller from 1633 to 1637, Willem Kieft from 1637 to 1647, and Peter Stuyvesant from 1647 to 1664. Irving's The Sketch Book contrasts English lengendary lore and traditions with that of New England. The three most important stories in The Sketch Book are "Rip Van Winkle," "The Legend of Sleepy Hollow," and "The Spectre Bridegroom."

61. Ringe, Donald A. "Irving's 'Mountjoy': Philosophy in the Comic Mode." Studies in American Humor NS3.4 (Winter 1984-85): 290-97.

    Sees Irving's "Mountjoy; or Some Passages out of the Life of a Castle-Builder" as being part of the "Quixote" tradition. The prevailing philosophy not only during Cervantes' day but during Irving's was that the reading of fantasies and adventure stories would clutter the mind and make it incapable of dealing with the real world. The satire in "Mountjoy" is so subtle that it requires a sophisticated reader. It is a very funny story about the adventures of a young man whose unrestrained imagination causes him many different embarrassments. The reason for Mountjoy's unrestrained imagination is that his mother had continually given him and his sister books to read that were filled with stories about fairies, giants, and enchanters. Mountjoy's mind was thus filled with the supernatural from an early age. He and his friends would try to outdo each other in the telling of extravagant stories, and on their way home from school they frequently had to pass a lonely pond at night. The sounds of birds, crickets, and bullfrogs would cause them to glance fearfully at each other and scamper through the woods in terror. Not only "Mountjoy" but also "Rip Van Winkle," "The Legend of Sleepy Hollow," and "The Spectre Bridegroom" contain glimpses of supernatural characters and events.

62. Robillard, Douglas. "Washington Irving." Encyclopedia of American Humorists. Ed. Steven H. Gale. New York: Garland, 1988, 236-42.

    Indicates that Washington Irving joined Peter Irving and James Kirke Paulding to write Salmagundi; or, The Whim-Whams and Opinions of Lancelot Langstaff, and Others. Salmagundi is "rich to the point of indigestiability unless the pieces are read, as they were meant to be read, singly and at intervals." A later, and more mature piece of writing is Knickerbocker's History of New York. Diederich Knickerbocker provided the inspiration for Knickerbocker Magazine, a leading literary magazine of the day. Irving undercuts his own purpose by creating not history but satiric parody. "Knickerbocker may be lovable and ambitious, but he is a fool." Although the book presumes to tell the history of New York, both the book, and

Diederich Knickerbocker are creations of Irving's comic mind. It has been said that Knickerbocker is an American Don Quixote. Washington Irving is most famous for two stories which appeared in The Sketch Book of Geoffrey Crayon Gent--"Rip Van Winkle," which appears early in the volume, and "The Legend of Sleepy Hollow," the final selection. These stories were so well written that they are said to establish the short story as a legitimate vehicle for narrative, able to compete successfully with the poem, the drama, the novel, and the essay.

63. Roth, Martin. Comedy and America: The Lost World of Washington Irving. Port Washington, NY: Kennikat, 1976, xiv + 205 pp.

Believes that Irving relied a great deal more on previous writers than critics have suggested. Irving needed models because of "his shortcomings in imagination and intellect." Roth examines Salmagundi for its derivative vocabulary, comic characters, tropes, and fictions. Roth suggests that Irving's History of New York does more to establish a particular style of American comedy than did The Contrast, Modern Chivalry, or even Salmagundi. Roth isolates and examines the paradigms and conventions of comedy that Irving relied on--polite satire, political satire, and domestic humor. Roth describes Irving's writing as "burlesque comedy" but suggests that "festive comedy" could equally well describe Irving's style, because in Irving's writing there is a balance of the reductive and negative vision of the world of words and ceremonial vision.

David Crockett (1786-1836)

64. Albanese, Catherine L. "David Crockett." Antebellum Writers in New York and the South. Detroit, MI: Gale, 1979, 94-96.

Feels that Crockett politically exploited his appeal as an ignorant, uncouth, and yet gentle backwoodsman in his autobiography and that his innuendos attacked Andrew Jackson and his "kitchen cabinet." In fact, Albanese feels that Crockett's Narrative may have been a campaign document designed to help Crockett establish his claim to wilderness innocence and exuberance and better endear him to his voting public. Albanese's article presents evidence that Crockett was not killed while fighting at the Alamo but that he either surrendered or was captured by the Mexicans and then executed with a group of other Texans. Ironically it is the legend that Crockett died fighting at the Alamo that solidified his reputation as a genuine and true American. Davey Crockett liked James Kirke Paulding's Nimrod Wildfire in Lion of the West, because Wildfire presented a sympathetic portrayal of Crockett's life. But Crockett didn't like the fact that James Strange French purchased his Sketches and Eccentricities of Colonel David Crockett of West Tennessee, and portrayed Crockett as something of a frontier lunatic. His irritation at French's portrayal, in fact, may have affected his decision to write the Narrative, which appeared the following year.

65. Blair, Walter. <u>Davy Crockett: Legendary Frontier Hero: His True</u>
    <u>Life Story and the Fabulous Tall Tales Told About Him</u>.
    Springfield, Illinois: Lincoln-Herndon Press, 1986, xii + 195
    pp.

    Contends that legend has so colored history that there is now
not one Davy Crockett but six, and it is a good idea to sort through
the evidence to discover which one is the statesman, which is the
humorist, which is the frontier hero, etc., for only by
understanding the real Davy Crockett will we develop an appropriate
understanding of the various legends. Blair compared the real-vs-
legendary Davy Crockett with the real-vs-legendary Abraham Lincoln.
Both used backwoods vernacular to state homely wisdom, and both
delighted in telling "wacky" stories. Crockett was respected by his
contemporaries for his courage, directness, and honesty. His
autobiography, <u>Narrative of the Life of David Crockett of the State</u>
<u>of Tennessee</u> was written to help him regain the political stature
that he had recently lost, and in it he refers a number of times to
"President Crockett." Blair considers Crockett to be the heir to
Benjamin Franklin and the ancestor of Henry Adams in the American
family of man. Already a legend when he died at the Alamo, he
became even more a legend by his martyrdom, and the famous Crockett
<u>Almanacs</u> continued to be published for twenty years after his death,
inspired by his ghost. Blair's accounts of Davy Crockett clearly
distinguish between the historical figure and the tall-tale
frontiersman but don't assume that the historical figure is any more
real or any more important than the legendary figure.

66. Blair, Walter, and Hamlin Hill, eds. "David versus Davy."
    <u>America's Humor: From Poor Richard to Doonesbury</u>. New York:
    Oxford University Press, 1978, 122-32.

    Picture Crockett as a politician whose backers and coat-tail
riders presented favorably, while his detractors reviled him. "When
he switched parties, everybody sashayed to the other side."
Crockett says that he has met hundreds of people who had already
formed their opinions about his appearance, habits, and language and
who were profoundly astonished to find him in human shape. At one
train stop in Pennsylvania, for example, the people had come out
expecting to see a wild man of the woods, clothed in a hunting shirt
and covered with hair. They were greatly surprised when the real
David Crockett appeared as a respectable looking gentleman, well
dressed, and wearing locks in the fashion of plain German farmers.
Crockett had a total of about 100 days of schooling, and the
Crockett legend portrayed Crockett in the tradition of <u>Alazon</u>, as
claiming more glory than he deserved. <u>Alazon</u> is the blustering,
swanking, cock-and-bull-story-telling boaster exemplified by Davy
Crockett. <u>Eiron</u>, on the other hand, makes himself out worse than he
is. Just as Crockett and Fink and Bunyan represent <u>Alazon</u>, Ben
Franklin's Poor Richard represents <u>Eiron</u>, a purveyor of dry and
understated humor.

67. Blair, Walter, and Raven I. McDavid, Jr., eds. "David
    Crockett." <u>The Mirth of a Nation: America's Great Dialect</u>
    <u>Humor</u>. Minneapolis: Univ of Minnesota Press, 1983, 42-47.

    Feels that Crockett's lack of education was more of an
advantage than a hindrance in frontier Tennessee politics, for there

was a general distrust of book learning at that time and place. Crockett's reputation was aided by the fact that this coon-skin cap frontiersman was an excellent hunter and militiaman, a genial drinker, and a great story teller. He was elected to a number of political offices, and was sent to Congress twice (1827-1831 and 1833-1835). Crockett's motto was "Be sure you're right and then go ahead," and the stories based on his life are based in part on reality. The legend was generated by many ghost writers, who imitated the speech and methods of the tellers of the Old Southwestern tall tales. The legend of Davy Crockett was further enhanced by his picturesque and heroic death at the Alamo.

68. Clark, William Bedford. "Col. Crockett's Exploits and Adventures in Texas: Death and Transfiguration." Studies in American Humor NS1.1 (June, 1982): 66-76.

Contends that General Santa Ana elevated Travis, Bowie, and Crockett to the state of martyrs when he ordered the cremation of enemy corpses at the Alamo on March 6, 1836. Santa Ana was tampering with American mythic legend, and his act enflamed Americans in their cause for Texas independence and American expansionism. The memory of Davey Crockett was especially elevated by this event because he had been a member of Congress and because he had become famous during his lifetime through the many stories that had been written and told about him. Crockett spoke in a number of voices, ranging from the backwoods blusterer to the homey eloquence of a crackerbarrel philosopher. He is most widely known from Col. Crockett's Exploits and Adventures in Texas (1836). This was advertised as his diary but was actually a fabrication assembled after the fall of the Alamo that became a best seller. It was the prototype of today's westerns, containing excellent indigenous humor. It was also a propaganda tool used against the Whigs' assault on Jackson and Van Buren in favor of American expansionism in the Southwest. And it changed Davey Crockett from a legend to a martyr.

69. Clark, William Bedford. "Davy Crockett." Dictionary of Literary Biography, Vol 11: American Humorists, 1800-1950. Ed. Stanley Trachtenberg. Detroit, MI: Gale, 1982, 89-94.

Agrees with Emerson Hough that Crockett was a paradox, a man who "lived like a savage and died like a hero." The first book attributed to Crockett, The Life and Adventures of Colonel David Crockett of West Tennessee (1833) was advertised as "strictly true," but a year later, Crockett repudiated the 1833 novel in a new book entitled A Narrative of the Life of David Crockett of the State of Tennessee. In the second book but not the first, he openly admitted his lack of formal education, but he did not apologize: "Big men have more important matters to attend to than crossing their t's, and dotting their i's--, and such like small things." The Life of Martin Van Buren (1835), a burlesque attributed to Davy Crockett "is of interest to the student of American humor as an example of vitriolic ad hominem satire." This book also anticipates "the more genial humor of later American political humorists." It was not until the later Almanacks, that Crockett's writing was taken to the limits of absurdity that would originate the popular frontier tall tale. In the Almanacks, "folklore and 'fakelore' mesh, and Davy

Crockett becomes "a forerunner of [such] later legendary figures as
John Henry, Paul Bunyan, and Pecos Bill."

70. Cohen, Hennig, and William B. Dillingham, eds. "David
    Crockett." Humor of the Old Southwest. 2nd ed. Athens: Univ of
    Georgia Press, 1975, 15-27.

    Consider the appeal of Davey Crockett to have mainly derived
from his reputation as a shrewd frontiersman and Indian fighter.
Crockett was born in Eastern Tennessee, where his grandparents had
been killed by Creek and Cherokee Indians. He was born into severe
frontier life, where survival was very difficult and where a man was
measured more by his skill in hunting and taming the wilderness and
spirit of freedom and independence than by his refinement and
education.   Crockett lacked the refinement and education.
Crockett's life is the basis of the Crockett legend both in his
deeds and his recounting of the deeds, but the books attributed to
Crockett's pen were heavily edited. His autobiography, A Narrative
of the Life of David Crockett, was edited by Thomas Chilton, and
even though it may not contain any of Crockett's actual writing, it
does contain his own stories and reflects his spirit and wit. "The
content is his even though the actual words are not."

71. Dorson, Richard Mercer. Davy Crockett: American Comic Legend.
    New York: Arno, 1977, xxvi + 171 pp.

    Considers Davy Crockett America's first superman, "grinning
with the silent humor of the day." Dorson traces the Crockett
legend through The Sketches and Eccentricities of Col. David
Crockett (1833) through Narrative of the Life of David Crockett
(1834) to the series of Crockett almanacs that followed. Dorson
says that between 1835 and 1856 a great many almanacs were published
in Nashville, New York, Boston, and elsewhere. These "quaint little
almanacs, with their grotesque woodcuts and eye-straining print"
provided a magic source of epic frontier lore filled with pioneer
heroes, fantastic adventures, imaginative sketches of nature and
wildlife, frontier anecdotes, and the development of characters of
legendary proportions.

72. O'Connor, Robert H. "David [Davy] Crockett." Encyclopedia of
    American Humorists. Ed. Steven H. Gale. New York: Garland,
    1988, 104-08.

    Claims that Crockett as a stump orator had the ability (which
Lincoln would develop later) of exploiting pithy anecdotes, homely
metaphors, and homespun jokes to win over his audiences. He was a
clever but uneducated backwoodsman. Davy Crockett of public
imagination was both the clown who drank from finger bowls at a
formal banquet and the sly politician who lured the electorate to
the local tavern before his opponent could speak. The legend of
Davy Crockett developed in parallel fashion to that of Mike Fink.
Furthermore, James Kirke Paulding's character, Nimrod Wildfire, was
modeled after Davy Crockett, even to the extent that Wildfire was a
candidate for reelection to Congress. So here we have a strange
blend of history and fiction. An Account of Col. Crockett's Tour to
the North and Down East, The Life of Martin Van Buren, and Col.
Crockett's Exploits and Adventures in Texas were all published
under Crockett's name, though he was not actually the author of any

of them. Davy Crockett had only about a hundred days of formal education; therefore everything he wrote required a great deal of editing and revision. But Crockett was a convenient persona for the several political satirists who published their works under his name.

73. Seelye, John. "A Well-Wrought Crockett: Or, How the Fakelorists Passed Through the Credibility Gap and Discovered Kentucky." Toward a New American Literary History. Eds. Louis J. Budd, Edwin H. Cady, and Carl L. Anderson. Durham, NC: Duke University Press, 1980, 91-110.

Indicates that in 1939 critics like Walter Blair and Richard Dorson and Constance Rourke considered Crockett to be a true hero of folklore, but that James Atkins Shackford's David Crockett: The Man and the Legend (1956) presents evidence that undermines Crockett's status as a legendary hero, changing the term "folklore" into the term "fakelore" by suggesting that Crockett's reputation sprung much more from printer's fonts than from Crockett's actual life. In 1973 Joseph Arpad added fuel to Shackford's fire by tracing The Lion of the West not back to an oral source but rather to Paulding's own Letters From the South (1817). Seelye's article discusses the general tradition of how legends are made through the strange blend of fact and fiction--but mostly fiction.

74. Shackford, James Atkins. "David Crockett, The Legend and the Symbol." The Frontier Humorists: Critical Views. Ed. M. Thomas Inge. New York: Archon Books, 1975, 208-18.

Explains that Davy Crockett was symbolic of the American frontier because he was extraordinarily strong, perseverant, courageous, and determined, four essential qualities for an American frontier hero. Crockett so excelled in these qualities that when an incredible story was to be told, it was attributed to Crockett lending it an "air of reality and credibility which made the story delicious to its hearers." Also, people could see their own qualities in the Davy Crockett legends, thereby appealing to "the self-interest of the conventional patriot of my town, my state, my section, my nation, and all of the other multitudinous ramifications of me." The qualities of Davy Crockett the backwoodsman, and David Crockett the politician formed an interweaving upward spiral, both contributing to the legend. The stories helped him become prominent in Tennessee politics, and his prominence in Tennessee politics, in turn, stimulated the imaginations of everybody who was contributing to the legend. Finally, Davy Crockett's heroic death at the Alamo symbolized extreme courage against overwhelming odds. Although the populace and the politicians were exploiting Davy Crockett, he was exploiting them as well. The best practical joke that Davy Crockett ever played upon posterity was to make it swallow the Crockett myth whole.

James Fenimore Cooper (1789-1851)

75. Kennedy, J. Gerald. "Cooper's Anti-Intellectualism: The
     Comic Man of Learning." Studies in American Humor. 3.2
     (October 1976): 69-75.

        Portrays Cooper as a writer who considered himself a gentleman
and a man of learning.   Nevertheless, Cooper had a suspicion of
learning and a mistrust of men committed to ideas. This is clear in
his portrayal of the "ludicrous man of learning," the "comic savant"
in his various novels, who was incredibly garrulous, verbose,
pedantic, and fond of intellectual subtleties and multi-syllable
expressions. These characters tend to be impractical and incapable
of performing mundane tasks; despite their learning, they are naive
about human nature and are easily deceived by outward appearances.
These characters are contrasted with the uneducated frontiersman,
who is witty and wise, as exemplified by Cooper's frontier hero,
Natty Bumppo, who acts decisively in difficult situations.
"Persistently, the scout ridicules the schooling of his comic
counterparts and defends the values of what he calls 'natural
l'arning,' a wisdom derived from experience, common sense, and
humility."   This ambivalence of Cooper toward education can be
explained.   Cooper was a student at Yale but was dismissed at the
age of fifteen. He was therefore unable to appreciate the value of
any education more extensive than his own.

76. Krauth, Leland. "Laughter in The Pioneers." Studies in
     American Humor NS1.2 (October 1982): 79-89.

        Agrees with Mark Twain that Cooper's humor is marginal at best
and suggests that this is why his humor didn't have as much effect
in the shaping of civilized life in the frontier West as Cooper
would have hoped.   Cooper's humor tends to be ponderous and
contrived, and it lacks subtlety.   His characters shift from
unbridled freedom to total "civilized" constraint. He writes not
just about the taming of the wilderness but more importantly about
the taming of the wildness in human nature. Of the five novels in
the Leatherstocking series, The Pioneers has by far the lightest
tone, and Cooper said he wrote it in order to "please himself." The
Pioneers is a novel of manners, containing simple caricatures rather
than fully developed characters, with each character representing a
distinct comic perspective.   Billy Kirby is probably the most
laughable of the characters; he is a ring-tailed roarer who claims
to have chopped down thousands of acres of forest land in the New
England area and who plans to live long enough to finish the job for
the entire country. Cooper considers him to be "human life in its
first stages of civilization." Ironically, Cooper's most civilized
characters are the least humorous. Given Cooper's attitudes toward
civilization, this may be one of the reasons that Cooper failed as
a humorist.

77. Twain, Mark. "Fenimore Cooper's Literary Offences." Satire:
     from Aesop to Buchwald.   Eds. Frederick Kiley and J. M.
     Shuttleworth. New York: Macmillan, 1971, 234-36.

        Begins with lauditory quotes about Cooper's writing from
Professor Lounsbury, Professor Matthews, and Professor Collins.
Then Twain continues that it didn't seem right for these three

professors "to deliver opinions on Cooper's literature without
having read some of it. It would have been much more decorous to
keep silent and let persons talk who have read Cooper." Twain
continues that in a certain two-thirds of a page in Deerslayer,
Cooper has scored 114 offenses agains literary art out of a possible
115. "It breaks the record." "Every time a Cooper person is in
peril, and absolute silence is worth four dollars a minute, he is
sure to step on a dry twig." In fact, the Leatherstocking Series
ought to have been called the Broken Twig Series." After commenting
on numerous details of the novels, Twain ends his criticism by
taking a broader perspective. He asks if Deerslayer is a work of
art and then answers: "A work of art? It has no invention; it has
no order, system, sequence, or result; it has no life-likeness, no
thrill, no stir, no seeming of reality...; its humor is pathetic;
its pathos is funny; its conversations are--oh! indescribable; its
love-scenes odious; its English a crime against the language." But
Twain ends on a positive note: "Counting these out, what is left is
art. I think we must all admit that."

78. Wittmer, George B. "James Fenimore Cooper, M*A*S*H, and the
    Origins of TV Drama." Teaching English in the Two-Year
    College. 14.2 (May 1987): 93-96.

    Presents evidence that Cooper was a major contributor to the
first episode of M*A*S*H. First, Cooper was quoted in a number of
M*A*S*H episodes. Second, Cooper wrote a play by the name of Mingos
and Soldiers at Ft. Henry, in which the two male surgeons are named
Lt. Hawkes (cf. Lt. "Hawkeye Pierce") and Trappman (cf. Lt.
Trapper"), and a beautiful nurse is named Margaret Flanagan (cf.
Nurse "Margaret Houlihan"). In another of Cooper's novels, entitled
The Spy, there is a doctor by the name of Archibald Sitgreaves, who
can easily be compared to Dr. Charles Emerson Winchester of M*A*S*H.
Kennedy describes Dr. Sitgreaves as a battlefield physician who
occupies a potentially heroic position. "Yet he functions primarily
as a buffoon," because of his long-winded speeches and eccentric
theories. What makes Sitgreaves preposterous, however, is his
passion for knowledge. He describes simple events in ponderous
terms. Furthermore, he regards combat as a source of bodies on
which to experiment, and when the novel's hero, Harvey Birch, the
spy, contemplates execution, Sitgreaves says, "I intend making as
handsome a skeleton of him as there is in the States of North
America--the fellow has good points, and his bones are well knit."
Could this be the skeleton in Colonel Potter's office?

Asa Greene (1789-1838)

79. Keller, Mark A. "Asa Greene." Dictionary of Literary Biography,
    Vol. 11: American Humorists, 1800-1950. Ed. Stanley
    Trachtenberg, Detroit, MI: Gale, 1982, 156-59.

    Proclaims Greene's A Yankee among the Nullifiers, a book which
"attacks Southern attitudes toward nullification, slavery, dueling,
and Northerners" to be "blatantly didactic." "Most of the satire is
heavy-handed and depends on a stereotyped view of Southerners.
Nonetheless, Greene anticipated humorous episodes and character
types that became common in later Down East and Old Southwest
humorous literature." The most humorous episode in the book

portrays a battle between planters and a group of slaves who
"attempt to 'nullify' their owners and 'secede' from the
plantations." Greene writes the novel in a mock-heroic style.
Greene's second book, The Life and Adventures of Dr. Dodimus
Duckworth, tells how the protagonist decided he was destined to
become a doctor, "when normally quiet ducks belonging to his parents
give out a series of inexplicable 'quacks' at the very moment of his
birth." The protagonist of Greene's third book, Travels in America,
by George Fibbleton, Esq., Ex-Barber to His Majesty, the King of
Great Britain, takes a condescending attitude toward the Americans
he meets because of his pride at having served as a barber to the
king of England. Fibbleton is shown to be a simpleton when he
confuses facts concerning American history, geography, and politics.

80. Royot, Daniel G. "Asa Greene." Encyclopedia of American
    Humorists. Ed. Steven H. Gale. NY: Garland, 1988, 181-86.

    Compares Asa Greene's "Israel Icicle" and "Cornelius Cabbage"
to Benjamin Franklin's Silence Dogwood and Poor Richard. Greene's
favorite targets were lawyers, doctors, sentimental literature,
phrenology, bloodletting, and feminism. Angellia was the heroine of
the "Cornelius Cabbage" stories. Greene's description of Angellia
is an excellent parody of the sentimental literature of the day:
"Her head was cast in the most delicate mould--being neither so
round as a cocoanut, nor so long as a cucumber" (Constellation, June
19, 1830). Although Greene graduated as a doctor from Brown Medical
School, he was critical of the medicine of his day, and in 1833 he
wrote The Life and Adventures of Dr. Dodimus Duckworth, A. N. Q.
"A.N.Q." stands for "a notorious quack," and reinforces the doctor's
name--"Duckworth." Another of his novels, A Yankee Among the
Nullifiers, spoofed romantic adventure novels and the Southern ideas
and mannerisms that are frequently displayed in these novels. Still
another of Greene's novels is The Perils of Pearl Street, written as
the autobiographical adventures of a New York mercantile salesman.
The novel satirizes both village greenhorns and city slickers and
hyperbolizes the shams and trickeries of the latter on the former.
Greene's main contribution was that "he helped bridge the gap
between popular culture and the literature for and by the elite."

Chapter 3
Nineteenth Century

(1790-1870) TO (1809-1858)

Augustus Baldwin Longstreet (1790-1870)

81. Cohen, Hennig, and William B. Dillingham. "Augustus Baldwin Longstreet." Humor of the Old Southwest. 2nd ed. Athens: Univ. of Georgia Press, 1975, 28-59.

Consider Longstreet's Georgia Scenes to have been the first in an impressive number of stories and books about southern humor to have come off the presses before the Civil War. Longstreet was the president of four southern colleges--Emory, Centenary, the University of Mississippi, and the University of South Carolina. Although he wrote many books and pamphlets, Georgia Scenes is his only work of current interest. Edgar Alan Poe reviewed the book for the Southern Literary Messenger and praised it highly; he said that he had perhaps laughed more immoderately over this book than over any other. Georgia Scenes is a remarkably varied collection of sketches that contains something for almost every reader of the 1830s. There is the sentimentality and didacticism of "The Charming Creature as a Wife" for the gentle reader. There is "The Debating Society" for the less domestically inclined urbane reader; this was Poe's personal favorite. There are the grotesque details of vivid imagery--down to the description of a horse's enormous sore in "The Horse Swap" for the macho reader. And "The Fight" contains not only the gory details of a bloody encounter, but also the realistic characterization of Ransy Sniffle, the troublemaker. And in all of the sketches, there is the distinction between the accounts themselves and the aristocratic narrator, who describes the scenes from a superior social and moral viewpoint.

82. Gribben, Alan. "Mark Twain Reads Longstreet's Georgia Scenes." Gyascutus: Studies in Antebellum Southern Humorous and Sporting Writing. Ed. James L. W. West III. Atlantic Highlands, NJ: Humanities Press, 1978, 103-11.

Places Mark Twain clearly in the tradition of Southwestern Humor both in his subject matter, and his attitudes. Twain was clearly heavily influenced not only by Augustus B. Longstreet but also by George W. Harris, Joseph M. Field, William T. Thompson, Johnson J. Hooper, Joseph G. Baldwin, Thomas B. Thorpe, and Richard M. Johnson. "Georgia Theatrics," the first sketch in Longstreet's collection, describes a young farmer giving a thorough thrashing to

an opponent who is not there. Walter Blair has noted the
similarities between Longstreet's story and Twain's having Tom
Sawyer struggle with an imaginary opponent in Chapter 18 of The
Adventures of Tom Sawyer. "The Horse Swap" is another of
Longstreet's short stories that had an influence on Twain. The
story involves a boastful horse trader who trades an ornery swayback
named Bullet for a gentle sorrel named Kit. A short time after the
trade, the horse trader discovers that Kit is both blind and deaf.
It takes little imagination to relate this to one of Twain's story
about a horse trader. When Twain edited his Mark Twain's Library of
Humor, he had numerous marginal notes indicating that he wanted to
include some of Longstreet's work. These notes even related to the
types of illustrations that would accompany Longstreet's
contribution. In the final version, however, Longstreet was totally
omitted from the work.

83. Justus, James H. "Augustus Baldwin Longstreet." Encyclopedia of
    American Humorists. Ed. Steven H. Gale. New York: Garland,
    1988, 289-92.

    Points out that the writing in Longstreet's Georgia Scenes is
very formal, with "balanced sentences..., arch asides, literary and
historical allusions, Latin tags, apostrophes, and direct addresses
to the 'gentle reader.'" Both of Longstreet's narrators, Hall and
Baldwin, "are patronizing observers whose language is correct,
formal, and ponderous, particularly when it is directly juxtaposed
against the linguistic raciness of the country characters."
Longstreet was a "reluctant humorist." Realizing that much of the
popular success of Georgia Scenes was on account of its humor,
Longstreet said that it was not primarily intended for entertainment
and that the public had misread his intentions. Because he was
embarrassed that his popularity was due to his humor, later in his
life he vowed that he would "henceforth publish only works that
would be received as unambiguously serious: orations on education
and defenses of slavery based on biblical study and historical
precedent." Ironically, these serious works are not considered
important by present-day critics. In his writing, Longstreet
presents two points of view "The first is crude and opportunistic,
the second materialistic and pretentious." Longstreet feels that a
synthesis of the two points of view is impossible.

84. King, Kimball. "Augustus Baldwin Longstreet." Antebellum
    Writers in New York and the South. Ed. Joel Myerson. Detroit,
    MI: Gale, 1979, 204-10.

    Considers Longstreet's compassionate treatments of simple,
uneducated characters to have broken the ground for both the local-
color movement and the literary realism and naturalism which would
follow. Longstreet's tales were told by chatty narrators and
suggested that in 1835 there were actually two Georgias--the rough
Georgia of illiterate pioneers and the Georgia of a newly prosperous
middle class with genteel interests and social pretensions.
Longstreet seemed to favor a synthesis of the two cultures,
suggesting that educated men needed to keep their pride in check
through contact with plain rural people still in possession of the
frontier spirit. Longstreet was a Southern humorist, a social
historian, and an innovative stylist who used candor to describe a

value system unique to his region.   His racial attitudes make it difficult for a modern reader to appreciate his skill and effectiveness as a stylist, because much of what he wrote was social and political pre-Civil-War propaganda.

85. Lilly, Paul R. Jr. "Augustus Baldwin Longstreet." Dictionary of Literary Bibliography: Vol 11: American Humorists, 1800-1950. Ed. Stanley Trachtenberg, Detroit, Michigan: Gale, 1982, 276-83.

Indicates that Georgia Scenes "did more to shape the style and subject matter of Southwestern humor" than any other book.   This novel went through eleven editions between 1835 and 1897. Georgia Scenes was an instant success both in the North and in the South, and "it had a lasting influence on an entire generation of Southwestern writers."   "Nothing he wrote, from the passionate arguments for nullification to the high-minded orations he delivered as a college or university president, will last as long as the ribald and earthy voices of a handful of his characters from Georgia Scenes."   Longstreet was fascinated with the contrast between backcountry dialects and the genteel speech of his own class, and Paul Lilly places such Longstreet characters as Ransy Sniffle, Billy Curlew, Ned Brace "in a rich tradition of colloquial speakers that includes George Washington Harris's Sut Lovingood, Mark Twain's Huck Finn, and William Faulkner's V. K. Ratliff."   "Thompson's Sammy Stonestreet, Hooper's Simon Suggs, and Harris's Sut Lovingood, all...trace their ancestry back to Ransy Sniffle."

86. Poe, Edgar Allan. "Georgia Scenes." The Frontier Humorists: Critical Views. Ed. M. Thomas Inge. New York: Archon, 1975, 85-93. Originally in Southern Literary Messenger. 2 (March 1836), 287-92.

Written anonymously, Georgia Scenes was still anonymously authored when Poe wrote in his review that "The author, whoever he is, is a clever fellow, imbued with a spirit of the truest humor." Poe's praise became even more intense: "Seldom--perhaps never in our lives--have we laughed as immoderately over any book as over the one now before us."   Poe then goes on to review each of the scenes individually--"Georgia Theatrics," "The Dance," "The Fight," "The Song," "Turn Out" "The Gander Pulling," "The Ball," "The Mother and Her Child," "The Debating Society," "The Militia Company Drill," "The Turf," "An Interesting Interview," "The Fox-Hunt," "The Wax Works," "A Sage Conversation," and "The Shooting Match." Poe said that these anecdotes are "told with a raciness and vigor which would do honor to the pages of Blackwood." Poe concludes his evaluation with "Altogether this very humorous, and clever book forms an aera in our reading. It has reached us per mail, and without a cover. We will have it bound forthwith, and give it a niche in our library as a sure omen of better days from the literature of the South."

87. Snipes, Wilson. "The Humor of Longstreet's Persona Abram Baldwin in Georgia Scenes." Studies in American Humor NS4.4 (Winter 1985-86): 277-89.

Contrasts two of Longstreet's characters. Abram Baldwin was a tragic figure and became Longstreet's vehicle for social satire. Lyman Hall, on the other hand, was a realist, a romantic, and a

humorist. Longstreet devised the idea of having two different
narrators with two distinct voices as a method of distancing himself
from the anonymously-written sketches and concealing the fact that
he [Longstreet] had been the author. In 1835 Longstreet revealed
that Lyman Hall was the narrator of those sketches where men were
the main characters, while Abram Baldwin was the narrator when women
characters were more prominent. Snipes points out that the subjects
and situations of the Baldwin sketches are also much more limited in
scope than are the Hall sketches. In "The Dance," "The Song," and
"The Ball," Baldwin is himself the subject of the humor. In "The
'Charming Creature' as a Wife" the focus is the "fatal marriage" of
his nephew George Baldwin, but his voice as narrator is still
prominent in both selection of detail and in style. In "A Sage
Conversation" the narrator's attitudes again determine the direction
of the piece. "The Mother and Her Child" is the most autonomous and
objective of the Baldwin-narrated sketches, but even here Baldwin
establishes the perspective and evaluates the situation.   So
Baldwin's voice dominates the Baldwin-narrated sketches, and this
accounts for much of the pathos and tragedy. The message of these
sketches is probably that human nature and the human condition are
very superficial but at the same time are "amusing, funny,
ridiculous, satirical, and ironic.   These effects are achieved
because of Baldwin's subjectivity, his describing his own thoughts
and feelings, and his making his own judgments.

88. Wade, John Donald. "Augustus Baldwin Longstreet: A Southern
    Cultural Type." The Frontier Humorists: Critical Views. Ed. M.
    Thomas Inge. New York: Archon. 1975, 94-104.

   Demonstrates the ambivalence that Longstreet felt for humor.
Although Longstreet realized the importance of humor, he had
difficulty admitting that what he wrote was humorous. Nevertheless,
Longstreet said that the way a politician could be elected to office
was to "treat liberally, ape dignity here, crack obscene jokes
there, sing vulgar songs in one place, talk gravely in another." It
may have been because of this perception that Longstreet did not
enter politics, for Longstreet also had a very serious bent. "When
Longstreet began nagging, his contemporaries soon found
instinctively what to do with him; they put him at the head of a
boys' school where nagging is held salutary, and where it cannot be
resented." Longstreet was always fascinated with the frontier West.
He felt that if only he could move west, he could become rich, so
Longstreet moved west in a way consistent with his own value system-
-by becoming president of universities that were to the west of
Georgia. In addition to the geographical westness of these moves,
"the business of being head of a state school lay somewhat west of
the business of being head of a church school." Longstreet was
president of Emory College and the University of Mississippi, and
the University of South Carolina.

Seba Smith (1792-1868)

89. Blair, Walter, and Raven I. McDavid, Jr., eds. "Seba Smith."
    The Mirth of a Nation: America's Great Dialect Humor.
    Minneapolis: Univ of Minnesota Press, 1983, 3-10.

    Indicate that Smith invented Jack Downing of Downingville,
Maine, in order to increase the interest, the popularity, and the
circulation of the Portland Daily Courier. Downing used plain
language in his letters to the folks back home. His letters were so
lifelike and Jack Downing was so well developed as a character that
many of Smith's readers believed both Jack Downing and Downingville
to be real. Another evidence of Smith's popularity is the number of
authors and playwrights who imitated his style, some of them
stealing his name as well. Jack Downing is the first in a long
line of nationally admired vernacular commentators that includes
Davy Crockett, Hosea Biglow, Josh Billings, Mr. Dooley, Mark Twain,
Will Rogers, and others.

90. Pettengell, Michael. "Seba Smith." Encyclopedia of American
    Humorists. Ed. Steven H. Gale. New York: Garland, 1988, 402-
    05.

    Indicates that Smith was the original creator of the character
"Major Jack Downing," a character which became the symbol not only
of the Yankee shrewd businessman but the prototype of "Uncle Sam."
Smith became a humorous novelist not only to increase the size of
his audience but also to be able to present more than a single point
of view. In order to do this, he gave each member of the fictional
Downing family a voice. There are letters from "Cousin Ephraim,
Uncle Joshua, Cousin Nabby, and Jack's mother, each supplying a
separate point of view." Smith's later letters became "heavy-handed
with reform," and as a result, they became much less effective. It
is ironic that Smith's epigraph mentions nothing about his
contributions to the field of American humor. It says simply, "Poet
and Scholar." These were "two things that Smith approached with
vigor but never accomplished successfully." Despite the fact that
his later letters were less humorous and less effective and despite
the fact that Smith wanted to become a poet and scholar rather than
a humorist, Pettengell concludes that his humorous work "is worth
careful study in itself, and is the egg from which late nineteenth-
century humor hatched."

91. Waldron, Edward E. "Seba Smith." Dictionary of Literary
    Biography, Vol 11: American Humorists, 1800-1950. Detroit,
    Michigan, 1982, 459-66.

    Alludes to the fact that "one of the problems that accompanied
Seba Smith's success with Jack Downing was the rash of imitators who
assumed his character's name and epistolary mode." Charles Augustus
Davis was the most famous of these imitators; the best way "to
distinguish the Smith and the Davis letters is by the signatures:
Smith always signed his letters 'Captain [or Major] Jack Downing,'
while Davis signed his letters 'J. Downing, Major.'" Nevertheless,
even now there is confusion concerning the authorship of many of the
"Jack Downing" letters. Smith is said to be "the creative force
behind the comic literary Yankee character." Smith, popular not
only with his contemporaries but also with modern-day critics, made

two major contributions to American humor. "First, he gave us a record...of a "genuine" Yankee from Down East, in a subtle and gentle form; second, he set a new pattern for American humor in his political satire issuing from the pen of a simple country philosopher." Smith had an important influence on such contemporaries as Thomas Chandler Haliburton and James Russell Lowell and on such later writers as Finley Peter Dunne and Will Rogers. These other writers "might often have surpassed him in literary style or wit, but they--and we--owe a great debt to the man who started it all."

John Neal (1793-1876)

92. Fiorelli, Edward A. "John Neal's Use of 'Comic' Material During the Formative Years of American Literature (1812-1835)." WHIMSY 1 (April 1983): 38-39.

Feels that Neal has an "almost Dickensian flair for comic description." For example, Neal describes "Mr. Major Jeremiah Davison" as "little, odd, and lumpish." He was "never still--his teeth projected frightfully--his ears were uncommonly large--his hair white. He was barefooted; half naked.... His arms and legs were too long; his head to large for his body." Fiorelli says that this sketch of the "unappetizing Yankee stage driver" in Volume II of Brother Jonathan is "one of those tiny but precious diamonds often found among the vast, cretaceous coal deposits of Neal's work." Fiorelli considers Neal to be one of the first not only to use the vernacular but also one of the first to use effectively the elements of the tall tale. In Brother Jonathan, for example, Winslow and his companion, Walter Harwood, are at a campfire when a bear attacks. Winslow grabs the bear around the middle and tries to hold him, while yelling at Walter to shoot the bear. "The narrative has all the ingredients of the classic tall tale, including the straight-faced narrator frustrating his listeners by long-winded circumlocutions, interruptions, and preposterous understatement."

Joseph Gault (1794-1879)

93. Meats, Stephen. "Joseph Gault, Cobb County Humorist." Studies in American Humor. NS4.4 (Winter 1985-86): 290-304.

Believes that Joseph Gault is very much underrated as an author in the tradition of Southwestern humor. Gault's Reports of Decisions in Justice's Courts, in the State of Georgia, from the Year of our Lord 1820 to 1846 was published in Marietta, Georgia, in 1846 and went through four printings during his lifetime and two after his death. The book was written in the form of a series of legal decisions, and which so convincing that they were often used as precedent in actual court cases; however, they were not based on fact and were originally written as satires. Gault fits well into the tradition of Southwest humorists that includes Harris, Longstreet, Thorpe, Hooper, Thompson, Lewis, and others. Gault became famous for his caustic wit and outspoken opinions on the mid-nineteenth-century American court system. He wrote anonymously for the Marietta Journal and was the most famous man in Cobb County for a while. His tongue-in-cheek writing in Reports is highly interesting and amusing. It is dedicated to James McGee, a Murray County justice of the peace who is the butt of much of Gault's ridicule. Gault writes as a witty and sarcastic attorney, not as a polished author. His writing is firmly grounded in realism, and it lacks characterization, dialogue, situation, and other literary qualities. But Gault has a keen idea for detail, and his portraits of backwoods attorneys and justices of the peace ring true. "His accounts of the rough-and-tumble chaos of the justices' courts are both funny and horrifying." Gault also continued the tradition of ludicrous portrayals of backwoods preachers popularized by Hooper and George Washington Harris. These accounts are so similar as to suggest that none of the accounts was very far removed from the actual truth.

Charles Augustus Davis (1795-1867)

94. Simms, L. Moody. "Charles Augustus Davis." Encyclopedia of American Humorists. Ed. Steven H. Gale. New York, NY: Garland, 1988, 111-13.

Indicates that Davis was established as a member of New York's "silk-stocking community" by the time he published his first "J. Downing, Major" letter in 1833. Simms feels that Davis drew heavily from Seba Smith's Jack Downing in developing his own J. Downing, Major. Davis' character attacked Jacksonian Democracy and became an official spokesman for the Whig Party. The letters were written to be read by a largely uneducated audience; therefore Davis relied heavily on homespun logic and spiced his stories with slang and ungrammatical vernacular language. Smith's Jack Downing was one of the first widely read "unlettered philosophers" in the American comic tradition. Many American authors attempted to cash in on the popularity of Smith's Jack Downing, but Davis' J. Downing, Major was Smith's only serious competitor. Although the letters were all signed "J. Downing, Major," rather than "Jack Downing," few readers were aware of any difference. Readers during this period would as soon read a good counterfeit as the original. Smith's Downing was a rustic bufoon who was very naive about politics. Since he was portrayed as Jackson's close friend, Jackson came off as arrogant and narrow minded in Davis' sketches.

95. Turner, Craig. "Charles A. Davis." Dictionary of Literary Biography, Vol 11: American Humorists, 1800-1950. Detroit, MI: Gale, 1982, 103-08.

Differentiates Davis' "J. Downing, Major" from Seba Smith's original "Major Jack Downing." "Davis, in sharp contrast with the lightly satirical and typically nonpartisan Seba Smith, was deeply involved in partisan politics." Turner concurs with Jennette Tandy that Davis' "J. Downing, Major, tended...to excel and to overshadow his original." This is supported by David Crockett's frequent allusions to Davis' "J. Downing, Major" in his writings. Like Smith, Davis placed "Major Downing" as a close advisor to the president, but Davis went one step further. J. Downing "is presented as closer to Jackson--they even sleep together." Prior to 1833, Davis was not an author. He was a member of a book club which included "Bryant, Cooper, Irving, and other members of the Knickerbocker set." But on June 25 of 1833, Davis' "strong interest

in current political events," his "irrepressible humor" and his
friendship with the Jackson adversary Nicholas Biddle prompted Davis
to write a letter to the New York Daily Advertiser. This letter
established the Davis character of "J. Downing, Major" by denying
"the reported death by drowning of President Jackson's fictional
friend and advisor, Major Downing, in the collapse of the bridge at
Castle Garden during the 'Gineral's Grand Tower of the Northeast.'"

Thomas Chandler Haliburton (1796-1865)

96. Blair, Walter, and Raven I. McDavid, Jr. eds. "Thomas
     Chandler Haliburton." The Mirth of a Nation: America's Great
     Dialect Humor. Minneapolis: Univ of Minnesota Press, 1983, 11-
     16.

     Points out that for years Haliburton's Sam Slick was the best-
known character in American fiction for ludicrous "Down East"
sayings. Between 1836 and 1860 the books about Sam Slick ran
through more than 200 editions in Canada, the United States, and
England. Haliburton also edited two important anthologies that
popularized Yankee dialect humor--Traits of American, by Native
Authors and Americans at Home. Sam Slick was a shrewd and alert
peddler who sold clocks and other items. He had a sharp eye, a keen
brain, and wide experience that had taught him many notable
aphorisms. Sam's speech was rich in Yankee provincialisms, however,
later in Haliburton's career, Sam's speech became purer and less
provincial.

97. Engle, Gary. "Thomas Chandler Haliburton." Encyclopedia of
     American Humorists. Ed. Steven H. Gale. New York, NY: Garland,
     1988, 189-91.

     Considers Haliburton's fame as a humorist to have been
international, especially in Canada, England, and the United States.
Haliburton developed the character of Sam Slick from Slickville for
a rural Canadian newspaper named the Novascotian. Slick was a
Yankee clock peddler who developed a sales pitch known as "soft
sawder." This pitch reflected a keen understanding of how human
behavior is affected by greed, envy, and vanity. Each sketch was in
the frame-tale tradition, contrasting the stodgy and urbane
narrative of the Squire with the glib outspoken vernacular of Sam
Slick. In the tradition of the picaresque novel, Sam Slick and the
Squire travelled throughout Nova Scotia. The sketches were so
entertaining that they soon appeared in book form and were issued
"in literally hundreds of editions" before the end of the nineteenth
century. The first series of clockmaker sketches (1836) emphasized
the fact that hard work can pay off in a developing democracy. The
second series (1838) ridiculed democratic reform proposals in Nova
Scotia. The third series (1840) was intended for a British
audience, and it argued against the movement in England to give Nova
Scotia the rights and privileges of self-government. Haliburton was
considered by many an American Charles Dickens. Sam Slick's
shrewdness, his thrift, and his laconic insights into human nature
made interesting reading.

98. Waldron, Edward E. "Thomas Chandler Haliburton." Dictionary
    of Literary Biography, Vol 11: American Humorists, 1800-1950.
    Detroit, Michigan: Gale, 1982, 169-75.

Disputes title given to Haliburton by early reviewers as "the
father of American humor" but nevertheless claims that Haliburton is
"a central figure in the formation of an American humor character
and approach." Haliburton created the character of a "Yankee clock
peddler of uncommon insight into the foibles of humankind,
especially Nova Scotians" by the name of "Samuel Slick, of
Slickville." Waldron considers Sam Slick to be closer to the
traditional stage Yankee than to the "'true Yankee' developed in the
person of Hosea Biglow by James Russell Lowell." The "sayings and
doings" of Sam Slick had a large audience both in America and
abroad. "Despite the parochial character of some of their
contemporary political concerns, Haliburton's works still convey a
laugh to modern readers." Nevertheless, Haliburton has his
detractors. For example, Professor C. C. Felton of Harvard says
that Sam Slick's language "is a ridiculous compound of provincial
solecisms, extravagant figures, vulgarities drawn from distant
sources, which can never meet in an individual...; he is an
imposter, an impossiblity, a nonentity."

Hamilton C. Jones (1798-1868)

99. Blair, Walter, and Raven I. McDavid, Jr., eds. "Hamilton C.
    Jones." The Mirth of a Nation: America's Great Dialect Humor.
    Minneapolis: Univ. of Minnesota Press, 1983, 33-36.

Consider "Cousin Sally Dilliard" to have been the the only
piece of Haliburton writing to have become really well known. This
sketch surfaced in a North Carolina newspaper in 1830 and was
reprinted extensively. The sketch illustrates the shaggy-dog
technique, a popular rhetorical device of the time in which the
narrator rambles from point to point until he gets lost and loses
the thread of the story. "Cousin Sally Dilliard" targets the
informality of frontier courts, a favorite topic in the new country.

100. Hendrick, Willene, and George Hendrick. "Hamilton C. Jones."
     Encyclopedia of American Humorists. Ed. Steven H. Gale. New
     York: Garland, 1988, 243-46.

Thinks that Jones' humor is subversive, "for in his stories
the rational, ordered world yearned for by the well-to-do Whigs is
replaced by an irrational world in constant disorder." One of his
first stories, "Cousin Sally Dilliard" was published in Atkinson's
Saturday Evening Post in 1831, and "it became, with variations, a
staple in the repertoire of nineteenth-century American raconteurs,
including Abraham Lincoln." In the 1830s Jones made contributions
to Carolina Watchman in a column entitled "Salisbury Omnibus."
These pieces were unusual, because Jones' observations range from
comic events in Salisbury to literary spoofs. Some of his jokes are
about politics, others are about race. "At their best, these
humorous "Omnibus" pieces are similar to today's "The Talk of the
Town" items in The New Yorker." Jones' language might be racy, "but
he generally avoids violence and overtly sexual subjects." Not many
of Jones' stories, sketches, and anecdotes survive, however, those

that do "capture the vitality of this region in the decades before
the war."

Thomas Kirkman (1800-1864)

101. Cohen, Hennig, and William B. Dillingham. "Thomas Kirkman."
     <u>Humor of the Old Southwest</u>. 2nd ed. Athens: Univ of Georgia
     Press, 1975, 60-65.

     Feel that Kirkman is a better author than his place in history
suggests.   Kirkman was born in Ireland but spent his youth in
Nashville, Tennessee. He owned a plantation in Mississippi, an iron
works, and a stable of race horses in Tennessee; he imported
expensive thoroughbreds from England. Kirkman's reputation would
have been adversely affected by publishing humor under his own name;
he therefore wrote anonymously. He published a sketch in <u>Spirit of
the Times</u> entitled "A Quarter Race in Kentucky," which William T.
Porter later chose as the title story of his anthology on
Southwestern humor.   Kirkman's "Jones' Fight" also appeared
anonymously in <u>Spirit of the Times</u> and was then selected as one of
the inclusions in Porter's <u>The Big Bear of Arkansas and Other Tales</u>.
Kirkman undoubtedly published many other pieces anonymously that
have unfortunately not become quite so famous.

Caroline Matilda Stansbury Kirkland (1801-1864)

102. Walker, Nancy, and Zita Dresner. "Mrs. Mary Clavers [Caroline
     Kirkland]." <u>Redressing the Balance: American Women's Literary
     Humor from Colonial Times to the 1980s</u>. Jackson: University
     Press of Mississippi, 1988, 39-45.

     Categorizes Caroline Kirkland with Sara Willis Parton as
significant women authors who helped develop the genre of realistic
fiction in American literature and who stood in direct opposition to
the idealized images created by James Fenimore Cooper and others.
Kirkland countered sentimentality and romanticism with commonsense
satire, and she encouraged her readers to look insightfully at
subjects as disparate as fashions and the frontier.   Kirkland's
grandfather had been a satirist during the Revolutionary War, and
Kirkland was raised in a literary environment. In <u>A New Home</u>,
Kirkland made fun both of pretentiousness and of the lack of manners
and polish of her Michigan neighbors. Like her contemporary Frances
Whitcher, many people of her day resented her satiric portrayals of
silly or crude behavior, because they saw themselves in Kirkland's
portraits. These critics failed to see that Kirkland also made fun
of her own unrealistic attitudes about the frontier. She discovers,
for instance that her china soup tureen is much more practical as a
chamber pot, and when her mahogany cabinet will not fit into her
tiny log cabin she converts it into a corn crib.   Much of the
significance of Kirkland's contribution in <u>A New Home</u> rests in her
portrayal of women's rather than men's experiences on the frontier.
Rather than land speculation and town boosterism, she discusses
having to raise children on dirt floors.

Solomon Franklin Smith (1801-1869)

103. Cohen, Hennig, and William B. Dillingham, eds. "Solomon
      Franklin Smith." Athens: Univ. of Georgia Press, 1975, 66-77.

      Indicates that Smith became the proprietor and occasional
actor of a local theater in 1822 and that in 1823 he formed his own
troupe and functioned as theatrical manager and actor. His company
performed in the Ohio and Mississippi river valleys as well as in
Georgia and South Carolina. In the 1840s his company dominated the
theatre in St. Louis and Mobile and, to some extent, even in New
Orleans. Both as an actor and as an author, Smith was best known
for his comic portrayals. His sketches and anecdotes are mainly
based on his experiences as an actor and manager. Sol Smith's
Theatrical Apprenticeship was published in 1845 and initiated the
popular Carey and Hart series, "Library of American Humorous Works."
This was followed by Sol Smith's Theatrical Journey Work in 1854.
The year before Smith died, he combined and expanded the two books
into Theatrical Management in the West and South. Instead of being
divided into chapters, this book was divided into five "acts." In
a postscript, he suggested the inscription of his gravestone by
quoting some suitable lines from Shakespeare, followed by the stage
directions, "Exit Sol." When Smith died, he was almost as legendary
in the theater as was Mike Fink on the river, and Davy Crockett on
the Southwestern frontier.

104. Oehlschlaeger, Fritz. "Solomon Franklin Smith." Encyclopedia
      of American Humorists. Ed. Steven H. Gale. New York: Garland,
      1988, 405-08.

      Praises the quality of Smith's treatment of hoaxes, swindles,
odd or eccentric characters, and cases of mistaken identity. Like
other Southwest humorists, Smith uses the "frame story" to develop
various types of comic incongruity between the formal, literary
language of the frame and the vernacular language of the story;
between the situation at the time the yarn was told and the
situation described by the yarn itself; and between the realism of
the frame and the often fantastic quality of the tale itself. Like
other Southwest humorists, Smith's humor was of "a distinctively
masculine brand." Typical subjects of Smith's frontier humor
sketches were hunting, fighting, racing, electioneering, gambling,
drinking, and swindling. The legislature, the courtroom, the camp
meeting, the riverboat, and the stage also frequently provided the
subjects of frontier humor, as did portrayals of dandies, bumpkins,
and eccentrics of all kinds. For many years, Smith was a theatre
manager, and the three works which were most responsible for Smith's
contribution to the development of humor of the Old Southwest all
deal with the theatre: Theatrical Apprenticeship (1845), Theatrical
Journey-Work (1854), and Theatrical Management in the West and South
(1868).

Alexander Gallatin McNutt (1802-1848)

105. Cohen, Hennig, and William B. Dillingham. "Alexander G.
      McNutt." Humor of the Old Southwest. 2nd ed. Athens: Univ of
      Georgia Press, 1975, 78-90.

Portrays McNutt as a controversial figure in history. Some of
his contemporaries considered him to be intemperate, cowardly, and
even murderous, while others praised him as capable, moral, and
courageous. During his time he was well known as a witty story
teller but was largely unknown as a writer because he wrote his
sketches and stories anonymously. The pen name he used for
submitting manuscripts to The Spirit of the Times was "The Turkey
Runner." Probably, only William T. Porter, editor of the Times and
a few close friends knew that this was McNutt's pen name. McNutt
wrote about two backwoods frontiersmen named Jim and Chunkey. Jim
tells stories about killing deer or wrestling bears and especially
enjoys telling tales about his friend, Chunky. Chunky loved
talkin', singin', and whistlin', and when he was doing one of these
he got lost in his work. "Why, I have knoed him to whistle three
days and three nights on a stretch." Cohen and Dillingham feel that
McNutt developed exaggerated but convincing characters in the bold
masculine humorous tradition of the Old Southwest.

106. Craig, Raymond C. "Alexander Gallatin McNutt." Encyclopedia
      of American Humorists. Ed. Steven H. Gale. New York: Garland,
      1988, 308-09.

Presents McNutt as a humorist of the Old Southwest. Writing
under the name of "The Turkey Trotter," McNutt published a series of
eight humorous sketches in various issues of The Spirit of the
Times. McNutt's stories often concern two frontier characters, Jim
and Chunkey. These characters lived on his plantation, and are
among the most original and funniest rustic characters to emerge in
this genre of humor. Not only are they hunting and fishing pals,
but they are also frontiersmen of the "ring-tailed roarer" variety,
and their vernacular accounts are full of irrelevant ramblings,
exaggerations and homemade words. McNutt's sketches frequently
appear in anthologies of frontier humor as examples of the very best
of that particular genre.

107. Howell, Elmo. "Governor Alexander G. McNutt of Mississippi:
      Humorist of the Old Southwest." The Journal of Mississippi
      History, May 1973: 153-65.

Considers McNutt's sketches in the Spirit of the Times to have
been an important contribution to the humor of the Old Southwest.
They added interest and excitement to Old Southwestern literature
and recalled a spacious time when the South was still young and
teeming with "primordial life." The humorists who contributed to
Old Southwestern literature were not well-read scholars; rather they
were doctors, soldiers, journalists, and lawyers, who wrote their
stories down in their spare time. McNutt was trained as a lawyer
and was governor of Mississippi for two terms. He was also
something of an opportunist. McNutt may have been involved in the
murder of a Warren County farmer. On the farmer's death, the estate
fell into McNutt's possession, and seven months later he married the
farmer's widow. Henry S. Foote, McNutt's arch political enemy,

accused McNutt of being involved, and McNutt made no effort to reply to the accusation, nor did he deny Foote's charge that on an earlier occasion McNutt had been physically assaulted by another attorney in Natchez and had failed to retaliate in kind--a clear expectation in Southern culture at the time. McNutt's never fighting a duel was just one example of his ability to turn a personal weakness into an advantage by ignoring or by making fun of it.

108. Keller, Mark A. "Th' Guv'ner Wuz a Writer"--Alexander G. McNutt of Mississippi." Southern Studies 20.4 (Winter, 1981): 394-411.

Suggests that McNutt had the ability to make people angry. His verbal assaults were often answered by physical assaults. When he called a former president of the Union bank "king devil of the bank thieves," the accused banker accosted McNutt in Jackson, Mississippi, and hit him over the head several times with his walking cane. Another Jackson resident became so angry at McNutt that he cursed McNutt publicly and vowed to do so again whenever he got the chance. A tavern owner became so upset over McNutt's anti-credit banking policy that he forced McNutt to pay his hostelry bill in coins rather than in bills, causing McNutt great inconvenience and embarrassment. McNutt became something of a folk hero in Mississippi with many stories to illustrate both his wit and his cowardice. During the Senate race of 1846 a General Quitman was running against McNutt and challenged him to a public fight. McNutt responded that if this is the way political races were to be determined, he had a Durham Bull on his plantation which he would propose as the candidate for the Senate seat. One piece of legislation which McNutt was famous for was "McNutt's Gallon Law." This was designed to curb alcohol flow by eliminating over-the-counter liquor sales by the glass. McNutt was one of the eighteen U.S. Congressmen who were regular contributors to Porter's Spirit of the Times.

Ralph Waldo Emerson (1803-1882)

109. Loving, Jerome. "'A Well-Intended Halfness': Emerson's View of Leaves of Grass." Studies in American Humor 3.2 (October 1976): 61-67.

Maintains that Emerson's essay, "The Comic" has been largely overlooked by Emerson scholars because it does not appear in Emerson's collected works till 1875. Nevertheless, this is an important essay, because it presents Emerson's theory of humor. In "The Comic," Emerson observes that man is the only joker in nature, and he suggests that this is because only man can use Reason to be able to perceive the difference between "the Whole and the Part." Whenever one of these is missing, the result is "halfness," and "halfness" is what causes humor. Emerson's prime example of "halfness" is Shakespeare's Falstaff, because "the courtier gives himself unreservedly to his senses, cooly ignoring the Reason, whilst he invokes its name." For Emerson, Whitman at his worst became a mirror of Falstaff. As the poet of the Body and the Soul, he frequently gave himself wholehearted to his senses while falsely invoking the name of Reason. In 1855, Emerson wrote a letter to Whitman saying, "I greet you at the beginning of a great creer."

Whitman "emblazoned the praise of his 'benefactors' in gold on the
spine of the second edition of <u>Leaves of Grass</u> (1856)" thereby
appealing to his own Senses, rather than Reason, for Emerson had not
given him permission to make the letter public.

Jim Bridger (1804-1881)

110. Blair, Walter, and Hamlin Hill. "Jim Bridger and William
     Wright." <u>America's Humor: From Poor Richard to Doonesbury</u>. New
     York: Oxford University Press, 1978, 238-48.

     Indicates that Bridger (known as "Old Gabe") was a great story
teller but that his stories took a long time to get into print; they
were not published until 1860 or even later, and they were as much
the creation of other authors as of Bridger. In one story Jim was
chased by six indians to the rim of the Grand Canyon. He killed
five of them, but the sixth was the tallest and fiercest he had ever
seen. They battled back and forth at the edge of a deep gorge where
a fall to the bottom meant certain death. Sometimes Bridger was
winning, sometimes the indian. At this point in the story Bridger
would pause to catch his breath and his audience would quickly ask
him, "How did it end?" Bridger would take a long breath and reply,
"The Injun killed me." Thirty years later, William Wright continued
the Jim Bridger tradition of leg-pulling stories. Wright was a
reporter for the Missouri <u>Enterprise</u>, and he used the pen name "Dan
De Quille." De Quille's lies differed in one respect from Bridger's
lies--they were scientifically plausible. He wrote about such
things as refrigerated solar armor, a perpetual-motion machine, and
a silver-petrified man found in an abandoned mine between Esmeralda
and Owens river.

Nathaniel Hawthorne (1804-1864)

111. Bense, James. "Nathaniel Hawthorne's Intention in "Chiefly
     about War Matters." <u>American Literature</u> 61.2 (May 1989): 200-
     14.

     Points out the irony that this essay was written as a
censorship <u>hoax</u> but has been interpreted by many critics as an essay
demonstrating legitimate self censorship. In this essay Hawthorne
developed a satirical dialogue between his narrator and an imaginary
editor. Hawthorne was attempting to demonstrate that freedom of
speech is most important when it is being most severely tested--in
times of the passions of national turmoil, times when a survival
mentality somehow impinges on freedom of speech. The opposite
interpretations of this essay result both from the "ventroliquism"
of the dialogue and from the possibility of interpreting the essay's
footnotes as having been written by either the author or by an
editor. There are also textual disjunctions that can be interpreted
either as satire or as missing passages. The "editor's comments"
alluding to these missing passages have the effect of enhancing the
reader's desire to find the missing passages, but of course, none
has ever been found.

112. Vanderbilt, Kermit. "Hawthorne's Ironic Mode: with Side-Trips into Emerson." Thalia: Studies in Literary Humor. 4.1 (Spring/Summer 1981): 40-45.

Investigates the irony in Hawthorne's "The Maypole of Merry Mount," "Young Goodman Brown," and "The Minister's Black Veil," suggests that "Hawthorne relished irony in many guises," and proposes a number of ways that Hawthorne's irony can be effectively taught. Vanderbilt also suggests that many of the subtleties in Hawthorne's irony remain hidden until they are seen through the light of Emerson's writing: "Hawthorne's colonial America offers the tough-minded reader some deliciously morbid encounters and occasional anti-Puritan ironies, but a comic spirit hardly presides here. Or so it appears until we detour through the pages of Emerson's Nature, a different outlook on man in the new world, and then return to Hawthorne's action." "Emerson's epigrams... upended in Hawthorne's fiction awaken us to a mood of pervasive irony, created with a variety of techniques and suggestions. Hawthorne works much of the mischief through his playful narrative method."

William Gilmore Simms (1806-1870)

113. Guilds, John C. Ed. Long Years of Neglect: The Work and Reputation of William Gilmore Simms. Fayetteville: University of Arkansas Press, 1988, 241 pp.

Presents the observations of James Meriwether, Anne Blythe, Linda McDaniel, Nicholas Meriwether, James Kibler, David Moltke-Hansen, Mary Ann Wimsatt, Rayburn Moore, William Shillingsburg, John McCardell, and Louis Rubin on the writings of William Gilmore Simms. Meriwether, Blythe, McDaniel, and Meriwether write explications of various Simms pieces. Kibler, Moltke-Hansen, and Wimsatt view Simms' writings in terms of which genres are best and worst for Simms as a writer. Moore and Shillingsburg consider the social contexts of various Simms pieces. And McCardell and Rubin take the broadest perspective, placing Simms into the tradition of Southern authors offering their perspectives on American history. McCardell feels that critics should stop trying to judge Simms by twentieth-century political and literary standards; they should instead allow Simms his own time and place. Mary Ann Wimsatt agrees and points out that Simms' most effective humor used devices that were developed in the traditions of early American frontier humor. Simms was a master at such devices.

114. Meats, Stephen E. "Bald-Head Bill Bauldy: Simms' Unredeemed Captive." Studies in American Humor NS3.4 (1985): 321-29.

Indicates that between 1700 and 1900 one of the most important literary genres in America was the Indian captivity narrative. This genre was so popular, however, that a large number of writers began publishing fraudulent narratives, that weren't even well written. They were filled with obvious literary pretension, trite and clichéd use of language, very little vivid realistic detail, and many sentimental interjections. The stage was now set for an openly fictional, often tongue-in-cheek type of captivity narrative in particular, and for the development of Southwestern humor in general in the frontier and backwoods areas of the South and Southwest.

William Gilmore Simms was one of the authors who wrote in this new
tradition. His "'Bald-Head Bill Bauldy,' And How He Went Through
the Flurriday Campaign!" was subtitled, "A Legend of the Hunter's
Camp." Simms inverted the religious and heroic traditions of the
authentic captivity narratives by creating a fantastic and satiric
tall tale. The "hunter's camp" referred to in the subtitle alludes
to the establishment of ritual lying by professional hunters. In
the various hunters' camps, there was only one rule--All stories
must be lies. "Sticking too close to the truth makes the teller
liable to a severe penalty." Bill Bauldy, the cook of one such
camp, was never in any danger of receiving this penalty. He steals
some rum and cigars from the officers and goes off into the woods to
enjoy them, but he is captured by a single indian and taken to the
indian camp, where he becomes a slave. He escapes by riding on two
giant alligators which use their tails to keep him captive on their
backs, one after the other. He is tried for desertion when he
returns to camp but is found innocent because he is such a good
cook.

115. Wimsatt, Mary Ann. "Native Humor in Simms's Fiction and Drama."
     Studies in American Humor 3.3 (January 1977): 158-64.

        Considers Simms "the antebellum South's foremost man of
letters" but suggests that American readers agree with Lewis Gaylord
Clark that one might as well look for a smile in the jaws of an
alligator as for humor in Simms." Nevertheless, in his various
writings, Simms helped to develop three humorous traditions: The
trickster or confidence man, the frontiersman in the Davy Crockett
vein, and hunting yarns and tall tales. Simms' humor "shows his
responsiveness to a vital, vigorous mode of expression of oral and
printed derivation and his skill at using this material, itself
robust and rowdy, in books that are essentially formal, serious, and
genteel." Wimsatt presents material to prove that Clark was as
wrong about Simms's comic talents as he was right about alligators.

116. Wimsatt, Mary Ann. "Simms and Southwest Humor." Studies in
     American Humor 3.2 (October 1976): 118-27.

        Traces Simms's use of frontier-related humor from his early
Revolutionary War novels and Border Romances through later
miscellaneous pieces and Mountain fiction, pointing out where his
work seems merely analogous to southwest writing and where it
borrows directly from that genre. Wimsatt describes those aspects
of Simms's taste and temperament that connect him to the humorists.
She also discusses certain cultural experiences he shared with them,
suggests some relationships of his early comedy to the romance
tradition, and outlines the professional and personal experiences in
mid career that caused him to increase his use of frontier humor in
his writing. Wimsatt proposes that Simms began using frontier humor
early in his career, with the tall tales he stuck into his early
correspondence, and continued throughout his writing career. These
tall tales permeate his short novels As Good as a Comedy and Paddy
McGann, each of which leans heavily on frontier and folk materials.
Wimsatt suggests that frontier humor persists in Simms's character
types, his episodes, and his structural patterns. It is "something
which future laborers in the vast and varied Simms vineyard might do
very well to explore."

Henry William Herbert (1807-1858)

117. Sloane, David E. E. "Henry William Herbert." Encyclopedia of
     American Humorists. Ed. Steven H. Gale. New York: Garland,
     1988, 220-22.

     Summarizes the life of Herbert as a writer. Herbert
specialized in light humor that depicted scenes of northeastern
hunting life in the 1830s and 1840s. He wrote mainly under the pen
name of Frank Forester. His reputation as a sporting writer is more
significant than his work as an amusing depicter of the
peculiarities of hunters and the values of New Jersey and New York.
Herbert deserves modest recognition as a humorous sporting writer;
in fact, Herbert used a persona before such a practice became common
during the Civil War. Another technique which Herbert used was to
barely disguise the truth, and make humorous changes in portraits of
actual New Jersey and New York sporting figures and local characters
in his sketches. This made for amusing reading for Herbert's
contemporary readers because they could recognize the real people
that Herbert was basing his caricatures on. Herbert would
frequently refer to jokes and conversations, but he would omit them
from his writing because he considered them inappropriate to this
genre.

Joseph C. Neal (1807-1847)

118. Sloane, David E. E. "Joseph C. Neal." Dictionary of Literary
     Biography, Vol 11: American Humorists, 1800-1950. Ed. Stanley
     Trachtenberg. Detroit, MI: Gale, 1982, 344-49.

     Explains why Joseph Neal was popular with contemporaries but
was quickly forgotten after his death. "Given Neal's limited canon
and the unobtrusiveness of his brief life in Philadelphia as
newspaper editor and urban comedian, it is understandable how later
anthologists could so easily confuse his work with that of John
Neal, the Yankee humorist." Furthermore, Neal wrote many of his
pieces for the Philadelphia Pennsylvania anonymously. "Peter Brush,
the Great Used Up," the most famous of Neal's sketches, originally
appeared in the Gentlemen's Vade Mecum. Neal's importance in the
history of American humor is diminished by the slimness of his
contribution and his reticence to write personal journals or
letters. The "Peter Brush" sketch, along with "The Black Maria,"
"The Newsboy," and "Orson Dabbs," have a kind of Hogarthian realism,
but without more exposure for his type of Northern urban comedy,
Neal is likely to continue to be a modest and unrecognized figure in
the development of American humor.

Oliver Wendell Holmes (1809-1894)

119. Hart, James D. "Oliver Wendell Holmes." The Oxford Companion
     to American Literature. 4th edition. New York: Oxford Univ
     Press, 1965, 377-78.

     States that Holmes' collection of witty occasional Poems
appeared in 1836 and continues that "As a witty, urbane
conversationalist, he reigned supreme in Boston society and club

life, and became the unofficial poet laureate of all important
gatherings in the intellectual 'hub of the Universe.'" Holmes
attacked the religion of the founding fathers in such pieces as "The
Deacon's Masterpiece," and the more vituperative "The Moral Bully,"
"which satirizes the preacher's hypocritical virtues." Other
notable humorous Holmes pieces include "'Dorothy Q' (1871) a
sentimentally humorous piece on a family portrait," "'Contentment,'
a humorous poem on 'simple pleasures,' from the _Autocrat_," and "'The
Ballad of the Oysterman' (1830), a parody of romantic balladry."

120. Hoyt, Edwin P. The Improper Bostonian: Dr. Oliver Wendell
     Holmes. New York: William Morrow, 1979, 319 pp.

     Presents Oliver Wendell Holmes as "the improper Bostonian."
Holmes was a little deaf, so at formal dinners he talked more than
he should have, because he could not hear what was said to him. In
a chapter entitled "Mark Twain's Fateful Night at the Atlantic
Club," Hoyt tells of the tradition of The Atlantic Monthly to host
very formal and proper dinners to honor their famous authors. They
decided to honor Whittier with such a dinner on December 17, 1877,
and decided to have Mark Twain as the after-dinner speaker. Hoyt
compares Holmes style to that of Twain: "He [Twain] had studied the
art of after-dinner speaking so well that he was as good at it in
his way as Dr. Holmes was at making bright conversation." Twain
wanted to honor Whittier and Howells, but he also wanted to
recognize the other notables in the audience--Lowell, Emerson, and
Longfellow, so he told of a trip in California. He said he had
approached a lonely miner's cabin, said he was Mark Twain, and asked
for lodging. The miner denied him lodging because three tramps had
visited the miner the night before, had drunk his whiskey, eaten his
food, and cheated at cards. They identified themselves as Emerson,
Longfellow, and Holmes. Boston never forgave Twain for blaspheming
their deity. Twain and his family picked and went to Germany. They
did not return for a whole year. That's how bad it was that night
in Boston.

121. Leary, Lewis. "Oliver Wendell Holmes." The Comic Imagination
     in American Literature. Ed. Louis D. Rubin, Jr. New Brunswick,
     New Jersey: Rutgers Univ. Press, 1983, 113-26.

     Describes Holmes as "a pert, bubbling little man," who was
noted for his conversation and sparking wit. He was trained as a
physician and held the chair (he preferred to call it the "setee")
of anatomy at Harvard University. Many of Holmes' patients were
puzzled or annoyed at his constant humor. He would use such
inappropriate greetings as "the smallest of fevers are gratefully
accepted." Leary's article then goes on to exemplify and discuss
some of Holmes' light verse.

George Wilkins Kendall (1809-1867)

122. Cohen, Hennig, and William B. Dillingham, eds. "George Wilkins Kendall." Humor of the Old Southwest. 2nd ed. Athens: Univ. of Georgia Press, 1975, 91-95.

Indicates that on January 25, 1837, George Wilkins Kendall and Francis A. Lumsden bought out the New Orleans Picayune and decided to increase the readership by avoiding political controversy and by increasing the number of human interest and local color stories. Soon thereafter, however, the Picayune had become involved in politics by agitating against Mexico. When war broke out in May of 1846, Kendall immediately went as a reporter to Point Isabel, near the mouth of the Rio Grande, where General Zachary Taylor had his troops. Kendall's newspaper reports and military exploits made him the most famous newspaper correspondent in America at the time. Kendall was a witty and convivial newspaper reporter; even his account of the Santa Fe disaster had many light moments and so much prankishness that he wrote an apology in the preface. Much of his fame as a reporter was due to his ability to determine the flavor of a locale, his cleverness with graphic detail, his eye for the peculiar, and his sense of the ridiculous.

Abraham Lincoln (1809-1865)

123. Billington, Ray Allen. "Foreword." Abe Lincoln Laughing. Ed. Paul M. Zall. Berkeley: Univ of California Press, 1982, ix-xii.

Praises Zall as "a well-known student of English literature with a special interest in Anglo-American humor" and praises his anthology as "true, rich in humor, invaluable for its insights into the life of nineteenth-century America, and an uproarious delight to read. But it's also a work of impeccable scholarship, designed with one basic purpose: to separate the authentic from the apocryphal Lincoln stories." These stories "shed light on Lincoln as a warm, compassionate, witty, and earthy human being--a man who possessed that greatest of all virtues: the ability to laugh at himself."

124. Jennison, Keith W. The Humorous Mr. Lincoln. New York: Bonanza Books, 1965, 163 pp.

Feels that Abraham Lincoln was greatly influenced by his father, Tom Lincoln. Abe's father taught Abe how to work but could never teach him to love it. Abe said he would rather "read, tell stories, crack jokes, talk, laugh--anything but work." The only humor that existed in the wilderness was what people put there, and both Tom and Abe Lincoln did their best to provide humor in the form of their yarns and tall tales. Their motto was "the only way to fight a wilderness is to cultivate it," and they practiced this motto both physically and intellectually. Abe Lincoln's humor changed over his lifetime. "During the wilderness years he told jokes and stories without trying to prove anything at all," but after he became a lawyer, then a politician, and then the President, he found that humor was an effective tool to use in the courtroom and on the political trail. "As a politician he handled the weapon

of satire as a stiletto or a broadax as the occasion demanded."
During his presidency, he used humor often as an indirect way of
saying "no."   Lincoln effectively used humor as to manipulate
people's opinions without making them angry.

125. O'Gorman, Kathleen. "Review of <u>Abe Lincoln Laughing</u>."
      <u>Studies in American Humor</u>. New Series 3.4 (Winter 1984-85):
      351-53.

        Describes the variety and richness of the humor in Zall's
anthology as sometimes bawdy and slapstick, sometimes piercing and
black, and says that this humor helped our country through one of
the most difficult periods of its history. In the anthology,
Lincoln is presented as a masterful teller of earthy and urbane
stories. These stories helped Lincoln as a lawyer to establish a
rapport with judges and juries, and it sharpened his rhetorical
effectiveness when he shifted his energies to the political realm.
Furthermore, they "indicate the political and social sensibility
nineteenth-century American life as no mere chronicle could."
Zall's anthology details more than three hundred Lincoln stories
that date as far back as 1839. O'Gorman feels that Zall is thorough
in his research and scrupulous in his documentation, noting
different versions of many stories in the collection and citing the
sources of all of them.   Since many of the stories allude to
previous events or to previous tellings of the stories, Zall
arranges the stories in chronological order to preserve the impact
each story must have had on its original listeners.

126. Zall, Paul M. <u>Abe Lincoln Laughing: Humorous Anecdotes from
      Original Sources by and about Abraham Lincoln</u>. Berkeley: Univ.
      of California Press, 1982, xii + 193 pp.

        Explains the occasions on which Lincoln told his famous
anecdotes. When he practiced law, he employed them as tools of the
trade; and when he entered politics, these anecdotes became weapon
for satire and ridicule. In the early presidency, they provided an
indirect way of disagreeing with someone else's position, and later,
as the responsibilities of the office became intense, they provided
therapy to lessen the tensions in himself and those around him.
Lincoln habitually told stories that were probably already familiar
to those who heard them. It was because of this practice that his
name became a lodestone for the hundreds of old jokes that expanded
in time to become the mass of "Lincoln stories" now part of our
national heritage. Nevertheless, Zall's anthology includes "only
those sayings and stories having some semblance of authenticity
along with a mere sampling of apocryphal 'Lincoln stories' that have
been attached to his name because of his reputation as a funny
fellow."

Edgar Allan Poe (1809-1849)

127. Clendenning, John. "Anything Goes: Comic Aspects in 'The Cask
      of Amontillado." <u>American Humor</u>. Ed. O. M. Brack, Jr.
      Scottsdale, AZ: Arete, 1977, 13-26.

        Contends that Poe intended much of his writing to be both
comic and tragic. In the Preface to his <u>Tales of The Grotesque and</u>

Arabesque (1840), Poe was fascinated by the interrelationships between the crude and the fantastic, the comic and the serious. In Tales he juxtaposed "Morella" with "Lionizing," William Wilson" with "The Man That Was Used Up," with "The Fall of the House of Usher" and "The Duc De L'Omelette." The first story of each pair is arabesque (serious, gothic, psychological, featuring terror of the soul), and the second story is grotesque (comedic, satiric, featuring exaggerated ridicule). Poe sometimes combined and harmonized the arabesque with the grotesque, as in "A Cask of Amontillado," which uses irony to blend these two countervaling features. Montresor performs his ritualistic murder in a way that grotesquely mocks the Holy Mass. He wears a roquelaire, which is a knee-length cape that slips over his head and hangs over his shoulders, covering up both the front and the back. It is nearly indistinguishable from the chasuble, the vestment of the Mass. The death theme is reinforced by the fact that the Holy Mass is the symbolic reenactment of the cruxifixion of Christ. The murder takes place in the churchly trappings in the catacombs, a burial place of early Christians who had gone underground to escape persecution from the Roman Emperors. The rituals surrounding the murder started during Mardi Gras and ended on the first day of Lent. The ringing of the bell, and the words are reminiscent of the ceremony of sacrament, culminating in the imperative, "Drink!"

128. Lacayo-Salas, Demarys. "The Prevailing Humor in Edgar Allan Poe's 'The Facts in the Case of M. Valdemar.'" WHIMSY 6 (April 1, 1988): 19-21.

Agrees with critic G. R. Thompson that almost all of Poe's work is controlled by prevailing irony. Nevertheless, there are few studies of Poe's humor, and the existing ones mostly focus on the obviously comic or satiric tales. "The Facts in the Case of M. Valdemar has been basically ignored by critics mainly because of its ending, which has caused this tale to have been called "Poe's most horrific story." The ending is certainly powerful, but it is not horrific if it is viewed as humor. Poe loved to practice literary hoaxes, not merely of false events but of the reality of false literary intentions and circumstances as well. Lacayo-Sales feels that the amusement of a literary hoaxer such as Poe is rather private, and is intended for a rather limited circle. The narrator of the story says that he has reached a point of his narrative at which every reader will be startled into absolute disbelief, and then he goes on to give a gross and gruesomely exaggerated account of the decaying-but-alive body of M. Valdemar. This exaggeration makes the horrible ridiculous, and turns terror into smiles. After all, the gruesomeness of the story is not dwelt on in some cruel way, but is rather saved and presented in the last scene--briefly and rapidly and with great economy of words.

129. Lewis, Paul. "Poe's Humor: A Psychological Analysis." WHIMSY 6 (April 1, 1988): 130-31.

Suggests that in most of Poe's Gothic and mock-Gothic work, the collapse of humor is visceral and direct, and is essential to the effective experiences of both readers and characters. Again and again when humor fails the reader is left with images of fear: the raven's shadow, the howling cat, the putrescent corpse, or the fallen house. Humor yields to terror in such otherwise diverse works as "The Premature Burial," "Hop-Frog," "The Black Cat," "Ligeia," "Facts in the Case of M. Valdemar," and Pym. It may well be that the perception of witty but obscure allusions and subtle puns undermines a unified sense of deepening terror. And this is why the pattern of collapsing humor at the surface of these narratives supports the typical reader's response to Poe as a writer of tales of deepening terror.

130. Nilsen, Don L. F. "Parodies of Poe: A Study in the Nature of Grounding." Massachusetts English Teacher, May 1989: 4-6.

Discusses the features of Poe's poetry which make it such an excellent target for parody, especially "Bells," "Annabel Lee," and "The Raven." Nilsen suggests that ironically "The Raven" may have been itself a parody or, even worse, possibly an example of blatant plagiarism. Before Poe wrote "The Raven," Thomas Holly Chivers had written a poem entitled "Isadore." The poem scanned and rhymed the same as "The Raven." It employed very similar imagery and metaphors. Both poems were dark--even macabre, and both had a dialogue between a man and a transformed spectre. Later, Holly Chivers wrote a parody of Poe's "The Raven," entitled "Humpty-Dumpty: A La Poe," which began as follows: "As an egg, when broken, never / Can be mended but must ever / Be the same crushed egg forever...." Chiver's parody is more than a parody; it is an accusation. Chivers felt that Poe had stolen his poem. Ironically, Poe went on to become a major author, while Chivers' fame relates almost entirely to his parody of Poe, a parody which is actually much darker than it appears to be on the surface.

131. Pierstorff, Don K. "Poe as Satirist: An Apology." Studies in Contemporary Satire, 10 (1983): 32-34.

Explains that the principal reason that much of the eighteenth century was rich in satire is that it also adhered to a ludicrously rigid social and moral code. Men and women knew when and to what extent they were deviating from that code. That is why the so-called Age of Satire is also called the Age of Exuberance; one is not possible without the other. You do not look for satire unless you suspect it exists, which is why "we have more eighteenth century satire now than readers had in the eighteenth century." Poe was born close enough to the eighteenth century for its "satiric lance" to have had the glancing effect that it had. Therefore, his "The Philosophy of Composition" can be viewed not only as poetry or methodology but also as satire. There are many statements in this piece that are puzzling if it is read as poetry or as methodology. Once we begin to see what Poe was masking, once the figurative reading that Poe intended for his "Philosophy of Composition" is disregarded, the sentences beg for a satiric interpretation. Furthermore, Poe provides some overt clues that the piece was written as satire. For example, Poe said that he had thought of using a parrot in "The Raven," but was prevented from doing so because of the poem's title.

132. Winder, Barbara D. "Two Poe Stories: The Presentation of Taboo Themes through Humorous Reversals" Thalia: Studies in Literary Humor. 1.2 (Fall 1978): 29-33.

Compares Poe's "The System of Dr. Tarr and Professor Fether" with "A Predicament" and states that these are significant as literary experiences, especially as examples of a humorous treatment of a special theme, whereby these particular forms engage the reader's fantasy, and at the same time allows the reader to recognize the themes of the stories. Reversal predominates in the stories, both in their presentation as parody and in the changeover in the characters' behavior to unconventional rather than expected roles. Winder describes the reversal in tone in Tarr and Fether, as the narrator approaches the mental hospital which he has proposed to visit. He describes the decaying old mansion in language similar to that in Gothic novels. The subsequent humorous handling of the tale, however, removes it from the pure Gothic tradition. In this same piece there is a tendency for the reader to be afraid; however, Winder feels that the reversal of patient and staff, the comic antics of the inmates, and the naive responses of the narrator, offset any tone that would function to create horror.

William T. Porter (1809-1858)

133. Dasher, Thomas E. "William T. Porter." Antebellum Writers in New York and the South. Ed. Joel Myerson. Detroit, MI: Gale, 1979, 298-300.

Indicates that two printers, James Howe and William Porter, first began printing Spirit of the Times on December 10, 1831. The Spirit soon began emphasizing realistic, humorous sketches written by amateur authors who resided mainly in the American South and Southwest. Porter's first anthology, The Big Bear of Arkansas, and Other Sketches contained only sketches which had previously appeared in the Spirit. It was published in 1845, and contained twenty-one sketches, one of which had originally appeared as early as 1832. In his "Preface," Porter focused on the "new vein of literature" which was appearing in America, a vein that was inexhaustible in its source. His second anthology was entitled A Quarter Race in Kentucky, and Other Sketches (1846). Both in the Spirit and in his anthologies, Porter championed that distinct genre of American literature that was developing at the time. This second volume illustrates that the humorous and realistic literature of America was not confined to only one area of the country. While The Big Bear had concentrated on humor of America's South and Southwest, A Quarter Race had sketches illustrating scenes, characters, and incidents throughout "The Universal Yankee Nation."

134. Yates, Norris W. William T. Porter and the "Spirit of the Times": A Study of the BIG BEAR School of Humor. Baton Rouge: Louisiana State Univ. Press, 1957, xii + 213 pp.

Attempts to determine "the part played by the 'Tall Son of York,' as Porter came to be called, and by the Spirit in promoting the regional writing of the Old Southwest." Chapters include "Porter, the Man, and His Magazine," "The Sporting Editor as Critic," "The Spirit and Its Writers," "Planters and Poor Whites,"

"Jugs, Jokers, Fights, and Frolics," "Tall Tales in the _Spirit_," and
"Disintegration."   Porter edited New York's _Spirit of the Times_,
which had the subtitle _A Chronicle of the Turf, Agriculture, Field
Sports, Literature and the Stage_. From this list, Yates' chooses to
concentrate on "literature."

John Brougham (1810-1880)

135. Armitage, Shelley. "John Brougham." <u>Dictionary of Literary Biography: Vol 11: American Humorists, 1800-1950</u>. Ed. Stanley Trachtenberg. Detroit, Michigan: Gale, 1982, 56-59.

Presents Brougham as an American actor and dramatist who brought a copious number of farces, burlesques, curtain pieces, adaptations of novels, and stories to the stage. Brougham is primarily known as a humorous playwright whose keen sense of audience allowed him to lampoon a wide array of social types and mores prevalent at the time. During Brougham's time, there were many dramas sentimentalizing the "noble savage" so Brougham wrote <u>Po-ca-hon-tas</u> to satirize the Pocahontas legend and the romantic Indian theme that was then so prevelant in American drama. This burlesque was so successful that David Hawes claimed it was largely responsible for the waning of the genre. In this piece, Brougham spoofed the sameness of plot, exaggeration of motive, and unrealistic treatment American Indian. Clues to the parodic nature of Brougham's writing include digressions of plot, minor travesties, puns, and double entendres. Many of Brougham's comic pieces are filled with allusions to nineteenth century events, ideas, and people, and his Armitage feels that his diction falls short of the standards of the best dramatic literature, because, in order to meet deadlines of stage production, he composed much of his work in haste.

Joseph M. Field (1810-1856)

136. Cohen, Hennig, and William B. Dillingham. "Joseph M. Field." <u>Humor of the Old Southwest</u>. 2nd ed. Athens: Univ. of Georgia Press, 1974. 96-107.

Considers Field to have been a successful actor, playwright, and journalist, who divided his talents between the theatre and newspaper writing in the New Orleans area. In 1832 he traveled the Southwestern circuit under the management of Sol Smith, playing in Cincinnati, St. Louis, Mobile, Montgomery, and other cities. Although he enjoyed playing Shakespearean roles and considered himself a tragedian, he found out that he was best at eccentric comedy. He married Eliza Riddle, Sol Smith's leading lady, and together they played a number of Southwestern theatres. Field wrote a number of humorous sketches and poetry about New Orleans life and published much of his work in the <u>Picayune</u>. In 1844, Field was involved in founding and editing the St. Louis <u>Reveille</u>, a newspaper noted for its sprightliness and originality. Field wrote <u>Such As It Is</u>, a social satire, and <u>Family Ties</u>, a comedy which won a $500 prize. His writings for the <u>Reveille</u> were collected in <u>The Drama in Pokerville, The Bench and Bar of Jurytown, and Other Stories</u>. Field also contributed to the Mike Fink legend and collected some of his sketches into the melodramatic and sentimental novel, <u>Mike Fink, the Last of the Boatmen</u>, which was printed serially in the <u>Reveille</u> in June of 1847.

137. Oehlschlaeger, Fritz. "Joseph M. Field." <u>Encyclopedia of</u>
     <u>American Humorists</u>. Ed. Steven H. Gale. New York: Garland,
     1988, 154-58.

     Considers Field to be typical of the nonprofessional authors
who shaped the humor of the Old Southwest. Field was an actor, a
theater manager, a playwright, a journalist, and an editor. Field's
significance to American humor lies in three areas: his editorship
of the <u>St. Louis Reveille</u>, his contribution to the Mike Fink legend,
and his authorship of <u>The Drama in Pokerville</u>. Field edited the
<u>Reveille</u> from 1844 until 1850, and during his editorship the
magazine specialized in humorous sketches of frontier life, and
these issues comprise an important part of the body of work known as
the humor of the Old Southwest. Field's "Mike Fink: 'The Last of
the Boatmen,'" published in the <u>Reveille</u> in 1847, was a melodramatic
novel filled with "typical claptrap"--wild coincidences, disguises,
sentimental characters, and maudlin observations. All of Field's
humor was characteristic of humor of the Old Southwest. There were
tall tales, stories of hoaxes and swindles, sketches of eccentric
characters, and satiric views of the life of the theater, courtroom,
and riverboat.

Charles Fenton Mercer Noland (c1810-1858)

138. Cohen, Hennig, and William B. Dillingham, eds. "Charles F.
     M. Noland." <u>Humor of the Old Southwest</u>. 2nd ed. Athens: Univ.
     of Georgia Press, 1975, 108-20.

     Contends that Noland was one of the earliest and most prolific
writers for the <u>Spirit of the Times</u>, contributing over 200
Southwestern sketches. In 1929 Noland was active in politics and
was writing for the Little Rock <u>Arkansas Advocate</u>. He attacked
Governor John Pope in one newspaper article so violently that the
governor's nephew responded by publicly insulting Noland. Noland of
course had to challenge the nephew to a duel and ended by killing
him. As Noland's life progressed, he added more dialect, sketched
his characters more carefully, and wrote more and more picturesque
detail, local color, and tongue-in-cheek exaggeration.   He
published the first of the forty-five Pete Whetstone letters early
in 1837.   They were carelessly composed and contained much
repetition, but Pete Whetstone was a fresh creation, a Southwestern
character who spoke his own language without benefit of a gentleman
standing alongside for contrast. The name "Pete Whetstone" was the
actual name of a commercial hunter in Arkansas who became something
of a legend in Texas, but the rest of the detail of the sketches was
supplied by Noland.

139. Fienberg, Lorne. "C. F. M. Noland." <u>Dictionary of Literary</u>
     <u>Biography, Vol 11: American Humorists, 1800-1950</u>. Ed. Stanley
     Trachtenberg. Detroit, Michigan: Gale, 1982, 360-63.

     Laments the fact that Noland's "entire body of work consists
of a series of 250 brief sporting epistles and humorous sketches
which appeared under three pseudonyms in William T. Porter's New
York <u>Spirit of the Times</u>." Feinberg also laments the fact that
Noland never attached his name to his works, and that his work never

appeared in book form until almost 100 years after his death. Noland was "not only the first contributor of original humorous sketches in the _Spirit of the Times_," but he was also "for several decades the most prolific and most flatteringly imitated correspondent to that journal." Noland was a pioneer not only in the realistic depiction of local color and in the accurate depiction of frontier dialect but also in the use of the framing device that was later to become an important feature of American frontier humor.

140. Feinberg, Lorne. "Colonel Noland of the _Spirit_: The Voices of a Gentleman in Southwest Humor." _American Literature_ 53.2 (May 1981): 232-45.

Considers Colonel Noland to have been not only the first of the "gentleman correspondents" who wrote for the _Spirit_ but also the most prolific such writer, contributing more than 250 sketches under such pseudonyms as "N. of Arkansas," "Pete Whetstone," and "Jim Cole." But Noland's contribution to the _Spirit_ was even greater than this, for his writing also was responsible for numerous imitations, parodies and flattering responses. Noland was a respected Southern gentleman who influenced the _Spirit_'s elitism. The _Spirit_ was always more expensive than its competitors, and it in fact was meant to imitate the manner, diction, and cultivation of the English gentlemen's magazines of the period such as _Bell's Life in London_, _Punch_, and _Blackwood's_. Before 1837 the _Spirit_ spent much of its space on sporting pastimes, such as turf racing; however, the economic depression which began in 1837 forced Porter and the _Spirit_ to broaden its readership and to concentrate on fictional humorous writing from the frontier Southwest. It was at this time that the influence of Noland and other like-minded writers greatly increased.

141. Milner, Joseph O. "Charles Fenton Mercer Noland." _Encyclopedia of American Humorists_. Ed. Steven H. Gale. New York: Garland, 1988, 337-40.

Describes the enigmatic Noland as a Virginia gentleman and friend of president on the one hand but a teller of tall tales and a legendary desperado of the Old Southwest on the other hand. He published frequently in the _Spirit of the Times_, and William T. Porter, the editor called him "our favorite correspondent," "a 'household word,'" and the "most popular correspondent of the _Spirit of the Times_." Noland also published humorous pieces in England's _London Sporting Magazine_, and he was even described as "the only American writer who figures to manifest advantage in the English Sporting Magazines." Noland has also been included in a number of humor collections. Pete Whetstone was his main protagonist, and Whetstone's robust frontier life as it related to the raucous folk of the new settlement was full of fun and frontier wisdom. For a long time Noland was the best-known contributor to the _Spirit of the Times_, and his work "provides a foretaste of Twain and Faulkner."

Ann Sophia Stephens (1810-1886)

142. Hart, James D. "Ann Sophia Stephens." *The Oxford Companion to American Literature*. 4th edition. New York: Oxford Univ. Press, 1965, 803.

   Indicates that Stephens' *High Life in New York* (1843), was "written under the pseudonym of Jonathan Slick," and that it is an example of Down East humor.

143. Walker, Nancy, and Zita Dresner. "Ann Stephens." *Redressing the Balance: American Women's Literary Humor from Colonial Times to the 1980s*. Jackson: University Press of Mississippi, 1988, 51-61.

   Describes Stephens as a prolific contributer to *Peterson's*. In fact Stephens wrote more than twenty-five domestic sentimental novels that were originally published in serial form in that magazine. Parton's *High Life in New York by Jonathan, Slick, Esq.* was published in 1843, and autobiographically told of Stephens' transition from rural life to urban life. Walker and Dresner consider this to be Stephens' only humorous novel. But it is important, since it carries on the tradition of Jonathan originally established in Royall Tyler's play, *The Contrast* (1787) and continued by Seba Smith in the Jack Downing letters. Like Smith, Stephens adopted the letter format to develop an uneducated but sensible crackerbarrel philosopher writing to the folks back home about the strange customs of city dwellers. The humor of *High Life* comes from the contrast between Jonathan's perceptions of reality and what the reader knows to be actual reality; nevertheless, Jonathan is not the only butt of the joke, since Stephens also uses his voice to satirize the pretenses and shallowness of urban high society.

Sara Willis Parton (1811-1872)

144. Walker, Nancy, and Zita Dresner. "Fanny Fern." *Redressing the Balance: American Women's Literary Humor from Colonial Times to the 1980s*. Jackson: University Press of Mississippi, 1988, 46-50.

   States that Parton was enormously popular during the 1850s with her "Fern Leaves" column that appeared in *The Boston True Flag* and *The New York Ledger*. Beginning in 1851, Parton wrote this column for more than twenty years, and she commented frequently on literature, manners, and the sexes. Her collected volume was named *Fern Leaves from Fanny's Port-Folio*, and was published in 1853. Sometimes Parton wrote monologues, at other times conversations, and her tone, which varied according to the topic being discussed ranged from mildly amused to sharply satiric.

Harriet Beecher Stowe (1811-1896)

145. Blair, Walter, and Raven I. McDavid, Jr., eds. "Harriet
     Beecher Stowe." The Mirth of a Nation: America's Great Dialect
     Humor. Minneapolis: Univ. of Minnesota Press, 1983, 169-80.
     Establishes Stowe as a "leader in the local color movement" as
the result of The Minister's Wooing (1859), The Pearl of Orr's
Island (1862), Oldtown Folks (1869), Oldtown Fireside Stories
(1872), and Poganuc People (1878). James Russell Lowell agreed with
Blair and McDavid in this assessment. Because Stowe's humor in
these books is based on reminiscences of earlier times, it tends to
be very positive and uncritical in tone. This may have decreased
the "historical accuracy" of her work, but it also helped create
"genial comedy." Sam Lawson is Stowe's protagonist. He is similar
to Irving's Ichabod Crane--"a tall, shambling, loose-jointed man,
with a long, thin visage, prominent watery blue eyes..., a man who
wouldn't be hurried, and won't work, and will take his ease in his
own way."

146. Walker, Nancy, and Zita Dresner. "Harriet Beecher Stowe."
     Redressing the Balance: American Women's Literary Humor from
     Colonial Times to the 1980s. Jackson: University Press of
     Mississippi, 1988, 86-97.

     Recounts an alledged meeting between Harriet Beecher Stowe and
Abraham Lincoln after Uncle Tom's Cabin had set sales record in the
United States. Lincoln is said to have referred to Stowe as "the
little lady who made this great big war." Stowe had a keen eye for
detail and a keen ear for dialect, and thus her astute observations
made her anti-slavery novels compelling and also contributed to the
appeal of her New England narratives in which she writes about her
protagonist, Sam Lawson, as the stereotypical lazy-but-kind story
teller. The stereotype is promoted further by Sam's nagging wife,
who reminds the reader of the nagging Dame Van Winkle in Washington
Irving's novel. The tone of most of Stowe's writing is droll. The
humor is indirect and understated, yet the comments on women's
domestic lives and their relationships with men are sometimes sharp
and incisive.

Sara Payson Willis (1811-1872)

147. Hart, James D. ed. "Sara Payson Willis." Oxford Companion to
     American Literature. Fourth Edition. NY: Oxford Univ. Press,
     1965, 930-31.

     Indicates that Willis wrote under the pseudonym of "Fanny
Fern." Willis' first book, Fern Leaves from Fanny's Portfolio, and
the several books which followed were popular because of their
"sharp, playful sketches" and because of Stowe's "style of feminine
wit plus blood-curdling melodrama and touchingly tender tales."
Willis was so infuriated at the actions of her playboy brother that
she wrote a scurilous fictional satire entitled Ruth Hall (1855).

Charles Napoleon Bonaparte Evans (1812-1883)

148. Bickley, R. Bruce, Jr. "From North Carolina to Nova Scotia:
     On the Bibliographical Trail of the Fool-Killer." _Southern_
     Folklore Quarterly 45 (1981): 163-71.

Traces major American and Canadian allusions to Jesse Holmes,
the fool-killer from his inception in the North Carolina _Chronicle_
in 1841 to a _Cosmopolitan_ article in 1971. Jesse Holmes carried
with him a club, which he used to knock the brains out of
ignoramuses, opportunists, hypocrites, and other fools. This club
was not a weapon to be used for self-protection or combat but was
instead used to thrash some sense into people who had misguided
notions, crassness, or pretense. Jesse Holmes is said to be
equivalent to Paul Bunyan, Pecos Bill, Mike Fink, and John Henry,
and his club is said to be equivalent to David's sling.

149. Parramore, Thomas C. "Charles Napoleon Bonaparte Evans."
     Encyclopedia of American Humorists. Ed. Steven H. Gale. New
     York: Garland, 1988, 145-46.

Characterizes Evans' protagonist, Jesse Holmes as "a
pugnacious little character in a long-tailed coat and floppy hat."
Jesse Holmes carried a club with which he would beat up "cheats,
cowards, faithless lovers, overbearing parents, heavy drinkers,
brutal slave-patrollers, and rascally public officials." Evans was
very staunch and unyielding in his attitudes, but his fame rises not
from this, but rather from "his rollicking good humor." Evans was
a North Carolinian, and his character, Jesse Holmes, is in the
tradition of two other North Carolina protagonists--Hamilton C.
Jones' "Cousin Sally Dillard," and Johnson Jones Hooper's "Simon
Suggs." However, Jesse Holmes was more physical in his awarding of
punishments than were the protagonists of the other North
Carolinians. Jesse Holmes was called "The Fool Killer," and is the
inspiration of a play entitled "The Fool Killer" written by William
Sydney Porter (O. Henry). "The Fool Killer" and his one-man-
vigilante mentality, as he carried his club and took justice into
his own hands and dealt with "scoundrels and scapegraces," was very
popular in the middle of the nineteenth century when people
preferred "frontier directness" over institutionalized impersonality
in the dispensing of punishments.

William Tappan Thompson (1812-1882)

150. Blair, Walter, and Raven I. McDavid, Jr. eds. "William
     Tappan Thompson." _The Mirth of a Nation: America's Great_
     Dialect Humor. Minneapolis: Univ. of Minnesota Press, 1983,
     90-98.

Considers some of Thompson's narratives to be humorous
masterpieces. Thompson used humor as a way of popularizing the
Madison, Georgia, _Southern Miscellany_, a newspaper he edited. His
most popular character was Major Jones of Pineville, Georgia. Major
Jones ran a small Georgia plantation with little education but with
interest and skill in letter writing and story telling. Jones was

a pious major in the militia who was a doting family man and keen-eyed observer who liked to use salty dialect in his recounting of his adventures. Blair and McDavid consider "A Coon Hunt in a Fency Country" to be Thompson's most amusing piece. The narrator is not Major Jones but has Major Jones' tendency to moralize and to use amusing vernacular. Mark Twain very much liked Thompson's sketches and imitated them in his own writing.

151. Cohen, Hennig, and William B. Dillingham, eds. "William Tappan Thompson." _Humor of the Old Southwest_. 2nd edition. Athens: Univ. of Georgia Press, 1964, 121-41.

Feels that much of the humor of William Tappan Thompson is the result of cacography--incongruous spellings, incongruous grammar, and incongruous situations. There is an important element of Down East humor in Thompson's works. His protagonist, Major Jones, was strongly influenced by Royall Tyler's Jonathan and Seba Smith's Major Jack Downing. Cohen and Dillingham contrast Thompson's Major Jones with such ring-tailed roarers as Thorpe's Jim Doggett, and McNutt's Jim and Chunkey on the one hand and with such tricksters and con men as Harris' Sut Lovingood, Hooper's Simon Suggs, and Warren's Billy Fishback on the other hand. They also contrast Major Jones with the poor whites so common in the Southwestern sketches. Major Jones is a teetotaler, a devoted family man, and a loyal Whig. Cohen and Dillingham feel, in fact, that his respectability makes him "much less interesting than many other figures from Southwestern humor." They further point out, however, that Thompson's ability to develop humorous situations makes him well worth reading.

152. Lilly, Paul R., Jr. "William Tappan Thompson." _Dictionary of Literary Biography: Vol 11: American Humorists, 1800-1950_. Detroit, Michigan: Gale, 1982, 485-90.

Describes Thompson's protagonist, Major Joseph Jones, as "a whimsical, vernacular-speaking, upper-middle class planter from Pineville, Georgia, who is in turn a buffoon and a wise man." Jones is so much a Whig that he names his first son Henry Clay. Thomson was greatly influenced by Augustus Baldwin Longstreet and even studied law in Longstreet's law office. He was an enthusiastic supporter of Longstreet's writing style and political views. Thompson was also greatly influenced by Seba Smith, and in fact, in the 1844 edition of _Major Jones's Courtship_, the twelve illustrations by F. O. C. Darley portray Major Jones in top hat, cravat, waistcoat, and tails, all reminiscent of the portrayal of Seba Smith's Jack Downing. Major Jones' speech was also like Jack Downing's, exhibiting "homespun wit and semiliterate, picturesque speech." Lilly quotes Jay Hubbell as having said that Thompson's women characters are "better drawn than those in most books by Southern humorists." Lilly also quotes another critic, this time Hamlin Hill, who says, "There are practical jokes and good-nature high-jinks in the Major's Pineville--but not an eye-gouging in his county." Lilly editorializes that "Pineville seems the less for that."

153. Shippey, Herbert P. "William Tappan Thompson." <u>Antebellum</u>
      <u>Writers in New York and the South</u>. Ed. Joel Myerson. Detroit,
      MI: Gale, 1979, 332-35.

      Attributes Thompson's interest in humor partially to the fact
      that he studied law under Augustus Baldwin Longstreet. Although
      Thompson had been born in Ohio, he lived most of his adult life and
      became a famous humorist and journalist in Georgia. Thompson's <u>Major</u>
      <u>Jones's Courtship</u> was one of the most popular humorous books
      published in America during the nineteenth century.   This book
      became famous throughout the country. The book contains a series of
      gossipy letters to the editor of the <u>Miscellany</u> by Major Joseph
      Jones of Pineville Georgia. Thompson has the Major use plainspoken,
      ungrammatical language in developing his commonsense views about
      coon hunting, the militia muster, school commencements, parlor
      games, proposing, and the reading tastes of middle-class Americans.
      Thompson's <u>Chronicles of Pineville</u> contrasts formal narration with
      humorous dialogue to present comical situations. Thompson wanted to
      record the characters of the Georgia backwoods before education had
      polished away their peculiar traits.

154. Shippey, Herbert P. "William Tappan Thompson as Playwright."
      <u>Gyascutus: Studies in Antebellum Southern Humorous and</u>
      <u>Sporting Writing</u>. Ed. James L. W. West III. Atlantic
      Highlands, NJ: Humanities Press, 1978, 51-80.

      Reports that although Thompson is presently remembered
      basically as a writer of dialect letters, he was also during his
      time an important playwright. He wrote three plays, only one of
      which has survived to the twentieth century--<u>Major Jones' Courtship:</u>
      <u>or Adventures of a Christmas Eve</u>. This play was probably the first
      sympathetic treatment of Georgia backwoods dialect and backwoods
      attitudes in American drama.   This farce was based on the book by
      the same name and was written to entertain through its humorous
      situations and colorful speech. Shippey says that this may be the
      only play written and performed before the Civil War which depicted
      the rural middle-class life and language in Georgia.

155. Simms, L. Moody, Jr. "William Tappan Thompson." <u>Encyclopedia</u>
      <u>of American Humorists</u>. Ed. Steven H. Gale. New York: Garland,
      1988, 434-36.

      Says that Thompson makes Major Jones a vessel for Whig
      propaganda, as he satirizes such subjects as women's fashions, the
      features and clothing of ladies' men, and heavy drinking. <u>Major</u>
      <u>Jones's Courtship</u> also satirizes the rituals of flirting, proposing,
      and marrying. Longstreet and Thompson were unique as Southwestern
      humorists in dealing with tender domestic scenes, and of the two,
      Thompson's style is much less coarse or brutal. Major Jones is a
      crackerbarrel philosopher who "emphasized the virtues of family
      ties, respect for women [as long as they acted like women], and
      community stability."   The first set of letters were the most
      popular, and his later letters became somewhat didactic.

Matthew Franklin Whittier (1812-1883)

156. Royot, Daniel G. "Matthew Franklin Whittier." Encyclopedia of American Humorists. Ed. Steven H. Gale. New York: Garland, 1988, 482-84.

Contrasts Matthew Whittier's writing style, which "combines the exuberance of frontier humor with deadpan sarcasm," with the writing style of his brother, John Greenleaf Whittier, which explored "holiness and spiritual truth." Ethan Spike, Matthew Whittier's protagonist, is a "Yankee bumpkin" who, during his picaresque adventures, is tarred and feathered, loses his scalp, a toe, and an ear and has a ring placed in his nose, and is almost lynched by a mob in Virginia. His appearance becomes so bizarre that he is offered a dollar to become a part of Barnum's museum in New York. Although he is fully aware of his various failings, Ethan Spike remains totally and constantly optimistic. He is a free spirit immersed in "hilarious nihilism." He is boastful and cynical and reminiscent of the Southern ringtailed roarer. He loves fighting, gambling, and women, though he is a total failure at dealing with all three. Royot considers Spike's "uninhibited virulence and racy comments on antebellum America" to be "a significant landmark in the history of American humor."

Henry Ward Beecher (1813-1887)

157. Randel, William Peirce. "The Humor of Henry Ward Beecher." Studies in American Humor. 3.3 (January 1977): 166-73.

Portrays Beecher as something of a preacher-clown. Both admirers and critics note that Beecher would frequently introduce amusing anecdotes and sly quips into his sermons. Beecher had a free-wheeling style that allowed him to electrify and sway his audiences. He could move people to tears or to laughter, and Lewis Brastow condemned him for his sudden shifts in mood. After describing human miseries with moving pathos, so that all readers were melted to tears. At this point would come those jests and witticisms that were almost never lacking in his preaching. Brastow lamented the fact that "this irrepressible humor, this lack of reverence in the treatment of sacred things" was what brought so many people to Beecher's Plymouth Church. Even Eunice, his wife, was not amused by what she called his "pulpit horseplay" and "crude, sometimes almost vulgar, humor." Ironically, Beecher had developed his facility at "horseplay" as a boy in reaction to "the stern and uncompromising Calvinism of his father." Although many critics wrote of Beecher's vulgar humor, Randel himself finds little evidence of it. The most offensive humor Randel finds was in a speech Beecher delivered in Liverpool, where he compared a particularly difficult chore to "driving a team of runaway horses and making love to a lady at the same time."

John S. Robb (Solitaire) (c1813-1856)

158. Blair, Walter, and Raven I. McDavid, Jr. eds. "John S.
      Robb." The Mirth of a Nation: America's Great Dialect Humor.
      Minneapolis: Univ. of Minnesota Press, 1983, 83-89.

      Indicates that Robb wrote a very popular story entitled
"Nettle Bottom Ball" about a respectable woman who is in a loft
strapping on a cushion where a bustle is customarily worn when she
slips from the loft into a crowd of people "without a thing on earth
on her but one of those stearn cushions." She dropped right through
the floor and ended up sitting in a pan of mush. Blair points out
that this story is reminiscent of a similar story by Madison Tensas.
Robb also wrote "The Standing Candidate," a comic monologue about an
old Missouri character named Sugar. Robb worked on The St. Louis
Reveille, a newspaper famous for its humorous sketches, and in 1846
a number of his sketches were collected in Streaks from Squatter
Life, and Far-West Scenes.

159. Cohen, Hennig, and William B. Dillingham. "John S. Robb."
      Humor of the Old Southwest. 2nd edition. Athens: Univ. of
      Georgia Press, 1964, 142-155.

      Indicates that Robb began writing for the St. Louis Reveille
in 1844 and moved into the editorial office in 1846. John Robb,
Joseph Field, and Sol Smith worked together to make the Reveille
into one of America's leading humor journals. Although Robb's humor
was less creative than that of Longstreet or Harris, he did a good
job of developing the "perennial humor of innocence." His Streaks
of Squatter Life, and Far-West Scenes is uneven in quality, varying
from its "dull opening narrative...to lively accounts of frontier
drinking, courting, hunting, and politicking."

160. Oehlschlaeger, Fritz. "John S. Robb." Encyclopedia of
      American Humorists. Ed. Steven H. Gale. New York: Garland,
      1988, 371-74.

      Points out that "Swallowing an Oyster Alive" was published in
the St. Louis Reveille in 1844. This story contrasts an innocent
country protagonist who speaks in the vernacular with a
sophisticated narrative voice. When the protagonist swallows an
oyster, he is told that the oyster is alive and will eat clean
through him. The protagonist gulps half a bottle of strong pepper
sauce in an effort to kill the oyster and ends up by gasping,
blowing, pitching, and twisting wildly. Although Robb pokes fun at
the protagonist's innocence, he still has genuine empathy. In
Streaks of Squatter Life, Robb makes a distinction between genuine
settlers, and "border harpies," who are worthless criminal types,
outcast from polite society; they prey on red men and white men
alike. Robb's humorous events are typically based on such frontier
pastimes as "drinking, courting, and politicking." In "Nettle
Bottom Ball" Jim is planning to take Betsy to the ball at Nettle
Bottom, and Betsy goes upstairs to dress. Betsy, scantily clad,
falls through the ceiling into the pan of hot mush sitting on the
supper table. Jim throws a pan of cold milk on Betsy's behind to
cool her down. Robb provides comic record of the customs and people
in early frontier America, and his work has influenced such major
American authors as Mark Twain and William Faulkner.

George Washington Harris (1814-1869)

161. Arnold, St. George Tucker, Jr. "Sut Lovingood, the Animals, and
     the Great White Trash Chain of Being." Thalia: Studies in
     Literary Humor 1.3 (1979): 33-41.

        Suggests that Sut may be as much an animal as he is a human.
     Sut may have been conceived when a pet sand-hill crane chased Sut's
     mother under a bed. When Sut says "durn my skin," he corrects
     himself to "no, my haslets," which suggests an afinity between him
     and a hog. He also claims kinship to a giraffe because of his long
     ungainly appearance. Sut sees every animal as having a particular
     place in the "Great Chain of Being," "whar...the big childer roots
     little childer outen the troff, an' gobbils up thar part. Jis' so
     the yeath over; bishops eats elders, elders eats common peopil, they
     eats sich cattil es me, I eats possums, possums eats chickins,
     chickens swallers wums, an' wums am content to eat dus." Throughout
     the Sut Lovingood yarns, there is a strong feeling that every action
     of every being is prescribed by the position that being has in the
     pecking order. There are creatures which act in unpredicted ways;
     however they are rare, and they count as exceptions which prove the
     rule. Throughout the yarns, Sut has a strong sense of what "ought
     to be," and this provides "the major thread joining the Yarns into
     a firm artistic fabric."

162. Bain, Robert. "George Washington Harris." Antebellum Writers in
     New York and the South. Ed. Joel Myerson. Detroit, MI: Gale,
     1979, 138-43.

        Considers Harris to be like other Southwestern humorists in
     being an adventurer and a jack-of-all-trades; he was a metal worker,
     journalist, steamboat captain, farmer, politician, and railroader.
     And like other Southwestern humorists, Harris is mainly remembered
     for a single book--Sut Lovingood, Yarns Spun by a "Nat'ral Born
     Durn'd Fool." Bain portrays Sut as a Yankee-baiting, whiskey-
     drinking jokester with an aversion to pomposity, always on the
     lookout for revenge, willing girls, and ready widows. Bain says
     that Harris' attitude in presenting grotesque tales about sex,
     religion, and violence is similar to what Mark Twain would later
     call the "damned human race." Bain, in fact, feels that Sut
     Lovingood is "one of the liveliest vernacular characters in American
     literature before Huckleberry Finn." Paradoxically, it is Harris'
     vigorous use of vernacular language and dialect spelling that made
     him so popular in the nineteenth century, and it is this same
     vernacular language and dialect spelling that makes him so
     unattainable in the twentieth century. This problem has been
     partially resolved by Brom Weber, who edited a 1954 collection of
     tales with modernized spellings and M. Thomas Inge who included a
     glossary of 350 special Harris usages with his Harris collection.

163. Blair, Walter, and Hamlin Hill. "Sut Lovingood and the End of
     the World." America's Humor: From Poor Richard to Doonesbury.
     New York: Oxford University Press, 1978, 213-21.

        Contrasts Edmund Wilson's evaluation of Sut Lovingood with
     that of William Faulkner. Wilson said that Sut was not a pioneer

dealing with the wilderness, but was rather a "peasant squatting in his own filth." On the other hand, William Faulkner said of Sut that he had no illusions about himself. He did the best he could (which wasn't all that good), and he wasn't ashamed. He never blamed his misfortunes on anyone else or on God. Blair and Hill suggest that what Wilson abhorred and what Faulkner admired was the same thing--"the earthy celebration of an amoral universe and the reprehensible carrying on of Sut." Mark Twain accurately predicted that the Sut Lovingood tales would sell well in the West but would not sell well in the East, where people would call them coarse or be offended by them.

164. Blair, Walter, and Raven I. McDavid, Jr. eds. "George Washington Harris." The Mirth of a Nation: America's Great Dialect Humor. Eds. Walter Blair and Raven McDavid. Minneapolis: Univ. of Minnesota Press, 1983, 115-24.

Indicates that Mark Twain felt that Sut Lovingood's Yarns were too coarse for Easterners to read; however, the book remained constantly in print for more than seven decades. By the time the book had gone out of print, Franklin Meine had included Harris in his anthology Tall Tales of the Southwest, and the "Sut Lovingood yarns" have thus remained available to readers to the present day. Meine praises Harris for his "vivid imagination, comic plot, Rabelaisian touch, and sheer fun." And even feels that the Sut Lovingood tales "surpass anything else in American humor."

165. Cohen, Hennig, and William B. Dillingham, eds. "George Washington Harris." Humor of the Old Southwest. 2nd ed. Athens: Univ. of Georgia Press, 1975, 156-202.

Feels that Harris infused his sketches with satire and hints that humans have a predilection for devilment. Harris was largely self educated, but he was not unsophisticated. He was a careful observer and a good listener. In 1854 he created Sut Lovingood in a Spirit-of-the-Times sketch entitled "Sut Lovingood's Daddy, Acting Horse." The Sut stories were published frequently in various Tennessee newspapers of the 1850s, and Sut Lovingood: Yarns Spun by a "Nat'ral Born Durn'd Fool" was reviewed by Mark Twain. Some of the Sut tales were written as Democratic Party political propaganda. Sut is not merely a trickster like Till Eulenspiegel or Pedro Urdemales. He is rather the victim of a bad cosmic joke. Sut's targets are carefully selected as the dregs of society--drunkards, adulterers, lechers, sadists, bigots, and hypocrites. The sketches are designed to show the animal nature of us all. In "Sut Lovingood's Daddy, Acting Horse," the father removes his filthy rags and divests himself of the last shred of decency and humanity as nakedly he acts the horse. In "Parson John Bullen's Lizards," a lecherous preacher is tricked into exposing both his nakedness and his hypocrisy. Cohen and Dillingham compare these sketches to the story of mad King Lear who talks of nakedness and tears off his clothes.

166. Day, Donald. "The Humorous Works of George W. Harris." American Literature 14 (January 1943): 391-406.

Feels that Harris, like the other boisterous authors of the humor tradition of the Old Southwest, relied more on his experiences than on reading about the experiences of others. Day agrees with Augustus B. Longstreet that Harris was prototypical for this group, which supplied entertaining and insightful information about the manners, customs, amusements, wit, and dialect of all grades of Old Southwestern society. In his earlier writings, Harris was content merely to amuse, but his later sketches add "lusty licks at the foibles of mankind."   Harris' chief target in his sketches is hypocrisy, especially the hypocrisy of women and circuit riders, two groups that he feel have a special responsibility not to be be hypocrites.   Whiskey plays an important part in Sut's world.   He considers it to be "the best thing in life," but it is not "to be enjoyed by those who damn other amusements." Day considers Harris to have reached "the highest level of achievement before Mark Twain," because Harris uses the same material and the same forms as the other humorists of the Old Southwest, but he uses them better.

167. Inge, M. Thomas. "The Satiric Artistry of George W. Harris." Satire Newsletter. 4.2 (Spring 1967): 63-72.

Commends Harris for his effective characterization, his eye for detail in both action and environment, his appropriate imagery, and his excellent depiction of Southern vernacular. Harris used three main types of satire in his works--invective, burlesque, and irony. His Menippean satire was achieved through the development of an animal fable or allegory. Like Rabelais, Harris used the rhetorical device of "abusive catalogue," as when he presents the participants in a political convention as various kinds of cats and rats as well as coons, ground hogs, minks, weasels, bats, owls, buzzards, dogs, boars, possums, moles, grub-worms, and tumble bugs. Harris also uses "meiosis" or "belittling" satire, as when he tells about catching a frog, driving a nail through its lips, tying two rocks to its hind toes and leaving it there to dry. When he returned to the same spot two weeks later and looked at the dried and stretched out frog he said it looked just like Abe: "...same shape, same color, same feel (cold as ice) an I'm d--d ef hit aint the same smell." Some of Harris' strongest satire was aimed at the Northerner. "As the dorg vomits, as the mink sucks blood, as the snail shines, as the possum sham's death, so dus the Yankee cheat, for every varmint hes hits gif'." The satires in Harris' four-part series "The Early Life of Sut Lovingood, Written by His Dad" are elaborate enough to be considered "travesty."

168. Keller, Mark A. "That George Washington Harris 'Christmas Story'--A Reconsideration of Authorship." American Literature 54 (1982): 284-87.

Presents evidence that disagrees with William Starr's assumption in Gyascutus: Studies in Antebellum Southern Humorous and Sporting Writing that George Washington Harris wrote "Home-Voices--A Take for the Holy-Tide." In the first place, this is an inferior piece of writing, far below the quality of George Washington Harris' other writing. Keller suggests in fact that it is "in the worst tradition of nineteenth-century sentimentalism."   Although the piece was signed G.W.H., Keller points out that two writers for the Spirit of the Times signed their pieces G.W.H. Although Porter usually assigned one set of initials to each contributor to the Spirit, there are a number of exceptions to this rule, and this is

one of them. Finally, Harris has an alibi, for Porter's notes refer
to G.W.H. in a location different from Harris' at the time.

169. Lenz, William E. "Sensuality, Revenge, and Freedom: Women in
     Sut Lovingood's Yarns." Studies in American Humor. 1.3
     (February 1983): 173-180.

Alludes to Henry Adams observation that puritan Americans
considered sex to be sin while "in any previous age, sex was
strength." Nineteenth-century American literature was in need of an
"American Venus." This American Venus would be a natural and direct
descendant from Eve, whose sexuality was sensual, vital, and
forceful. George Washington Harris' Sut Lovingood was in constant
search for this American Venus, and "sensuality and revenge are
major forces in this [Lovingood's] world," a world of stark frontier
humor, and a world which strived more for freedom than for anything
else. The women in Harris' stories were aware that "sex is a power
before which men are helpless" and is a balance in a power system
which is normally dominated by males.

170. McClary, Ben Harris. "George Washington Harris's New York Atlas
     Series: Three New Items." Studies in American Humor 2.3
     (Winter 1983-84): 195-99.

Reveals three important short stories written late in George
Washington Harris' writing career. On September 5, 1858 an article
appeared in the Athens, Tennessee, Banner entitled, "Coved in and
Done." The article was the obituary of William S. Miller, "who had
provided Harris with the original characterization of Sut." With
the death of his inspiration, Harris turned to writing stories with
other protagonists. The three stories dealt with in this article
were entitled, "She Had the Slows," "How to Gain Your Seed Oats,"
and "A Strange Breed of Cats." None of them had Sut Lovingood as a
protagonist. These items are nevertheless important, because they
demonstrate Harris' ability to use language as a method of
characterization. One of the stories involves a stutterer, and one
character speaks in an Irish brogue. Harris' later stories are
heavier in political satire than are the earlier stories involving
Sut. Is it possible that in these later stories we have not
actually lost Sut but have instead witnessed a metamorphosis whereby
George Washington Harris and Sut Lovingood are no longer
distinguishable?

171. Micklus, Robert. "Sut's Travels with Dad." Studies in American
     Humor NS1.2 (October, 1982): 89-102.

Considers Harris' plots in the Sut Lovingood tales to be quite
trite and repetitious, but this is a plus rather than a minus, for
it allows Harris to concentrate on the telling of the tale rather
than the plot. Harris' humor is more process than product. He
relies on his good ear for dialect, and he develops wild, yet
appropriate, simile, and vivid, yet comic, metaphors. Harris has
"astonishingly apt imagery, cadence, and dialect." Brom Weber feels
that no one has developed a style that equals that of Harris in its
concentrated richness. So although the plots repeat themselves, the
accompanying imagery is always fresh and unique. The repetitiveness
of the plots not only provides a constant for readers, allowing them
to concentrate on the poetry of the piece, but this repetitiveness

also reinforces Harris' basic message--that Sut is indeed a "nat'ral born durn'd fool." Furthermore, the episodes are not only repetitive and digressive, they are formulaic as well. First there is the prelude to the "skeer" where someone pretends to be someone or something he is not. Next some sucker is physically or psychologically trapped. Then the "skeer" begins and chaos erupts resulting in ludicrous skirmishes. The "skeer" finally runs its course, and the dupe finds himself acting like an animal. He seeks relief by running for cover. And finally, Sut does his best to salt the wounds of the dupe and "runs away before getting his butt kicked." By telegraphing not only the plots but the plot developments as well, Harris can concentrate on his real task--the poetry of his writing.

172. Polk, Noel. "The Blind Bull, Human Nature: Sut Lovingood and the Damned Human Race." Gyascutus: Studies in Antebellum Southern Humorous and Sporting Writing. Ed. James L. West III. Atlantic Highlands, NJ: Humanities Press, 1978, 13-49.

Suggests that both M. Thomas Inge and Milton Rickels failed to consider Sut as a three-dimensional character. They both interpreted Sut literally when he proclaimed that he was a "natural born durn'd fool," assuming that Sut had said this with a straight face. But Polk gives evidence that Sut Lovingood is as much of a storyteller as is his creator, George Washington Harris. In fact calling himself a "natural born durn'd fool" is the type of rhetorical device that storytellers of the time would use to signal that what followed was an exaggeration--a tall tale of some sort. There are other clues as well that Sut was himself a storyteller rather than just one of the characters in the Yarns, such as the elaborated detail, the exaggerated violence, and the farfetched metaphors. In "Hen Bailey's Reformation," for example, a mole chases a lizard up Hen's pants leg, into his anus, through his stomach and esophagus, and out of his mouth. This violent imagery cannot have been provided solely by Harris; Sut also had to have been a contributor, for, if he was not, then he had to believe that all of this actually happened.

173. Rickels, Milton. George Washington Harris. New York: Twaine, 1965, 159 pp.

Believes that only now is Harris being given due credit for his significant achievements as a writer. Harris was a careful editor and painstaking reviser of his work. He constantly changed his imagery to increase the frequency and power of his metaphors and similes. In the original "Sut Lovengood Blown Up," for example, Sut observes Sicily's figure and proclaims, "Oh sich a buzum--but thar aint no use trying to describe her." The revision contains a strong metaphor: "Sich a buzzim! Jis' think ove two snow balls wif a strawberry stuck but-ainded intu bof on em." Harris' plots are carefully developed, and more than half of the sketches in the Yarns are practical jokes. The anecdotes are elaborate and fantastic with an element of carelessness and spontaneity. There is limited cruelty in the tales, but none of Sut's jokes are fatal or permanent. Probably the most grotesque imagery Harris develops is when Mrs. Yardley dies and Sut is calling for help "tu salt ole Missis Yardley down." Later, he fixes her "comfortably" in the grave and covers her up with soil "to keep the buzzards from cheatin

the wurms." In the sketches which are not practical jokes, the
language and the characterization become especially effective, as
Harris creates "comic fables of poor backwoods mountain life that
will express, through the ambiguity of comedy, the yearning for
unrestrained existence."

174. Rickels, Milton. "George Washington Harris." Dictionary of
     Literary Biography: Volume II: American Humorists, 1800-1950.
     Ed. Stanley Trachtenberg. Detroit, MI: Gale, 1982, 180-89.

     Points out that twentieth-century admirers of Sut Lovingood
include Flannery O'Connor, Robert Penn Warren, and William Faulkner.
Even though Sut was grotesque in appearance, with his "long-legged,
short-bodied, small-headed, white-haired, hog-eyed, funny sort of
genius," he was nevertheless a dominant figure among mountaineers.
Harris' first satire involving Sut was developed as a dream allegory
in which Presidential candidates Fillmore, Fremont, and Buchanan
were playing cards. In Sut's dream, Buchanan won the card game, and
a few weeks later Buchanan actually won the presidency. Harris was
viewed as some sort of prophet. Sut rejects the traditional
constraints of religion, politics, education, and family and
represents a free spirit. As such, he degrades not only himself but
also those he comes into contact with, so he correctly considers
himself to be "a nat'ral born durn'd fool." Sut believes that the
most important function of men is to eat, drink and stay awake, and
he believes that the function of women is to "cook the vittils, mix
the sperits, an help the men du the stayin awake." Harris believed
in the superiority of Southern culture, and after the North had won
the War Between the States, he was shattered and never finished
another book.

175. Rickels, Milton. "The Imagery of George Washington Harris."
     American Literature. 31 (May, 1959): 173-87.

     Compares George Washington Harris to Mark Twain in terms of
the darkness of his vision and to Jonathan Swift in terms of his
preoccupations with physical ugliness. Harris would be classified
in the tradition of the frontier humorists, including A. B.
Longstreet, T. B. Thorpe, William Tappan Thompson, Johnson Jones
Hooper, and others. However Harris' work stood apart from the rest
because of its artistry. Harris may have been one of the least
interesting writers in the group in terms of the variety of his
plots, but he was one of the most interesting in terms of the
intensity of his vision. Sut is merely a fun seeker; however Sut's
visual images are powerful, lifting him to something in between the
comic and the mythic. He hopelessly desires an impossible freedom;
he obsessively and irrationally pursues experiences of the flesh; he
has large hopes of what man might be on the frontier of the new
world but is bitterly disappointed in what man actually is. Sut is
hard and cruel because of the moral void of the American backwoods.
He can express his individuality only through violence. Harris'
yarns recount crude and cruel practical jokes; the imagery supplies
the counterpoint, reflecting a world that is only sometimes
satisfying and that is more often harsh, hypocritical, wicked,
transitory, and meaningless.

176. Weber, Brom. <u>Sut Lovingood</u>. New York: Grove Press, 1954.

Quotes Franklin J. Meine as saying, "For vivid imagination, comic plot, Rabelaisian touch, and sheer <u>fun</u>, the <u>Sut Lovingood Yarns</u> surpass anything else in American humor." Harris evokes laughter and exposes our animal natures by depicting the events of the Great Smoky Mountain folk in racy detail and faithful vernacular language. But Harris has a generous sympathy for the characters he writes about. Most authors during the pre-Civil War period when Harris wrote were New Englanders who looked askance at an author whose main stress was ribald humor, whose central figures were common folk speaking as common folk really speak. For Harris there were "no taboos on the robust expression of the funny and the pleasurable," but for the New England authors there were many taboos. Harris' writings in a way mocked and ridiculed the sentimentality and gentility of New England; they were the epitome of Jacksonian democracy. They flaunted coarseness, ignored the canons of good taste, seemed to be unaware of respectable culture and education as well. Despite his coarseness and lack of education, Sut is portrayed displaying love, joy, truth, and justice even though he is a "nat'ral born durn'd fool." Weber sees this irony as representing "humor on a grand scale."

177. Wenke, John. "Sut Lovingood's Yarns and the Politics of Performance." <u>Studies in American Fiction</u> 15.2 (1987): 199-210.

Describes Sut Lovingood of the <u>Yarns</u> as engaging in four types of performance--actor, director, polemicist, and story-teller. As actor and director, Lovingood tends to control the action. As polemicist and story-teller, he enters into intimate dialogue with the reader, usually about his friend and transcriber, George. In "Eaves-Dropping" an antithesis develops between literate George and illiterate Sut. The antithesis pits east against west, and "book-larnin" against "mother-wit." Characters are frequently playing roles in the <u>Yarns</u>. In one sketch Sut dresses up as a lawyer thinking it will somehow make him smarter. He puts on a fancy starched shirt, hoping this will make a lawyer out of him, but it doesn't work. Sut's Dad tries to make up for the death of the family horse, Tickeytail by becoming a horse himself; this way the field could still be plowed. In another sketch, Sut's Dad puts on the skin of a cow in order to teach the family dog how to drive away foreign animals. In taking on the character of animals, Sut's Dad reverts to animal behavior. In all of these cases, the taking on of a role is intended to solve some specific problem. What results, however, is that rather than becoming solved, the problem is always exacerbated by the role playing.

178. Wilson, Edmond. "Sut Lovingood." <u>New Yorker</u> 31 (May 7, 1955): 150-59.

Claims that Sut can be as outlandish and as oafish as and as cruel as he pleases, because he can always claim that his father sired him as "a nat'ral born durn'd fool." George Washington Harris, a Tennessee journalist, exploited the character of Sut Lovingood as a mouthpiece for his political satire. Harris made many friends, but he also made many enemies. In 1869 Harris took a trip to Lynchburg, Virginia, to do some railroad business and to

arrange for the publication of his second Sut Lovingood book. On
his train trip back home, he became so ill that the conductor
thought he was drunk. He was carried off the train at Knoxville,
and there he died. His manuscript disappeared. The cause of his
death is not known, but it is reported that immediately before he
died, he whispered the word "Poisoned!"

179. Young, Thomas Daniel. "A Nat'ral Born Durn'd Fool." Thalia:
     Studies in Literary Humor 6.2 (Fall-Winter 1983): 51-56.

     Indicates that Mark Twain was correct in his prediction that
Harris' Sut Lovingood yarns would be popular on the frontier but
would be regarded by Easterners as coarse and vulgar. Young
contrasts the reaction of William Faulkner, a Southerner, with that
of Edmund Wilson, an Easterner. Faulkner liked Sut Lovingood
because he had no illusions or pretentions. He just plugged along,
doing the best he could. He was a coward and he knew it, but he
never blamed any of his misfortunes on anyone else, and he never
cursed God for his difficulties. Edmund Wilson, on the other hand,
did not consider Sut to be a pioneer fighting against the
wilderness; rather he was "a peasant squatting in his own filth."
Like other authors in the tradition of Old Southwest Humor, Harris
violated the Victorian code of ethics and morality of his day. Like
Longstreet and Baldwin, Harris depicted the cruelty, trickery,
knavery, and practical jokes that were rampant on the frontier, and
just as happened in real life, many of the practical jokes of
Harris' sketches ended in tragedy. But it is clear from reading the
sketches that Harris considered sin to be basically comic rather
than tragic. Sut's humor exposes hypocrisy, guile, and fraud, and
the targets are frequently important authority figures--pretentious
preachers, stupid or corrupt sheriffs, and dishonest lawyers, for
Sut is indeed a fool killer.

Benjamin Pendleton Shillaber (1814-1890)

180. Royot, Daniel G. "Benjamin Pendleton Shillaber." Encyclopedia
     of American Humorists. Ed. Steven H.Gale. New York: Garland:
     1988, 393-98.

     Discusses Shillaber's most important protagonist, Mrs.
Partington, who was born to puritan parents and lived in Beanville,
Massachusetts, until her husband died and her home was demolished by
the railroad. She moved to Boston with her nephew Ike. Mrs.
Partington was an unlettered and parochial lady who ignored the
conventions of genteel society. She was the first well-developed
female crackerbox philosopher. Shillaber uses the her persona to
parody the dogmaticism, to satirize the intellectual fads, and to
reveal the snobbery and the cultism of the day. Mrs. Partington is
herself very literal minded, being something of a rustic innocent
transplanted into a cosmopolitan and intellectual city. Shillaber
has a number of important characters in his novels besides Mrs.
Partington. Old Roger attempts utopian projects with his friends,
Philanthropos and Poo-Poo. Old Roger thrives on puns and
spoonerisms, but he also suffers from gastric disorders that force
him to judge his fellow man harshly. Wideswarth and Blifkins are
blundering scapegoats. Wideswarth (like Wordsworth) writes lyrical

verse. Blifkins was one of the first "little men" (in the Charlie
Chaplin tradition). Ike Partington plays practical jokes, lies,
steals, and tortures cats.

181. Wade, Clyde G. "B. P. Shillaber." Dictionary of Literary
     Biography, Vol II: American Humorists 1800-1950. Detroit, MI:
     Gale, 1982, 434-38.

     Indicates that Shillaber, a compositor for the Boston Post,
became famous when he slipped one of his sketches into that
newspaper. Shillaber founded and edited the shortlived Carpet Bag,
which published the work of some of the best humorists of the day
and included the work of two unknowns by the names of Artemus Ward
and Mark Twain. To Shillaber's protagonist, Mrs. Partington, it
"made no difference...whether flour was dear or cheap, as she always
had to pay just so much for a half-dollar's worth." The Mrs.
Partington novels concentrate on the problems encountered by a
person from Beanville trying to live in Boston. "Blifkins's Summer
Retreat" is an ironic reversal of this situation. Blifkins, a city
man, is "hopelessly and sometimes humorously out of place in a rural
setting." Shillaber was a newspaper man, and he wrote like a
newspaper man. Life and Sayings of Mrs. Partington is very loosely
structured. It contains random anecdotes, one-liners, and other
pieces that were obviously first used as newspaper filler.
Shillaber's writing is good natured and sensible, not provoking much
deep thought or contemplation but rather creating a smile and giving
people a momentary sense of pleasure. The cruelty in the stories is
very soft, as when Mrs. Partington decides to drown some kittens but
has to "take the chill off the water" first.

Frances Miriam Berry Whitcher (c1814-1852)

182. Blair, Walter, and Raven I. McDavid, Jr., eds. "Frances
     Miriam Whitcher." The Mirth of a Nation: America's Great
     Dialect Humor. Minneapolis: Univ. of Minnesota Press, 1983,
     27-30.

     Tells us that gossipy Widow Bedott, tart Aunt Maguire, and
other female chatterboxes created by Frances Whitcher were among the
most popular nineteenth-century American characters. The twenty-
five editions of the Widow Bedott Papers sold in excess of 100,000
copies, and in addition there were long runs of dramatizations of
the books in playhouses. Blair and McDavid feel that Whitcher was
one of the first successful developers of the Shaggy-dog story later
to be made famous by Mark Twain and others. The Widow Bedott's
"meandering reminiscences" of her husband Hezekiah are prototypical
exemplifications of a genre Mark Twain describes as bubbling gently
along, and spinning out and wandering around, and arriving "nowhere
in particular."

183. Butler, Michael D. "Frances Miriam Berry Whitcher."
     Encyclopedia of American Humorists. Ed. Steven H. Gale. New
     York: Garland, 1988, 470-75.

     Explains that the language of Permilly Spriggins, the Widow
Bedott, and Aunt Maguire is filled with "comic misspellings,

malapropisms, coined words, and indecorous combinations of lofty
diction and slang characteristic of vernacular humor." The letter
"e" becomes "i" in "gintle," and "poitry;" final "g"s are dropped;
strange spellings of strange words occur, as in "billy dux (that
are's the French for loveletter)," and the sketches are replete with
such words as "eny," "agin," "heerd," "knowd," "kinder," and "enuf."
Whitcher's malapropisms often look like translations rather than
words created in ignorance as her half-educated characters attempt
to ornament their lives with elogance and sophistication. Permilee
is trying to talk like a lady when she "condescends" the stairs or
refers to male heroes as "swine" rather than "swain." Such
instances lead Butler to conclude that the humor of Whitcher's
vernacular writing comes from a strange appropriateness rather than
an inappropriateness of their language. The errors are made by
characters who may be ignorant but who are attempting to be
something other than what they are, something new and exciting in
their own eyes but perhaps not so admirable or attractive in the
eyes of the reader. These characters are upwardly mobile. As
Permilly Spriggins said, "I was called the biggest genyus in
Podunk."

184. Morris, Linda A. "Frances Miriam Whitcher: Social Satire in
     the Age of Gentility." Last Laughs: Perspectives on Women and
     Comedy Ed. Regina Barreca. New York: Gordon and Breach, 1988,
     99-116.

        Relates the Seneca Falls women's rights conference to the
Elmira sewing-society conference. Both of these conferences took
place in New York in 1848. Furthermore, Morris contends that they
both had to do with women's rights. Seneca Falls is often regarded
as the birthplace of women's rights in America because of the 1848
conference. 300 women and men traveled to Seneca Falls to debate
for two days the merits of a document entitled "The Declaration of
Sentiments and Resolutions." It was Elizabeth Cady Stanton who drew
up and presented this document at the convention. It was patterned
on the "Declaration of Independence, and was the Seneca Falls
response to what its authors called "the degradation of women in
American society." Five months later, the Elmira Sewing Society
met, and Miriam Whitcher, wife of an Episcopal minister and a member
of the sewing society, satirized the meeting in Godey's Lady's Book.
This satire was responding to the same social ills that had prompted
the convening of feminists in Seneca Falls--the increasingly
restricted roles of women in mid-nineteenth-century American
society. Whitcher was indignant and frustrated, and she held women
largely responsible for much of the degradation that women suffered.

185. Wade, Clyde G. "Frances Miriam Whitcher." Dictionary of
     Literary Biography, Vol II: American Humorists, 1800-1950.
     Detroit, MI: Gale, 1982, 560-67.

        Portrays Whitcher as a writer with great powers of observation
and a gift for satiric ridicule. She herself observed, "I received
at my birth the undesirable gift of a remarkably strong sense of the
ridiculous." This gift was undesirable, because it got Whitcher
into a great deal of trouble. Her husband was a preacher, and many
of his parishoners objected because they saw themselves and their
loved ones ridiculed in Whitcher's novels. From her earliest years,
Whitcher used humorous ridicule in her artistic sketches and in her

writing to communicate her objections to aspects of village life, church, and education that bothered her. She recalls that she cannot remember a time when neighbors were not afraid that she would make fun of them. But in her novels, Whitcher made fun only of the sanctimonious, the hypocritical, and the powerful folk who inflicted needless injury on the weak and defenseless. Although her writing career was short (only five and a half years), she succeeded in creating the first fully developed humorous women characters in American literature. In addition, she parodied the lugubrious poetry that filled the village newspapers and journals of the day. She is the writer of "some of the best and funniest bad verse in American literature."

186. Walker, Nancy, and Zita Dresner. "Frances Miriam Berry Whitcher. Redressing the Balance: American Women's Literary Humor from Colonial Times to the 1980s. Eds. Nancy Walker, and Zita Dresner. Jackson: Univ. Press of Mississippi, 1988, 68-81.

Praises Whitcher for concentrating on "women's culture" which was in Whitcher's day the sewing circles of New York villages. Although women were Whitcher's chief targets, what she was actually satirizing was "frivolity and sentimentality that detracted from women's potential to be viewed as rational, capable people." Whitcher's women are controlled by what Walker and Dresner term the "cult of domesticity." Whitcher's rejection of the gentility that was expected of women, and her use of her husband's parishioners as models for her characters caused Miriam and her husband to move from Elmira to Whitesboro. Miriam died three years after her only child was born.

Joseph Glover Baldwin (1815-1864)

187. Cohen, Hennig, and William B. Dilingham. "Joseph Glover Baldwin." Humor of the Old Southwest. 2nd edition. Athens: Univ. of Georgia Press, 1975, 250-66.

Considers Baldwin's humor to be sometimes earthy but never crude, and there is never any horseplay. Baldwin's jokes sometimes have targets, but the target is always someone who deserves to be--a braggart, a bully, a pedantic individual, or a con man. No one is ever really hurt by Baldwin's humor, and justice always wins out. Baldwin's wrote humor about the law, and lawyers enjoyed reading his works. Abraham Lincoln, who was at one time a circuit lawyer, enjoyed reading Flush Times aloud, and Washington Irving, a one-time judge, also enjoyed reading that novel.

188. Current-Garcia, Eugene. "Joseph Glover Baldwin: Humorist or Moralist? The Frontier Humorists: Critical Views. Ed. M. Thomas Inge. Hamden, Connecticut: Archon, 1975, 170-86.

Makes the point that The Flush Times of Alabama and Mississippi was so popular that it may have detracted from Baldwin's considerable achievement as social historian, jurist, and moralist. Scholars have thoroughly evaluated Baldwin's place in history as a Frontier Southern Humorist; however Current-Garcia feels that this may not have been Baldwin's most significant contribution to history. The judges and lawyers who lived during Baldwin's time felt that Baldwin's best writing was not his humorous anecdotes but rather his essays about political theory. Nevertheless, Flush Times was an informal record of "the age of litigation in a lawless country." Flush Times was obviously written to entertain, but Current-Garcia feels it also had a didactic purpose--to correct. Baldwin's position as moralist can be better seen in Party Leaders, where he states his aim as being "to unite biography with political..., [and] by placing rival leaders in antagonism, to make events and principles stand out in bold relief."

189. Keller, Mark A. "The Transfiguration of a Southwestern Humor Sketch--Joseph Glover Baldwin's "Jo. Heyfron." American Humor: An Interdisciplinary Newsletter. 8.2 (Fall 1981): 19-22.

Considers "Jo. Heyfron" to be the most popular sketch in Baldwin's The Flush Times of Alabama and Mississippi. This sketch relates to an Irish lawyer and wit by the name of Jo. Heyfron, who outwitted a stern Mississippi judge in a courtroom confrontation. The sketch is important enough to have been included in two significant collections of antebellum humor, Cohen and Dillingham's Humor of the Old Southwest and Mody Boatright's Folk Laughter on the American Frontier. Baldwin maintained that the incident was a true one and even insisted that his account was meant to correct some of the errors of the newspaper accounts which had run previously. Also, the earlier accounts had portrayed the lawyer as something of a buffoon, while Baldwin's account was about a confrontation between Jo. Heyfron, who "knew too much law, and a judge too little, for an equality of advantages." Baldwin's account is superior both factually and aesthetically, for he cast Heyfron's retort into the dialect of an Irish brogue.

190. Simms, L. Moody, Jr. "Joseph Glover Baldwin." Dictionary of Literary Biography: Vol II: American Humorists, 1800-1950. Detroit, MI: Gale, 1982, 12-17.

Attributes Baldwin's success as a leading humorist of the Old Southwest to the writing of The Flush Times of Alabama and Mississippi, a book which describes boom times in two frontier states (Alamaba and Mississippi) before the Louisiana Purchase had moved the frontier further west. It contains anecdotes and humorous sketches related to law, but it also includes serious biographies of lawyers and judges. "Baldwin sketched authentic and vivid portraits of slippery clients, shifty lawyers, inept prosecutors, unlettered judges, and other frontier types [as they came into contact with the law]." There is no single protagonist and no careful organization. What holds the book together is the central theme of "what happens in court." In the most famous sketch, "Ovid Bolus, Esq," the protagonist lies, charms, and cons everyone he meets, and finally finds himself in court because of the huge bills he has run up. A sketch entitled "Simon Suggs, Jr., Esq: A Legal Biography" is probably based on an actual South Carolina lawyer of Baldwin's time. It tells about a lawyer who rises to the top of his profession by packing juries, subverting the state's criminal laws, and other chicanery. Flush Times is a high-spirited farce, but it also is the dilemma of an author who has difficulty reconciling his conscience with the excesses of his peers.

191. Stewart, Thomas H. "Joseph Glover Baldwin." <u>Encyclopedia of
     American Humorists</u>. Ed. Steven H. Gale. New York: Garland,
     1988, 23-24.

     Claims that Baldwin's primary audience was contemporary
attorneys who had time to read light literature as they traveled
from courtroom to courtroom across the country.   Therefore,
twentieth-century readers, especially those without special legal
training, have difficulty with "Baldwin's free use of Latin, his
allusion to contemporaneous court cases, and his use of attorneys'
cant." Thomas Stewart suggests that Baldwin's humor may be lively
and unrestrained, but it is also very localized in time and space
because of the many local allusions. As the frontier moved further
west, Baldwin moved to San Francisco and was writing <u>Flush Times in
California</u> at the time of his death.

192. Wimsatt, Mary Ann. "Baldwin's Patrician Humor." <u>Thalia: Studies
     in Literary Humor</u> 6.2 (Fall-Winter 1983): 43-50.

     Considers Baldwin to be the most neglected and underrated of
the major antebellum southern humorists and suggests that a major
reason for this lack of critical attention relates to Baldwin's
writing style.   The pace is leisurely; the presentation is not
exciting; there are frequent digressions; and there is a lack of
structure and unity.   These features of Baldwin's style are the
result of the fact that under the pressure of deadlines, he often
composed pieces rapidly and at odd times, hurrying to or from his
office, picking up convenient scraps of paper on which to write down
his ideas.   And he seldom had time for revision.   Another problem
with Baldwin's style is that it was too formal.   Other writers
during Baldwin's time wrote in dialect, and their vernacular writing
was regarded by most critics to be fresh, true to life, and
engaging.   The frontier was making a break from the genteel
tradition, and therefore vernacular writing was regarded as more
valuable than was Baldwin's more literate style.   But Baldwin is
important, because unlike most writers of his day, Baldwin linked
two aspects of southern culture, the Tidewater or patrician
mentality and the frontier or rural southern mentality.   Wimsatt
feels that Baldwin's writing should be praised for the very
qualities it has been blamed for.   Baldwin's digressions allow him
"to range whimsically over diverse topics, viewing them from a
number of angles." The genteel style was realistic, for it was the
way that some, but not all, southerners actually talked and thought.

Johnson Jones Hooper (1815-1862)

193. Bain, Robert. "Johnson Jones Hooper." <u>Antebellum Writers in
     New York and the South</u>. Ed. Joel Myerson. Detroit, MI: Gale,
     1979, 161-63.

     Attributes Hooper's fame to the creation and development of
Captain Simon Suggs of Tallapoosa, Alabama, a character both
engaging and despicable.   The character Simon Suggs was tall and
skinny; he had a muscular neck, and he was about fifty years old.
Suggs had the ability to "detect the soft spots in his fellow." W.
Stanley Hoole is Hooper's biographer, and he indicates that the

character Simon Suggs is based on a real-life person by the name of Bird H. Young. William Makepeace Thackeray believed Hooper to be one of the best writers of his day, and Norris Yates has suggested that Hooper's book is the only effective picaresque novel written by a pre-Civil-War Southwest humorist. Furthermore, Hooper wrote one of the most frequently quoted sentences in Southwest humor: "It is good to be shifty in a new country."

194. Blair, Walter, and Raven I. McDavid, Jr., eds. "Johnson Jones Hooper." The Mirth of a Nation: America's Great Dialect Humor. Minneapolis, Minnesota: Univ. of Minnesota Press, 1983, 69-78.

Says that Mark Twain imitated Hooper by modeling the twentieth chapter of the Adventures of Huckleberry Finn after Hooper's protagonist, Simon Suggs. Some of Simon Suggs' characteristics also can be seen in James Russell Lowell's Yankee character, Birdofredum Sawin. Simon Suggs was a crude con-man, whose motto was "It is good to be shifty in a new country." Simon remains a confidence man from his youth, when he cheats his minister father at cards, to his middle age, when he outwits fellow swindlers and cynically becomes a candidate for public office.

195. Cohen, Hennig, and William B. Dillingham, eds. "Johnson Jones Hooper." Humor of the Old Southwest. 2nd edition. Athens: Univ. of Georgia Press, 1975, 203-49.

Compares Hooper's Simon Suggs to the King in Twain's Huckleberry Finn by saying that neither of these characters is a lovable rogue nor a detested villain. Suggs is Robin Hood but without a conscience. The reader wants to hate Suggs but is too busy laughing at his antics to be able to do so. Suggs is a comic opportunist who is successful as a rogue because he knows human nature so well and is able to profit by the selfishness, affectation, and greed that he knows are qualities of everybody he meets.

196. Justus, James H. "Johnson Jones Hooper." Encyclopedia of American Humorists. Ed. Steven H. Gale. New York: Garland, 1988, 227-31.

Describes Simon Suggs as illiterate but perceptive in interpersonal relationships. Suggs believes that people's characteristics are what get them into trouble, so he sees no problem in being available to benefit from other people's misfortunes. For example, when he fixes the cards in a poker game and then tricks his father into playing with him, he applies the theological doctrine of predestination when he wins. As a rebellious teenager, Suggs slips a thimbleful of gunpowder into his mother's pipe before he leaves home. Suggs lives by the adage, "Mother-wit kin beat book-larnin, at any game." Hooper portrays the antics of Simon Suggs with rambunctious humor and subtle satire as he develops the character. Justus feels that Simon Suggs has only one rival in complexity and vividness among the many comic protagonists of the Old Southwest--George Washington Harris' Sut Lovingood.

197. Keller, Mark A. "Johnson Jones Hooper." Dictionary of
      Literary Biography: Volume II: American Humorists 1800-1950.
      Detroit, MI: Gale, 1982, 211-19.

      Claims that Simon Suggs' sardonic brand of humor is echoed in
      the writings of Herman Melville, Mark Twain, William Faulkner, and
      Guy Owens. Hooper's character Simon Suggs became so popular in
      William T. Porter's The Spirit of the Times that Porter found a
      publisher to publish Hooper's sketches as Some Adventures of Captain
      Simon Suggs. This book was dedicated to William T. Porter and went
      through eleven editions in the same number of years. The character
      of Simon Suggs appears to have been based on an actual person--Bird
      H. Young by name. Both Suggs and Young were rogues and inveterate
      gamblers. Two of the sketches in A Ride with Old Kit Kuncker are
      about Simon Suggs. The best sketch in the book is entitled "A Night
      at the Ugly Man's." This story alludes to a tradition of the times
      whereby all of the ugly people have to carry a horn-handled knife,
      but they are obliged to pass these knives on to any people they meet
      who are uglier than they are. This sketch is about Bill, whose
      flatboat is nearly capsized by a steamboat. The steamboat
      passengers crowd to the side of the boat to get a look at Bill, and
      then Bill is struck by a storm of what he thinks is huge hail
      stones. But when he comes around, he discovers that the steamboat
      passengers had hit him with "a level peck of buck-horn-handled
      knives."

198. Rachal, John. "Language and Comic Motifs in Johnson Jones
      Hooper's Simon Suggs." The Alabama Historical Quarterly 38.2
      (Summer 1976): 93-100.

      Refers to Harry West's unpublished thesis which quantified
      Hooper's metaphors (including similes) as being thirty-nine percent
      "animal," and twenty-one percent "farm," with the rest being
      "miscellaneous. Hooper's Adventures of Captain Simon Suggs is
      typical of the frame tales that exemplified the work of southern
      humorists. The realistic and earthy language of the character,
      Simon Suggs, is contrasted with the dignified and "Addisonian"
      language of the narrator, to achieve a special ironic effect. Simon
      Suggs is the quintessential backwoods con man, and since his nature
      is a bit animalistic, it is no surprise that his images are
      animalistic as well. Paradox and comic irony can be found
      throughout Adventures of Captain Simon Suggs, and perhaps the most
      ironic paradox of all is the ability of Simon to impress his victims
      with his empathy and his honesty.

199. Smith, Winston. "Simon Suggs and the Satiric Tradition."
      Essays in Honor of Richebourg Gaillard McWilliams. Ed. Howard
      Creed. Birmingham, Alabama: Birmingham Southern College, 1970,
      49-56.

      Disagrees with those critics who believe that Hooper broke
      with earlier European traditions to declare a kind of literary
      independence in developing a fresh vein of frontier realism.
      Instead, Smith feels that Hooper's Simon Suggs is squarely in the
      tradition of the European picaresque novel. The picaresque novel is
      an adventure story of a rogue's life. It is typically told in the
      first person. Furthermore, it is an episodic account of the rogue's
      wanderings, his adversities, and his ingenious role-playing that

gets him out of various difficulties. The picaresque novel presents
a satiric view of society. Smith concludes that in both structure
and characterization, Hooper's Simon Suggs is picaresque.

200. Treadway, James L. "Johnson Jones Hooper and the American
     Picaresque." Thalia: Studies in Literary Humor 6.2 (Fall-
     Winter 1983): 33-42.

     Considers the frontier South to have been a spawning ground
for picaresque characters.   This was the land of robust and
undisciplined pioneers, and the qualities of the pioneer were
virtually the same as the qualities of the picaro--"nomadism,
insensibility to danger, shrewdness, nonchalance, and gaiety."
There are many picaresque settings and picaresque characters in
Southern frontier humor, but only Johnson Jones Hooper wrote a
single sustained work that depicted picaresque elements throughout,
in the tradition of the picaresque narrative. Treadway feels that
Hooper's Some Adventures of Captain Suggs, Late of the Tallapoosa
Volunteers can be considered a traditional picaresque novel in the
best sense of the genre. Simon Suggs, the central character in the
book is "a rogue second to none," and the depicting of his roguery
provides the novel's main substance.   The novel presents episode
after episode to account for Captain Suggs' epithet of "Shifty."
Like other picaros, Simon Suggs has been educated by experience or
what he calls "human natur'." And like other picaros, he does not
progress; he is a rogue from the beginning to the end of the novel.

Thomas Bangs Thorpe (1815-1878)

201. Bain, Robert. "Thomas Bangs Thorpe." Antebellum Writers in
     New York and the South. Ed. Joel Myerson. Detroit, MI: Gale,
     1979, 335-39.

     Indicates that between 1839 and 1843 Thorpe published some
thirty-four tales and sketches in Spirit of the Times and in the
Knickerbocker Magazine.   In 1843 and 1844 Thorpe wrote a series of
"Letters from the Far West" first published in the Intelligencer,
and later reprinted in the Spirit of the Times.   These letters
burlesqued the letters which Mat Field was writing for the Picayune
about the Western hunting expedition of Sir William Drummond
Stewart, a wealthy Scotchman.   Thorpe's burlesque letters were
signed "P. O. F."   In 1845 Thorpe published The Big Bear of
Arkansas, and Other Sketches, which Walter Blair feels contained
"new possibilities for a vernacular style, comic characterization
and imaginative invention." The hyperbole and fresh language of
Thorpe's prose has been compared favorably to the prose of
Washington Irving.

202. Blair, Walter. "'The Big Bear of Arkansas': T. B. Thorpe and
     His Masterpiece." The Frontier Humorists: Critical Views. Ed.
     M. Thomas Inge. New York: Archon, 1975, 105-17.

     Portrays Thorpe as "short and pudgy, with a big flat nose,
auburn hair and a sour phiz; he resembled a pug dog with russet
sideburns." One of Thorpe's friends contrasts Thorpe's "grave and
saturnine countenance" with "the kind and playful spirit that seems

to live in light and loveliness beneath the madness and gloom of his character." Thorpe's character, Jim Doggett, the narrator who tells the story of "The Big Bear of Arkansas" has a great eye for significant detail. "Although his [Doggett's] story (in large part because of its salty style) seems artless, it steadily mounts to its climax and then ends." At the end of the story, Jim shoots the bear and the bear walks away and groans in a nearby thicket "like a thousand sinners." When Jim reaches the bear, he is dead. But Jim doesn't feel that it was his shot that killed him. He rationalized that the bear was an "unhuntable bar, and died when his time come." Blair conjectures that the blending of the earthy with the fantastic is what makes it typically frontier American, and what makes it an entertaining and believable tale. It is so well told that it fools not only the listeners on the Mississippi steamboat, but even fools Jim Doggett himself.

203. Blair, Walter, and Hamlin Hill. "The Big Bear of Arkansas." America's Humor: From Poor Richard to Doonesbury. New York: Oxford University Press, 1978, 200-12.

Points out that the similarities between Thorpe's "The Big Bear of Arkansas" and Faulkner's "The Bear" are impressive and then go on to discuss Thorpe's "The Big Bear of Arkansas" in detail. Jim tells the story in salty language, and after he is finished, the story shifts back to the stuffy style of the first narrator which contains latinate words, apologetic quotes, and long sentences. At this same point in the story, both Jim and the audience are plopped down again in the mundane cabin. The final sentence contrasts Jim's world with the world of the writer. The shift in style, tone, and subject mark an anticlimax.

204. Blair, Walter, and Raven I. McDavid, Jr., eds. "Thomas Bangs Thorpe." The Mirth of a Nation: America's Great Dialect Humor. Minneapolis: Univ. of Minnesota Press, 1983, 48-59.

Confirms that it was Bernard DeVoto who named the antebellum Southern comic writers "the Big Bear School" in recognition of Thomas Bangs Thorpe's most important sketch. The sketch is a tale within a tale. It takes place in the social hall of a Mississippi River steamboat during a trip north from New Orleans. There is a crowd of story tellers that is joined by Jim Doggett who tells about "The Big Bear of Arkansas." This bear is a "creation bear," and in this sketch there are many narrative complexities, and there is a great deal of mythic significance. One of William Faulkner's graduate students asked Faulkner about the resemblances between Thorpe's "Big Bear of Arkansas," and Faulkner's own "The Bear," and Faulkner looked surprised, and responded, "That's a fine story. A writer is afraid of a story like that. He's afraid he'll try to rewrite it. A writer has to learn when to run from a story."

205. Cohen, Hennig, and William B. Dillingham, eds. "Thomas Bangs Thorpe." Humor of the Old Southwest, 2nd edition. Athens: Univ. of Georgia Press, 1975, 267-95.

Suggests that "The Big Bear of Arkansas" has much in common both with Melville's Moby-Dick (1851), and with Faulkner's The Bear (1942). Thorpe's realistic and humorous yarns about the American frontier have been translated into German, Italian, and French.

Thorpe's importance as an author is a result of his "originality, earthy comedy, realism, and the sense of the dignity which he saw in the life and people of the Southwestern frontier."

206. Keller, Mark A. "T. B. Thorpe's 'Tom Owen, the Bee-Hunter': Southwestern Humor's 'Origin of Species.'" Southern Studies 18.1 (Spring 1979): 89-101.

Contends that during the 1840s and 1850s Thorpe's "Tom Owen, the Bee-Hunter" surpassed "The Big Bear of Arkansas" in popularity, even though modern critics and modern audiences are familiar with the second but not with the first. "Tom Owen" was published in Spirit of the Times in 1841, and in 1859 Thorpe wrote a sequel for Spirit of the Times entitled "Reminiscences of Tom Owen the Bee Hunter." Keller feels that both of these works deserve a wider readership and more critical attention than they are getting.

207. Keller, Mark A. "Thomas Bangs Thorpe." Dictionary of Literary Biography, Volume II: American Humorists, 1800-1950, Ed. Stanley Trachtenberg. Detroit, MI: Gale, 1982, 497-505.

Contrasts Thorpe's "The Big Bear of Arkansas," which has lasted well over time, with "Tom Owen, the Bee-Hunter," which was "perhaps the most popular single frontier humor sketch of the antebellum period" but didn't last so well through time. "Tom Owen, the Bee-Hunter," Thorpe's first important sketch, describes a single incident. Tom Owen follows a bee to its hive in a tree and then cuts the tree down. The humor comes from the mock-heroic tone reminiscent of Washington Irving's sketches and also of Cervantes' Don Quixote. Thorpe compares Tom Owen to Davy Crockett and Nimrod Wildfire in their hunting ability. As Tom begins to chop down the honey-laden tree, he is attacked by a swarm of bees and changes from hunter to heroic fighter. He wins the battle by confusing his enemies with a thick cloud of smoke. The humor in "The Big Bear of Arkansas" is based on incongruities: the incongruity between the polished rhetoric of the gentleman narrator and the frontier dialect of Jim Doggett and the incongruity between the time and place of the story and the time and place of the event itself. Leo Lemay suggests that Doggett's killing of the bear symbolizes the fall of man as it marked "the end of the reign of the Eden-like wilderness of the Old Southwest."

208. Keller, Mark A. "Thomas Bangs Thorpe." Encyclopedia of American Humorists. New York: Garland, 1988, 442-45.

Considers Thorpe's "The Big Bear of Arkansas" to be the most famous sketch to come out of the comic and realistic backwoods tradition of the humorists of the Old Southwest. Keller further considers Thorpe's first story, "Tom Owen, the Bee-Hunter," to have been Thorpe's most widely read sketch during his own day. The Tom Owen story describes in mock-heroic tone the courageous exploits of a backwoodsman in a quest to find and do battle with ferocious bees. The characterization and setting of the story are southern, but the style is more reminiscent of that of Washington Irving. Keller feels that this sketch provides an important bridge between the genteel humor of the nineteenth century and the more realistic, racy humor of the Old Southwest. In 1843 and 1844, Thorpe wrote "Letters from the Far West" for the Concordia Intelligencer in Louisiana. In these letters, Thorpe developed the character of "Little Woeful" to satirize the romantic depiction of travel literature in general and western sport literature in particular. Thorpe satirically develops romantic metaphors and ludicrous images of prairie artifact collection and eastern views of indians and wildlife. Thorpe also satirizes James Audubon and other natural history enthusiasts who viewed nature from what Thorpe considered to be an "overly intellectual stance." Thorpe's two most important collections of sketches are The Mysteries of the Backwoods (1846), and The Hive of 'The Bee-Hunter' (1954).

Henry David Thoreau (1817-1862)

209. Hodges, Robert R. "The Functional Satire of Thoreau's Hermit and Poet" Satire Newsletter. 8.2 (Spring 1971): 105-08.

Indicates that the twelfth chapter of Thoreau's Walden functions as a transition from the "Higher Laws" of the previous chapter to the relaxed and passive observation of nature of the following chapter. The Hermit's dilemma of whether to go to heaven or to go fishing points up the transitional element of this chapter, but the tone of the dialogue between Hermit and Poet at the beginning of "Brute Neighbors" suggests that there is more than just a simple transition involved here. The dialogue of chapter twelve seems to have a "comic" or "whimsical" or "mock-pastoral" tone. Hodges feels that the shift from the "austere spirituality of 'Higher Laws'" to the "descriptions of nature in the rest of 'Brute Neighbors'" has coherence only if it is read as satire. Hodges feels that the rich paradox of the title when coupled with the "sterile antipathy between the exploitable realm of the brutes and the pretentious spirituality of the humane realm of neighbors" should convince the reader to read the passage as satire.

210. Williams, Ned B. "Thoreau's Healing Humor in The Maine Woods." WHIMSY 4 (1986): 31-32.

Stipulates that The Maine Woods, Thoreau's final book, contains some of the finest humor of nineteenth-century New England literature. The book's effectiveness as a travel account is largely the result of Thoreau's nimble wit, ironic innuendo, comical aphorisms, clever exaggerations, and whimsical anecdotes, of which he is often the center of the joke. On a deeper level, however, Thoreau's humor softens and ultimately conquers his personal dejection and instability concerning his declining health and his erratic moodiness. The vehicle of humor, therefore, brings Thoreau back from the center of his personal wilderness after he recognizes for the first time the dark, irrational, and destructive side of nature--a view which nearly spoiled his early celebration of transcendentalism. Williams feels, therefore, that Thoreau effectively used humor as a healing force over his own despair.

Orlando Benedict Mayer (1818-1891)

211. Kibler, James. "'The Innocent Cause, Or How Snoring Broke
     Off a Match': A Sketch from the Dutch Fork School of Humor."
     Studies in American Humor NS2.3 (Winter 1983-84): 185-194.

     Presents Mayer as a jolly extrovert and practical joker in
ways similar to his own character, Belt Seebub. Mayer is a recently
discovered humorist, and his "The Innocent Cause, Or How Snoring
Broke Off a Match" appeared in the January 25, 1848, issue of the
South Carolinian. Mayer was a native of Dutch Fork as was Adam
Summer, the editor of the South Carolinian. "The Innocent Cause" is
vintage Southern humor, and one of Mayer's best pieces of humorous
writing. It contains well-handled dialect, comic misspellings,
incongruous comic situations, precise and concrete descriptions, and
the creation of a lively and believable protagonist. Kibler feels
that O. B. Mayer's Belt Seebub and G. W. Harris' Sut Lovingood must
be first cousins. They were born six years apart (1848 and 1854,
respectively). They both have the same amorous nature, and they
both run away whenever their predicaments get too scary. Mayer also
uses the "sut" of the stove-pipe as a central object in the plot of
this particular sketch. Seven months after "The Innocent Cause,"
Mayer published his realistic humorous novel, John Punterick: A
Novel of the Old Dutch Fork, a humorous folk history of Mayer's
community, written to preserve customs, dialect, and manners.

212. Kibler, James E. Jr. "Orlando Benedict Mayer." Encyclopedia
     of American Humorists. Ed. Steven H. Gale. New York: Garland,
     1988, 315-20.

     Characterizes Mayer as having a keen eye for detail, a keen
ear for dialect, and an appreciation for the quaint customs of the
Dutch immigrants he wrote about. Mayer wrote for the Columbia South
Carolinian, for Russell's Magazine, and for Southern Bivouac. His
comic backwoods tales were in the mainstream tradition of southern
frontier humor. Mayer uses the frame device which contrasts the
allusive, stilted, sometimes lyrical language of the narrator with
the earthy dialect, exaggerated descriptions, and physical humor of
the characters the narrator is telling about. Under the pseudonym
of "Haggis," he wrote "The Innocent Cause, Or How Snoring Broke Off
a Match," in which Belt Seebub must compete for a country girl's
affections. Belt must share a room for the night with his
competitor and describes how his competitor sleeps on his back with
his mouth open; it "looked like a steel trap set for a otter and
baited with a piece of dried beef." "Snip--A Tale" was Mayer's
second humorous work. The story was about the role that a horse,
"Snip," played in a wedding and other Dutch Fork family life. "The
Easter Eggs" also involves Dutch Fork courting customs as does "The
Corn Cob Pipe," the plot of which is similar to that of Irving's
"The Legend of Sleepy Hollow."

Henry Wheeler Shaw (1818-1885)

213. Blair, Walter, and Hamlin Hill. "Shaw, Locke, and Smith."
     America's Humor: From Poor Richard to Doonesbury. New York:
     Oxford University Press, 1978, 284-99.

     Compares three important "phunny phellows" (Henry Wheeler
Shaw, David Ross Locke, and Charles Henry Smith) and their
respective narrators (Josh Billings, Petroleum Vesuvius Nasby, and
Bill Arp). Charles Farrar Browne through his narrator, Artemus
Ward, had blazed the trail for these other three phunny phellows to
follow. Shaw wrote ten successful books bearing Josh Billings'
name. Josh Billings' Farmer's Allminax developed the illiterate
comic aphorism and sold more than a million copies in a single
decade. David Ross Locke's writings, which relied on rhetorical
devices developed earlier by Browne, were also well read. Locke's
works contained horrible spelling, delinquent grammar, and other
verbal acrobatics. Finally, there were the writings of Charles
Henry Smith. Like Shaw and Locke, Smith also found Browne's formula
highly profitable. These four "phunny phellows" brought laughter to
a much larger audience than the earlier "local colorists" had done.
By coining cynical aphorisms and by combatting sentimentality and
pretentiousness, they helped express and popularize the changed
attitudes that had resulted from the Civil War.

214. Blair, Walter, and Raven I. McDavid, Jr., eds. "Henry Wheeler
     Shaw." The Mirth of a Nation: America's Great Dialect Humor.
     Minneapolis: Univ. of Minnesota Press, 1983, 154-56.

     Points out that Shaw was an explorer of the west, a farmer, a
river boat captain, an auctioneer, and a real estate salesman before
he became a full-time humorist and that all of these occupations
helped Shaw become a homespun philosopher. When Shaw read some
popular "letters" written in some newspapers by Artemus Ward, he
remembered that he himself had written some similar pieces. He dug
out and published his "Essa on the Muel" and signed it with the pen
name of Josh Billings. It was an instant success, and Josh
Billings' sayings were published in ten books. Abraham Lincoln very
much liked Shaw's aphorisms and considered Josh Billings to be
second only to Shakespeare as a judge of human nature.

215. Kesterson, David B. "Henry Wheeler Shaw." Dictionary of
     Literary Biography: Volume II: American Humorists, 1800-1950.
     Detroit, MI: Gale, 1982, 429-84.

     Suggests that Shaw was a model for Twain and illustrates the
many features which Shaw and Twain had in common. They were both
homespun philosophers on the comic circuit who liked to coin clever
aphorisms, write popular essays, sketches, and burlesque almanacs.
Shaw said, "When a feller gets a goin down hil, it dus seem as tho
evry thing had bin greased for the okashun." Shaw was restless and
prankish rather than scholarly as was his alter ego, Josh Billings.
Billings, the narrator in Shaw's frame tales, wrote in a rustic and
ungrammatical way. His sayings exhibited many different literary
devices such as understatement ("I found the ice in a slippery
condition"), anticlimax ("Buty is power; but the most treacherous
one i kno ov"), and antiproverbialism ("Give me liberty, or giv me

deth--but ov the 2 I prefer the liberty"). Josh Billings had a
talent for squeezing a great deal of folk wisdom into a few words.
In 1867 he began writing a column for the New York Weekly. The
column was so successful that it continued running the remaining
eighteen years of his life and "was even rerun for several years
posthumously. (The publishers simply did not announce Shaw's death
in 1885)." Josh Billings' Farmer's Allminax was Shaw's most
successful piece of writing.

216. Myers, James E., ed. America's Phunniest Phellow, Josh
     Billings: The Delightful. Springfield, IL: Lincoln-Herndon
     Press, 1986, x + 235 pp.

     Considers Shaw not to have been much of a scholar. He loved
fishing and hunting, and he especially loved pranks and practical
jokes. At the age of fifteen he entered Hamilton College in
Clinton, New York. On Sundays, the students were awakened and
beckoned to church services by the clanging of the bell that hung in
the campus chapel. Shaw was so annoyed by this weekly noise that he
climbed up the lightning rod next to the bell tower and removed the
bell's clapper. Then he climbed back down and went back to bed.
From his childhood, Shaw had lusted to see the frontier West first
hand, so he moved to Toledo, Ohio, where he and two friends
developed a lecture and show based on a form of hypnotism called
"mesmerism." Shaw's hilarious and entertaining delivery probably
established him as America's first important stand-up comic. Shaw
wandered around from 1835 to 1845 experiencing life and developing
a kind of healthy skepticism about both the noble and the less-than-
noble aspects of the American frontier that would later be evident
in his writing. Shaw's biographer, Cyril Clemens, is correct in
saying that "Josh Billings is as American as apple pie or the
corncob pipe." Many of Shaw's phonetic spellings have been altered
by his editors; however, Myers feels that they are an important
aspect of his humor and that they are as funny now as they were
then. Shaw's own attitude on the subject is that he had just as
much right to spell words the way they sounded as the dictionary had
to spell them the way they didn't sound.

Hardin Edwards Taliaferro (c1818-1875)

217. Blair, Walter, and Raven I. McDavid, Jr., eds. "Harden E.
     Taliaferro." The Mirth of a Nation: America's Great Dialect
     Humor. Minneapolis: Univ. of Minnesota Press, 1983, 110-14.

     Presents Taliaferro as a preacher and editor of the
Southwestern Baptist. He published only one book during his
lifetime, Fisher's River (North Carolina) Scenes and Characters, by
"Skitt," Who was Raised Thar, but this book contained his best
writing. It is now read for "its social history, its
characterizations, and the oral tales that it recorded." Larkin
Snow is Taliaferro's narrator, as he tells the "Story of the Eels."
Blair says that this story conforms to the tradition of the tall
tale as formulated by Norris W. Yates, being "a fantastic yarn
rendered temporarily plausible by the supporting use of realistic
detail."

218. Cohen, Hennig, and William B. Dillingham, eds. "Harden E.
      Taliaferro." Humor of the Old Southwest. 2nd edition. Athens:
      Univ. of Georgia Press, 1975, 296-309.

      Indicates that Taliaferro worked on his farm all week and then
preached on Sundays. When he was about nineteen, he moved to
Alabama where he became a Baptist minister, but he kept in touch
with North Carolina residents and collected proverbs, superstitions,
and folkways of Surry County. A reviewer of his work for Harper's
New Monthly Magazine said that while the rest of the United States
were practicing "bland conformity," the people of Surry County that
Taliaferro wrote about "clung to their individualism and went their
own way."   Taliaferro's stories are about "fantastic snakes and
fabulous hunters whose adventures were close to those of Baron
Munchausen."   Because of Taliaferro's incredible eye for detail,
folklorists consider him an excellent source for North Carolina back
country folkways and folklore.

219. Craig, Raymond C., "H. C. Taliaferro." Encyclopedia of
      American Humorists. Ed. Steven H. Gale. New York: Garland,
      1988, 422-24.

      Feels that the Civil War was a turning point in Taliaferro's
career. It overwhelmed him to the extent that he did not return to
writing humor after the war. During Taliaferro's time, story
telling was a significant form of recreation, and in North Carolina
each community boasted excellent story tellers. Taliaferro was an
excellent collector of these folk tales, identifying the story
tellers by name, and capturing "their storytelling styles as well as
their best tales." There were eight-six real-life persons so named
in Fisher's River, and thirty-three real places, including
mountains, passes, river forks, creeks, and camping sites. Fisher's
River even included the names of favorite horses, guns, dogs, and
pocket knives. Since Taliaferro was a preacher himself, he
especially enjoyed collecting stories about preachers.   "His
favorite target was Parson Bellows, the local 'Mathodiss' preacher."
Although he collected stories about women, blacks, and cripples, he
always treated his targets with kindness and empathy compared with
his contemporaries.   His favorite stories were about hunting,
courting, religion, fighting, quilting, weddings, and encounters
with the genteel manners of "quality" folks.

220. Craig, Raymond C., ed. The Humor of H. E. Taliaferro.
      Knoxville: Univ. of Tennessee Press, 1987, xii + 259 pp.

      Goes into detail concerning Taliaferro's life, his collection
techniques, his writing style, and especially, his humor. He would
visit with his old friends in Surry County, eat at their tables, sit
with them in their small cabins in the evening to swap stories and
just talk. In order to relate to the people better, he would preach
in the local churches, and walk up and down the steep trails he had
walked as a boy. He had an advantage in his collecting in that his
family was still influential in the community. He would visit Surry
County for a couple of weeks, and then return to Tuskagee, Alabama,
and write down the anecdotes he had heard during his trip, "hoping
to record their idiosyncracies and capture some of their charm."
Taliaferro enjoyed eccentric behavior and eccentric speech, and
somehow, Surry County had more than its share of odd and colorful

characters: "Uncle Davy Lane, the local gunsmith, lazy, garrulous, rarely separated from his hunting rifle, Old Bucksmasher; poor gullible Uncle Billy Lewis, who got into trouble for shooting horses instead of deer on a night hunt...; Oliver Stanley, who'd been to sea and told tall tales about his exploits there; and Bob Snipes; and Josh "Hash Head" Jones; and a whole string of Snows--Larkin, Dick, Johnson, Frost, John--most of them good for a story." A mild criticism of Taliaferro's work is that he made the county appear a little too Utopian.

221. **Penrod, James H. "Harden Taliaferro, Folk Humorist of North Carolina." The Frontier Humorists: Critical Views. Ed. M. Thomas Inge. Hamden, CT: Archon, 1975, 187-93.**

Considers Taliaferro to have been important for his portrayal of folk character, his treatment of dialect, his transcription of local color in detail, and his recording of the social history of the Old South. Penrod feels that the quality of Taliaferro's work would place him among the distinguished humorists of the Old Southwest, except for the geographical location of his stories, which is not strictly the Southwest. Penrod also distinguishes Taliaferro from other yarn spinners of his day by one other feature--his sympathy. Penrod feels that the reason that Taliaferro was more sympathetic than Longstreet, Baldwin, Hooper, and others is that Taliaferro was writing about his own people. He therefore didn't strike the superior pose that the others had assumed. Taliaferro was also writing about the stable, well-rooted elements of society, whereas other Southwestern humorists tended to write about the "fluid frontier" with its wide assortment of "opportunists" or "rapscallions." Conspicuously absent in his work are such swindlers as Hooper's Simon Suggs, and Baldwin's Ovid Bolus; hypocrites like Sheriff Doltin and Parson Bullen of Sut Lovingood's Yarns. Taliaferro writes about unqualified preachers, insincere converts, and an idler, but these are not hurtful people, and even these characters are treated in a sympathetic manner.

William C. Hall (c1819-c1865)

222. **Anderson, John Q. "Mike Hooter--The Making of a Myth." Southern Folklore Quarterly 19 (March 1955): 90-100.**

Considers the evolution of Mike Hooter from a real man to a legend to be a good example of the myth-making process. The oral tale coupled with the printed story increased Mike Hooter's fame from regional to national, thereby entering him in as a legitimate member into American folklore. There were several other legendary heroes of the Old Southwest who underwent this same process, including Davy Crockett, Mike Fink, and Paul Bunyan. Mike Hooter was a bear hunter and lay preacher in Mississippi. He was changed from man to myth primarily by two writers, William C. Hall and Henry Clay Lewis. In selecting an actual man as the basis for the humorous yarns, Hall and Lewis were following a long tradition in frontier humor. During the time of Hall and Lewis, Mike Hooter's exploits were very popular in Yazoo County. Hall and Lewis realized that something old in speech might look like something new in writing, so they dramatized Mike's most obvious eccentricities and surrounded him with characteristic actions and attitudes, some of which might not have originally belonged to Hooter. But Lewis died at the early age of twenty-five, and Hall stopped writing about Mike Hooter, so Hooter therefore never attained the sustained popularity of Crockett, Fink, or Bunyan.

223. Blair, Walter, and Raven I. McDavid, Jr., eds. "William C. Hall." The Mirth of a Nation: America's Great Dialect Humor. Minneapolis: Univ. of Minnesota Press, 1983, 99-105.

Explains that Hall's five "Yazoo Sketches" were named after the county in which Hall was born--Yazoo County, Mississippi. The sketches portray the life of a cotton planter of Yazoo county. Mike Hooter was Hall's protagonist, "a profane, tall-talking, guzzling backwoodsman." One of the sketches was entitled "How Sally Hooter Got Snake-bit" and describes a fire and brimstone sermon by Parson James, during which Sally Hooter started fidgeting more and more until finally she was "a-rearin and a-pitchin, a-rippin and a-tearin, and a-shoutin like flinders." The whole congregation gather around her, figuring that Sally had "done got 'ligious," but then they discovered that a snake had crawled up under Sally's coat. The visual imagery of Brother Potter fumbling around trying to get hold of the snake's tail was very racy in Hall's time, especially the part about Potter carrying on his search "sorta like he didn't like to do it at first, and then, sorta like he did." Blair and McDavid feel that Hall had a tendency to be "unfashionably frank," and says that one of sketches which graphically describes a whorehouse in Natches, isn't even very funny.

224. Cohen, Hennig, and William B. Dillingham, eds. "William C. Hall." Humor of the Old Southwest. 2nd edition. Athens: Univ. of Georgia Press, 1975, 310-321.

Explains that Hall's Mike Hooter and Henry Clay Lewis's "Mik-Hootah of 'The Indefatigable Bear-Hunter'" were both based on the life of the same real-life person, "a well-known cotton planter and devout Methodist of Yazoo County," Mississippi. When he's on his own, Mike "hunts, drinks, brags, preaches, and swears with extraordinary vitality," but he is a domestic coward who fears that his wife, Sally, "might raise pertickler hell" if he doesn't come home in time for supper.

225. Keller, Mark A. "The Cowardly 'Lion of the [Old South] West'--Mike Hooter of Mississippi." Mississippi Folklore Register 18.1 (Spring 1984): 3-18.

Indicates that between 1849 and 1850 Hall published five stories in the New Orleans Delta later to become known as the "Yazoo Sketches." These stories were based on the life of an actual resident of Yazoo County, Mississippi, by the name of Mike Hooter, and the eccentric character which Hall wrote about bore the same name. Hall's sketches have action-filled plots and strong characterization with Mike Hooter sometimes relating the narratives himself in his own vernacular. Mike is portrayed as a garrulous old backwoods type, who wore a coonskin cap and a buckskin coat, chewed tobacco, and often interrupted his narratives at their most dramatic points and digressed in all directions in the tradition of Southwestern humor. Mike Hooter is often referred to as "Uncle

Mike" or "Ole Preach," this last name referring to the fact that he was a preacher and ruling elder in the Methodist church. But Mike's religion didn't keep him from hunting on Sunday, cussing when the situation warranted, and drinking liquor. In fact, the Hooter stories frequently concluded with the exhortation, "Come boys, let's liquor."

226. **Keller, Mark.** "'How Mike Shouter "Cotch" the Bar': Another 'Yazoo Sketch.'" Southern Folklore Quarterly 41 (1977): 65-72.

Considers it noteworthy that interest in the Mike Hooter stories has been sustained despite the fact that these five stories in "The Yazoo Sketches" represent all of William Hall's known literary output. Keller feels that Mike Hooter continues the tradition of the ring-tailed roarers such as Davy Crockett and Mike Fink. Keller feels that Mike Hooter lacks "the bravado of Mike Fink, the shiftiness of Simon Suggs, and the diabolic genius of Sut Lovingood," but he notes that Hooter nevertheless manages to survive in the wild environment of the Mississippi frontier. Four of the five Yazoo sketches rely on the "framing" structure which contrasts the literate narrator with the vernacular character, but there is one tale which Mike Fink tells directly and in the tradition of Southwest humor. This tale departs from the straight narrative line into a series of seemingly endless digressions. These digressions may delay the action of the story and cause the reader to become frustrated, but the digressions also arouse the readers' interest and make them impatient to hear the end of the story.

James Russell Lowell (1819-1891)

227. **Blair, Walter, and Raven I. McDavid, Jr., eds.** "James Russell Lowell." The Mirth of a Nation: America's Great Dialect Humor. Minneapolis: Univ. of Minnesota Press, 1983, 17-30.

Acknowledges that Lowell was a Harvard professor, a learned scholar, an outstanding editor, an influential writer on politics, a profound literary critic, and a serious poet. It is therefore ironic that most of Lowell's writings have not stood the test of time, and that he is remembered today almost entirely because he created two illiterate Yankees--a disreputable rascal and a pious hayseed. Early on, Lowell realized that his serious writings were almost unread. Furthermore, he had many models from Poor Richard's day to his own to prove that some of the most effective satirists had been uneducated, horse-sensible commentators, so he decided to let such characters be his mouthpieces. Lowell was a Professor of Romance Languages and Linguistics at Harvard University, and he therefore not only knew and respected regional and social dialects but also had a good ear for them. The authentic language was an important aid both to the vivid characterization and to the comedy of his writing. Birdofredum Sawin was a patriotic farm boy who enlisted in the army. He lost an arm, a leg, and an eye and then decided to cash in on his disfigurements by going into politics.

228. Royot, Daniel G. "James Russell Lowell." Encyclopedia of American Humorists. Ed. Steven H. Gale. New York: Garland, 1988, 296-301.

Portrays Lowell as an incisive and sometimes impertinent critic. His "Fable for Critics" singled out the mannerisms of such major figures as James Fenimore Cooper, Edgar Allan Poe, Ralph Waldo Emerson, Margaret Fuller, Nathaniel Willis, and John Neal, among others. Margaret Fuller had earlier criticized Lowell, so Lowell got even in "Fable for Critics" by offering the harshest of his criticisms. Lowell summed up Poe's contribution with the line, "three fifths...genius and two fifths sheer fudge." The southern writers are general missing from "Fable for Critics"; it's difficult to know whether they mind being excluded or not. The Biglow Papers are a satire in Yankee dialect on the campaign to recruit troops in Massachusetts to fight the Mexican-American war and the Civil war. Many of Lowell's critics accused him of being unpatriotic in a national crisis. The "casual use of Yankee dialect often seemed inappropriate to people who were too much in earnest to appreciate mock-heroic satire." Lowell was strongly opposed to both wars, and he used humor and incisive irony to keep his didacticism and perhaps fanaticism from showing. "Biglow is a shrewd crackerbox philosopher, Homer Wilbur a pedantic parson encumbered with his profuse quotations from the classics, and Birdofredum a Yankee rogue in the image of the peddler."

229. Royot, Daniel. "James Russell Lowell: Un humoriste Yankee face au sud et à l'esclavage." Etudes Anglaises 39.1 (1986): 26-36.

Explains the Biglow Papers as a Yankee view of slavery and the South, and suggests that this may be because Lowell was born and raised in the "bourgeoisie intellectuelle" New England atmosphere of Cambridge, Massachusetts. Lowell's satiric style is more like that of Juvenal than that of Horace.

230. Wortham, Thomas. "James Russell Lowell." Dictionary of Literary Biography, Volume II: American Humorists, 1800-1950. Ed. Stanley Trachtenberg. Detroit, MI: Gale, 1982, 291-303.

Suggests that Charles Eliot Norton, Lowell's literary executor, didn't have a sense of humor. Even so, humor is never absent from Lowell's best poetry, even that edited by Norton. Lowell was not a cynic, but he was indeed a skeptic and one with a strange angle of vision. He characterized humor as "that modulating and restraining balance-wheel." In assessing the contribution of Cervantes, Lowell said that his sense of humor had made him capable of seeing that there are "two sides to every question" Lowell was a didactic satirist. He wrote to entertain, but he also wrote to convince, and his views on transcendentalism, abolition, woman's rights, and temperance were clear from his writings. Fellow abolitionist John Greenleaf Whittier said that the world-wide laugh caused by Hosea Biglow was enough to "have shaken half the walls of Slavery down." Lowell himself was amazed at how popular Hosea Biglow became. "I held in my hand a weapon instead of the mere fencing-stick I had supposed." He found verses of Hosea Biglow copied everywhere and often would hear arguments as to the authorship of the Hosea Biglow statements. Wortham feels that

Lowell's satires have earned him inclusion in every responsible anthology of American literature, humorous or otherwise, ever compiled.

Herman Melville (1819-1891)

231. Bickley, R. Bruce, Jr. "The Triple Thurst of Satire in Melville's Short Stories: Society, The Narrator, and the Reader." Studies in American Humor 1 (January 1975): 172-79.

Indicates that at the end of the nineteenth century Herman Melville had the reputation of a comic writer. Harper's Magazine ran an article in 1890 listing him as one of America's literary comedians. Robert Louis Stevenson described him as a "howling cheese." Edward Rosenberry, a more recent critic, says that there is a marvelous range in Melville's humor. There is the "jocular-hedonic" humor of Typee and Omoo. There is the imaginative, psychological, and intellectual humor of Mardi, Moby Dick, and The Confidence-Man. And there is always Melville's irony and satire. Melville uses his satire to achieve social revenge in a rather sophisticated way. Through his narrators, Melville chastises social groups for their failures and inadequacies. However, he also chastises his own narrators for inadvertently doing the things they find reprehensible in society. Finally, he develops his narrators as engaging characters the readers will identify with. Readers, therefore, are sympathetic and develop a rapport that forces them to fall into the same trap as the narrators are falling into--becoming objects of the satire they think is being directed elsewhere.

232. Brucker, Carl. "Review of Melville's Humor: A Critical Study by Jane Mushabac." Studies in American Humor 2.3 (Winter 1983-84): 215-216.

Indicates that Mushabac supports Edward Rosenberry's contention that "comedy was Melville's 'true milieu'." Mushabac suggests that critics have been reluctant to approach Melville's writing from the comic perspective because of "the modern critical fear of the 'contagion of sentimentality'." Mushabac feels that this is an unwarranted fear, for she feels that humor "plays off" sentimentality, and "moves through" sentimentality "to achieve its effects." Mushabac's book sees Melville's humor as in the European macho tradition, stressing "braggadocio and defeat," "grand pointless quests," and a verbal energy that "undoes itself with measured illogic, folly, and ultimate wisdom." Mushabac suggests that Melville uses humor as a means for "'hugging' the contraries of existence." Mushabac feels that The Confidence-Man and Israel Potter represent the two extremes of Melville's comic method. Brucker feels that Mushabac's book forces us to reconsider the significance of humor in the development of the American novel.

233. Kern, Alexander C. "Melville's The Confidence-Man: A Structure of Satire." Ed. O. M. Brack, Jr. American Humor. Scottsdale, Arizona: Arete, 1977, 27-41.

Postulates the paradox that Melville's The Confidence-Man can be viewed either as an optimistic or as a pessimistic novel and further postulates that this paradox is resolved if the novel is read as a satire. The book contains much intentional ambiguity. It was published on April 1st. And the action of the novel takes place on "April Fool's Day." Kern feels that Melville "so effectively befooled his readers that there is still disagreement as to his intent." In Anatomy of Criticism, Northrop Frye indicates that Menippean prose satire is more abstract and intellectual than the regular novel, that it "deals less with people than with attitudes, uses stylized rather than realistic characterizations, and presents people as mouthpieces of the ideas they represent." The Confidence Man displays these characteristics. It also displays ambiguity and paradox. The Confidence-Man has been variously identified as the Devil, God, and Everyman. Furthermore, the novel has "no obvious hero, no plot, no resolution, and an ironic ending." It is not a novel, but an anti-novel, like Gulliver's Travels. Finally, while Moby Dick gives us Ishmael, through whose eyes the reader is able to see the unfolding of events, The Confidence-Man offers us no such consistent viewpoint. For these reasons, the satiric reading is the most plausible.

234. Latchaw, Joan S. "Beyond Nationality: Ishmael as a Comic Force." WHIMSY 6 (1988): 21-22.

Contrasts Ahab, who exhibits the mask of tragedy, with Ishmael, who exhibits the mask of comedy. Susanne Langer says that comedy "celebrates the victory of the witty man over the obstacles of chance and fortune." Latchaw therefore wonders if this is why Ishmael, the humorist, is the sole survivor in the novel, the only person left to tell the tale. Ishmael was able to use humor as a tool for survival because it allowed him "the distance that is required of the comic intelligence." He remembers and recounts events without self-pity, self-consciousness, or obsession but with psychological acuity. Ahab also has knows a great deal about the events; however, Ahab insists on controlling the events, and, ironically, Ahab is the person who in the end is most controlled by the events he is trying too hard to control.

235. Raff, Heather. "Review of Melville's Humor: A Critical Study by Jane Mushabac." Thalia: Studies in Literary Humor. 7.1 (1984): 51-52.

Gives evidence that Melville's writing was influenced from a number of humorous traditions: "the Renaissance extravaganzas of Rabelais, Cyrano de Bergerac, Bayle, and Burton," "the romantic and amiable humor of Sterne, Lamb, and DeQuincey," and "the American style of Washington Irving, Davy Crockett" and others. From these come both the tone: "erotic, expansive--and grim," and the forms for Melville's wit: "the tall tale, the melancholy anatomy, the humorous novel, the essay of sensibility, the cock-and-bull story, and the almanac sayings." The tragicomic element can be seen by contrasting the comradeship and bed-sharing of Ishmael and Queequeg at the Spouter-Inn with the deathly embrace of Ahab and the Great White Whale in their final encounter. Flippancy is also a clue to the humor of the novel, as when Queequeg's birthplace is described as "not down in any map; true places never are." Mushabac feels that Melville's humor "releases the tension of man's predicament in an ideal democratic society."

Anna Cora Mowatt (1819-1870)

236. Walker, Nancy A. "Anna Cora Mowatt." A Very Serious Thing:
     Women's Humor and American Culture. Minneapolis: Univ. of
     Minnesota Press, 1988, 74.

Compares the prologue to Mowatt's satiric play Fashion with
the prologue to Anne Bradstreet's The Tenth Muse. In both cases
there is a plea for readers to regard women's humorous writing as
significant. Just before Mowatt's Fashion was first presented
W. A. Jones published an article entitled "The Ladies' Library" in
Graham's Magazine (volume 21, 1842) that had categorically denied
the possibility that women might have a sense of humor. It said
that while women may have sprightliness, cleverness, and smartness,
they have little wit. True wit has a "body substance" and a
"reflectiveness" that is usually found only in the masculine
intellect. Jones knows of not a single female writer who has "a
high character of humor," and concludes that "the female character
does not admit of it." In reaction to this and other similar
statements, Epes Sargent writes in the prologue that Mowatt's play
is suspect on two grounds: "that it was written by a woman, and that
it was written by an American." Mowatt herself continues the
irony: "What! from a woman's pen?   It takes a man/To write a
comedy--no woman can."

Walt Whitman (1819-1892)

237. Crisler, Jesse S. "Gay Walt: 'Wit' in Song of Myself."
     WHIMSY 2 (1984): 20-23.

Quotes Whitman as having said "I pride myself on being a real
humorist underneath everything else." This quote appears in Richard
Chase's Walt Whitman Reconsidered. Emerson also found Whitman to
have exhibited "extraordinary wit" in Song of Myself. The wit can
be physical or visceral, as he dives beneath the new-mown clover and
timothy, his hair flying and filled with wisps. Whitman is at times
quite ribald, as when he says he will "...make short account of
neuters and geldings, and favor men and women fully equipt."
Whitman also uses seven different types of intellectual, or
linguistic wit, as follows: 1. abrupt beginnings, 2. individual
words, 3. punning, 4. parody, 5. litotes, 6. hyperbole, and 7.
association. The poem begins abruptly, "I celebrate myself, and
sing myself,/ And what I assume you shall assume." During a scene
of utter chaos and despair, Whitman understates: "It is generally
thought we are sinking." Whitman overstates when he describes
"landscapes projected masculine, full-sized and golden." Whitman is
almost in rapture as he affirms his worship of and devotion to one
particular body part. "Rhythmically, the lines are reminiscent of
the antiphonal readings between clergymen and parishioners which
obtain in many higher church services."

238. Safer, Elaine B. "Whitman's Leaves of Grass and the
     Twentieth-Century Comic Epic." The Contemporary American Comic
     Epic. Detroit: Wayne State Univ. Press, 1988, 39-49.

Considers the novels of Barth, Pynchon, Gaddis, and Kesey to
be largely a reaction to Whitman's celebrative, enthusiastic tone in

Leaves of Grass. Whitman celebrates richness of America where no one ever needs to go hungry as long as corn grows from the ground, the orchards drop apples, and the bays contain fish. For Whitman, "Manhattan participates in an Edenic dance of life: the conductor beating time for the band; the peddler sweating with his pack on his back; the bride unrumpling her white dress; the prostitute dragging her shawl; the crowd laughing; the men jeering and winking." The twentieth-century writers of the absurd present a darker, more derisive, satiric picture. For them, Manhattan is the wasteland. For them the land of milk and honey has become "the Street, home of the Whole Sick Crew." Whitman's innocent enthusiasm for America is repeatedly mocked in the twentieth-century novel. The twentieth century writers of the absurd recall Whitman's optimism, enthusiasm, and primal innocence to say that the American dream has turned into a nightmare. Whereas Whitman saw the ideal wherever he looked, the twentieth century absurdists force the reader to "combine laughter and pain, farce and horror, causing the reader to recognize the ideal and confront its absence."

239. Tanner, James T. F. "Four Comic Themes in Walt Whitman's Leaves of Grass 5 (1986): 62-71.

Describes the four comic themes of Leaves of Grass as four types of antithetical equality--body vs. soul, animal vs. human, male vs. female, and good vs. evil. Whitman illustrates the equality of body and soul by saying that the scent of his own arm- pits provides an "aroma finer than prayer." Whitman illustrates the equality of animal and human by addressing the oxen and telling them that what they express in their eyes is "more than all the print I have read in my life." Whitman illustrates the equality of male and female by addressing a prostitute and saying, "Not till the sun excludes you do I exclude you." Whitman illustrates the equality of good and evil by suggesting that since God made everything, one thing is just as good as another. For Whitman, evil is a part of God. Whitman says he is as propelled by evil as he is by good; he concludes, "I stand indifferent." Tanner claims that the more serious is Whitman's theme, the more apt he is to make his presentation comic or at least provocative.

240. Wallace, Ronald, ed. "Walt Whitman: Stucco'd with Quadrupeds and Birds All Over." God Be with the Clown: Humor in American Poetry. Columbia: Univ. of Missouri Press, 1984, 52-75.

Places Whitman into the tradition of the backwoods "ring- tailed roarers." In section 24 of Song of Myself, for example, we see the the swagger and braggadocio of the humorous backwoodsman, as he calls himself "a Kosmos, of Manhattan the son,/ Turbulent, fleshy, sensual, eating, drinking and breeding." Whitman like Davey Crockett and Nimrod Wildfire is a frontiersman, a man of excesses whose principal targets are "gentility, social pretense, culture, and personal anemia." By saying, "I do not press my fingers across my mouth,/ I keep as delicate around the bowels as around the head and heart," Whitman is satirizing "those ultrarefined people who reject bodily function by displays of polite shock or fear of sexuality." Whitman did not want people to get too comfortable in the easy, the conventional, and the secure; rather he wanted them to "explore wildernesses of the self." Jorge Luis Borges said that Whitman needed a hero like Achilles, Ulysses, Aeneas, Beowulf,

Roland, The Cid, and Sigurd. "Whitman's response was an amazing
one: he himself would be the hero of the poem." Wallace claims that
Whitman affirmed the backwoods character's excesses and
eccentricities by setting them to poetry, and he legitimitized their
aberrancy by putting himself in as subject.

Francis James Robinson (c1820-c1870)

241. Cohen, Hennig, and William B. Dillingham, eds. "Francis James Robinson." Humor of the Old Southwest. 2nd edition. Athens: Univ. of Georgia Press, 1975, 322-35.

Explains that Kups of Kauphy was Robinson's collection of letters and sketches and that the title is an allusion to Governor George Matthews of Oglethorpe County, Georgia. Governor Matthews always read aloud with all of the confidence of a person who knows he is doing everything very well. But he would fully pronounce the l in would, should, and the ed of expressed, and he spelled "coffee" as "kauphy." Robinson was a little-known writer; however he was firmly in the tradition of Old Southwest humor. Robinson ranges from tall tales to the Negro humor of "Old Jack C." He filled his sketches with dialogue in vernacular language, saying "wherever it has been possible we have let our characters use their own language in portraying their individuality." Rance, the protagonist of Robinson's sketches can kill twelve Comanches with six bullets, and Lije Benadix is a lazy and gluttonous member of the lowest poor white class. Robinson was a country doctor, and, therefore, his favorite targets include body disfunction and doctors who have difficulty figuring out what is wrong with their patients.

Edward Everett Hale (1822-1909)

242. Bellman, Samuel I. "Edward Everett Hale." Dictionary of Literary Bibliography: American Short-Story Writers Before 1880, Vol. 74. Ed. Bobby Ellen Kimbel, 1988: 109-23.

Suggests that "My Double and How He Undid Me" is Hale's first important story. Rev. Frederic Ingham is unable to perform all of the numerous and varied duties of a minister, so he asks another person, a person who looks very much like the minister, to be his "alter ego." But the double is dull witted and lazy. Reverand Ingham legally changes this man's name to his own and teaches him four cliche responses that should suffice for most occasions: "Very well, thank you. And you?," "I am very glad you liked it," "There has been so much said, and, on the whole, so well said, that I will not occupy the time," and "I agree, in general, with my friend on the other side of the room." The reverend further advises his double never to give speeches and always to vote with the minority. Of course the double soon finds himself in a situation where the four set responses will not work, and the clergyman is discovered. He is banished to open a new parish in Maine, where his only parishioners there are his wife and his daughter. Hale's short stories reveal his love of American history and his interest in developing science and technology. Hale has a wild imagination and a vibrant sense of humor. His prose was dull when he wrote about commonplace events and ordinary people, but when he allowed his fantasy to reign, he became witty and effective.

George Horatio Derby (1823-1861)

243. Blair, Walter, and Hamlin Hill. "Derby, Alter Egos: Phoenix
    and Squibob." America's Humor: From Poor Richard to
    Doonesbury. New York: Oxford University Press, 1978, 229-37.

    Considers Derby to have been a natural practical joker. At a
Sonoma party he sneaked into a room where the babies had been placed
and switched their blankets. The parents discovered the prank only
after they had returned home from the party. Before introducing his
bride to his mother, Derby had told each of them that the other was
deaf. He then listened to their shouting for ten minutes before
admitting that he had lied. Another time, when he was acting editor
of the San Diego Herald, he reversed the newspaper's politics,
ferociously attacking the candidate the paper had been backing and
praising highly the man the paper had been opposing. In San
Francisco there were regular meetings of a free-and-easy group of
literary men, mainly officers, journalists, editors, artists,
actors, politicians, and others with a strong sense of play, who
gathered in a particular saloon on Montgomery street, and Derby
frequently attended these gatherings. The group was aware of
Derby's great sense of humor and encouraged him to write his
material down. He wrote for newspapers and magazines first and
later collected his material in two popular books, Phoenixiana; or,
Sketches and Burlesques by John Phoenix, and Squibob Papers by John
Phoenix.

244. Lang, John. "George Derby and the Language of Reasoned
    Absurdity." Publications of the Missouri Philological
    Association 3 (1978): 61-70.

    Disagrees with those critics who believe that Artemus Ward was
the first American practitioner of the art of "reasoned absurdity."
Ward was inspired to become a humorist by reading George Derby's
Phoenixiana, and "it is Derby, not Ward, who first introduced to
America that zany comedy characteristic of Perelman, Benchley, and
the other New Yorker humorists whom Walter Blair labels 'crazy
men'." It is true that Derby's narrators don't exhibit the same
sense of helplessness and humiliation that is seen in the neurotic
"Little Man" of the New Yorker genre. Nevertheless, his humor
depends on the same attention to language and instinct for the
absurd. Derby is concerned with the limits of language, and with
"language's tendency to exhuast itself through cliche." Lang notes
that Derby was at one time considered a better writer than George
Washington Harris, James Baldwin, and Augustus Longstreet. Lang
feels that Derby deserves to be better known by both readers and
literary critics.

245. Lang, John. "George Horatio Derby." Dictionary of Literary
    Biography, Volume II: American Humorists, 1800-1950. Ed.
    Stanley Trachtenberg. Detroit, MI: Gale, 1982, 114-23.

    Affirms that Derby earned the nickname of Squibob at West
Point because of his numerous pranks and practical jokes. When
asked to write an essay on man's greatest virtue, he wrote on
"Impudence," for this is what got people furthest in life. On

another occasion he used complicated drawings and the jargon of ballistics to convince a senior general that a cannon had been invented which could shoot around corners. He also recommended to the War Department that the cavalry uniforms should have metal rings installed to the seats of the pants so that terrified recruits could be brought back onto the battlefield by sergeants with long hook-end poles if they attempted to flee. He became so famous as a sketch writer under the pen name of "Squibob" that many other authors also adopted this pen name. To silence them Derby published Squibob's obituary in the Herald and thereafter wrote under the name of John Phoenix. He spoofed the illustrated newspapers in "Phoenix's Pictorial" by repeating in various issues of the Herald the same wood block drawing of a house and labeled it as the home of Shakespeare, Sir Walter Scott, Governor Bigler, and John Phoenix, Esq. Below a picture of several ships he ran the caption, "The Battle of Lake Erie,...fought in 1836 on Chesapeake Bay."

246. Maguire, James H. "George Horatio Derby." Encyclopedia of American Humorists. Ed. Steven H. Gale. New York: Garland, 1988, 122-27.

Says that Derby is described as one of America's most famous writers in Mark Twain's Library of Humor. Early in life, Derby was a discipline problem and was sent to the School for Moral Discipline in his hometown, Dedham (near Boston). There he developed the reputation of a bad boy and a prankster. He later entered West Point where he continued as a prankster; he nevertheless graduated seventh in his class of fifty-nine. He became a famous humorous writer almost overnight as the result of a well-orchestrated prank. When J. J. Ames, the editor of the San Diego Herald, left town to do some political campaigning, he placed Derby in charge of the paper. Derby "transformed a sober, Democratic, small-town weekly into a riotous conglomeration of wit, burlesque, and satire, devoted to the Whig party." Derby used both high burlesque (in which an elevated style is used for a trivial subject), and low burlesque (in which a low style is used to treat an important subject). To explain why Twain's reputation still grows, while Derby's has waned almost to oblivion, George Stewart wrote that "to be a great humorist, a writer must be something much more, and a humorist secondarily."

Phoebe Cary (1824-1871)

247. Walker, Nancy, and Zita Dresner, eds. "Phoebe Cary." Redressing the Balance: American Women's Literary Humor from Colonial Times to the 1980s. Jackson: Univ. Press of Mississippi, 1988, 62-67.

Cites Mary Clemmer Ames as Cary's biographer and indicates that Ames considers Cary to be "the wittiest woman in America." In The Wit of Women (1885), Kate Sanborn indicated that Cary's dialogues are "most brilliant sallies...[which] came like flashes of heat lightning, like a rush of meteors, so suddenly and constantly you were dazzled while you were delighted." Cary's wit is often compared with that of Dorothy Parker. The main subject of her wit in her Poems and Parodies is society's expectations about the prescribed roles and images of women and the difficulties women have

in the socialization process. Sample titles of her poems include,
"Girls Were Made to Mourn," "The Wife," "A Psalm of Life," and "When
Lovely Woman." The poems tend to be ironic in tone.

Charles G. Leland (1824-1903)

248. Sloane, David E. E. "Charles G. Leland." Dictionary of
      Literary Biography, Volume II: American Humorists, 1800-1950.
      Ed. Stanley Trachtenberg. Detroit, MI: Gale, 1982, 156-66.

States that the most important event in Leland's career as a
humorous author occurred in 1857 when he published a burlesque in
Low-German-American dialect entitled "Hans Breitmann's Party" in
Graham's Magazine. This was a rollicking story of a "bier-trinken
low Dutchman" who was in love with Madilda Yane. Many of Leland's
mock-German lieder feature Breitmann and are typically burlesques of
German sagas and folktales. Meister Karl's Sketch-Book was
published in 1855. Sloane describes it as "an exuberant melange of
arcane speculations and quotations, travel descriptions, and light
verse." Leland wrote mock ballads in low-German for amusement and
said he originally had not intended to publish them. He composed
"De Maiden mit Nodings on" in his own mind on a train in 1864, but
it was not written down on paper until more than a year afterward.
The mermaid of this poem becomes "dis wasser maiden / Vot hadn't got
nodings on." In his Memoires, Leland compared P.T. Barnum, Abraham
Lincoln, and Rabelais, as all using "the brief arithmetic of the
joke to express their humanity." It is reported that one of
Leland's humor books was found on Lincoln's bedside table after the
assassination.

William Penn Brannan (1825-1866)

249. Blair, Walter, and Raven I. McDavid, Jr., eds. "William Penn
      Brannan. The Mirth of a Nation: America's Great Dialect Humor.
      Minneapolis: Univ. of Minnesota Press, 1983, 106-09.

Quotes Henry Watterson as having said that Brannan's mock
sermon "The Harp of a Thousand Strings" was one of "the most notable
stories which have gone the rounds of the American press the last
forty years,...thoroughly characteristic, in tone, color, and action
of the era." Brannan wrote a number of burlesque sermons and
published under the pen names of Bill Easel and Vendyke Brown.

250. Cohen, Hennig, and William B. Dillingham. "William Penn
      Brannan." Humor of the Old Southwest. 2nd edition. Athens:
      Univ. of Georgia Press, 1975, 355-59.

Indicates that Brannan's "The Harp of a Thousand Strings" was
frequently performed by Alf Burnett, an entertainer who became
famous in Union Army Camps. The sketch is an allusion to a Biblical
passage. The preacher doesn't know exactly where his text is to be
found in the Bible, but it is somewhere between the first chapter of
the book of "Generations" and the last chapter of the book of

"Revolutions." And the preacher informs the reader that if he searches the Scriptures he'll find not only this text, "but a great many other texes as will do you good to read." His quote reads, "And he played on a harp uv a thousand strings--sperits of jest men made perfeck." The preacher talks about the meaning of "spirits" and says what he means by the word is "HELL FIRE." Then he talks about how the "Piscapalions," the "Methodis," and the "Baptists" interpret this scripture, finally siding with the Baptists who are "likened unto a possum on a 'simmon tree" during a thunder storm and an earth quake. When one foot gets shaken loose, another one holds on. When all of the feet are shaken loose, "he laps his tail around the limb, and clings and he clings furever, for 'He played on a harp uv a thousand strings, sperits uv jest men made perfeck.'"

251. **Kummer, George.** "Who Wrote 'The Harp of a Thousand Strings'?" Ohio Historical Quarterly 67 (July 1958): 221-31.

Questions the authorship of the "The Harp of a Thousand Strings." During the first half of the nineteenth century the American backwoods flourished with Hardshell Baptist preachers who chewed tobacco and drank whiskey in public. They were called "Ten-Gallon Baptists" or "Whiskey Baptists" and were a great amusement to outsiders. These Hardshell clergymen spent only part of their time preaching, and they were therefore poorly trained in sermon delivery. But what they lacked in skill, they made up for in exhuberance and fantastic imagery to the extent that people were constantly mimicing them. Perhaps the best- known burlesque of this tradition is "The Harp of a Thousand Strings" published under William Penn Brannan's signature. Joshua S. Morris, editor of the Port Gibson (Mississippi) Reveille also claimed to have written the piece, however, and in response, Brannan asked Morris to produce a list of "the thousand and one wonderful productions of his able and witty pen." Of course Morris was unable to produce anything significant. Then Brannan sarcastically thanked Morris for not claiming to have written all of the other pieces that had appeared over his [Brannan's] signature and pen name [Bill Easel]. Brannan then proceeded to write an effective sequel to "The Harp" just for good measure.

Henry Clay Lewis (1825-1850)

252. **Blair, Walter, and Raven I. McDavid, Jr., eds.** "Henry Clay Lewis." The Mirth of a Nation: America's Great Dialect Humor. Minneapolis: Univ. of Minnesota Press, 1983, 60-68.

Says that Lewis published his sketches first in newspapers and magazines, and they were later collected into his one book, Odd Leaves from the Life of a Louisiana "Swamp Doctor." The book is mainly autobiographical, dealing with Lewis's medical practice among the planters, swampers, backwoodsmen and blacks in northeastern Louisiana. Lewis's most popular piece is entitled "Cupping on the Sternum," which tells about an incident in his medical training when his teacher was not precise in giving him instructions, and he misunderstood the word "sternum" and "applied the scarifactor and the blister in the wrong area" with the results being "both painful and highly irrelevant." Many of Lewis's medical sketches give details that are "too agonizing or too macabre for lay readers to enjoy." A sketch entitled "A Tight Race Considerin" is one of the many frontier stories in which a prim and proper lady somehow finds herself horribly embarrassed by ending up stark naked in front of a large crowd of people. Such sketches had a "racy devilishness" about them.

253. Cohen, Hennig, and William B. Dillingham, eds. "Henry Clay Lewis." Humor of the Old Southwest. 2nd edition. Athens: Univ. of Georgia Press, 1975, 336-54.

Explains that Lewis's pen name, Madison Tensas, was derived from the place where the Tensas River joins Bayou Despair in Madison Parish (northeastern Louisiana). Lewis led a difficult and grisly life as a doctor in the Louisiana bayous, and his sketches in Odd Leaves from the Life of a Louisiana "Swamp Doctor" are mainly autobiographical. His sketches deal with Louisiana customs, pleasures, and pastimes. Cohen and Dillingham feel that Lewis's writing is a good illustration of "the element of cruelty and degradation...the underside of comedy." The holdings of the "swampers" were frequently flooded, and the medical histories of Lewis's fever-ridden patients were often grotesque and crude. Lewis made his medical rounds clothed in "mud boots, 'swamp broadcloth,' and coonskin cap," and he lived in a log cabin with few amenities. In the summer of 1850 he was drowned on his return through the swamp after visiting the bedside of one of his patients.

254. Keller, Mark A. "'Aesculapius in Buckskin'--The Swamp Doctor as Satirist in Henry Clay Lewis's Odd Leaves." Southern Studies 18.4 (Winter 1979): 425-448.

Feels that Lewis packed a lot of living into his brief life. At the age of ten he ran away from his family. He worked as a cabin boy on a steamboat and later became a farmer. By the age of sixteen he had received his medical degree from the Medical Institute in Louisville, Kentucky, after which he became a frontier doctor in Louisiana and wrote his only volume of stories--Odd Leaves from the Life of a Louisiana "Swamp Doctor." This is an enigmatic work that includes many physical and even cruel elements. Lewis was fascinated with the morbid and the grotesque, and the Gothic horror of his writing is very similar to the Gothic horror of Edgar Allan Poe's writing. Lewis used surreal humor to artistically develop violent episodes and images and to portray a life of chaos, alienation, injustice, and despair. Odd Leaves presents the world of the Swamp Doctor, a world where a boy can journey into manhood, where humor can be used to relieve tragedy, and where man's goodness can triumph over his baser instincts. At the age of twenty-five, Lewis drowned while attempting to cross a swollen bayou.

255. Mace, Jennings R. "Henry Clay Lewis." Antebellum Writers in New York and the South. Ed. Joel Myerson. Detroit, MI: Gale, 1979, 202-03.

Describes Lewis' tales as exposing the physical and mental flaws in human nature. Lewis' stories had a kind of raw realism, which stood in contrast to the writing of many mainstream American authors during this period of Romanticism. During his first year of medical school, Lewis published "Cupping on the Sternum" in the

Spirit of the Times, the premier humor and sporting journal of the day. After getting his medical degree, Lewis practiced medicine in Madison Parish, Louisiana, a town located on the Tensas River. Lewis quickly published five more pieces in the same journal under the pen-name of Madison Tensas, and in May of 1847 he published "A Leaf from the Life of a 'Swamp Doctor'" in The Spirit. This was the first public mention of the term "swamp doctor" by Lewis. Although Lewis was young, his protagonist was an "old swamp doctor," who recounts his experiences as a young medical student and beginning doctor. Therefore, the young doctor being described in the various episodes is very close in age to that of the author himself, and indeed many of the accounts are largely autobiographical. On August 5, 1850, Lewis met his death while attempting to ford a flooded bayou. His horse apparently became entangled in some submerged underbrush and carried Lewis to his death.

256. Piacentino, Edward J. "Henry Clay Lewis." Encyclopedia of American Humorists. Ed. Steven H. Gale. New York: Garland, 1988, 280-84.

Places Lewis into the tradition of Southwestern humor not only by his birthplace (South Carolina), and the location of his sketches (Louisiana), but also by his writing style: the frame, dialectal speech, folkloric perspective, tall-tale exaggeration, and incongruous juxtaposition of fact and fantasy. Lewis's "The Indefatigable Bear Hunter" is a retelling of the Mike Hooter legend. In Lewis's tale, he becomes "Mik-hootah," and his sole ambition is to become the best bear-hunter of "ameriky." One of Mik's legs is seriously mauled in a fight with a bear and the swamp doctor has to replace it with a wooden leg. In a later fight, Mik uses the wooden leg as a weapon to kill still another bear. Lewis's humor is grotesque--even sardonic. A black woman who feigns illness to avoid work in the fields is prescribed a liberal flagellation as a cure. "She has never had trouble with fits since." In another sketch, a boy has three fingers bitten off when he tries to steal a plug of tobacco from the mouth of a sleeping swamp squatter. Lewis's frank and realistic tone were in reaction to the widely popular convention in antebellum American literature of stressing gentility of language and subject matter. Lewis's humor was earthy and grotesque in reaction to the other literature's "mawkish sentimentality and obtrusive didacticism."

Bayard Taylor (1825-1878)

257. Hazen, James. "Bayard Taylor." Encyclopedia of American Humorists. Ed. Steven H. Gale. New York: Garland, 1988, 425-27.

Considers humor to be virtually absent from Taylor's poetry, where "the high-mindedness, the quasi-religious view of nature, and the idealized conception of women characteristic of the genteel tradition leave little room for a humorous treatment of any subject." The humor in Taylor's prose, however is "good-natured and mild, never wild or extravagant, and often at his own expense." Hannah Thurston, Taylor's first novel, was a humorous account of the women's rights movement. Hannah, the heroine, is a well-developed and sympathetic character, but her involvement in the movement is viewed as a flaw in an otherwise charming lady. And she corrects the flaw at the end of the novel by marrying a "conventional suitor" and "taking her place in the home." The novel satirizes not only the feminist movement but other reform movements as well such as spiritualism, temperance, and abolitionism. Taylor's second novel, John Godfrey's Fortunes, is also a satire. It presents an amusing picture of the New York literary scene and is loosely autobiographical. Taylor's other books are not humorous; there are, however a number of humorous passages in his many travel books. Taylor also wrote a number of poetic parodies, and these are the main reason he is remembered today.

Charles Henry Smith (1826-1903)

258. Blair, Walter, and Raven I. McDavid, Jr., eds. "Charles H. Smith." The Mirth of a Nation: America's Great Dialect Humor. Minneapolis: Univ. of Minnesota Press, 1983, 136-42.

    Compares Smith's stance with that of Charles Farrar Browne as he poses as a friendly advisor to Abraham Lincoln. In one sketch Bill Arp (Smith's fictional narrator) writes a letter to Artemus Ward (Browne's fictional narrator). Bill Arp's letter presents the Southern point of view to a supporter of Northern causes, Artemus Ward. Many of Smith's letters (published under the pseudonym of Bill Arp) are addressed to "Abe Linkhorn." His letters are filled with misspellings, faulty grammar, and other signs of a poor education. In the early letters, Bill Arp claimed to be sympathetic to the Union's causes, but he kept saying dumb things that suggested that Lincoln was a fool and that the Union was doomed to failure. In Arp's later letters (as illustrated by the one written to Artemus Ward), Arp is a quite different person--sympathetic to Confederate causes rather than Union causes. This later Arp is closer in mind to Charles H. Smith. The later Bill Arp had more common sense, mother wit, and good humor than did the earlier one.

259. Lenz, William E. "Charles Henry Smith." Dictionary of Literary Biography: Volume II: American Humorists, 1800-1950. Ed. Stanley Trachtenberg. Detroit, MI: Gale, 1982, 447-52.

    Contends that Smith's misspellings and bad grammar were funny during Smith's time because so many people had recently become literate. Reading the misspellings, bad grammar, and strange allusions, and weird logic of the "wise fools," these readers could "feel superior to the uneducated and unsophisticated comic persona." Bill Arp buoyed the spirits and the hearts of the Confederates by reminding them of their triumphs and made them laugh by trivializing their defeats. In other words, Smith used humor to present the middle-class Southerner's point of view. During the dark days of the Civil War, Smith "kept southern hearts from breaking," and when he died in 1903, many newspapers both in the North and in the South wrote that he was "the best loved man in all the Southland."

260. **Simms, L. Moody, Jr.** "Charles Henry Smith." <u>Encyclopedia of American Humorists</u>. **Ed. Steven H. Gale. New York: Garland, 1988, 398-400.**

Claims that between 1861 and 1903 Smith published more than 2,000 humorous letters in various Southern newspapers. Charles Henry Smith (Bill Arp) joined the ranks of Henry Wheeler Shaw (Josh Billings), David Ross Locke (Petroleum V. Nasby), and Charles Farrar Browne (Artemus Ward) as a "literary comedian." These literary comedians "capitalized on caricatures, with the tortured dialects of illiterate individuals, and comic misquotations and misspellings." Bill Arp was a semi-literate Georgia cracker, who maintained a tone of skeptical inquiry. Targets of the letters include high taxes, corrupt officials, and draft dodgers. In <u>Bill Arp's Scrap Book</u>, Smith tells how he selected the pseudonym of Bill Arp. Before submitting his first "Abe Linkhorn" letter to a newspaper, he read it aloud to several friends. One member of the audience was William Arp, "the town wag." After he had finished, Arp asked, "Squire, are you gwine print that?" Smith replied that he was going to try to have it published. Arp asked if he was going to put a name on it, and Smith said he didn't know; he hadn't thought of a name. "Well, 'Squire,' I wish you would put mine, for them's my sentiments." Smith always wrote from a Southern point of view; however he changed through time from a "timely satirist" to a "country sage."

<u>George William Bagby (1828-1883)</u>

261. **Watson, Richie D.** "George William Bagby." <u>Encyclopedia of American Humorists</u>. **Ed. Steven H. Gale. New York: Garland, 1988, 18-21.**

Suggests that Bagby's whimsical and at times outrageous humor is perhaps the most vivid, pungent, and accurate depiction of plantation life in antebellum Virginia. Many of his sketches are based on real-life characters and incidents. One sketch, entitled, "The Virginia Editor" tells about a particular editor who was a "young, unmarried, intemperate, pugnacious, gambling gentleman." The editor of Bagby's sketch ended his life with "half an ounce of lead...honorably and satisfactorily adjusted in his heart or brain." The sketch was so realistic, that the Virginia editor on whose life the sketch was based challenged Bagby to a duel; a mutual friend had to step in to stop the duel. Bagby wrote letters to the <u>Southern Literary Messenger</u> under the pen name of Mozis Addums. They were addressed to a farmer friend by the name of "Billy Ivvins" in "Curdsville, Virginia." Mozis was patterned on the people Bagby had grown up with in Southside Virginia. Bagby's most successful lecture was "Bacon and Greens." The greens in Bagby's title refers to cabbage. Bagby reasons that although people across the United States may eat bacon and greens, the only <u>perfect</u> bacon, and the only <u>perfect</u> greens are found in Virginia. So Virginians are therefore a very remarkable (if not perfect) people.

Charles Graham Halpine (1829-1868)

262. Hart, James D. ed. "Charles Graham Halpine." The Oxford
     Companion to American Literature. 4th edition. New York:
     Oxford University Press, 1965, 344.

States that although Halpine was born in Ireland, he came to
the United States at the age of twenty-two, where he became a
brigadier-general in the Union army. He became famous for his
humorous depiction of Civil War events in The Life and Adventures,
Songs, Services, and Speeches of Private Miles O'Reilly (1864).

Kittrell J. Warren (1829-1889)

263. Cohen, Hennig, and William B. Dillingham, eds. "Kittrell J.
     Warren." Humor of the Old Southwest. 2nd edition. Athens:
     Univ. of Georgia Press, 1975, 360-75.

Considers Warren to have been one of the last of the
Southwestern humorists. His three books are based on his life as a
soldier. They are entitled, Ups and Downs of Wife Hunting, History
of the Eleventh Georgia Vols, and Life and Public Services of an
Army Straggler. Billy Fishback, the protagonist in the last novel,
portrays the most despicable of military types--the deserter. He is
a clever scavenger, who, "like Simon Suggs, capitalizes on other
people's greed, stupidity, or misfortune." Sometimes he teams up
with Captain Slaughter in his cons, and this makes the cons more
effective because of Captain Slaughter's ability to use educated
language. "Together, they prefigure the Duke and the Dauphin of
Mark Twain's Huckleberry Finn."

264. Piacentino, Edward J. "Kitrell J. Warren." Encyclopedia of
     American Humorists. Ed. Steven H. Gale. New York: Garland,
     1988, 458-62.

Indicates that Warren's Life and Public Services of an Army
Straggler was published under the pseudonym of Chatham. The novel
portrays the adventures of picaro Billy Fishback, one of the
"grosser elements of human nature." Fishback was "ignorant,
unpatriotic, and persistently deceitful...a fictional portrayal of
a large number of soldiers who actually deserted from the
Confederate Army." Piacentino describes Jezebel Huggins in Warren's
Ups and Downs of Wife Hunting as having a "hideously comical
appearance." As Jezebel himself says, "I have black hair, heavy red
whiskers, squint pop eyes, sharp cheek bones, one club foot, and a
nose which describes the arc of a parabola." Jezebel misinterprets
the stare of one woman he is courting as physical attraction, but
when he asks why she has been watching him so intently, she
exclaims, "bekase...you was so tarnashun ugly, I couldn't help it."
Jezebel's courting attempts are also thwarted by the fact that he is
a fool. He reads romantic novels and fails to distinguish between
fantasy and reality. He uses "flowerly, pretentious, and pedantic
rhetoric...[that] requires three days for a school teacher to
'translate' into comprehensible English."

William Wright (1829-1898)

265. Berkove, Lawrence I. "Dan De Quille." Encyclopedia of American
     Humorists. New York: Garland, 1988, 119-21.

     Indicates that Dan De Quille is the "nom de plume" (In this
case "nom de quille") of William Wright. Wright was a master of the
literary hoax. Wright was Mark Twain's roommate, and when Twain got
a swollen nose in a boxing match, Wright wrote a sketch saying
Twain's nose became so swollen that whole towns turned out to
witness the spectacle. Wright was a master at picturesque
vernacular and almost believable tall tales, which he called
"quaints." These "quaints" were made credible through "a wealth of
corroborative detail, a serious tone, and cleverly specious
rationalization." Wright reported the discovery of a "Silver Man,"
said to have been found in a remote part of Nevada. Mark Twain's
"Petrified Man" may have been influenced by Wright's earlier hoax.
Wright also reported the discovery of "traveling stones" in the
Pahranagat Mountains of Nevada, which were said to have magnetic
properties. P. T. Barnum is said to have offered Wright $10,000 for
samples of the traveling stones. Wright also announced the
invention of "Solar Armor" designed to keep people cold in the
desert, but the inventor perished by freezing to death when he
couldn't turn the armor off during a Death Valley demonstration.
Wright also told about the discoveries of mountain alligators, a
five-headed snake, and eyeless fish, all of which evoked serious
inquiries from Eastern scientists.

266. Berkove, Lawrence I. "Dan De Quille and 'Old Times on the
     Mississippi.'" Mark Twain Journal 24.2 (Fall 1986): 28-34.

     Explores the nature and the extent of Dan De Quille's
influence on the writings of Mark Twain. For a while they were
roommates and close friends, and they also shared a number of high-
spirited escapades with each other. Both of them started out with
paranomastic pen names; Mark Twain started out as "Josh," and of
course De Quille is a pen name par excellance. They also both
practiced a tongue-in-cheek sense of humor, and enjoyed playing
hoaxes on their contemporaries. Their hoaxes involved deadpan
delivery, specious rationalization, and elaborate details, these
details often relating to actual individuals and events. Even more
specific influence may be possible. Dan De Quille wrote a piece
entitled "Pilot Wylie: Life on the Old Massasipp" which very well
may have influenced the composition of Twain's Life on the
Mississippi. Twain's pilot was based on a real-life pilot as De
Quille's sketch had been--Strother Wiley. Twain gave his captain
the name of "Stephen W___." It could have been that both De
Quille's sketch and Mark Twain's sketch were merely based on similar
observations and similar writing styles. But it is entirely
possible that De Quille's influence on Twain was more than this.

267. Berkove, Lawrence I. "Dan De Quille's Narratives of Ohio:
     Lorenzo Dow's Miracle." Literary Images 60.2 (Spring 1988):
     47-56.

     Indicates that Mark Twain helped Dan De Quille on his first
major work, The Big Bonanza. The first sketch in this book was

entitled "Lorenzo Dow's Miracle" and originally appeared in the San Francisco Examiner. This piece is full of delightful humor in the form of a tall tale. De Quille had an excellent eye for and an excellent memory of detail and his resultant sketches sounded plausible if a bit fantastic. Many of his readers read his sketches as true accounts. "Lorenzo Dow's Miracle" is a good example of how appropriate detail and excellent story-telling techniques can make a story appear to be true even though it isn't.

268. **Berkove, Lawrence I. "Dan De Quille Revives the 'Traveling Stones' Hoax." Mark Twain Circular 4.5-6 (May-June 1990): 1-4.**

Explains that William Wright, under the pen name of Dan de Quille, first published his pseudo-scientific report of the "traveling stones" in an 1865 or 1866 issue of Virginia City, Nevada's Territorial Enterprise. In scientific language De Quille claimed that these stones had magnetic properties that made them move closer and closer to each other, and P. T. Barnum was so convinced by the hoax that he offered De Quille $10,000 for some samples. On November 11, 1879, De Quille published a disclaimer in the Enterprise, confessing that the whole story was a hoax, and after fifteen years, it was becoming a little bit monotonous. Then, on March 6, 1892, De Quille revived the hoax in Salt Lake City, Utah's Daily Tribune. Here he confessed that the original story had been a fake, but he had since found a university professor who said that the stones actually did travel and huddle together. De Quille admitted that he had previously lied, but now he was telling the truth. He supplied copious detail, some of it true and some of it only with the ring of truth. He cited corroborative evidence and testimonies of knowledgeable people. Most of this hoax was in fact true and verifiable, but the hoax as a whole was nevertheless a put-on. De Quille's candor and scientific verisimilitude thus reestablished the hoax of the traveling stones.

Emily Elizabeth Dickinson (1830-1886)

269. **Armitage, Shelley. "Emily Dickinson's Crackerbox Humor." Thalia: Studies in Literary Humor 3.1 (1979): 11-15.**

Proposes that Dickinson was a female counterpart of the frontier crackerbox philosopher. Dickinson's ironic humor has been variously labeled "wit," "riddle," and "metaphysical mirth," but in American Humor, Constance Rourke said that Dickinson was a "comic poet in the American tradition," and this was the tradition of the crackerbox philosopher. There is even evidence that Dickinson is something of a "Ringtailed Roarer," as she chides her uncle Joel Norcross for not writing, "You villain without rival, unparalleled doer of crimes, scoundrel, unheard of before, disturber of public peace, creation's blot and blank, state's prison filler, magnum honum promise maker, harum scarum promise breaker," and so on. In another letter Dickinson wrote "No one has called so far, but one old lady to look at the house. I directed her to the cemetery to spare expense of moving." Like other ringtailed roarers, Dickinson is mostly bluster. Mrs. Partington tells Ike to drown some kittens, but then adds, "I'll take the chill off the water. It would be cruel to put them in stone cold." Armitage concludes that a recognition of Dickinson's crackerbox stance is necessary in order to appreciate the ironic drama of Dickinson's work.

270. **Kiley, Frederick, and J. M. Shuttleworth, eds.** "Emily Dickinson: Five Poems." Satire from Aesop to Buchwald. New York: Macmillan, 1971, 284-86.

Feels that Dickinson's short poetry concentrates on aphorism, irony, and paradox. These poems pretend to be small, but they raise universal questions about life and religion. A device which Dickinson uses especially effectively is "slant rhyme." This device constantly echoes the imperfection in the world Dickinson is writing about. But Dickinson also uses slant rhyme as a dramatic device--a way to demonstrate her offbeat perspective and a way to catch people's attention. Dickinson's poetic philosophy is summed up in the first line of one of her poems--"Tell all the truth but tell it slant."

271. **Walker, Nancy, and Zita Dresner.** "Emily Dickinson." Redressing the Balance: American Women's Literary Humor from Colonial Times to the 1980s. Jackson: Univ. Press of Mississippi, 1988, 82-85.

Admits that much of Dickinson's poetry shows an obsession with death and unrequited love but point out that much of her other poetry is light, playful, irreverent, and satiric. All of her poetry demonstrates an active intelligence that frequently reminds the reader of the poet's very private and insulated life. Dickinson's style is cryptic and filled with metaphors. Her tone changes from anguished to detached to amused. Her humorous poetry is skeptical of the patriarchal conception of God and presents the natural world in minute detail. Like Frances Whitcher before her, Dickinson satirizes the "cult of gentility" that defined the roles of the "gentlewoman" of her day. She refused to be categorized, and wrote "I'm Nobody! Who are you?" Much of Dickinson's poetry is enigmatic.

272. **Wallace, Ronald, ed.** "Emily Dickinson: A Day! Help! Help! Another Day!" God Be with the Clown: Humor in American Poetry. Columbia: Univ. of Missouri Press, 1984, 77-105.

Cites Constance Rourke, George Whicher, Richard Chase, Charles Anderson, and others as having discussed Dickinson's humor, her playfulness, her wit, but most critics "prefer the dark Dickinson to the lighter one, reserving their highest praise for her tragic sense, for her poems of anguish, pain, despair, grief, agony, and death." Wallace contrasts the poetry of Emily Dickinson with that of Walt Whitman, one of her contemporaries. "If Walt Whitman is often accused of lacking a sense of humor, Emily Dickinson is often accused of having one." Walt Whitman was a teller of tall tales. His method was self-mockery and exaggeration--consciously claiming to be more than he is. "He knows he is not the mythic character he claims to be, and we know that he knows it." Dickinson like Whitman used self-mockery, but the self-mockery of understatement; she claimed to be less that she is. "She knows she is not the simpleminded character she poses as, and we know that she knows it." Dickinson said, "Tell all the Truth but tell it slant," and later,

"As Lightning to the Children eased / With explanation kind / The Truth must dazzle gradually / Or every man be blind."

Mary Abigail Dodge (1831-1905)

273. Walker, Nancy, and Zita Dresner. "Gail Hamilton." Redressing the Balance: American Women's Literary Humor from Colonial Times to the 1980s. Jackson: Univ. Press of Mississippi, 1988, 107-14.

Suggests that Mary Abigail Dodge lived in a time when feminist issues were not publicly discussed and therefore had to separate her self from her alter-ego, Gail Hamilton, a personna she used in writing for the National Era, the Atlantic Monthly, and the New York Times. In the meantime, Mary Abigail Dodge avoided publicity and "adhered to the dictates of 'true womanhood' in her personal life." Feminist issues were still in flux during Dodge's time, and although she espoused many liberal causes, especially abolition, she opposed female suffrage, feeling that giving women the right to vote "would lower women to the level of men rather than allowing them to exert the influence of their finer natures." In her writing, she made fun of both genders for excessive or intolerant behavior. Dodge took her pseudonym from her birthplace, Hamilton, Massachusetts. She wrote mainly about religious matters and country life. Her Twelve Miles from a Lemon anticipates Betty MacDonald's The Egg and I in depicting the difficulties of living in a remote rural area.

Mortimer Neal Thomson (1831-1875)

274. Piacentino, Edward J. "Mortimer Neal Thomson." Encyclopedia of American Humorists." Ed. Steven H. Gale. New York: Garland, 1988, 437-41.

Indicates that Thomson was popular during the 1850s under the name of Q. K. Philander Doesticks, P.B. Q.K. stood for "Queer Kritter," and P.B. stood for "Perfect Brick." Thomson's first book, Doesticks: What He Says satirizes the absurdities of metropolitan life by placing a tenderfoot (Doesticks) into the New York environment. His Plu-ri-bus-tah mimics the trochaic meter of Longfellow's Hiawatha, as it debunks the American love for the ALMIGHTY DOLLAR. It is written in mock heroic style and pictures the Revolutionary War as a seven-year prize fight. Regarding the Civil War, Thomson predicts defeat for both the North and the South. The climactic ending of the poem occurs when Yunga-Merrikah (son of Plu-ri-bus-tah) is crushed by an enormous dollar that falls on him. Thomson's The History and Records of the Elephant Club consisted of sketches that take place in police court. The title comes from the characters who want to view New York City as an enormous "Metropolitan Elephant" from many different angles. Thomson's Nothing to Say is a parody of Allen Butler's satire on women's clothing entitled Nothing to Wear. Thomson's The Witches of New York contains revealing satirical sketches of New York fortune-tellers, sorceresses, and clairvoyants, exposing their exploitation techniques.

275. Piacentino, Edward J. "'Seeing the Elephant': Doesticks' Satires of Nineteenth-Century Gotham." Studies in American Humor NS 5.2-3 (Summer-Fall 1986): 134-44.

Says that Mortimer Neal Thomson wrote three satiric novels on New York City life, Doesticks: What He Says (1855), The History and Records of the Elephant Club (1856), and The Witches of New York (1858). Doesticks: What He Says is Thomson's most popular and most famous book. Thomson describes it as "a series of unpremeditated literary extravaganzas." The History and Records of the Elephant Club is a burlesque social history and ludicrous satire of New York culture. It parodies Longfellow's Hiawatha by being written in the same trochaic meter and is an account of a group of newcomers to New York City who want to explore Gotham, which they describe as the "Metropolitan Elephant," in both its wild and domestic states. The Witches of New York is a critical and satiric exposure of witchcraft and spiritualism. This theme is a continuation from Thomson's first book, Doesticks: What He Says. Thomson targets the quirks and shortcomings, the various social classes, and the cultural, religious and political institutions of New York City in his satires. Piacentino considers Thomson to be one of the more important literary humorists of nineteenth-century American Gotham and one of the best writers in the tradition of urban literary humor, especially between 1855 and 1860.

276. Sloane, David E. E. "Mortimer Thomson." Dictionary of Literary Biography: Volume II: American Humorists, 1800-1950. Detroit, MI: Gale, 1982, 491-97.

Portrays Thomson as a prankster who was a student in the College of Literature, Science, and the Arts at the University of Michigan until his pranks finally caught up with him. He was finally dismissed during the spring semester of 1850 for "too much eagerness in getting specimens for dissection." Thomson's first Doesticks sketch was written while he was visiting Niagara Falls; it was entitled "Doesticks on a Bender," and its publication in the New York Tribune brought Thomson to immediate fame. Thomson was a very good writer, who could transform the vulgar details of city life into strong images with ironic social ramifications. Thomson's optimism and sense of humor both diminished as the result of the Civil War and the death of two talented wives.

Louisa May Alcott (1832-1888)

277. Walker, Nancy, and Zita Dresner. Redressing the Balance: American Women's Literary Humor from Colonial Times to the 1980s. Jackson: Univ. Press of Mississippi, 1988, 115-30.

Considers Jo in Little Women to be an autobiographical reflection of Alcott's own rebelliousness. Alcott writes masculine qualities into Jo's character, and she also creates strong women characters who live out their passions. Her "Transcendental Wild Oats" is a satiric reverie about the Alcott family's short stint of communal living at Fruitlands, a naturalistic environment that Henry David Thoreau was also tangentially involved in. Louisa May Alcott's mother, Abba, endured the hardships of Fruitland with stoic

patience in this story. Mrs. Hope in the same story has an ironic
name, for there is in fact little hope for her.

Horatio Alger (c1833-1899)

278. Shepard, Douglas H. "Nathanael West Rewrites Horatio Alger,
      Jr." Satire Newsletter 3.1 (Fall 1965): 13-28.

      Contends that Nathanael West's third novel, A Cool Million is
a satire aimed at the All-American Horatio Alger success story. In
A Cool Million, Horatio Alger's style is parodied, and the plot is
an inversion of the typical Alger plot. But Shepard feels that the
satire fails because the plot is inverted and also because West
quoted directly from Alger's earlier novels but did not give Alger
credit. Much of West's material therefore consists of direct quotes
rather than parodies of the original Horatio Alger novels. It's
difficult to tell quote from parody here.

David Ross Locke (1833-1888)

279. Blair, Walter, and Raven I. McDavid, Jr. eds. "David Ross
      Locke (Petroleum Vesuvius Nasby)." The Mirth of a Nation:
      America's Great Dialect Humor. Minneapolis: Univ. of Minn.
      Press, 1983, 144-53.

      Indicates that Locke used the persona of Petroleum Vesuvius
Nasby to discredit the Copperheads and Rebels. Nasby discredited
the opposition by being a member of the opposition, since he was
portrayed not only as a bigot but also as a hypocrite, a sluggard,
an alcoholic, a coward, a bigamist, a thief, a corrupt politician,
and a traitor. Boutwell, a member of Lincoln's cabinet, attributed
the overthrow of the Rebels to three forces: 1) the Army and the
Navy, 2) the Republican party, and 3) the letters of Petroleum V.
Nasby. Lincoln is quoted as having said that he would have given up
his presidency to have been able to write satiric letters as well as
Locke had done. Blair and McDavid feel that one attribute which
made Locke especially effective as a satirist was his genuine
bitterness and partisanship. They add that modern readers of Locke
do not, however, easily discover these attributes.

280. Engle, David. "David Ross Locke." Encyclopedia of American
      Humorists. Ed. Steven H. Gale. New York: Garland, 1988, 286-
      88.

      Considers Petroleum Vesuvius Nasby to be "one of the most
vividly drawn grotesques in all of American humor." Nasby was
offensive, racist, frequently drunk, cowardly, lazy, and barely
literate, but he also had intelligence and cunning. Both Lincoln
and Grant admired Locke's writing enough to offer him political
appointments; he turned them both down. Locke's Swingin Round the
Cirkle was the first of many Locke books to be illustrated by Thomas
Nast. Locke was not so much of a humorist as he was a propagandist
and satirist. His wit was sharpest when he used it to further such
causes of the Republican party as abolition of slavery and

preservation of the Union. After the Civil War was over, however, Locke's effectiveness as a satirist gradually declined, for his writing lacked the venom of earlier times.

281. **Minor, Dennis E.** "David Ross Locke." <u>Dictionary of Literary Biography: Volume 11: American Humorists, 1800-1950</u>. Ed. Stanley Trachtenberg. Detroit, MI: Gale, 1982, 270-75.

   Says that in 1862 Locke wrote his first Nasby letter--"Letter from a Straight Democrat." Lincoln was fond of quoting this particular letter. Although Lincoln was heavily criticized in Nasby's letters, Lincoln realized that the criticisms were not actually directed at him or his government but were rather designed to expose the weaknesses of the Democratic Party. Nasby's character is designed to prompt laughter at the same time he "arouses distaste for all the real-world vices he personifies." Like Walt Whitman, Nasby is something of a ring-tailed roarer: "I am a steamboat captin with a full load, a doggry keeper on a Saturday nite, a sportin man with four aces in his hand./All these am I, and more." Locke's Nasby parodies Shakespeare's Hamlet in "The times is out uv joint, oh cussed spite,/That I wuz ever born to set em rite." Locke continued to write Nasby letters until February 15, 1888 when he died of tuberculosis; some letters were written on his death bed. There has been a revival of Locke's Nasby letters in the second half of this century, because of a renewed interest in the civil rights movement.

282. **Minor, Dennis E.** "The Many Roles of Nasby." <u>The Markham Review</u> 4.1 (October 1973): 16-20.

   Portrays Nasby (Locke's character) as a bum, a lecher, a drunk, and a draft-dodger but also as a preacher, an editor, and a teacher. Nasby was a low-life, but he also had a legitimate sense of his own worth, and Minor feels this is what makes the character important. Nasby has enough good qualities to keep him from being sinister or evil incarnate. Locke created Nasby as a "bumbling role-player," whose ignorance and intolerance were the result of limited horizons rather than evil intent.

Charles Farrar Browne (c1834-1867)

283. **Abrams, Robert E.** "Charles Farrar Browne." <u>Dictionary of Literary Biography: Volume 11: American Humorists, 1800-1950</u>. Ed. Stanley Trachtenberg. Detroit, MI: Gale, 1982, 60-68.

   Feels that Browne dominated American humor during the Civil War period. Browne integrated the techniques of Down-East humorists with those of the Old Southwest humorists in the development of his protagonist, Artemus Ward, modeled to some extent on P. T. Barnum, one of Browne's contemporaries. Ward was a garrulous itinerant circus showman; Ward's circus contains a California bear, two snakes, tame foxes, and a wax works. Browne's humor also provided a link between the regional and unpolished humor of a frontier nation, and the sophisticated humor of developing urban and cosmopolitan centers. Browne first wrote under the pseudonym of

Lieut. Chubb, which was a clipping of his name, Charles Browne, and
an ironic description of his skinny stature. Browne had some
difficulty on the lecture circuit, because he was "thin and lank,
with delicate hands and elegantly coiffured hair" whereas he was
portraying Artemus Ward as earthy, corpulent, and crude.
Furthermore, the letter-writing Artemus Ward was a flamboyant
boaster, whereas the humor of the stage Artemus Ward was delivered
deadpan. Therefore the Artemus Ward on stage had to differ in many
respects from the Artemus Ward of print.

284. Blair, Walter, and Hamlin Hill. "Charles Farrar
      Browne/Artemus Ward." America's Humor: From Poor Richard to
      Doonesbury. New York: Oxford University Press, 1978, 274-84.

      Considers the Civil War to have been the dividing time between
two important humor movements in America. Before the Civil War
there were the "local colorists," who looked wistfully back at the
past. After the Civil War there the the "phunny phellows"
(including Charles Farrar Browne), who joked about a nation limping
toward unity. The local colorists were very regional in their
outlook and their appeal, but the "phunny phellows" were more
national in their outlook and appeal. The distinction can be seen
by two contrasting magazines. The Spirit of the Times was part of
the local-color movement, and it concentrated on regional sketches.
In 1861, after a life of thirty years, The Spirit suspended
publication. In contrast, the Yankee Nation concentrated on
language rather than on place, time, and people. The April 1861
issue of Yankee Nation contained nine cartoons, an ample number of
wisecracks and jokes, and comments on various controversies of the
day. Furthermore, it contained numerous intentional misspellings,
puns, malapropisms, assaults on grammar, weirdly formed sentences,
dialect distortions, parodies, and burlesques. The humorist who was
most responsible for this change of direction was Charles Farrar
Browne and his narrator, Artemus Ward.

285. Blair, Walter, and Raven I. McDavid, Jr., eds. "Charles
      Farrar Browne." The Mirth of a Nation: America's Great Dialect
      Humor. Minneapolis: Univ. of Minn Press, 1983, 127-35.

      Considers Browne to have been the first full-time writer in
America to have made a decent living as a humorist. Signing his
pieces as Artemus Ward, Browne wrote for the Cleveland Plain Dealer,
and Vanity Fair, and later sailed to England, where he wrote for
Punch. He died in London in 1867, at the height of his fame.
Browne's writings were filled with various kinds of cacography
precisely because the principal aim of the schools of his day was
the teaching of traditional spelling and proper grammar as symbols
of cultural achievement.

286. Dahl, Curtis. "Artemus Ward: Comic Panoramist." New England
     Quarterly 32 (Winter 1959): 476-85.

      Indicates that during the 1840s gigantic panoramas were very
popular along the Mississippi River. Banvard, Egan, Lewis, and
others made journeys into the wilderness and came back to display
their adventures in panoramic fashion. Charles Farrar Browne made
a similar journey to the West and created a panoramic display of his
adventures, but Browne's panorama was a burlesque, a parody, a

caricature not so much of his adventures as of the gigantic panoramas that had been prepared by other panoramists. Browne's parody of a panorama was a comic criticism of its serious predecessors. It was a three-dimensional tall tale full of exaggerated satiric humor, targeting those subjects that had long appealed to New Englanders and other Americans at this period in time--miners, Mormons, and Indians of the West. And the program that Browne (in the character of Artemus Ward) prepared was just as satiric as the panorama itself, crediting in traditional fashion all of the people who had helped with the panorama from the "crankist" and "assistant crankist" on to the "moppist," the "doortendist," and the rest. Browne identified himself as the "gas man."

287. **Jessup, Emily.** "Teaching and Preaching While Doing Neither: Artemus Ward, Mark Twain, and Garrison Keillor." WHIMSY 3 (1985): 23-25.

Suggests that the longevity of humorous work depends on its ability to operate at a number of different levels simultaneously. The title of Jessup's article alludes to a Twain statement that "Humor must neither teach nor preach yet it must do both if it is to last forever." By "forever" Twain means 30 years. Artemus Ward, Mark Twain, and Garrison Keillor all accept a humble self-effacing stance. On the surface, their characters are rustic, unschooled, and lacking in refinement; however, beneath the surface their characters all exhibit genuine worth and genuine common sense. Thus these writers are all continuously making specific points about how society treats its individuals, and they are also all making the more general point that people must not allow surface appearances to keep them from trying to discover deep worth.

288. **Pullen, John J.** Comic Relief: The Life and Laughter of Artemus Ward, 1834-1867. Hamden, CT: Archon, 1983, ix + 202 pages.

Presents the writings of Charles Farrar Browne as politically profound. In a chapter entitled "The Man Who Made Lincoln Laugh," for example, Pullen tells of a cabinet meeting on the morning of September 22, 1862, during the battle of Antietam. The battle had been long and bloody, and no one had won. The war showed no signs of being resolved. These were tragic times. Lincoln asked his cabinet if they had ever read anything by Artemus Ward. Of course they all had. Then Lincoln read a chapter from Artemus Ward, His Book entitled "High Handed Outrage at Utica." A big burly native of Utica was visiting Artemus Ward's wax figure museum, and when he came to the figure of Judas Iscariot in the depiction of the Lord's Last Supper, the Utican grabbed Judas by the feet and dragged him out of the exhibit and began pounding him mercilessly. When Artemus told the man from Utica that Judas was a wax figure, the Utican replied that Judas Iscariot can't show himself in Utica with impunity, and at that point he caved in Judas's head. After telling the story, Lincoln said to the cabinet that they were all under such strain, both night and day, that if they didn't all laugh, they would all die. He next took up a paper from in front of him and read it to the cabinet. It was the Emancipation Proclamation.

Samuel Langhorne Clemens (1835-1910)

289. Anderson, Frederick, ed. **A Pen Warmed-Up in Hell: Mark Twain in Protest**. New York: Harper/Colophon, 1972, viii + 211 pages.

   Discusses Twain's later works as more critical and more biting than his earlier works. Anderson's title is taken from a letter Twain wrote to his editor, William Dean Howells, to accompany his submission of **A Connecticut Yankee** in 1889. The letter laments the fact that he had to leave out many things he wanted to say. In order to add these things he would have to have access to a library "and a pen warmed-up in hell." As Anderson said, "He warmed his pen often in the twenty years that remained of his life." Twain had a divided mind on many issues; however one theme was constant throughout his writing--that we all should have the right to form our own opinions and that persons or groups should not impose their views onto other persons or groups. Twain had an ability to see issues from more than a single perspective. "The War Prayer" points out that success for one cause often results in disaster for a competing cause. In "Pudd'nhead Wilson's New Calendar," Twain argued that in war, negotiation or withdrawal is often better than counterattack. As Twain stated, "It is easier to stay out than get out." Targets of Twain's satire during his later years included wars, racial injustice, the fraudulent distribution of wealth, and governmental exploitation of individuals.

290. Arnold, St. George Tucker, Jr. "Mark Twain's Birds and Joel Chandler Harris's Rabbit: Two Modes of Projection of Authorial Personality in Comic Critters." **Thalia: Studies in Literary Humor** 11.1 (1990): 34-41.

   Considers Mark Twain and Joel Chandler Harris to be master artists in the mode of humorous writing whereby animals are depicted as having human traits. This tradition arose out of the plantation humor of the Black oral culture of deep southern slave folklore, but these earlier animals all had very negative qualities. Twain and Harris were extending the tradition of animal personifications developed by Augustus Baldwin Longstreet (animals depicting Whig opponents), Thomas Bangs Thorpe (The Big Bear of Arkansas), and Alexander McNutt (who showed empathy with the animals he portrayed). But Twain and Harris showed more than empathy with the animals they portrayed. Maxwell Geismar said of Mark Twain that he wrote about animals as though he were one. But the animals of Twain and of Harris are not the same. Twain, whose animals are the result of a more liberal, more socially secure southern upbringing, edits out much of the cruelty and equality that relates to the slave culture of the South, while Harris' animals often portray the meanest and most shocking animal characteristics that were present in the slave tales.

291. Arnold, St. George Tucker, Jr. "The Twain Bestiary: Mark Twain's Critters and the Tradition of Animal Portraiture in Humor of the Old Southwest." Southern Folklore Quarterly 41 (1977): 195-211.

Remarks even though Twain critics have investigated almost every aspect of Twain's life to determine his true psyche or his true view of politics, they have left his animal figures largely unevaluated, tending instead to sit back and merely enjoy his animal characterizations figures of speech. The Southwestern Humorists tend to use animal figures either to ridicule backwoods simplicity, or to demonstrate a kind of animal cunning that places them on a par with humans. This second group would view the hunter and the hunted in a sort of game in which either one could win. Twain fits into this second category. Twain's Indian crow clearly has empathy. His blue jays and frogs and coyotes are as human as most humans. Arnold quotes Maxwell Geismar as saying, "Twain wrote of animals as though he was one." Twain had a special genius for animal depiction because of his rare talent for precise description and because of his genuine affection for the creatures he was describing. The resulting caricatures provide the reader with a pathos of the opposing aspects of the human condition--comedy and tragedy.

292. Austin, James C. "The Age of Twain." American Humor in France: Two Centuries of French Criticism of the Comic Spirit in American Literature. Ames, IA: Iowa State Univ. Press, 1978, 69-73.

Considers Madame Bentzon to have dominated French criticism of American literature in the last three decades of the nineteenth century. In her two 1872 articles that appeared in Revue des deux mondes Madame Bentzon treats Charles Farrar Browne (Artemus Ward), Henry Wheeler Shaw (Josh Billings), Charles Godfrey Leland (Hans Breitmann), and Samuel Langhorne Clemens (Mark Twain). Although Samuel Clemens was clearly a better writer than were the other authors discussed in detail, Benzon nevertheless enjoyed reading the works of Leland more than the works of the other three American authors. Bentzon liked Leland's mixture of good sense, honest mirth, and fine humor accented with a pinch of Yankee salt. She didn't like Artemus Ward's writing because it exhibited a gross mirth that relied on pranks and portrayed the Americans as being somewhat childish. On the other hand, she liked Leland because he was very good at ridiculing the Germans. Austin also discussed the French critic Charles de Varigny, who was the first French critic to note the difference between Yankee humor and Southwestern humor. He said that Southwesterners' humor was less bitter or hostile. Their mirth is more naive and free. Their laughter is more contagious.

293. Barksdale, Richard K. "History, Slavery, and Thematic Irony in Huckleberry Finn." Mark Twain Journal 22.2 (Fall 1984): 17-20.

Discusses the irony of Huck Finn's relationship with Jim. During this period in American history the poor white trash both hated and disrespected blacks, for it was only the blacks that they could feel superior to. The Finn family was poor white trash. Jim was a runaway slave. The only way Huck and Jim could have developed a friendship was as outcasts (both were runaways), and totally

removed from society (they were on a raft in the middle of the
Mississippi River, America's biggest and longest river). At the
present time Huckleberry Finn is on many censorship lists. Many
blacks don't like the book because it reminds them of a time when
blacks were treated as subhuman and had to behave as subhuman. Many
whites don't like the book because it reminds them of a time when
whites were mean and cruel to blacks. Barksdale suggests that
neither the blacks nor the whites would want to censor Huckleberry
Finn if they read the book as irony, for this reading would stress
the ambivalence in Huck's comments about blacks and would provide a
ray of hope for the future. But in order to read the novel as
ironic, the readers must achieve considerable ethical distance from
the novel, and this is not an easy posture to achieve.

294. Berkove, Lawrence I. "Mark Twain and Horace Greeley:
     Penpals." Thalia: Studies in Literary Humor 11.2 (1990): 3-11.

     Suggests that whenever Twain wrote about Horace Greeley he
treated him with gentle humor, even though Greeley was very
opinionated and partisan, took controversial stands, and had many
enemies who mocked him cruelly during his lifetime and even after
his death. But Twain's treatment of Greeley was much more friendly,
as he playfully spoofed Greeley's handwriting and in general
produced a light view of Greeley by which he could be remembered
affectionately. Twain recognized Greeley to be an authentic
personality. For Twain, Greeley may have been eccentric, but at the
same time he was genuine and interesting, and he was forceful and
colorful, and sincere. In short, he was an ideal target for satire,
and Twain chose gentle satire to caricature him, thereby ensuring
Greeley a place in the living tradition of American humor.

295. Berkson, Dorothy. "Mark Twain's Two-Headed Novel: Racial
     Symbolism and Social Realism in Pudd'nhead Wilson." Studies in
     American Humor 3.4 (Winter 1984-85): 309-20.

     Criticizes "Those Extraordinary Twins" as having ambivalent
discordance. In Pudd'nhead Wilson, Twain says, "a duet that is made
up of two different tunes is a mistake; especially when the tunes
ain't any kin to one another." Berkson concludes that "the problem
with Pudd'nhead Wilson is that it is a two-headed novel, a duet,
made up of two themes that 'ain't any kin to one another'." Twain's
twins are named Angelo (Angel), and Luigi (Lucifer). Angelo is
light and Luigi is dark. Angelo is described as "the blonde one;"
he is "as good as gold" with "kind blue eyes, and curly copper
hair." Luigi is "the dark-skinned one." In all of their tastes,
Angelo and Luigi are opposites; Berkson feels that Twain has
developed a "schizophrenic dualism symbolized by their dark and fair
complexions."

296. Bickley, R. Bruce, Jr. "Humorous Portraiture in Twain's
     News Writing." American Literary Realism 3 (Fall 1970): 395-
     98.

     Believes that the 1860s gave Mark Twain more literary freedom
and journalistic latitude than any other period of his life. During
this period Twain, as a journalist for a number of different
newspapers, covered marriages, balls, homicides, agricultural fairs,

dramatic productions, fires, and attempted seductions. As a paid correspondent he wrote about his travels and sight-seeing experiences from Hawaii to the Near East, and his writings ranged from legitimate heavy documentation to facetious fantasy in a tone of ironic displacement. Bickley discusses the humorous portraits in Twain's news coverage during the 1860s, a time when news writing not only allowed but encouraged the merging of genuine reporting with humorous elaboration.

297. Bier, Jesse. "'Bless You, Chile': Fiedler and 'Huck Honey' a Generation Later." Mississippi Quarterly, Fall 1981: 456-62.

Criticizes Leslie Fiedler's article entitled "Come Back to the Raft Ag'in, Huck Honey" which placed Huckleberry Finn with Moby Dick as novels that avoided heterosexual love and substituted a covert and idealistic "chaste male love." Fiedler had used Jim's statements of endearment, his dressing in a woman's gown, his general depiction throughout the novel as a sort of virgin bride. To this evidence, Fiedler adds the watery setting and the dream-like structure of the novel, both of which authorized a partial release of inhibitions. Finally, Fiedler noted that Huck Finn was fourteen, an age which coincides with latent adolescent homosexuality. Bier suggests, however, that Fiedler was stacking the cards a bit in order to make his point. For example, he conveniently omitted Huck's getting into drag disguised as Sarah Mary Williams, and in retrospect, Bier feels that the article is filled with "ellipses, non-sequiturs, and stretches." Fiedler also ignored the universal nature of the term "honey" in southern culture. Finally, Bier suggests that all of Fiedler's evidence could point in a different direction. Bier agrees with Kenneth Lynn that Jim's function in the novel is a substitute father rather than a bride or lover. This interpretation is equally compatible from a psychoanalytic point of view, and it matches the evidence of the novel just as well.

298. Blair, Walter, and Hamlin Hill. "Mark Twain's Chestnuts." America's Humor: From Poor Richard to Doonesbury. New York: Oxford University Press, 1978, 303-63.

Feels that Twain downplayed reading and upplayed experiences. Twain boasted that his "wide culture" was the result of living, not the result of reading about living, "I don't know anything about books." He did have a wide range of experiences, all of which influenced his books in one way or another. He spent his boyhood on the Mississippi. He later worked as a traveling printer, a Mississippi steamboat pilot, a Western miner and prospector, a newspaper reporter, a lecturer, an entrepreneur, and a publisher. He once confessed to having been an author for 20 years and an ass for 55.

299. Blair, Walter, and Raven I. McDavid, Jr., eds. "Mark Twain." The Mirth of a Nation: America's Great Dialect Humor. Minneapolis: Univ. of Minnesota Press, 1983, 257-75.

Claims that Twain had ties with every movement of nineteenth-century American humor. First, he read the antebellum authors. Later he put their stories into print. Still later, he echoed them in his own writing. And finally, when he edited Mark Twain's

<u>Library of Humor</u> he included them along with the "phunny phellows."
On the lecture circuit he was frequently joined by George Washington
Cable, a local colorist, and he often used the techniques of the
local colorists both in his lectures and in his writings. As an
example, "Jim Baker's Blue-Jay Yarn" "has touches of pathos that
give it warm humanity."

300. Branch, Edgar M. **"Did Sam Clemens Write 'Learning Grammar'?"**
     <u>Studies in American Humor</u> 2.2 (Winter 1983-84): 201-05.

Explains that the citizens of Warsaw, Illinois, have had a
long tradition that Sam Clemens spent a few weeks there in the
winter of 1855. In the middle of January 1856, a sketch appeared in
the Warsaw <u>Express and Journal of the People</u> entitled "Learning
Grammar," and many people feel that Twain wrote that sketch. The
sketch is signed by Thomas Jefferson Sole. Less than a year later,
Twain would use the pseudonym of "Thomas Jefferson Snodgrass." The
"Thomas Jefferson" part is the same, and "Sole" like "Snodgrass" is
developed as a country bumpkin--"garrulous, naive, opinionated,
self-revealing, and sometimes crudely direct in his actions." The
name "Sole" also brings to mind another penname that Twain would use
later--"Soleather," and "Sole" may have been still more significant
for when Twain was in Warsaw he was separated from his brothers
Orion and Henry, who were in neighboring Keokuk. He was indeed,
therefore, the "sole" Twain resident of Warsaw. The sketch involves
a father observing a grammar lesson in which the verb "to love" is
being conjugated. "I love!...Thou lovest; He loves;...." By the
time the teacher gets to "I might could or would love," the father
is incensed, and breaks off the grammar lesson as obscene. Twain
often conjugated verbs in his sketches to show the disparity between
book learning and real life.

301. Brunsdale, Mitzi M. **"A Punster with a Tear in His Eye: Mark
     Twain and the Russian Dissenters."** <u>WHIMSY</u> 1 (1983): 41-42.

Feels that the group of satirists known as the "Russian
Dissenters" read and were influenced by the writings of Mark Twain.
Many of Twain's asides that have remained as aphorisms to the
present day have the structure of a beginning statement with an
idealistic tone and then the provocative shock as this idealistic
statement is turned on its head by giving it a cynical twist. The
Russian Dissenters used this same technique. For example, Twain
said, "Truth is the most valuable thing we have. Let us economize
it." In <u>The Yawning Heights</u> Zinoviev said, "Internationalism is
when a Russian, a Georgian, a Ukrainian, a Chuvash, an Uzbek and all
the rest get together to go out to beat up a Jew."

302. Budd, Louis J. <u>**Our Mark Twain: The Making of His Public
     Personality**</u>. Philadelphia: Univ. of Pennsylvania Press, 1983,
     xv + 266 pages.

Describes the ubiquitousness of Mark Twain. Although he wrote
mainly in the nineteenth century, he is constantly in our minds
today. There is a crater on Mercury named after him. Some jokes
cannot be understood by anyone who is not fairly familiar with his
works. He is often alluded to both in literature and in everyday
life. His images invade our brains--Tom's whitewashing the fence,
Huck and Jim's floating down the Mississippi observing the stars,

the Connecticut Yankee's working miracles in Arthurian England, a cub-pilot at the wheel of a riverboat nervously trying to avoid sand bars, and even Mark Twain himself on the lecture circuit brushing cigar ashes from his white suit. Twain made such a lasting impression because his writing "reinforced qualities crucial to the happiness and perhaps survival of humankind: delight in experience, emotional spontaneity, and irreverence toward pomposity, petrified ideas, injustice, and self-pride."

303. Budd, Louis J. "Who Wants to Go to Hell? An Unsigned Sketch by Mark Twain?" Studies in American Humor 1.1 (June 1982): 6-16.

Explains that on Friday August 22, 1884 William Laffan, the business manager of the New York Sun wrote a letter to Sam Clemens which said that he had "put her into type" and that the sketch "is going in on Sunday." Although the Sun on Sunday, August 24, was huge, Twain scholars have searched it thoroughly to try to find Twain's contribution. They have finally zeroed in on a piece entitled "Hunting for H____" on page 2, the editorial page. Although the sketch was unsigned, there is further evidence that Twain wrote it. Twain had earlier written a poem entitled "To Miss Katie of H____" and later explained that H____ referred to "Hannibal." But the best evidence is that the sketch employed many of the literary devices which Twain used so often--"colloquial tone, emphatically direct address, an underlying violence of diction, dashes of slang, impudent exaggerations, deadpan metaphors, and even one of his tag-phrases ('you know')." In characteristic Twain style, the sketch was the piling of absurdity on absurdity, with an abrupt ending.

304. Budd, Louis J., and Edwin H. Cady, eds. On Mark Twain: The Best form American Literature. Durham, NC: Duke Univ. Press, 1987, x + 303 pages.

Contains articles explaining Mark Twain's treatment of science (by Hyatt Waggoner, and John Tuckey), his treatment as children (by Albert Stone), his indebtedness to John Phoenix (by Gladys Bellamy), his German translations (by Dixon Wecter), one of his lecture tours (by Fred Lorch), the style of Huckleberry Finn (by Leo Marx), the composition and structure of Tom Sawyer (by Hamlin Hill), the form of Innocents Abroad (by Bruce Michelson), his tone (by Clinton Burhans), his subjects (by George Spangler), and his personality (by Paul Baender and Stanley Brodwin).

305. Bush, Sargent, Jr. "The Showman as Hero in Mark Twain's Fiction." American Humor. Ed. O. M. Brack, Jr. Scottsdale, Arizona: Arete Publications, 1977, 79-98.

Considers the second half of the nineteenth century to have been the age of showmanship in America. There were traveling dramatic companies, minstrel shows, circuses, rodeos, menageries, and lecturers, not to mention circuit-riding preachers and traveling salesmen who would also try to develop showman techniques. This was the age of Buffalo Bill and of P. T. Barnum, and Twain caught this era of the showman very well in his novels in the development of such characters as Beriah Sellers, Tom Sawyer, Hank Morgan, Pudd'nhead Wilson, and Satan/44. All of these characters were showmen-heroes, very much in the tradition of Buffalo Bill and P. T. Barnum.

306. Busskohl, James. "Mark Twain's Humorous Use of Linguistic Naivete." WHIMSY 1 (1983): 42-43.

Suggests that Twain used Huck Finn's linguistic naivete as a rhetorical device. A Connecticut Yankee is a story about Hank Morgan's education in the poetic use of language. But Hank nevertheless has a tendency throughout the novel to interpret things literally. He describes the knight's helmet as having "the shape of a nail-keg with slits in it," and when he is told that Clarence is a page, Hank responds that that can't be right; he can't be more than a paragraph. The Adventures of Huckleberry Finn is a story of Huck's education in the realistic use of language. When the Widow reads to Huck about "Moses and the Bullrushers," he is at first very worried about what will happen to Moses. But when he is told that Moses is dead, he totally loses interest, because he "don't take no stock in dead people." Later in the novel, when Huck tells the slave hunters that the man on his raft is white, he is finally able to turn black into white. But this is because he has also learned to break with a society that condemns the spoken lie while condoning the silent lie.

307. Caron, James E. "The Comic Bildungsroman of Mark Twain." Modern Language Quarterly 50.2 (June 1989): 145-72.

Proposes that when three of Twain's pieces are read together as a single piece they can be viewed not as an example of the Bildungsroman genre, but rather as a parody of this genre. These three pieces are "Old Times on the Mississippi," Roughing It, and The Innocents Abroad. While the Bildungsroman genre takes the protagonist from earlier to later life, and shows how he or she grows and develops as a result of experiences, Twain's "Bildungsroman," which Caron chooses to call "The Adventures of Mark Twain" start later in life and recall earlier events. And the protagonists don't necessarily learn or progress as a result of their experiences. Caron cites the Horatio Alger stories as prototypical examples of the Bildungsroman genre, and suggests that the genre implies such concepts as learning, progress, science, the truth of facts, the reliability of narration, and the freedom implied by individuality. Mark Twain's "Bildungsroman" is not based on such concepts themselves, but it is based on the mocking of such concepts, and the tall tale self-contradition, and other comic devices are used to parody this genre which was central to the literary climate in nineteenth-century America. For example, in his writings, Twain clearly resents travel books which tell the traveler where to go and what to do; nevertheless, at the end of Innocents Abroad, he filters out the negative memories and presents a "Currier and Ives" recollection of the whole experience.

308. Caron, James E. "Pudd'nhead Wilson's Calendar: Tall Tales and a Tragic Figure." Nineteenth Century Fiction 36.4 (March 1982): 452-470.

Suggests that most critics have misread Twain's "Pudd'nhead Wilson's Calendar." The first misunderstanding is based on the incorrect assumption about the relationship between the aphorisms and the narration. Most critics feel that the aphorisms are spoken by the author; however, Caron feels that they are spoken by the character (David "Pudd'nhead" Wilson). This reading is supported by the book's complete title, The Tragedy of Pudd'nhead Wilson. It is furthermore supported by a tradition rampant during Twain's time known as the "Tall Tale." The Tall Tale represents a "tragedy" of some kind. It is characterized by authorial intrusions and implausibilities of plot and fantastic and fabulous images. The narration of a tall tale proceeds with progressively exaggerated detail until finally a preposterous climax--the "snapper" is reached. The credibility of the listener is stretched and stretched until he finally realizes his own gullibility. But most critics of Pudd'nhead Wilson have read it not as a tall tale but as a novel. They criticize it for lacking veriscimilitude, for wandering around, for authorial intrusions, an implausibible plot, unrealistic images, and a preposterous conclusion, all of these bad qualities in a novel but very good qualities in a tall tale.

309. **Cohen, Hennig, and William B. Dillingham.** "Samuel Langhorne Clemens." Humor of the Old Southwest. Athens: University of Georgia Press, 1975, 387-410.

Considers Mark Twain's works to be the culmination of the tradition of Southwestern humor in that Twain derived his raw material for his novels, stories, and lectures from this tradition and also because his writing reflects the tradition in its narrative techniques and his orientation toward realism. Cohen and Dillingham feel that "The Celebrated Jumping Frog," the "Blue-Jay Yarn," and the "Old Ram" are Southwestern yarns once removed. It is only geography, time, and writing skill that separate them from the earlier tradition.

310. **Couser, G. Thomas.** "Mark Twain as Humorist and Autobiographer." WHIMSY 5 (1987): 21-22.

Compares the life of P. T. Barnum with that of Mark Twain, suggesting that both of them spent their entire lives preoccupied with humor, duplicity, and autobiography. Twain's name denotes duplicity, since Mark means "sign," and Twain means "duplicity." Couser argues that duplicity not only underlies Twain's humor but is essential also to his autobiography.

311. **Covici, Pascal Jr.** "Mark Twain." Dictionary of Literary Biography: Volume 11: American Humorists, 1800-1950. Detroit, MI: Gale, 1982, 526-55.

Lists sixty books, sixteen articles, and eight collections of letters written by Mark Twain as well as ten biographies of Twain and twenty-two edited volumes of his works, indicating as a final entry that most of Twain's papers are presently housed at the Bancroft Library of the University of California in Berkeley. Covici devotes thirty pages to discussing Twain's significance as an author of humorous materials and concludes that his readers would have liked to know him personally. He had a passion for billiards and a fascination with gadgets, psychic phenomena, tempered by a healthy skepticism. He was self-educated, courageous, optimistic, and he rose to fame and fortune. These qualities, and especially his sense of humor, made him for many an archetypal American. He

made humor not just reputable but even necessary as an aspect of
expected and effective behavior.

312. **Covici, Pascal Jr.** "**Mark Twain and the Failure of Humor:
The Puritan Legacy.**" South Central Review 4.5 (Winter 1988-
89): 2-14.

Links Mark Twain with the Puritans by discussing his
Presbyterian guilt and early religious upbringing and states that
Twain shared with most of his readers the idea that the function of
humor is merely enjoyment and that taking it seriously or
considering it important was somehow not part of the Puritan ethic.
Covici lists as important Puritan influences on Twain's attitudes in
this regard not only the doctrine of Puritan determinism (including
the sense of God's chosen community and personal guilt) but also
three important writers: first, the mid-seventeenth-century
Nathanial Ward; second, the mid-eighteenth-century Benjamin
Franklin; and third, the mid-nineteenth-century Nathaniel Hawthorne.

313. **Covici, Pascal Jr.** Mark Twain's Humor: The Image of a World.
Dallas, TX: Southern Methodist Univ. Press, 1962, xvi + 266
pp.

Discusses Twain as a humorist, a satirist, and a philosopher,
and discusses his literary forms--the frontier anecdote, the parody,
and the hoax. This book offers new insights into the interpretation
of Huckleberry Finn, "The Man That Corrupted Hadleyburg," and The
Mysterious Stranger. Covici feels that the ending of Huckleberry
Finn should be read as a hoax to be properly appreciated. "Tom
Sawyer's ridiculous high jinks in the pretended rescue of Nigger Jim
communicates more than boyhood's fascination with burlesque, just as
the Mysterious Stranger's condemnation of humanity is not the final
word with which Mark Twain leaves us." Although Twain has often
been classed as a frontier humorist by various critics, Covici takes
him out of this category and classes him instead with Herman
Melville and Henry James because of his sophisticated literary
development.

314. **Cox, James M.** "**Mark Twain: The Height of Humor.**" The Comic
Imagination in American Literature. Ed. Louis D. Rubin, Jr.
New Brunswick, NJ: Rutgers University Press, 1983, 139-48.

Discusses Mark Twain's humor from the point of view of tension
and from the point of view of aesthetic perception. Cox feels that
the humorist must develop the right amount of tension. If there is
not enough tension, then the piece is viewed as too safe--there is
not enough wildness, incongruity, absurdity, or madness. If there
is too much tension, the security and pleasure of the humor are
lost. Twain maintained a nice balance. Another difficulty for
Twain, however, was that the humorist--especially an American
humorist--occupied a relatively low position in the hierarchy of
aesthetic values. Twain resolved this problem by getting to the
tragedy, the seriousness, and the vision beneath the humor. Twain
was a likely candidate to become the prototypical American humorist,
for he was more than a non-conformist; he was an outlaw. First of
all, Samuel Clemens joined the Confederate army, thus becoming a
traitor to his country. After about two weeks, he "resigned" from
the army, Twain's word for referring to his desertion. Finally, he

left Virginia City en route to San Francisco because he was on the verge of a dual with a rival reporter, because he had played fast and loose with the truth in reporting an incident involving a contribution to the American Sanitary Society.

315. Cox, James M. **Mark Twain: The Fate of Humor**. Princeton, NJ: Princeton Univ. Press, 1966, x + 321 pp.

Points out that Mark Twain criticism mainly revolves around three people. Albert Bigelow Paine provided Twain with a kind of genteel protection; Van Wyck Brooks attacked Twain's personality and art; and Bernard De Voto defended Twain and presented a kinder countertheory. Cox's book responds to these three Twain critics as well as to other Twain critics. But the book does more. It investigates the relationship between Mark Twain and Sigmund Freud. In Cox's opinion, Freud did for the Comic what Aristotle had done for the Tragic. Freud sought to describe, analyze, and define three critical categories--wit, comedy, and humor. For Freud, humor was the "highest" joke, though in Freud's own writings he concentrated more on wit and comedy. Twain specialized in humor, and, in fact, Freud cited Twain's humor as a perfect example of the economy of expenditure of effort. Twain was fascinated with repression, censorship, dreams, the conscience, and self-approval, the very things that Freud was also fascinated with. In fact, Freud's psychoanalytic theory was a culmination of nineteenth-century thought and sensibility, to which Mark Twain was one of the major contributors.

316. Cox, James M. "Mark Twain: The Triumph of Humor." **The Chief Glory of Every People**. Ed. Matthew J. Bruccoli. Carbondale, IL: Southern Illinois Univ. Press, 1973, 211-30.

Considers both Twain and Whitman to have been outside of the genteel tradition as they both related the idea of "voice" to the act of writing "as if the voice had literally embodied the writer." Twain, however had a larger audience than did Whitman. Whitman tried to reach all people and failed; Twain tried to reach all people and succeeded. The difference is that Twain was determined to please. He wrote what the people wanted to hear, and some critics have considered this to be a betrayal of his genius. Nevertheless, Twain's style of writing is so direct, so clear, and so transparent that it is in effect an implied criticism of all literary language which preceded him. In addition, Twain had a great sense of humor. He could both tell a joke and take one. Justin Kaplan has observed that much of his life is a joke. After all, "he began with a publisher named Bliss and ended with a biographer named Paine."

317. Davis, Betty J. "Mark Twain and the Parisians." **WHIMSY** 5 (1987): 22-23.

Points out that Halley's Comet appeared in 1835, the year that Twain was born, in 1910, the year he died, and in 1986, the one hundredth anniversary of the publication of Huckleberry Finn. Davis investigates Twain's observations of the Americans in contact with the French in The Innocents Abroad. Twain observed that Americans try to speak French just to torture the natives. Twain translates "The Jumping Frog" from English into French, and then back into

English again. The result contains literal idioms, French word order and adjective agreement, literal grammar (as double negatives), and various parenthetical comments such as "If that isn't grammar gone to seed, then I count myself no judge." As a youth Twain had dreamt of being shaved in a luxurious French barber palace, but when this actually happened, and the barber was just about to comb his hair he remarked that it was sufficient to be skinned; he declined being scalped as well. In Paris he met a guide who said "I speaky ze Angleesh pairfaitemaw." They named the guide Ferguson and told him they wanted to see the Louvre. He kept taking them to silk shops that were "on the way," in hopes of earning a commission, and each time the doctor would say something like "At last! How imposing the Louvre is; and yet how small." After the fourth silk shop the guide said it was too late to to see the Louvre anyway since it would be closing in ten minutes.

318. DeCiccio, Albert C. "Mark Twain's Comety: A Look at a Great American Humorist." WHIMSY 5 (1987): 24-25.

Exploits a pun in the title whereby "Comety" and "Comedy" are superimposed in the context of Mark Twain. DeCiccio applies Wayne Booth's rhetorical stance to Mark Twain, indicating that Twain was able to discover and maintain a proper balance between "the available arguments about the subject itself, the interest and peculiarities of the audience, and the voice, the implied character, of the speaker." DeCiccio investigates the quality of Twain's rhetorical skills and then concludes with a story about one of Twain's visits to London. He was to have been the main guest at a dinner to be given by a literary club, and a rumor reached the literary club that Twain had died. Mrs. Clemens was contacted about the rumor and got in touch with Twain, who telegraphed the literary club that "Rumor of my death has been greatly exaggerated." DeCiccio concluded that in 1986, 100 years after the publication of The Adventures of Huckleberry Finn," rumor of Twain's death has indeed been greatly exaggerated.

319. Gibson, William M. "Mark Twain's 'Carnival of Crime.'" American Humor. Ed. O. M. Brack, Jr. Scottsdale, Arizona: Arete, 1977, 73-78.

Explores the relationship between Mark Twain and Sigmund Freud. Freud was born in 1856 and was therefore twenty years Twain's junior. Freud suggested that where the id is there shall the ego be as well. Twain suggested the opposite--where the superego is, there shall the ego be as well. Twain's "Carnival of Crime" is an illustration of George Bernard Shaw's dictum that "telling the truth is the funniest joke in the world." The "Carnival of Crime" is told in first-person colloquial as something of a confessional. A door opens and in walks a two-foot-tall dwarf covered with a fuzzy greenish mold. Twain is amazed that the dwarf has an intimate knowledge of all of the misdeeds which Twain has long been ashamed of. The accusations become stronger and stronger until Twain throws a poker, books, inkstands, and chunks of coal at the dwarf. The dwarf is actually Twain's Conscience, and he says that he used to be seven feet tall and pretty as a picture. Finally, Twain grabs Conscience by the throat, tears him into pieces, and burns the pieces in a fire. Then Twain, a man without Conscience throws his Aunt Mary out of the house, kills thirty-eight people, burns down a building that blocks his view, swindles a widow and orphan out of their only cow, and generally enters into his carnival of crime.

320. **Gibson, William M.** **"TR and Mark Twain"** **Theodore Roosevelt Among the Humorists: W. D. Howells, Mark Twain, and Mr. Dooley.** Knoxville, TN: Univ. of Tennessee Press, 1980, 24-42.

Considers both Theodore Roosevelt and Mark Twain to have been men of intense moral commitment, but Twain's moral commitment was unconventional while Roosevelt's was traditional. Roosevelt believed in and lived the strenuous life; Twain insisted that he had never engaged in exercise except for sleeping and resting. Roosevelt had a passion for hunting, especially big game hunting. He hunted for sport, for food, and for museum collections. Twain, on the other hand, hated cruelty to animals and wrote A Horse's Tale and A Dog's Tale to protest bullfighting and vivisection respectively. After he had read about Roosevelt's killing of a bear in Louisiana, Twain wrote that it hadn't been a bear at all but a cow. Roosevelt was contrapuntally different from Twain in almost every respect. Roosevelt liked romantic and epic literature; he had reverence for great men and great deeds of bygone eras. Twain preferred the real and the irreverent or iconoclastic. Roosevelt spoke and wrote simply and in a straightforward manner. Twain's speech and writing were ironic. Twain once remarked that Roosevelt was "still only fourteen years old after living half a century."

321. **Greenagle, Frank Louis.** **"The Irony of Mark Twain: An Analysis of a Rhetorical Strategy."** Ph.D. dissertation, University of Minnesota, 1965, x + 154 pp.

Feels that before 1965, Twain's irony had been studied from a much too restricted point of view--as a trope rather than as a rhetorical strategy. For Twain, irony is not ornamentation; it is a writing style. Twain's writings contain many different types of irony, and furthermore, Twain's irony is "generative" as well as "illustrative." Twain's irony was not just an aspect of his writing: It was part of his life, and it was part of his interaction with his audience. He wanted to involve his readers in the literary process. He wanted to intrigue them. He wanted to ingratiate them, and he even wanted to outrage them. Greenagle feels that Twain had an understanding and control of the symbolic functions of irony that lay the groundwork for many contemporary authors.

322. **Gribben, Alan.** **"The Importance of Mark Twain."** American Quarterly 37.1 (Spring 1985): 30-49.

Contends that Twain had a great deal of difficulty establishing himself as an important writer once he was branded as a humorist. Many critics have attacked Twain's credentials and achievements; however other critics have brushed aside the attacks, claiming that although they may have been good critics, they didn't have a sense of humor. Twain was attacked not only because of his sense of humor but also because of his immense popularity. In Who Are the Major Writers?, Jay Hubbell explains, "This [popularity] disturbs the modern critics who seem to value only those writers whom they regard as alienated from society." Twain had his supporters. The American Literature Group of the Modern Language Association has classed him as one of the eight best American authors; the others are Poe, Emerson, Hawthorne, Thoreau, Melville, Whitman, and James. In his own time, Twain received three honorary degrees, one of them from Yale. He was also one of the first seven individuals selected for membership into the American Academy of Arts and Letters. Although he was well known and had a distinctive writing style, Twain was not frequently parodied. Gribben feels this is because Twain had a balance and flexibility not found in Poe, Cooper, Whitman, James, Crane, Hemingway, or Faulkner. Twain was one of the few humorists of his time to survive and to significantly influence such authors as Cheever, Vonnegut, Berg, and Barth.

323. **Gribben, Alan. "Mark Twain, Business Man: The Margins of Profit."** Studies in American Humor **NS1.1 (June 1982): 24-43.**

Investigates Mark Twain's business sense both in his personal life and in his writings. In one installment of "Old Times on the Mississippi," for example, he tells about a fellow named Stephen who got a job as a steamboat pilot for half-wages ($125 a month). By continually steering the boat directly into the river's current, this pilot convinced the captain who had hired him that a $250 pilot was needed. Twain also wrote "The Million Pound Bank-Note," which told about how an American gets financial credit in London on the basis of possessing such a note. Of course the note couldn't be cashed, and he thereby saves his friend's investments, gets a good job for himself, and wins the hand of a lovely heiress. "The $30,000 Bequest" is another Twain sketch that concerns money. In this sketch a couple are destroyed by an old man's promise to leave them a lot of money. In their dreams, they put the money into stocks in an attempt to improve their capital and their social standing and wake up in a nightmare with someone shouting "Sell! Sell! For Heaven's sake sell." The next day came the historic crash.

324. **Gribben, Alan. "That Pair of Spiritual Derelicts": The Poe-Twain Relationship."** Poe Studies **18.2 (December 1985): 17-21.**

Recalls V. S. Pritchett's 1940s claim that everything really American originated from a "pair of spiritual derelicts" by the name of Edgar Alan Poe and Mark Twain. This article explores the literary parallels betwen Poe and Twain, especially with reference to their dark or satiric modes, their doubles (dopelgängers), and their detective stories. Gribben concludes that although these authors have vastly different literary reputations, there are many curious intersections of situation, mood, theme, symbol, and phrase. He states that in recent years Twain's writings have been viewed as more somber, brooding, even "Gothic," than had been previously assumed--much more like the writings of Poe.

325. **Hayden, Bradley. "The Legacy of Mark Twain."** WHIMSY **6 (1988): 16.**

Considers Mark Twain to be archetypically American. His style includes the brashness of the tall tale, a great deal of local color, and a vernacular style that came out of the almanac and newspaper traditions of the literary comedians. He also had a strong sense of morality and developed the comic incongruity between the naive right and the sophisticated wrong. His tone was used to satirize the common folk. Twain's humor explores the conflict between new-world aspirations, and old-world realities.

326. **Hellwig, Harold. "A Psycholinguistic Analysis of Twain's A Connecticut Yankee." WHIMSY 1 (April 1983): 43-45.**

Agrees with Henry Nash Smith that Twain had a constant fascination with volcanoes and that for Twain the volcano (especially the one in A Connecticut Yankee) was symbolic of Twain's oscillation between enthusiasm for the exciting world of science and technology and the simple and peaceful agrarian world that the Industrial Revolution was destroying before his very eyes. Hellwig suggests that Twain's rhetorical style is determined to some extent by whether he is talking about a fictional volcano (England), or a real volcano (Hawaii). The passage describing the fictional volcano uses the passive construction and prepositional phrases of location, while the real volcano passage uses active verbs. The fictional uses possessional verbs, while the real uses positional and identificational verbs. The Connecticut volcano is threatening because it is static, personal, and powerful. The Hawaiian volcano is active, natural, and almost friendly. The contrast is begween the malignant, smouldering, deadly, metaphoric volcano of the mind and the benign but powerful force of nature.

327. **Hill, Hamlin. "Mark Twain's Roughing It: The End of the American Dream." WHIMSY 1 (April, 1983): 45-47.**

Claims that it was not the years that Twain actually spent in the West that provided him with the basic tensions explored in Roughing It, but it was rather his courtship and early marriage to Olivia Langdon. Roughing It is an example of what W. D. Howells calls "the nether-side of tragedy" and is Twain's renunciation of his free and footloose bachelorhood. It was Twain's rejection of the wonderful and fantastic frontier West that controlled the American imagination in the nineteenth century. It was his "autopsy of the American Dream." The novel is full of chance deaths, chance fortunes, and dramatic failures. Freedom is only an illusion. Independence and self-reliance are shattered over and over again by harsh reality. The humorous portrayal only adds to the drama. Failure is the theme throughout Roughing It, and the novel ends with Twain as the butt of a practical joke in which his "friends" stage a mock hold-up and deprive him of his watch, money, and other possessions. Throughout the novel, the humor is presented in deadpan--in such a way as to suggest that the narrator doesn't have even the slightest suspicion that there is anything funny about the stories he is recounting.

328. **Hiscoe, David W. "The 'Abbreviated Ejaculation' in Huckleberry Finn." Studies in American Humor NS1.3 (February 1983): 191-197.**

Proclaims that one of Twain's most effective dramatic devices was the "abbreviated ejaculation," used to show a change in the train of thought of a speaker. In the last chapter of Huckleberry Finn Tom Sawyer suddenly comes to a realization: "What! Why Jim is--

." Huck explains that he has Jim and is going to steal him, and
Tom's eyes light up as he says, "I'll help you steal him!" Jim can
hardly believe his ears, "Tom Sawyer, a nigger stealer!" In his
Mark Twain's Humor Pascal Covici says that Huck becomes convinced of
Tom's sincerity and that in the process the reader becomes convinced
as well. Covici calls this "Tom's hoax," and understanding his
statement as a hoax greatly improves the quality of the ending of
Huckleberry Finn. To support Covici's stance and in fact to suggest
that Twain's hoaxing stance is more common than is usually believed,
Hiscoe gives other examples of the "abbreviated ejaculation" as when
the wife of the slave hunter is explaining to Huck about runaway
Jim, and he exclaims, "Why he--" and then stops. At another point,
the Duke is telling Huck about Jim's location, "A farmer by the name
of Silas Ph--." "...Abram Foster--Abram G. Foster." Huck knows that
Jim is at the Phelps' place. Readers had better take note whenever
Twain uses the "abbreviated ejaculation," for it always reflects the
twinkle in his eye.

329. **Inge, M. Thomas, ed. Huck Finn among the Critics: A
Centennial Selection.** Frederick, Maryland: University
Publications of America, 1985, xi + 465 pp.

Claims that Twain's strength in Huckleberry Finn and his other
works is his cutting humor. The book is divided into four sections:
Backgrounds, Early Response, Modern Criticism, and Appendix. In a
book review that appeared in Thalia, David L. Vanderwerken says,
"Inge surveys the critical reputation of the novel [Huckleberry
Finn] as well as its controversial nature--interdicted in 1885 for
alleged 'vulgarity,' in 1985 for alleged 'racism.'" Vanderwerken
further feels that Inge's section on Modern Criticism is one of the
most provocative, perceptive, and enduring critiques that we have.

330. **Keough, William. "Round Two: The Painted Fire of Mark Twain."
Punchlines: The Violence of American Humor.** New York: Paragon
House, 1990, 15-60.

Considers Mark Twain to be the fulcrum of American humor
because Twain was attuned to the violent paradoxes of American
culture. Twain witnessed much violence, and much violence made it
into his novels--frequent corpses, dead cats, starving Indians, open
coffins, graveyards, pig-guttings, child-whippings, an impressive
and terrifying list. Twain used comic-deflation devices as
invective, parody, travesty, burlesque, and hoaxing to deal with the
violence he encountered and wrote about. When he was young, Twain
viewed the violence with amusement, but when he got older he viewed
it with misgivings and disgust, and he finally fell into
misanthropic despair. During his prime, Twain's answer to all of
the violence was to escape. In Huck's words, "It's lovely to live
on a raft." For Twain, the raft was symbolic of a hard-earned
peace; the raft was part of Twain's legacy, his plea for peace in a
world racked by continuous and uncontrollable violence.

331. **Kesterson, David B. "Mark Twain and the Humorist Tradition."
Samuel L. Clemens: A Mysterious Stranger.** Ed. Hans Borchers
and Daniel E. Williams. NY: Verlag Peter Lang, 1985, 55-69.

Proposes that Twain could not have made such an impact on the
American humorous tradition if he had not relied heavily on the

humorous American writers who wrote before him, and whom he read and learned from. Twain was well versed in the great humorous classics, and had read enough works in the picaresque tradition to be able to effectively control the structure, scope, and style of The Adventures of Huckleberry Finn. Twain was also well versed in the social satires of Charles Dickens and knew Shakespeare's comic creations as well. Kesterson suggests three humor traditions which had a significant effect on Twain's writing. Twain was familiar with such Down East Humorists as Seba Smith, whose characters spoke in wise sayings and proverbs, and used dialect to discuss government, politics, and society. Twain was also familiar with the Old Southwestern Humorists like William Trotter Porter. These humorists came from Georgia, Alabama, Mississippi, Arkansas, Louisiana, and Tennessee, and their (like many of Twain's stories) have backwoods settings, bold, rough-hewn characters, and a love of boisterousness and exaggeration. Twain was also influenced by the literary comedians like Charles Farrar Browne (Artemus Ward), and like the literary comedians, Twain adopted a pen name that almost eclipsed his real name.

332. Kolb, Harold H., Jr. "Mere Humor and Moral Humor: The Example of Mark Twain." American Literary Realism: 1870-1910 19.1 (Fall 1986): 52-64.

Feels that Twain accepted the prevailing nineteenth century view that humor (like sex) was to be privately enjoyed but publically denounced. But Twain felt that he had a special talent for humor, and he decided to follow his instincts even though he considered humor to be "literature of a low order" and that writing it "is nothing to be proud of." The nineteenth century view was that literature should be didactic; it should teach moral values. Many of Twain's defenders, therefore, demonstrated Twain's significance as a writer by showing that Twain was indeed teaching moral lessons in his writings. Ironically, then, these defenses distorted not only the significance of humor and the significance of Twain's writing but augmented Twain's own perception that humor was unimportant unless it was being used to expose vice and folly.

333. Krauth, Leland. "Mark Twain Fights Sam Clemens' Duel." Mississippi Quarterly 30.2 (Winter 1980): 141-53.

Explains why in 1863 when Samuel Clemens was the acting editor of the Virginia City Territorial Enterprise he stated that the Virginia City Daily Union would not make good on their pledges to the Sanitary Fund. Clemens later said that this was "a hoax, but not all a hoax." In fact, the Enterprise and the Union were in a bidding war, each attempting to bid the most money to the sanitation fund, and the Enterprise lost. Clemens was embarrassed and first attacked the Union and then challenged the Union to a dual (a strong Southern tradition) and finally moved to the mountains of Nevada. It is Krauth's contention that Samuel Clemens used the personna of Mark Twain to change himself from an aggressor to a victim. Krauth compares this personal incident with the tendency of sentimental Southern writers to describe the Civil War as the march of Northern aggression over Southern weakness, and concludes that in both cases the pen proved to be mightier than both the dueling pistol and the sword.

334. Krauth, Leland. "Mark Twain: The Victorian of Southwestern Humor." American Literature 54 (1982): 368-84.

Claims that Twain's move to Hartford's Nook Farm, New England, in 1871 greatly influenced his attitudes. He moved there from the West and brought with him free drinking, free smoking, and colloquial speech. To the New England attributes of morality, sentiment, and seriousness, Twain added humor, burlesque, and play. Twain had a billiard table in his study. He was an invader of New England Victorian values. But Twain soon absorbed New England values, and by the time he wrote Huckleberry Finn he had developed a strong sense of propriety. The novel is affected by Victorian values in three major ways: First, some of the stock situations and characters were reshaped; second, only certain subjects were selected for discussion, and other subjects were discarded as inappropriate; and third, his character development transcends the tradition of Southwestern Humor.

335. Krauth, Leland. "The Whimsical Mark Twain." WHIMSY 1 (April, 1983): 47-50.

Contends that though Twain's early writings were carefree and frolicsome and his late writings were tortured and dire, both early and late writings are marked by whimsy. When Twain worked for The Enterprise, for example, he described the arguments of Nevada lawyer determined to prevent the taxing of mines. The lawyer's argument was that "mine" is only a "pronominal adjective" and that there is nothing in the Constitution that allows the State to tax English grammar. Another time, bored by legislative speeches Twain suggests that a particular representative either add something fresh to his speech or else say it backwards. As a reporter he tells about an old two-story house that got loose from its moorings and drifted down Sutter street and then suggests that that is OK because there is no law against houses loafing around public streets at night. In Mark Twain's Letters from Hawaii Twain describes a horse that resembles a sheep and then goes on to give a fanciful account of his first ride. In Roughing It he tells about a western drunk whose speech has more hiccups than syllables in it and about a Tenderfoot who falls prey to an auctioneer to convinces him to buy a "Genuine Mexican Plug." Throughout Twain's late writings there is cynicism and bitterness, but there is whimsy as well.

336. Logan, Darlene. "A Metaphor of Duality: Twain's Literary Caesarean Operation." WHIMSY 2 (April 1984): 23-26.

Disagrees with most Twain critics who feel that Twain did well when he separated The Tragedy of: Pudd'nhead Wilson from The Comedy: Those Extraordinary Twins. In publishing them together, Twain was commenting on the duality of human nature, but later he performed a kind of literary Caesarean operation. In both pieces, Twain was fascinated by the concept of unity vs. duality. In Pudd'nhead he tells the townspeople that he wished he owned half a dog so that he would be able to kill his half. In Twins the townspeople hung one half of a Siamese twin. Twain was also fascinated with the duality that existed within himself, feeling that he was two spirits bound in a single body.

337. **Lynn, Kenneth S.** **Mark Twain and Southwestern Humor.** Boston, MA: Little, Brown and Co, 1959, 300pp.

Is saddened by the fact that many critics have taken Twain at his word when he remarked in the Preface of Huckleberry Finn, "Persons attempting to find a motive in this narrative will be prosecuted; persons attempting to find a moral in it will be banished; persons attempting to find a plot in it will be shot." Mark Twain was being ironic. Motives, morals, and plots are all well developed in Twain's writings. Twain was in the tradition of the Southwestern humorists, who did more than write about the backwoods mind; they exemplified it. Southwestern humor at its best is characterized by its careful craftsmanship and artistic expression.

338. **McCullough, Joseph B., and Donald Malcom.** "Mark Twain's Creation Myths: 'Captain Stormfield' and Letters from the Earth." Studies in American Humor 5.2-3 (Summer-Fall 1986): 168-76.

Presents Twain's Letters from the Earth as a scathing portrayal of the creation myth. God is presented as an absent-minded mad scientist; Satan is a skeptic; and mankind is some sort of a botched experiment. In 1868, before he had written Tom Sawyer, or Huckleberry Finn, Twain had written "Captain Stormfield's Visit to Heaven." This was later expanded into Letters from the Earth. From 1868 on, Twain was intensely interested in religious and moral subjects and early on wrote such sketches as "Adam's Expulsion" "Methuselah's Diary" "Papers of the Adam Family," and "Adam's Diary." Nevertheless he couldn't publish the "Stormfield" text because of its scandalous contents. Twain was also not satisfied with the text and later effected a serious tone to be undercut by the satire. The original version could not maintain the serious tone because of the Southwestern vernacular idioms that pervaded the dialogue. Twain also moved the creation myth to the beginning of the work rather than have it as a random item in the reminisences of a scuffy old sailor. Twain's instincts were correct. He published the manuscript as Letters from the Earth in 1881.

339. **Madigan, Francis V.** "Review of At Home Abroad: Mark Twain in Australasia by Miriam Jones Shillingsburg." Studies in American Humor 5.2-3 (Summer-Fall 1986): 207-11.

Indicates that this is the last of Twain's travel books. Twain found the humor of the Australasians to be much more consistent with his own humor than was the humor of England. Much Australasian humor was based in absurdity. Twain granted an interview to a group of reporters during the loading of a ship. The interview took place amidst the commotion of winches, hawser pipes, and other clanking and grating. One reporter, Herbert Low, became so frustrated in his taking of notes that he shouted to Twain that he would have to just imagine the interview. Twain responded "Go ahead, my boy; I've been there myself." While he was in Australasia, Twain adapted his material to suit his listeners. The members of his audiences were so familiar with his work that they often laughed in anticipation--before the punch line of a joke had been reached. The Australasians also enjoyed Twain's blending of humor and pathos as in a story Twain told about the reuniting of a slave woman with her son or some of the excerpts from <u>Huckleberry Finn</u>.

340. Moser, Kay. "Mark Twain and Ulysses S. Grant." <u>Studies in American Humor</u> NS1.2 (October 1982): 130-141.

Suggests that Mark Twain's love and admiration for Ulysses S. Grant was ironic and somewhat irrational. Twain respected Grant as a leader. He liked Grant's abilities as a self-sacrificing good citizen. He was especially impressed by Grant's personal qualities. But Grant was the General of the enemy (Union) forces. And Grant had a great many failings and shortcomings. Moser believes that Twain viewed Grant as something of a father figure and that this perception clouded his vision. Twain's real father, John Clemens, was unapproachable. Grant, on the other hand, had offered his outstretched hands to Twain with love and understanding. Grant was to Mark Twain the father he never had.

341. Neider, Charles. <u>The Comic Mark Twain Reader</u>. Garden City, NY: Doubleday, 1977, xxx + 489 pp.

Feels that Twain has an innately clear, precise, deep, and empathetic comic perspective both on his own life and on that of other people. His vernacular and idiomatic writing is rich in slang and is vital in its reverberances. Twain was not the originator of the humorous vernacular style; rather, he was its culminating point. He frequently stopped in the middle of a narrative to recount a favorite yarn, such as "Buck Fanshaw's Funeral" and "His Grand-Father's Old Ram" in <u>Roughing It</u>, "The Jumping Frog" in <u>Huckleberry Finn</u>, or "Jim Baker's Bluejay Yarn" in <u>A Tramp Abroad</u>. The yarns were luxurious in the telling but were not intended to arrive at a conclusion. In 1895 Twain published, "How to Tell a Story," where he posited that the homespun yarn is to Americans what the comic story is to the English and the witty story is to the French. The success of the American yarn depends on the manner of telling--the timing, the pausing, the mimicry, the suggestion, and the self control. It is spun out to great length, wanders as it pleases, and ends up no place in particular. It is told gravely and in deadpan style, while the British comic story and the French witty story are often told with eager delight and sometimes with guffaws of laughter.

342. Neider, Charles, ed. <u>The Outrageous Mark Twain: Some Lesser-Known but Extraordinary Works, with "Reflections on Religion."</u> New York: Doubleday, 1987, 348 pp.

Argues that many Twain readers are not aware of his extreme side. They consider Twain to be a pleasant and genial spirit and remarkable humorist and not much more. Others believe his principal contribution to have been two children's classics, both dealing with life on the Mississippi River and in the Mississippi Valley setting. The purpose of this book is to disturb such notions by showing the unsettling, far-out side of Twain. Twain is shown to be sacrilegous ("Reflections on Religion"), bawdy ("1601"), shocking ("Science of Onanism"), irreverent ("Extract from Captain Stormfield's Visit to Heaven"), outraged ("Goldsmith's Friend Abroad Again"), obstreperous ("Is Shakespeare Dead?"), and infuriating ("Christian Science").

The book also illustrates Twain uproariously gifted use of invective ("Open Letter to Commodore Vanderbilt").

343. Nilsen, Don L. F. "Mark Twain's Coping Techniques." The Study of Humor Eds. Harvey Mindess and Joy Turek. Los Angeles, California: Antioch University, 1980.

Suggests that an important function of humor for Twain was as a device to deal with everyday frustrations. He was frustrated by the exploitation of salesmen and describes a burglar alarm he had bought as having all that is objectionable about a fire, a riot, and a harem, with none of the compensating advantages. In talking about the late Benjamin Franklin Twain said that he was twins born simultaneously in two different houses in Boston, adding that these two houses remain to this day and have signs on them describing Franklin's birth. He was frustrated by the exploitation of religion, saying that our forefathers gave us the religious liberty to worship and vote as the church required. He was frustrated by the exploitation of government and tells about a bluejay that hadn't any more principles than a Congressman. He was frustrated by traveling and told about many humorous incidents that resulted from contacts with Germans, Frenchmen, Italians, etc. He was frustrated by other authors and said that the difference between a Cooper Indian and a cigarshop indian is not great. He was frustrated by death, and in A Tramp Abroad when he was forced to fight a duel, he chose axes as the weapon, but his request was denied because the inevitable result would have been bloodshed.

344. Rogers, Franklin R. Mark Twain's Burlesque Patterns, as Seen in the Novels and Narratives 1855-1885. Dallas, Texas: Southern Methodist University Press, 1960, x + 189 pp.

Concentrates on the works written from the beginning of Twain's writing career and 1885. Rogers attempts to dispell the notion that burlesque is an inferior art form unworthy of serious or extended attention and also to dispell the notion that Twain's burlesques were merely a training ground for his development as a "realist." Rogers considers literary burlesque to be a humorous exaggerated imitation of the plot, characterization, and/or style of a particular genre, author, or piece. Although "burlesque" and "parody" both generally connote a critical attitude on the part of the writer, Rogers does not imply that Twain was in any way being critical in the burlesques in question. Rogers contends that Twain developed a new type of travel narrative in Roughing It and in Tom Sawyer, The Prince and the Pauper, and Huckleberry Finn Twain developed an effective writing style by first writing burlesques, and then transforming these burlesques into skeletons that later became well-crafted novels.

345. Rogers, Franklin R., ed. Mark Twain's Satires and Burlesques. Berkeley: Univ. of California Press, 1967, 465 pp.

Realizes that Twain may not have wanted to have these materials from his personal files published, because he chose not to publish them during his life time. But Rogers feels that these materials are important because they dispel a myth about Twain's creative process which Twain himself had established and constantly promoted. The myth was that Twain did not have to work very hard to write his novels. On one occasion, for example, Twain embroidered a pair of slippers for Elsie Leslie Lyde, and when he presented the slippers to her he presented a letter as well that said that he had made the slippers without design or plan of any sort "just as I would begin a Prince and Pauper, or any other tale." In the letter, Twain suggested that all he had to do was invent two or three characters and set them loose in the manuscript, and from that point on, something exciting was bound to happen which the author has no pain in developing. The book writes itself out of the "natural consequences," and "first thing you know, there's your book all finished up and never cost you an idea." But the files suggest that the truth is very different. Actually, Twain experienced great pain and trouble in delimiting his fictional world, establishing its nature, and maintaining control over the characters in the novels.

346. Royot, Daniel. "The Fantastic Record of a Maniac: King Leopold's Soliloquy Revisited." An American Empire: Expansionist Cultures and Politics, 1881-1917. Ed. Serge Ricard. Aix en Provence, France: Grena, 1990, 237-43.

Considers King Leopold's Soliloquy to have been the most scathing of Twain's polemical writings. It is an ironic defense of Congo rule written in the same manner as Swift's "A Modest Proposal." The essay is crude, and was apparently written on the spur of the moment. It has loose narrative structure, grounded to reality by allusions to newspaper headlines, photographs of mutilated natives taken by Kodak cameras, missionary reports, and official documents of the Congo government. Although the subject of the discourse was the Belgian Congo, the piece was also a criticism of other systems of terror that were spreading around the world during Twain's time. For Twain, Leopold is our own alter egos and as such is protected by our indifference and cowardice. The Leopold piece is a harsh caricature and exemplifies Freud's belief that humor is the most economic expenditure of the emotions.

347. Schmitz, Neil. Of Huck and Alice: Humorous Writing in American Literature. Minneapolis: University of Minnesota Press, 1983, 269 pp.

Selects Mark Twain and Gertrude Stein as the two best representatives of non-conformist thought in American literature. In Huckleberry Finn Twain culminates the nineteenth-century tradition of the crackerbarrel philosopher by developing what he calls "Huckspeech." This vernacular language does not contain as many mistakes as is found in earlier nineteenth century authors, but the mistakes which do appear are carefully calculated. Huckspeech is the speech "of the preliterate, of the poor, and of children." It is charming, but it is held to be inadequate and wrong, the language of the excluded classes, the ignorant. It is "emotionally rite and socially rong." An example of Huckspeech is the word "nigger." The word bristles throughout the novel. Another example--this time ironically appropriate--is the word "sivilize." The word "sivilize" is the first misspelling in Huckleberry Finn and the last. Huckleberry Finn also investigates the problems of two-value logic--thinking in black and white. When Huck is asked whether the man on the raft is black or white, he responds, "He's white...he's my father." Schmitz feels that this is a "white lie" and compares it to the "whitewash" in Tom Sawyer.

348. Seelye, John. "The Craft of Laughter: Abominable
Showmanship and Huckleberry Finn." Thalia: Studies in Literary
Humor 4.1 (1981): 19-25.

Proposes that Mark Twain had originally had a different ending
for Huckleberry Finn. He had originally intended a dramatic climax
where Jim would have been tried for Huck's murder but would be saved
at the last minute by Huck's showing up at the trial. But then
Twain realized that he had already squandered this plot in Chapter
23 of Tom Sawyer when Muff Potter is saved from hanging by Tom's
testimony. Seeley suggests that the ending to Huckleberry Finn is
the best ending possible for the novel. It is good because it is
bad. It is an ending that develops art as entertainment, as Twain
does his best to amuse his readers. It is also an ending that is
good for Twain's critics, as "it provides one of those critical
enigmas upon which academic careers are built."

349. Shugg, Wallace. "The Humorist and the Burglar: The Untold
Story of the Mark Twain Burglary." Mark Twain Journal 25.1
(Spring 1987): 2-11.

Suggests that Albert Bigelow Paine, Mark Twain's biographer
was misleading and incomplete when he suggested that Mark Twain was
untouched by the break-in of his home on September 18, 1908. Paine
was probably attempting to reinforce the public image of Twain as an
aging cynic with a twinkle in his eye and a warm underlying
sympathy. Twain himself was attempting to reinforce this same
image. He posted a notice that was run in both American and
European newspapers that read: "To the next Burglars. There is
nothing but plated ware in the house--now & henceforth...." He
received a telegram from Melville Stone, President of the Associated
Press, asking if he would be willing to pay carfare and other
expenses for two efficient and trustworthy burglars. Twain replied
in kind "No. I can get burglars here at club rates and they pay
their own fare." The Baltimore Morning Sun ran a piece entitled
"BURGLARIZED AT LAST!" The piece said that Mark Twain had realized
one of his life's ambitions, since he had been waiting for more than
50 years in hopes of some burglar deeming his possessions of
sufficient value to steal. But Shugg claims that under this veneer
of frivolity, Twain deeply resented the theft of his dead wife's
silver and the resultant disruption of his household.

350. Simpson, Claude M., Jr. "Huck Finn after Huck Finn."
American Humor. Ed. O. M. Brack, Jr. Scottsdale, Arizona:
Arete, 1977, 59-72.

Contrasts the Huckleberry Finn of Tom Sawyer with the
Huckleberry Finn of Huckleberry Finn and says that the dangers in
Tom Sawyer are mainly make-believe, while those in Huckleberry Finn
are real. There is also a significant change in point of view
between these two novels. In the first novel Tom Sawyer is in total
command. Huck Finn could not have developed as an individual in the
presence of Tom's aggressiveness and managerial instincts. The
advantage of Huckleberry Finn is its colloquial vigor directness of
impression and unconscious irony provided by Huck's first-person
innocent but shrewd narration. In 1902 Twain was working on a
manuscript in which Huck and Tom were old men looking back over
their lives and dwelling on the triumphs and tragedies of their

existence. But the manuscript was abandoned, and the thirty-eight
thousand words that had been written were destroyed "for fear I
might some day finish it." The real problem may have been that in
that manuscript neither Tom Sawyer nor Huckleberry Finn could have
emerged as a truly dominant character.

351. Sloane, David E. E. **Mark Twain as a Literary Comedian**. Baton
     Rouge: Louisiana State University Press, 1979, 221 pp.

Disagrees with Twain critics who place him into the category
of Southwestern humorists by placing him instead into the category
of literary comedians. Twain's humor was not based on local color
(as that of the Southwestern humorists was) but was instead based on
his egalitarian vision, his jokes, his ironic inversions, and his
burlesques, writing features not of the Southwestern humorists but
rather features of the literary comedians of the 1850s and the Civil
War era.

352. Sloane, David E. E. "Samuel Langhorne Clemens." Encyclopedia
     of American Humorists. Ed. Steven H. Gale. New York: Garland,
     1988, 83-91.

Contrasts Mark Twain with the Civil War literary comedians.
Twain avoided the superficial tricks of spelling and other
mechanical humor devices that the literary comedians had used, and
concentrated more on satiric and sarcastic devices. When the
Connecticut Yankee looks at Camelot, he asks if it is "Bridgeport,"
alluding to the home of P. T. Barnum's castle, Iranistan. The
Innocents Abroad satirized the hypocrisy of old Europe and
uneducated Americans who had developed the bad manners of the
"nouveau riche." Roughing It, an account of a tenderfoot's journey
across the frontier to Nevada, was filled with social sarcasm. Tom
Sawyer satirized Southwestern roughness with incidents like feeding
the cat medicine or teasing the schoolmaster. A Tramp Abroad is an
account of a walking tour taken by Twain and Twitchell and is a
burlesque of travel records of the day. In fact, all of Twain's
writing seems to be doing more than merely entertaining. It is at
the same time making important social observations.

353. Smith, Janet, ed. **Mark Twain on the Damned Human Race**. New
     York: Hill and Wang, 1962, xx + 259 pp.

Presents some of the strongest of Mark Twain's writings.
Smith points out that The Innocents Abroad was considered vulgar and
even immoral to most European critics, while American critics saw it
as good clean fun. Both American and European critics have claimed
that Mark Twain's patriotism forced him to be too uncritical,
however, Soviet critics have long felt that he was a fearless critic
of his own country, and in fact they have claimed that much of what
Twain wrote was so critical that it had to be censored. One of the
pieces they refer to is his autobiography which originally appeared
in two milder versions. When the third, stronger, version appeared,
the Soviet critics claimed censorship; however the actual case was
that Twain had left instructions that it should not be published
while it could still cause pain to living persons. Twain was
unaware of how soon his ideas would become commonplace and how soon
his writing would become tame by comparison to other writing.

354. Sousa, Raymond J. "'Be It What It Will, I'll Go To It Laughing': Mark Twain's Humorous Sense of Life." Thalia: Studies in Literary Humor 2.1-2 (1979): 17-24.

Points out some of the catastrophes that Twain had to endure during his lifetime. Before his mid-teens, his father, sister, brother, and numerous friends and acquaintances had died; he had to take on a man's job as a boy. Within two more decades he had lost a job he loved and a very close brother. Soon afterward, his wife's father died, and his wife (Livy) had a nervous breakdown. Then came the death of his son and of numerous friends and relatives, and then came his financial collapse and the death of his favorite daughter, Susy, and the illness of Jean, and then Livy's collapse. But Twain used humor as a device for coping with all of these misfortunes. In Following the Equator he said, "The secret source of humor is not in joy but in sorrow." When Twain's wife collapsed, the doctor prescribed silence as essential for her recovery, so Twain pinned notes to the trees around their home ordering the birds to be silent. Twain was not like Sisyphus or Job who did not use laughter to cope with their miserable states; rather he was like Stubb in Melville's Moby Dick, who said, "Be it what it will, I'll go to it laughing."

355. Sousa, Raymond J. "Mark Twain and Frontier Humor: Liberation through Laughter." WHIMSY 3 (April 1985) 25-26.

Suggests that all the rigors of the frontier forced all frontiersmen to become laughing philosophers in order to survive the stress of the wilderness and provides examples of Twain's ability to turn something horrid and deadly into a plaything for laughter. Jim Blaine in Roughing It tells about a woman who was "considerable on the borrow." This particular woman was only a trunk of her former self because of all of the parts of her body that either didn't work or had just plain fallen off. In order to receive company, she would borrow Miss Higgin's wooden leg, and Miss Jacops's wig. She would also borrow Old Miss Jefferson's glass eye, but it was too small, so it would get twisted around in the socket and look off in various directions while the good eye was looking straight ahead. Blaine said that grown people didn't mind, but it usually made the children cry.

356. Steinbrink, Jeffrey. "Mark Twain and Hunter Thompson: Continuity and Change in American 'Outlaw Journalism.'" Studies in American Humor NS 2.3 (Winter 1983-84): 221-34.

Places some of the writings of Mark Twain and Hunter Thompson into the category of "Gonzo Journalism." The first assumption of the Gonzo journalists is that except for box scores, race results, and stock market tabulations, there is no such thing as objective reporting, which they deride with such terms as "traditional," "Eastern," or "straight" journalism. And they contend that such journalism is rooted in a lie--and a barren lie at that. They consider the expression "objective reporting" to be a contradiction of terms. Once this is established, they develop the genre of Gonzo Journalism, which is "aggressively subjective, intensely imaginative, determinedly iconoclastic, and almost unremittingly 'literary'." This tradition is picaresque, in that it normally

follows a comic central character (often the author himself) through
a series of episodic adventures.

357. **Vonnegut, Kurt.** **"Speech Delivered on April 30, 1979, at the
One-Hundredth Anniversary of the Completion of Mark Twain's
Fanciful House in Hartford, Connecticut."** A Propos 4 (1986):
132-33.

Discusses Twain's veriscimilitude by equating it with the
elegant Missouri verb "to calculate." Twain was familiar with the
verb "to calculate." On the frontier a person who calculated this
or that was asking that his lies be accepted, because they had been
arrived at by means of the science of arithmetic. He wanted the
listener to acknowledge that although the facts might not be
accurate, the arithmetic was in fact logical. Vonnegut contends
that the art of good story telling is based on keeping the
arithmetic sound. A story teller starts with an initial lie, and
this lie will suggest other lies and elaborations as he goes along.
The good story teller has learned how to choose from the many lies
that come to his mind only those that are the most believable--those
which keep the arithmetic sound.

358. **Wade, Clyde.** **"Twain's Psychic Farce."** Publications of the
Arkansas Philological Association 13.1 (Spring 1987): 59-66.

Contends that such sketches as the jumping frog, the blue jay,
and the old ram should best be categorized as farces. Twain himself
says that a humorous story "may be spun out to great length and may
wander around as much as it pleases and arrive nowhere in
particular." Wade feels that this is in fact a good description of
farce, which is generally held to be a string of incongruities and
absurdities. There are two reasons that previous Twain critics have
not categorized these Twain pieces as farces. The first is that
Twain didn't call them farces; he called them stories. And the
second is that the farce is considered by many critics to be almost
exclusively within the realm of theatre.

359. **Zall, Paul M., ed.** **Mark Twain Laughing: Humorous Anecdotes
by and about Samuel L. Clemens.** Knoxville: University of
Tennessee Press, 1985, xxiv + 200 pp.

Collects a wide number of discrete, self-contained bits and
pieces of Twain's writings which had previously been scattered
widely in his notes, letters, books, newspapers, magazines, and
private collections. Zall explains that during frontier days, the
cowboys on the open range were so starved for literature that they
frequently read the labels on the cook's tin cans--so frequently
that they learned them by heart. They would frequently sing out a
key word, and everyone would join in to sing the remainder of the
label in unison. They could always determine who was a tenderfoot,
because he didn't "know his cans." Twain knew this and was doing
what he could to provide as many good short selections for people to
read as possible, but until recently, these short selections have
not been available for modern audiences. Twain was a major part of
the transition of American culture from an oral culture to a print-
oriented culture. His writings reflected the spirit of frontier
America--"irreverent, independent, bold, brash, big-hearted,
exuberant, and awfully noisy."

Thomas Bailey Aldrich (1836-1907)

360. Bellman, Samuel I. "Thomas Bailey Aldrich." Dictionary of Literary Biography: Volume 74: American Short-Story Writers Before 1880. Detroit, MI: Gale, 1988, 3-74.

Considers Aldrich's short stories, popular verse, sketches, and novels to be witty and charming, with frequent domestic misunderstandings and ironic twists, and with surprise endings in the manner of Edgar Alan Poe. Aldrich also wrote satires, such as "Mademoiselle Olympe Zabriski," which is a satire on the old Knickerbocker aristocracy gone to seed; and parodies, such as "Two Bites at a Cherry," whose protagonist, Marcus Whitelaw, is an unsubtle parody of an earlier Henry James character. Aldrich's characters came to life in his own mind and actually took over. In one notebook he wrote that in his first drafts, his characters talked more than they ought to but that he later goes back through and cuts out about four fifths of the long speeches. He then added that he assumes that that makes his characters pretty angry.

(Francis) Bret Harte (1836-1902)

361. Morrow, Patrick D. "Bret Harte, Popular Fiction, and the Local Color Movement." Western American Literature, 1974: 123-31.

Considers Bret Harte not only as a writer of scathing satires and parodies of contemporary literary figures but also as the originator of the local color movement in American literature. Morrow disagrees with Hamlin Garland's contention that local-color writing "has such quality of texture and background that it could not have been written in any other place or by anyone else than a native." Morrow points out that Harte spent less time in the location where his stories took place than an enthusiastic tourist would have. He lived only eighteen of his sixty-six years in California, and he spent almost all of that time in the metropolitan San Francisco Bay area. "Harte, then, was anything but a native." Harte was nevertheless a master at local color with his emphasis on social and linguistic texture--dialect speech, folkways, and local lore. He emphasized the "background" in his stories, including distinctive landscapes and picaresque character types. The reason that Harte's local-color writings were so popular from the 1860s on was that in the period after the Civil War, the nation needed an identity, needed grounding, needed reconciliation. Americans retreated to nostalgia and simplification in reaction to an uncertain future.

362. Tokarczyk, Michelle M. "(Francis) Brett Harte." Encyclopedia of American Humorists. Ed. Steven H. Gale. New York: Garland, 1988, 209-13.

Classifies Harte as a local color writer skilled in depicting California dress, values, and dialect. His stories exhibit a mixture of pathos, sentimentality, and social criticism, and incongruity of situation is one of his especially effective rhetorical devices, as in "The Luck of Roaring Camp" where a bunch of ruffian prospectors find themselves domesticated by having to rear an orphan Indian baby. Harte describes the finding of the infant as a novel and exciting event. The miners who saw the commotion of the discovery were certain that it was not just an ordinary event, like a fight or a killing, since birth in this settlement was a great deal less common than death. "The Outcasts of Poker Flat" is filled with sentimentality and didacticism but irony as well as a group of outcasts sit around a campfire and have "square fun," that is, fun without whiskey or other unclean entertainment. Margaret Duckett feels that Harte was a major influence on Mark Twain (especially Twain's Roughing It). Tokarczyk also feels that Harte had an important influence on Twain, especially in the development of the "outcast," and he cites as examples Huck Finn and, to a lesser extent, Tom Sawyer. The outcast tradition continues to this day with Woody Allen's various characterizations.

Marietta Holley (1836-1926)

363. Armitage, Shelley. "Marietta Holley: The Humorist as Propagandist." Rocky Mountain Review of Language and Literature 34.4 (Fall 1980): 193-200.

Agrees with Walter Blair that Marietta Holley is primarily a propagandist. In her twenty novels, she wrote about race and religion, women's rights, temperance, fashion, manners, and travel. She scrutinized these issues from the standpoint of a crackerbox philosopher named Samantha Allen, who used wisecracks to button-hole her logic as well as entertain the reader. Because of her topicality and her formula novels, Holley was largely forgotten ten years after her death but during her lifetime she was tremendously popular and insightful. She used a comic approach to address crucial issues. Her humor made her an especially effective feminist, because the usual voice of the feminists of the time tended to be either too shrill or too intellectual. Holley's rustic homilies were accepted because they were grounded in religious respectability and everyday experience. Her arguments were simple and credible. She used figurative language, malapropisms, exaggerations, understatments and other humorous rhetoric not only to proselyte but also to expose and challenge certain traditions. Samantha Allen is a wise, active, self-reliant leader, organizer, and adviser--qualities typical only of the male protagonists of her day.

364. Cracroft, Richard H. "Samantha Smith Takes on Elder Judas Wart: Marietta Holley and "the Mormon Question." WHIMSY 5 (1987): 177-79.

Considers Marietta Holley's humor to have had a greater effect on the Mormon practice of polygamy than did the lighter, less pointed, and more good-hearted anti-Mormon humor of Artemus Ward, Max Adeler, and Mark Twain. In My Wayward Pardner, for example, Holley's humor was more confrontational as the early feminist protagonist, Samantha Allen, takes on Elder Judas Wart, a hard-cider drinking, tobacco-chewing Elder in the Mormon church. Samantha is stunned to learn that Elder Wart had added the Widdow Bump to his "wifery," claiming that all of his other wives were either ill, disabled, bed-ridden, or with young children, and he needed another wife to take charge of things.

365. Curry, Jane A. "Marietta Holley." Dictionary of Literary Biography: Volume II: American Humorists, 1800-1950. Detroit, MI: Gale, 1982, 206-10.

Speculates as to why Marietta Holley's work was so immensely popular during her lifetime (she was regarded as the female Mark Twain) and why she was so little read after her death. While she was writing she was the only humorist whose female main character spoke vehemently on women's rights. The subjects which Holley treated, sufferage, temperance, race, war, the white-slave traffic, imperialism, the conflict between labor and management were all women's rights issues and as such had a wide interest among potential readers. The times were right for Holley's writing. However the ideas that were so dramatic and novel while Holley was writing had become commonplace in 1926 (the year of her death) because of the passage of the Nineteenth Amendment.

366. Curry, Jane, ed. Samantha Rastles the Woman Question. Urbana: Univ. of Illinois Press, 1983, xviii + 235 pp.

Indicates that even though Marietta Holley took a strong stance in favor of women's rights, she nevertheless wrote under the name of Josiah Allen's Wife. Most of her books were published between 1873 and 1914. During this period women characters were predictable--Yankee marms, superstitious swamp dames, or settlement snoops. They tended to be vain, scolding, capricious, coquettish, unpredictable, curious, impractical, loquacious, gullible, muddle-headed, gossipy, gushy, back-biting, jealous, vindictive, or other equally undesirable qualities. They were portrayed as guardians of the home, of the family, and of cultural mores in general. During this period, male characters may have shortcomings; they may be vain, foolish, shortsighted, pompous, etc., but these qualities are not so closely tied to their maleness as the female qualities are tied to the femaleness of the female characters. At any rate, Samantha Allen was liberated. She had gumption and she also had mother wit. She suggests that men and women should sit down side by side as they tackle all of the problems that life deals them. Marietta Holley was the first humorist whose main character was a woman who spoke specifically about women's rights, and she had a large following. In 1905, a writer for The Critic wrote that Marietta Holley had entertained as large an audience as had Mark Twain.

367. Graulich, Melody. "'Wimmin is my theme, and also Josiah' The Forgotten Humor of Marietta Holley." The American Transcendental Quarterly 47-48 (Summer-Fall 1980): 187-97.

Traces Holley's writing from My Opinions and Betsey Bobbet's, written in 1873 to Samantha on the Woman Question, written in 1914. Samantha Allen, Holley's protagonist, displays a common sense, a quick wit, and a sharp tongue in her arguments that women should receive equal treatment before the law and in society. Samantha is something of a country bumpkin, but Graulich states that "Samantha is wise even when she is ignorant, and through her voice, Holley effectively attacks conventional and narrow thinking." Marietta Holley led the charge of women humorists like Eliza Calvert Hall, Gail Hamilton, Grace Greenwood, Kate Wiggins, and others in proving that that women indeed <u>do</u> have a sense of humor. And many men also had to arrive at this same conclusion for they constantly wanted to publish her articles and books. Kate Sanborn asks, "As they rattle the gold and caressingly count the bills from twentieth editions, do they still think of women as sad, crushed, sentimental, hero-adoring geese who can't see the humorous side?" In the final analysis, Graulich concludes that Holley's work is uneven and that her satire is often topical and outdated; nevertheless, her central concern--women's rights--is ironically not outdated at all.

368. **Templin, Charlotte.** "Marietta Holley's Comic Critique of a Nineteenth-Century Idiology of Gender." <u>Thalia: Studies in Literary Humor</u> 11.2 (1990): 28-33.

Explains why Marietta Holley should be a significant figure in the feminist movement. First, Holley was a contemporary of Mark Twain, and while she was alive, her writing was almost as popular as that of Twain. Second, Holley firmly established a female character, Samantha Allen, into the tradition of the cracker-barrel philosopher, and this had not been done previously for any female characters. And third, Holley and her character Samantha Allen took a straightforward feminist stance, and this had not been done previously. Templin suggests that "the humorist as story-teller occupies a position of superiority, and few women have claimed such a position for themselves." But Holley's delightful character Samantha Allen does take such a position. She knows, for example that she has a stronger head than her husband, for Josiah has a small, and delicate brain.

369. **Walker, Nancy, and Zita Dresner.** "Josiah Allen's Wife." <u>Redressing the Balance: American Women's Literary Humor from Colonial Times to the 1980s</u> Jackson: University Press of Mississippi, 1988, 98-106.

Contends that at the turn of the century Marietta Holley's character Samantha Allen was as popular as any figure in American humor. Between 1873 and 1914, Holley published twenty books about Josiah Allen's wife, and Samantha's blend of homespun common sense and outspoken feminism amused and educated the readers of her day. Holley wrote about fashions, race relations, temperance, and female suffrage. Her protagonist, Samantha, speaks a rural New York dialect as she pits her wit, her intelligence, and her 204-pound body against the sexist and silly notions of her husband and other men. In real life, Marietta Holley was very shy. She never married and despite many opportunities to present publically her views on women's rights, she always refused. Holley shows the falseness of Betsy Bobbet's traditional and sentimental stance by exposing the shallowness of her behavior. Samantha Allen's use of the term "Josiah Allen's Wife" to refer to herself is an ironic jibe at the traditional notion that men own women.

370. Williams, Patricia. "The Crackerbox Philosopher as Feminist: The Novels of Marietta Holley." <u>American Humor: An Interdisciplinary Newsletter</u> 7.1 (1980): 16-21.

Feels that feminist humor began before the end of the nineteenth century and that Marietta Holley initiated this strong tradition. Williams classes Holley as a "literary comedian," who criticized religious hypocrisy and political skulduggery. Since she satirized male chauvinism of the time, Holley was sometimes considered a radical and subversive feminist humorist, but in terms of literary tradition she was totally conventional, being firmly planted in the tradition of the literary comedians and using the rhetorical devices of this tradition--rural dialect, cacography, domestic images, proverbs, wise saws, and extraordinary metaphors. In her last novel Holley switched her first person-narrative from Samantha to Josiah's perspective. Of course Josiah takes the opposite point of view from that of Samantha, but Holley skillfully continues to make the same points about women's rights, for Samantha's arguments are clearly superior to those of Josiah's, even when the reader sees them from Josiah's perspective. Ironically, Samantha represents the <u>Eiron</u> character, even though <u>Eiron</u> is usually male and Samantha is a 210-pound woman. Ironically again, Josiah represents the <u>Alazon</u> character, for although he is a man, both his body and his arguments are skinny and weak.

371. Winter, Kate H. "Marietta Holley." <u>Encyclopedia of American Humorists</u>. Ed. Steven H. Gale. New York: Garland, 1988, 225-27.

Considers Marietta Holley to be "the female Mark Twain," saying that she followed in the male tradition of the literary comedians--Twain, Billings, Ward, and Nasby. Holley's writing style, like that of others in the tradition of crackerbox philosophy, depended on upcountry dialect, proverbs, maxims, and extravagant images. She incorporated three important American literary traditions--the regional detail of the local colorists, the sentimentality of the domestic novelists, and the vernacular comedy that had been made popular by such writers as Ann Stephens and Frances Whitcher. Earlier comic writers had presented woman's rights advocates as the butt of their humor. In contrast, Holley's Samantha Allen (Josiah Allen's Wife) was the first important humorous female protagonist who made temperance and suffrage issues accessible and palatable. Her twenty-four Samantha books over forty-one years developed domestic humor, giving credence to the home as a legitimate site for humor and providing an awareness of seasons and landscapes as well.

Robert Henry Newell (1836-1901)

372. Butler, Michael. "Robert Henry Newell." <u>Dictionary of Literary Biography: Volume 11: American Humorists, 1800-1950</u>. Detroit, MI: Gale, 1982, 350-59.

Indicates that during the Civil War Newell was one of the North's most widely read humorists and further indicates that Abraham Lincoln read his letters often and once declared that anyone

who had not read them was a heathen. Newell wrote under the
pseudonym of Orpheus C. Kerr, a pun based on the fact that he [Kerr]
was attempting to find employment in Washington, D.C., and was
therefore an "Office Seeker." Kerr is portrayed as intelligent,
well educated, and well read. Since the spelling, syntax, and
grammar are correct, and not in dialect, Kerr is one of the easiest
nineteenth century humorists for twentieth-century readers to read
but nevertheless pretty obscure today. Butler feels that an
important reason for this is that contemporary critics tend to judge
the significance of nineteenth century authors by how much influence
they had on Mark Twain's The Adventures of Huckleberry Finn, and
Newell had very little influence on this work. Butler feels that
The Orpheus C. Kerr Papers are important for two reasons--one, their
literary merit, and two, their cultural and political observations.

373. Engle, Gary. "Robert Henry Newell." Encyclopedia of American
     Humorists. Ed. Steven H. Gale. New York: Garland, 1988: 336-
     37.

     Places Robert Henry Newell (Orpheus C. Kerr) into the category
of "Civil War Satirists," especially David R. Locke (Petroleum V.
Nasby), and Charles Henry Smith (Bill Arp). Newell's characters
include an Irish volunteer fireman, blacks modeled on minstrel
clowns, Down East Yankees, drunks, and roughnecks. Kerr went to war
mounted on his gothic steed, Pegasus, accompanied by his dog,
Bologna. Kerr's letters are erudite and witty and reveal that
Newell himself was well read in literature. Newell's humor devices
run the gamut from dialect humor to bilingual puns.

William Dean Howells (1837-1920)

374. Gibson, William M. "TR and W. D. Howells: 'I am faint
     thinking of him.'" Theodore Roosevelt Among the Humorists: W.
     D. Howells, Mark Twain, and Mr. Dooley. Knoxville: University
     of Tennessee Press, 1980, 9-23.

     Suggests that throughout their lives Theodore Roosevelt and W.
D. Howells shared an interest in good literature, not only in terms
of what they read but also as a result of Howells' reviewing several
of Roosevelt's books and commissioning several articles by Roosevelt
while he [Howells] was editor of The Cosmopolitan. When the sinking
of the American battleship Maine in Havana harbour early in 1898
resulted in war with Spain and Cuba and a new era of armed
conflicts, Roosevelt's and Howells' intellects parted company,
however. There was now a division between the politician and the
humorist on two major issues--warfare and the size of American
families. Teddy Roosevelt was proud of himself as a hunter, having
bagged lions and elephants and other big game; however, Howells
could not understand why the prolongation of infancy into permanent
boyhood should be anything to be proud about. Nevertheless, Howells
was in awe of Roosevelt's zest for life. After sitting beside
Roosevelt at breakfast and noting his unbridled enthusiasm, Howells
exclaimed that Roosevelt is "so strenuous that I am faint thinking
of him."

375. Krauth, Leland. "The Mysterious Stranger of William Dean Howells." Ball State University Forum 24.1 (Winter 1983): 30-37.

Considers Howells' A Traveler from Altruria to be a basically serious book, but Howells nevertheless uses humor as a buffer in his criticisms of American life. In this book, Mr. Twelvemough is a typical American, and Mr. Homos is the mysterious stranger from Altruria. These are considered by Krauth to be mild versions of Alazon and Eiron, respectively. The Mysterious Stranger is a mock innocent. His questions provoke choral explanations from anyone who hears them. The Stranger is neither self-deprecating nor obviously superior, yet his questions seem at times to be so pointed that Mr. Twelvemough begins to suspect that the Stranger is more than he seems. Indeed the earnest and simple manner reinforce the deadpan tradition of frontier humor. In "Through the Eye of the Needle," in The Altrurian Romances Howells resolves the enigma of the Mysterious Stranger by stating that Altrurians view America as a "gigantic joke." By saying that, Howells uncloaked the mystery of the Mysterious Stranger and never wrote of him again.

376. Murphy, Brenda. "Laughing Society to Scorn: The Domestic Farces of William Dean Howells." Studies in American Humor NS1.2 (October 1982): 119-29.

Focuses on the quality of the farce in Howells' twelve Campbell-Roberts plays. Murphy indicates that in his twelve farcical plays Howells chose social occasions that gave him an opportunity to use wit and satire to display the peculiarities of society. Although some critics have contended that farce is not an effective device for making social commentaries, Murphy disagrees and suggests that Howells uses farce to make revelations about society, about the nature of people's interactions with other people, and about the writer's view of the world. Howell's 1882 "The Sleeping Car" is the first in this series of farces, and its main function is to introduce the farcical characters who will be present throughout the entire series. Edward Roberts is a literary man who goes around in a daze. He is married to Agnes, a loving but sometimes hysterical wife who chatters endlessly. Edward and Agnes are actually burlesqued representations of the Howellses themselves. Willis Campbell is the outsider to the group and embodies good sense and practicality. He bears a striking resemblance to Mark Twain. All twelve of the Campbell-Roberts farces are about the interactions of the characters in "Proper Boston Society," and all of the farces contain a great deal of veiled (perhaps ambivalent) aggression.

Francis Hopkinson Smith (1838-1915)

377. Blair, Walter, and Raven I. McDavid, Jr. "Francis Hopkinson Smith." The Mirth of a Nation: America's Great Dialect Humor. Minneapolis: University of Minnesota Press, 1983, 203-207.

Portrays Smith as a local colorist who was most famous for his protagonist, Colonel Carter, a proud old-time Virginian. Smith became a full-time writer late in life. He published "Ginger and the Goose" in 1882. There were earlier versions of this story in

nine different countries; however, Smith's version differs
remarkably from the others. For example, the narrator in the
fourteenth-century Italian version is much less of an individual
than is Smith's narrator. Furthermore, the characters and the
family relationships of the Italian version have no specific
counterparts in Smith's version.

Kate Sanborn (1839-1917)

378. Sheppard, Alice. "From Kate Sanborn to Feminist Psychology:
     The Social Context of Women's Humor, 1885-1985." Psychology of
     Women Quarterly 10 (1986): 155-70.

     Considers Sanborn's 1885 anthology The Wit of Women to have
been a pioneering book proving that American women had a genuine
sense of humor. The book was casual, almost conversational in
style, ranging from informal anecdotes to literary quotations. The
lead article, written by Alice Rollins, used literary works to
establish women's sense of humor. The second article reinforced the
findings of the first article but made the stronger claim that women
not only had a sense of humor but that this sense of humor was a
distinct and more intellectual sense of humor than men had.
Sanborn, a published author in her own right, solicited
contributions from important nineteenth-century women humorists of
her acquaintance.

Charles Heber Clark (1841-1915)

379. Engle, Gary. "Charles Heber Clark." *Encyclopedia of American Humorists*. Ed. Steven H. Gale. New York: Garland, 1988: 81-83.

Attributes Clark's reputation as a humorist mainly to *Out of the Hurly-Burly; or, Life in an Odd Corner*, his first book (1874), which sold more than a million copies worldwide. In the persona of Max Adeler, Clark writes about the problems of suburban life--the difficulties and frustrations of inconvenient commuting, time-consuming gardening and lawn care, dangerous home repair, noisy neighbors, and unpredictable children and pets. Max Adeler is portrayed as learned, amiable, and modest. Clark's second novel, *Elbow Room* (1876), develops a regular cast of characters, including the patriarchal Fogg family. His third novel, *Random Shots* (1879), satirizes simple-minded cracker barrel philosophy and the American business mentality. Clark was a leading Literary Comedian of the 1870s.

380. Lang, John. "Charles Heber Clark." *Dictionary of Literary Biography 11: American Humorists, 1800-1950*. Ed. Stanley Trachtenberg. Detroit, MI: Gale, 1982, 77-81.

Indicates that Clark, like the other Literary Comedians, enjoyed exaggeration, literary burlesque, and the desire to arouse laughter in every paragraph. Lang considers *Out of the Hurly Burly* to be highly episodic, even anecdotal. Clark's humor ranges from satirical to zany. His satirical targets include politicians, poetasters, undertakers, and inventors. He considers many inventions, for example, to be more problems than solutions to problems, and tells about the "Patent Combination Step-Ladder" which can also serve as an ironing board, and a settee for the kitchen. The main difficulty with this invention is its tendency to change from one thing to the other without warning, thereby grinding shirts to rags or hurling guests against the furniture. One of Clark's strengths is his ability through his persona [Max Adeler] to implicate himself in the absurdities he describes. Despite Clark's immense popularity among his contemporaries, he has received very little attention by recent critics.

Ambrose Gwinett Bierce (1842-c1914)

381. Field, B. S., Jr. "Ambrose Bierce as a Comic." *Western Humanities Review* 31.2 (Spring 1977): 173-80.

Contends that Bierce's contribution to American literature is much greater if he is viewed as a comic rather than a serious writer. Many critics consider Bierce to be a philosophical writer who is striving to make his audiences aware of the absurdist-tragic quality of their lives. But Bierce's work does not measure up well when compared with genuinely philosophical writing, and it therefore appears to be weaker than it really is. When compared with American

comic writing, where it belongs, Bierce's work fares much better.
The grotesque joke, for example, is an important element in Bierce's
fiction, and in fact, Bierce is something of a black humorist.
Bierce's characters seem to be the helpless targets of some kind of
cosmic sadistic practical joke. The blackness of Bierce's humor can
be seen in titles such as "The Parenticide Club," "Killed at
Resaca," "Coup de Grace," and The Devil's Dictionary. In
"Occurrence at Owl Creek Bridge" for example, the central character
escapes death by hanging because the rope breaks, and he falls into
the river, swims to the other bank, and runs cross-country to his
home before discovering these are just events passing through his
condemned mind.

382. **Fowler, Douglas**. "Ambrose Gwinett Bierce." Encyclopedia of
     American Humorists. Ed. Steven H. Gale. New York: Garland,
     1988: 44-47.

Lists Mark Twain, William Dean Howells, Bret Harte, Hamlin
Garland, Frank Norris, Theodore Dreiser, and Ambrose Bierce as
important writers who developed their humor skills in newspaper
offices. Bierce's two most anthologized short stories,
"Chicamauga," and "An Occurrence at Owl Creek Bridge" both relate to
war and both have dramatically ironic trick endings. His humor was
cynical and biting. His fame rests mainly on his first book, The
Cynic's Word Book, later renamed The Devil's Dictionary. It was
written in the tradition of Dr. Samuel Johnson, who sometimes got
bored as a lexicographer and gingered up his dictionary with entries
like the one for "oats," which he defines as "the food of horses in
England, but in Scotland, that of men." Bierce's witty epigrams
were precise and insightful. Often they were separated by what he
called "Telegraphical Dottings," a rhetorical device Bierce used to
indicate that there was no logical progression or linkage between
his various entries. Bierce's legacy of black comedy continues in
the writings of Thomas Pynchon, Joseph Heller, Kurt Vonnegut, Robert
Coover, and John Barth. Throughout his life, Bierce loved war, and
he died at seventy two as a reporter in a firestorm of the Mexican
revolution.

383. **Highsmith, James Milton**. "The Forms of Burlesque in The
     Devil's Dictionary." Satire Newsletter 7.2 (Spring 1970): 115-
     27.

Indicates that Bierce was known in California as "the
wickedest man in San Francisco" and in London as "Bitter Bierce."
In The Devil's Dictionary, he defines "dictionary" as "A malevolent
literary device for cramping the growth of a language and making it
hard and inelastic," a definition which ironically could not be
applied to his own dictionary. The Devil's Dictionary was at first
named The Cynic's Word Book because when the book was published the
word "Devil" was considered too strong to be part of a book title.
In a letter to George Sterling on May 6, 1906, Bierce explained,
"Here in the East, the Devil is a sacred personage (the Fourth
Person of the Trinity, as an Irishman might say) and his name must
not be taken in vain." Bierce was frequently attacked by his
readers who took his writing to be literal, or at least serious, so
he proposed a new mark of punctuation, the snigger point. The
snigger point was in the shape of a smiling mouth and would be
appended to the period whenever a sentence was to be taken jocularly

or ironically. Bierce considers his work not to be humorous (tolerant, tender, almost caressing) but rather witty (stabbing, begging pardon, and then turning the weapon again on the wounded). He considered polish to be important, saying that good writing is not a gift but a gift and an accomplishment.

384. Keough, William. "Round Three: The Bottled Bile of Ambrose Bierce." Punchlines: The Violence of American Humor. New York: Paragon House, 1990, 61-77.

Traces Bierce's humor to his first job, ironically that of a printer's devil for the Northern Indianian. He left this job to volunteer as a soldier in the Civil War, where he collected in his memory the many grotesque scenes he would later write about. While directing a charge at Kenesaw Mountain, he suffered a head wound. He later recalled that his head felt as if it had cracked like a walnut. Bierce was never the same after this accident. A piece of the shell stuck in his brain and afterward Bierce became bitter, suspicious, and cynical. In The Devil's Dictionary he described a "cynic" as "a blackguard whose faulty vision sees things as they are, not as they ought to be. Hence the custom among the Scythians of plucking out a cynic's eyes to improve his vision." Bierce wanted men to stand up and keep standing. He noted that it is only Christians and camels who receive their burdens while kneeling. Bierce used violent language to attack his violent society. But as an author, he needed violence as a stimulant. He asks what life would be like without its mullahs and its dervishes. And then he answers that it would be a bunch of merchants and camel drivers, and that there would then be no one in the world to laugh with--or at.

385. Martin, Jay. "Ambrose Bierce." The Comic Imagination in American Literature. Ed. Louis D. Rubin, Jr. New Brunswick, NJ: Rutgers Univ. Press, 1983, 195-205.

Considers Bierce's writing to contain the four constituents of humor outlined by Jean Paul in his Vorschule der Asthetik. Paul says that humor obliterates distinctions between the great and the small, the pathetic and the ludicrous, the beautiful and the horrific. Paul says that it inverts values, so that what is good becomes damnable, or vice versa. Paul says that it exploits subjectivity whereby the reader can be drawn into the same vision as the author. And finally, Paul says that humor deforms, making things incongruous or even grotesque. Bierce's basic comic stance was one of attack, assault, invective. His secular curses are one of the oldest forms of satiric writing. The idea is to obliterate the offending object through verbal abuse. Bierce was able to mingle innocence with crime, the beautiful with the horrible, the sacred with the profane. His vision of the world was surrealistic, almost insanely grotesque. He once remarked to a friend as they observed the happy scene of a midwinter fair, "Wouldn't it be fun to turn loose a machine gun into that crowd?"

386. O'Brien, Matthew. "Ambrose Bierce." Dictionary of Literary Biography 11: American Humorists, 1800-1950. Ed. Stanley Trachtenberg. Detroit, MI: Gale, 1982, 38-48.

Feels that Bierce is underrated as a humorist mainly because he tended to focus on grim and macabre tales of the war. Bierce was a versatile and prolific satirist, writing in such widely divergent genres as the editorial, essay, tale, fable, epigram, and lyric. Bierce follows the tradition of Swift and La Rochefoucauld, is the sardonic equivalent of such contemporaries as Twain and Harte, and influenced such twentieth-century authors as Mencken, Benchley, Thurber, and the "black humorists." Much of Bierce's humor was locally bound; furthermore, he had a tendency to expend a great deal of energy criticizing relative nonentities. Every definition in The Devil's Dictionary is an epigrammatic deflation of some cherished belief. He was generally misunderstood in his own age but can be seen now as an accurate visionary. His writing had many flaws, among them the belaboring of the same targets, oversimplifications of the complications of human behavior, and self-contradiction. Nevertheless, he is one of our preeminent satirists.

387. Suhre, Lawrence R. "A Consideration of Ambrose Bierce as Black Humorist." Ph.D. dissertation. University Park, PA: Pennsylvania State University, 1972. 232 pp.

Deems Bierce to have been the first notable writer of "black humor" in American literature. Bierce's parents were strict Calvinists, and they ruled their family with an iron hand. Bierce was the youngest of ten children and had a strong spirit of rebellion. He was among the first to volunteer to fight in the American Civil War and among the last to depart from military service. Bierce, like Hemingway, was a member of the "Lost Generation," and he considered his life itself to be something of a cruel joke. The black humor of Bierce's writings deals with the abnormal and grotesque aspects of society and evokes the nervous laughter of human despair and failure.

John Habberton (c1842-1921)

388. Kollar, Stuart. "John Habberton." Encyclopedia of American Humorists. Ed. Steven H. Gale. New York: Gale, 1988, 186-88.

Considers Habberton's strongest features as a writer to have been his fast pacing, clear visual description, and ability to capture dialect. Habberton was mildly ashamed of being a humorous writer and was almost apologetic at the fact that his own comic writings were more widely read than were those of clearly better writers. Critics didn't much like his writing, but his readers found it irresistible. A favorite technique was to introduce Bible stories first accurately and later distorted by children, rustics, or hypocrites. Habberton was able to characterize his miners, schoolmarms, law men, widows, and deacons through his use of appropriate dialect, in such stories as "Old Twitchett's Treasure," "Jim Hockson's Revenge," and "The Meanest Man at Blugsey's." In Helen's Babies, Habberton develops the relationship between Uncle Harry and Helen's children. The children made mud pies and "poison," and ran across rooftops. When he caught up with them, they sat on him, pounded his chest, and made him pray, sing, and tell stories. When he grew angry, they would revert to innocence, repentant crying, and baby talk.

Charles Bertrand Lewis (1842-1924)

389. Armitage, Shelley. "Charles B. Lewis." Dictionary of
      Literary Bibliography 11: American Humorists, 1800-1950.
      Detroit, MI: Gale, 1982, 267-69.

      Agrees with William Clemens' classification of Lewis as a late
nineteenth-century "phunny phellow" and explains his broad public
appeal as stemming from his ability at burlesque and verbal
caricature. He was fully identified with his comic personna, M.
Quad, and almostly uniquely associated with one newspaper, The
Detroit Free Press. In fact, Lewis' whimsical rollicking style may
have been the most important reason for the success of the Free
Press. Lewis' style depended heavily on a particular type of
understatement called "Litotes," which is understatement through
negation. His 1875 Goaks and Tears, for example contains Lewis'
comic biography, stating that Lewis was born of humble parents, that
his father had never been on jury duty, delivered an important
oration, or been sued for slander. Likewise, his mother had never
rescued anyone from drowning or made a presentation on women's
rights. He said that at the age of eighteen he was invited to go up
in a balloon. He didn't. In Quad's Odds he gives the "Wisconsin
Method," the "Rochester Method," and the "New Jersey Method" of
"Keeping the Boy in at Nights." With the "Wisconsin Method," for
example, the father simply spikes the boy down to the kitchen floor.

390. Engle, Gary. "Charles Bertrand Lewis." Encyclopedia of
      American Humorists. Ed. Steven H. Gale. New York: Garland,
      1988, 278-80.

      Suggests that Lewis became known as a Western humorist in the
style of Mark Twain and Bill Nye with the writing of "How It Feels
to Be Blown Up." This sketch is based on a true incident
experienced by the author as he was traveling to Jonesboro,
Tennessee, on the Ohio River steamer, Magnolia. The steamer
exploded, seriously injuring Lewis and killing a number of
passengers. Lewis' droll telling of the catastrophe and his
subsequent hospitalization in Cincinnati, Ohio, developed a broad
readership for Lewis. In 1875 he published a collection of self-
effacing pieces from the Detroit Free Press, where he wrote under
the pen name of M. Quad. The pen name is a play on the blank slug
in a line of type, which is called an "em quad." The collection is
named Quad's Odds. Lewis was best when he tied together an extended
community of regular characters as in the "Lime Kiln Club," a series
of sketches about a black Detroit fraternal lodge presided over by
Brother Gardner. Characters in the sketches were given such names
as Waydown Beebe, Givadam Jones, Pickles Smith, and Elder Toots.
The sketches were blatantly racist, containing black stereotyping
about such things as chicken stealing and comfortable shoes, but
they were very popular at the time.

391. Masson, Thomas L. "C. B. Lewis." Our American Humorists
      Freeport, NY: Books for Libraries Press, 1931, 230-37.

      Feels that Lewis has made a million American homes rock with
laughter with his Bowser stories, his Lime Kiln Club philosophy, and

the escapades of the "Arizona Kicker." Lewis was a reporter, editor, advertising salesman, and humorist for the <u>Detroit Free Press</u>. Lewis described a typical day: "I wrote my regular column of humor in the morning, edited copy and drummed advertising in the afternoon, and worked as an all-round reporter in the evening up to midnight." Lewis became a humorist while he was convalescing in a hospital after having been blown up on a Mississippi steamboat. His first piece was entitled "How It Feels to Be Blown Up," and that story was picked up by newspapers all around the world and made Lewis famous as a humorous writer. Lewis' side-splitting humor was "robust in its primitive revelings." Lewis remained cheerful to the end despite the fact that he had rather severe rheumatism for the last fifteen years of his life.

<u>Henry James, Jr. (1843-1916)</u>

392. Core, George. "Henry James and the Comedy of the New England Conscience." <u>The Comic Imagination in American Literature</u>. Ed. Louis D. Rubin, Jr. New Brunswick, NJ: Rutgers University Press, 1983, 179-93.

       Considers James' brilliance as a comic writer to have been the reason that most of James' fiction has stood the test of time. James is an ironic comedian who interspersed humor throughout his comedies, his tragicomedies, and even his tragedies. Core concentrates on <u>The Europeans</u> (1878), <u>The Bostonians</u> (1886), and <u>The Ambassadors</u> (1903) to illustrate T. S. Eliot's observation that the books of Henry James must be read as a bunch rather than individually. These are all three comedies. All three present man in an essentially sympathetic light, accepting humans with all their defects and shortcomings. All three are celebrations of man's folly. <u>The Europeans</u> is a comic pastoral, an allegory, a dramatic poem. The comedy results not so much from the confrontation of European and American ideologies as from the misconceptions about both ideologies. <u>The Bostonians</u>, like <u>The Europeans</u>, is a satirical comedy, but it is more ironic and more profound. James once said that Boston meant absolutely nothing to him; "I don't even dislike it." <u>The Ambassadors</u> explains life by what is missing--our reserves, omissions, and suppressions.

393. Leyburn, Ellen Douglass. <u>Strange Alloy: The Relation of Comedy to Tragedy in the Fiction of Henry James</u>. Chapel Hill: Univ. of North Carolina Press, 1968, xviii + 180 pp.

       Feels that from his first short story ("A Tragedy of Error") to his last novel (<u>The Golden Bowl</u>), Henry James' fiction always exhibited a pervasive fusion and intermingling of the good with the bad, the comic with the painful. Leyburn uses the metaphor of the "strange alloy" to describe this mixture. For James, man's virtues sometimes turn into vices, and great wrongs sometimes produce right. James sees sometimes a tragedy in man's events, and sometimes he sees comedy, and sometimes he sees an "irony so complex as to seem comic and tragic at once, as if he were showing both sides of the medal at the same time." For James, tragedy is the material world, and comedy is the angle of vision on the material world, and often James' characters have to develop a kind of wry or sardonic humor in

order to deal with their plights. For James, comedy can be found
both in the situation and in the presentation of the situation, and
it often intensifies the distress.

394. **Villa, Virginia Barrett.** "Nobody Tells Fibs in Boston: The
     Comic Significance of Selah Terrant in Henry James's The
     Bostonians." WHIMSY 1 (1983): 51-53.

     Considers Selah Terrant to be a more significant character
than most other critics have believed. Other critics see Terrant as
merely a crook, a charlatan faith healer, a very shady character.
James' readers all realize that the "Dr." in front of Tarrent's name
is bogus. But Villa believes Selah Terrant is more than just this.
She sees him as a symbol for humanity and suggests that through
Selah Terrant James is suggesting that Boston is alive with liars,
and that in a way we're all Bostonians--all liars. She feels that
James takes a perverse consolation in this "sweet grotesqueness."
For Villa, Selah Terrant is a vampire. Pointing out that Terrant
shows his teeth in a "large joyless smile," Villa suggests that "a
laugh is man's way of showing his fangs."

395. **Villa, Virginia Barrett.** "Vampire Metaphors in Selected
     Works of Henry James." WHIMSY 2 (1984): 19-20.

     Suggests that James uses many vampire metaphors for both comic
and tragic effects. Throughout his fiction, there is a recurrent
theme of possession, both physical and spiritual. There are also
many references to teeth, hands, wings, cloaks, carrying away,
bearing aloft, soaring, etc., and these references are used to
foreshadow, to characterize, to reinforce theme, to describe
setting, and to advance plot. Such vampire allusions appear in
stories, such as "Professor Fargo," as well as in novels, such as
The Bostonians, The Turn of the Screw, The Ambassadors, The Golden
Bowl, and Portrait of a Lady." The Dracula figure is portrayed by
James as inordinately genteel, delicate, refined, fastidious, and
elitist. This Dracula image fits nicely into James' "comedy of
manners" and is not as incongruous as one would suppose.

396. **Wallace, Ronald. Henry James and the Comic Form.** Ann Arbor:
     Univ. of Michigan Press, 1975, 202 pp.

     Examines comedy in James' fiction as it relates to
characterization, plot, style, and development, and concludes that
James' novels are some sort of a hybrid of tragedy, comedy, and
irony. Wallace states that many James critics have the feeling that
the greatest literary art is necessarily tragic, and recognizing
James as a great novelist, they are forced to conclude that his
novels must therefore be tragic rather than comic. But Wallace
feels that such a view on the part of James' critics lacks a clear
perception of the seriousness of high comedy and furthermore fails
to give give full credit to James as a writer of very successful
high comedies. In a letter to Howells, James wrote that he
suspected it was the tragedies in life that most caught his
attention and imagination, but Leon Edel points out that in spite of
this viewpoint, James' greatest fame is built in his comedies. In
The Princess Casamassima James himself sheds some light on the
issue, "The tragedy and comedy of life, are things of which the
common air...seems pungently to taste."

Robert Jones Burdette (1844-1914)

397. Engle, Gary. "Robert Jones Burdette." Encyclopedia of
      American Humorists. New York: Garland, 1988, 67-69.

      Considers Burdette to be the leading literary comedian of the
1870s and 80s. He was a lecturer and a Baptist minister whose
contributions to newspapers employed a genial wit. Most of his
writings are short. He wrote filler pieces and verse parodies, and
his best work tended to be 1000-word sketches. He was a local
colorist who emphasized friendly caricature and family situations
and sentimentality. In his first collected volume, The Rise and
Fall of the Mustache, and Other Hawkeyetems (1877), his favorite
subjects were the mundane frustrations of middle-class life--lawn
care, pets, school pranks, commercial transactions, house cleaning,
and overbearing neighbors. His second volume, Hawk-Eyes (1879) was
mostly about his life on the Lyceum circuit, including pieces about
train travel. His Robert J. Burdette, His Message (1922) continued
to have vivid accounts of his life as a professional lecturer. "The
Brakeman at Church" was an extended metaphor, in which Burdette
described various Protestant denominations by comparing them to
various types of railroads. The Presbyterian church, for example
was described as "narrow gauge." The Presbyterians followed a very
straight track, but the cars were a little narrow, the people had to
sit one person to a seat, and there was no room in the aisle to
dance.

George Washington Cable (1844-1925)

398. Blair, Walter, and Raven I. McDavid, Jr. eds. "George Washinton
     Cable." The Mirth of a Nation: America's Great Dialect Humor.
     Minneapolis: Univ. of Minnesota Press, 1983, 181-96.

      Considers Cable to have been a pioneer local colorist for the
New Orleans region in which he lived for forty-one years of his
life. He wrote The Grandissimes in 1880, Madame Delphine in 1881,
Dr. Sevier in 1885, and a number of other fictional works that
caught the exotic romance and realism of Louisiana life in an often
humorous and satiric manner. His "Posson Jone'" is typically rich
in localized detail and plays on the incongruities between Creole
French culture and the culture of Anglo-Saxon Protestants. All of
his work exhibits English and French culture in conflict and
displays French pronunciations, constructions, and wordings.

Edward Noyes Westcott (1846-1898)

399. Blair, Walter, and Raven I. McDavid, Jr. "Edward Noyes
     Westcott." The Mirth of a Nation: America's Great Dialect
     Humor. Minneapolis: Univ. of Minnesota Press, 1983, 241-253.

      Feels that Westcott was a one-book author. He wrote David
Harum, A Story of American Life after he had retired as a business

man. He finished it on his deathbed, and it was published the year after he died. It was successful as it sold one and a quarter million copies, was translated into a number of different languages, and did well both as a play and as a motion picture (with Will Rogers playing the leading role). This novel was the New York version of the most popular of all nineteenth-century stereotypes-- the slightly educated country man whose keen insights and practical experience allowed him to understand human nature better than people with more education.

Julia Moore (1847-1920)

400. Hayden, Bradley. "In Memoriam Humor: Julia Moore and the Western Michigan Poets." English Journal 72.5 (September 1983): 22-28.

Considers Julia Moore to have been a bad poet but a great inspiration. He feels that the only reason she is remembered today is the result of an obscure allusion to her work in Mark Twain's Following the Equator, and Emmaline Grangerford's "Ode to Stephen Dowling Bots, Dec'd" which appeared in The Adventures of Huckleberry Finn. Twain said that he studied the poetry of Julia Moore in order to learn how to be funny. Twain felt that Moore had a rare organic talent for humor, adding, that she had the ability to make "an intentionally humorous episode pathetic and an intentionally pathetic one funny." Moore did not intend to be a humorous poet; she was striving for high seriousness.

Joel Chandler Harris (1848-1908)

401. Arnold, St. George Tucker, Jr. "Joel Chandler Harris." Encyclopedia of American Humorists. Ed. Steven H. Gale. New York: Garland, 1988, 194-203.

Places Harris's Uncle Remus into historical perspective. After the Civil War Blacks were no longer slaves. As a staff writer for the Atlanta Constitution, Sam Small had developed the character of an old-time Atlanta Black by the name of Old Si to comment on politics and the local scene. In 1876 Small resigned from the paper, and Harris was assigned to write his columns. At first, Harris' Uncle Remus was very similar to Small's Old Si; however, Uncle Remus soon began to evolve into the type of figure common in the Afro-American story-telling tradition, by which story tellers repeated and refined the fables of the oral tradition. The trickster figure was a common figure in the African tradition. Although the early Uncle Remus had chosen not to return to the plantation, the later Uncle Remus decided to return, and there he would tell stories to the little white boy while he was working in the garden, cleaning the cabin, or patching a hole in a shirt. The stories were mostly motivated by actions of the child, like throwing rocks at chickens, and they usually had morals. A common theme was that might doesn't make right, as Brer Rabbit (representing the out of power) continually outwits Brer Fox and Brer Bear (representing power).

402. Arnold, St. George Tucker Jr. "The Joker in His Jays, the Writer in His Rabbits: Authorial Personality as Projected into the Humanized Animals of Two American Humorists." WHIMSY 5 (1987): 19-21.

Compares Joel Chandler Harris and Mark Twain not only in their abilities to create animal protagonists with human characteristics but also in their reliance on antebellum plantation humor of the deep southern slave culture for the ambiance of their writings. But Twain's animals were light in tone, while Harris' were much darker. Twain's "totem" was the Indian Crow, who is joyous rowdy, scolding, scoffing, laughing, ripping, and cursing. Twain's animals have the ability to laugh at themselves; Harris' animals laugh instead at each other. In "Mr. Rabbit Nibbles Up the Butter," Br'er Rabbit, Br'er Fox, and Br'er Possum have decided to store their food in the same shanty. Br'er Rabbit gets hungry and eats up all of Br'er Fox's delicious butter--all that is except enough to smear some on Br'er Possum's paws. When they wake up, Br'er Fox discovers his butter missing, and further discovers some butter on Br'er Possum's paws. Br'er Possum says he didn't steal the butter, so Br'er Rabbit suggests "Trial by Fire," saying that the guilty person will be weighted down by his guilt. All of the nimble critters jump over the fire, but Br'er Possum can't do it and is burned to death. When the shocked listener objects to the ending, Uncle Remus merely explains "Hit's des dat way."

403. Bickley, R. Bruce, Jr. "Joel Chandler Harris." Dictionary of Literary Biography 11: American Humorists, 1800-1950. Ed. Stanley Trachtenberg. Detroit, MI: Gale, 1982, 189-201.

Refers to Harris' five reputations as a writer. He was a "paragrapher" for Georgia newspapers, editor of the Atlanta Constitution, recreator of a large body of Afro-American folklore, important southern local colorist, and author of children's books. Harris felt that a culture's sense of humor was an indication of its health and vitality. He further felt that a culture's oral humorous literature is very dear to that culture because it is based on its unique experiences, is part of its personality, is an accurate representation of history, and is a declaration of "independence and strength, of sanity and wisdom, of honesty and simplicity." Harris was short; he had red hair and freckles and a severe stammering problem. He was so self-conscious about his stammering that he refused to read in public; he was so self-conscious about his hair that he wore a hat even indoors. In compensation for these problems, Harris became an incorrigible prankster and practical joker, and some of his practical jokes were quite cruel. He once knocked a wasps' nest into a boy's face; the boy was so severely strung that he carried the scars to his adult life. Harris tricked another friend into jumping into a muddy pig pen swarming with fiercely biting hog fleas.

404. Bickley, R. Bruce, Jr. "Two Allusions to Joel Chandler Harris in Ulysses: "Wusser Scared" and "Corporosity" Redux." English Language Notes 17 (September 1974): 42-45.

Concedes that James Joyce might not have had copies of Harris' books on his desk as he wrote Ulysses but nevertheless contends that Joyce's remarkable auditory memory allowed him to recall the rhythms and inflections of Harris' vernacular writing as he worked on the novel. Weldon Thornton identified two allusions to Harris' writing in Ulysses. "Your corporosity sagaciating OK?" from "Oxen of the Sun" is highly reminiscent of Br'er Rabbit's question, "How duz yo' sym'tums seem ter segasuate?" in Harris' "The Wonderful Tarbaby Story." Elijah's speech, "I don't never see no wusser scared female." also echos Harris' vernacular writing. "Wusser" appears frequently in Harris' books, and appears next to "skeer'd" in "dey ain't been no wusser skeer'd beas'" than Br'er Rabbit when he found himself trapped in a descending well bucket.

405. **Blair, Walter, and Raven I. McDavid, Jr.** "Joel Chandler Harris." The Mirth of a Nation: America's Great Dialect Humor. Minneapolis: University of Minnesota Press, 1983, 197-202.

Considers Harris' vernacular writing to be poetic speech, rhythmic, vivid, and imaginative. The hero in his stories is the weakest and most harmless of all of the animals, yet the hero, Br'er Rabbit, is always victorious in contests with Br'er Bear, Br'er Wolf, and Br'er Fox. It is not virtue that triumphs but helplessness, not malice but mischievousness. Walter Blair and Raven McDavid agree with John Herbert Nelson who says that the ideals of the animals in the Uncle Remus tales are the ideals of the Negroes--"their neighborliness, their company manners, their petty thefts, their amusements." Br'er Rabbit "likes the same kind of food, the same brand of fun, as his interpreter does; he has the same outlook on life."

406. **Budd, Louis J.** "Joel Chandler Harris and the Genteeling of Native American Humor" Critical Essays on Joel Chandler Harris. Ed. R. Bruce Bickley, Jr. Boston: G. K. Hall, 1981, 196-209.

Characterizes Harris' humor as tender, sympathetic, and gracious as he tells about the Black, the Georgia Cracker, and the aristocratic planter. Harris' Uncle Remus stories reached to the heart of race relations in the South. The stories had romance, humor, and pathos. Harris brought the Black and the poor white a long way toward literary visibility. Since Faulkner was a devout reader of the Joel Chandler Harris writings, it should be no surprise that scholars often spot echoes of Harris in Faulkner's writings.

James Whitcomb Riley (1849-1916)

407. **Blair, Walter, and Raven I. McDavid, Jr.** "James Whitcomb Riley." The Mirth of a Nation: America's Great Dialect Humor. Minneapolis: University of Minnesota Press, 1983, 230-34.

Indicates that Riley began as a Hoosier dialect poet, working for the Indianapolis Journal. He wrote under a number of different pen names for various newspapers and later published a collection of a dozen sketches in The Old Swimmin'-Hole and 'Leven More Poems in 1883. He used "Benj. F. Johnson of Boone" as his pen name; however, he placed his name in brackets after Johnson's name to make sure that he got full credit. Riley was such a good writer that Mark

Twain used his "The Old Soldier's Story" in his "How to Tell a
Story" to illustrate the difference between a comic story ("a short
joke with a snapper than anybody can tell") with a humorous story
("a work of art--high and delicate art--that only an artist can
tell"). In "The Old Soldier's Story" the narrator is a dull-witted
old farmer who has just heard a really funny joke and tries to
retell it. But he can't remember it, and he gets mixed up and
wanders helplessly all over putting in tedious details that don't
belong and leaving out other details that are necessary to the
telling. The joke itself is relatively unimportant. What is
important is the excruciatingly inept way of Riley's unfolding the
narrative.

408. Wade, Clyde G. "James Whitcomb Riley." Encyclopedia of
      American Humorists. Ed. Steven H. Gale. New York: Garland,
      1988, 367-71.

      Feels that Riley created a new genre of American literature
that Wade calls "the Middle western pastoral." Wade feels that
Riley transformed the details of small town life into a kind of Eden
with the nostalgic tone of "In Wortermelon Time," "When the Frost is
on the Punkin," "A Summer's Day," and "Little Orphant Annie." Riley
used dialect, the rhythms of oral speech, and homely figures to
create a comic but utopian past. He was capable of a wide range and
variety in his verse, but his expressive images are what he is
remembered for, refrains like "An' the Gobbl-uns 'at gits you/ If
you/Don't Watch/Out." Despite his popularity during his time,
Riley's writings are too sentimental for present-day readers or
critics. For example, in 1961, Louis Leary classed James Whitcomb
Riley with Oliver Wendell Holmes, Henry Wadsworth Longfellow, and
James Greenleaf Whittier as the "short-order cooks of literature,"
saying that these writers write "simple fare that easily consumed
and easily forgotten." Riley liked to sign his letters with such
whimsical names as "James Popcorn Riley," "Old E.Z. Mark," "An
Adjustable Lunatic," and "James Hoosier Riley, the Whitcomb poet."
Riley's was the voice of the rustic folk at the time when America
was changing from a predominantly rural to a predominantly urban
culture.

Eugene Field (1850-1895)

409. Wade, Clyde G. "Eugene Field." Encyclopedia of American
      Humorists. New York: Garland, 1988, 150-54.

      Considers Field to have been a writer in transition from
rustic to urbane humor. Field's early humor expressed the broad
comedy of the Midwest and frontier America; his later Chicago
writings laid the groundwork for the more sophisticated humor that
flourishes in urban America today. Walter Blair and Hamlin Hill
refer to Field as "the spiritual father of Chicago's humorists."
Field's early writings from the Denver Tribune were later collected
and published under the title of The Tribune Primer. It contained
witty responses to newspaper life, mischievous children,
politicians, wayward fathers, and nagging wives; it was comedy in a
grim domestic setting. At one time twenty papers imitated Field's
style of dark humor. In Chicago, Field's humor developed a kind of

understatement; however the zaniness remained. Field often attributed pieces to other authors that he himself had written. He wrote at length about a child prodigy who existed only in his own imagination. And he reviewed the biography of Florence Bardsley--a non-existent book.

410. Williams, Kenny J., and Bernard Duffey. "Eugene Field." Chicago's Public Wits: A Chapter in the American Comic Spirit. Baton Rouge: Louisiana State University Press, 1983, 122-49.

Considers Field's poetry to have been of the humorous-sentimental type that was very popular in his day. Field liked to imitate Horace, and he also used a kind of mock-Middle-English spelling. He wrote some bawdy verse which was very popular with his newspaper friends; however, most of this has not been published. His prose was generally short, ranging from topical squibs (which were staples in his columns) to developed short tales--comic, sentimental, and/or romantic (which he used to fill his entire two-thousand-word columns). Fields' "An Auto-Analysis" was a biographical summary of his publications, his tastes, and his habits. The Tribune Primer contained grim domestic squibs about naughty children, errant fathers, nagging mothers, politicians, bill dodgers, etc.

Mary Noailles Murfree (1850-1922)

411. Fisher, Benjamin Franklin IV. "Mary Noailles Murfree's 'Special' Sense of Humor." Studies in American Humor NS 4.1-2 (Spring-Summer 1985): 30-38.

Proposes that the humor in Murfree's writing is constant and substantial because she was influenced by the writings of Irving, Poe, and Dickens and by the "Big-Bar" writers in the tradition of humor of the Old Southwest. Murfree's writing is significant not only because she relied on and modified earlier humor traditions but also because she was a woman writing in a man's domain. Murfree wrote under the male pseudonym of Charles Egbert Craddock, and she dealt with such male topics as gander pulls, horse swaps, gambling, drinking, and moonshining. These were common subjects in various sporting and racing journals of the day such as W. T. Porter's The Spirit of the Times, but they were subjects confined to male authors and male audiences. Much of Murfree's writing is social satire, and she enjoys playing with language. In "My Daughter's Admirers" the Reverend is named "Mr. Yawn-Your-Head-Off" and is the foil to the witty "Mr. Sparkle." "Jack Olwell" is attempting to win the friendship and influence of "Mr. Regulus." The name and the behavior of "Olwell" brings to mind the expression, "oil well," and "Mr. Regulus" has a name that means "Little King," appropriate for a person who is a "petty tyrant." Although Murfree was influenced by earlier humor traditions, her tone tends to be more subtle than that of earlier humorists.

Edgar Wilson Bill Nye (1850-1897)

412. Kesterson, David B. Bill Nye: The Western Writings. Boise,
     Idaho: Boise State University, 1976, 48 pp.

     Portrays Nye as a literary realist who scoffs at Easterners
who, expecting the frontier to be wild and dangerous, come West
wearing cowboy dress and guns at each hip. Nye explains that the
only trouble the Yankee finds is his own doing as he shoots off his
own thumb. In response to a New York Police Gazette illustration of
two Laramie girls dragging a masher behind their horses, Nye
responds that life in New York must be so dull that the people there
have to concoct preposterous images of the West in order to
entertain themselves. Nye is so provoked at the arrogance of an
Eastern Major named F. G. Wilson that he vows that the next time the
major passes through he will pick up a chunk of quartz and "spread
his intellectual faculties around the building till it looks like
the Custer Massacre."

413. Kesterson, David B. "Bill Nye." Dictionary of Literary
     Biography: Vol.11: American Humorists, 1800-1950. Detroit, MI:
     Gale, 1982, 364-69.

     Considers Nye to have been such a prominent humorist during
his time that his reputation rivaled that of Mark Twain. Twain was
even said to have been jealous of the younger man's talents. Nye
mostly wrote short items--newspaper columns, comic essays, sketches,
and fictional vignettes; however he also wrote two books of
burlesque history, an almanac, and two Broadway plays. He was
editor of the Laramie Boomerang (named after his pet mule), for
which he wrote a humor column. He was admired for his wit and
joviality and became chair of the "Forty Liars Club." Even under
newspaper deadlines, Nye wrote careful copy. His work had an
informal structure and a relaxed tone. Nye made droll, inane
observations about bizarre situations. He used understatement and
anticlimax effectively, and his satiric and ironic writing
occasionally contained violent or sick humor. He treated such
topics as Indians, Mormons, Chinese labor, mining and miners, the
landscape and the weather, and regional customs. Nye was blatantly
prejudiced in some of his critical commentaries on Indians and
Mormons. Nye derives his pen name from Bret Harte's character--Bill
Nye--in his famous poem, "Plain Language from Truthful James."
After the poem, the name "Bill Nye" was so famous that it couldn't
easily be changed back to "Edgar Wilson Nye."

414. Larson, T. A., ed. Bill Nye's Western Humor. Lincoln:
     University of Nebraska Press, 1968, xxii + 183 pp.

     Feels that Bill Nye wrote his best humor during the seven
years from 1876 to 1883 when he lived in Laramie, Wyoming. Nye
became the assistant editor of the Laramie Daily Sentinel in May of
1876, where he remained until 1877. In Wyoming, Nye enjoyed
fishing, picnicking, mining, and social events, and within a year he
had not only gained the reputation of an outstanding wit but he had
passed the Wyoming bar as well. In 1877, therefore, he hung up his
shingle and began to practice law. While waiting for law clients,
Nye wrote humorous pieces for the Laramie Times, the Cheyenne Sun,

and the <u>Denver Tribune</u>. Then in 1881 he became the full-time editor of the <u>Laramie Boomerang</u>. Nye published his two funniest books before leaving Laramie--<u>Bill Nye and Boomerang</u> (1881), and <u>Forty Liars and Other Lies</u> (1882). These were both collections of newspaper columns. In 1884 he published <u>Baled Hay</u>, and in 1886 <u>Remarks by Bill Nye</u>, both relying heavily on his Laramie experiences. In all, Nye published fourteen collections, two plays, a burlesque history of the United States, and a burlesque history of England. His <u>Bill Nye's History of the United States</u> (1894) was his best seller. Nye liked to use puns, anti-climax, incongruities, exaggeration, homely details, and absurd foreign phrases as he deflated   pomposity   and   debunked   individuals,   ideals,   and institutions.

415. Wade, Clyde G. "Bill Nye." <u>Encyclopedia of American Humorists</u>. New York: Garland, 1988, 340-44.

Considers language to be the major source of Nye's humor. Nye likes catch phrases like "olive oil" (for "au revoir"). He blends Biblical language with the vernacular as in "Pride goeth before destruction and a haughty spirit before a plunk." Nye loved playing with Latin and other languages and developed a crest that consisted of a "towel-rack penchant, with cockroach regardant, holding in his beak a large red tape-worm on which was inscribed 'spiritus frumenti, cum homo tomorrow." Even though Nye loved to play with words, he did not go in for the comic misspellings and substandard grammar of some other humorists of his day. Bill Nye's son, Jim, once estimated that Bill Nye wrote more than three million words for publication. He was always funny and always prolific. He was a good writer who controlled his mixing of metaphors, anticlimaxes, and comic catalogs carefully. Nye's material, however, related to the interests and events of the day, and he never developed an immortal character like Tom Sawyer or Huck Finn. Nye, therefore, unlike Twain, was not able to transcend his own era.

Grace Elizabeth King (c1851-1932)

416. Bonner, Thomas Jr. "Grace Elizabeth King." <u>Encyclopedia of American Humorists</u>. Ed. Steven H. Gale. New York: Garland, 1988, 256-59.

Considers King's views on women to have been liberal while her views on racial matters were conservative. King was a daughter of the South and defended its customs just after the Civil War. King is a local colorist, whose humor and wit give her works grace and charm. Often her non-fiction prose turns on amusing anecdotes. In "Bayou L'Ombre" the Yankee and Rebel soldiers exchange uniforms, and the resultant confusion of identies causes the wrong soldiers to be released from bondage. In <u>The Pleasant Ways of St. Medard</u> the dialogue between Mr. Talbot and Mademoiselle Mimi about Catholic and Protestant history is typical drawing-room comedy. In <u>La Dame de Saint Hermine</u> the dialogue between the <u>casquette</u> girl, Annette, and her husband the morning after the mass wedding is burlesque. In addition, there are traces of the tall tale in King's fiction.

Mary Eleanor Wilkins Freeman (1852-1930)

417. Blair, Walter, and Raven I. McDavid, Jr. "Mary E. Wilkins Freeman." _The Mirth of a Nation: America's Great Dialect Humor_. Minneapolis: University of Minnesota Press, 1983, 208-218.

Considers Freeman to be a New England local colorist. She lived in Massachusetts (near Boston), Vermont, and New Jersey, and set all of her fiction in New England. She wrote in a laconic understated Yankee style, appropriate for the frugal, pious, repressed, often comic New Englander. Freeman's women may be rebellious, but they are not demonstrative. In "The Revolt of Mother," for example, Sarah Penn quietly moves into a new barn that was built in place of the new house that she had wanted, saying, "We've got jest as good a right to live here as new horses and cows." Likewise, Lucy Tollet in "Gentian" behaves in a similarly rebellious but undemonstrative way. Blair and McDavid feel that Freeman is a "primordial feminist."

418. Robillard, Douglas. "Mary Eleanor Wilkins Freeman." _Encyclopedia of American Humorists_. Ed. Steven H. Gale. New York: Garland, 1988, 160-64.

Considers Freeman to have been a New England local colorist and further feels that nineteenth-century New England local color fiction is basically a woman's genre, citing the writings not only of Mary Eleanor Wilkins Freeman (1852-1930), but those of Harriet Beecher Stowe (1811-1896), Rose Terry Cooke (1827-1892), Elizabeth Stuart Phelps (1844-1900), and Sarah Orne Jewett (1849-1909) as well. Because Freeman has the ability to record the smallest details of daily life in her writings, it would be very easy for her writings to become sentimentalized. In order to avoid sentimentality, Freeman's writings are carefully orchestrated with irony. The protagonist in "A Village Singer" is Candace Whitcomb, who has sung in the village church for forty years and is replaced by a younger woman with a better voice. To rebel at her dismissal, Candace mistreats the picture album given to her at her retirement, and she loudly plays and sings from her home during church services to drown out her rival. But on her death bed, she requests her rival to sing for her, and she listens with "a holy and radiant expression" but remarks after the song is finished, "You flatted a little on 'soul'." Freeman's characters are gentle and silent as they live their uneventful lives, but they possess an ironic tenacity and have ways of making their points.

Henry Cuyler Bunner (1855-1896)

419. Bellman, Samuel I. "H. C. Bunner." _Dictionary of Literary Biography 78: American Short-Story Writers, 1880-1910_. Detroit, MI: Gale, 1989, 32-39.

Considers Bunner, the editor of _Puck: The Comic Weekly_, a refined humorist in his own right. Bunner's best writing genre was the well-developed story of an event or an incident equivalent to the French "conte." In such a genre character development is less important than a suspenseful conflict which is quickly resolved and causes the reader to smile at what Thomas Hardy called "life's little ironies." Bunner's reputation is based on such provocative and memorable short stories and on his ability to parody the styles of other writers.

Simeon Ford (1855-1933)

420. Masson, Thomas L. "Simeon Ford." Our American Humorists. Freeport, NY: Books for Libraries, 1931, 124-27.

Evaluates Ford's A Few Remarks (1904), in which Ford writes about patriotism, George Washington, automobiles, clams, hotel proprietors, and experiences in a Turkish bath. Masson laments the fact that Ford has spent so much of his time as a hotel proprietor rather than spending all of his time writing, for Masson feels that Ford, with his acute mind and native shrewdness, is one of America's best humorists.

Edward Waterman Townsend (1855-1942)

421. Masson, Thomas L. "E. W. Townsend." Our American Humorists. Freeport, NY: Books for Libraries, 1931, 295-98.

Considers Townsend to be the only writer who lived down his reputation as a humorist long enough to be elected to Congress. Townsend was a star reporter on the New York Sun, and author of the Chimmie-Fadden tales about the New York Bowery during the time of the "Bowery Boys." Townsend's stories were Irish in origin and flavor. In addition to Chimmie, Townsend's major characters were "de Duchess," her mistress, "Miss Fannie," and Miss Fannie's father, whom Chimmie referred to as "His Whiskers." One of the drollest of the Chimmie tales is about the festivities of the Rose Leaf Social Outing and Life Saving Association. Chimmie and other members of the Bohemian Club spent most of their free time cruising around on their yacht, calling themselves the "Rose Leaf Social and Outing Club." On one of their outings they rescued the crew of a boat that had been capsized in the bay, and shortly thereafter they added "Life Saving" to the name of their club.

Elbert Green Hubbard (1856-1915)

422. Capra, Douglas R. Encyclopedia of American Humorists. Ed. Steven H. Gale. New York: Garland, 1988, 232-36.

Considers philosophical humor and biting wit to have been Hubbard's trademarks. Hubbard and two of his friends founded the Philistine: A Periodical of Protest, and this literary magazine soon became a vehicle for his sarcastic wit. They called the magazine Philistine because its primary target was the "Chosen people in literature." It attacked William Dean Howells, Mark Twain, and others. When Mark Twain said he was writing "Joan of Arc" anonymously in <u>Harper</u> because if he signed it people would insist it was funny, Hubbard responded "Mr. Twain is worried unnecessarily." When Hubbard appointed himself the "General Inspector of the Universe," he expanded his targets to ministers, doctors, lawyers, teachers, and anyone else expounding establishment views. Of education, he said, "You can lead a boy to college, but you can't make him think." Hubbard was an eccentric not only in his writing but in his dress as well. He sported a curly, shoulder-length pageboy, and wore a Buster Brown cravat, baggy corduroys, a flannel shirt, farmer's brogans, and a cowboy's Stetson hat. His vernacular usage makes him difficult to read. Moreover, whenever he could not think of a word, he would invent one. "Gabbyjack" was an over-zealous talker, and "cabthought" was a witty response.

Henry Augustus Shute (1856-1943)

423. Masson, Thomas L. "Henry A. Shute." <u>Our American Humorists</u>. Freeport, NY: Books for Libraries Press, 1931, 285-89.

Feels that Shute's <u>Real Diary of a Real Boy</u> (1904) illustrates the principle that in terms of writing, it is necessary to become fifty before you can become fifteen. <u>Real Diary of a Real Boy</u> met with huge success because it dealt with actual occurrences, and the characters went by their real-world names. Furthermore, there was an appendix which gave the addresses of all of the characters, and a short history of their subsequent achievements. Shute served his writing apprenticeship preparing obituary notices with garish delight. Following the principle of "De mortuis nil nisi bonum," Shute was lavish with praise in his panegyric eulogies. This, of course, pleased Shute's editor, for the friends and relatives of the deceased always bought hundreds of papers and sent them around the world to other friends and relatives. The subscribers who were not friends or relatives of the deceased merely snorted with disgust. In April of 1883 Shute wrote his first story for the <u>Exeter News-Letter</u>, "The Story of Josh Zack." The story was based on the actual disappearance of a "locally popular colored boy," but Shute invented a few more characters and a great many details in order to make the story more interesting. One of the particulars that Shute added was about two stained and weather-beaten tablets in the old cemetery. Sunday was the day that most people of this area went to the cemetery to pay homage to the deceased, but on the Sunday following Shute's story, there was an unusually heavy turnout of people at the cemetery, all of them looking for the tablets in the story--which in fact did not exist.

Charles Waddell Chesnutt (1858-1932)

424. Blair, Walter, and Raven I. McDavid, Jr. "Charles W. Chesnutt." The Mirth of a Nation: America's Great Dialect Humor. Minneapolis: University of Minnesota Press, 1983, 219-29.

Indicates that Chesnutt was one of the first American Blacks to have succeeded as a fiction writer. His formative years were spent in North Carolina, the setting for his best novels. Chesnutt's first book, a collection of short stories, is entitled The Conjure Woman. Uncle Julius, the narrator, was well developed, and his dialect stories informed readers of Black superstitions and race relationships. "The Conjurer's Revenge" contrasts the narrator's stuffy diction with the raconteur's vernacular speech. The wry ending shows that despite Uncle Julius' innocent appearance, he is a shrewd operator.

425. Mann, Joanna Sanders. "Charles Chesnutt." WHIMSY 6 (1988): 23.

Uses Chesnutt's The Conjure Woman to show how an author explains the values, symbols, folk narratives, music, dance, and visual arts of a people through humor. The character Uncle Julius gives the reader a revealing glimpse into the soul of Black folks.

Alfred Henry Lewis (c1858-1914)

426. Blair, Walter, and Raven I. McDavid, Jr. "Alfred Henry Lewis (Dan Quin). The Mirth of a Nation: America's Great Dialect Humor. Minneapolis: University of Minnesota Press, 1983, 235-42.

Describes Lewis as a Far-Western local colorist. Lewis contributed to magazines from the late 1890s until his death in 1914. These stories were later collected and published in six books, Wolfville, Sanburrs, Wolfville Days, Wolfville Nights, Wolfville Folks, and Faro Nell and Her Friends. The stories take place in Arizona's cattle and mining country and are yarns told by the old cattleman to the tenderfoot writer (narrator). Blair and McDavid chose to reprint "Jaybird Bob's Joke," a story about two serious events--a stampede and a killing--but although the subject of the story is dark, the tone of the story teller is very light.

Agnes Repplier (c1858-1950)

427. Hart, James D. "Agnes Repplier." The Oxford Companion to American Literature. 4th edition. New York: Oxford University Press, 1965, 704.

Considers Repplier's scholarly essays to be graceful and witty. These essays are collected in Books and Men, Points of View, Essays in Miniature, Essays in Idleness, In the Dozy Hours, The

Fireside Sphinx, Compromises, Americans and Others, Counter Currents, Under Dispute, To Think of Tea!, and Eight Decades. Repplier's In Pursuit of Laughter is a historical study of the various types of humor.

428. Walker, Nancy, and Zita Dresner. "Agnes Repplier." Redressing the Balance: American Women's Literary Humor from Colonial Times to the 1980s Jackson: University Press of Mississippi, 1988, 207-20.

Considers Repplier to have been immensely popular during her day although now almost forgotten. Between 1888 and 1937 she published more than twenty-five books including biographies, histories, and collections of essays on literature and current events. Repplier had to educate herself because she was dismissed from two different private schools for "independent behavior." Repplier's life was a paradox if not a contradiction. She was a devoted Catholic who wrote biographies about three American Catholic leaders; nevertheless, she believed in the feminist cause and argued against American neutrality in World War I. In 1920 Repplier published Points of Friction. This collection included "Woman Enthroned" and other pieces originally published in the Atlantic Monthly. "Women Enthroned" explores the relationship between women and power and is written in a witty tone. In this piece Repplier repudiates the idea that women are inherently "purer" than men. Repplier's In Pursuit of Laughter (1936) is an informal treatment of the importance of humor in Western culture. Walker and Dresner feel that in this book elegance of style took precedence over accurate documentation.

Chapter 4
Twentieth Century

(1860-1935) TO (1879-1955)

Charlotte Perkins Gilman (1860-1935)

429. Walker, Nancy, and Zita Dresner, eds. "Charlotte Perkins Gilman." Redressing the Balance: American Women's Literary Humor from Colonial Times to the 1980s. Jackson: Univ. Press of Mississippi, 1988, 169-75.

Indicates that Gilman used humor and irony to investigate the vast discrepancies between the rights and freedoms of men and women at the turn of the twentieth century, and that this is especially developed in her utopian novel, Herland. In the beginning of "If I Were a Man," Gilman treats her protagonist, Mollie Mathewson, as a "true woman," as she ironically treats the "appropriate" behavior that is expected of women. Later, Mollie imagines what it would be like to be wearing her husband's clothes. As soon as she imagines herself to be dressed like a man, she has a feeling of exhilaration and great freedom.

John Kendrick Bangs (1862-1922)

430. Cox, Virginia Lee. John Kendrick Bangs and the Transition from Nineteenth to Twentieth-Century American Humor. Ph.D. dissertation. Columbus: Ohio State University, 1970, 233 pp.

Feels that although Bangs enjoyed enormous popularity during the 1890s and 1900s, writing some sixty books, there is no recognized critical standard that would rate him as one of America's truly great humorists. His material now reads as bland and outdated. Compared to the New Yorker school, Bangs' humor is mediocre, and it lacks vitality. It also strikes the reader as "just too polite." But Cox nevertheless feels that in order to have attained the achievements of the 1920s and 1930s it had to pass through the nineteenth-century genteel phase which Bangs epitomized, and Bangs was therefore important as a transitional humorist.

179

431. Hoffa, William C. "John Kendrick Bangs." <u>Dictionary of
     Literary Biography, Volume 11: American Humorists, 1800-1950</u>.
     Ed. Stanley Trachtenberg. Detroit, MI: Gale, 1982, 17-22.

     Agrees with other critics that Bangs is basically an
entertainer, not a reformer in his gentle humorous writing. His
writing displays wit, erudition, irony, and urbanity. His humor is
pleasant and amusing but never sharp and cutting. Bangs became the
first literary editor of <u>Life</u> in 1884, using the comic spirit to
fight for justice, cheerfulness, and charity. <u>Lorgnette</u>, his first
book, was a collection of satirical sketches about obsessions with
money, nationalism, and other topical matters. Bangs later became
editor of <u>Munsey's Weekly</u>, of "Facetiae" for <u>Harper's Bazaar</u>, and
the humor department of <u>Harper's Young People</u>, and <u>Puck</u>. The best
of what he wrote for these various magazines generally reemerged
later in book form. Bangs enjoyed collecting folklore, myth, fairy
tales, balladry, and stories of the supernatural, and much of his
writing related to these themes. Bangs wrote not only satiric
books, sketches, and stories, but he was also a prominent and
popular playwright and a prolific composer of excellent light verse.

432. Masson, Thomas L. "John Kendrick Bangs." <u>Our American
     Humorists</u>. Freeport, NY: Books for Libraries Press, 1931, 26-
     46.

     Considers Bangs to have been one of the principal authors in
the development of comic journalism. This is the journalism of
<u>Vanity Fair</u>, of <u>Puck</u>, and of <u>Life</u>. For many years, Bangs was the
editor of <u>Puck</u>, and before that, he was the editor of "The Drawer,"
a regular column in <u>Harper's Magazine</u>. During this time, Bangs also
had charge of the back page of the old <u>Harper's Bazaar</u>, famous in
its day as publishing the very best of short humor pieces.

433. Pettengell, Michael. "John Kendrick Bangs." <u>Encyclopedia of
     American Humorists</u>. Ed. Steven H. Gale. New York: Garland,
     1988, 24-27.

     Demonstrates that Bangs tended to write in thematic clusters.
As a collector of folklore and fairy tales he wrote tales for his
three boys in the style of Lewis Carroll. These include
<u>Tiddledywink Tales</u>, <u>The Tiddledywink's Poetry Book</u>, <u>In Camp with a
Tin Soldier</u>, <u>Half-Hours with Jimmieboy</u>, and <u>The Mantel-Piece
Minstrels</u>. These books showed a quick wit and a fertile
imagination. For adult readers Bangs wrote a series on the
supernatural, including <u>The Water Ghost and Others</u>, and <u>Ghosts I
Have Met</u>, dealing with encounters between Bangs and various shades.
He extended the supernatural theme into such later novels as <u>The
Houseboat on the Styx</u>, <u>The Pursuit of the House-Boat</u>, and <u>The
Enchanted Typewriter</u>, in which he described what life was probably
like for an assortment of famous ghosts who are freqently seen at a
club on the river Styx. One of these ghosts is Hamlet, who is
depressed by the way actors are portraying him on the stage. In
retaliation, Hamlet plays the actors playing Hamlet, taking certain
liberties in the portrayal. Bangs also wrote an "idiot" series,
including <u>Coffee and Repartee</u>, <u>The Idiot</u>, <u>The Idiot at Home</u>, <u>The
Genial Idiot</u>, and <u>Half Hours with the Idiot</u>, portraying actually
more of an "innocent" than an "idiot." Bangs' <u>Peeps at People</u>

involves satiric views of such famous people as Emile Zola, Andrew Lang, and Rudyard Kipling.

434. Yates, Norris W. "John Kendrick Bangs, University Wit." The American Humorist: Conscience of the Twentieth Century. Ames, Iowa: Iowa State University Press, 1964, 49-60.

Considers Bangs to have been one of the most prolific and popular of the "university wits." Bangs used the solid citizen to exemplify decorum and morality. His A House-Boat on the Styx and The Idiot are still found in even the smallest of college and public libraries. Bangs' humor was more urbane and cultivated than that of Mark Twain and other newspaper humorists, who had received their training in print shops and in real life. Bangs' schooling had been more formal, and his humor exemplified this. Bangs poked fun at high society, but at the same time he was not above engaging in occasional racial or rural snobbery. Bangs felt that his values were those of an earlier and purer America, and he was therefore concerned with the encroachments of the upper crust from above and of the unwashed masses from below. Bangs felt that it was not necessary to be vulgar in order to be amusing. He wrote more than sixty volumes of essays, tales, fantasies, parodies, plays, and verse, and constantly fought for the status quo of an earlier generation. His most entertaining chapter in A House-Boat on the Styx is an attack on Darwinian evolution. He used reductio ad absurdum to reason that Adam and Eve must have had tails, and that their first sin was to swing by these tails in the forbidden tree. He further reasoned that the serpent must have evolved from Adam's tail.

William Sydney Porter (1862-1910)

435. Hart, James D. "William Sydney Porter." The Oxford Companion to American Literature. 4th edition. New York: Oxford University Press, 1965, 668-69.

Indicates that Porter founded The Rolling Stone, a humorous weekly magazine in 1894 and that he also wrote for a Houston newspaper a daily column of humorous anecdotes. Under the pen name of O. Henry, he had a gift for ingenious depiction of ironic circumstances. His plots frequently depended upon coincidence, and his forte was episodic vignettes displaying the whims and whirlygig of fortune. His characters were plain, simple folks, and his plots frequently relied on a surprise, often fatalistic, ending. He seemed to be incapable of writing any longer unified works, but his vignettes are timeless. They include "The Gift of the Magi," "The Ransom of Red Chief," and "The Furnished Room." Porter's The Four Million includes observations on the four million ordinary everyday run-of-the-mill New Yorkers who are neglected by other writers.

436. Weiss, Helen S., and M. Jerry Weiss. "O. Henry." The American Way of Laughing. Eds. Helen S. Weiss and M. Jerry Weiss. New York: Bantam, 1977, 64-76.

Considers the ironic surprise ending the hallmark of O. Henry's short stories. Porter also has a sympathy for the underdog

and a strong sense of coincidence. In 1896 he was indicted for
embezzling funds from the bank at which he worked. He escaped to
Honduras, where he joined two famous outlaws, the Jennings brothers
in their travels and exploits throughout Mexico and South America.
He returned to the United States to find his wife dying and a three-
year prison sentence awaiting him. It was in prison that Porter
developed his reputation as a story teller under the pen name of O.
Henry. Ironically, when his body was imprisoned his mind became
filled with flightful fancy.

Oliver Herford (1863-1935)

437. Masson, Thomas L. "Oliver Herford." Our American Humorists.
     Freeport, New York: Books for Libraries, 1931, 154-61.

     Considers Herford to have been a unique combination of
philosopher, wit, poet, and artist and indicates that Herford "has
been, and still is, the most quoted man in America." Herford had
such a reputation for never keeping appointments that he began to
believe it himself. At a particular dinner party the hostess
pointed out that there was an empty seat near where Herford was
sitting. Herford remarked, "Yes, if I weren't here I should know
that seat was mine." Herford was famous for such epigrams as "Many
are called but few get up," and "Actresses will happen in the best
regulated families." This Giddy Globe "can easily be read through
in half an hour, yet it contains practically all that is known about
this world." At one point Herford resolved to stop smoking. When
a friend asked him if he had kept his resolve, he responded that he
was obliged to smoke occasionally so as not to fall into the habit
of not smoking. Masson compares Herford's ability with words to
that of Shakespeare. He feels that Herford plays with words the
same as a kitten plays with a ball of yarn, raveling it and
unraveling it with delicate touch, nimble wit, and unerring insight.

Raymond Weeks (1863-1954)

438. Wixson, Douglas C. "Raymond Weeks." Encyclopedia of American
     Humorists. Ed. Steven H. Gale. New York: Garland, 1988, 462-
     66.

     Considers Weeks' The Hound-Tuner of Callaway to be filled with
whimsical humor about human vanity and perfidy. Weeks wrote gentle
but pointed satire about false piety, dogmatism, vanity, and
hypocrisy. A favorite target was Missouri State University in
Columbia, where he once taught. Many of his short stories are based
on his recollections of the old times he spent in Missouri. He was
fascinated by the eccentricities of speech and character and was
trained as a phonetician. His depictions of Missouri speech
patterns were both accurate and entertaining. Even though Weeks was
tolerant of human foible, he nevertheless liked to poke fun at moral
blindness and obsessive behavior. Weeks held a firm conviction that
both the quantity and quality of humor in education should be
increased. In his The Boy's Own Arithmetic he advocates teaching

arithmetic by turning exercises and rote memorizations into imaginative and fanciful stories. He was proposing a revolution in teaching based on the effective uses of laughter.

George Ade (1866-1944)

439. DeMuth, James. "George Ade." Small Town Chicago: The Comic Perspective of Finley Peter Dunne, George Ade, and Ring Lardner. Port Washington, NY: Kennikat Press, 1980, 46-68.

Contrasts the Chicago writings of George Ade, who moved to Chicago late in life, with those of Finley Peter Dunne, who was a native Chicagoan. In his daily columns and in his three comic novels of Chicago, Ade was never able to create a sustained comic character like Mr. Dooley, who could encompass the intimacies of Chicago and the typical experiences of his neighborhood. Ade's characters were usually fresh immigrants to Chicago from either Europe or rural America, who were confused and lonely in a strange city but generally hopeful that they would be able to succeed. There was an element of autobiography in these stories. "A Young Man in Upper Life" from Stories of the Streets and Town is a typical Ade story which shows how the intimidating city can be tamed. Arthur Ponsby is an office worker in a Chicago high rise with a magnificent view of Chicago and Lake Michigan beyond. But his view is interrupted by a workman on a steel pillar and then by many workmen on narrow beams spitting tobacco juice and straddling girders for lunch and beer. Finally, a terra-cotta wall is attached to the building, and Mr. Ponsby goes back to his neglected work.

440. Goldstein, Kalman. "George Ade." Encyclopedia of American Humorists. Ed. Steven H. Gale. New York: Garland, 1988, 4-7.

Considers Ade to have been an amiable cynic. His characters display a misplaced hopelessness, a sort of stoic endurance. Goldstein feels that although Ade wrote acrid burlesque, he was incapable of truly savage or vulgar satire. Ade is most remembered for his "Fables in Slang." The vividness of expression of these "fables" results from the neologism and argot usage along with strangely juxtaposed words and unconventional capitalization. There are also jarring incongruities, ironic inversions, and the use of archaic forms to portray modern culture. The satiric tone is reinforced through parody, pun, anticlimax, wisecrack, and non sequitur. Lee Coyle considered Ade to be a "literary Rotarian who wrote too quickly and in too many genres to sustain quality or depth of characterization." Ade's appeal is mainly to three groups of readers--literary realists, who find his detail enlightening, linguists and punsters who delight in his wordplay, and social historians, who receive important historical insights. Ade's humor synthesized the frontiersman's tall tale with the Yankee's moral jest. Along with Field and Dunne, Ade helped establish a distinctively midwestern genre of American humor. Nevertheless, Ade will go down in history merely as a local colorist.

441. Hoffa, William W. "George Ade." <u>Dictionary of Literary
Biography, Volume 11: American Humorists, 1800-1950</u>. Ed.
Stanley Trachtenberg. Detroit, MI: Gale, 1982, 3-12.

Considers Ade to have been the most important American
humorous author between Mark Twain and James Thurber. S. J.
Perelman once lamented that his place in history has become assured
only in the form of a question in the <u>New York Times</u> Sunday
Crossword Puzzle: "A three letter word meaning 'Indiana Humorist.'"
Hoffa points out the important relationship between authors and
newspapers during Ade's time. Just as George Ade wrote for <u>The
Chicago Record</u>, Theodore Dreiser wrote for the <u>Boston Globe</u>, Eugene
Field wrote for the <u>Daily News</u>, Bert Leston Taylor wrote for the
<u>Tribune</u>, and Finley Peter Dunne wrote for the <u>Evening Post</u>. Against
this talented field, the Ade and McCutcheon column nevertheless
received extensive readership and praise. Ade's plays were clean
and fresh and free of slapstick and heavy dialect that was typical
of his day, but these plays were also locally grounded and therefore
ephemeral. His fables dealt with more universal themes. His
tradition of witty understatement, and his inept and victimized
targets influenced the writing of both Robert Benchley and James
Thurber.

442. Kelly, Fred C. <u>George Ade: Warmhearted Satirist</u>.
Indianapolis: Bobbs-Merrill, 1947, 282 pp.

Points out that George Ade has only one limb on his family
tree. His father was named John Ade, and his mother, Adeline, was
an Adair. "According to the geneologists, who can become excited
over the various kinds of fruit hanging on family trees, the names
of Ade, Adee, Adie, Adey, Aide, Ader, Yde, Ide, and others of
phonetic similarity are all variations of the Scotch name of Adair.
The name became variously twisted and abbreviated because no
one...knew how to spell." Commenting on the fact that all of his
ancestry was British, George concluded that that is why he always
felt that he had a right to take liberties with the English
language. When John was a child the Ade family moved to Morocco,
Indiana, to take charge of a general store. This was a time when
men wore whiskers and women sang old-time hymns in high, piping
tremolo. Both men and women walked to church barefoot and put their
shoes on before they went inside. Even though the town was small
and remote it was the home of The Bank of North America. Ade said
that they could have named it the "Bank of the Western Hemisphere"
or the "Bank of the Solar System," but they were being modest. The
founders chose Morocco because they wanted the bank to be far enough
away from the depositers that they would have difficulty stopping by
to withdraw their money.

443. Lazarus, A. L. "George Ade: A Humor That Is Truly American."
<u>The Purdue Alumnus</u> 74 (September 1986): 7-25.

Considers George Ade, the author, and John T. McCutcheon,
Ade's illustrator, two of Purdue's most famous alumni. At Purdue,
Ade studied German literature, and, of course knew the German rules
of capitalization. Later, his own writing exhibited a heavy use of
capitalization, to some extent conforming to the German pattern of
capitalizing all nouns and to some extent following his own
conventions for emphasis, for slowing down readers and forcing them

to take notice of the form, and for creating an individualistic writing style. Ade was born in Kentland, Indiana, a town targetted by temperance leaders because it had more saloons than churches (an anomaly in Indiana). Ade went with his mother to Methodist meetings and went with his father to Campbellite meetings but ended up by gravitating to agnosticism.   During 1904 three of his most successful plays were running simultaneously. With his royalties he paid off the mortgage of his estate, Hazelden, and held picnics, barbecues, and ice cream and lemonade socials that attracted such celebrities as Warren Harding, William Howard Taft, Charles Dawes, Booth Tarkington, James Whitcomb Riley, Franklin P. Adams, John Studebaker, Jesse Lasky, and May Robson. His only friend who did not attend was George Barr McCutcheon, whom he had satirized in The Slim Princess.

444. Lazarus, A. L., ed. The Best of George Ade. Bloomington: Indiana University Press, 1985, xxii + 254 pp.

Points out that in 1890 George Ade moved to Chicago to live with John McCutcheon, a cartoonist for the Chicago News. While in Chicago, Ade wrote Artie, about the exploits of a brash and opportunistic office boy named Artie Blanchard; Pink Marsh, about a shrewd bootblack who received his education by rapping with his affluent customers; and Doc Horne, about a retiree who enjoyed recounting stories in his new home--a European hotel. Ade also wrote a series of fable books, including Fables in Slang, More Fables in Slang, Forty Modern Fables, and The Girl Proposition: A Book of He and She Fables. These books were Aesopian in nature, but the morals at the ends of the fables were often ironic. Ade's most humorous and best collection of stories and essays is entitled In Babel. This book published in 1903, sold 70,000 copies within the first few months of its appearance.   In Pastures New, (1906) recounts some of Ade's experiences in Cairo, London, Paris, and Naples and is written in the style of Twain's Innocents Abroad but with even more irreverence and even greater satirizing of the idiotic behavior of certain types of American tourists. This tradition of satirizing American tourists continued in Ade's The Sultan of Sulu, a comic operetta satirizing jingoism and gunboat diplomacy in the Philippines written in the style of Gilbert and Sullivan.

445. Masson, Thomas L. "George Ade." Our American Humorists Freeport, New York: Books for Libraries Press, 1931, 1-20.

Considers George Ade and Finley Peter Dunne to be America's two leading humorists both in achievement and in intrinsic merit. Masson further feels that the reputations of these two humorists are quite restricted and unified. Dunne is famous mainly for his creation of Mr. Dooley. Ade is famous mainly for his Fables in Slang. But they both were broader than their reputations. Ade wrote good rollicking operas with a truly American flavor, the best being entitled, The Sultan of Sulu. He wrote many other meritorious works; but his reputation as a dramatist and novelist is closely linked to his reputation as a fablist. Ade was American to the core, and his writings reflected this fact. His ear for slang could only have been developed in the American heartland--the middle western soil.

446. Shepherd, Jean, ed. <u>The America of George Ade</u>. New York: G. P. Putnam's, 1961, 284 pp.

Describes the Midwest in which George Ade wrote as the land of futility. It was filled with Toledos wanting to be Detroits, and Detroits wanting to be Chicagos, and Chicagos wanting to be New Yorks. Surrounding these large metropolitan areas were hundreds of hamlets whose only ambitions were to become incorporated and to beat the County Seat in softball. The only exciting events in Monan, Indiana, for example, were the roar of trucks rushing toward Chicago to the north or the clatter of trains rushing toward Cincinnati to the south. People only stopped in Monan for gas or to visit ailing relatives. Monan had hard midwestern winters and languid midwestern summers and was a typical Indiana town. This was the Indiana that George Ade wrote about. In an essay on Indiana, Ade wrote about the humorists that could be found everywhere--not professional humorists but practicing humorists--and theirs was the humor of futility and the humor of evil triumphing over good--a special kind of midwestern realism. For Ade, there are no heroes or noble figures. Everybody is subjected to the same trivial emotions and tiny frustrations. "Ade, as has no one, before or since, chronicled the Great Unchronicled." He wrote about the totally unimportant, the profoundly insignificant, people without romances or great loves-- people who were not capable of profound emotions either tragic or comic.

447. Williams, Kenny J., and Bernard Duffey, eds. "George Ade." <u>Chicago's Public Wits: A Chapter in the American Comic Spirit</u>. Baton Rouge: Louisiana State University Press, 1983, 154-76.

Feels that Ade was an attentive observer and that his writing is unparalleled in showing the variety of personalities to be found in a city like Chicago. He wrote a lively column for the <u>Chicago Record</u> and later published more than twenty-five books. His fables began their book appearance in 1899 and continued until 1914. "The Fable of the Two Mandolin Players" was his personal favorite, and it remains the most often reprinted today.

448. Yates, Norris W. "George Ade, Student of 'Success'." <u>The American Humorist: Conscience of the Twentieth Century</u>. Ames IA: Iowa State University Press, 1964, 61-80.

Feels that the first fifteen years or so of the 1900s was an important time of development for American urbane wit and humor. In the East there were John Kendrick Bangs, Clarence S. Cullen, Miles Bantock, Frank Moore Colby, and Harry Thurston Peck. In the West there were George Ade, Finley Peter Dunne, Kin Hubbard, Will Rogers, Ring Lardner, H. L. Mencken, and Don Marquis. College degrees were common among the Eastern humorists, but among the Western humorists, George Ade was the only major author of this period to hold a university degree. Ade, Dunne, and Hubbard wrote satire in dialect and slang. They continued the crackerbox tradition, but their characters also had as many traits of the solid citizen as they had of the crackerbarrel philosopher. By the end of the 1920s there would be a new crop of humorists, some from the Midwest and some from the East, but all with university degrees and all with backgrounds of writing for big magazines in the East. Ade began writing a two-column feature in the <u>Record</u> entitled <u>Stories of the</u>

Streets and of the Town" in 1893 and continued for seven years. During this time he accumulated a large quantity of straight news, parodies, verse, dialogues, and fictions, which were later published as Artie (1896), Pink Marsh (1897), Doc' Horne (1899), In Babel (1900), and Bang! Bang! (1928).

Frank Gelett Burgess (1866-1951)

449. Cruse, Irma R. "Frank Gelett Burgess."Encyclopedia of American Humorists. Ed. Steven H. Gale. New York: Garland, 1988, 69-73.

Mentions that Burgess published "The Purple Cow" in the first issue of The Lark. The poem reads: "I never saw a Purple Cow./ I never hope to see one;/ But I can tell you, anyhow,/ I'd rather see than be one." This poem became Burgess' trademark and was recited back to him on so many occasions that in 1900 a sequel appeared in Cinq Ans Apres that reads: "Oh, yes, I wrote the "Purple Cow"--/ I'm sorry now, I wrote it!/ But I can tell you, anyhow,/ I'll kill you if you quote it." In 1900 Burgess also published Goops and How to Be Them, designed to teach proper manners by showing negative examples. This book was followed by other Goop books like More Goops and How Not to Be Them, Blue Goops and Red, The Goop Directory of Juvenile Offenders, and New Goops and How to Know Them. Parents liked the books for their didacticism, children enjoyed the Goops and their behavior. Burgess often coined words in his writings, and such coinages as blurb, goop, and bromide have become popular American words. Burgess' The Maxims of Methuselah is a collection of biting epigrams, and his Burgess Unabridged is an exploration of the sounds and meanings of words. Burgess felt that "Humor is the most serious subject in the world and it's impossible to discuss it without being solemn."

450. Masson, Thomas L. "Gelett Burgess as a Humorist." Our American Humorists. Freeport, New York: Books for Libraries, 1931, 53-72.

Indicates that when Burgess was an instructor in topographical drawing at the University of California he enjoyed playing practical jokes and in general didn't take his job very seriously. In San Francisco there was a cast-iron statue of the famous Dr. Coggswell that many San Franciscans considered to be an eyesore. Burgess agreed with this assessment of the statue, and one midnight he pulled the statue down. This action made Burgess a hero among the University of California students, but the administration was not so impressed and indicated to Burgess that his resignation from the Faculty would be accepted. This was the beginning of Burgess' literary career. With Bruce Porter, he founded The Lark. It contained little satire, parody, or criticism but was rather devoted to nonsense, serious verse, essays, fiction, drawings, and inventions. Its creed was optimism and "joie de vivre." Burgess did most of the writing himself, and a typical example is "The Window has four little Panes--But One have I./ The Window Panes are in its Sash--I Wonder Why." One issue of the Lark contained an essay entitled "Interchangeable Philosophical Paragraphs." The six paragraphs could be interchanged haphazardly in any combination resulting in an infinite number of logical permutations.

451. Schwartz, Richard Alan. "The Lark." American Humor Magazines
     and Comic Periodicals. Ed. David E. E. Sloane. Westport, CT:
     Greenwood Press, 1987, 135-39.

Describes a nonsense magazine founded by Gelett Burgess and
Bruce Porter entitled The Lark. The magazine was published in San
Francisco between May of 1895 and April of 1897. There was a
single-issue sequel in 1897 named The Epilark, and another single-
issue April-Fool sequel in 1898 entitled Enfant Terrible! Since one
of their targets was the commercialism of journalism, they sold
single issues of the magazine for a nickel and an annual
subscription (12 issues) for a dollar; nevertheless many people paid
the extra 40 cents for the annual subscription. The cover of The
Epilark continues to advertise the yearly one-dollar subscription
rate, even though only one issue was ever printed or was even
planned. The Lark contains such Goop poems as "I'd never dare to
walk across/ A Bridge I could not see,/ For much afraid of falling
off,/ I fear that I should be." There were also nonsense stories,
long narrative poems like "The Ambitious Shepherd," spurious
ballads, like "Tyrante" sung to the tune of "Lord Randal," and
impure maxims like "A Lark in the Hand gathers no Moss." The Lark
had a circulation of about 5,000. The Lark joined The Chap-Book,
the Philistine, and other nonsense magazines as copy for the
intellectually elite at the end of the century and probably
foreshadowed the Dada and existential movements.

452. Wenke, John. "Gelett Burgess." Dictionary of Literary
     Biography, Volume 11: American Humorists, 1800-1950. Ed.
     Stanley Trachtenberg. Detroit, MI: Gale, 1982, 68-76.

Describes Burgess' Goops as "boneless, mischievous, ill-
mannered creatures with oval heads." Burgess led an avant-garde
group that included Bruce Porter, William Doxey Oliver Herford, and
Carolyn Wells and was called "Les Jeunes." They founded the Lark,
known for its whimsy, spontaneity, eccentricity, imagination, and
especially for its spirit of adventure. The magazine contained
poems like "I wish that my Room had a Floor!/ I don't so much care
for a Door,/ But this crawling around/ Without touching the Ground/
Is getting to be quite a Bore." The poem is illustrated by a
gooplike creature awkwardly suspended between a cot and the mantel
of a fireplace trying to keep from falling through the bottom of the
room into endless space. Burgess also founded Le Petit Journal des
Refusees, a magazine designed to accept only manuscripts rejected
from other, better magazines. It was published on wallpaper cut
into trapezoidal shapes but did not continue past the first number.
Burgess also invented a nonsense machine, which didn't do anything
but run and make noises. Burgess' place in history remains mainly
confined to Bohemian circles; however Walter Blair and Hamlin Hill
feel that the Lark is a forerunner of such lunatic-fringed
periodicals as Mad and National Lampoon.

Finley Peter Dunne (1867-1936)

453. Blair, Walter, and Raven I. McDavid, Jr., eds. The Mirth of a
     Nation: America's Great Dialect Humor. Minneapolis: Univ. of
     Minnesota Press, 1983, 156-66.

     Represents Dunne as a newspaper reporter who moved from one
paper to another in Chicago and who developed the character of Mr.
Dooley, a Chicago sixth-ward saloon keeper who delivered political
sermons in heavy Irish brogue.   In addition to being a saloon
keeper, Mr. Dooley was a traveller, an archaeologist, a historian,
a social observer, an economist, and a philosopher.   He is
perceptive of human ways, cynical, and detached because of his
advanced age (sixties) and his bachelorhood. He speaks as a member
of an ethnic and religious minority, and his compassion contributes
to his charm.   Despite Dooley's thick brogue, Dunne's books were
well read from the late 1890s until the late 1920s and for decades
following the 20s. Dunne was so much read and so well beloved that
the second book written about him was entitled Mr. Dooley in the
Hearts of His Countrymen (1899).

454. DeMuth, James. "Finley Peter Dunne." Dictionary of Literary
     Biography, Volume 11: American Humorists, 1800-1950. Ed.
     Stanley Trachtenberg. Detroit, MI: Gale, 1982, 123-33.

     Lists Dunne's favorite satiric targets as the Spanish-American
War, the Philippine insurrection, and the general clumsiness of
American imperialism. Mr. Dooley's motto is, "Thrust ivrybody, but
cut th' cards."   Mr. Dooley is frank and honest in his opinions and
has a brash self-confidence. He is a working-class Irish-American
saloon keeper who is an active Democrat in Chicago's sixth ward.
When Dooley's brogue is translated into standard English, as
anthologizers often do, his voice loses its edge of cocky impudence.
In discussing why he developed the character of Mr. Dooley and the
thick Irish brogue, Dunne said that he felt it might be dangerous to
call an alderman a thief in standard English, but that "no one could
sue if a comic Irishman denounced the statesman as a thief." Mr.
Dooley learns about the politics of the day by reading the daily
newspapers; he then shows the significance of these events by
relating them to the daily lives of Hennessy, Hogan, and the other
drinkers. The incongruity of the comparisons are often comical, but
there is also a strange logic. DeMuth concludes that if the world
continues to hold the values which Dunne cherished--personal
integrity, plain speaking, catholic tolerance, compassion for the
weak, good humor, and salty wit, Dunne will surely continue to be
read.

455. Demuth, James "Finley Peter Dunne." Small Town Chicago: The
     Comic Perspective of Finley Peter Dunne, George Ade, and Ring
     Lardner. Port Washington, New York: Kennikat Press, 1980, 24-
     31.

     Explains the origin of the name "Whitechapel Club."   The
inspiration for the name came from the section of London where Jack
the Ripper committed his crimes.   Dunne and the other young
journalist members of the "Whitechapel Club" met in two Chicago

taverns both located on "Newspaper Alley" (Calhoun Place) to drink,
argue, and carouse. The decorations of these taverns were macabre.
On the walls were weapons from local crimes, and centerpieces on the
tables were skulls. One of the bars was coffin shaped. Some of the
pranks of the club were as ghoulish as the ambience in which they
met. Their most extreme escapade involved the cremation of the body
of "Club Member Collins." The story has it that Collins was an
impoverished poet, and in a particularly melancholy mood he proposed
to his friends in the Whitechapel Club that they have a protest mass
suicide to dramatize the evils of capitalist exploitation. The
practical joke was worked out down to the last detail, including the
last will and testament of Collins requesting that the Whitechapel
Club cremate his body, and of course a gaudy ceremony actually took
place. The favorite sport of the Whitechapel Club was witticism,
and they especially enjoyed "sharpshooting" an honored guest or an
ambitious member. On the staff of The Evening News Dunne worked
with Eugene Field and learned the fine balance of sentiment and
irony. In 1887 he was assigned by the Herald to cover White Sox
baseball games with Charles Seymour, and introduced a light and
slangy style of reporting that has lasted until the present day.
The term "southpaw," for example derives from the fact that left-
handed pitchers at Comiskey Park threw from the South side.

456. DeMuth, James. "Hard Times in the Sixth Ward: Mr. Dooley on the
     Depression of the 1890s." Studies in American Humor 3.2-3
     (Summer-Fall 1984): 123-37.

     Portrays Dunne's protagonist, Mr. Dooley, as a forty-year
resident of Chicago, making him more of a Chicagoan than most
natives of the city. Dooley was active in his Democratic precinct
and an active debater of political issues. Mr. Dooley kept bar in
the Sixth Ward or Bridgeport area of Chicago that had originally
been settled by Irish canal and railroad workers, and whose sons now
worked in the lumber yards and packing plants. During the
depression of the 1890s Bridgeport suffered a disproportionate
number of layoffs and evictions because most of the laborers in the
area were unskilled. Mr. Dooley was a skeptic who saw the irony of
the fact that hard times usually caused people in privileged
positions to "exert their authority more arbitrarily, flaunt their
wealth more ostentatiously and oppress their fellowmen more
shamelessly." Mr. Dooley's charm comes out when he ridicules people
whose ideas are not quite ordinary. He satirizes new-fangled ideas
and self-important people. But he has a deep understanding of how
a community works, and he has a love and sympathy for his neighbors.
And these facts make his biased political views a bit more
palatable.

457. Gibson, William M. "TR and Finley Peter Dunne, 'Mr. Dooley'"
     Theodore Roosevelt Among the Humorists: W. D. Howells, Mark
     Twain, and Mr. Dooley. Knoxville: University of Tennessee
     Press, 1980, 43-65.

     Points out that Finley Peter Dunne, who was thirty years
younger than Howells and Twain, was nevertheless very popular from
the time he first created Mr. Dooley in 1890 until the beginning of
World War I, twenty-five years later. Dunne wrote about seven
hundred "Mr. Dooley" sketches, and they became widely syndicated.

Dunne referred to Teddy Roosevelt as "Tiddy Rosenfelt." He attacked him relentlessly, and in 1907 he sent him an apology, saying that in fact TR had been his most valuable asset. In his inventory of assets he listed Teddy Roosevelt at 75 percent, and Taft, the German emperor, current topics, and the rest only at 25 percent. Mr. Dooley's dramatic political monologues could take many forms-- satire, droll mimicry, fables, tales, rollicking comedy, or witty maxims. They were peppered with delectable puns such as "Anglo-Saxon 'liance.'" Mr. Dooley would say, "War is a fine thing." Then he would correct himself to "Or perhaps I'm wrong. Anyhow, it's a strange thing," but then he would go on to say that it didn't matter whether it was fine or strange; what mattered was how we conducted war. Mr. Dooley's way of conducting war was to keep the common people out of it. He would prefer to match up Nick Romanoff and the Mikado, or Roosevelt and the Emperor of Germany, and continues, "Whenever I'm called on to fight for God and my country, I'd like to be sure the senior partner had been consulted."

458. Goldstein, Kalman. "Finley Peter Dunne." Encyclopedia of American Humorists. Ed. Steven H. Gale. New York: Garland, 1988, 139-44.

Feels that Mr. Dooley (if not Finley Peter Dunne) has earned a firm place in the history of American literature and folklore. His philosophical aphorisms are frequently quoted by politicians, lawyers, political scientists, and historians. Edward Asner portrayed Mr. Dooley in a skit as recently as the 1976 Democratic National Convention. But many people who quote Mr. Dooley have no idea that they are really quoting Finley Peter Dunne. It is somehow appropriate, though also ironic, that Dunne's creation, Mr. Dooley, has swallowed up his creator, for Dunne fathered a strong and historically significant protagonist. The "Phunny Phellows" who had preceded Dunne has used cacography and misspellings for comic effect, but Dunne's dialect writing was more; he carefully reproduced the argot of Chicago's Irish-speaking Sixth Ward. In creating Mr. Dooley, Dunne borrowed from a number of literary traditions. The saloon keeper was a crackerbox philosopher, a dialectician, a tall-tale raconteur, and an Irish story teller who had an ear for drama, for culture, and for language as well as a keen wit and a strong sense of irony. Dooley effectively used malapropisms, unorthodox spellings, repetition, paradoxical leveling, transformed cliche, absurd juxtaposition, and double entendre to create charming and provocative speech.

459. Masson, Thomas L. "Finley Peter Dunne." Our American Humorists. Freeport, New York: Books for Libraries Press, 1931, 110-19.

Believes that between 1898 and 1910, Dunne's protagonist, Mr. Dooley, anticipated just about everything that was going to happen in America. Masson goes on to say that if somehow all of the newspaper files and all of the histories were destroyed for this period, and nothing remained but Mr. Dooley's observations, that would be enough. Mr. Dooley's observations are unerring, philosophical, and true; and they are also witty. Masson feels that there is no "Port of Humorists" in American history to compete with Chicago, because of H. L. Mencken, Eugene Field, George Ade, and especially Finley Peter Dunne. Even Boston with Oliver Wendell Holmes, Samuel McChord Crothers, and Calvin Coolidge, and

Philadelphia with Benjamin Franklin and George Horace Lorimer are
out of the competition.

460. Rees, John. "An Anatomy of Mr. Dooley's Brogue." Studies in
     American Humor NS5.2-3 (Summer-Fall 1986): 145-57.

     Considers Dunne's vernacular to have deserved more praise by
critics than it has received. Many of Dunne's contemporaries found
the shanty-Irish brogue offensive and wanted Dunne to write in
"decent English." More recent critics have not damned the
vernacular writing, but they haven't praised it very much either,
and the function of Rees' article is to investigate the linguistic
abilities that Dunne exhibited in writing Mr. Dooley's brogue. Rees
disagrees with Dunne's biographer, Elmer Ellis, his son Philip
Ellis, and other critics who contend that if the Mr. Dooley sketches
had been written in standard English very little would be lost. In
fact, some of the sketches have indeed been published in standard
English, and Rees concedes that much of Dooley's humor, humanity,
and salutary skepticism does come through unscathed. But he still
feels that some of the sketches need to be presented in vernacular
in order to be effective.

461. Schaaf, Barbara, ed. Mr. Dooley: Wise and Funny--We Need Him
     Now. Springfield, Illinois: Lincoln-Herndon, 1988, xvii + 286
     pp.

     Suggests that Dunne's views were often at odds with those of
the newspaper for which he worked, and that he therefore developed
the voice of Mr. Dooley, an Irish saloon-keeper in Chicago's
working-class neighborhood to distance himself from his own writing.
The Irish brogue provided the buffer that kept Dunne from being shot
or assaulted as had happened to other critics of his day. Schaaf
feels that Mr. Dooley symbolized the tragicomedy of modern life and
that his trenchant sayings are as appropriate now as they were when
Dunne penned them. She also feels that Dunne would appear on any
critic's short list of America's greatest humorists, and she points
out that J. C. Furnas has even declared that Dunne was more
deserving that was Twain to be regarded as America's national
humorist because Dunne "touched on a far wider spectrum." Dunne's
favorite targets were politics and business, and he once wrote that
whenever he saw an alderman and a banker walking down the street
together he knew that the Recording Angel would have to "ordher
another bottle iv ink." Dunne was a relentless foe to hypocrisy,
pomposity and arrogance. Philip Dunne points out that the knowledge
that he was there served as a deterrent to many who would abuse
political or financial power. Schaaf feels that the Mr. Dooley
essays were not only very relevant to their times but to other times
as well.

462. Thogmartin, Clyde. "Mr. Dooley's Brogue: The Literary Dialect
     of Finley Peter Dunne." Visible Language 16.2 (Spring 1982):
     185-98.

     Explains that Theodore Roosevelt read from Finley Peter
Dunne's columns at Cabinet meetings in the same way that Abraham
Lincoln had read from Petroleum V. Nasby's columns a half-century
earlier. Finley Peter Dunne, Mark Twain, and Stephen Crane all

wrote in dialect. Thogmartin suggests that there are a number of reasons why Twain's and Crane's work is presently much more widely read than is the work of Dunne. First, many of the names and events mentioned by Dunne no longer have any significance to the general reader, especially the references in Dunne's earlier pieces which refer to specific Chicago political events and specific Chicago politicians. Second, the vernacular which Twain and Crane were representing may have been colloquial and slangy, but it was nevertheless a genuine native American dialect. The language which Dunne was representing was the Anglo-Irish spoken by the Chicago Irish working class. It was a dialect that has no roots in popular American English but instead belongs to a different dialect system. Dunne's writing was also localized by a strong sense of time and place--the Bridgeport area of Chicago during the 1890s. Still, Mr. Dooley is currently more salient than Hosea Biglow, Artemus Ward, or Petroleum V. Nasby, because he is a much more fully developed character who has been placed in a particular social and geographical context. When compared to Dooley, Thogmartin feels that Biglow, Ward, and Nasby are "isolated and shadowy figures-- little more than disembodied rural voices."

463. Thomson, Woodruff C. "Mr. Dooley Attends to the 'Nice Little War.'" WHIMSY 4 (1986): 29-31.

Contends that it was Henry Cabot Lodge who called the Spanish-American War of 1898 "the nice little war." Lodge was comparing it with World Wars I and II. This nice little Spanish-American war, and the later Philippine insurrection which it caused, were frequent targets of Finley Peter Dunne's humor. Mr. Dooley, Dunne's protagonist, liked to take the macrocosmic insights of the world and reduce them to the microcosmic insights of Archey Road, a literary device that was not exactly a parable and not exactly a fable but had elements of both. Mr. Dooley sides with those who would keep the Constitution of the United States bound to her shores. He reasons that you can't expect the constitution to fit everywhere in the world just because some American has gone there and planted an American flag. And in typical fashion, Mr. Dooley has a clincher for this Dooleyistic argument: "...No matter whether th' constitution follows th' flag or not, th' supreme coort follows th' iliction returns." This may be a non sequitur, but it's a non sequitur that somehow exhibits a special kind of logic.

464. Yates, Norris W. "Mr. Dooley of Archey Road." The American Humorist: Conscience of the Twentieth Century. Ames, Iowa: Iowa State University Press, 1964, 81-100.

Considers Finley Peter Dunne's Mr. Dooley a culmination of a long line of humorous characters who talked in the dialect of recent immigrants to America, including Charles Godfrey Leland's Hans Breitmann and Charles Follen Adams' Yawcob Strauss, representing the German-American dialect, and Edward Harrigan's Private Miles O'Reilly, representing the Irish-American dialect, and Wallace Irwin's Hashimura Togo, representing the Japanese dialect. Finley Peter Dunne was raised in an immigrant American family. His father was a self-made Catholic who had been born in Ireland and came to America to work first as a carpenter and later as manager of some Chicago real estate. Dunne's attitudes often seem ambiguous and inconsistent. He was skeptical of reformers, yet he himself

crusaded against municipal and financial evils. He slashed out at
various vices, yet he also ridiculed Theodore Parkhurst, himself a
crusader against vice. He compared business to murder and highway
robbery but also said that business was the bulwark of progress.
Yates concludes that Dunne was not being inconsistent; rather, he
was being skeptical, and skepticism tends to aim in all directions.
Yates feels that Dunne's writings exhibit irony and pity but not
sentimentality. Dooley, the solid citizen, gives advice to
Hennessy, but there is little hope that Hennessy will follow the
advice, and even if he does, there is no guarantee that that advice
will be sound.

Harry Leon Wilson (1867-1939)

465. Masson, Thomas L. "Harry Leon Wilson." Our American Humorists.
      Freeport, NY: Books for Libraries, 1931, 303-304.

      Indicates that Wilson was the editor of the old Puck from 1896
to 1902. Wilson coauthored the highly successful The Man from Home
with Booth Tarkington. Masson considers Wilson to have been one of
the few humorists in America who does not write totally from the
first-person perspective and considers Merton of the Movies,
Wilson's last book, his best.

Beatrice Herford (c1868-1952)

466. Masson, Thomas L. "Beatrice Herford." Our American Humorists.
      Freeport, NY: Books for Libraries, 1931, 145-53

      Considers Herford to be a master in the writing of humorous
monologues that succinctly and effectively delineate characters.
These monologues have appeared in America's leading magazines and in
occasional books. Herford's monologues exemplify the old saw that
the best satire is only truth in a thin disguise. Herford gets
material for her monologues almost everywhere--shops, railway
stations, employment agencies, street cars. But the lines which
Herford writes are not funny by themselves. They become funny only
in the context of the specific characterization and situation that
Herford is developing. And after you are familiar with her
monologues, you remember people who fit her descriptions perfectly:
"Mrs. Chaney, or Cousin Abbie, or that woman in the apartment upstairs." There are also portraits of the readers themselves.
However, readers are apt to say, "Well, if that isn't just like that
Mrs. What's-her-name."

Frank McKinney (Kin) Hubbard (1868-1930)

467. Hawes. David S., ed. The Best of Kin Hubbard: Abe Martin's
    Sayings and Wisecracks. Bloomington: Indiana University Press,
    1984, x + 145 pp.

    Feels that there was something special about the grounding of
Kin Hubbard's books in the local Indiana scene. In May 1932 the
state of Indiana dedicated Brown County State Park as a memorial to
Kin Hubbard. They built the rustic Abe Martin Lodge out of native
hardwoods and Brown County stone and filled it with Kin Hubbard
memorabilia. Near the lodge they constructed cabins and named them
after Abe Martin's "neighbors"--Fawn Lippincut, Constable Newt Plum,
Uncle Niles Turner, and the others. Hubbard had gotten his material
by listening for hours to the palaver at the General Store. He knew
most of the roads and villages of Brown County, including Hornettown
Road, Possum Trot Road, Gnaw Bone, Story, and Bean Blossom. Some of
the citizens of Brown County felt offended at Abe Martin's
wisecracks. Others got caught up in Abe's fanciful world and tried
to guess which of Hubbard's characters related to which Brown County
real people. "So and so fits Fawn Lippincut to a T." Hawes used
the reactions to his own presentations in the personna of Abe Martin
to determine which material to include in a book entitled The Best
of Kin Hubbard's Sayings and Wisecracks. He included what he felt
to be the most effective, relevant, and compelling of his humor.

468. McNutt, James C. "Kin Hubbard." Dictionary of Literary
    Biography, Volume 11: American Humorists, 1800-1950. Ed.
    Stanley Trachtenberg. Detroit, MI: Gale, 1982, 219-23.

    Indicates that between 1906 and 1930 Kin Hubbard published a
book of Abe Martin's sayings every year. Eight of these books were
published by commercial publishers, the other sixteen by Abe Martin
Publishing Company. James Whitcomb Riley wrote of the impish Kin
Hubbard, who had never had the patience to finish seventh grade let
alone take formal art training: "The artist, Kin Hubbard's so
keerless/ He draws Abe most eyeless and earless." Hubbard was a
prolific satirist who selected many targets of the day. The
emerging automobile was one of his favorite targets, and he said "It
looks like th' ortomobile wuz goin' t' do way with hoss sense ez
well ez th' hoss." Ironically, in 1919 Kin Hubbard's third child,
a one-year old boy, was killed when their car went out of control
and ran into a creek. Kin Hubbard, like Finley Peter Dunne, was a
Democrat who worked hard for his party. After the Democrats lost a
particularly important election, Hubbard, as a practical joke,
entered the News office heavily bandaged and on crutches. There was
an even more important similarity between Finley Peter Dunne and Kin
Hubbard. Just as Dunne used the personna of Mr. Dooley to express
thoughts he could not have expressed himself; Hubbard used Abe
Martin to do the same.

469. Masson, Thomas L. "Kin Hubbard." Our American Humorists
    Freeport, NY: Books for Libraries Press, 1931, 162-63.

    Indicates that Kin Hubbard took a position on the Indianapolis
News in 1891 as a caricaturist and created the character of Abe
Martin, a small-town philosopher representing the sentiment of a

wild and hilly country without telegraph or railroad in the southern
part of Indiana named Brown County. Hubbard's feature was
syndicated for about eleven years, and at one point the syndication
reached 195 American and Canadian newspapers. Typical Kin Hubbard
aphorisms include "Th' first thing t'turn green in th' spring is
Christmas jewelry" and "Women are just like elephants t' me. I like
t' look at 'em, but I wouldn' want to have one." "Abe Martin's
Sayings" were published every November for sixteen consecutive
years.

470. Yates, Norris W. "Kin Hubbard of Brown County, Indiana."
     The American Humorist: Conscience of the Twentieth Century.
     Ames, Iowa: Iowa State University Press, 1964, 101-112.

     Proves that crackerbox humor still flourished in America in
the 1960s by citing such syndicated columnists as Sydney J. Harris
("Strictly Personal"), Fletcher Knebel ("Potomac Fever"), William E.
Vaughan ("Senator Soaper"). There were also important non-
syndicated crackerbox philosophers, like "Spider" Rowland, who wrote
for the Arkansas Gazette in Little Rock, and Harry Golden, who wrote
for the Carolina Israelite, and Langston Hughes, who wrote for the
Chicago Defender. But the prototypical crackerbox philosopher
during this period was Frank McKinney (Kin) Hubbard, whose "Abe
Martin" was an important feature of American newspapers from 1904
until the author's death in 1930. James Whitcomb Riley wrote an
enthusiastic poem in praise of his fellow Hoosier, Kin Hubbard.
Brander Matthews, E. V. Lucas, George Ade, and Will Rogers all
praised him highly. Kin Hubbard's style was to draw a picture of
Abe, with a caption under him of two or three unrelated sentences,
like "There goes old Ez Pash. By ginger, he's a old timer. He kin
remember when it wuz all right t'be a Dimmycrat." Beginning in 1906
a yearly collection of Hubbard's drawings and sayings began to be
published in the form of a comic almanac reminiscent of the
nineteenth-century "Allminax" of Josh Billings.

Ellis Parker Butler (1869-1937)

471. Masson, Thomas L. "Ellis Parker Butler." Our American
     Humorists. Freeport, NY: Books for Libraries Press, 1931, 73-
     90.

     Indicates that Butler was born in Kansas City but soon moved
to Flushing, New York, a city that "enables a man to escape from New
York with great rapidity." Butler's first attempts at writing were
poetry. He was living in Muscatine at the time, and when a cyclone
hit that city he wrote a serious parody entitled "Blow, Bugles,
Blow." Butler's high school had the tradition of punishing students
for minor infractions by making them write a five-hundred to one-
thousand-word essay and then reading it aloud in class. Butler's
essays on "Trees" or "Prohibition" made the teacher and the students
giggle so much that Butler became addicted to humor. He had wanted
to become a doctor, because that was a profession that made a
college education necessary, and he liked school. He feels that he
would have been a very popular doctor but a very ineffective one.
Because of his love for words, he would have had a great bedside
manner, but he would have too often prescribed arsenic for quinine.

The graveyards would have been full of his patients. Butler's inspiration for <u>Pigs Is Pigs</u> lies partly in the fact that his grandfather was a pork-packer. After writing <u>Pigs Is Pigs</u>, Butler set up residence in Paris, France, to broaden his horizons.

Anne Richmond Warner French (1869-1913)

472. Walker, Nancy, and Zita Dresner, eds. "Anne Richmond Warner French." <u>Redressing the Balance: American Women's Literary Humor from Colonial Times to the 1980s</u>. Jackson: Univ. Press of Mississippi, 1988, 144-62.

Points out that Anne Richmond Warner French wrote as Anne French, Anne Richmond Warner French, and Anne Warner. Susan Clegg, the protagonist in <u>Susan Clegg and Her Friend, Mrs. Lathrop</u> quickly established Warner in the same "local color" tradition as Harriet Beecher Stowe. All five Susan Clegg books are stories about the spinster Susan chatting with her neighbor, Mrs. Lathrop, about men, duty, and the social events of their small town. Since Susan is an excellent gossiper, many of these stories become more monologues than dialogues.

Strickland W. Gillilan (1869-1954)

473. Masson, Thomas L. "S. B. Gillilan." <u>Our American Humorists</u>. Freeport, NY: Books for Libraries, 1931, 127-32.

Traces Gillilan's earliest writing of humorous pieces to the <u>Jackson Herald</u> and the <u>Athens Herald</u>, both newspapers in Ohio. Here he would write squibs and sketches from "Cove Station." Gillilan later wrote light verse and prose sketches for the <u>Sunday Indianapolis Journal</u>. In Richmond, Virginia, he wrote for the <u>Richmond Palladium</u>, and for <u>Life</u>, and in 1897 he published a collection of his pieces in a book entitled, <u>Finnigin</u>, a very funny book.

Edwin Arlington Robinson (1869-1935)

474. Hart, James D. "Edwin Arlington Robinson." <u>The Oxford Companion to Literature</u>. 4th Edition. New York: Oxford University Press, 1965, 718-19.

Quotes one reviewer of Robinson as having said, "The world is not beautiful to him, but a prison house." To this, Robinson responded, "The world is not a 'prisonhouse,' but a kind of spiritual kindergarten where bewildered infants are trying to spell God with the wrong blocks." Robinson's <u>Van Zorn</u> (1914) was a comedy in which the protagonist had the mysterious ability to learn other people's secrets and use this information to help them in solving their personal problems. <u>The Porcupine</u> (1915) was a tragedy based on this same ability.

Carolyn Wells (c1869-1942)

475. Dresner, Zita Zatkin. "Carolyn Wells." _Dictionary of_
      Literary Biography, Volume 11: American Humorists, 1800-1950.
      Ed. Stanley Trachtenberg. Detroit, MI: Gale, 1982, 556-60.

      Considers Carolyn Wells to have been one of America's favorite
parodists and the foremost woman humorist during the first two
decades of the twentieth century. One reviewer remarked that simply
beginning a sentence with "Carolyn Wells says..." would attract
total attention and complete cessation of chatter by any tablefull
of people during this period. At first Frank Gelett Burgess
rejected her nonsense submissions to Lark, but she later became one
of its most important contributors. She had learned from Burgess
the difference between "silliness" and "nonsense." Silliness is
random and personal, while nonsense is "organic, well-ordered, and
almost mathematical in its precision, and in its certainty to hit
the reader or listener straight between the eyes." Wells' A
Phenomenal Fauna and Folly for the Wise offered six- and eight-line
rhymes about such imagined creatures as the Humbug, Feather Boa,
Bookworm, Shuttlecock, Welsh Rabbit, Jail-Bird, Clothes Horse, and
Wall Street Bulls and Bears. As a librarian for the Rahway Library
Association she was a passionate collector for anthologies such as
A Parody Anthology, A Satire Anthology, A Whimsey Anthology, and
many others.

476. Hayward, Malcolm. "Carolyn Wells." _Encyclopedia of American_
      Humorists. Ed. Steven H. Gale. New York: Garland, 1988, 466-
      69.

      Considers the limerick to have been Carolyn Wells' favorite
form. One of her best is "A tutor who tooted the flute,/ Tried to
teach two young tooters to toot;/ Said the two to the Tutor,/ 'Is it
harder to toot or/ To tutor two tooters to toot?'." Her technical
skill in poetry and her well-developed sense of the absurd made
Wells an excellent parodist. She distinguished between "form
rendering" and "sense rendering." Sense rendering "utilizes not
only the original writer's diction and style, but follows a train of
thought precisely along the lines that he would have pursued from
the given premise." For Wells, sense rendering is superior.
Nevertheless, much of Wells' wit lies close to the surface--in the
entanglements of language and wit and wordplay. The irony in her
satires, parodies, nonsense verse, and mixed maxims is noteworthy.
There is a special truth in "A word to the wise is the root of all
evil" or "The course of true love waits for no man" or "A friend in
need is the thief of time." In "The Two Automobilists" she tells
about a "Bold and Audacious" young man who drives his car very fast
and recklessly; he crashes and is killed. Another driver is
"Timorous and Careful"; he drives slowly and cautiously. He gets
hits from behind by two automobiles and an ice wagon; he is also
killed.

477. Masson, Thomas L. "Carolyn Wells." _Our American Humorists_.
      Freeport, NY: Books for Libraries Press, 1931, 305-23.

      Recalls receiving a manuscript from Carolyn Wells when he was
the literary editor of Life. The manuscript contained a number of

amusing satiric verses lampooning ladies who wore ornate hats while
attending the theater. Masson had the article illustrated by Allan
Gilbert and published it, which was a coup for Wells, who had
struggled for years to be accepted. Wells considers her most
important mentor to be Gelett Burgess. Wells started reading
Burgess's Lark and fell in love with the nonsense which it
contained. She wrote to Burgess that she would like to submit
something, and his response was sarcastic and not encouraging. She
sent him a contribution nevertheless, which he criticized severely,
saying that her writing was not up to the mark and that she should
give up trying to write good nonsense. Wells continued to submit
items regularly, and Burgess continued to criticize and ridicule her
work. Burgess never failed to load up her manuscripts with red ink
before returning them. Wells' persistence finally paid off, and
Burgess started publishing her work regularly. Burgess had taught
Wells the difference between silliness and nonsense. Silliness is
chaotic, while nonsense is organic, well ordered, and manufactured
with almost mathematical precision.

478. Walker, Nancy, and Zita Dresner. "Carolyn Wells." Redressing
     the Balance: American Women's Literary Humor from Colonial
     Times to the 1980s. Jackson: Univ. Press of Mississippi 1988
     133-38.

     Considers Wells one of the most acclaimed turn-of-the-
twentieth-century American parodists and also the most significant
female humorist of the first two decades of the 1900s. Wells' was
inspired by the writings not only of Lewis Carroll and Edward Lear
but also of her contemporaries, Gelett Burgess and Oliver Herford.
In Idle Idylls, her best-selling collection of verse, she parodied
the classics, like The Rubayiat of Omar Khayyam, Hamlet's soliloquy
"To Be Or Not To Be," and she also parodied popular songs of the day
like "The Old Oaken Bucket" and the sentimental and nature poetry of
the period. She wrote with a light touch, a lively fancy, and
fluent rhythm. Love, courtship, women's fashions, the images of the
ideal woman, and feminine frailties were frequent targets. She
delighted in verbal wit, word play, puns, and incongruous visual
images. She also published books of games, puzzles, and brain
teasers; poetry and stories for children; two burlesque novels; and
eighty-one mystery novels.

Frank Norris (1870-1902)

479. Caron, James E. "Grotesque Naturalism: The Significance of
     the Comic in McTeague." Texas Studies in Literature and
     Language 31.2 (Summer 1989): 288-317.

     Considers McTeague to be basically a comic novel despite the
abuse and murders of Trina and Maria, the suicide of Zerkow, the
death of Marcus, and the suicidal acts of McTeague himself. It is
a kind of grotesque comedy that leaves McTeague handcuffed to a
corpse in the middle of Death Valley, because McTeague presents the
intriguing relationship between laughter and naturalism.
Furthermore, McTeague is humorous in both senses of the word; it is
peculiar as well as laughable. When read as a comic text, McTeague
suggests how naturalism functions with laughter in both its European

and American variants.   Such a reading furthermore invites a
rereading of the work of Zola and Hardy as comic texts.   But the
most interesting question that such a reading suggests is why Norris
uses laughter in <u>McTeague</u> but not in his other works.   In fact, is
the grotesque naturalism of <u>McTeague</u> actually comic, or is it only
a kind of macabre incongruity?

Stephen Crane (1871-1900)

480. Bellman, Samuel Irving. "Stephen Crane's Vaudeville
Marriage: "The Bride Comes To Yellow Sky." <u>Selected Essays:</u>
<u>International Conference on Wit and Humor, 1986</u>. Ed. Dorothy
M. Joiner. Carrollton, GA: West Georgia College, 1988, 14-19.

Investigates the vaudevillian features of "The Bride Comes To
Yellow Sky" and suggests that Crane had these vaudevillian features
in mind as he wrote the story.   The story can be imagined as
happening on a vaudeville stage, and there are appropriate stage
settings and orchestrated scenes.   There are also a number of comedy
skits--on the train from San Antonio, in the saloon in Yellow Sky,
and on the streets of the town.   The visual imagery of the awkward,
embarrassed couple about to set sail on the sea of matrimony is
comical, and the audience's mind would of course begin to play out
the inevitable comic scenarios.   The stage set for the lavishly
appointed parlor car would be very theatrical--sea-green figured
velvet, shining brass, silver, and glass, gleaming wood, a bronze
figure holding a support for the enclosed lavatory, an olive-and-
silver ceiling fresco--vaudevillian all the way.   Other skits
include the "Newlyweds'Games Number," and the "Showdown between
Potter and Scratchy Wilson Number," and the "Weary-Gentleman-Saloon
Number"--a one-man show performed by a newcomer, a stand-up comic of
sorts, who tells funny stories.

481. Kiley, Frederick, and J. M. Shuttleworth, eds. "Stephen
Crane: Seven Poems." <u>Satire: from Aesop to Buchwald</u>. New York:
Odyssey/Bobbs-Merrill, 1971, 279-301.

Points out that in the 1890s Crane wrote many brief light
verses, about fifty of which were satiric.   "Do Not Weep, Maiden,
for War is Kind" ironically contrasts battlefield reactions to war
with domestic reactions.   "A Newspaper is a Collection of Half-
Injustices" says that a newspaper is a court, a market, a game, a
symbol, and in all of these features it makes up its own rules.
Other poems comment on the pomposities, the religious beliefs, and
the philosophical absurdities of man.   Crane's style and tone can be
summed up in a short poem: "A man said to the universe:/ "Sir, I
exist!"/ "However," replied the universe,/ "The fact has not created
in me/ A sense of obligation."

482. Moseley, Ann. "Dark Laughter: The Comic Spirit in Stephen
Crane's Whilomville Stories." <u>WHIMSY</u> 1 (1983): 53-55.

Discusses the humor in the Crane's "Whilomville Stories."   One
example is "The Stove."   When Jimmie's cousin Cora and her family
come to Whilomville, they bring Cora's play stove with them, a
large, workable, iron stove.   One evening, the mothers are giving a

tea party, so they send the children outside to play. When it begins to snow, the children take the stove down into the cellar, and there they begin to cook "dozens and dozens of puddings for the thousand people at our grea' big hotel." But these "puddings" are really frozen turnips, and before long the strong smell of the cooking turnips wafts upstairs and overpowers the dainty perfumed smells of the tea party. Another example is "Lynx Hunting." In this story Jimmie shoots a cow because he thought it was a lynx. On being told this, Fleming and the Swede roll helplessly with laughter. An important point that Mosely makes in this article is that the lighter humor of the earlier Whilomville stories turns bitter and sardonic. "The laughter darkens; the comedy becomes almost black."

Thomas Augustine Daly (1871-1948)

483. Williams, Patricia Owens. "T. A. Daly." <u>Dictionary of Literary Biography, Volume 11: American Humorists, 1800-1950</u>. Detroit, MI: Gale, 1982, 100-102.

Considers Daly's greatest skill as a writer to be his humorous dialect. He wrote humorous and patriotic verses in Italian, Irish, Negro, and even French dialect, and he frequently added a section of more serious love poems in standard English at the ends of his books. Daly's organ-grinders, fruit peddlers, and barbers use their wit in coping with the joys and sorrows of everyday living. <u>Canzoni</u> is mainly a book of dialect poems. <u>Carmina</u> is rhymed verse about Italian and Irish immigrants doing their best to become good Americans; many of the poems have surprise endings. <u>McAroni Ballads and Other Verses</u> treats the fruit peddler Tony McAroni and his Italian friends with humor, pathos, and sympathy. Daly's warm, humorous tone in his treatment of his large family can be seen in the long title of <u>Herself and the Houseful: Being the Middling-Mirthful Story of a Middle-Class American Family of More than Middle Size</u>. Daly was criticized for being a versifier rather than a poet. His work was often described as comic and clever, ironically, qualities which Daly did not consider positive for humorous verse. Daly was a sentimentalist in a time when the <u>New Yorker</u> was developing the style of acerbic wit. He has been described as the "poet laureate of the peanut peddler."

Arthur Guiterman (1871-1943)

484. Terrie, Philip G. "Arthur Guiterman." <u>Dictionary of Literary Biography, Volume 11: American Humorists, 1800-1950</u>. Detroit, MI: Gale, 1982, 165-68.

Considers Guiterman's humorous verse to have been the cause of his popularity while he was writing and his sole attraction today, even though Guiterman also wrote contemplations on nature, patriotic ballads, philosophical aphorisms, and love poems. His serious poetry is superficial and uninspired and mostly ignored by critics. Guiterman felt that the critics disliked him because he "defended the values of traditional verse against radicals and pessimists."

His humorous verse was at times filled with jingoistic militancy or romantic sentimentality, but it also sparkled with clever rhymes and wry comments.   In 1916 he was awarded the dubious distinction of being judged by Joyce Kilmer to be "the most American of all poets." The Laughing Muse, Guiterman's first collection of humorous verse, contained clever poems assaulting modern life such as "The Quest of the Car," and "Auto-Buy-O-Graphic Mode."   In his later years Guiterman joked that he could become president of the United States any time he wanted to. He may have half-heartedly actually believed this.

Clarence Shepard Day, Jr. (1874-1935)

485. Schwartz, Richard Alan.   "Clarence Day." Dictionary of
      Literary Biography, Volume 11: American Humorists 1800-1950.
      Detroit, MI: Gale, 1982, 108-13.

      Considers Day to have been unconventional in a number of respects, such as eating breakfast at 9:00 P.M. and entertaining guests in the middle of the night. Women were attracted to him though he treated them badly. When they brought him flowers, he would toss them out of the window. The Simian World explains the ramifications of man's evolution from apes. Humans like vaudeville and slapstick humor. If we had evolved from eagles, such humor would merely bore us. If we had evolved from felines, the resultant super-cat city at night would be sparkling with jewels and filled with aquariums; mice would be raised by cat-farmers rather than chickens; and parks would contain lush fields of catnip. The Crow's Nest and After All contain mostly essays and comic parables in the style that James Thurber later perfected. Thoughts Without Words and Scenes from the Mesozoic consists of Day's humorous drawings and light verse satirizing human nature, social conventions, and civilizations.   There is, for example, a drawing of Adam and Eve towering over God and the Devil. The caption reads, "So Adam created two beings, Jehovah and Satan. Yea, in his own image created he them." Thoughts also contains excellent examples of "little man humor" which Benchley and Thurber were developing at the same time.

486. Schwartz, Richard Alan. "Clarence Shepard Day, Jr."
      Encyclopedia of American Humorists. Ed. Steven H. Gale. New
      York: Garland, 1988, 113-17.

      Feels that Day's writing represented a transition between the robust tall tale humor of the American frontier and the witty, cynical, self-deprecating humor of twentieth-century American cities. As an early contributor to the fledgling New Yorker, Day's early humor is witty and philosophical, satirizing human frailties and shortcomings.   In these early writings, Day's work is characterized by puns, incongruities, and clever word play, as well as excessive punctuation and overstatement, but these devises were replaced by a more subtle and understated style in his later works. This Simian World fantasizes about alternative evolutions. If we had evolved from cats our love making would be fierce and capricious and sudden. "How hostile, how ecstatic, how violent." If we had evolved from cows, on the other hand, our lives would be much more pastoral. We would be able to contemplate a single thoughts for hours or days. "Our minds would not possess the simian's short attention span."

487. Yates, Norris W. "Life with Clarence Day, Jr." The American Humorist: Conscience of the Twentieth Century. Ames: Iowa State University Press, 1964, 229-40.

Traces Day's beginnings as a humorist when he was secretary of the Yale Class of 1896 and had charge of writing the Decennial Record. To make the Record more interesting Day was frequently candid and satirically droll. By 1914 Day was writing for Metropolitan and the New Republic. He developed the ability to both satirize and defend the reformers who wrote for and read these two magazines. Day's drawings appear in The Crow's Nest, After All and Scenes from the Mesozoic; and in Thoughts Without Words the drawings virtually took the place of the words altogether. Day liked to draw the bumbler or henpecked husband with a face very like his own.

Robert Frost (1874-1963)

488. Gage, John T. "Humour En Garde: Comic Saying in Robert Frost's Poetic." Thalia: Studies in Literary Humor 4.1 (Spring/Summer 1981): 54-61.

States that readers of Frost's poetry are well aware of Frost's wit and whimsy and his direct and indirect humorous assault. In "The Mountain," Frost tells about a magic brook that's always cold in the summer but warm in the winter. He explains later in the poem that the water is actually the same temperature and that actually it's only warm compared with cold, or cold compared with warm. He concludes the poem, "But all the fun's in how you say a thing." In "U.S. 1946 King's X" Frost tells about America's inventing a new kind of Holocaust. He continues that after we have used this new invention to win the war, we cross our fingers and cry out, "King's X--no fair to use it anymore." Frost developed the humorous genre of the "rigamarole," a combination of unrelated ideas that can be merged into a single statement, but his poetry is non-conventional. He himself remarks, "It takes all sorts of in- and outdoor schooling/ To get adapted to my kind of fooling." When one of Frost's pious friends remarked "Love thy neighbor as thyself," Frost rejoined, "And hate thy neighbor as thyself." This seems to be an illustration of Frost's most famous poem, "Forgive, O Lord, my little jokes on Thee/ And I'll forgive Thy great big one on me."

489. Kiley, Frederick, and J. M. Shuttleworth, eds. "Robert Frost: Three Poems." Satire: from Aesop to Buchwald. New York: Odyssey, 1971, 341-344.

Notes that Frost seldom satirizes individual people, events, or institutions. He rather prefers to write more general satire, often understating and suggesting rather than railing forth. His "Departmental" is a low burlesque about bureaucracy. His "The Bear" ridicules certain human attitudes by contrasting the bear and man. His "Forgive, O Lord" is a poem about "the big one"--"the cosmic joke."

490. Wallace, Ronald. "Robert Frost." <u>God Be with the Clown:</u>
      <u>Humor in American Poetry</u>. Columbia: University of Missouri
      Press, 1984, 107-39.

      Considers Frost's most effective quality as a humorous poet
his ability to embrace contradictory feelings, affirming and
questioning both of these feelings at the same time. Frost's
sentimentality, his conservative politics, his conventional verse
form appeal to popular readers who prefer the comfortable and the
familiar. But his skepticism about God and religion, his feelings
of isolation, limitation, and ignorance, and his awareness of the
difficulties of human communication appeal to the more serious
critics. Frost's humorous images are delightful. In "A Hillside
Thaw" the sun frees ten million lizards out of the snow, breaking
them into a run, and finally into a stampede, a wet stampede of
slithering wiggling lizards. He says that the sun is a wizard and
the moon is a witch, for the moon casts her spell and turns the
lizards to stone: "The swarm was turned to rock." Frost considered
humor to be an expression of fear and inferiority. He felt that the
world is not a joke, but that we joke about it to avoid
confrontation.   He felt that humor was a way of engaging in
cowardice and admitted that he himself had used humor frequently to
hold his enemies in play and far out of gunshot. Wallace, however,
feels that Frost used humor not merely as a strategy to avoid
confrontation but as a strategy to <u>win</u> confrontations.

<u>Alice Duer Miller (1874-1942)</u>

491. Walker, Nancy, and Zita Dresner. "Alice Duer Miller."
      <u>Redressing the Balance: American Women's Literary Humor from</u>
      <u>Colonial Times to the 1980s</u>. Jackson: Univ. Press of
      Mississippi, 1988, 202-206.

      Portrays Miller as having deep feminist convictions despite
the lighthearted and often satiric tone of her novels, stories, and
newspaper columns. "Are Women People?" ran in the <u>New York Tribune</u>
from 1914 until 1917, and in 1915 a collection of her satiric verses
appeared under the same title. Miller continues the tradition of
Marietta Holley and other nineteenth-century feminist writers who
found women's oppression patently absurd.

<u>Gertrude Stein (c1874-1946)</u>

492. Isaak, Jo-Anna. "Gertrude Stein: The Revolutionary Power of
      a Woman's Laughter." <u>WHIMSY</u> 3 (1985): 32-35.

      Laments that so much Stein criticism has focused on the person
rather than on her work. There are reasons for this, however.
Stein was an interesting person, led an interesting life, and was a
close   acquaintance   to   a   lot   of   other   interesting   persons.
Furthermore, her writing is boring, repetitious, nonsensical, and
very difficult to read. But struggling with Stein can nevertheless
be rewarding. Much of Stein's writing investigates what she calls
"the recreation of the word." She once did an experiment with words

to find out if it is possible for them to be pure nonsense--for them not to have any meaning at all--and she discovered that this was not possible. Once a person uses a word, it has meaning. Furthermore, Stein discovered that when individual words are put down next to other words there is no such thing as putting them together without sense. She made many efforts to put words together in a way that made no sense and found it impossible. "Any human being putting down words had to make sense of them." Stein played with the sounds, the rhythms, the repetitions of words and discovered a regenerative power. Her "A rose is a rose is a rose" was the result of her frustration with the flatness of overworked nouns. She considered a noun to be completely uninteresting unless it is revitalized. She placed her nouns into a ring and made poetry by addressing and caressing the nouns.

493. Schmitz, Neil. Of Huck and Alice: Humorous Writing in American Literature. Minneapolis: University of Minnesota Press, 1983, 269 pp.

Presents an enigmatic title. The "Huck" is clearly "Huck Finn," and it would seem that the "Alice" refers to "Alice in Wonderland." In fact, the "Alice" being referred to is "Alice B. Toklas," Gertrude Stein's lover, for whom Stein wrote an "autobiography" entitled Tender Buttons. That title was chosen because it was Alice's job to take care of Gertrude Stein or, in other words, to "tend her buttons." Richard Bridgman describes Stein's writing as "rather like listening to an interminable tape recording made secretly in a household." B. L. Reid was even less kind. He considers Stein to be a vulgar genius who is talking to herself and therefore offers insurmountable difficulties for the reader and the critic. He suggests, therefore that she be "defined out of existence as an artist." Janet Hobhouse says that her writing is strewn with irksome nettles and recounts the story of Ernest Hemingway's sending a copy of his recently published Death in the Afternoon along with a circular inscription reading "A bitch is a Bitch is a Bitch." The inscription was signed, "Your pal, Ernest Hemingway."

494. Walker, Nancy, and Zita Dresner. "Gertrude Stein." Redressing the Balance: American Women's Literary Humor from Colonial Times to the 1980s. Jackson: University Press of Mississippi, 1988, 163-68.

Describes Stein as a literary pioneer, who argues against traditional narrative and borrows heavily from cubism, cinema, and the theories of William James. Stein used repetition to achieve immediacy and to communicate essences. Beginning in her Tender Buttons in 1914, Stein developed a writing style that employed enigmatic linguistic structures and extravagant lexical experiments. She was both praised and condemned for these innovations. In 1933 Stein published The Autobiography of Alice B. Toklas, which is in truth an autobiography, because it presents the life of Gertrude Stein as seen through the eyes of Alice B. Toklas as perceived by Gertrude Stein. Alice B. Toklas was Stein's companion from 1911 until Stein's death in 1946. This autobiography was celebrated for its wit and was Stein's first commercial success. Neil Schmitz suggests that Stein's humorous style developed out of the double-talk that was present in Tender Buttons and further suggests that

Stein's linguistic innovations are intended to deconstruct, through irony, the traditional sex roles of men and women. Stein's work is a parody of both the domestic speech of mothers and the philosophical writing of fathers.

Helen Rowland (1875-1950)

495. Walker, Nancy, and Zita Dresner. "Helen Rowland." Redressing the Balance: American Women's Literary Humor from Colonial Times to the 1980s Jackson: Univ. Press of Mississippi, 1988, 251-56.

Traces the beginning of Rowland's writing career to a satiric dialogue that she sold to the Washington Post at the age of sixteen. When her first marriage ended, Rowland began writing a weekly satiric column for the World, and this article became syndicated when it was seen by S. S. McClure, the founder of the first newspaper syndicate in the United States. Rowland's column changed from "Widow Wordalogues," to "The Sayings of Mrs. Solomon," to "Meditations of a Married Woman," to "Marry-go-Round" while it was under syndication, but the themes remained constant: "Men are vain and faithless," "women are at their mercy," and "marriage is an inherently unequal relationship." Rowland's "It Must Be Thrilling to Be a Man" is reminiscent of Charlotte Perkins Gilman's "If I Were a Man." Both assume that men's clothes and bodies and lives are more comfortable than are those of a woman. Rowland's "Why Can't a Woman be 'Middle-Aged'?" attacks the requirement in our culture that women must retain at all cost their youthful beauty.

Sherwood Anderson 1876-1941)

496. Krauth, Leland. "Sherwood Anderson's Buck Fever; or, Frontier Humor Comes to Town." Studies in American Humor 3.4 (Winter 1984-85): 298-308.

Indicates that in the summer of 1925 Anderson moved to Virginia, purchased two country newspapers (the Smyth County News, and the Marion Democrat), became their editor, and started the southern phase of his writing. By the third issues of his two weekly newspapers, Anderson had created the comic character, Buck Fever, and by the sixth issues of these papers Buck Fever had his own column--"Buck Fever Says." Anderson explained that he invented Buck Fever and provided him with a full personal history, a distinct voice, and an idiosyncratic perspective, because he couldn't afford to pay for a live reporter. The regional personna of the oral storyteller, Buck Fever, was transitional between the predominately rustic humor of the nineteenth century to the predominately urbane humor of the twentieth. In order to get material for the Buck Fever column and improve on the presentation of the material, Anderson made his newspaper office in Marion, Virginia, a gathering place, where local citizens of both townsman and farmer variety could sit around and chat. The resultant humor was Southwestern in character with its awareness of the nation, its perception of the frontier, and its feelings of the importance of newspapers as a cultural medium.

497. **Weber, Brom.** Sherwood Anderson. Minneapolis: University of
     Minnesota Press, 1964, 48 pp.

     Feels that Anderson was influenced by Gertrude Stein's experimentation with language in Tender Buttons. In his Marching Men, Anderson says that it is terrible how humans have been defeated by their inability to use words effectively. We go through life as "...socialists, dreamers, makers of laws, sellers of goods and believers of suffrage for women and we continuously say words, worn-out words, crooked words, words without power or pregnancy in them." Anderson feels that the brown bear in the forest is not reduced to such a state. Because the bear is not defeated by the words he uses, it has a kind of nobility that is lacking in man.

Sarah Norcliffe Cleghorn (1876-1915)

498. **Kiley, Frederick, and J. M. Shuttleworth, eds.** "Sarah
     Cleghorn: Quatrain." Satire from Aesop to Buchwald. New York:
     The Odyssey Press, 1971, 291.

     Contrasts the quiet irony on the surface of the following poem with the bitter social satire that lies beneath the surface: "The golf links lie so near the mill/ That almost every day/ The laboring children can look out/ And see the men at play."

Irvin S. Cobb (1876-1944)

499. **Engle, Gary.** Encyclopedia of American Humorists. Ed. Steven
     H. Gale. New York: Garland, 1988, 91-93.

     Portrays Cobb as a prolific author of humorous short stories, travel books, and familiar essays, who, during the first half of the twentieth century, was America's most famous after-dinner speaker. Cobb's books were mostly collections of his magazine pieces, and he averaged about two books per year. He developed the character of Judge Priest whose wit was dry and kind. Cobb continued the simplistic conventions of the nineteenth-century local color movement. His Roughing It Delux was influenced by Twain's Roughing It and treated such topics as western topography, Mormonism, curio vendors, and trail guides. One of the better sections was a satire about California boosterism. Cobb's Some United States was another travel book; it contains seventeen comical essays on various regional stereotypes. His Europe Revised is based on the notion of the American innocent abroad, with a witty criticism also of the European tourism industry. The book Cobb is most remembered for is Speaking of Operations... which describes his rather severe surgery. This book is conversational, witty, and well focused. Cobb had a photographic memory, and most of his books have a rambling and long-winded style though they are also humorous, witty, and insightful. Cobb's autobiography, Exit Laughing was published in 1941 and was his last major work.

500. Lieb, Sandra. "Irvin S. Cobb." Dictionary of Literary
      Biography, Volume 11: American Humorists, 1800-1950. Detroit,
      MI: Gale, 1982, 82-88.

      Considers Cobb to have been one of the most versatile and
successful humorists of his day. He was an author, journalist,
after-dinner speaker, lecturer, radio personality, screenwriter, and
Hollywood actor. He wrote hundreds of short stories and nearly
sixty books. For the Louisville Evening Post he wrote a humor
column entitled "Kentucky Sour Mash," which included political
satire, comic verse, and portraits of Kentucky stereotypes. Later,
for the World he wrote a daily column entitled "Through Funny
Glasses," a humor page for the Sunday section, and another popular
column entitled "Hotel Clerk." At this same time he was also
writing comic pieces for the McClure syndicate. When his friend
Charles Chaplin fell ill, the witty curmudgeon Cobb quipped, "Let's
hope it's nothing trivial." In the Cobb's Anatomy, he made comic
observations about tummies, teeth, hair, hands, and feet. His
Cobb's-Bill-of-Fair talked about vittles, music, art, and sports.
And his Speaking of Operations gives a witty account of the
indignities of being in a hospital for an operation. Cobb continued
the tradition of Southwestern story telling and local color; however
a more important contribution was the early development of "the
little soul at the mercy of the twentieth century." setting the
stage for Thurber, Benchley, and black comedy.

501. Masson, Thomas L. "Irvin Cobb." Our American Humorists.
      Freeport, NY: Books for Libraries, 1931, 91-103.

      Disagrees with Cobb who described himself as fat and homely.
"I don't know of any man that I would rather look at than Irvin
Cobb, and I am not joking about this." Although Cobb's Speaking of
Operations appears to be impersonal, it is actually just the
opposite. People who read the book get the impression that Cobb is
not writing about himself; he is writing about them. They are
amazed that Cobb knows so much about their operations.

502. Yates, Norris W. "The Crackerbarrel Sage in the West and
      South: Will Rogers and Irvin S. Cobb." The American Humorist:
      Conscience of the Twentieth Century. Ames: Iowa State Univ.
      Press, 1964, 113-36.

      Traces   the   nineteenth-century   sit-around-the-hot-stove
tradition of crackerbarrel philosophy to have continued in America
in the Western writings of Will Rogers and the southern writings of
Irvin S. Cobb.   This tradition is associated with rugged
individualism, conservative politics, and stability in the home.

Josephine Dodge Dascam (Bacon) (1876-1961)

503. Walker, Nancy, and Zita Dresner. "Josephine Dodge Dascam Bacon." Redressing the Balance: American Women's Literary Humor from Colonial Times to the 1980s. Jackson: Univ. Press of Mississippi, 1988, 139-43.

Considers Dascam to have been a prolific author of short stories, novels, articles, and poems. Her married name was Josephine Bacon, but she mostly wrote under her maiden name of Josephine Dascam. Dascam's The Memoirs of a Baby is a satire on the various theories of child raising. It is grounded in the fact that Dascam raised three children of her own. Dascam wrote much poetry, and she edited two books of verse, one a book of nonsense verse, and one a more serious book entitled Truth o' Women: Last Words from Ladies Long Vanished. Dascam's Fables for the Fair is an early book and one which demonstrates her feminist stance. It is subtitled, Cautionary Tales, and is addressed to the "new woman." Dascam warns the reader that although there is indeed a "new woman" in her reading audience, they are not likely to find a corresponding "new man," which Dascam defined as "one ready to accept her education, independence, and ambitions." This "new man" is contained in the moral of each of Dascam's fables as a concept that has unfortunately not yet come to fruition.

Mary Roberts Rinehart (1876-1958)

504. Walker, Nancy, and Zita Dresner, eds. Redressing the Balance: American Women's Literary Humor from Colonial Times to the 1980s. Jackson: Univ. Press of Mississippi, 1988, 176-201.

Considers the protagonist, Tish, to have been a unique and vibrant character in American humor and one of Rinehart's greatest achievements. The first "Tish" story was published in The Saturday Evening Post, and stories appeared from 1910 until 1937. They were later collected into seven volumes. They all dealt with the humorous adventures of the indomitable spinster, Letitia Carberry, a character who has many traits in common with Miss Rachel Innes, the narrator of Rinehart's mystery, The Circular Staircase. Both characters present a strange mixture of old-fashioned ideals and independent behavior, of genteel mannerisms coupled with an irresistible attraction to adventure. In addition to the Tish series, Rinehart wrote children's verses, satiric poems, and stories of all kinds--comic, romantic, and grotesque.

Frederick Irving Anderson (1877-1947)

505. Fisher, Benjamin. "Frederick Irving Anderson's Godahl: Con Man Extraordinaire." WHIMSY 3 (1986): 26-29.

Portrays Anderson's Godahl as devil-like in his ability to hoodwink unsuspecting antagonists and then walk away without a

rumple to his arrogant elegance. From the beginning of <u>Adventures</u>,
Godahl is associated with games and game-playing. Godahl has a
veneer of gentility which covers his core of violence. He is
constantly ready to explode into unforeseen horrors, thereby
mingling the terror with the comedy. "The infallible Godahl" is
actually a thief and a murderer who attempts to obtain the great
white ruby from Mrs. Wentworth, appropriately named because she is
a collector of valuable <u>objets d'art</u>. Godahl is able to con people
and play jokes on them because he is aware of their human vanity.
In "The Night of a Thousand Thieves," Godahl plays such a joke, as
he cajoles a crackpot inventor into springing a burglar-alarm
system. The inventor, ironically named "Merwin" believes that he
has just won a wager; however, Godahl uses the diversion to purloin
the valuable Bentori crucifix from Old Ludwig Telfens's
depositories. Anderson underscores the joking nature of the story
with the repetitions of "He-he..." and then in the next line, "He!
He! Yes--he. Who was he?"

Arthur Folwell (1877-?)

506. Masson, Thomas L. "Arthur Folwell." <u>Our American Humorists</u>.
     Freeport, New York: Books for Libraries Press, 1931, 120-123.

          Portrays Folwell as a "schlemiel." Folwell submitted a poem
to <u>Collier's Weekly</u>. The editor wrote him that his poem was
accepted for publication and that he would be paid for the poem.
Folwell immediately wrote back accepting the offer but then waited
a long time without receiving the money. Finally, he got a letter
from <u>Collier's Weekly</u>, returning his manuscript with a note saying,
"You have delayed so long answering our letter, we are compelled to
return your poem." Folwell edited a paper for five years, the first
contribution of which was a parody on "The Charge of the Light
Brigade." He later worked on the <u>Eagle</u> for six years--on sports
first, then as a general reporter, and finally as the city editor.
This last position allowed him to write funny stories and to compose
humorous verse and humorous specials for the Sunday paper
(anonymously and without extra pay). At this time he wrote
burlesque country news items, one of which was called "This Week's
Brooklyn Budget," which he sent to America's <u>Puck</u>. He sent
everything to <u>Puck</u>, and whatever they turned down he would submit to
the <u>Eagle</u>. He finally became the literary editor of <u>Puck</u>. In 1904
he was fired by John Kendrick Bangs and later rehired for a lower
salary, but eventually he succeeded Bangs as editor.

Montague Glass (1877-1934)

507. Masson, Thomas L. "Montague Glass." <u>Our American Humorists</u>.
     Freeport, New York: Books for Libraries, 1931, 133-44.

          Indicates that Glass has made more people genuinely laugh than
anyone else he knows. Masson says that if he were cast away on a
desert island with the <u>Encyclopedia Britannica</u>, and he could
exchange the encyclopedia for anything he wanted, he would exchange
it for Montague Glass. "Mr. Glass has all of the information

contained in the 'Encyclopaedia,' and besides this, he has a highly developed sense of humor and likes to talk about Max Beerbohm." Glass portrays the Jews as the most introspective and imaginative class of people in the world. He accurately interprets the Jew through humor. He does not use satire; rather he uses "atmosphere." Glass is a reporter, and he has reported on the Jews so that people no longer laugh at them but rather with them. Masson says that Glass is a good humorist and that a good humorist can soften down our prejudices and give us all a sort of community spirit. He feels that for humorists, age is a great mellower--that a really good humorist just gets going good at the age of a hundred or so, which is why really good humorists should never be allowed to die.

508. Simms, L. Moody, Jr. "Montague Glass." Encyclopedia of American Humorists. Ed. Steven H. Gale. New York: Garland, 1988, 175-78.

Feels that one of Glass's favorite subjects was mannerisms and the speech of Jewish immigrants working in the garment trade. He used warm and affectionate humor to describe these immigrants. Glass wrote a series of stories featuring Potash and Perlmutter that editors were reluctant to publish because they felt that the one-dimensional ethnic stereotypes could offend both Jewish readers and Jewish advertisers. Nevertheless, in 1910 he published his masterpiece, Potash and Perlmutter, a book about two Jewish cloak and suit salesmen in New York's garment district in the early 1900s. Perlmutter was an idealist while Potash was a pessimist. The book relies heavily on dialect writing, including misspellings, shifts of syntax, apostrophes, and other rhetorical devices. People in the book drive "oitermobiles" and drink "tchampanyer." In 1911 Glass published a sequel to Potash and Perlmutter entitled Abe and Mawruss. In 1928 he published a poetic farce entitled A Full and True Account of the Prodigious Experiment Brought to Perfection in Boston at Father Burke's Academy. This book was published under the pseudonym of Theophilus Cossart and was written in the spirit of Benjamin Franklin's Poor Richard, but it was nevertheless based to a large extent on his own life.

509. Sojka, Gregory. "Montague Glass." Dictionary of Literary Biography, Volume 11: American Humorists, 1800-1950. Detroit, Michigan: Gale, 1982, 151-55.

Portrays Glass as essentially a humorist intent on softening the prejudices and suspicians that many Americans and British felt toward the Jews in the early twentieth century. His play about Morris ("Mawruss") Perlmutter and Abraham ("Abe") Potash ran on Broadway for a twenty-five year period. Glass studied law at New York University and published both humorous prose and humorous poetry in the school's literary journal, Item. In 1909 when his income from writing exceeded his salary, he resigned as a lawyer to devote full time to his writing. He wrote for the Saturday Evening Post, Cosmopolitan, Life, Hampton's Broadway Magazine and other slicks of the time. Potash and Perlmutter, Glass's protagonists, upheld the Protestant work ethic by working long hours and by being honest and humble. Glass's schlemiel characters resemble Isaac Bachevis Singer's "Gimpel," Paul Goodman's "Jonah," Bernard Malamud's "Fidelman," Saul Bellow's "Herzog," and Philip Roth's "Portnoy." In all of these cases the comic situations derive from

the need to bridge the chasm between the spiritual claim that Jews
are the "Chosen People" and their actual humble material and social
situations.

Burges Johnson (1877-1963)

510. **Masson, Thomas L. "Burges Johnson."** Our American Humorists.
Freeport, NY: Books for Libraries, 1931, 182-83.

Considers Johnson to be both a humanist and a humorist. Many
Johnson pieces have been published in Harper's and Everybody's
magazine, and for a year, Johnson was editor-in-chief of Judge.
Johnson published a number of books, including volumes of verse and
essays.

Don Marquis (1878-1937)

511. **Arnold, St. George Tucker, Jr. "Don Marquis, Archy and
Mehitabel, and the Triumph of Comic Vitality: Cats and
Cockroaches on the Darkling Plain"** Thalia: Studies in Literary
Humor 5.2 (Fall & Winter 1982-83): 3-13.

Describes Marquis' mehitabel as a cat who once lived in the
body of Cleopatra and who now must live up to the erotic standards
set for her by the temptress of the Nile. In order to do this,
mehitabel must ignore a great deal of her present degrading and
mundane environment. Arnold describes Marquis' archy as also having
a human soul--this time transmigrated into the body of a cockroach
as punishment for having written such awful free verse when he was
a human. But despite his lowly state, archy still maintains the
highest of aesthetic standards. As an insect, archy must keep
constantly moving on icy nights to keep from freezing to death, and
as a poet he translates this into lyric, into dance, and into song.
When the reader sees his poetry, he quickly realizes why archy had
to be changed from a poet to a bug. Archy writes of mehitabel,
"Whirl mehitabel whirl / flirt your tail and spin / dance to the
tune your guts will cry / when they string a violin." The poet
archy is trying very hard to work his way from bug back up to poet,
and that is why his poetry is so intense, alternating between crying
with rage and weeping with self-pity.

512. **Jaffe, Dan. "Don Marquis."** Dictionary of Literary
Biography, Volume 11: American Humorists, 1800-1950. Ed.
Stanley Trachtenberg. Detroit, MI: Gale, 1982, 309-16.

Indicates that Don Marquis was born at 3 PM on July 29, 1878,
during an eclipse of the sun. Marquis feels that being born during
an eclipse left him with sort of a "cosmic caul" covering his life.
Archy was Marquis' cockroach character, and he wrote messages on
Marquis' typewriter addressed to "dear boss," for Marquis to publish
in his column, "The Sun Dial." Marquis attributed to archy the
cockroach and mehitabel the cat so much vitality that they couldn't
die. He tried to kill them off a number of times, and each time he
did there was such a public outcry that he had to resurrect them.

Reviving them was easy, though, for all he had to do was transmigrate their souls into other cockroach and cat bodies losing hardly any literary momentum in the process. During his lifetime, Marquis published twenty books, many of them collections of his poems, parodies, vignettes, commentaries, and epigrams originally published in newspapers and magazines. In addition to archy and mehitabel, he developed the character of Hermione to attack pseudo-intellectuality, superficiality, and the tendency to self congratulation. Marquis' works are not enjoyed by the people who know things absolutely, the fanatics, the too easily enthusiastic, in short, by many of those who are in charge.

513. **Masson, Thomas L. "Don Marquis." Our American Humorists.** Freeport, NY: Books for Libraries, 1931, 247-260.

Indicates that many non-American critics of Don Marquis have contended that he is the best writer of humor in America. To some extent, Masson agrees with this evaluation, but he feels that Marquis is uneven and adds, "I think, at his best, he is the best." Marquis is very readable. He has the uncanny ability to express what we all feel. And he is especially adept in portraying the struggle of the soul. Nevertheless, Masson also feels that the reader of Marquis reads on and on, knowing that what he is reading is nonsense and possibly not the best of nonsense. But it is more. it is subtle satire--satire about people's interractions and satire about how we express ourselves about those interractions.

514. O'Connor, Robert H. "Don Marquis." **Encyclopedia of American Humorists.** Ed. Steven H. Gale. New York: Garland, 1988, 309-14.

Feels that most of Marquis' humor developed out of the American urban experience. Marquis created Hermione to display the hatred he had of intellectual and artistic pretensions, the epitome of which were to be found in the clubs and coffee houses of Greenwich village. Hermione is constantly "taking up in a serious way" things like Russians, purification through suffering, the exotic in poetry and art, and prison reform. Hermione's short attention span "is exceeded only by the extent of her hypocrisy." Much of Marquis' characterization of Clem Hawley is achieved through dialect humor. Clem's observations about Prohibition are told in the style of a cracker-barrel philosopher with a great deal of first-hand knowledge. Archy the cockroach writes poetry by diving headfirst onto the keys of Marquis' typewriter, and his inability to hit the capital key results in poetry setting the stage for the poetry of e. e. cummings. Archy appears to be writing about mehitabel the cat but is instead writing about the troubled lives of all suffering creatures who live in New York's tenements and back alleys. Many people might have objected if Marquis had written about the sexual adventures of a liberated woman; however, no one could object to his writing about the promiscuities of an alley cat. "Mehitabel is not a one-tom feline."

515. Yates, Norris W. "The Many Masks of Don Marquis." The American
    Humorist: Conscience of the Twentieth Century. Ames, Iowa:
    Iowa State University Press, 1964, 195-218.

    Compares Marquis' career with that of George Ade, Will Rogers,
Irvin S. Cobb, and Ring Lardner, in that they all came from a small
town in the Midwest, and all achieved much success in the big city.
In 1907, Joel Chandler Harris hired Don Marquis as the assistant
editor of Uncle Remus's Magazine. During this period, Marquis wrote
a personal column entitled, "A Glance in Passing." Marquis later
wrote a Broadway hit entitled The Old Soak, which was a
dramatization of the crackerbarrel philosopher in his column.
Marquis created Archy and Mehitabel while he was still writing for
Uncle Remus's Magazine as a way of justifying his use of free verse
as column filler. Marquis' reincarnation of Archy was in the
tradition of John Kendrick Bangs, George Ade, and Wallace Irwin, who
had already made fun of spiritualism, transmigration, and other
occult phenomena. In "The Coming of Archy," Marquis explains how he
one day entered his office earlier than usual to find a cockroach
jumping up and down on his typewriter's keys. On looking more
closely at what the bug had written, Marquis discovered the
following message: "expression is the need of my soul / i was once
a vers libre bard / but i died and my soul went into the body of a
cockroach." Marquis' only regret is that he will be remembered
through history as the author who created a cockroach.

William Pen Adair Rogers (1879-1935)

516. Gragert, Steven K. Ed. "How To Be Funny" and Other Writings
    of Will Rogers. Stillwater, OK: Oklahoma State Univ. Press,
    1983, xv + 187 pp.

    Claims that during his lifetime Will Rogers published more
than two million printed words. The present volume was supported by
Oklahoma State University and the Will Rogers Memorial Commission.
It contains a funny analysis of both humor and of humorists. Other
subjects are politics, aviation, heroes, show business, geographical
chauvinism, running, diplomacy, the presidency, prohibition,
boosterism, and many more.

517. Heller, Terry L. "Will Rogers." Dictionary of Literary
    Biography, Volume 11: American Humorists, 1800-1950. Detroit,
    MI: Gale, 1982, 404-09.

    Considers Rogers to be the last of the cracker-barrel
philosophers, the rural tradition of a bunch of guys gathered around
the crackerbarrel all transfixed on the witty talker who keeps them
all laughing while he sums up their thoughts, tells amusing tales,
and occasionally creates a pungent aphorism like "All I know is what
I read in the papers." Rogers loved to travel. He sailed to South
America and from there worked his way to South Africa, where he
joined Texas Jack's Wild West Show as a trick rider. He later
toured New Zealand and Australia in circuses. Much later in life,
Rogers went to Europe, where he wrote a column for the New York
Times entitled "Will Rogers Says." This ran as a syndicated wire
until his death. Rogers also traveled to Russia and wrote There's

not a Bathing Suit in Russia. His travel pieces are much more unified than his earlier works and show his ability to sustain humorous narrative and present a cohesive world view. In 1931 when Will Durant asked Rogers about his philosophy, he replied "There ain't nothing to life but satisfaction" and then added that the American Indians were the most civilized, because they were the most satisfied. Rogers was an enthusiastic supporter of air safety, and ironically, he died with Wiley Post while attempting to find a safer route to Russia for delivering air mail.

518. Heller, Terry. "William Penn Adair [Will] Rogers." Encyclopedia of American Humorists. Ed. Steven H. Gale. New York: Garland, 1988, 374-76.

Suggests that when Rogers started adding humorous comments to his tricks in circuses and Wild West shows his popularity increased and that when he died in an airplane crash with Wiley Post in 1935, he was generally considered the most popular man in America. Rogers' popularity was mainly due to his facile wit; however, he also expressed a point of view that was consistent with mainstream American attitudes, and he commented on particular events that were happening at the time. Ironically, these last two qualities of his humor have made Rogers mainly inaccessable to today's readers. Rogers was probably the last humorist to have the entire nation as his audience. Rogers was good at distilling folk wisdom into wit. He liked to puncture the pompous and extol common sense as a cure for the "bunk" that was being passed on by American intelligencia. Rogers' ironic barbs tended to be painfully true. In The Illiterate Digest he said that if a farmer's hog has Cholera the whole country knows it, and everyone is helping to deal with the problem. But if your five children all have Infantile Paralysis, no one seems to know or care. Rogers' Ether and Me is more readable than most of his other writings because it is more autobiographical than political and has not become so dated. Rogers' greatest ability was to gauge the public mind and speak in its behalf.

519. Linneman, William R. "Language Technique in Will Rogers and Art Buchwald" WHIMSY 1 (1983): 72-74.

Applies Schopenhauer's explanation of "incongruity" to the work of both Will Rogers and Art Buchwald. In both cases, the faculty of wit forces two very different types of real objects under a single concept, and the sudden understanding of this incongruity causes laughter. As an example of this type of incongruity, consider Will Rogers' comment in Daily Telegrams that he loved the desert so much that when he retired from active life he would retire either to the Senate or to the desert. In Weekly Articles, Rogers alluded to three active and prominent figures in the banking industry--J. P. Morgan, Andrew Mellon, and Jesse James. Rogers could even be incongruous when describing a good meal, as he would talk about people who would take a piece of bread and harvest all of the left-over gravy on the plate. He added that if a person is that hungry he should be fed out of a horse's nose bag. Another of Will Rogers' incongruities is the disparity between the seriousness of his subjects and the casualness of his stance and his grammar. Will's wife, Betty Rogers, commented that Will's careless manner and careless speech softened the sharpness of his spoken words and made his message much more palatable.

520. Linneman, William R. "Will Rogers: The Cowboy Philosopher on
     Economics" WHIMSY 4 (1986): 23-24.

    Explains that during the First World War, Rogers' monologues
at the Ziegfeld Follies gave him the reputation of a "Cowboy
Philosopher." Although he commented on everything from agriculture
to zeppelins, he especially liked to target politics, so when the
Great Depression came, economics became one of his favorite
subjects. In Weekly Articles he said that Wall Street was only a
few blocks long, but that you still couldn't see the whole length of
it; that's how crooked it was. Rogers also criticized Herbert
Hoover's theory of "trickle-down economics." He speculated that
Hoover was trained as an engineer and had learned that water flows
downhill. But Rogers felt that money followed a different law; it
flows from the bottom to the top. He said that if you give a lot of
money to the people at the bottom, it will be in the hands of the
people at the top by nightfall. Will attributed the downfall of the
National Recovery Administration (NRA) to its overcomplicated
structure. He said it could have been written as a single
commandment, "Thou shalt pay so much. And thou shalt work men only
so much." Will felt that America was in a depression because of our
gambling instincts. He therefore facetiously suggested that we
establish a lottery to raise money for government. Ironically,
Will's suggestion has since become a reality.

521. Linneman, William R. "Will Rogers and the Great Depression."
     Studies in American Humor NS3.2-3 (Summer-Fall 1984): 173-86.

    Describes Rogers as favoring the causes of Jeffersonian
Democracy and populism and lists Rogers' satiric targets as the
rich, the Congress, industry, and banking. During the 1920s Rogers
warned about the dangers of American indebtedness almost as if he
knew that the Depression was sure to come. Rogers couldn't
understand how it is possible for people to be starving in the midst
of plenty. About the American banking industry he said that every
international banker should have a sign printed for his office door
reading, "Alive today by the grace of a nation that has a sense of
humor." Rogers praised F. D. R.'s limiting the trading sessions in
the stock market to three hours per day. He told his audiences that
this was Roosevelt's way of telling the brokers they would only have
three hours a day to work on the suckers. "The other twenty-one
hours they were under the protection of the fish and game laws."
Rogers never bought stocks himself. If he had money to invest, he
always put the money into land, because "You could always walk on
it." Rogers didn't believe that it was possible to get something
for nothing, and he once told Eddie Cantor that he never made a
dollar in his life without having to chew gum for it.

522. Linneman, William R. "Will Rogers: The Metaphor of Common
     Experience." WHIMSY 2 (1984): 28-30.

    Feels that metaphors are as much a tool of humorists as of
poets and that humorists' metaphors reveal their personalities,
backgrounds, and purposes. Will Rogers' metaphors and similes are
realistic, rural, and against pomposity, but they are not
necessarily incongruous. Very often they state the obvious in a
witty way. He calls the Panama Canal a "Big Gully," a dirigible is
a "floating bladder," and the stalactites at Carlsbad Caverns are

church steeples hanging upside down. When Mahatma Ghandi was
pictured in the papers in a loin cloth, Rogers commented that he had
just blown into London with nothing on but a diaper. Rogers used
down-home comparisons and common sense metaphors to humanize his
subjects and make them more understandable. His metaphors stripped
the sham and deceit and idealism away from the legislative process
and exposed the pretense. He referred to the capital as the
"National Fun Factory" and to the Congress as the "hired help." He
also compared the activities of Congress with a Hollywood production
company. He referred to the House of Representatives as the
"Scenario Department" and the Senate as the "Cutting and Titling
Department." In both houses of congress there were the "Gag Men,"
who would "furnish some little Gag, or Amendment as they call it,
which will get a laugh."

523. Rollins, Peter C. Will Rogers: A Bio-Bibliography. Westport,
     Connecticut: Greenwood, 1984, xiv + 282 pp.

     Considers the full range of available Will-Rogers materials
from memorabilia and bric-a-brac to book-length works and feature
films. Chapters 1 and 2 list his major accomplishments and discuss
important interpretations of Rogers and his life. Chapter 3
discusses Rogers' humor, with short quotations analyzed in close
detail to highlight specific humor strategies. Chapter 4 is a
biographical essay written in the style of Dr. Johnson. In Chapter
5 the material is presented more factually and clerically, with
authors, dates, films and filmmakers, audiovisual presentations, and
recordings both by and about Will Rogers. Chapter 7 is a listing of
Will Rogers' papers at Claremore Memorial.

524. Rollins, Peter C. "Will Rogers and the Saturday Evening Post.
     The Chronicles of Oklahoma 68 (1990): 38-53.

     Compares Will Rogers to George Horace Lorimer, editor of the
Saturday Evening Post, for whom Rogers was a prolific writer,
suggesting that they are kindred spirits. The major goal of both
Rogers and Lorimer was to interpret America to itself. They were
both tired of political muckraking and felt that the readership of
the Post was tired of it as well. They both wanted to celebrate
America's past. The Post covers traditionally carried traditional
American symbols like Benjamin Franklin, George Washington, or
Independence Hall. Norman Rockwell's covers celebrating hometown
American values were also frequently used. Both Rogers and the Post
celebrated the frontier spirit of the American West, and they
weren't above ridiculing stereotypes of effete dudes as they honored
virile cowboys and the girls from the East who gave their hearts to
their unaffected manliness. In 1926 Lorimer invited Rogers to tour
a number of European capitals and discuss various foreign policy
issues from a humorous American point of view. Rogers agreed, and
wrote up the trip in a series of epistles in tone very similar to
Mark Twain's earlier Innocents Abroad (1879). Rogers, like Twain,
emphasized the human side of the stories, employing an informal
style and stressing personal observations and feelings rather than
abstractions. During the 1930s Rogers and Lorimor drew apart
because Rogers was much more sensitive to the feelings of minority
groups than was Lorimor.

Wallace Stevens (1879-1955)

525. Wallace, Ronald. "Wallace Stevens: The Revenge of Music on
     Bassoons." God Be with the Clown. Columbia: Univ. of Missouri
     Press, 1984, 141-70.

     Describes Stevens' poetry as filled with contradictions,
coinages, archaic usages, intellectual complexity, exuberant
playfulness, and willful obscurity and adds that poetry with such
qualities will keep the critics busy for a very long time. Stevens
didn't like to see poetry analyzed or explained, because he said
that ruined the poetry. He felt that poetry must have an element of
obscurity or mystery for it to be interesting, and he further said
that once people are perfectly sure of a poem they no longer have
any interest in it, and the poem loses its potency: "The poem must
resist the intelligence / Almost successfully." Many literary
critics have commented on the humor in Stevens' poetry, especially
that in Harmonium, his first book. Harriet Monroe considered
Stevens to be a "great humorist, using the word in its most profound
sense." Daniel Fuchs and Robert Pack have written articles on
Stevens' comedy, and Samuel French Morse and Fred M. Robinson have
both traced the humor connections between Stevens and Bergson.
Stevens especially enjoyed developing comedy character types--
comedian, buffo, fop, scaramouche, sophomore, and egotist. He also
favored comic images like bananas, buttocks, spring, paramour, and
motley.

(1880-1956) TO (1894-1961)

Henry Louis Mencken (1880-1956)

526. Baer, John W. "The Great Depression Humor of Galbraith,
Leacock, and Mencken." Studies in American Humor NS3.2-3
(Summer-Fall 1984): 220-27.

Feels that during the Depression Mencken reported American
politics as a bluster of hypocrisy and buffonery. For Mencken, one
of the major traits of the politicians was the exploitation of human
frailties. This was probably a trait of the professions and of the
business world as well, but they tend to be more insulated from
exposure. In the "Monday Articles" which he wrote for the Baltimore
Sun from 1920 to 1936, Mencken saw Hoover as a prohibitionist and
despised his inadequacies in handling the Depression. As a believer
in Social Darwinism, Mencken strongly opposed the Roosevelt's New
Deal. When Mencken ended his "Monday Articles" in 1936, he sank
into public obscurity as a humorist for a number of years. He later
emerged during World War II to write his humorous autobiographical
series, and he returned to political reporting in the 1948 election
campaign, thereby regaining some of his former prestige. However,
it was short lived, because his stroke in 1948 ended his writing
career.

527. Buitenhuis, Peter. "The Value of Mencken." The Western
Humanities Review. 14.1 (Winter 1960): 19-28.

Maintains that Mencken came onto the scene exactly when he was
needed. During the first three decades of the twentieth century,
America was suffering from complacency, conformity, moralism,
saccharine religiosity, and political inertia. Buitenhuis views
Mencken as a "literary arsonist" who could burn the trash heap of
intellectual dead wood. Mencken was a dynamic crusader against
crusaders. He got his early training from reading Mark Twain,
especially Huckleberry Finn. He delighted in Friedrich Nietzsche's
anti-Christianity and contempt for the herd and in George Bernard
Shaw's suspicion of emotionalism and his love for ideas and even
wrote important books about Nietzsche and Shaw. Mencken's most
successful writings were his collections of short essays with their
grace, their toughness, and especially their originality, zest, and
humor.

528. Bulsterbaum, Allison. "Henry Lewis Mencken." Encyclopedia of
American Humorists." New York: Garland, 1988, 320-29.

Points out that in 1901 Mencken began writing a humorous
opinion column for the Baltimore Herald entitled "Rhyme and Reason."
Bulsterbaum adds that if news about a particular event or issue was
scarce, Mencken would sometimes invent details to make the reporting
more interesting. Mencken's lifelong goal as a journalist was to
invert conventional prejudices. Mencken's "Monday Articles" covered
every national convention held between 1920 and 1948 except for
1944. His reporting was as rowdy as were the conventions
themselves; he called them the "Carnival of Buncombe." Although he
criticized this mass of writhing humanity, he very much enjoyed
219

jumping into the middle of it. While working for the Sun, Mencken
did some free-lancing with George Jean Nathan on The Smart Set. By
1914 they were co-editors, encouraging young authors, and attacking
the forces of genteel, Victorian Puritanism, a movement which Nathan
and Mencken felt was a major hindrance to the development of a
viable national literature. In 1924, both Mencken and Nathan co-
founded The American Mercury (published by their friend, Alfred A.
Knopf), regaining the goals they had had while co-editing The Smart
Set. Mencken's cutting satire was achieved through comic
exaggeration, outlandish diction, and incongruous juxtapositions of
ideas and visual images. His fame reached its height during the
roaring twenties.

529. Love, Glen A. "Stemming the Avalanche of Tripe: Or, How H. L.
     Mencken and Friends Reformed Northwest Literature." Thalia:
     Studies in Literary Humor 4.1 (Spring and Summer 1981): 46-
     53.

Contends that the Pacific Northwest was the last area in
America to develop a viable written literature and that there is
practically no pre-1920 literature worth reading today. This is in
contrast to the Northeast, the Old Southwest, the Middle West, and
the West which all have rich traditions of worthy pre-1920
literature. Love feels that the reason for this lack of development
is that Northwesterners tended to be smug and aloof. They were not
interested in folk life or folk art or anything bawdy or humorous.
And in their Rocky Mountain splendor they felt they had everything
and didn't have to look anywhere else for inspiration. But then
along came a breath of fresh air in the form of a pamphlet entitled
Status Rerum... written by James Stevens and H. L. Davis. Both
Stevens and Davis were from rural and working-class backgrounds. H.
L. Mencken influenced this pamphlet in a number of important ways.
First, he provided a model of cock-sure audacity for free-swinging
assaults on establishment values and institutions. Mencken
virtually redefined the American literary canon during the 1910s and
1920s developing the colloquial tradition of Mark Twain. Second,
both Stevens and Davis published in Mencken's The American Mercury.
Third, he provided a model for their prose style.

530. Miles, Elton. "H. L. Mencken." Dictionary of Literary
     Bibliography, Volume 11: American Humorists, 1800-1950.
     Detroit, Michigan: Gale, 1982, 323-31.

Explains that Mencken was born in Baltimore, Maryland, where
he lived his entire life, most of it in the same house. During his
ten years of formal schooling, he was a voracious reader. Later, as
literary critic and editor of Smart Set, he wrote biting humor
defending naturalists like Theodore Dreiser and satirists like
Sinclair Lewis, while sarcastically criticizing defenders of the
genteel tradition like William Dean Howells and Henry James. In
1926 Mencken made the national press by getting himself arrested for
publicly selling the outlawed issue of American Mercury that
contained Herbert Asbury's story, "Hatrack" about a small-town
prostitute. His reputation was further tarnished because of his
opposition to F. D. Roosevelt's New Deal. He called it "a milch cow
with 125,000 teats." Mencken also opposed England and supported
Germany during World War I. He tended not to go along with
traditional thinking. Mencken was like Swift in his ability to

expose naked pretension, quackery, and stupidity. He was like
Voltaire in his ability to amuse and entertain on a multitude of
subjects. But unlike Swift and Voltaire, Mencken left the world no
creative masterpiece like Gulliver's Travels or Candide.

531.   Olivar-Bertrand,   R.   "Mencken's   This-World   Satire."
       Contemporary Review 223.1293 (October 1973): 202-06.

    Considers Mencken to have been a conservative but not a
radical conservative. Mencken did not believe that God, the United
States flag, and the President form an immutable trinity. Olivar-
Bertrand describes Mencken as "the heretic in the Sunday School."
He had a contempt for the mob and despised what he called the "100
percenters." Mencken was interested in the "truth" and he delighted
in telling the truth in the face of traditional thought. Like
George Bernard Shaw, Mencken was effective in stating old truths but
wrapping them in vigorous expression. Mencken didn't like actors,
especially those who pretended intellectuality. Mencken's cogent
satire often hit very close to home and offended many people. This
is one of the reasons that he had such a significant impact.

532.   Rubin, Louis D., Jr. "If Only Mencken Were Alive...." The
       Comic Imagination in American Literature. Ed. Louis D. Rubin,
       Jr. New Brunswick, New Jersey: Rutgers Univ. Press, 1983, 217-
       30.

    Describes the Menckeniana, which is published periodically by
the Baltimore public library. The Menckeniana not only publishes
articles about Mencken but also attempts to document all of the
public references made to him throughout the country. In a way, the
Menckeniana is constantly asking what America would be like if
Mencken were still alive and writing. The assumption is that
someone of Mencken's insights and abilities is needed to expose the
confusion and chicanery presently on the American scene. Rubin
points out that Mencken stopped writing during World War I because
he had been so extensively criticized for his lack of patriotic
fervor, failing to make angels of the Britons and devils of the
Germans. Mencken had not joined in on the suppression of German
courses in our schools or the banishment of Friedrich Nietzsche and
Theodore Dreiser from curricula because of their Teutonic names or
the sanctions against performing music by Richard Wagner or Richard
Strauss for the same reason. For Mencken, value is value, and fraud
is fraud. He was later vindicated in his judgments, and the 1920s
became a happy time for him. It was a time of urban prosperity,
popular   pleasure-taking,   a   time   of   cosmopolitanism   and
sophistication, a time when the Mencken philosophy was welcomed.

533.   Walling, William. "Agape at Dayton: The Humor of H. L.
       Mencken." WHIMSY 1 (1983): 55-56.

    Considers Mencken's "In Memoriam: W. J. B." to be Mencken's
most outrageous and best-known essay. The year before his death,
William Jennings Bryan had directed the prosecution of a young man
named Scopes in Dayton, Tennessee. Scopes was accused of violating
state law by teaching the theory of evolution to his high school
students. Clarence Darrow was the defendent's attorney, and he had
heaped much ridicule on Bryan, but Darrow's ridicule was light

compared to that of H. L. Mencken. In "In Memoriam," which was
published on the day immediately following Bryan's death, Mencken
called Bryan a charlatan, a mountebank, and a zany and said that
Bryan's position had brought him into contact with the top people of
his time but that "he preferred the company of rustic ignoramuses."
Mencken continued by saying that Bryan was motivated by simple
ambition, "the ambition of a common man to get his hand upon the
collar of his superiors, or, failing that, to get his thumb into
their eyes."

534. Yates, Norris W. "The Two Masks of H. L. Mencken." The
American Humorist: Conscience of the Twentieth Century. Ames,
Iowa: Iowa State Univ. Press, 1964, 142-64.

Feels that authors such as Howe, Bierce, Lardner, and Marquis
blend iconoclasm with bitterness and that this is a common blend.
In contrast, Mencken blends iconoclasm with cheerfulness and gusto.
In Only Yesterday, Frederick Lewis Allen suggests that Mencken gives
the reader the same intense viscereal pleasure as gained by throwing
baseballs at crockery at an amusement park. Mencken was raised by
a family that gave him little help or encouragement with his
writing. Yates feels that his pulling himself up by his own
bootstraps played a role in fixing his ambivalent attitudes. He
tried to write satirical fables in slang as George Ade had done but
failed. He himself called the results "miserable botches." His own
effective style involved invective, oversimplification,
exaggeration, hoax, and grotesque metaphor. He would show his
support of a person or idea by charging full tilt at the opposition.
Mencken considered himself a gentleman, and his criticisms of
Woodrow Wilson, William Jennings Bryan, and Theodore Roosevelt were
based on the fact that these men were not gentlemen. Yates contends
that it is easy to determine what Mencken's satiric targets were.
Determining what Mencken was in favor of, however, is not so easy.

(Alfred) Damon Runyon (c1880-1946)

535. Grant, Thomas. "Damon Runyon." Dictionary of Literary
Biography, Volume 11: American Humorists, 1800-1950. Ed.
Stanley Trachtenberg. Detroit, MI: Gale, 1982, 419-29.

Compares Damon Runyon to Mark Twain, Ring Lardner, and James
Thurber: all entered the field of comic writing from journalism.
Runyon was one of the most popular journalists and writers during
the first half of the twentieth century. His Guys and Dolls opened
in 1950, after his death, and ran 1,200 performances. It was then
made into a movie starring Marlon Brando and Frank Sinatra. As a
sports reporter for the Denver Post he was encouraged to embellish
the facts and color the news with human interest angles in order to
take readers away from the Rocky Mountain News, a competing paper.
He overdid it, however, and was fired by the Post, only to be picked
up later by the Rocky Mountain News. Runyon himself was an
outsider, and the characters in his fiction also tend to be
outcasts, undesirables and misfits but with a strong sense of
camaraderie. Their nicknames reflect not only a sense of intimacy
but also give clues as to their roles in underground society and

their positions in the underground hierarchy. Runyon's <u>The Tents of Trouble</u> (1911) is a book of ballads written about wanderers, beachcombers, and hoboes. It earned him the title of "The Kipling of Colorado."

536. Jones, Veda. "(Alfred) Damon Runyon." <u>Encyclopedia of American Humorists</u>. Ed. Steven H. Gale. New York: Garland, 1988, 384-87.

Considers Runyon to have been a good listener and feels that this is why he was able to incorporate so much effective local color into his writing. He embellished the slang which he heard and developed his own literary dialect, "Runyonese." He would call men "guys" and women "dolls," "sweethearts," "broads," or "pancakes" with affection, but also with a touch of condescension. He also liked alliterative nicknames like "Dave the Dude," "Hot Horse Herbie," or "Tobias the Terrible." His Broadway pieces were also spiced with gangster terminology. Guns might be called "rods," "betsys," "old equalizers," or "rooty-toot-toots." Runyon referred to a yes-man as a "nod guy," and he referred to a lawyer as "a tongue." Runyon also developed some trademark expressions like "No little and quite some" and "more than somewhat." He had a genuine empathy for the gangsters he wrote about; he felt that the underworld had a code of ethics based on loyalty and trust. The Broadway stories were sentimental, humorous, and ironic. His endings can be compared to those of O'Henry. Runyon's writing is frequently based on emotions. For dramatic tension, it is common to find loneliness, failure, and disappointment throughout a piece of writing but never at the end. Runyon's endings are always upbeat and optimistic.

537. Rees, John O. "The Last Local Colorist: Damon Runyon." <u>Kansas Magazine</u> 7 (1968): 73-81.

Points out that few readers of Runyon's Broadway stories realize that Runyon was actually a Westerner and that as a Westerner his writing carries on the local-color tradition of Bret Harte and others. The epitome of the local-color movement occured during the last third of the nineteenth century in New England, the South, the Midwest, and the West. Bret Harte was probably the most distinctive of local-color writers with his California stories, and Harte was idealized in Kansas and Colorado printing shops and newspaper offices where Runyon grew up. Runyon's Broadway stories exhibit much influence from Harte, even though Harte tended to be more sentimental and Runyon more comic. Local-color stories tended to be short, blending realism and romance, emphasizing the speech, customs, and physical setting of a particular provincial or backwoods community, and they implied that all of this local color was fading and would soon be gone. Runyon's writing followed this formula completely. Like other local colorists, Runyon's material is too grounded in the here and now to be considered great literature. To the modern reader, Runyon's vernacular writing, labeled "Runyonese" soon becomes tiresome.

Franklin Pierce Adams (1881-1960)

538. Drennan, Robert E., ed. "Franklin Pierce Adams." <u>The
      Algonquin Wits</u>. Secaucus, New Jersey: The Citadel Press, 1983,
      23-38.

      Describes Adams as "the cigar-smoking, pool-playing little
gargoyle with the long neck and the big nose and the bushy
mustache." Adams was considered to be the "father" of the Algonquin
Round Table. He published his column, "The Conning Tower," in three
different New York newspapers, the <u>Herald Tribune</u>, the <u>World</u>, and
the <u>Post</u>. He wrote in the genteel tradition, excelling in urbanity,
wit, and erudition. His favorite targets were hat-check girls,
paper towels, illegible house-numbers, and his wife's salad
dressing. He was fond of light verse with a satiric bite, and his
<u>The Book of Diversion</u>, and <u>Half a Loaf</u> contained poetry and short
prose sketches. He also wrote a literary parody entitled <u>The Diary
of Our Own Samuel Pepys</u>. Adams was also a master of the epigram,
like "Money isn't everything, but lack of money isn't anything," and
"What this country needs is a good five-cent nickel." Adams had a
quick wit, and during one particular poker game he was able to
determine how good a hand his opponent, Herbert Ransom, was holding
by reading his body language. Finally, he proposed a new poker rule
for the club, "Anyone who looks at Ransom's face is cheating."

539. Schwartz, Richard Alan. "Franklin Pierce Adams."
      <u>Encyclopedia of American Humorists</u>. Ed. Steven H. Gale. New
      York: Garland, 1988, 1-4.

      Places Adams into the tradition of the mid-nineteenth-century
literary comedians. These writers specialized in quick wit,
wordplay, and satiric parody. As a member of the "Algonquin Wits,"
Adams invented a game called "I Can Give You a Sentence," where one
member of the group suggests a word and challenges another member of
the group to respond with a witty sentence containing the word.
When asked to provide a sentence for "meretricious," Adams responded
by wishing everyone a "meretricious and a Happy New Year." When
Dorothy Parker, another member of the Algonquin Wits was asked to
use "horticulture" in a sentence, her response was "You can lead a
horticulture, but you can't make her think." The Algonquin wits
engaged in many such word games, designed to increase camaraderie,
enliven spirits, and produce cutting, sarcastic, and cynical
observations. When a particular Alexander Woollcott book appeared,
he boasted, "What is so rare as a Woollcott first edition." Adams
retort was "A Woollcott second edition." Schwartz feels that Adams'
arrogant cynicism was responsible not only for his success but for
his lack of success as well. Although he was talented and witty, he
remained emotionally aloof, expressing an occasional brilliant
insight or <u>bon mot</u> rather than writing a truly great sustained work.

Florence Guy Seabury (1881-1951)

540. Walker, Nancy, and Zita Dresner. "Florence Guy Seabury."
Redressing the Balance: American Women's Literary Humor from
Colonial Times to the 1980s. Jackson, Mississippi: Univ. Press
of Mississippi, 1988, 234-43.

States that Seabury was a member of Greenwich Village's
"Heterodoxy Club" from 1912 until 1940. This was a club for
unorthodox women that included as members radical feminists,
artists, and suffragettes. Seabury published satiric articles in
Harper's, McCall's, and The New Republic, and some of these were
printed in her The Delicatessen Husband and Other Essays (1926).
Seabury used mock case studies, and parodied the scientific method
to write about changes in sex roles, morals, and manners, suggesting
some of the causes and effects of the confusions and resentments
that are felt relating to changing sex roles in our society.
Seabury suggests that an egalitarian society is not something to be
feared but rather welcomed by both men and women as it can provide
greater opportunites for personal fulfillment of both sexes.

Jessie Redmon Fauset (1882-1961)

541. Walker, Nancy, and Zita Dresner. "Jessie Redmon Fauset."
Redressing the Balance: American Women's Literary Humor from
Colonial Times to the 1980s. Jackson, Mississippi: Univ. Press
of Mississippi, 1988, 248-50.

Explains that the characters in Fauset's third novel, The
Chinaberry Tree (1931) had backgrounds similar to Fauset's own.
They were Blacks who spoke good English. They were self-supporting
and idealistic. Fauset was named literary editor of The Crisis from
1919 to 1926. In this position, she promoted the careers of Jean
Toomer, Countee Cullen, Langston Hughes, and other Harlem
Renaissance writers. In addition to The Chinaberry Tree, Fauset
wrote three other novels--There Is Confusion (1924), Plum Bun
(1929), and Comedy: American Style (1933). Fauset's writings
exhibit a sense of irony rather than outrage. She feels that racial
prejudice is patently absurd--from everyone's point of view. Her
last novel, Comedy: American Style, explains the dilemma of
mulattoes, who are able to "pass" for being white and who are
therefore discriminated against by other Blacks.

Homer Croy (1883-1965)

542. Masson, Thomas L. "Homer Croy." Our American Humorists.
Freeport, NY: Books for Libraries, 1931, 104-10.

Considers Croy's best humor to be in his short pieces rather
than in his novels. Croy has written a book about the motion
pictures and laments the fact that even though the reviews were
good, the royalties were not. Croy has written two realistic and
humorous novels that deal with life in the Middle West.

Will Cuppy (1884-1949)

543. Castle, Alfred L. "Naturalist Humor in Will Cuppy's How to
     Tell Your Friends from the Apes." Studies in American Humor
     NS3.4 (1988): 330-36.

     Places Cuppy into the naturalist tradition of Dreiser, London,
and Dos Passos. This tradition was a reaction to an age dominated
by scientific metaphors, survival of the fittest, historicism, and
materialism. Scientists during this period were investigating
determinism through instinct, heredity, and/or environment, the
insignificance of man in the overall scheme of things, and the
perception of man as as a part of nature, that is, as an animal.
How to Tell Your Friends from the Apes, written shortly after the
Scopes "Monkey Trial," investigates the uncanny similarities of
animals to man, and vice versa. Cuppy says you can prove that a
Wren loves you by forcing its paws around your neck and asking if it
loves you. If it bites you, get another Wren. He says the sweet
bubbling song of the Wren is communicating that it has just
punctured the eggs of a Chipping Sparrow and torn up the home of a
Yellow Warbler, and it is now thinking of murdering a couple of baby
Titmice. He observes about Penguins that only an expert can tell a
live one from a stuffed one. He says that the Beaver has solved the
problem of the work ethic. He works to survive, not because he
thinks that work will make him a better beaver.

544. Feldcamp, Fred, ed. The Decline and Fall of Practically
     Everybody. New York: Holt, Rinehart and Winston, 1950, 230 pp.

     Describes Will Cuppy's The Decline and Fall of Practically
Everybody as describing the personal events surrounding all of the
famous men and women throughout history. When he died in 1949 he
had been working on the book for sixteen years, off and on, and
Feldcamp edited and published the book. Cuppy was a devoted author
a dedicated scholar, and a hermit. He would stay for weeks at a
time in his Greenwich Village apartment, arranging for food to be
brought in when he got hungry. The apartment overflowed with books.
They were in bookshelves, stacked up against walls to the ceiling.
They were even on his cupboards, above his refrigerator, and on top
of the stove in his kitchen. Cuppy hated noise and did much of his
writing during the quiet hours around midnight. But his apartment
was next to a school playground, and when the noise became
especially unbearable, he would take out his New Year's Eve
noisemaker, the kind that uncoils when you blow into it, and blow it
in the direction of a noisy child. He had a different strategy for
annoying adults. He would write a devastating letter to the
offensive party, address the envelope, apply stamps, and then place
the letter on the table near his door. In the morning, he would
tear up the letter and throw it away.

545. Johnson, Eric W. "Will Cuppy." Encyclopedia of American
     Humorists. Ed. Steven H. Gale. New York: Garland, 1988, 109-
     11.

     Explains that during the 1920s Cuppy lived in a cabin on
Jones' Island, off Long Island, New York. He wrote How to Be a

Hermit as a record of his solitary life on this island. Cuppy was
a dedicated researcher and prodigious note taker. After he did, his
friend and literary executor, Fred Feldkamp, edited and published two
more Cuppy books utilizing the more than 200 boxes full of note
cards. These formed The Decline and Fall of Practically Everybody,
which treated famous historical figures with the same tone of
disrepect that he had used to treat animals in an earlier book, and
How to Get from January to December, a humorous almanac containing
a comic entry for each day of the year. Whether writing about
animals or people, Cuppy was not sentimental or charitable or
malicious. His humor is similar to that of Robert Benchley, James
Thurber, and Thorne Smith, though rays of Mark Twain also sometimes
come streaming through. Richard Armour later emulated Cuppy's mock-
scholarly style, footnotes and all. Cuppy was a crusty but gentle
misanthropist. He felt that neither the animals nor the humans he
wrote about had much chance for improvement as long as the humans
were in charge.

546. Lieb, Sandra. "Will Cuppy." Dictionary of Literary
      Biography, Volume 11: American Humorists, 1800-1950. Detroit,
      Michigan: Gale, 1982, 94-99.

      Portrays Cuppy as a slow and painstaking writer who produced
only one book of college stories, six books of comic essays, and
three collections of mystery stories. He used the persona of the
scientific investigator to satirize human foibles. For a long time
Cuppy pursued a Ph.D. at the University of Chicago. Burton Rascoe,
one of his fellow students, felt that Cuppy's long duration in
graduate school was not so much the result of his passion for
scholarship as from his terror of the "real world." Both How to
Tell Your Friends from the Apes and How to Attract the Wombat are
parody field manuals for amateur naturalists. Cuppy approached
nature with a mixture of delight and fascination on the one hand and
irreverence, ridicule, and repulsion on the other. He noted that
orangutans have solved the problem of work. They don't work and
they don't worry about it. Then Cuppy adds that they nevertheless
have wrinkles. Cuppy explains that in zoos it is very easy to
distinguish one's friends from the apes. "The Apes are in cages."
But then Cuppy continues, "Yes, but when you are not at the Zoo,
what then?" Cuppy's pithy epigrams, comic footnotes, non sequiturs,
and whimsical style are close to the mock-naturalist essays and
fables of Benchley and Thurber.

547. Yates, Norris W. "Will Cuppy: The Wise Fool as Pedant." The
      American Humorist: Conscience of the Twentieth Century. Ames,
      Iowa: Iowa State Univ. Press, 1964, 321-30.

      Remarks that Cuppy received his B.A. from the University of
Chicago in 1907 and then stayed on at the University for seven more
years, taking courses in whatever he wanted to know about, and
frequently failing to show up to take the examinations. His first
book was entitled Maroon Tales (1909). The university authorities
had asked Cuppy to make up some "traditions" for the newly
inaugurated fraternity system there. It contained a bunch of short
stories about fraternity life at the University of Chicago. Cuppy
developed the reputation of the wise fool as pedant in his writings.
His wit and his pessimism rivaled Ring Lardner's. He could see no
way of alleviating the human condition and suggested that the only

solution would be for us all to become extinct. He said that any
other solution was a mere palliative.

Ring(gold Wilmer) Lardner (1885-1933)

548. Blair, Rebecca S. "Ring(gold Wilmer) Lardner." Encyclopedia
      of American Humorists. Ed. Steven H. Gale. New York: Garland,
      1988, 263-67.

      Indicates that Lardner wrote a column for the Chicago Tribune
from 1913 to 1919 entitled, "In the Wake of the News." This column
consisted of short stories, satires, sports gossip, and poems about
Lardner's children. In 1914 Lardner introduced Jack Keefe to the
column as a "wise boob." Keefe was an egotistical semi-literate
baseball player who was later to author the You Know Me, Al letters.
The image that Keefe wanted to project was that of a brash,
swaggering, worldly-wise star athlete. The image that Keefe
actually projected was an arrogant, vain, gullible, bush-league
fool--a "wise boob." And the language which Keefe speaks has been
dubbed "Ringlish." It reflects his character flaws, his
psychological makeup, and his life style. Although all of the long
and difficult words are spelled correctly, many of the common words
are misspelled, because Keefe is certainly not going to look up the
easy words in the dictionary. In 1917, Lardner wrote Gullible's
Travels, Etc., satiric pieces narrated in Midwestern vernacular by
a semi-literate person named Gullible. In 1919, he wrote Regular
Fellows I have Met, satiric descriptions of socially prominent
Chicagoans. In 1920, he wrote The Young Immigrants, a parody of the
Lardner's move east from his perspective as a child.

549. DeMuth, James. "Ring Lardner." Small Town Chicago: The
      Comic Perspective of Finley Peter Dunne, George Ade, and Ring
      Lardner. Port Washington, New York: Kennikat Press, 1980, 69-
      75.

      Considers Lardner's view of his popular audience to be
ambivalent. Lardner could be their best advocate or their severest
critic. Lardner wrote for such mass-circulation periodicals as
Saturday Evening Post, Collier's, and The American Magazine. The
syntax of his vernacular writing appears to be careless and lax, but
it is a carefully developed satiric device. Beneath the surface of
Lardner's fiction there is always a muffled belligerence that
sometimes breaks through as abuse, complaint, or even obscenity.
His characters violate traditional rules of courtesy, modesty, and
good taste. Their sense of humor runs from sarcasm to rude
practical jokes. In You Know Me, Al, Lardner makes a distinction
between the "bushers" (always fictional characters), and the
"regulars" (always actual baseball players). It is the function of
the manager ("Cal" Callahan), the coach ("Kid" Gleason), and a
veteran pitcher (Ed Walsh) to help season Jack Keefe, a "busher."
In one game against Detroit, Keefe yields sixteen runs in seven
innings. Ty Cobb steals four bases; Keefe walks half a dozen
batters and bobbles a couple of bunts, so they pull Keefe. When he
says his arm isn't sore, the pitching coach responds that they're
more worried about the outfielders' legs.

550. Drennan, Robert E. "Ring Lardner." The Algonquin Wits.
      Secaucus, New Jersey: Citadel Press, 1983, 95-108.

      Suggests that Lardner's early reputation as a humorist came as
a result of his "Letters of a Bush-League Ball Player," a sporting
column in the Chicago Tribune. He is considered by many to be one
of the best American writers of the short story; he's especially
good at writing rural Western idiomatic speech. In social events he
tended to remain silent for long periods and then issue a well-timed
dry or witty remark. When he saw an ostentatious actor with wild,
unruly, hair at a party, for example, he asked, "How do you look
when I'm sober?" Lardner says that wives think that when the
telephone rings, it is against the law not to answer it. When a
husband asks a wife if he needs to shave she says "No, you look
alright." But then at the party she will remark that her husband
didn't have time to shave.   Lardner's readers were constantly
asking him on whom the protagonist in You Know Me, Al was based.
Lardner finally started responding that he was not based on a
baseball player at all but on Jane Addams, a former Follies girl.
When Harold Ross of the New Yorker asked Lardner how he wrote his
short stories, Lardner responded that he wrote some widely separated
words on a piece of paper and then went back and just filled in the
spaces.

551. Evans, Elizabeth. "Ring Lardner." Dictionary of Literary
      Biography, Volume 11: American Humorists, 1800-1950. Detroit,
      MI: Gale, 1982, 242-56.

      Considers Lardner one of America's most successful writers of
humor even when placed among the competition of his day--S. J.
Perelman, Don Marquis, Robert Benchley, Franklin P. Adams, and
Dorothy Parker. Lardner wrote parody, comic verse, satiric fairy
tales, nonsense plays, and one-liners, but his stories were his best
genre. His sardonic examination of middle-class America never fails
to be amusing. In a single year, 1925, Scribner published You Know
Me Al, Gullible's Travels, Etc., The Big Town, and How to Write
Short Stories. This was so noteworthy that it was mentioned on the
first page of the April 19, 1925, issue of the New York Times Book
Review. Lardner based three of his books as well as a cartoon strip
with cartoonist Dick Dorgan, on his "wise-boob" protagonist Jack
Keefe. In the 1920s Lardner's close neighbors included Grantland
and Kate Rice, Zelda and Scott Fitzgerald, Gene Buck, and Ed Wynn.
Even though Lardner died at the early age of forty-eight, he had
already written one 120 short stories, 9 nonsense plays, numerous
magazine columns, parodies and burlesques, and hundreds of newspaper
columns.

552. Geismar, Maxwell. Ring Lardner and the Portrait of Folly.
      New York: Thomas Y. Crowell, 1972, 167 pp.

      Observes that Lardner had a brilliant wit and a totally
sophisticated brand of humor and comedy. It is unfortunate that
many people in our culture perceive humor through puritanical and
middle-class prejudices, feeling that it is not quite respectable
and may even be dangerous. Geismar suggests that this view may
indeed be correct, for he feels that once a person has read a great
comedy or a great tragicomedy by a Mark Twain, or a Ring Lardner, he
will never be quite the same again. He will probably be happier and

more interesting. He will see life more freshly, and he will no
longer be able to endure life without humor. Geismar feels that
Lardner's humor has great range--from comedy to farce to devastating
satire, to surrealism, and dada, and even nonsense. Geismar
considers Lardner to have been one of our sharpest cultural
historians during the gaudy the Roaring Twenties.

553. Keough, William. "Round Four: Ring Lardner: Sad Sack in the
      Fun House." Punchlines: The Violence of American Humor. New
      York: Paragon House, 1990, 78-100.

      Investigates the paradoxical nature of Lardner's writings.
His sardonic writings are quite dark, but his lighter pieces come
off as almost silly. Lardner was the rare writer who confessed to
a happy childhood. His writing style is quirky and colloquial and
contrasted the tight and hard rules of baseball itself with the
loose, flaky players of the game. Lardner's writing is often witty
and humorous, but Lardner himself tended to be profoundly
melancholic. His problem was that he refused to accept the Jazz-Age
society that surrounded him. Lardner tried to wear a party
lampshade, but his Puritan spirit was bothered by the frantic hustle
and the boosterism that was everywhere he looked. He was, in
effect, a sad sack living in a fun house. Lardner wrote about the
slimy and the detestable underbelly of life, but he had a compassion
for the characters he depicted, and this made him one of our best-
loved humorists. Lardner's characters do violence to the world, to
each other, and to the English language, but Lardner wrote about
them with charity and compassion. His message seemed to be that we
all need better manners if we are to keep from hurting each other,
but acquiring better manners is not all that easy.

554. Masson, Thomas L. "Ring Lardner." Our American Humorists.
      Freeport, NY: Books for Libraries Press, 1931, 186-208.

      Deems Lardner's success as a writer to be based on his ability
to "listen hard." Lardner used the language of the people to
produce a humor with a gentle glow of freshness and gaiety.
Lardner's writing is so convincing that we can actually smell the
soil of the baseball diamond. Masson feels that Lardner's sentiment
is what makes him a good humorist. It allows him to write a story
that really grabs the reader. "It is low-brow stuff. But it is the
best of low-brow stuff."

555. Moseley, Merritt. "Ring Lardner and the American Humor
      Tradition." South Atlantic Review 46.1 (January 1981): 42-60.

      Considers Lardner to be more of a humorist than a satirist.
Moseley feels that Lardner's critics have attempted to make him more
of a satirist, because these critics tend to feel that a satirist
makes more of a contribution to literature than does a humorist. In
order to establish Lardner as a satirist, critics tend to stress his
negative and critical view of mankind. Allan Nevins writes that
Lardner's work is a "merciless exposure of the American moron."
Otto Friedrich feels that Lardner had a "deep hatred" for the world
in which he lived. H. L. Mencken said that Lardner's characters
share the same "amiable stupidity," the same "transparent vanity,"
and the same "shallow swinishness" as a bunch of Methodist
evangelists. Maxwell Geismar considers him to be "one of the most

savage and merciless satirists and social critics of his period."
Such critics as these feel that all of Lardner's work is to some
extent satirical. Moseley points out that Lardner sometimes wrote
satire, and he sometimes wrote humor, and he did both on purpose.
Lardner's "Champion" and "The Love Nest" are almost pure, bitter
satire. His "The Story of a Wonder Man and "Clemo Uti (The Water
Lilies)" are almost pure humor. In general, the work done before
1920 is more "humor."

556. Pellow, Ken. "Mixed Metaphor in Baseball Fiction." WHIMSY 2
     (1984): 176-78.

     Feels that Lardner's baseball fiction was prototypical and
that it laid the groundwork for such later baseball fiction as James
Thurber's "You Could Look It Up" (Saturday Evening Post, 1935), Jim
Bouton's Ball four (1970), and Mark Harris' Henry Wiggin's Books
(1977), his The Southpaw (1953), his Bang the Drum Slowly (1956),
and his A Ticket for a Seamstitch (1956). Lardner's protagonist was
Jack Keefe, and he developed a language of his own with his
"Keefisms." He said things like "right off the real" and "I will
pay two fairs." He accrues many "dedts," refers to a hangover from
drinking "ginger ail," and many times refers to the "World Serious."
In a similar manner, Thurber's Magrew holds the midget in the
"crouch" of his arm; his "Doc" accuses the team of playing like the
"intimates" of a school for the blind. The lead-off hitter, Whitey
Cott, "crotches down" in a "fearsome stanch." The St. Louis manager
makes signs and faces as if he were a "contorturer." And the
umpires huddled together as if they were doctors discussing the
"bucolic plague." Mark Harris also develops the mixed metaphor, the
malapropism, the non-sequitur, and the misremembered cliche in such
expressions as "listening out of the corner of her eye," "let the
cat out of the barn," "should of seen the handwriting in the cards,"
"time will weed out the punks from the ivory," and "it rolled off my
back like a duck out of water."

557. Williams, Kenny J., and Bernard Duffey, eds. "Ring Lardner."
     Chicago's Public Wits: A Chapter in the American Comic Spirit.
     Baton Rouge: Louisiana State Univ. Press, 1983, 223-35.

     Feels that Lardner was a writer of remarkable originality.
During his years in Chicago, Lardner developed two types of
characters. Some of his characters were farcical and repellent,
like Jack Keefe. Others were likable but at the mercy of others who
had limited vision and futile ambitions, like Gullible. All of his
characters were lowbrow. Sometimes they are sardonic, sometimes
comic, sometimes they even elicit pathos. Often they live in a
nihilistic world in which hope seems to be largely abandoned.
Lardner was a merciless debunker of the average man. He was
extremely popular in his day despite the hardness of his tone. His
writing influenced both Sinclair Lewis and Ernest Hemingway. A more
complete account of his life and work can be found in Jonathan
Yardley's Ring (1977).

558. Yates, Norris W. "The Isolated Man of Ring Lardner." The
     American Humorist: Conscience of the Twentieth Century. Ames,
     Iowa: Iowa State Univ. Press, 1964, 165-94.

     Postulates that there is a remarkable similarity between
Lardner's various characters. On the surface, they can be athletes,
salesmen, clerks, barbers, nurses, newspapermen, song writers, or
whatever. They can range in age from teenagers to elderly and/or
retired. But they are all variations on a single type--middle-
class, blue-collar Americans. Lardner largely ignored the more
sensitive or more intelligent character types. Yates feels that
Lardner often shared the values and the interests of the character
types he developed. In 1913 Lardner began writing a humorous
sporting column for the Chicago Tribune named "In the Wake of the
News." This was such a popular column in Chicago that people quoted
it constantly. Ernest Hemingway and James T. Farrell both imitated
the Lardner dialect in their high-school papers. F. Scott
Fitzgerald was Ring Lardner's neighbor and close friend in Great
Neck, Long Island from 1922 to 1924. In fact, Abe North, in
Fitzgerald's Tender Is the Night may have been based on the life of
Lardner, and his frustrating career of only fragmentary
achievements.

Sinclair Lewis (1885-1951)

559. Friedman, Allan Philip. "Babbit: Satiric Realism in Form and
     Content." Satire Newsletter 4.1 (Fall 1966): 20-29.

     Agrees with Sinclair Lewis' first wife who said that Main
Street was not considered by Lewis so much of a satire until critics
started calling it that. He then began seeing himself more in the
role of a satirist, and it is possible that Babbitt was his first
intentional satire. The name "Babbitt" is significant. It alludes
to a kind of frictionless buffer metal--a metal that doesn't get
involved with other metals. George Follansbee Babbitt didn't
produce any tangible product. He was only good at selling houses
for more than people could afford to pay. Babbitt was kind of a
neutral buffer somewhere between the top and the bottom rungs of the
social ladder, not having much effect in either direction. His idea
of a "sensational event" was wearing a button proclaiming "Boosters-
-Pep!" To Babbitt, it was like a Legion of Honor ribbon or a Phi
Beta Kappa key. It was "of eternal importance, like baseball or the
Republican Party." Friedman feels that Lewis is telling us that
Babbitts are not merely funny or somewhat pathetic characters; they
are "dangerous to the future of civilization." They are not passive
or ineffective but are rather active, even violent, in their
"conformism" and "phillistinism."

560. Kishler, Thomas C. "'The Sacred Rites of Pride': An Echo of
     'The Rape of the Lock' in Babbitt." Satire Newsletter 3.1
     (Fall 1965): 28-29.

     Considers the satire in Lewis' Babbitt and Elmer Gantry to be
of the same hard-driving type as in Swift and Voltaire. Lewis'
satire exposes not only the folly but also the hypocrisy of mankind.
Kishler points out many details of Chapter V, Section 3, of Babbitt

that are similar to Canto I, lines 121-128 of "The Rape of the Lock." This refers to the section of <u>Babbitt</u> in which Paul Riesling entered the Zenith Athletic Club, and the section of "The Rape of the Lock" where Belinda prepares for the sacred rites of her toilet. Not only are the subjects and treatments similar but in both the tone is light and the authors use the technique of mock epic, whereby low actions are described in elevated and pompous language. Also, in both cases the religious imagery is comic and serious at the same time, as supreme values are interpreted in terms of individual perceptions.

561. Witkowski, Paul. "Bathroom Humor: Plumbing Some Depths of Satire in <u>Babbitt</u>." <u>Literary and Linguistic Aspects of Humour</u>. Barcelona, Spain: Univ. of Barcelona English Department, 1984, 291-96.

Suggests that fancy plumbing and bathtub gin were American obsessions in 1922 when Sinclair Lewis' <u>Babbitt</u> was published. Lewis made bathrooms an important part of the satiric portrait of real estate agent George F. Babbitt's life. In <u>Babbitt</u> bathrooms are idols; they are shrines. They are to be worshipped in the way that all modern appliances are to be worshipped. The reader laughs at Babbitt for worshipping his tub and his taps, but the reader must realize that Lewis wasn't opposed to progress. He only feared some of the social consequences of that progress. Lewis was afraid of a culture that said, "By their bathtubs shall ye know them." Babbitt's customers are described as "joining him in the worship of machinery," Babbitt himself is a "pious motorist" who is somehow "fortified by the familiarity of the rite of having his gasoline tank filled." Lewis is fascinated by the silliness of the worship of technology in general and of plumbing in particular, and this adds to the humor of Lewis' <u>Babbitt</u>, by exposing the sterility of Babbitt's existence.

<u>Edna Ferber (1887-1968)</u>

562. Drennan, Robert E. "Edna Ferber." <u>The Algonquin Wits</u>. Secaucus, New Jersey: Citadel Press, 1983, 151-55.

Indicates that when Edna Ferber and George S. Kaufman collaborated to produce <u>Minick</u> (1924), <u>The Royal Family</u> (1927), <u>Dinner at Eight</u> (1932), and <u>Stage Door</u> (1937), Ferber brought sentimentality, moralism, and family melodrama into the collaboration. As a member of "The Algonquin Wits" Ferber had a ready wit. When a reporter said of her novel <u>Ice Palace</u> that the canvas was rather large, Ferber responded that she didn't do miniatures. One afternoon, Ferber showed up at the Round Table wearing a tailored suit very similar to one which Noel Coward was wearing. Coward remarked to Ferber that she looked almost like a man, to which Ferber responded, "So do you." Ferber invited George Kaufman up to her suite at the Algonquin hotel one night so they could work together on <u>The Royal Family</u>. About midnight, a desk clerk telephoned and asked if Ferber had a gentleman in her room. Ferber responded, "I don't know. Wait a minute and I'll ask him." When a <u>New Yorker</u> critic reviewed a movie based on a Ferber novel, he leveled some criticism at Ferber, who responded that she had not

written the movie <u>Classified</u> any more than Moses had written the
movie <u>The Ten Commandments</u>.

Alexander Humphreys Woollcott (1887-1943)

563. Drennan, Robert E. "Alexander Woollcott." <u>The Algonquin
     Wits</u>. Secaucus, New Jersey: Citadel Press, 1983, 129-49.

     Describes Woollcott as a literary critic, a drama critic, an
essayist, and an arbiter of taste and fashion. <u>Long Long Ago</u> and
<u>While Rome Burns</u> are his collected works. Ben Hecht called him "a
persnickety fellow with more fizz than brain," and Thurber called
him "Old Vitriol and Violets." He loved life, especially the
yapping, scrapping, laughing, eating, romping, and exploration of
it. But he was not comfortable with the intimate or the sexual side
of life. His wit was cutting and sarcastic, but it was also
poignant and entertaining. When George and Beatrice Kaufman
celebrated their fifth wedding anniversary, Woollcott could not at
first find an appropriate wooden gift. He finally presented them
with "Elsie Ferguson's performance in her new play." When he first
saw <u>Our Town</u> he was so touched that when the producers found him he
was sitting on a fire escape in the theater alley, sobbing. When
asked if he would endorse the play, he said, "Certainly not! It
doesn't need it. I'd as soon think of endorsing the Twenty-third
Psalm." Not all of his evaluations were so positive. When he
reviewed <u>And I Shall Make Music</u> for <u>The New Yorker</u>, he said simply,
"Not on my carpet, lady."

Heywood Broun (1888-1939)

564. Drennan, Robert E. "Heywood Broun." <u>The Algonquin Wits</u>.
     Secaucus, New Jersey: Citadel Press, 1983, 61-74.

     Considers Broun to be an ardent crusader for the underdog.
Broun had a clever wit, a reflective and philosophical personality,
and a huge physique. Broun said that he had been a child prodigy.
"By the age of five, he already required twelve-year-old pants."
Broun was a paradoxical person. He was soft-hearted yet
steelminded. He was brave yet terrified. He was considerate yet
tough. He was gregarious yet solitary. He once described Geoffrey
Steyne as the worst actor on the American Stage. Steyne sued, but
the case was dismissed. After the law suit, Broun reviewed another
of Steyne's performances, saying, "Mr. Steyne's performance was not
up to its usual standard." Broun enjoyed fishing and was bothered
when people told him it was an unkind act. Broun responded that he
had been told that fish were cold-blooded and felt no pain, but then
as an afterthought, he added, "But they were not fish who told me."

Raymond Chandler (1888-1959)

565. Melnick, Jane. "The 'Femme Fatale' in Tough Novels as a
      Metaphor of Evil." WHIMSY 2 (1884): 30-33.

      Considers the "femme fatale" of Raymond Chandler's and
Dashiell Hammett's novels to be prototypical in influencing the
"femme fatale" characters in the novels of Ernest Hemingway, James
M. Cain, David Madden, and John O'Hara. The "femme fatale" in
novels by all of these authors tends to be a mysterious but
hardboiled heroine who is held up to ridicule by selective and
exaggerated narration. Melnick suggests that there is something
enigmatically dangerous about sex, and is sort of a paradoxical
representation of the misogyny in most of American literature from
the 1930s on.

566. Tanner, Stephen L. "The Function of Simile in Raymond
      Chandler's Novels." Studies in American Humor NS3.4 (Winter
      1984-85): 337-46.

      Maintains that the profusion of fresh similes and metaphors is
a hallmark of Raymond Chandler's style. These are not unobtrusive
similes but are rather "as easy to spot as a kangaroo in a dinner
jacket." They include "as rare as a fat postman," "a brain like a
sack of Portland cement," "tasted like a plumber's handkerchief,"
"about as inconspicuous as a tarantula on a slice of angel food," "a
tongue like a lizard's back," "a face like a collapsed lung,"
"feeling like a short length of chewed string," and "as restful as
a split lip." The similes are strained and bizarre and therefore
perfectly appropriate to Chandler's writing style. When other
writers try to copy Chandler's style the results do not seem natural
or original but only an imitation of Chandler. Chandler's similes
were thoroughly American. The contrived similes were perfectly
consistent with his idiomatic, slangy language, filled with
wisecracks, hyperbole, understatement, and tough talk. It actually
took British critics to recognize these as positive qualities in
Chandler's style and humor. Somerset Maugham praised Chandler for
his quick American mind and added that "his sardonic humor has an
engaging spontaneity."

T. S. Eliot(1888-1965)

567. Fleissner, Robert F. "About the Mews: Catching Up with
      Eliot's Cats." Thalia: Studies in Literary Humor 4.2 (Fall-
      Winter 1981-1982): 35-38.

      Shows there to be a number of significant religious allusions
in Old Possum's Book of Practical Cats. In the introductory poem,
"The Naming of Cats," there is "Old Deuteronomy," and this
particular poem is reminiscent of Adam's talent for naming in the
Book of Genesis. There are also cats named Jonathan, and Peter, and
Paul, and even George, which is the name of England's patron saint.
There is also Eliot's mystical cat named "Mr. Mistoffelees," which
derives from the devil-pact tradition of Marlowe and Goethe. But
Fleissner suggests that other important influences on Old Possum's

Book of Practical Cats included Edward Lear's nonsense verse, which
included "The Owl and the Pussycat," and Lewis Carroll's Alice in
Wonderland, which contains the Cheshire Cat that vanishes except for
its ubiquitous smile. There is also the Great Cham's cat Hodge in
Susan Coolidge's amusing "Hodge, the Cat" and Thomas Gray's "On the
Death of a Favorite Cat, Drowned in a Tub of Gold Fishes," and
Louella C. Poole's "Betsey Trotwood's Cat." And Fleissner suggests
that Eliot was even more indebted to Shakespeare's and Dickens' cats
in his writing of Old Possum's Book of Practical Cats.

568. Quick, Jonathan R. "'Ildiot': T. S. Eliot in Finnegans Wake".
      Thalia: Studies in Literary Humor 1.3 (Winter 1978-79):
      17-24.

    Agrees with William York Tindall who says that while Joyce was
writing Finnegans Wake he had T. S. Eliot in mind. Whenever Eliot
is alluded to in Finnegans Wake, his name is distorted to something
like "Misto Teewiley Spillitshops," or "Mr. MacElligut," or "Tame
Schwipps," or "Tansy Sauce," and these allusions are often
accompanied by fragmented quotations from Eliot's writing--often
from The Waste Land. Sometimes the effect is a parody of Eliot's
parody, taking a swipe at his "fastidiously dandyish appearance."
Many of Joyce's allusions to "tea" are also an allusion to the "T"
of T. S. Eliot. In fact, Quick feels that "any mention of tea in
Finnegans Wake is likely to evoke Eliot, his verse, and his complex
function as a character."

Anita Loos (1888-1981)

569. Grant, Thomas. "Anita Loos." Dictionary of Literary
      Biography, Volume 11: American Humorists, 1800-1950. Detroit,
      Michigan, Gale, 1982, 283-90.

    Proclaims that Loos became an internationally known satirist
by the time of the Great Crash, and a successful screenwriter when
the talkies invaded Hollywood. Loos had a tiny, childlike
appearance, and between 1912 and 1915 she wrote 105 movie scripts,
most of them slapstick comedies and romantic melodramas. In 1919,
Photoplay called her "the Soubrette of Satire." Loos had a crush on
H. L. Mencken, and when a particularly dumb blond bedazzled Mencken,
Loos wrote the sketch to what would later become her most important
novel, Gentlemen Prefer Blondes: The Illuminating Diary of a
Professional Lady. She sent the sketch to Mencken, who advised her
to send it to Harper's Bazaar, which published it as a serial. This
serial not only quadrupled the circulation of Harper's Bazaar, but
it also led to a best-selling book, a stage production (201
performances), a movie, a musical comedy (740 performances), another
movie, and another musical comedy (143 performances). Loos wanted
this piece to be a satire as well as a comedy. She saw Lorelei as
a symbol of "our nation's lowest possible mentality." Lorelei is an
ambling, uninhibited, pert, wide-eyed innocent. Her thoughts tumble
out of her mouth totally unpremediated and uncensored.

570. Randall, Phyllis R. "Anita Loos." <u>Encyclopedia of American Humorists</u>. Ed. Steven H. Gale. New York: Garland, 1988, 292-96.

Establishes Anita Loos' birth year as 1888 rather than 1893 as previous sources had suggested. When Loos died in 1981, some of her close friends reported that she was really ninety-three. Since Loos looked much younger than she actually was, she had simply knocked five years off from her age. Her <u>Gentlemen Prefer Blondes</u> was a huge literary success. It drew praises from H. G. Wells, Aldous Huxley, George Santayana, and James Joyce. Edith Wharton called it <u>the</u> American novel. H. L. Mencken was the original target (the gentleman who preferred blondes), and he wanted to publish it in <u>The American Mercury</u>, but it was too risque. The novel became a stage play in 1926 with June Walker, a movie in 1928 with Ruth Taylor, a musical comedy in 1949 with Carol Channing, and a movie musical in 1953 with Marilyn Monroe. Loos was a gourmet of the wisecrack, both her own, and other people's. The main wisecracker in <u>Gentlemen</u> is Dorothy, Lorelei's traveling companion. To some extent, the character Dorothy is autobiographical. Loos likes to satirize such ironies of our culture as Henry, the upper-class American, who likes to watch over and over again movies that he and other members of the censorship society have banned in order to protect the morals of the American public.

571. Walker, Nancy, and Zita Dresner. "Anita Loos." <u>Redressing the Balance: American Women's Literary Humor from Colonial Times to the 1980s</u>. Jackson: Univ. Press of Mississippi, 1988, 228-33.

Explains that Loos was born in California and was a child actor before she became famous as a screenwriter. By 1919 Loos had written witty scripts and/or titles for about 200 films. Such stars as Mary Pickford, Lionel Barrymore, Lillian and Dorothy Gish, Norma and Constance Talmadge, and Douglas Fairbanks all played in Loos films. Anita Loos' Lorelei Lee was a female version of H. L. Mencken's "boobus americanus." The novel in which she was a character, <u>Gentlemen Prefer Blondes</u>, had 83 American printings and was translated into 13 languages. It is probable that Lorelei was the original "dumb blonde" in American popular culture. Lorelei falls into the tradition of the wise fool popular in early American frontier humor. We laugh at Lorelei the same way that we laugh at the rubes who were her predecessors. But we also laugh with her at those who attempt to take advantage of her--the wealthy, the pompous, the sugar daddies and lotharios. In 1928 Loos wrote a sequel to <u>Gentlemen Prefer Blondes</u>, <u>But Gentlemen Marry Brunettes</u>.

Robert Charles Benchley (1889-1945)

572. Blair, Walter, and Hamlin Hill. "Benchley and Perelman." <u>America's Humor: From Poor Richard to Doonesbury</u>. New York: Oxford Univ. Press, 1978, 427-37.

Submits that Benchley first developed the concept of the non-hero confronting a hostile world--the "little-man" character--in his earliest books, <u>The Early Worm</u> and <u>20,000 Leagues Under the Sea, or,</u>

<u>David Copperfield</u>.   Benchley's writing expresses frustration,
uncertainty, passivity, and fear of failure.   He first met
illustrator Gluyas Williams while he was working on the Harvard
<u>Lampoon</u>; Williams' illustrations of the timid little man were later
to appear in all of Benchley's books. Together, they fleshed out
the bumbling idiot disguised as an expert.   He was timid and shy,
and he lacked confidence.   Confronted by any animate or inanimate
object--pigeons, parking meters, waitresses, french pastry, any
every day annoyance--he knew he was doomed.   Benchley found a
sympathetic audience for his characterization of the "little man"
among the middle-class moviegoers of the 1930s and 1940s.   Blair and
Hill feel that both Benchley and Perelman stop short of satire; they
both parody sentimentalism in literature; they both expose human
frailty in confronting a technological world; both concentrate on
the ridiculous aspects of man's fate.   And for both, their banter,
frivolity, and whimsy make it difficult for the reader to get
through to the real message.

573. Drennan, Robert E. "Robert Benchley." <u>The Algonquin Wits</u>.
      Secaucus, New Jersey: Citadel Press, 1983, 40-58.

      Depicts Benchley as a "sly wag" with an "inexact mustache," a
"burbling laugh," and a "warm wit."   Benchley was a drama critic for
the old <u>Life</u> magazine and later for the <u>The New Yorker</u>.   <u>Of All
Things</u>, <u>My Ten Years in a Quandary</u>, and <u>Chips Off the Old Benchley</u>
display a gently sardonic tone. Drennan feels that Benchley made a
clear break from the tradition of the "crackerbox philosopher"
choosing instead a persona that was both sophisticated and literate.
As a college undergraduate he edited the <u>Harvard Lampoon</u>.   He was
not good at handling his own finances, and it is reported that he
applied for a loan from his local bank, and the loan application was
approved.   At that point, he withdrew all of his money from savings
because he didn't trust a bank that would "lend money to such a poor
risk."   The story is probably apocryphal.   Benchley once wrote a
magazine article entitled, "I Like to Loaf."   He submitted the
article to the editor two weeks after the deadline along with a note
which read, "I was loafing."   Benchley acted in many movies, and at
one point the script required that he be strung up to some telephone
wires above a city street.   While in this ludicrous position he
asked his wife, Gertrude, who was on location, if she remembered how
good he had been in Latin when he was in school.   She responded that
she did remember, at which point Benchley said, "Well, look where it
got me."

574. McDiarmid, John F. "The Verbal Humor and Fantasy of Robert
      Benchley." <u>WHIMSY</u> 1 (1983): 61-63.

      Describes Benchley as a kidder. He is kidding in pieces like
"Carnival Week in Sunny Las Los" and in "The Treasurer's Report" and
in "The Social Life of the Newt."   We all picture ourselves as
serious, impressive, and capable beings, so Benchley is kidding us
when he, representing everyman, finds himself outclassed by a
typewriter ribbon, a candy wrapper, or a pigeon.   McDiarmid feels
that kidding around means loosening up. It means freeing our minds
from normal logical constraints and allowing our minds to play with
disconnectedness and free association.   Our minds can make logical
leaps rather than being confined to cause-and-effect, point-to-
point, early-to-later sequence.   Freed from logical constraints,

Benchley's writing is surrealistic. It gets us into a crazy but
pleasant world of relaxation and is therefore great bedtime reading.
His "Menace of Buttered Toast" is not one of his best stories but
the title encapsulates his style and illustrates that Benchley's
pieces are parodies of real life. "Buttered Toast" is not a
"Menace" in the real world, only in Benchley's surreal world.

575. Masson, Thomas L. "Robert C. Benchley." Our American
     Humorists. Freeport, NY: Books for Libraries, 1931, 47-52.

Considers Of All Things to be a remarkable volume of humorous
essays. Benchley was born in Worcester, Massachusetts, and
graduated from Harvard. When he moved to New York, he began writing
for Vanity Fair and then wrote reviews for the New York World and
later the old Life as their drama critic. Benchley had a large
readership and was one of the youngest humorous writers of his day.

576. Pinsker, Sanford. "Comedy and Cultural Timing: The Lessons
     of Robert Benchley and Woody Allen." The Georgia Review 52.4
     (Winter 1988): 822-37.

Considers 1910 to be a "watershed year" in American literary
history. It was the year that Mark Twain died, the year that T. S.
Eliot graduated from Harvard and wrote "The Love Song of J. Alfred
Prufrock." It was the period of transition from the Southwestern to
the Modernist new literary perspective. Virginia Woolf claimed that
it was the year that human nature changed and provided an audience
for Roger Fry's post-impressionism and Stravinsky's "Firebird." In
1910 Robert Benchley was elected to the Harvard Lampoon's editorial
board and began convulsing Harvard gatherings with comic monologues
that contained the embryonic stages of the "Little Man, our
country's most enduring comic persona." Benchley once recruited a
local Chinese laundryman to come to a Harvard football banquet as
Professor Soony of the Imperial University of China and make a
presentation (via Benchley's translation) on the history of Chinese
football. Benchley had such a reputation as a gifted speaker that
Harvard's president insisted that he not follow Benchley as an
after-dinner speaker. Benchley had a weird mustache on an
undersized head perched on top of a pear-shaped body. He was a
perfect picture of someone just a little out of control. He was a
phunny phellow without the fractured spelling.

577. Simms, L. Moody, Jr. "Robert Charles Benchley." Encyclopedia of
     American Humorists. Ed. Steven H. Gale. New York: Garland,
     1988, 36-44.

Notes the many offices Benchley held as a humorist. At
Harvard University he was elected a member of the Hasty Pudding
Club, known for its annual burlesque. He was also president of the
Signet Literary Society and a member of the presidency of the
Harvard Lampoon. In 1916 Franklin P. Adams made him associate
editor of the New York Tribune's Sunday Magazine, where he produced
such weekly features as "Do Jelly Fish Suffer Embarrassment?" He
was later fired for not conforming to the Tribune's political
ideologies. In 1919 Benchley became managing editor of Vanity Fair,
where he met such colleagues as Dorothy Parker and Robert E.
Sherwood. Dorothy Parker was dismissed because of a particularly

candid theatrical review, and Sherwood and Benchley both resigned in protest. Benchley worked as the drama critic of the humor magazine, Life, from 1920 to 1929, by which time he had developed "The Wayward Press" column for The New Yorker. "The Social Life of the Newt" demonstrates Benchley's pure nonsense, bordering on dadaism. He asks a rhetorical question and then provides an absurd answer. He parodies both the popularizers of science and their tendencies to attempt erudition by citing German sources. His Of All Things exhibits warmth, absurdity, whimsy, and satire at its best.

578. Solomon, Eric. "Robert Benchley." Dictionary of Literary Biography, Volume 11: American Humorists, 1800-1950. Detroit, Michigan: Gale, 1982, 22-37.

Lists the seventeen books and the forty-nine movie shorts which Benchley wrote. The movie shorts were written for 20th Century Fox, MGM, and Paramount, and Benchley himself starred in many of them. Solomon suggests that there are five reasons for Benchley's popularity. First, he was an author of superb comic essays; second, he wrote excellent parodies, mocking writers' excesses from Shakespeare to Galsworthy; third, he created the comic of the little man, the neurotic bumbler, the put-upon fool, the sweet inocent, the eiron of Greek comedy; fourth, he "luxuriated in the absurd"; and fifth, Benchley himself was an amiable, imbibing, anecdotal comic public figure. He acted in more than forty of the forty-nine movie shorts that were based on sketches he had written. Frank Sullivan said that everyone wanted to be Benchley's best friend and hear his booming laughter. Of All Things is "the paradigm of the Benchley canon." It exhibits what Wolcott Gibbs calls "almost logic." Love Conquers All is an example of strong Benchley parody. The best pieces in Pluck and Luck are again parodies. The Early Worm is Benchley's first attempt at long, connected humorous writing. The title piece of The Treasurer's Report, and Other Aspects of Community Singing is a treasure of cliches, repetitions, and non-sequiturs.

579. Solomon, Eric. "Notes Towards a Definition of Robert Benchley's 1930s New Yorker Humor." Studies in American Humor NS3 (Spring 1984): 34-46.

Points out that during the decade of the Depression, Benchley wrote more than seventy essays for the New Yorker, most of which have been collected in the five books he published in the 1930s--The Treasurer's Report, No Poems, From Bed to Worse, My Ten Years in a Quandary, and After 1903--What? Forty of these New Yorker essays appeared under the pseudonym of "Guy Fawkes," and many of Benchley's essays of this period demonstrated strong political commentary. He was preparing the way for A.J. Liebling to take over the "Wayward Press" column that Benchley had been writing. During the 1930s Benchley also wrote close to 350 drama reviews for the New Yorker, often demonstrating what Solomon calls the arts of "comic appreciation" and "wry rejection." Benchley reviews tend to be both comic and trenchant. His basic tone in all of his writing is ironic. In noting the political bias of the New York Times, for example, Benchley suggested that on the day that the Times published any pro-Soviet news, we could look for the entire Appalachian range to "get up and walk over to the ocean for a dip."

580. Yates, Norris W. "Robert Benchley's Normal Bumbler." The
American Humorist: Conscience of the Twentieth Century. Ames,
Iowa: Iowa State Univ. Press, 1964, 241-61.

Compares Robert Benchley to Clarence Day, Jr.; both grew up in
Victorian America.   In Benchley's case it was Worcester,
Massachusetts, where he started his training in Victorian morality.
Stephen Leacock was one of Benchley's models.   Both Leacock and
Benchley found fun in the little man in confrontation with
advertising, fads, tradition, sex, science, machinery and many other
"impersonal tyrannies."   Benchley goes so far as to say, "I have
enjoyed Leacock's work so much that I have written everything he
ever wrote--anywhere from one to five years after him."   Benchley's
acting career began when he produced a satirical review for the
"Vicious Circle" otherwise known as the "Algonquin Wits."   The
production was entitled "The Treasurer's Report," and the cast
included not only Benchley but also Jascha Heifetz, Alexander
Woollcott, Marc Connelly, Heywood Broun, George S. Kaufman, Franklin
P. Adams, and Donald Ogden Stewart.   Benchley narrated his own
piece. This performance led to a job at the Music Box Theater that
paid him $500 per week.   Five years later, he was invited to star in
this same piece in the movies, "in what may have been the first all-
talking picture ever made."

George S. Kaufman (1889-1961)

581. Drennan, Robert E. "George S. Kaufman." The Algonquin Wits.
Secaucus, New Jersey: Citadel Press, 1983, 77-92.

Considers Kaufman to be the "gloomy dean of American humor."
Kaufman collaborated on more than forty plays and musical comedies.
He won a Pulitzer Prize for Of Thee I Sing, written with Morrie
Ryskind, and another Pulitzer Prize for You Can't Take It With You,
written with Moss Hart.   Kaufman preferred to work with a
collaborator; the only successful play he wrote by himself was The
Butter and Egg Man.   Kaufman was the reigning king of Broadway for
more than twenty hears.   His comedies were fast-moving, gag-filled
farces.   The tone of his verbal wit was mocking, cutting, and often
cynical.   He enjoyed playing with language and was a master at
punning.   Kaufman was famous for his epigrams.   He said, for
example, that "satire is something that closes on Saturday night."
Kaufman once suggested that his own epitaph should read, "Over my
dead body!"

582. Miller, Tice L. "George S. Kaufman." Encyclopedia of
American Humorists. Ed. Steven H. Gale. New York: Garland,
1988, 246-51.

Explains that Kaufman's humorous verses began appearing
regularly in Franklin Pierce Adams' "Always in Good Humor" column in
the New York Evening Mail in 1909, and in 1915, on the
recommendation of Adams, Kaufman was hired to establish a new humor
column for the Evening Mail.   Kaufman collaborated with Morrie
Ryskind to write two musical comedies for the Marx Brothers,
Cocoanuts (1925), and Animal Crackers (1928).   Kaufman's
collaboration with George and Ira Gershwin resulted in Of Thee I

<u>Sing</u>, which ran for 446 performances and won a Pulitzer Prize. Kaufman also collaborated with Edna Ferber, Herman Mankiewicz, Ring Lardner, Alexander Woollcott, Howart Dietz, Katherine Dayton, Marc Connelly, and Moss Hart. Each collaboration resulted in a different tone. With Connelly it was flippant and satiric; with Ferber it was serious and melodramatic; with Hart it was humorous and whimsical but sentimental as well; with Ryskind it was fantastic and satiric. Kaufman determined the direction of American stage comedy from 1920 to 1950 with his witty and satiric dialogue and his crackling bon mots. At least twenty-five of his plays could be classified as hits.

Marcus Cook Connelly (1890-1980)

583. McIntyre, Carmela. "Marcus Cook Connelly." <u>Encyclopedia of American Humorists</u>. Ed. Steven H. Gale. New York: Garland, 1988, 94-98.

Describes Connelly as a member of the Algonquin Wits, who founded the "Round Table," otherwise known as the "Vicious Circle." Connelly was therefore in constant contact with Kaufman, Adams, Taylor, Benchley, Broun, Woollcott, Sherwood, Parker, and Ross. In 1925 Connelly became a member of the editorial board of <u>The New Yorker</u>. He wrote plays, short fiction, screenplays, a novel, and a memoir. His play, <u>The Green Pastures</u> won him a Pulitzer Prize in 1930. Connelly's writing is so closely bound to urban American life between World War I and World War II (1920 through 1940) that modern readers have difficulty appreciating his works. His plays <u>Dulcy</u>, and <u>To the Ladies!</u> as well as his playlet "Luncheon at Sea" poke gentle fun at conventional American businessmen. The playlet depicts a Rotary Club meeting at sea at which virtually nothing happens. Connelly's "The Guest" features a protagonist, Mercer, who is a forerunner of Thurber's Walter Mitty. He also represents Benchley's little man in that he is placed at the mercy of malfunctioning hotel snack machines. Connelly, a journalist, playwright, and humorist, coauthored four successful comedies with George S. Kaufman--<u>Dulcy</u>, <u>To the Ladies!</u>, <u>Merton of the Movies</u>, and <u>Beggar on Horseback</u>.

Samuel Goodman Hoffenstein (1890-1947)

584. Steege, David K. "Samuel Hoffenstein." <u>Encyclopedia of American Humorists</u>. Ed. Steven H. Gale. New York: Garland, 1988, 222-24.

Feels that Hoffenstein practiced the art of "humorous pessimism." His poems discuss courtship, love, and women from the perspective of comic realism. Hoffenstein also targeted certain impersonal qualities of the modern age, like business, advertising, science, and "progress" in general. "Oh, how my town-tried heart desires / To know the peace of Kelly Tires." Hoffenstein was the master of the comic couplet and the comic quatrain; he was labeled by Thomas Sugrue as "the star of the octosyllabic line." Hoffenstein's work was published during what Morris Bishop called "a joyous outburst of light verse." He interspersed humorous and serious poetry in his The Broadway Anthology in 1917. Hoffenstein gained little notice for his serious poetry but nevertheless became so famous for his witty verses and parodies that in 1928 he published a collection of satiric verses in his best work, Poems in Praise of Practically Nothing. This collection specializes in pessimistic poetry, but the first poem in the collection is actually a parody of such poetry, as he exults at how wonderful his sorrowful verse looks in print and worries that happy days might come along and prevent him from writing the kind of verse he does best.

585. Wermuth, Paul C. "Samuel Hoffenstein." Dictionary of Literary Biography, Volume 11: American Humorists, 1800-1950. Detroit, MI: Gale, 1982, 202-05.

Considers Hoffenstein's Poems in Praise of Practically Nothing to be a minor classic of American humor. It is witty and satirical, although some readers didn't appreciate Hoffenstein's tendency of "wise cracking." It was published in 1928 and caught the fancy of the Jazz Era; 200,000 copies were sold during Hoffenstein's lifetime. Hoffenstein is skilled at turning an appropriate phrase, at delivering an effective pun, at parodying his contemporaries, and at puncturing pretentions. Hoffenstein wanted to be a serious poet, but Life Sings a Song (1916) failed to stir up much attention. Later, when he started publishing his humorous poetry, a number of reviewers remarked that he showed genuine lyrical talent, implying, belatedly, that he should spend more time writing serious verse. His humorous collections always had serious poems interspersed among the humorous ones. This provided a change of pace but it was also his way of making sure that his serious poems would be read. Many reviewers have called Hoffenstein's work uneven. Harry Hansen said Year In, You're Out (1930) contained many witty, sparkling concepts, but it was like a vaudeville program, with a few good headliners and a lot of cheaper acts thrown in.

Christopher Morley (1890-1957)

586. Masson, Thomas L. "Christopher Morley." Our American Humorists. Freeport, NY: Books for Libraries, 1931, 261-75.

Holds that Morley has what Metchnikoff calls the "sense of life." Masson describes the "sense of life" as an intensity that is only possible in maturity; he says that such a concept is therefore usually associated with old age, since youth is normally a detached and fleeting hurry-scurry. But Morley matured earlier than most other writers and therefore developed his "sense of life" much sooner. It allowed him to develop the superb facility of being vitally interested in every person and in every topic, and this vital interest makes his writing humorous and amusing.

Katherine Anne Porter (1890-1980)

587. Gessel, Michael. "Katherine Anne Porter: The Low Comedy of
     Sex." American Humor. Ed. O. M. Brack, Jr. Scottsdale,
     Arizona: Arete, 1977, 139-52.

     Suggests that Porter uses "cruel satire," "grim comedy,"
"bristling humor," and "vituperative bursts of a burp-gun anger" as
weapons against those who pervert the low comedy of sex either with
obscenity or with the sentimentality of love. Gessel sees Porter as
a clown, as a fool, as a comic writer whose purest form of love is
"a good honest lusty fuck" and whose perception is real because it
is based on physical, chemical, and hormonal honesty. Other people
may see love attachments on a higher plane while Porter sees them as
comic exposures, revealing varying degrees of vulgarity and
perverted obscenity. The sanest and most fulfilling sexual moments
in Ship of Fools appear at the end of the novel. When the
Baumgartners have good sex, they release their pressure on Hans,
their anxiety-ridden son, and allow him to have a solid night of
sound sleep. The night after Johann has good sex, he feels warm and
easy, and makes "luxurious noises in his throat." The newlyweds are
the least sexually frustrated characters in the novel and are also
the most detached from the entanglements of the ship's panorama of
follies. Porter's message is that people shouldn't try to live
according to traditional illusions. The low comedy of sex may be
ludicrous, but it is sane and wise.

Zora Neale Hurston (1891-1960)

588. Walker, Nancy, and Zita Dresner. "Zora Neale Hurston."
     Redressing the Balance: American Women's Literary Humor from
     Colonial Times to the 1980s. Jackson: Univ. Press of
     Mississippi, 1988, 244-47.

     Judges Hurston to be one of the first Black writers to find
strength in her Afro-American heritage and judge her humor to be
warm and rollicking. Hurston studied anthropology with Franz Boas
at Columbia and later became a member of the Harlem Renaissance.
Walker and Dresner compare Hurston to Dorothy Parker during the same
period; they were both the resident female wits and both admired but
not always liked by their peers. Hurston set the stage for such
later Black women writers as Alice Walker, Paula Marshall, and Toni
Cade Banbara. Hurston consciously separated herself from what she
called the "sobbing school of Negrohood." The humor in her writings
exhibits pride and joy; a central theme is individual self-
fulfillment. Janie, the protagonist in Their Eyes Were Watching God
finds happiness with a man she can laugh with as her equal.
"Turpentine Love" is a story in I Love Myself When I Am Laughing, in
which Becky Moore finds herself with eleven children and no husband.
She says, ironically, that she "never stopped any of the fathers of
her children from proposing." Her autobiography, Dust Tracks on a
Road (1942) is, like her other novels, wry and witty.

Edward Streeter (1891-1976)

589. Cruse, Irma R. "Edward Streeter." Encyclopedia of American
      Humorists. Ed. Steven H. Gale. New York: Garland, 1988, 414-
      17.

         Tells how the "Dere Mable" letters got started. In 1916,
      Streeter was a member of Troop 1, of the First Cavalry, of the
      Twenty-Seventh Division of the New York National Guard. The Twenty-
      Seventh Division had a newspaper, and since Streeter had edited the
      Lampoon and had written for the Hasty Pudding show while he was at
      Harvard, the Guard asked Streeter to edit the humor column of the
      paper, "The Incinerator." Streeter inserted a letter from Private
      Bill Smith of Camp Wadsworth to his girl friend, Mable Gimp, of
      "Philopolis," New York. The letter was full of misspelled words,
      malapropisms, and strange French phrases. Streeter's fellow rookies
      were so enthusiastic about the "Dere Mable" letter that Streeter
      wrote more of them. In 1918, the letters were published as a book
      under the title of Dere Mable: Love Letters of a Rookie, and it
      received great acclaim as one of the few humorous books to come out
      during World War I. This book was soon followed by two more, That's
      Me All Over, Mable, and Same Old Bill, Eh Mable. Streeter would
      make such comments as "They say Cleanliness is next to Godliness,
      Mable. I say it's next to impossible." The letters in these three
      books were reprinted during World War II and were again widely read
      by service men and women.

590. Masson, Thomas L. "Ed Streeter." Our American Humorists.
      Freeport, NY: Books for Libraries, 1931, 290-94.

         Agrees with Streeter, who says that the best way to insure the
      success of a book written in a light tone is for the author to be
      unaware that he is writing it. Streeter was writing his "Dere
      Mable" letters strictly for fun. He had no idea they would ever
      appear in book form, and therefore he didn't try to be too funny.
      While Streeter was at Camp Wadsworth, South Carolina, when he was
      assigned to write "The Incinerator" column for the camp newspaper,
      the Camp Wadsworth Gas Attack. His orders were to write "short,
      witty paragraphs on Army Life." Streeter had difficulty getting his
      creative juices to flow, and he finally wrote a "Dere Mable" letter
      and presented it to Dick Connell, the editor of the paper. Connell
      read the letter, crumpled it up and threw it into the waste basket.
      When Connell went to lunch, Streeter retrieved the letter, smoothed
      it out, and shipped it off to the printer along with the rest of the
      manuscript. The letter looked better in print than it did when
      Streeter originally wrote it, so he repeated the process, and
      "Repetition quickly grew into habit." Streeter says that writing
      humor is difficult and elusive. He says that nobody will ever be
      able to discover "that mysterious drop which converts dead
      commonplace into warm, living reality," but he adds that the
      occasional sound of the "spontaneous gurgle" of someone reading one
      of his pieces keeps him at his difficult task.

591. Swanson, Roy Arthur. "Edward Streeter." Dictionary of
     Literary Biography, Volume 11: American Humorists, 1800-1950.
     Detroit, MI: Gale, 1982, 474-77.

     Classifies Edward Streeter with Robert Benchley and Ogden Nash
into a group of New England humorists who got their start at Harvard
University.   Streeter's New England upbringing gave him the
background he needed to produce gentle, restrained, charitable, and
witty humor. It is true that his "Dere Mable" books are filled with
raucous satire, as they exploit near illiteracy as a comic device.
Nevertheless, his post-Dere Mable humor is wry and sophisticated
with wisps of sadness.   Ham Martin, Class of '17 (1969) is a
reflection on the relationship between his business career and his
literary aspirations.   The humor is very muted.   The humor in
Streeter's masterpiece, Father of the Bride, is sophisticated and
flawless. Daily Except Sundays exhibits a Benchley-like humor, and
in fact is decorated with drawings by Benchley's illustrator, Gluyas
Williams. Streeter's last stage of humor is represented by Chairman
of the Bored (1961), a study of the trauma of retirement, with the
first part serious and the last part humorous, as the character
Crombie fails at country living and returns triumphantly to the
city.

Edna St. Vincent Millay (1892-1950)

592. Walker, Nancy A.   A Very Serious Thing: Women's Humor and
     American Culture. Minneapolis: Univ. of Minnesoa Press, 1988,
     55-56.

     Explains that the conflicts of Millay's Distressing Dialogues
range from such trivial items as leaving the cap off from a
toothpaste tube in "No Bigger Than a Man's Hand" to the serious
failure of a man to appreciate his wife's desire for a career in
"The Implacable Aprhodite."   Millay's characters are urbane,
privileged, world-weary socialites. Millay satirizes their "brittle
sophistication." Millay caricatures both men and women; however her
women are presented as even sillier and vainer than the men. These
unflattering stereotypes remind the reader of the women characters
of Frances Whitcher and Marietta Holley. In Millay's work, however,
they are transferred to an urban setting.

593. Walker, Nancy, and Zita Dresner. "Nancy Boyd." Redressing the
     Balance: American Women's Literary Humor from Colonial Times
     to the 1980s Jackson: Univ. Press of Mississippi, 1988, 221-
     27.

     Indicates that the Nancy Boyd pieces of Edna St. Vincent
Millay originally appeared in Vanity Fair and were later collected
in Distressing Dialogues (1924).   These pieces reveal Millay's
feminist leanings as they present with wit and humor the absurd
posturing between men and women. During the 1920s many American
humorous writers like Dorothy Parker, James Thurber, Florence Guy
Seabury, and E. B. White were targeting the war between the sexes,
and Millay added fuel to the fire.   The dialogue form of Millay's
Laughing Their Way derives from Millay's love for the theatre.

Millay's fourth book of poems, <u>Ballad of the Harp-Weaver</u> won a Pulitzer Prize in 1923.

James Thorne Smith (1892-1934)

594. Berkowitz, Gerald M. "Thorne Smith." <u>Encyclopedia of American Humorists</u>. Ed. Steven H. Gale. New York: Garland, 1988, 409-11.

Observes that Thorne Smith's writings tend to have titillating magical ghostfilled plots. <u>Topper</u>, for example contains many confusing and embarrassing moments, since the Kirbys can make themselves invisible at will, and Topper is left to explain whatever prank the Kirbys have just engaged in. Topper is rigid at first but starts to loosen up and enjoy the escapades as the novel progresses. In <u>The Bishop's Jaegers</u> a weird fog causes a commuter ferry to run off course into a nudist colony. In <u>Skin and Bones</u> the protagonist, Mr. Bland, ocasionally turns into a walking skeleton. The people in a particular speakeasy who see Mr.-Bland-the-skeleton are only mildly surprised, because they are tipsy at the time. One bar mate asks how Mr. Bland can see, without eyes, and Mr. Bland answers, "Search me." The bar mate responds that that wouldn't be hard, but it would be "damned unpleasant." <u>Turnabout</u> involves a married couple whose minds are in each other's bodies. In <u>Rain in the Doorway</u>, the protagonist takes refuge from a storm into an environment Berkowitz describes as a "bawdy <u>Alice in Wonderland</u>." Smith novels have a Rabelaisian quality. He writes ribald bawdy scenes, and naughty lines that frequently elicit a "wicked giggle."

595. Jitomir, Howard Steven. "Forgotten Excellence: A Study of Thorne Smith's Humor." Ph.D. dissertation. Collegeville, Minnesota: St. John's Univ., 1983, 232 pp.

Compares the writing of Thorne Smith to that of his contemporaries Robert Benchley, James Thurber, and Will Cuppy. All four were excellent writers, and all four dealt with common themes like the little man, the conflict between the sexes, advances in science and technology, and financial success. But of the four, only the writings of Thorne Smith do not still have a large readership. This is because Smith's writings were considered to be in bad taste, because of the following societal changes during the 1930s. First, there was an increase in violent attacks on innocent people, making Smith's violent scenes more disturbing than comic. Second, the increase in sexual permissiveness and resulting backlash made his sexual humor distasteful. Third, a patriotic entrenchment caused his satire of American morality and capitalism to be viewed as verbal attacks on the United States as a nation. Jitomar concludes that Smith was merely advocating maximum freedom and individual fulfillment.

Francis John (Frank) Sullivan (1892-1976)

596. Bartelt, C. J. "Francis John (Frank) Sullivan." _Encyclopedia of American Humorists_. Ed. Steven H. Gale. New York: Garland, 1988, 417-22.

Suggests that as a reporter for the _World_, Sullivan showed his ability for writing humor and his inability for factual reporting. Whenever he needed copy, he would make up interesting facts. He needed a paragraph in his coverage of the New York Democratic Convention and invented Aunt Sarah Gallup, a feisty, 104-year-old delegate who spent her milk and egg money to come from Holcomb Landing to support Al Smith. When other reporters started investigating the story, they discovered that neither Sarah Gallup, nor Holcolm Landing existed. Sullivan also wrote a front-page obituary of a prominent socialite of the day. Everything was perfectly accurate except for one detail. The lady had not yet died. The _World_ changed Sullivan's job from reporter to writer of his own humor column--"Out of a Clear Sky." Material from this column was the source of Sullivan's first book, _The Life and Times of Martha Heppelthwaite_. His second collection was _Innocent Bystanding_, which poked fun at the enterprise of writing. In the mock foreword Sullivan especially thanked Sir John Weether Brakemore, professor of philatotemy and don of Ephraem College, Ufton University, England, who had read the chapter on "Gladstone, Man or Myth?" and suggested certain revisions, one of which was to omit the chapter.

597. Erkkila, Betsy. "Frank Sullivan." _Dictionary of Literary Biography, Volume 11: American Humorists, 1800-1950_. Detroit, MI: Gale, 1982, 478-85.

Remarks on the length of Sullivan's contribution as a humorous writer--five decades--stretching from the zany antics of Aunt Sarah Gallup in the 1920s to the final Christmas greeting poem in the _New Yorker_ in 1974. P. G. Wodehouse described Sullivan as "America's finest humorist." Sullivan created such comic characters as the chandelier-swinging secretary, Miss Martha Hepplethwaite, and the fearless New York City street cleaner, Joseph Twiggle. Mr. Arbuthnot is Sullivan's Cliche Expert. It is his responsibility to "let the cat out of the bag," "take the bull by the horns," and "count his chickens before they're hatched." Sullivan's last Christmas greeting in the _New Yorker_ traced the Christmas greetings that he had written all the way from 1932 until "Why, hardly a prophet is now alive / Who thought we'd make it to '75." Erkkila feels that Sullivan's death marked the end of a particular school of American humor that included George Ade, Robert Benchley, Willy Cuppy, Will Rogers, Ring Lardner, Booth Tarkington, and Stephen Leacock.

598. Hutchens, John K. "The Happy Essense of Frank Sullivan." _Saturday Review_, September 12, 1970, 88-89.

Lists Leacock, Benchley, and Wodehouse as important influences on Sullivan's writing. He got busy every autumn from 1932 till 1974 to hunt the newspapers for prominent names to put in his next Christmas poem, "Greetings, Friends!" to appear in the Christmas

issue of the New Yorker. He was careful never to put in a name he
had already used. One of Sullivan's favorite rhymes appeared in a
New York Times article celebrating the New York Mets winning of the
World Series. It coupled "Tom Seaver" with "joie de vivre."

599. Sherman, Beatrice. "Bravo Once More, Frank Sullivan!" New
     York Times Book Review, November 27, 1938, 5.

     Surmises that Sullivan's writing is uneven in A Pearl in Every
Oyster. Sherman concludes that not all of Sullivan's oyster-poems
contain a pearl--"at least not a pearl of the first water." Sherman
goes on to say, however, that readers will nevertheless find
enjoyable and insightful poems if they carefully match the poems to
their own particular senses of humor. "Practically anybody will
find gems of crazy, nonsensical Sullivan humor" in the collection
which will tickle the fancy. Sherman doesn't like the Cliche Expert
but admits that it is practically impossible to resist playing the
cliche game.

Samuel Nathaniel Behrman (1893-1973)

600. Hoy, Cyrus. "Clearings in the Jungle of Life: The Comedies of
     S. N. Behrman. New York Literary Forum 1 (Spring 1978): 199-
     227.

     Contends that Behrman wrote high comedy in unpropitious times
and that his best plays were produced between 1927 when he wrote The
Second Man to 1939 when he wrote No Time for Comedy. His plays
reflect the manners and mores of a world in transition between the
high period of Coolidge prosperity through the Great Depression, and
up until the time of World War II. His No Time for Comedy displayed
brilliant wit and affirmation of the comic spirit even in
(especially in) times of world crisis. Ironically, 1939 was the end
of Behrman's writing for the theater, even though he would live
thirty-four more years--until 1973. Between 1939 and 1973 Behrman
was mainly concerned with adapting the works of other people to the
Broadway stage. Hoy concludes that Behrman struggled to write No
Time for Comedy during difficult times, and having written it,
Behrman must have felt that he had said all that he could say on the
subject.

601. Watt, Stephen. "Samuel Nathaniel Behrman." Encyclopedia of
     American Humorists. Ed. Steven H. Gale. New York: Garland,
     1988, 32-36.

     Suggests that Behrman was a successful essayist and
screenwriter but an even better playwright. From 1927 to 1939 he
wrote sophisticated and thoughtful comedy that many critics feel
resembles Restoration comedy of manners. Gerald Weales disagrees,
however, suggesting that Behrman's comedy is more comedy of ideas
than comedy of manners. George Jean Nathan felt that Behrman's The
Second Man (1927) exhibited his talent for "whipping the English
language into a sparkle." Behrman had twenty of his plays produced
on Broadway, all of them witty and urbane.

Morris Gilbert Bishop (1893-1937)

602. Hart, James D. "Morris Gilbert Bishop." The Oxford Companion
     to American Literature. 4th Edition. New York: Oxford
     Univ. Press, 1965, 82.

     Alludes to the many volumes of light verse which Morris wrote,
especially his A Bowl of Bishop (1954).

Dorothy Rothschild Parker (1893-1967)

603. Drennan, Robert E. "Dorothy Parker." The Algonquin Wits.
     Secaucus, New Jersey: The Citadel Press, 1983, 110-127.

     Describes Parker as a literary critic and drama critic for
Vanity Fair. Parker also wrote excellent humorous short prose, and
her Big Blonde won the O. Henry Prize. Parker is probably best
remembered, however, for her light, witty, and mocking poetry. For
a while, Parker wrote for the Marxist magazine New Masses; she
chided a number of different American personality types and also
satirized the nineteenth-century ideal of the vacuous, idle feminine
mystique. Among the members of the Round Table, Parker was probably
the most devastating master of the repartee and verbal put-down.
She had an acid wit and a ready tongue. Writing about a Yale prom,
she declared that if all of those sweet young things were laid end
to end, she wouldn't be at all surprised. When one of her female
acquaintances broke her leg while vacationing in London, Parker
exclaimed, "Probably sliding down a barrister." One evening during
a dinner party, Parker was in an especially festive mood, and a snob
told her that he couldn't join in the merriment because he couldn't
bear fools. "That's queer," responded Parker, "your mother could."
In reviewing Margot Asquith's long and boring autobiography, Parker
exclaimed that "The affair between Margot Asquith and Margot Asquith
will live as one of the prettiest love stories in all literature."

604. Grant, Thomas. "Dorothy Parker." Dictionary of Literary
     Biography, Volume 11: American Humorists, 1800-1950. Detroit,
     MI: Gale, 1982, 369-82.

     Points out that Parker was the first, and for quite some time
the only, member of the "Algonquin Round Table." Her acceptance
into the group pivoted on her ability to dryly deliver devastating
verbal blows. Of the members of the Round Table, Parker was most
often quoted in Addams' influential daily column, "The Conning
Tower." She was good at word games. When neither Benchley nor
Sherwood could provide a witty sentence containing the word
"horticulture," Parker remarked, "You can lead a horticulture, but
you can't make her think." Parker wrote for Vanity Fair until 1920
when she criticized a performance by Billie Burke. Burke's husband
was influential Florenz Ziegfeld, and Ziegfeld got Frank Crownin to
fire Parker from Vanity Fair. Parker's friends Robert Sherwood and
Robert Benchley both resigned in sympathy to Parker's cause. Parker
remained active, however, publishing in the next three years ninety-
one pieces in Life, a satirical magazine similar to England's Punch.

In 1929 Parker coauthored a domestic comedy with Elmer Rice named
Close Harmony. It was about two people whose fumbling attempts to
have an adulterous affair so frightened them that they returned to
their spouses. In Sunset Gun, published in 1928, Parker wrote a
cycle of daring epigrams. In "A Pig's-Eye View of Literature," she
took sort of a barnyard stance in reviewing some of the classics.

605. Kline, Virginia. "Dorothy Rothschild Parker." Encyclopedia of
     American Humorists. Ed. Steven H. Gale. New York: Garland,
     1988, 344-49.

     Agrees with Brad Darrach who said that Parker had done more
than anyone else to make the "wise guy" a predominent American
stereotype. Parker's poetry is brilliant, alive, and sparkling.
She was a good writer with a keen wit, and she understood the times
in which she lived. In 1935, Scholastic Magazine wrote that Parker
had such fame as a satirist and deadly wit that whenever a
particularly vitriolic phrase happened to be going around town, it
was always attributed to Parker. In 1944, J. Donald Adams wrote in
a New York Times book review that Parker's clever and polished
writing derived from what he called "an attitude." In 1947 received
a divorce from Alan Campbell, and she later wrote a poem to him
entitled "War Song," in which she encouraged him to asuage his
loneliness by developing a new friendship. The poem is ironic,
however, and ends with the hope that he will turn to his new lover
and call her by the name of "Dorothy." Kline indicates that Parker
suffered from periods of emotional highs and lows and that she
attempted suicide on three different occasions. She wrote a poem on
the discomforts of suicide and concluded that "You might as well
live." Parker was a survivor. She lived and wrote through the
"Roaring Twenties," the Depression, World War I, World War II, the
McCarthy trials, and the civil rights movement. He writing changed
with the times; she was a social and literary barometer.

606. Masson, Thomas L. "Dorothy Parker." Our American Humorists.
     Freeport, NY: Books for Libraries, 1931, 276-84.

     Considers Parker to be the best American humorous woman
writer, and justifies the hedge "woman" by saying that men's writing
and women's writing cannot be compared because they are different
genres. Masson disagrees with those critics who contend that women
have no sense of humor and suggests that these writers probably also
deny women the talent for having-children. Masson suggests that
Parker's talent lies in her ability to say the most cutting things
with a lamb-like air. She is a prima donna who will not do anything
she is ordered to. She makes all sorts of excuses not to do it
and then usually survives very well not doing it at all. Masson is
amused by the fact that Parker's critics accuse her of being a
cynic, adding that such a posture is unbecoming in a woman. Masson
suggests that some people find any action unbecoming if it is done
better than they could have done it. Masson feels that Parker could
have easily had her place in literary history if she would only
write, but she refuses to write. Every once in a while she turns
out something that is perfect in its way, but it is always only an
"aside." She has no sustained body of literature on which critics
can make an appropriate judgment of her merit.

607. Walker, Nancy, and Zita Dresner. "Dorothy Parker." Redressing
     the Balance: American Women's Literary Humor from Colonial
     Times to the 1980s. Jackson: Univ. Press of Mississippi. 1988,
     257-67.

     Regards Parker as one of the few female humorists whose work
frequently appears in anthologies and critical studies of American
humor, but lament the fact that her inclusion is based more on her
membership in the Algonquin Round Table than on a critical
appreciation of her writing. Mordecai Richler did not include her
explaining that her work was brittle, short on substance, and no
longer funny, but it is indeed still funny to feminists who are
amused by her bittersweet depiction of the sexual double standard
and strained relationships between men and women. "The Waltz" is a
classic story about the devastating effects of female socialization.
It constrasts a woman's private thoughts with her public statements
and is a study in male brutishness and female helplessness. Parker
was a master of light verse, but most of her writing is quite dark,
as can be seen in such titles as Enough Rope (1927), Laments for the
Living (1930), and Death and Taxes (1931). Parker was a paradox.
She often seemed witty and self-confident, but she was often
suicidal. Her turbulent personal life contrasted sharply with her
public image of being a successful writer for Vanity Fair and The
New Yorker.

608. Yates, Norris W. "Dorothy Parker's Idle Men and Women." The
     American Humorist: Conscience of the Twentieth Century. Ames,
     Iowa: Iowa State Univ. Press, 1964, 262-74.

     Notes that Parker used her facile wit as a coping device.
During a period of loneliness, she tacked a sign on her office door
reading, "Men." When Harold Ross asked her why she hadn't turned in
a certain piece to The New Yorker, she replied that somebody was
using the pencil. When she was told that Calvin Coolidge was dead,
Parker asked, "How can they tell?" And another time, Parker leaped
to her feet in an open cab and began shouting to passers-by that she
was being abducted. Robert Benchley, the other occupant of the cab,
whipped off his scarf and started in mock seriousness began to gag
her with it. Yates concludes from such incidents as these that
Dorothy Parker's personal conduct should be used to season any
history of America during the 1920s. Yates considers Parker's
Enough Rope (1926), Sunset Gun (1928), and Death and Taxes (1931) to
be light, sardonic, and, at times, hedonistic. Parker's
sentimentality was tempered with wit and irony. Alexander Woollcott
called her a combination of "Little Nell and Lady Macbeth."

E. E. Cummings (1894-1962)

609. Kiley, Frederick, and J. M. Shuttleworth. "e. e. cummings."
     Satire: from Aesop to Buchwald. New York: Odyssey, 1971, 344-
     47.

     Considers Cummings to be difficult reading at first, because
he arranges words in puzzling ways, coins words, uses little
punctuation, plays with capitalization, and creates wild metaphors
and similes, like "a fragment of angry candy." His "I Sing of

Olaf," "The Cambridge Ladies," and "My Sweet Old Etcetera" are all witty satires. "I Sing of Olaf" tells of a potential soldier who prefers to be a conscientious objector. "The Cambridge Ladies" is a sonnet which satirizes the shallowness and trivial activities of the ladies in a particular university city--Cambridge, Massachusetts. "My Sweet Old Etcetera" is another ironic war poem, this one telling of all of the things, etcetera, that are needed in the war effort, and how everyone must help, etcetera, in the war effort, and how everyone will be so proud when the protagonist is killed, etcetera, in the war.

610. Read, Donald R. "E. E. Cummings: The Lay of the Duckbilled Platitude." Satire Newsletter 3.1 (Fall, 1965): 30-33.

Considers verse satire, the genre in which E. E. Cummings wrote, to be something of a contradictory genre. Verse is often characterized as being compact, concise, and organically structured. For verse there is a close relationship between technique and content. Read feels that satire frequently lacks some or all of these qualities. Read feels that Cummings is successful in combining the devices of satire with the devices of poetry in a way that unites form and function. Read does not state that Cummings has resolved the paradox of verse satire, but he does believe that he has used the paradox to his own advantage. Read analyzes a Cummings poem entitled "Remarked Robinson Jefferson" to demonstrate how Cummings has used poetry as a vehicle for conveying trenchant satire of political hypocrisy. The symbolism of this poem is far ranging, from "Lydia E. Pinkham," to a "duckbilled platypus." The poem uses lampoon and parody to illuminate issues of obscenity. It is filled with verbal irony and ranges from low burlesque to high burlesque. There is such a strange juxtaposition of rhetorical devices and visual images that Read considers it not satire versified but rather pure poetry.

Dashiell Hammett (1894-1961)

611. Brenner, Gerry. "More Than a Reader Responding: Hammett's Refeathered Maltese Falcon." Thalia: Studies in Literary Humor 10.1 (1989): 48-56.

Insists that Item 638-663 (labeled "Miscellany, Unidentified) in Berkeley's Bancroft Library is actually correspondence between Dashiell Hammett ("Dash") and recently deceased Lillian Hellman ("Lilly"). Brenner's colleague suggested that he submit his find to a scholar who was preparing an anthology of reader-response criticism, but Brenner declined, saying that he was not in sympathy with new-fangled schools of literary criticism. Hammett had written to Hellman apologizing for a snarling criticism of her first play. Hammett had written, "It's worse than bad--it's half good." What had prompted Hammett to write to Hellman was that he had just reread his own Maltese Falcon and had determined, ironically, that his earlier criticism of Hellman's play was actually a very appropriate criticism of his own. He was in the process of revising the "Falcon" and was writing to thank Hellman for her inspiration.

Donald Ogden Stewart (1894-1980)

612. McNutt, James C. "Donald Ogden Stewart." Dictionary of
      Literary Biography: Volume 11: American Humorists, 1800-1950.
      Detroit, MI: Gale, 1982, 466-73.

     Classifies Donald Stewart with Ring Lardner, Robert Benchley,
and James Thurber developing the "little man." Stewart's first
humorous writing was a parody of Edward Streeter's Dere Mabel.
Stewart's piece, "Dere Queenie," was published in a local Navy
magazine. In 1921 Stewart published "The Secret of Success" in the
Smart Set. This story satirizes the Horatio Alger myth by telling
about Richard Kennedy who spent much time taking self-help courses
without success, but who then rose in the ranks by marrying the
daughter of the company president. His first book is entitled A
Parody Outline of History. In 1922 he wrote Aunt Polly's Story of
Mankind, a satire of middle-class American values. Stewart also
wrote etiquette parodies for Harper's Bazaar and Vanity Fair. These
were later collected and published in Perfect Behavior and enhanced
Stewart's reputation as a writer of light humor. Stewart's first
book of "crazy-humor," Mr. and Mrs. Haddock Abroad, was begun in
Paris in 1924. This book established his crazy-humor style with its
salient qualities of non sequitur and slapstick. The Crazy Fool was
a twist on a French novel Stewart had read about a young man who had
inherited a brothel. In Stewart's book, he inherits an insane
asylum.

James Grover Thurber (1894-1961)

613. Arner, Robert D. "'The black, memorable year 1929': James
      Thurber and the Great Depression." Studies in American Humor
      NS3.2-3 (Summer-Fall 1984): 237-52.

     Points out that Thurber's earliest writings coincide with the
decade of the Great Depression--1929-1939. About two weeks after
Black Thursday, he published a collaboration with E. B. White
entitled Is Sex Necessary? or Why You Feel the Way You Do (1929).
He also published a number of collections of "casuals" and cartoons
during this decade--The Owl in the Attic (1931), The Seal in the
Bedroom (1932), My Life and Hard Times (1933), The Middle-Aged Man
on the Flying Trapeze (1935), Let Your Mind Alone! (1937), and The
Last Flower (1939). This last book appeared shortly after the
invasion of Poland on September 1, 1939. One of the reasons that
Thurber wrote so diligently during this period is that he had a
painful fear that playful humor would be one of the casualties of
the Depression. He noted this concern as early as 1933 in "Preface
to a Life." In the middle 1950s Thurber reiterated the concern to
George Plimpton and Max Steele of the Paris Review and even went so
far as to say that the Depression had had more of an impact on
American humor than had Hitler and the war. Thurber felt that humor
is an American tradition. The "Declaration of Independence"
promises "life, liberty, and the pursuit of happiness." Thurber
considered unhappiness to be un-American. It is our patriotic duty
as Americans to be happy.

614. Arnold, St. George Tucker, Jr. "Stumbling Dogtracks on the Sands of Time: Thurber's Less-Than-Charming Animals, and Animal Portraits in Earlier American Humor." The Markham Review 10 (Spring 1981): 41-47.

Notes the symbiotic relationship between Thurber's visual and linguistic animal caricatures. The "Thurberhounds" are cartoon bloodhounds with dogly charm, composure, unaffectedness and sympathy for the males who are engaged in losing battles with their spouses. Although the "Thurberhounds" have dominated critical comment regarding animals, it should be noted that Thurber writes about a wide range of creatures with widely varying traits and relationships to the people around them. Thurber's animals tend to be innocent and appealingly ingenuous, but some of them are boring, sneaky, or even hypochondriacal. In "There's an Owl in My Room," Thurber cannot understand how Gertrude Stein could have written "Pigeons on the grass, alas!" For Thurber, pigeons are dull. Thurber cannot tolerate the total lack of personality in the pigeon and says the bird is not worthy of notice in any form, and is certainly not capable of evoking an "alas." Thurber notes that it is the docility of pigeons that allows them to be released in large numbers at "band concerts, library conventions, and christenings of new dirigibles" and suggests that there would be utter chaos if hens, owls, or eagles were released at such events. Arnold points out that Harris, Twain, and Thurber have all found laughter in animal-human interactions.

615. Black, Stephen A. James Thurber: His Masquerades: A Critical Study. The Hague: Mouton, 1970, 126 pp.

Postulates that Thurber's writing is transitional between the "native American humor" of the nineteenth century and the tragicomic fiction of such writers as Salinger, Bellow, Roth, Malamud, and Heller. Black feels that Thurber is virtually the only comic writer of his generation whose work is of consistently high quality and goes on to say that just as Twain defined the "native" humor of the nineteenth century, Thurber defined the comedy of the early twentieth century. Black feels that there is a basic similarity between the writing of Washington Irving and that of James Thurber. The desires and fantasies of Walter Mitty and those of Ichabod Crane are fundamentally the same. But Thurber does not share with Irving the contempt for the intellectual class. Thurber identifies with Mitty in a way that Irving does not identify with Crane. Emotionally, Thurber is a middle of the roader. He exhibits neither easy optimism nor bleak despair. In Thurber's world, the cultural stereotypes are reversed, and the world is operated for and by women. In Thurber's world the men are more prone to failure, frustrations, and neuroses than are the women.

616. Blair, Walter, and Hamlin Hill. "'The Secret Life of Walter Mitty.'" America's Humor: From Poor Richard to Doonesbury. New York: Oxford Univ. Press, 1978, 448-59.

Explains that Thurber's "The Secret Life of Walter Mitty" was first published in The New Yorker in 1939 and that it was reprinted in The Reader's Digest "for millions of readers, few of whom subscribed to The New Yorker or even liked it." Still later the piece was picked up in numerous collections of American humor and high school and college textbook anthologies. It became a radio playlet, a movie, a review sketch, an opera, an off-Broadway musical, and a segment of a one-man evening-long Thurber impersonation. One of Thurber's biographers who had access to his royalty statements speculated that the reprint permissions for this story had brought Thurber more money per word than for any other story, serious or humorous, ever written. "Walter Mitty" has become as well known as "Hercules," "Judas," "Romeo," "Don Quixote," "Don Juan," Mrs. Malaprop," "Frankenstein," "Scrooge," "Sherlock," "Pollyanna," and "Babbitt" in the English language, and "the Walter Mitty syndrome" is a common psychological term.

617. Carnes, Pack. "The Damp Hand of Melancholy: Thurber's Fabular Humor." WHIMSY 3 (1985): 28-29.

    Contends that a significant part of Thurber's reputation as one of America's paramount humorists is the result of Fables for Our Time (1939) and Further Fables of Our Time (1956). These two volumes are radically different, the first being fables written in traditional forms but with the traditional wisdom parodied and modernized. Most of the fables in Thurber's first book are light-hearted re-writes of earlier fables. Nevertheless, this first set of fables is also colored with the dark humor of Thurber's ability to visualize the impending World War. The second book contains pessimistic satires which carry the message that the traditional collected wisdom of the ages is simply not to be trusted. Further Fables exhibits the "damp hand of melancholy" as the fables are sharply critical of the McCarthy age in which they were written. Much of the humor of Thurber's fables derives from the fact that they are incongruent with twentieth-century life. All of Thurber's fables show a delight in the language he manipulates. They all contain perverted morals or twisted proverbial phrases.

618. Gale, Steven H. "Thurber and the New Yorker." Studies in American Humor NS3.1 (Spring 1984): 11-23.

    Declares that Thurber was a primary factor in determining the style of The New Yorker. He became a member of The New Yorker staff in 1927 and wrote a total of 365 signed items. He was even managing editor for a while. He contributed poetry, "casuals" (a term coined by Harold Ross to describe short humorous prose pieces), factual essays, photographs, cartoons, and profiles. He also contributed various regular columns such as "Famous Poems Illustrated," "Fables for Our Times," "Where Are They Now," "Onward and Upward with the Arts," and "The Tennis Court." Thurber developed the character of "the little man." He was a meek, badly dressed, physically small man, who had just had a fight with his wife. He is silent and prodding. One such "little man" got caught in a revolving door and remained there for four hours. As a result he received $100,000 worth of vaudeville and motion picture offers. His explanation of how he accomplished the feat is typically Thurber: "I did it for the wife and children." Thurber was a wordsmith who was meticulous and precise in word choice. Thurber had a penchant for clean copy. He never turned in a page with a mistake on it. He always copied it over, and when he did, he made revisions. As a result of constant revisions, his writing became relaxed and subtle. Thurber also had a remarkable memory and paid great attention to detail. His writing has a solid, realistic feel.

619. Heuscher, Julius E. "Humour and Fairy Tales: Quests for Wider
     Worlds." It's a Funny Thing, Humour. Eds. Antony J. Chapman
     and Hugh C. Foot. New York: Pergamon Press, 1977, 413-16.

     Uses Thurber's "The 13 Clocks" to demonstrate that both humor
and fairy tales lift us beyond the ordinary, mundane, practical real
world to a level of higher awareness. A common paradoxical theme of
the fairy tale is that only the person who risks everything in
performing an impossible task can succeed.   Thurber's "The 13
Clocks" illustrates this, for the protagonist must place his faith
in Golux, a bizarre, befuddled, amusing, completely unreliable
creature. Golux dresses and speaks weirdly. He speaks in limericks
and light ballads. His language is grotesquely exaggerated, with
ridiculous perversions of logic. His jokes are intended to elicit
tears, and he displays a cold, sardonic laughter. Heuscher relates
fairy tales to dreams, daydreams, art, philosophy, and psychotherapy
as well as to wit and folklore in that all of these situations are
ways of getting distance, stepping back in order to gain a broader
perspective detached from real life.   Heuscher feels that wit,
jests, laughter, jokes, and humor in general are probably the oldest
forms of gaining detachment from the dreariness that invades
everyday existence. Fairy tales and humor are like the smiling
Buddha, the jesting Zen Master, the tricked Trickster in that they
all achieve transcendence.

620. Kenney, Catherine McGeehee, ed. Thurber's Anatomy of Confusion.
     Hamden, CT: Archon Books, 1984, 235 pp.

     Characterizes Thurber's major theme as the clash between chaos
and order or, as Thurber himself sees it, "chaos recollected in
tranquility." "Thurber's work is the result of a systematic study
of chaos, delineating the structure of disorder." Kenney considers
Thurber's work "poetry." She feels that Thurber should have a place
not only in the tradition of American humor but in the tradition of
English-language fiction as well.   The four middle chapters of
Kenney's book are treatments of "anatomy." "Corpus Mundi" treats
the physical aspects of the human animal with such themes as the
battle of the sexes, the failure of science and technology, the
inadequacy of the family, and the horrors of history.   "Corpus
Mentis" treats the mental aspects of the human animal with such
sections as "Moonlit Merges of the Mind," and "The Language of
Confusion." "Homo Loquens" treats Thurber's long-time love affair
with words, whether spoken, seen, or heard. In a section entitled
"A Bright and Melancholy Spectacle: The Anatomist in a World of Time
and Death," Kenney explains what Thurber may have meant by the
statement, "The claw of the sea-puss gets us all in the end."

621. Nelson, F. William. "James Grover Thurber." Encyclopedia of
     American Humorists. Ed. Steven H. Gale. New York: Garland,
     1988, 445-51.

     Proclaims that Thurber published some twenty-eight books. His
play The Male Animal and such short stories as "The Secret Life of
Walter Mitty," "The Unicorn in the Garden," and "The Catbird Seat"
became motion pictures, the last one retitled "The Battle of the
Sexes." Together with E. B. White and Robert Benchley, Thurber set
the tone for The New Yorker, especially in the "Talk of the Town"
section.   Thurber's second book, The Owl in the Attic, was

originally eight episodes from the life of Mr. and Mrs. Monroe. Mr.
Monroe was a typical timid, unsure, bewildered and frustrated
"little man." Nelson points out that the nineteenth century
predecessors of "the little man" were brash and confident, while
Thurber's characters are overwhelmed by trivial matters. Nelson
suggests that much of Thurber's humor is merely an exaggerated
version of his own experience. The major conflicts involve the
battle of the sexes, the clash of romantic idealism with cold
reality, and the inability of males to cope with technological and
social complexities of the twentieth century. My Life and Hard
Times, The Seal in the Bedroom, and The Middle-Aged Man on the
Flying Trapeze illustrate these conflicts. The New Yorker's "Pet
Department" was originally a parody of the question-and-answer
columns in that were the rage in newspapers. "Guide to Modern
English Usage" was a parody of writing manuals.

622. O'Hearn, Carolyn. "James Thurber: Humorist as Linguist."
     WHIMSY 3 (1985): 29-32.

     Divides Thurber's work into three categories based on the
linguistic tendencies of the particular work--phonological,
syntactic, and semantic. O'Hearn feels that the works which
emphasize phonological devices are Thurber's least effective. They
result in a Whitmanesque catalogue of sounds. They tend to deal
with such subjects as insomnia in the middle of the night, or word
games at parties. "The Tyranny of Trivia" is an example of the
insomnia category. O'Hearn considers the syntactically based
stories to be of higher quality. In these pieces Thurber comments
on the craft of the writer. Almost all of Thurber's syntactic
pieces were published in 1929 in a New Yorker series entitled, "Our
Own Modern English Usage." These pieces were later collected into
a book entitled Ladies' and Gentlemen's Guide to Modern English
Usage. For O'Hearn, the richest of the three linguistic categories
is semantic. These pieces tend to center around a situation where
a man and a woman are attempting unsuccessfully to communicate with
each other, each of them falling back into his own linguistic system
and misunderstanding what the other is saying. An example is "What
Do You Mean It Was Brillig?" This third category also contains
Thurber's anti-metaphorical development, whereby businessmen who
tell their wives they are tied up at the office are shown to be
physically bound and gagged. All the businessmen in the city seem
to be tied up at around 5 o'clock in the afternoon.

623. Scholl, Peter A. "James Thurber." Dictionary of Literary
     Biography, Volume 11: American Humorists, 1800-1950. Ed.
     Stanley Trachtenberg. Detroit, MI: Gale, 1982, 505-26.

     Considers Thurber to be a transitional humorist, linking the
traditional horse-sense humorists of his predecessors with the black
humorists of the postatomic era. His most comfortable genre was the
short, almost conversational but at the same time elegantly crafted
"casual." Thurber developed a character type which E. B. White
called the "Thurber men." These characters are constantly
perplexed, frustrated and out of place. They are doing their best
to escape from a room, from a situation, or from a state of mind,
but they are too humble or too weak to be successful. Dorothy
Parker placed Thurber's characters into three classes, the playful,
the defeated, and the ferocious. "All of them have the outer

semblance of unbaked cookies." Thurber's Mr. Monroe, Mr. Mitty, Mr.
Martin, and Mr. Kinstrey forereshadow the spiritual drifters and
death-obsessed schlemiels of later <u>New Yorker</u> writers like Donald
Barthelme and Woody Allen. Scholl feels that these characters are
closer to the black humor characters who follow than they are to the
cracker-barrel philosophers who preceded. Chaos threatened the
protagonists of both Thurber's early and his late stories, and the
chaos increased as Thurber continued writing. But even at the end,
when there were more lances than lanterns, there was nevertheless
always the thread of hope.

624. Scholl, Peter A. "James Thurber." <u>Concise Dictionary of
      Literary Biography</u>. Ed. Stanley Trachtenberg. Detroit, MI:
      Gale, 1989, 336-59.

     Notes that Thurber won many literary awards, among them two
humor awards, the "Laughing Lions of Columbia University Award for
Humor" in 1949, and the "American Cartoonist's Society T-Square
Award" in 1956. While attending Ohio State University, Thurber was
most affected by Joseph Taylor, an English professor who introduced
him to the works of Willa Cather, Joseph Conrad, and, especially,
Henry James. But Thurber was also influenced by the comic strips of
his day, by melodramas, and later by movies and "nickel novels."
Thurber's own writings were most influenced by the stories of O.
Henry and Robert O. Ryder, editorialist for the <u>Ohio State Journal</u>.
Thurber developed the dry, deadpan style of the best oral yarn
spinners in his writings. Like the yarn spinners, Thurber realized
that comedy is enhanced by the contrast between the deadpan delivery
and the frenetic events being described in the story. This contrast
between the overstated events and the understated telling of the
events also became the essence of the <u>New Yorker</u>'s style of "studied
artlessness." <u>The Middle-Aged Man on the Flying Trapeze</u> is so
autiobiographical that upon reading it many of Thurber's friends
became concerned about his well-being. Walter Mitty is the
prototypical Thurber man, and in fact the expression "Walter Mitty"
is defined in a number of dictionaries.

625. Toombs, Sarah Eleanora. <u>James Thurber: An Annotated
      Bibliography of Criticism</u>. New York: Garland, 1987, xlx + 258
      pp.

     Maintains that mainstream critical opinion has been slow to
acknowledge the importance of Thurber's work to the field of
American literature and hopes that this annotated bibliography of
criticism will help to rectify the situation. The bibliography
contains newspaper notices, book reviews, and full-length studies of
Thurber's themes and techniques. In order to be included, a piece
had to be determined to be of critical, historical or biographical
importance. The bibliography contains biographical material,
criticism of books and articles, criticism of single collections,
criticisms of plays, films, stage productions, and television
productions. Toombs views Thurber's writing as paradoxical. His
moods range from playfully lighthearted to bleakly pessimistic. His
favorite theme is the battle of the sexes, but his affirmation of
women was a source of his strength and hope. His stories are brief
and anecdotal, yet there was a full range of genres--stories,
recollections, parodies, fables, essays, and "conversation pieces."
Toombs feels that Thurber criticism falls into three distinct time

periods.   The apprentice stage (1929-1945) started with <u>Is Sex
Necessary?</u> (coauthored with E. B. White) and ended with <u>The Thurber
Carnival</u>.   The virtuosity and versitility stage lasted from 1945
till 1963.   The posthumous stage of Thurber criticism (1964-84) is
still in process.

626. Yates, Norris W. "James Thurber's Little Man and Liberal
      Citizen." <u>The American Humorist: Conscience of the Twentieth
      Century</u>. Ames, Iowa: Iowa State Univ. Press, 1964, 275-98.

Indicates that Thurber felt that nobody had more influence in
shaping his style than did E. B. White.   In 1929 Thurber and White
collaborated on <u>Is Sex Necessary?</u> White convinced Thurber that he
should also prepare thirty or forty drawings for the volume.
Thurber did the drawings and they were submitted with the manuscript
to <u>Harper's</u>.   The editors at <u>Harper's</u> assumed that the drawings were
rough sketches and that the real drawings would be submitted later,
but White convinced them not only that the drawings were finished
but also that they were good and should go in the book.   Thurber and
White joined Robert Benchley and Clarence Day, Jr., in developing
the personna of the meek, bewildered white-collar character to be
called the "little man."   Only Thurber's "little man" is bothered
most of all by "SEX."   Thurber and White both claimed that there
were two subjects that had been overemphasized in American culture.
One was aviation, and the other was sex.   In satirizing sexual
inhibitions, Thurber and White are attacking the prudishness that
caused such a situation to develop.

Milt Gross (1895-1953)

627. Blackbeard, Bill. "Milt Gross." <u>Dictionary of Literary Biography, Volume 11: American Humorists, 1800-1950</u>. Detroit, MI: Gale, 1982, 160-65.

Lists Gross's books as <u>Nize Baby</u> (1926), <u>Hiawatta, Witt No Odder Poems</u> (1926), <u>De Night in De Front From Chreesmas</u> (1927), <u>Dunt Esk!!</u> (1927), <u>Famous Fimmales, Witt Odder Ewents From Heestory</u> (1928), <u>He Done Her Wrong</u> (1930), <u>Dear Dollink</u> (1945), and <u>I Shoulda Ate the Eclair</u> (1946). Gross had the ability to make both linguistic and visual presentations, and all of his books contain his evocative sketchy drawings as well as his fiction and/or poetry. Gross had the gift of a flawless memory and liked to exaggerate his parents' Bronx Yiddish dialect. He appealed to two widely disparate audiences--the sophisticated book-reading world and the readers of newspaper comic strips. Gross had a dry period from 1930 until 1940 when he returned to his dialect humor in a Hearst newspaper column entitled "Dear Dollink." Each column was a letter from a doting Jewish mother to her soldier son, giving him the home-front news in heavy dialect. Gross's last book, <u>I Shoulda Ate the Eclair</u> was not as heavily dialectal as his earlier books. The world would no longer accept the heavy dialect it had up until then applauded all the way from Mr. Dooley to Amos and Andy. After World War II, publishers would not publish the heavy dialectal writing from even such an established writer as Milt Gross.

Thomas Hornsby Ferril (1896-)

628. Kiley, Frederick, and J. M. Shuttleworth. "Thomas Hornsby Ferril: 'Freud on Football.'" <u>Satire: From Aesop to Buchwald</u>. New York: Odyssey, 1971, 437-40.

Shows "Freud on Football" to be a spoof of scientific analyses of social phenomena. The satire starts slowly and quietly but builds to its powerful conclusion. The satire has the effect of making readers more skeptical and reserved when they later read socio-scientific analyses. It gives them more balance in their critical judgment of such works. In order to do this, Ferril describes the game of football as it would be seen through the eyes of a psychologist. Thus seen, football is "a syndrome of religious rites symbolizing the struggle to preserve the egg of life through the rigors of impending winter." Ferril notes that the ceremony begins at the autumnal equinox and culminates on the first day of the New Year with great festivals and bowls of plenty. These festivals are associated with the harvest. Some are dedicated to flowers such as roses, others to fruits such as oranges, or farm crops such as cotton. There are even festivals dedicated to animals such as alligators. All of the festivals appear to be special celebrations in honor of the Sun God.

William Faulkner (1897-1962)

629. Blair, Walter, and Hamlin Hill. "William Faulkner." America's
     Humor: From Poor Richard to Doonesbury. New York: Oxford Univ.
     Press, 1978, 465-70.

     Explains the extent to which Faulkner used frame narratives
and mock oral tales. These devices are used throughout As I Lie
Dying, The Hamlet, The Town, The Mansion, The Reivers, as well as in
Jason's segment of The Sound and the Fury. Faulkner was much
indebted to the Southwest humorists. When it was pointed out to him
that his "The Bear" had great similarities to Thomas Bangs Thorpe's
"The Big Bear of Arkansas," Faulkner replied that that was such a
good story a writer should not read it for fear he will later
remember it and present it as his own. Faulkner was also greatly
influenced by Harris' Sut Lovingood, whom he ranked with Twain's
Huck and Jim as his three favorite characters in American
literature. Faulkner's library also contained many books by
humorists of the Old Southwest as well as compilations of jokes of
his day. He was a personal acquaintance of Benchley, Thurber,
Parker, and other writers for The New Yorker. Matthew Wood Little,
in his 1975 doctoral dissertation, demonstrated that the humor in
Faulkner's major novels ranges from black humor to crackerbox
philosophy, to local northern Mississippi color, to broad satire, to
tall tales, to sophisticated intellectual humor.

630. Collins, Carvel. "Faulkner and Certain Earlier Southern
     Fiction." The Frontier Humorists: Critical Views. Ed. M.
     Thomas Inge. New York: Archon, 1975, 259-65.

     Points out that Faulkner's fiction continues two Southern
literary traditions--the fiction tradition that glamorized the
antebellum and Civil War life of earlier times in the South and the
humorous tradition of the Old Southwest--where Faulkner spent his
life. A number of scholars have demonstrated the close parallels
that exist between episodes in Faulkner's novels and episodes in
Augustus Baldwin Longstreet's Georgia Scenes. In addition, there
are three more general influences of the Southwest humorists on
Faulkner's work--flamboyance, violence, and folk values. The
flamboyant humor can be illustrated by Faulkner's 1926 statement
that he had been born of a negro slave and an alligator. The
violent humor can be seen by comparing the gougings of Longstreet's
"The Fight" or the violent practical jokes and calamities of Harris'
Sut Lovingood with the violence in Faulkner's Sanctuary. The
folkloric quality of Faulkner's humor can be seen in The Hamlet
where Houston, the resident of a small unsophisticated town lies
naked with his wife in the moonlight believing that this will insure
her pregnancy.

631. Dimino, Andrea. "Why Did the Snopeses Name Their Son 'Wallstr-
     eet Panic'? Depression Humor in Faulkner's The Hamlet." Stu-
     dies in American Humor NS3.2-3 (Summer-Fall 1984): 155-72.

     Contends that the basic comic theme of Faulkner's The Hamlet
is the difference between northern and southern values, especially
their contrasting economic values. The novel discusses financial
struggles, class conflicts, mortgage foreclosures, and a general

lowered standard of living during the Depression. The novel is
filled with intriguing con men, including Stamper, whose eyes are
the color of a new axe blade, Flem Snopes, who is froglike in
appearance, and V. K. Ratliff, who sells sewing machines and is a
general raconteur. Ratliff's goat-trading scheme is a typical
episode designed to point up the difference between northern and
southern economics, as it demonstrates the South's identity crisis
following the Civil War, including the problems relating to the
industrialization of the "New South," and the northern domination of
the southern economy. The Snopeses name their son "Wallstreet
Panic" so he will be like Morgan, Hill, Harriman, Frick, and
Rockefeller, people who speculated ruthlessly on the stock market to
line their own pockets at the expense of the smaller fish. The
Snopeses felt that it was such speculators who both caused and
benefitted from the panic of 1907, and Eck Snopes named his son
"Wallstreet Panic" so the boy could get rich like these northern
millionaires had done.

632. Foster, Ruel E. "The Modes and Functions of Humor in Faulkner."
      Thalia: Studies in Literary Humor 6.2 (1984): 9-16.

      Contrasts Faulker criticism of 1984 with Faulkner criticism of
1954 when Harry Campbell and Ruel Foster wrote the first book-length
critical study of Faulkner and included a chapter on Faulkner's
humor. In 1954 there were only random comments on Faulkner's humor,
but in 1984 critics are in agreement that humor dominates the
majority of his work, and there is scarcely a critic who denies this
primacy of humor. Faulkner's favorite book was the comic novel Don
Quixote. His favorite fictional characters were Sarah Gump, Mrs.
Harris, Falstaff, Prince Hal, Don Quixote and Sancho Panza, Lady
Macbeth, Ophelia, Bottom, Mercutio, Huck Finn and Jim, and Sut
Lovingood. Faulkner used humor extensively not because he had some
complex theory about humor, but because he had a knack for humor and
because it fit well into what he was trying to do. The humor in The
Reivers served as a counterpoint to the the boy Lucius'
confrontation with evil, a catharsis, and a graceful, calm, relaxed
farewell to the world. Almost all of Faulkner's stories are salted
generously with a wide range of humor. It might be cruel and
sadistic, or genial and anecdotal, or it might be a little of both.
Faulkner was skilled in making humor an integral part of the
narrative. It was seldom exploited for its own sake.

633. Heck, Francis S. "Faulkner's 'Shingles for the Lord.'" WHIMSY
      1 (1983):   65-67.

      Classifies Faulkner's "Shingles for the Lord" as a farce but
only if the reader is able to view Pap's discomfort with the sense
of detachment that is indicated by the tone of the narrative. Pap
has volunteered to put in a day's work making shingles for the
church, but he needed to borrow a froe and a maul from old-man
Killegrew and therefore had to wait for him to return from an all-
night fox hunt. Pap was therefore two hours late getting to the
church. Solon and Homer had arrived on time, but they didn't start
work without Pap because three men were supposed to begin work
together, and they reasoned that no one person could begin before
the others. Pap and Tull each owned half interest in a dog that
Solon wanted, so Solon wanted to exchange some work units for Pap's
half interest. But Pap had a counter plan. He went to see Tull and

agreed to do Tull's work in return for full-interest in the dog.
And he decided to work all night. But in removing the shingles, he
took them off in large chunks rather than one shingle at a time, and
one chunk of shingles contained the nail that was holding Pap's
lantern. And the lantern broke and started a fire in the old wooden
church. Reverend Whitfield castigates Pap and calls him an
arsonist. Pap sums up the entire story--"Work units. Dog units.
And now arsonist. I Godfrey, what a day!" This story is pure
Faulknerian Yoknapawtawpha. It prefigures the cracker-barrel wisdom
of V. K. Ratliff, and the schoolboy antics of Gavin Stevens and
Manfred de Spain in relation to Eula Varner, and it even prefigures
the nefarious schemes of the phlegmatic Flem Snopes.

634. Heck, Francis S. "Faulkner's 'Spotted Horses': A Variation of
     a Rabelaisian Theme." Arizona Quarterly 37.2 (Summer 1981):
     165-72.

     Alludes to Joel A. Hunt's 1969 article in Contemporary
Literature entitled "William Faulkner and Rabelais: The Dog Story,"
in which he presents convincing evidence that an episode in
Faulkner's The Mansion and an episode in Rabelais' Pantagruel are
closely related.   In Pantagruel, Panurge gets revenge against a
Parisian lady who has spurned his advances in the same way that
Ratliff gets revenge against the politician Clarence Snopes in The
Mansion, by sprinkling their garments in dog urine and having the
neighborhood dogs do the rest. Heck contends that Faulkner is also
indebted to Rabelais for an episode in The Hamlet called "Spotted
Horses," which is similar to a Rabelaisian episode in Gargantua and
Pantagruel called "Sheep of Dingdong." In the Rabelais version
Panurge has a quarrel on board ship with the merchant Dingdong.
After the quarrel Panurge is nevertheless eager to purchase a sheep
from Dingdong, who sells Panurge the sheep, but at an exhorbitant
price. Panurge takes his sheep and throws it into the sea, and all
of the merchant's sheep follow the leader while the merchant and his
employees are also swept into the sea as they attempt to hold the
sheep back. Panurge uses an oar to keep them from returning to the
ship, and they are drowned with the sheep. Faulkner's "Spotted
Horses" is reminiscent of the Rabelais story in a number of details.
Flem Snopes has an auction of wild Texas horses. After the auction,
the buyers try unsuccessfully to round up their horses, but the
horses turn on the men, and scatter them and then run away. Henry
Armstid's leg is broken, and Tull has been knocked unconscious in
the melee, and Flem Snopes has escaped with the auction money.

635. Heller, Terry. "Misogynous Wit in Faulkner's Sanctuary." WHIMSY
     1 (1983):   67-68.

     Relates the episode in Faulkner's Sanctuary where the two
country boys live in a Memphis whorehouse while they attend barber
college, thinking that it is a cheap hotel. Ironically, they remain
unsuspicious of the nature of their new home even after they
patronize some of the rival establishments in the city. Heller
cites this an example of misogynous wit in Faulkner's Sanctury and
contends that the novel is full of such wit. Most of the characters
in Sanctuary are unable to find any good reason for living.
Furthermore, most of their despair is related to their failure to
establish a maaningful sexual relationship and the resultant
resentment against the opposite sex. Six obscene jokes are told in

Sanctuary, and all of them demonstrate the resentment of men toward women. An analysis of the jokes reveals a profound yet disappointed desire to love and be loved but also expresses a certain violence against women. The jokes provoke laughter among the characters of the novel, but to most readers, the jokes are grim and even terrifying. In the jokes, women are depicted either as mothers, who are sexually unavailable except for procreation, or as whores. Men are depicted either as eunuchs, as rapists, or as customers. In this situation, it is impossible for any man to love any woman. The reason for the misogynous wit in Sanctuary is that both the women and the men have narrowly defined roles that don't allow meaningful sexual relationships to occur.

636. Inge, M. Thomas. "William Faulkner and George Washington Harris: In the Tradition of Southwestern Humor." The Frontier Humorists: Critical Views. Ed. M. Thomas Inge. New York: Archon, 1975, 266-80.

    Credits Malcolm Cowley with first establishing the heavy debt that Faulkner owes to the material and techniques of the frontier humorists. Robert Penn Warren points out, however, that Faulkner and the frontier humorists may have developed these materials and techniques independently, for Faulkner's humor is the type that could be developed from the porches of country stores and the courthouse yards of county-seat towns by any good listener. Faulkner recognized that Americans have a priceless universal trait in humor. He further felt that an author should present the humorous as well as the tragic aspects of life in order to display the "whole fabric of existence," for the ultimate aim of the writer should be "to help man endure by lifting his heart." It is interesting that George Washington Harris stated this same aim of the writer in the preface to his Sut Lovingood's Yarns. Furthermore, the kinetic imagery of several passages of Faulkner's The Town is highly reminiscent of the kinetic imagery used by Harris, as when I. O. Snopes's mules escape and Old Het and Mrs. Hait chase them around the yard. But although there are similarities, there are also differences between Faulkner's use of humor and that of the frontier humorists. Faulkner always used humor for more serious artistic purposes, never merely for comic value. For Faulkner, humor was a means rather than an end.

637. Inge, M. Thomas. "William Faulkner." Dictionary of Literary Biography, Volume 11: American Humorists, 1800-1950. Ed. Stanley Trachtenberg. Detroit, MI: Gale, 1982, 134-46.

    Contends that for Faulkner the comic and the tragic are inextricably intertwined. Inge feels that it is impossible for a Faulkner critic to understand Faulkner completely without also understanding the history of American humor of the Old Southwest. The entire canon of Faulkner's works contains humor, and the humor ranges through sophisticated, subtle, and ironic. In Mosquitoes (1927) the humor is smug, while in The Reivers (1962) it is wild, raucous, bawdy, and vulgar. Faulkner utilized the same hyperbole and comic exaggeration that have been typical of American humor from William Byrd to John Barth. Some of Faulkner's humor is based on alienation, sadism, and cruelty, and this humor prefigures the absurdist and black humor that would follow. In Sanctuary, there is a macabre parody of a funeral scene, as the funeral takes place in

a nightclub, is attended by criminals and prostitutes, and is
officiated by a bootlegger. The funeral is for a gangster named
Red, and at the end of the funeral a drunken brawl leaves Red's body
lying half in the coffin and half on the floor. "A Rose for Emily"
is another examble of macabre humor. It is a story about a Southern
Lady who must resort to necrophilia in order to protect her genteel
reputation. Many critics have looked for symbolic meanings, but
Inge feels that Faulkner is mainly playing tricks on his gullible
readers. In his acceptance speech given when he received the Nobel
Prize, Faulkner said he used humor "to help man endure by lifting
his heart."

638. Jacobs, Robert D. "Faulkner's Humor." The Comic Imagination in
     American Literature. Ed. Louis D. Rubin, Jr. New Brunswick,
     New Jersey: Rutgers Univ. Press, 1983, 305-18.

     Suggests that Faulkner was using a favorite ploy of humorists
in The Hamlet when he has the horse trader Pat Stamper insert a
bicycle valve under the skin of a bony horse and pump him up and
then dye the horse's hair and sell him to Ab Snopes for a pretty
good price, for Abe Snopes had just sold the scrawny horse to Pat
Stamper for too much money. This, then, was the old formula of the
trickster tricked. Jacobs relates Faulkner's horse trading to the
horse trading in Longstreet's Georgia Scenes, since Longstreet's
horse swap was based on an equivalent situation. In The Hamlet,
Faulkner also gave the various members of the Snopes family humorous
names. There was Admiral Dewey Snopes, Colonel Sartoris Snopes,
Lancelot Snopes, Mink Snopes, Saint Elmo Snopes, Montgomery Ward
Snopes, Watkins Products Snopes, and, of course, Wallstreet Panic
Snopes. Faulkner enjoyed ironic practical jokes. In The Hamlet, he
succeeds in giving two country bumpkins almost mythic qualities, as
he exaggerates their physical and mental characteristics. In The
Mansion, V. K. Ratliff ruins Clarence Snopes's chances to be elected
to Congress when he gets two boys to brush Snopes's pants with bush
branches saturated with dog urine. The dogs in the neighborhood
come and urinate on Snopes's legs, and Snopes flees in disgrace.
Although most of Faulkner's humor is concentrated in the Snopes
trilogy, there is tragicomic humor as early as his first novel,
Soldiers' Pay. The humor in As I Lay Dying is also tragicomic and
somewhat macabre. Sartoris likewise has occasional comic relief,
though the general tone is serious.

639. Jie, Tao. "Faulkner's Humor and Some Chinese Writers." Thalia:
     Studies in Literary Humor 6.2 (1984): 57-60.

     Compares the teahouses in Chinese villages and towns to the
courthouse squares and village stores in Faulkner's stories. They
are the centers of activity, where news, gossip, legends, and tales
are swapped, and thereby handed down in the Chinese and American
oral traditions, respectively. Jie feels that Faulkner's humor is
very similar to that of a number of Chinese writers. In both cases
the oral tradition is paramount; in both cases some kind of trickery
is usually involved; and in both cases the humor reveals flaws in
human nature; often that flaw is avarice. Jie is not suggesting
that there is a direct relationship between Faulkner's humor and the
humor of the Chinese writers she considers. There is too much
distance in time, space, and opportunity. They are nevertheless
linked by their study of man's plight and human frailty.

640. Kane, Patricia. "What Could Be Funny in Faulkner's Serious
      Fiction?" WHIMSY 5 (1987): 25-27.

      Points out that even though Faulkner's fiction is
traditionally divided into the tragic and the comic works, even the
serious works have comic interludes. Sanctuary is a serious novel
about such serious topics as rape, perjury, and lynching. But there
are two funny episodes in Sanctuary. One is about a funeral held in
a speak easy for a dead gangster. Food, liquor, and music are all
part of the funeral. The proprietor worries about what kind of
music to play because he is afraid that the drunken guests will
start dancing and it will look bad. The leader suggests "The Blue
Danube," but the proprietor says he doesn't want him to play "the
blues." When the proprieter is told that "The Blue Danube" is not
the blues but a waltz by Strauss he responds that he doesn't want a
song by "a wop," because Red was a real American. He then suggests
that the leader play "I can't Give You Anything but Love," because
Red always liked that song. Faulkner's Go Down Moses contains a
story about a bear hunt, but the bear hunt is ritualistic and
symbolic. It actually represents the hunt for the runaway slave.
It is funny that when the slave owners have an argument, they settle
their differences in a poker game. The poker game is used to
determine the future of the slave families. The evils of slavery
are thus exposed first as a fine race between the fox and the
hounds, and then as a violation of the family. The humor here is
very dark and ironic.

641. Mellard, James M. "Soldiers' Pay and the Growth of Faulkner's
      Comedy." American Humor. Ed. O. M. Brack, Jr. Scottsdale,
      Arizona: Arete, 1977, 99-117.

      Traces the development of Faulkner's humor from his first
novel, Soldiers' Pay. There are three points that need to be made
about the humor of this novel. First, although Faulkner used most
conventional comic devices of his day, his most sustained
development of humor is in the comic characters, their entanglements
in various incongruous situations, and their comic verbal techniques
usually involving either hyperbole or understatement. Second, these
comic elements are developed functionally for characterization,
narrative texture, or theme development thus enhancing the impact
of the novel. Third, Faulkner's mind-set is both comic and tragic;
it allows a double vision showing not only what the world ought to
be but what it actually is. It is because of this double vision
that irony pervades most of Faulkner's work. It is also this double
vision that gives Faulkner's work its humanistic element.   In
reading Faulkner, there is always hope--hope of enduring and even
hope of prevailing.   Nevertheless, Faulkner's comedy was not
consistent. He went from "comedy" in his first novel through
periods of "tragi-comedy," and "tragedy" in his middle novels. And
then he returned to "comic romance" in his last novel. His humor
went full cycle.

642. Moseley, Merritt. "Faulkner's Dickensian Humor in The Sound and
      the Fury." Notes on Mississippi Writers 13.1 (1981): 7-13.

      Agrees with those critics who feel that Dickens' humor and
Faulkner's humor are strikingly similar. Leslie Fiedler has called
Faulkner "an American Dickens," pointing out that the humor of both

authors relies on an obsession with the grotesque, rich invention, and contempt for the platitudes of their day. Furthermore, both Faulkner and Dickens are essentially popular and sentimental writers. They both share a strong sense of humanism, have many characters in their novels, criticize the past, write about children and the law, write Gothic novels, and have similar techniques of characterization. The most humorous part of The Sound and the Fury is the third section, which Jason Compson narrates with a mordant wit. The scene where Jason chases Caddy and her friend with the red tie is richly comic and is reminiscent of the scene in The Pickwick Papers where Mr. Pickwick and his friend Wardle chase Alfred Jingle and Rachael Wardle. Evidence of borrowing can also be seen by comparing Uncle Maury of The Sound and the Fury with Mr. Micawber of David Copperfield. Both are leeches who pretend to be genteel; both believe strongly that something will turn up; and both have similar styles in their writing of letters. Faulkner, like Dickens, enjoyed telling a story "in an amusing, dramatic, tragic, or comical way," and Faulkner's humor is deeply rooted in the tradition of the comic English novel.

643. Trouard, Dawn. "Faulkner's Eula-la: The Irony of Misogyny." WHIMSY 1 (1983): 68-70.

Points out that in 1972 Faulkner's widow Estelle was interviewed, and that when she was asked about why he so disliked women, she responded that she wasn't aware that he disliked them. In fact, she was frightened that he liked them a little too much. Still, there are many evidences of Faulkner's misogyny. In The Hamlet, Eula fills the role of "mammalian ludicrosity," and when Faulkner offers physical descriptions of her these illustrate what Trouard calls "the irony of exess." "There was too much--too much of leg, too much of breast, too much of buttock; too much of mammalian female meat." She is "a kaleidoscopic convolution of mammalian ellipses." In The Hamlet, Eula is portrayed as lumpish and static, but in The Town she becomes an object of lust and envy. The Eula of The Town developed mythical proportions. She was not too much; she was merely too much for any one man. She was Junoesque. She became "too much of white, too much of female, too much of maybe just glory," so that at first sight of her a person was just happy to be alive and to be male.

644. Vanderwerken, David L. "Lost in the Whorehouse: The Comic Chapters of Sanctuary." Conference of College Teachers of English in Texas 54 (September 1989): 34-38.

Contends that Sanctuary is probably Faulkner's grimmest novel but further contends that Sanctuary contains the two funniest episodes in all of Faulkner. One involves young Virgil Snopes and his friend Fonzo who rent a room in Miss Reba's house of ill repute while they are attending a Memphis barber college. So far as they know, their landlady is a dressmaker with a large family of unmarried daughters--all living at home. The chapter illustrates the vastness of the human capacity for self deception. We all believe what we want to believe. The other humorous episode involves Red's gangland funeral in a Memphis night club. Both illustrate how Faulkner used comic relief to make the tragic vision of the novel stand out in bold relief, for the strategy of the novel is to blur the distinction we all make between good decent respectable Christian folk (the upperworld), and the disreputable hoodlums and hookers (the underworld). In fact, in Sanctuary, the underworld becomes a "parodic and grotesque mirror image of the upperworld." Faulkner uses both of these episodes to show how civilized society covers up the world's meanness with a thin vaneer of respectability.

645. Wade, Clyde. "The Irving Influence on Faulkner." WHIMSY 6 (1988): 30-31.

   Postulates that Faulkner has incorported every major comic device used in Irving's "Rip Van Winkle" into his comic Snopes trilogy. Wade considers Faulkner's Yettie Snopes to be a southern version of Irving's Dam Van Winkle, and he equates Mink's prison term in The Mansion with Rip Van Winkle's long sleep. Mink's paranoia is what establishes him as a comic character. Mink's death concludes the trilogy. After Mink has murdered Flem, Ratliff and Stevens find him hovering in a cave under his ruined home. They give him $250, and he carefully folds the bills and secures them with a safety pin. Before this point, Faulkner had established the pattern of Mink's repeatedly handling and then losing money, and the reader is expecting this pattern to repeat itself. This time, however, a reversal takes place. "Mink dies. He does not lose his money; it is lost to him." Irving's "Rip Van Winkle" and Faulkner's "Snopes trilogy" are both about gaining wealth, not in real life but in our dreams. In both cases there is an attempt to subvert the traditional proverb, "Early to bed and early to rise makes a man healthy, wealthy, and wise." Both stories are about greed and the humorous state of an unending moneyless sleep. The only major difference between the two stories is that what Irving tends to treat lightly, Faulkner tends to treat harshly.

Thornton Niven Wilder (1897-1976)

646. Vivion, Michael. "Thornton Wilder and The Farmer's Daughter." Thalia: Studies in Literary Humor 3.1 (1979): 41-45.

   Considers Wilder's Heaven's My Destination (1934) to be a modern American mythic quest based on the joke cycle about the travelling salesman and the farmer's daughter. In Wilder's novel, George Brush, a travelling textbook salesman, meets a farmer's daughter, makes love to her, and gets her pregnant. Brush's conscience gets to him, and he wants to find the girl and make an honest woman out of her, but he can't remember the location of the farm. Heaven's My Destination is a comic, mock heroic quest novel, which illustrates how religious form and moral principle become vacuous when they achieve mythic and legendary status. But the statement of the novel is more sophisticated than this, for there is also a criticism of those who would substitute material goals for spirituality. The message of the novel is that all viewpoints are vulnerable as soon as these viewpoints become excessive. Wilder is mocking the excesses of both the materialistic and of the spiritual world. In a way, the mock heroic is a smiling tribute to the heroic. George is part salesman and part evangelist; he represents both the material and the spiritual world and achieves mythic proportions because he represents two of America's most sacred beliefs--Money and God. George is part Willie Loman and part Elmer Gantry.

Bennett Alfred Cerf (1898-1971)

647. McKeen, William. "Bennett Alfred Cerf." Encyclopedia of
      American Humorists. Ed. Steven H. Gale. New York: Garland,
      1988, 73-75.

     Considers Bennett Cerf to be America's best-known publisher-
humorist during the middle part of the twentieth century. During
the 1930s James Joyce's Ulysses was banned in the United States. As
an activist publisher, Cerf attempted to smuggle a copy into the
country, and the copy was seized by customs officials. This is what
Cerf had wanted to happen, for that particular copy of Ulysses
contained reviews praising the book pasted on the inside cover.
These reviews became evidence when the book came to trial, and the
result was a landmark decision that opened the doors for much
literature that had previously been banned because of sexually
explicit content. Cerf eventually became the publisher of Ulysses
in the United States. Cerf also published such authors as William
Faulkner, Eugene O'Neill, Gertrude Stein, William Styron, Truman
Capote, Ayn Rand, John O'Hara, William Saroyan, James Michener, and
Dr. Seuss. Cerf also published his own writing. In 1944 his Try
and Stop Me became a "number-one best seller." Cerf collected and
published anecdotes, puns, and riddles for an audience that included
both children and adults. He wrote or edited The Pocket Book of War
Humor (1943), Laughing Stock (1945), Anything for a Laugh (1946),
Shake Well Before Using (1948), Laughter (1950), Good for a Laugh
(1950), An Encyclopedia of American Humor (1954), The Life of the
Party (1956), Reading for Pleasure (1957), Out on a Limerick (1960),
The Laugh's on Me (1960), Laugh Day (1964), A Treasury of Atrocious
Puns (1968), The Sound of Laughter (1970), and At Random (1977).

Melvin Beanorus Tolson (c1898-1966)

648. Flasch, Joy. "Humor and Satire in the Poetry of M. B. Tolson"
      Satire Newsletter 7.1 (Fall 1969): 29-36.

     Considers Tolson's Prologue to Harlem Gallery to be "funny,
witty, humoristic, slapstick, crude, cruel, bitter, and hilarious."
Flasch feels that Tolson is a Black poet whose humor and satire have
not been fully realized, even though his poetry has been acclaimed
by authors of such stature as Robert Frost, Allen Tate, John Ciardi,
William Carlos Williams, Theodore Roethke, and Selden Rodman.
Tolson is the author of three important books of poetry--Rendezvous
with America (1944), Libretto for the Republic of Liberia (1953),
and Harlem Gallery: Book I, The Curator (1965), and critics agree
that he has a difficult style. He is said to "outpound Pound" as he
shocks educated readers into a recognition of their own ignorance,
and because of the difficult style, many Tolson critics have failed
to comment on his delightful wit and humor. Libretto for example
contains many African proverbs like "A stinkbug should not peddle
perfume," "A mouse as artist paints a mouse that chases a cat."
Tolson's comic spirit is best explained by an anecdote. A former
student of Tolson's once went to the village where Tolson lived and

asked asked one of Tolson's neighbors what he was doing these days. The neighbor replied, "Doc Tolson? Oh, why he's still typin'."

Jack Conroy (1899-)

649. Wixson, Douglas C. "Jack Conroy." Encyclopedia of American Humorists. Ed. Steven H. Gale. New York: Garland, 1988, 98-104.

Feels that Conroy's characterizations are an important contribution to American humor. Conroy's Uncle Ollie is an eccentric and wily Missouri farmer; Slappy Hooper paints pictures of stoves on billboards which warm hoboes during the winter. Conroy's Sooner Hound outruns the Wabash Cannonball on three legs. Conroy's humor presents comic relief to the dreary conditions of a newly industrialized society. This comic relief is necessary in contrast to his blue-collar characters who are living in grime and sometimes pain. Conroy's The Disinherited is a picaresque novel about Conroy's growing up in Monkey Nest, Missouri, travelling around the country looking for work, and returning to Missouri during the Depression. The significance of The Disinherited lies in its ability to present the frontier point of view into new industrial settings. The "rough homespun humor of the frontier is grafted onto the caustic good-naturedness of Wobbly laughter." Conroy learned that one of the best defenses working people have during hard times is humorous storytelling. Through their stories they can remember the past in a half-bitter, half-joking way and view the universe as comically absurd rather than tragically hostile. The rollicking, gusty humor of Conroy's novels are an excellent representation of midland humor of the time. In addition to being an author, Conroy was also the editor of The Anvil, a democratic and humanistic magazine with the motto of "We prefer crude vigor to polished banality." He published such authors as Nelson Algren, Meridel Le Sueur, Erskine Caldwell, and Langston Hughes, all unknown at the time.

Ernest Hemingway (1899-1961)

650. Hinkle, James. "Some Literal Jokes in Hemingway's The Sun Also Rises." WHIMSY 1 (1983): 70-73.

Suggests that Hemingway critics have in general failed to notice Hemingway's jokes in The Sun Also Rises. These critics have commented on the free-associative banter of Bill Garton. They have commented on the fractured English of Count Mippipopolous. They have commented on the sardonic statements of the narrator, Jake Barnes. However, Hinkle claims that there are many more jokes in The Sun Also Rises than most readers realize, and he suggests that the reason such jokes go unnoticed is that the reader is not aware that playing with the multiple meanings of words is a pervasive feature of Hemingway's writing. Most of Hemingway's puns do not call attention to themselves. "Brett was radiant.... The sun was out and the day was bright"; "for six months I never slept with the electric light off. That was another bright idea"; "the publishers had praised his novel pretty highly and it rather went to his head";

they were "playing for higher stakes than he could afford in some
rather steep bridge games"; "in the dark I could not see his face
very well. 'Well,' I said, 'see you in the morning.'" Several
examples play on the word "hell," as in "she likes a lot of people
around." "Tell her to go to hell." Hemingway's puns tend to be
both literally and metaphorically true or literally true in more
than one way.

651. Raeithel, Gert. "Aggressive and Evasive Humor in Hemingway's
     Letters." HUMOR: International Journal of Humor Research 1.2
     (1988): 127-134.

     Refers to a letter written by Hemingway to Horace Liveright,
his publisher, in 1925 describing himself as a satirist and
describing his Torrents of Spring as an American satire. Raeithel
agrees that Hemingway is a satirist and finds many examples in
Hemingway's letters to illustrate each of Leon Feinberg's seven
aspects of satire--obvious aggression, unexpected truth, sexual
humor, scatological humor, black humor, nonsense humor, and word
play. To illustrate the category of obvious aggression Raeithel
points to Hemingway's witty insults, his invectives, his sadism, his
practical jokes, and his expressions of superiority. As sexual
humor he cites Hemingway's reference to Fitzgerald as a "brother
pederast." As scatological humor he lists some puns like
"masterpiss," "pissport," and "precipice." As black humor Raeithal
refers to a Hemingway poem, "So mote it be / So mote it be / So hang
yourself on a Christmas tree." As nonsense humor Raeithal refers to
an announcement that Hemingway was preparing a program of Fats
Waller and Mozart; Hemingway added, "They are really very good
together." As examples of word play, Raeithal refers to such
Hemingway coinages as "pooblishers," "bookadamunt," "Roosians,"
"liturary careeah," the "portable or potable Hemingway book,"
getting "embare-assed," and a reference to William Faulkner, "it's
too Faulking bad."

652. Smith, Paul, and Jacqueline Tavernier-Courbin. "'Terza
     Riruce': Hemingway, Dunning, Italian Poetry." Thalia:
     Studies in Literary Humor 5.2 (1983): 41-42.

     Recounts a true incident of when Ernest Hemingway and Ezra
Pound attempted to rescue the poet Ralph Cheever Dunning from death.
When Hemingway and Pound arrived on the scene, Dunning had been
smoking opium, had forgotten to eat, and had let his body become a
skeleton. He was lying on his cot, dying. As a poet, Dunning wrote
in terza riruce, a risque and scatological verse form. The term
terza riruce is a casual pronunciation of terza rimaccio, with the
accio ending denoting ugliness and dirtiness as well as being a
diminutive ending. Terza riruce, therefore referred to a dirty
little version of terza rima. Hemingway and Pound liked the genre,
and they felt that Dunning wrote good terza riruce. Hemingway
didn't want Dunning to die; therefore, to lift his spirits he said
that he had never known any man to die while speaking terza riruce,
and he doubted if even Dante, the originator of the form, could
accomplish such a feat.

653. Tavernier-Courbin, Jacqueline. "The Comedy of Interpretive
     Criticism, a Testcase: Ernest Hemingway and Jack London."
     WHIMSY 1 (1983): 56-58.

     Disagrees with those critics who consider Hemingway a
dedicated craftsman who would never write anything but a true and
well-documented sentence and consider Jack London a vendor of cheap
stories written for money, who would plagiarize, or buy plots in
order to turn out stories faster. Tavernier-Courbin criticizes
these two prevailing views, saying that in both cases the authors
themselves perpetuated the respective myths. Although he was not
the first to do so, Hemingway once talked about the iceberg theory,
where two-thirds of the meaning of everything he wrote was
submerged. Since that time, Hemingway critics have been working
hard to find significance in Hemingway's work, even where there is
none. Many of Hemingway's enigmatic statements, are just not well
thought out, and in fact, Hemingway sometimes got his own characters
mixed up. Both London and Hemingway use tricks, lies, and
borrowings as rhetorical devices, but such devices are praised in
Hemingway's writing but damned in London's writing. London and
Hemingway also used sources in similar ways, though London tended to
be more playful and less self-righteous, but again something good in
Hemingway was thought bad in London. Finally, both authors wrote
both good and bad stories, but critics tend to recall only
Hemingway's good stories and London's bad ones. Tavernier-Courbin
concludes that critics find what they are looking for.

654. Tavernier-Courbin, Jacqueline. "Ernest Hemingway's Humor in
     The Sun Also Rises: Difficulties in Translation." Contrastes
     2 (December 1985): 223-33.

     States that Hemingway often complained that his critics did
not consider him a humorist. They consider him to be a tough,
virile sportsman, a world traveler, a bon vivant, an exposer of sham
and arbiter of taste, a stoic and battle-scarred veteran, and a
heroic artist but not a humorist. About his critics, Hemingway said
"the bastards don't want you to joke because it disturbs their
categories." But Tavernier-Courbin suggests another reason why
critics don't like Hemingway's humor--it's simply not very
effective, and that is why Torrents of Spring did not become
recognized as a classic of satiric or even mildly amusing
literature. Nevertheless, Hemingway attempted humor frequently. He
played with words which were incongruous or had multiple meanings.
He made statements that were true in more than one way. He made
jokes based on ambiguities or jokes based on syllogisms with the
middle term unstated, left for the reader to supply. Hemingway's
humor is not more widely accepted for two main reasons. First, his
humor is deeply submerged into the text, and second, Hemingway never
presented himself as a humorist, and his readers were therefore not
expecting the humor. It is there, nevertheless.

655. Wilson, Mark. "Ernest Hemingway as Funnyman." Thalia: Studies
     in Literary Humor 3.1 (1979): 29-34.

     Feels that Hemingway's protagonist often bears a striking
psychic resemblance to Huck Finn. In his formative years, Hemingway
was very conscious of humor. As a reporter and editor for the
weekly newspaper at Oak Park High School, Hemingway wrote many

burlesques and much other humor epitomizing 20th-century emptiness
and despair.   Hemingway's column in that paper was consciously
modeled after the humor of Ring Lardner, who at the time was writing
for the Chicago Tribune.   Furthermore, Hemingway's first novel,
Torrents of Spring, was both a burlesque and a parody of the writing
of Sherwood Anderson.   Wilson claims that there are touches of humor
in virtually everything Hemingway wrote, with much of this humor
being in the tradition of Ring Lardner, Mark Twain, and other
Southwest humorists.   In Hemingway: The Writer's Art of Self-
Defense, Jackson Benson stresses the dark side of Hemingway's humor.
Hemingway also used humor as an escape valve to deal with such
topics as death, injury, romantic illusion, sentimental stereotypes,
impotence, and sexual perversion.   Many of these same themes are
present in the tradition of Southwest humor.   Hemingway also tends
to treat his doctors, critics, writers, politicians, inept athletes,
pseudo artists, homosexuals, and middle-aged women humorously; many
of these are again targets of the Southwestern humorists.

Vladimir Nabokov (1899-1977)

656. Pearce, Richard. "Nabokov's Black (Hole) Humor: Lolita and Pale
     Fire."   Comic Relief: Humor in Contemporary American
     Literature. Urbana: Univ. of Illinois Press, 1978, 28-44.

     Considers Nabokov diabolical in his strategy of first creating
a structured and recognizable world and then undermining or
deconstructing this world, taking away the reader's ability to form
judgments.   In the end, the reader is left with a tantalizing
surface suspended over something like a "black hole in space."
Pearce notes that Nabokov's writing is similar to the writing of
contemporary American novelists in this respect and extends the term
"black humor" to "black hole humor." Reading Lolita is like walking
on shifting sands, since the narrator's message is always just
beyond our grasp.   In Pale Fire the black hole that the reader
encounters is not metaphorical but literal and physical. Pearce
points out that the "black hole" in outer space is not merely empty
space; it is instead a star so massive that it has collapsed into
itself.   Lolita and Pale Fire also implode, but they do so
psychologically rather than physically.   Like the black hole in
space, they question rational explanation, but Nabokov also
questions human judgment.   The narrator in Lolita causes us to
laugh, and long, and love diabolically, at the same time suspending
our ability to measure love against traditional norms. The narrator
in Pale Fire separates the poem from the commentary, forcing the
reader to question physical, psychological, epistemological, and
aesthetic judgments.

657. Reierstad, Keith. "Most Artistically Caged: Nabokov's Self-
     Inclusive Satire on Academia in Pale Fire." Studies in
     Contemporary Satire 5 (Spring 1978): 1-8.

     Lists as satiric targets of Nabokov's Pale Fire brutes, bores,
class-conscious Philistines, Freud, Marx, fake thinkers, puffed-up
poets, frauds, and sharks but further indicates that the most
revealing target of Nabokov's satire is the academic world.
Nabokov's targets include Nabokov himself as well as the critics and

the readers of his works. Charles Kinbote feels that the entire poem, "Pale Fire" is a parody of the "scholarly edition." In the poem, the "Main Hall" of Wordsmith College is named "Parthenocissus Hall." Reierstad suggests that this is a coupling of the word "parthenos" with the word "Narcissus" creating the image of the virgin and the egotist.

658. Wallace, Ronald. "No Harm in Smiling: Vladimir Nabokov's Lolita." The Last Laugh: Form and Affirmation in the Contemporary American Comic Novel. Columbia: University of Missouri Press, 1979, 65-89.

Presents Lolita, Nabokov's nymphet protagonist, as more widely known than any other character in recent literature. One reason that the novel is so popular is that it is filled with eroticism, sexual perversion, and taboo. The very word "Lolita" is related in most American minds to forbidden pleasures and sensuously provocative young women. But Wallace argues that the novel is not pornographic and argues further that its popularity is not so much related to the subject matter as it is related to the structures, intricate patterns of literary allusion, whimsical game-playing, and lyrical eccentric style in which it is written. Furthermore, Lolita is a double parody. It is a parody both of Shakespearean romantic comedy and of Meredithian satiric comedy. It is the parody form that complicates the character of Humbert Humbert and determines the thematic focus of the novel. In the tradition of the romantic comic hero, Humbert Humbert idealizes his lover, protects her "purity," and defends her "chastity." This is absurd, however, for Humbert protects her chastity from everyone but himself, and he himself is the worst threat to her chastity. Humbert's delicate and pure language is contrasted with his uncivil and ugly actions. The discrepancy between his descriptions of his acts and the acts themselves is ludicrously funny.

659. Zall, Paul M. "Lolita and Gulliver." Satire Newsletter 3.1 (Fall 1965): 33-36.

Explains that the reason that Nabokov has been so widely maligned and misread is that he wrote in the tradition of Swiftian satire. Zall feels that anyone who writes satire is begging to be misunderstood and anyone who writes Swiftian satire should expect to be maligned as well. Satire is a departure from conventional standards because it is indirect; satiric authors don't mean what they say. Swiftian satire is an even further departure from conventional standards because it is "double, even triple, dealing." There is an initial inversion of meaning and value. Then there is the distortion in the medium itself. Nabokov, in the tradition of Swift, makes his readers accept the persona as real even while presenting much evidence that this persona is actually phony. And in Swiftian satire, there is a final twist--the distortion provided by the reader. Zall reminds us that it wasn't Swift who told us that Yahoos are People; we readers came to that assumption on our own. What Swift did with Gulliver, Nabokov did with "Lolita." These authors engage the reader by making him/her an organic part of the novel. The reader becomes a satiric hero in the novel. In both Gulliver's Travels and Lolita, the central figures of the book first delude themselves and then go on to delude the reader. This is why these books are so misunderstood and so maligned; it is also why they are so engaging.

Elwyn Brooks White (1899-1985)

660. Blair, Walter, and Hamlin Hill. "White and Thurber." America's
     Humor: From Poor Richard to Doonesbury. New York: Oxford Univ.
     Press, 1978, 437-47.

     Considers Thurber and White to have been the most durable
writers on the New Yorker staff. White did the routine reporting
and rewrote captions for various comic drawings, including some of
Thurber's. During his stay with the New Yorker, White contributed
to almost every department; he even painted a cover. White's calm,
quiet and introspective personal style caused some of his colleagues
to consider him aloof, but his writing style was very informal.
Nowhere in White is there a display of the contempt that a book-
learned city man often has for the rural and frontier ways of
learning and of reaching decisions. White's writing has a homespun
quality reminiscent of earlier vernacular writers. But while he was
appreciative of rural values, he had no patience with
sentimentality, pretense, regimentation, parochialism, prejudice, or
exploitation, and like many earlier satirists he used humor to
attack such targets. Blair and Hill call his approach "Truth in
Sheep's Clothing." Like Thoreau and other New England humorists,
White relied on dry, Yankee wit. And like them, he also utilized
paradox, homely figures of speech, understatement, anticlimax,
humanized animals, and vernacular speech for color and for emphasis.

661. Bulsterbaum, Alison. "E[lwyn] B[rooks] White." Encyclopedia of
     American Humorists. Ed. Steven H. Gale. New York: Garland,
     1988, 476-81.

     Considers White one of America's finest essayists. However,
White has also written important poetry, short stories, editorials,
children's books, and even cartoon captions. Along with Thurber, he
developed the genre of the "casual," a short, humorous informal
piece that became an important fature of the New Yorker. White's
writing is gentle, modest, lyrical, and honest. It is seldom
slapstick, nor is it biting, though in later life he developed more
of a sting. His tone was colloquial but precise. It assured his
readers that he was one of them, an ordinary guy, trying to find
sense in a difficult world. White was especially skilled at finding
and commenting on "newsbreaks." These were grammatical,
typographical, or editorial errors in newspapers. Some newsbreaks
would be published without comment; others would be introduced by
such headings as "Department of Understatement," "Neatest Trick of
the Week," or "How's That Again? Department." White also invented
another type of column filler which he called, "Answers to Hard
Questions," a device he also included in Is Sex Necessary? Or Why
You Feel the Way You Do, which White co-authored with Thurber in
1929. White's Every Day Is Saturday is a collection of some of his
earlier "Notes and Comment" paragraphs. His The Lady Is Cold is a
collection of poems which had originally appeared in The New
Yorker's "Conning Tower."

662. Grant, Thomas. "The Sparrow on the Ledge: E. B. White in New York." Studies in American Humor NS3.1 (Spring 1984: 24-33.

   Compares White's feelings with those of two sparrows which White wrote about. In a New Yorker piece entitled, "Interview with a Sparrow," White asks a sparrow why he chooses to live in New York when he could easily fly to the surrounding countryside if he preferred. The sparrow answered that New York offers everything that the country offers plus drama. Additionally, in New York there is much more of an opportunity for interesting contacts. Like the sparrows he wrote about, White liked to range far and wide but feed near the ground. Like the bird in another sparrow piece, "The Wings of Orville," White "will gape at anything queer." And, like this sparrow, a White essay meanders about, sentence by sentence, allowing the windy cross-currents to determine direction and destination. Like the sparrow, White figures out the facts and the significance as he goes along. A White essay is a way of traveling light. White described Thoreau's Walden as "a ramble." Each of White's essays is also "a ramble." In "The Wings of Orville," the sparrow is trying to prove the feasibility of towing a wren from Madison Park to 110th street; it is trying to do something that hasn't been done before. Here again, White is like the sparrow he describes.

663. Sampson, Edward C. "E. B. White." Dictionary of Literary Biography, Volume 11: American Humorists, 1800-1950. Ed. Stanley Trachtenberg. Detroit, MI: Gale, 1982, 568-83.

   Describes White's first book, The Lady Is Cold as a collection of light verse. Nevertheless, Sampson indicates that many of White's best poems are not humorous and that even his humorous ones often have an ironic twist that allows them to leave a serious message. Is Sex Necessary?, which White wrote with Thurber, is a lighthearted spoof of the myriad of sex manuals published in the 1920s. The serious point beneath the humor is that the sex manuals tended to be glib oversimplifications of a complicated issue. Thurber and White parodied the authoritative stance and its use of case histories and definitions to resolve problems. White's Ho-Hum (1931) and Another Ho-Hum (1932) were collections of his "newsbreaks," unintentionally humorous items that had been taken from newspapers and magazines that White read. Every Day Is Saturday (1934) and Quo Vadimus? (1939) are mostly collections of his "Notes and Comment" column in the New Yorker. Since these items are local color, they tend to be ephemeral, but they are nevertheless still interesting to read. In his Introduction to White's One Man's Meat (1942), Morris Bishop said that White had developed a new genre, creating a mid-form between "light verse" and "heavy verse," "between the determined comic conviction of the one and the pretentious obscurity of the other."

664. Tanner, Stephen L. "E. B. White and the Theory of Humor." HUMOR: International Journal of Humor Research 2.1 (1989): 43-53.

   Recounts some of White's statements about humor. White says that like a frog, humor can be dissected, and like a frog it dies in the process, and the "innards are discouraging to any but the pure scientific mind." White insists that humor is fragile and evasive,

that it won't take much blowing up or poking. He says that
basically, it is a complete mystery. White says that explaining
humor is as futile as attempting to explain a spider's web in terms
of its geometry. But ironically, all of these statements are made
in a chapter that attempts to shed insight on the nature of humor.
White claims that humorous writing, like poetic writing, has an
extra content, and White's writing is a blend of the comic and the
cosmic. White says that humorists are commonly perceived as sad
people--clowns with broken hearts, but there is a deep vein of
melancholy running through everyone's life, and humorists, who are
trained in dealing with emotions, perhaps sense it more deeply as
they attempt to deal with it. Thoreau's Walden was the single most
important book in White's life, and in One Man's Meat he makes the
statement that the first person singular is the only form that he
can use without cutting himself in two. This is reminiscent of
Thoreau's statement that he would not talk about himself if there
were anyone else he knew nearly as well. White writes that Thoreau
makes him laugh "the inaudible, the enduring laugh."

665. Tanner, Stephen L. "The Humor of E. B. White." WHIMSY 5 (1987):
     27-29.

    Feels that White has the humorous mannerism of treating
abstract matters with concrete metaphors, and the result is both
amusing and insightful. White is repelled by watching America's
champion soap-bubble blower, who would make enormous bubbles and
then jump in and out and perform various unattractive tricks. Then
White compares humor to blowing bubbles. It can't stand too much
blowing up or poking. It is fragile and evasive, and these
characteristics need to be respected. White is uncomfortable with
the word "humorist," because that label limits the author. White
admits that the world loves a humorist, but it nevertheless treats
humorists patronizingly. "It decorates its serious artists with
laurel, and its wags with Brussels sprouts." In Second Tree from
the Corner White states that the world feels that if something is
humorous it is necessarily second rate, for it if were truly great
it would be entirely serious. Of the humorist, he says, "the sharp
brim of the fool's cap leaves a mark forever on his brow." During
his lifetime White experienced much illness and depression. His
doctor once described him as having a Rolls-Royce mind in a Model-T
body.

666. Yates, Norris W. "E. B. White, 'Farmer/Other.'" The American
     Humorist: Conscience of the Twentieth Century. Ames, Iowa:
     Iowa State Univ. Press, 1964, 299-320.

    Lists White with Don Marquis, Ring Lardner, Dorothy Parker,
and James Thurber as authors who made important contributions to
Franklin Pierce Adams' "The Conning Tower." In 1921 White drove to
Seattle, Washington, in his Model T Ford, where he began writing for
the Times. His feature articles were quaint, contained much
colorful detail, and helped White develop his highly personalized
writing style. Most of White's million words for the New Yorker's
"Talk of the Town" were written anonymously, but he has written
thirteen books of prose and poetry which do bear his name. In 1926
Katharine Sergeant Angell hired White to work for the New Yorker for
thirty dollars a week. She later became White's wife, and co-
authored with him A Subtreasury of American Humor. White made

important contributions to the <u>New Yorker</u>. He edited the "Talk of the Town" and wrote the "Notes and Comments" part of that column. He convinced Harold Ross to hire James Thurber. He encouraged Thurber to publish his drawings. He wrote most of the one-line captions for the section entitled "Slips That Pass in the Type." Finally, he contributed many poems and "casuals" to the magazine. White's poetic and lyrical style of writing and his interest in nature contributed to the tone of the <u>New Yorker</u> and kept it from becoming just another battle with the "booboisie" a la H. L. Mencken and Sinclair Lewis.

Arthur Kober (1900-1975)

667. Pinsker, Sanford. "Arthur Kober." <u>Dictionary of Literary Biography, Volume 11: American Humorists, 1800-1950</u>. Detroit, MI: Gale, 1982, 237-41.

Feels that Kober had a sharp ear for distinctive speech patterns. He wrote such books as <u>Thunder over the Bronx</u>, <u>Having Wonderful Time</u>, <u>Pardon Me for Pointing</u>, <u>My Dear Bella</u>, <u>Parm Me</u>, <u>That Man Is Here Again</u>, <u>Bella, Bella Kissed a Fella</u>, <u>Ooooh, What You Said!</u>, and <u>A Mighty Man Is He</u>, this last written with George Oppenheimer. Kober married Lillian Hellman in 1925, and they were divorced seven years later. Nevertheless, Kober dedicated <u>Bella, Bella Kissed a Fella</u> to Lillian in 1951, twenty years after their divorce. Bella Gross, Kober's protagonist, is an indefatigable husband hunter, who speaks in the domesticated idiom of first-generation Jewish immigrants in the Bronx. Kober wrote about Bella Gross and her parents and her friends in the Bronx with fidelity, compassion, warmth, and humor. Dorothy Parker wrote in the Introduction to <u>Thunder over the Bronx</u> that "In the annals of such as the Grosses, there are no trivia. Everything is tremendous, and most things are terrible." Kober's play, <u>Having Wonderful Time</u> won the Roi Cooper Megrue prize for Best Comedy of 1937. S. J. Perelman described Kober as only eighteen inches high and carrying a tiny umbrella to beat off any cats if they tried to attack him. Kober's characters could be described in exactly the same way.

Thomas C. Wolfe (1900-1938)

668. Idol, John L., Jr. "Angels and Demons: The Satire of <u>Look Homeward, Angel</u>." <u>Studies in Contemporary Satire</u> 1.2 (Spring 1975): 39-46.

Cites <u>Welcome to Our City</u>, an early Wolfe novel, and <u>The Hills Beyond</u>, Wolfe's last novel, as evidence that satire was an important aspect of Wolfe's writing from beginning to end. Wolfe's main target was Philistinism, and this can be best seen in <u>Welcome to Our City</u> and <u>Look Homeward, Angel</u>. Wolfe develops his satire in two ways. First, he creates characters as members of the Gant family and their associates. Second, he weaves satire into his fiction by putting the author in the role of the confessor. But in reading Wolfe, the reader must always be careful to keep Thomas Wolfe separate from Eugent Gant, because Wolfe as narrator is laughing at

Gant whenever Gant goes off into absurd fantasies or threatens to
become a romantic escapist. Wolfe felt hurt when his family and
other people from Asheville or other nearby cities expressed shock
and anger at Look Homeward, Angel. What hurt Wolfe was not that
they found his characters to be so well grounded in real-life
Asheville characters but rather the assumption that Wolfe had
written himself out of the novel. The novel was purely
autobiographical, and Wolfe intended it to be read so.

669. McElderry, B. R., Jr. "The Durable Humor of Look Homeward,
     Angel." The Merrill Studies in "Look Homeward, Angel." Ed.
     Paschal Reeves. New York: Charles E. Merrill, 1977, 91-96.

     Suggests that Wolfe's early death at the age of thirty-eight
may have prevented him from being recognized as one of America's
finest humorists, perhaps even better than Mark Twain in range and
variety. McElderry considers Look Homeward, Angel Wolfe's best
novel. It has gallery of wonderfully comic characters, especially
Eugene Gant, who struggles throughout the novel to escape from
family and environment. McElderry considers Wolfe to be more
detached than Twain. He feels that Twain's writing shows more
malice and less tolerance. Twain attempts to bludgeon his way
through life, while Wolfe's writing is more natural and more varied.
Eugene Gant is one of the most varied comic characters in American
literature. His wife Eliza is literal minded, obsessed with greed,
and a marvelous foil for Eugene. Then there are the teachers, the
stuttering Mr. Leonard, and the pompous Rhodes Scholar, Doc
Professor Torrington. And there are Bruce Glendenning, the
beachcomber, and Doc Maguire and Horse Hines, the undertaker. But
it is the character of Eugene that is the masterpiece. Eugene was
a youthful daydreamer years before Thurber had developed the
character of Walter Mitty.

Cornelia Otis Skinner (1901-1979)

670. Walker, Nancy, and Zita Dresner. Redressing the Balance:
     American Women's Literary Humor from Colonial Times to the
     1980s. Jackson, MS: Univ. Press of Mississippi, 1988, 271-78.

     Traces Skinner's writing of humorous essays and light verse to
her marriage in 1928. Her writings for The New Yorker, Harper's
Bazaar, and Ladies' Home Journal present the roles of wife and
motherhood in an amusing and self-deprecating style that
foreshadowed such later domestic humorists as Shirley Jackson and
Jean Kerr. Kerr, in fact, adapted Skinner's and Emily Kimbrough's
Our Hearts Were Young and Gay (1942) for the stage. The book
recounts the humorous escapades of Skinner and Kimbrough on a trip
to Europe, and in 1944 it was also released as a film. Skinner's
humorous essays have been collected in such volumes as Tiny Garments
(1932), Dithers and Jitters (1938), and Soap Behind the Ears (1941).
What Skinner wrote was not exactly essays. It was more like the
"casuals" of the New Yorker, or the "sketches" of earlier
traditions. "The Body Beautiful" is an example. In this sketch,
Skinner makes fun of herself for her bodily flaws and her ineptitude
in dealing with them. But at the same time, she is satirizing the
lengths to which women go for their appearance and the impossible,

arbitrary, and absurd standards that society places on women in this regard.

Corey Ford (1902-1969)

671. Day, Patrick. "Corey Ford." <u>Dictionary of Literary Biography, Volume 11: American Humorists, 1800-1950</u>. Detroit, MI: 1982, 147-51.

Considers Ford's most productive period to have been 1926 to 1931, but throughout his writing career, Ford wrote more than thirty books and more than five hundred articles and stories. Ford wrote his monthly parodies for <u>Vanity Fair</u> under the pen name of John Riddell. He parodied not only writers like Dreiser, Anderson, Faulkner, Hemingway, O'Neill, Lewis, and Frost but also popular figures like Rudy Vallee, Mae West, Will Durant, Calvin Coolidge, and Osa and Martin Johnson. These parodies were later collected into three books--<u>Meaning No Offense</u> (1928), <u>The John Riddell Murder Case</u> (1930), and <u>In the Worst Possible Taste</u> (1932). Hemingway did not take kindly to Ford's parody of him in "Corto y Derecho." It is clear that in Ford's judgment Hemingway was better at writing short stories than he was at writing novels, and in "Corto y Derecho" Ford may have made his point too strongly. In 1926 Ford introduced a series of "Impossible Interviews" for <u>Vanity Fair</u>, in which such unlikely pairs as Rockefeller and Stalin, or Garbo and Coolidge were presented as interviewing each other. In 1926 Ford also published his <u>The Gazelle's Ears</u>, a collection of pieces that had appeared earlier in <u>Life</u>, <u>Judge</u>, <u>The New Yorker</u>, and <u>Vanity Fair</u>.

672. Simms, L. Moody, Jr. "Corey Ford." <u>Encyclopedia of American Humorists</u>. Ed. Steven H. Gale. New York: Garland, 1988, 158-60.

Characterizes Ford as a humorist who aimed at deflation not annihilation. Ford's humor was happy and wholesome. Simms describes it as the custard pie in the face or the snowball aimed at the top hat but for Ford there was never a rock in the snowball. For Ford there was only one reason for fun--to be funny. Humor was its own reward. Ford wrote two humorous plays, the comedy <u>Hunky Dory</u> with Russell Crouse (1922) and the musical comedy <u>Hold Your Horses</u> (1933). Ford's most successful book was <u>Salt Water Taffy</u> (1929), a parody of Joan Lowell's <u>The Cradle of the Deep</u>. In this parody, Ford follows the incidents of Lowell's book rather closely. Ford parodied dramatist Thornton Wilder in his "The Bridge of San Thornton Wilder," in which he transforms Wilder's characters into public figures like George Nathan (George Jean Estaban), and H. L. Mencken (H. L. Manuel). In the late 1930s Ford became a screenwriter, and during this time no humorous books by him were published. The humor books published after that period were quite short. Late in his writing career Ford became an associate editor for <u>Field and Stream</u>, where he wrote a column entitled "Lower Forty," a series of humorous sketches about the "Lower Forty Shooting, Angling and Inside Straight Club."

673. Sullivan, Frank, ed. <u>The Time of Laughter</u>. Boston: Little,
     Brown, and Company, 1967, xxii + 232 pp.

     Portrays Ford's <u>The Time of Laughter</u> as an account of New York
and Hollywood during the 1920s and early 1930s, concentrating on the
fun-makers and the humorists of the day and the circles they moved
in. It is about W. C. Fields, Robert Benchley, Harold Ross, Heywood
Broun, Marc Connelly, and their friends at the Players Club, the
Coffee House, the Dutch Treat Club, Chasen's, the Garden of Allah,
the Algonquin Hotel, Bleeck's, Moriarty's, and "21." Sullivan says
that Ford's <u>How to Guess Your Age</u> was not only widely read, it was
also widely stolen and published as if the thiefs had written it
themselves with not a single word of credit to Ford.

Wolcott Gibbs (1902-1958)

674. Grant, Thomas. "Wolcott Gibbs." <u>Encyclopedia of American
     Humorists</u>. Ed. Steven H. Gale. New York: Garland, 1988, 171-
     75.

     Asserts that Gibbs' influence on the <u>New Yorker</u> was immense.
He joined the <u>New Yorker</u> as a copywriter in 1927 contributing both
humorous poetry and humorous columns to Katharine Angell White. For
the twenty-five years, Gibbs was <u>The New Yorker's</u> most prolific
writer. He quickly rose to become an editor and was described by
James Thurber as "the best copy editor the <u>New Yorker</u> has ever had."
As a copy editor for the <u>New Yorker</u>, Gibbs anonymously edited his
colleagues' manuscripts, and in so doing, he absorbed their styles
and turned into a skilled parodist. In "Topless in Ilium" he
parodied the pretentious style of Aldous Huxley, and in "Primo, My
Puss," he parodied annoying mannerisms of Alexander Wollcott. In
"Death in the Rumble Seat" he parodied the machismo phase of Ernest
Hemingway. In 1929 Gibbs wrote "Pal, A Dog," a parody of the
sentimental style and moralizing tone of the <u>Saturday Evening Post</u>.
In 1931 he published <u>Bird Life at the Pole</u> under the pseudonym of
"Christopher Robin," a burlesque not only of polar expeditions but
of the writings of A. A. Milne as well. In 1938 he succeeded E. B.
White as writer of "The Talk of the Town," and in 1940 he succeeded
Robert Benchley as drama critic. His "The Secret Life of Myself"
(1946) is a parody of Thurber's "The Secret Life of Walter Mitty."

Harry Lewis Golden (1902-1981)

675. Goldstein, Kalman. "Harry Lewis Golden." <u>Encyclopedia of
     American Humorists</u>. Ed. Steven H. Gale. New York: Garland,
     1988, 178-81.

     Considers Golden's fame to rest on his <u>Only in America</u> and the
sixteen books which followed. For a number of years, Golden's
writing achieved almost cult status. "Only in America" became the
name of a race horse, and "Enjoy, Enjoy!" became an ad slogan for a
beer company. Golden used gentle humor and folksiness to reach
hostile minds. Golden said, "I will always believe that if Galileo

had used humor, the Inquisition and the Popes would have left him alone." Early in his career, Golden was literally a "cracker barrel philosopher." He would jot ideas, lead sentences, and short paragraphs onto scraps of paper and throw them into a barrel. When a deadline approached, he would fish the scraps out of the barrel and flesh out the ideas depending on the amount of space the newspaper had available for him. Even after his success allowed him to have filing cabinets and secretaries, he still continued to publish non-sequiturs both in the Israelite and in his collections. He did this so he would be considered a "fellow tarheal" and not a stereotypical New York liberal Jew. In his "Why I Never Bawl Out a Waitress," Golden considers the cosmos with its myriad of planets, stars, and galaxies and then concludes that with such things to think about it is silly to worry about whether the waitress brought you string beans instead of lima beans.

James Langston Hughes (1902-1968)

676. Mintz, Lawrence E. "Langston Hughes's Jesse B. Semple: The Urban Negro as Wise Fool." Satire Newsletter 7.1 (Fall 1969): 11-21.

    Considers Langston Hughes's Jesse B. Semple to be in the tradition of Josh Billings, Mr. Dooley, Artemus Ward and other crackerbox philosophers, even though the crackerbox has been replaced by the bar stool. There is a common sense, a natural nobility and a penetrating wit for all of these wise fools. Hughes began publishing the "Simple" sketches in 1943 in The Chicago Defender, a newspaper for Blacks, and in 1962 continued the tradition in The New York Post. Hughes's stories are noted for their satiric humor and their delightful characterizations. Hughes chose to write in a light tone because he considered the prejudices that whites have about Blacks to be very funny. In "White Folks Do the Funniest Things," Hughes writes about being served through a hole in the wall of a segregated restaurant and about finding himself in a whites-only waiting room and being told by an officer of the law that he couldn't leave through the front door because that also was for whites only. Hughes considered the whole issue of Jim Crowism to be ludicrous and patently absurd. In The Book of Negro Humor, Hughes says that humor is laughing at what you don't have when you should have it and then adds that you're really laughing at the other guy's deficiencies and not your own. Hughes considers humor to be a form of psychotherapy.

677. Williams, Kenny J., and Bernard Duffey, eds. "[James] Langston Hughes." Chicago's Public Wits: A Chapter in the American Comic Spirit. Baton Rouge: Louisiana State Univ. Press, 1983, 261-67.

    Considers Hughes to have been an established writer before he introduced the "Simple" stories into his column in the Chicago Defender in 1943. Before this he had published three books of poems, a novel, a book of short stories, an autobiography, and established three theatrical groups mainly to produce his own plays. His Jesse B. Semple sketches would later be published in five separate volumes. Hughes mingled broad humor and wit with realism and social criticism in commenting on the evils of segregationism in

the Black sections of Chicago. His writing is very similar to Peter
Finley Dunne's portrayal of the Irish sections of the same city.

678. Williamson, Juanita V. "Langston Hughes' Wry Humor in the
     Semple Stories." WHIMSY 6 (1989): 31.

Characterizes Hughes' humor in the Semple stories as "wry."
Hughes uses humor as a weapon to cut through what would otherwise be
considered an unhumorous condition. In most of the Semple stories,
there are only two characters, Semple, and one other person. In the
exchange between Semple and the other character, Semple usually
emerges as the person with "uncommon common sense," and the other
character, often more educated, emerges as being dominated by
cliches and class thinking. Williamson notes that Hughes has been
compared by some critics to Mark Twain and to Sholem Aleichem. His
stories have been translated into French, Danish, and German.

Frederick Ogden Nash (1902-1971)

679. Arnold, St. George Tucker, Jr. "Ogden Nash." Dictionary of
     Literary Biography, Volume 11: American Humorists, 1800-1950.
     Detroit, MI: Gale, 1982, 331-44.

Notes that Nash was born in Rye, New York, and that he was the
most famous, appreciated, and imitated writer of light verse during
his lifetime. He wrote such jewels as "If called by a panther, /
Don't anther," and "In the vanities / No one wears panities," and
"Candy / Is dandy, / But liquor / Is quicker." Nash combined poetic
buffoonery, wit, and imagination to create memorable rhymes. While
working for Doubleday-Doran, Nash collaborated with Christopher
Morley and another writer to create his first published piece of
comic writing, some parodies entitled Born in a Beer Garden. Nash
was still working for Doubleday-Doran when he started scrawling
brief verses on scraps of paper during meetings. These verses later
appeared in a collection of humorous verse, Hard Lines (1931).
Nash's style was whimsical, as he would unconventionalize
conventional syllables, pronunciation, stress, and rhyme. His
extended straggling line has been compared to a horse which runs up
to a hurdle that the rider doesn't know if it will jump or not.
Major sources of Nash's inspiration were Dorothy Parker, Samuel
Hoffenstein, Peter Mark Roget, and Julia Moore, the "Sweet Singer of
Michigan." Nash seldom discussed his comic patterns, but he did
once explain his use of cliche. It must be someone else's cliche,
not your own.

680. Hasley, Louis. "The Golden Trashery of Ogden Nashery." The
     Arizona Quarterly 27.3 (Autumn 1971): 241-50.

Contends that the verses of Julia Moore inspired Nash's
"artfully distorted syntax, gnarled rhythms, and mangled rhymes."
Both Julia Moore and Ogden Nash were noted for their irregular
rhythms, their cliched expressions, their awkward inversions, and
their inept rhymes. But Nash, unlike Moore did not deal in homely
sentimentality, and Nash's irregularities are more exaggerated and
wilder than Moore's. Furthermore, they are intentional. Nash saw
the oxymoronic inconsistencies in such modern concepts as the

structured society, ritual entertainment, and organized leisure. He
satirized food, taxis, cocktails, language, love, the common cold,
the theater, travel, conscience, money, birthdays, card games,
weather, football, and marriage. His treatments were exuberant but
not bubbly. He was skilled at closely observing those objects which
are normally considered unimportant. He was able to put a lot of
philosophy into very little space, as in "It is easier for one
parent to support seven children than for seven children to support
one parent," or "Never befriend the oppressed unless you are
prepared to take on the oppressor." Hasley feels that no poet since
Lewis Carroll has gathered such a universal readership, both among
the common people and among discriminating readers. Hasley also
feels that there is probably no other poet who has had so many
imitators.

681. Robillard, Douglas. "Ogden Nash." Encyclopedia of American
     Humorists. Ed. Steven H. Gale. New York: Garland, 1988, 333-
     335.

        Points to the irony of the discrepancy between Nash's extreme
popularity among all classes of Americans, and the small amount of
criticism about his works. Nash published more than fifteen books
for children, edited a number of collections, worked on Broadway,
and contributed a large body of humorous poetry over his writing
career. He was immensely popular. Nevertheless, critical
assessments of Nash's writings are "limited to a few pages by Morris
Bishop, an excellent article by Louis Hasley, and an attractive
introduction by Archibald MacLeish." None of his work has been
analyzed through the eyes of Marxist, psychoanalytic,
phenomenological, or deconstructive criticism. Nash was aware of
the healing powers of the ludicrous perceptions of human frailty
when he wrote Bed Riddance, A Posy for the Indisposed. The poems
are about illness, insomnia, dieting, discomfort, doctors, germs,
and getting well. Nash ridicules all of those things that we're not
supposed to ridicule and praises those things that we're not
supposed to praise. He attacks "ganders, grackles, Philo Vance,
current news, Lord Byron, cold bath water, parsnips, and wasps."
And he praises "monsters, wealth, smelts, the ocean, turtles, and
Hippolyte Adolphe Taine." His titles are often miniature epigrams
or tiny poems. And his poems are delivered with equanimity and
aplomb.

John Steinbeck (1902-1968)

682. Owens, Louis. "Steinbeck's Sweet Thursday: Hanged God as Dead
     Metaphor." WHIMSY 2 (1984): 34-36.

        Considers Sweet Thursday to be a funny novel and even goes so
far as to say that while writing it, Steinbeck was thinking of it as
a musical comedy. He was right, for it was later adapted into a
musical comedy by Rogers and Hammerstein. The term "Sweet Thursday"
refers to the day before "Good Friday," and the book is a gentle jab
at the necessity for sacrifice and commitment, but at the same time
uses humor to describe what the Western World would be like without
its most significant symbol--Christian sacrifice. Sweet Thursday is
also a self-parody which mocks the characters, the symbols, the

themes, and the seriousness of Steinbeck's earlier fiction, all the way from his first novel <u>Cup of Gold</u> (1926) to <u>Cannery Row</u> (1945). Since Steinbeck country had rejected Steinbeck's serious writings, he decided to retaliate with the ironic novel, <u>Sweet Thursday</u>. The inhabitants of the original Cannery Row are all changed, or they are gone. Mack had been a deep thinker on matters of pleasure and survival; he had been a social dropout. In <u>Sweet Thursday</u>, he became "painfully literary, dispensing fragments of Latin and verse with abandon." Doc, who had been a lonely man in <u>Cannery Row</u> changed to a catalyst in a lightweight love story. In <u>Sweet Thursday</u>, Joe Elegant is a posturing effeminate writer, suggesting a young Truman Capote and, even more, a young John Steinbeck.

Erskine Preston Caldwell (1903-1987)

683. Jacobs, Robert D. "The Humor of <u>Tobacco Road</u>." <u>The Comic Imagination in American Literature</u>. Ed. Louis D. Rubin, Jr. New Brunswick, NJ: Rutgers Univ. Press, 1973, 285-94.

Depicts Caldwell's characters as "scarcely human creatures lost in the rural background of an increasingly industrialized, urbanized society." Tragic things happen in <u>Tobacco Road</u>, but <u>Tobacco Road</u> is no tragedy, for in a tragedy the characters must have the sensibility to comprehend their own predicaments. Caldwell's characters continue the American humor tradition of the Old Southwest developed over a century earlier. Caldwell's <u>Tobacco Road</u> can be compared to Longstreet's <u>Georgia Scenes</u>, both of which contain scenes of horror that are intended to be interpreted as comic. In fights, the backwoodsmen are animals or automatons as they hit and claw each other. They bite off ears and noses and maim their opponents for life. But the backwoodsmen don't view themselves tragically. They are incapable of both fear and pity. They regard an eye as a trifling price to pay for the prestige of being a frontier champion. To these backwoodsmen, a really violent fight is merely a form of entertainment. Even the loser is a winner if he has fought a good fight. And the violence represented here belongs to the tradition of frontier humor that probably dates back to the earliest days of frontier America.

Nathanael Wallenstein Weinstein West (1903-1940)

684. Nichols, James W. "Nathanael West, Sinclair Lewis, Alexander Pope and Satiric Contrasts." <u>Satire Newsletter</u> 5.2 (Spring, 1968): 119-22.

Contends that West's <u>A Cool Million</u> satirizes Horatio Alger's <u>Andy Grant's Pluck</u> and <u>Joe's Luck, or Always Wide Awake</u> by borrowing extensively from both novels. Nichols feels that there is no better way to satirize the Horatio Alger myth than to use Horatio Alger's own words. In both <u>A Cool Million</u> and <u>The Rape of the Lock</u>, West and Pope use the effective satiric technique of playing one set of ideas or values against another, showing that something is wrong or blameworthy by presenting it as ridiculous. Satiric contrast is a prevailing technique in the writings not only of West but also of

Lewis and Pope. In fact, Nichols claims that even though satires differ greatly in style, period, place, and target, most satires have one thing in common--contrast. This device is especially effective in mock-heroic satires, however, Nichols cautions that the contrast, not the heroic ethos, is essential in achieving the satiric tone.

685. Shepard, Douglas H. "Nathanael West Rewrites Horatio Alger, Jr." <u>Satire Newsletter</u> 3.1 (Fall 1965): 13-27.

Contends that West's third novel, <u>A Cool Million</u> (1934), is a satire aimed at the All-American Horatio Alger success story. Horatio Alger was only one of many authors who wrote in this you-can-be-successful-if-you-work-hard genre, and West's novel is, in fact, a parody of all of these books. However, West's novel especially parodies Alger's prose style at the same time as it parodies the theme by inverting a typical Alger plot. In his parody West lifts considerable portions from a number of Alger's novels without putting the material in quotes or in any way acknowledging that the material is being quoted. Shepard provides a side-by-side comparison of material from Alger that later appeared in West's novel.

Moss Hart (1904-1961)

686. Florey, Kenneth. "Moss Hart." <u>Encyclopedia of American Humorists</u>. Ed. Steven H. Gale. New York: Garland, 1988, 204-209.

Considers Hart to have been one of the most important writers for Broadway from 1930 to 1950. Hart collaborated with George S. Kaufman on <u>Once in a Lifetime</u>, a satire about "the garish opulence, the lack of creative talent, and the generally fickle and arbitrary nature of the movie industry." Although the humor may be heavy handed, it is generally not offensive. Sam Harris criticizes the play as being too noisy and too busy. It contains less of a plot than a satiric account of a rapid series of encounters with various Hollywood stereotypes. Many characters represented real-life people. A brash composer named Sam Frankel and a sharp-tongued alcoholic writer named Julia Glenn bore striking resemblances to George Gershwin and Dorothy Parker, respectively. Hart again collaborated with Kaufman in writing <u>You Can't Take It with You</u>, a wild and funny domestic comedy in which all the characters could do whatever they wanted to do. It ran 837 performances and became a movie which won the 1938 Academy Awards for Best Picture. In 1937 its winning of the Pulitzer Prize disturbed many critics who felt that the award should have been given to a serious drama rather than a comedy. The central character in Hart's <u>The Man Who Came to Dinner</u>, Sheridan Whiteside, was modelled after Alexander Woollcott. The play is based on Hart's actually having had insensitive Woollcott as a house guest.

Abbott Joseph Liebling (1904-1963)

687. Simms, L. Moody, Jr. "A. J. Liebling." Encyclopedia of
      American Humorists. Ed. Steven H. Gale. New York: Garland,
      1988, 284-86.

      Describes Liebling as "the gadfly of American journalism."
Harold Ross liked Liebling's irreverent and unpretentious style and
hired him to write for the New Yorker. He remained on the New
Yorker staff from 1935 until his death in 1963 and became famous for
his column, "The Wayward Press," in which he used biting wit and
lampoon to criticize editors, publishers, reporters, politicians,
and even the general public. Liebling's style was witty yet
serious, defiant yet cheerful. All of his books are collections of
New Yorker pieces, but they are frequently drastically revised.
Back Where I Came From presents an amusing perspective of Liebling's
beloved New York. The Telephone Booth Indian exposes the devices of
a number of different types of tricksters. The Wayward Press uses
humor and incisive quotations to expose newspaper writers. Some of
the sharpest barbs in The Second City are aimed at Colonel Robert
McCormick of the Chicago Tribune. Liebling critics have noticed the
influence of Rabelais, and the American tellers of tall tales in The
Honest Rainmaker. Liebling's style is skeptical but warm-hearted.
His satire is sharp, but it comes from the underlying understanding
and empathy that Liebling had for his targets.

Sidney Joseph Perelman (1904-1980)

688. Barrow, David. "Robbins' Robbings: Ay Chihuaha! What a
      Coincidence!" WHIMSY 5 (1987): 31-32.

      Points out that there are a number of passages in Tom Robbins'
Still Life with Woodpecker which rely very heavily on S. J.
Perelman's works. Robbins writes "The dyed hair on his neck stood
up with him. Beneath him was the beloved Chihuahua. He had sat on
it. And broke its neck." Earlier in "Don't Blench, This Way to the
Fantods" Perelman had written, "He spun around to discover Mrs.
Drumright's pet chihuahua outspread on the seat, flattened as neatly
as a flounder."   This coincidence cased Barrow to do a closer
comparitive analysis of Robbins' text, and he discovered a clear
pattern of borrowing. The borrowing includes not only squashed
chihuahuas, but also spilled inkwells, ruined carpets, apologetic
houseguests, and dubious domestic servants. Furthermore, these
allusions occur in identical sequence in the Perelman and Robbins
texts and over approximately the same number of pages. Barrows
concludes that this is more than a mere coincidence.

689. Fowler, Douglas. "Sidney Joseph Perelman." Encyclopedia of
      American Humorists. Ed. Steven H. Gale. New York: Garland,
      1988, 354-59.

      Traces Perelman's interest in humor to his college days, when
he edited the Brown Univ. humor magazine. In 1925 Perelman moved to
Manhattan's Greenwich Village and started contributing cartoons and
prose sketches to Judge, College Humor, and other similar

publications. During this time he also co-authored a novel with Quentin Reynolds, Jr., entitled Parlor, Bedlam and Bath. In 1931 he co-authored with Will Johnston a screenplay for the Marx Brothers named Monkey Business. Perelman later wrote another movie, Horse-feathers, for the Marx Brothers, but he didn't like what the Marx Brothers did to his scripts. Their movies were so filled with shenanigans and chaos that it prompted Perelman to remark that writing for them was like "shaving with a piece of glass" or "removing a coat of tar and feathers." Perelman contributed 278 comic sketches during the 45 years he wrote for the New Yorker, and during the 1940s, '50s, and '60s, Perelman published a collection of his pieces from The New Yorker and other magazines every two or three years. Like Tobias Smollett, Jonathan Swift, Samuel Johnson, Lewis Carroll, Mark Twain, Jules Verne, Evelyn Waugh, and Vladimir Nabokov, S. J. Perelman found that travel is one of the richest sources available to the writer. Other sources of inspiration for Perelman included stimulation by other writers, like James Joyce, Jules Verne, and Edgar Rice Burroughs; show business; and the domestic terrors of owning a house and property with the associated problems with maids, cooks, hired hands, domestic animals, plumbing, and visiting relatives. In addition to being a careful observer, Perelman took pride in his writing and was a skilled stylist.

690. Gale, Steven H. "S. J. Perelman: 'The Keenest Hatred of Chickens.'" Studies in American Humor NS3.23 (Special Issue on "Humor in Economic Depressions," Summer-Fall 1984): 228-36.

Contends that Perelman's writing philosophy was very much influenced by his earliest childhood memories. Perelman grew up in Providence, Rhode Island, where his father worked as a machinist and attempted to raise chickens. In a 1969 interview with William Zinnser for the New York Times Magazine Perelman said that his early life was an example of the "American Dream." Perelman explained that if a person owned a few acres and a chicken farm there was no limit to the financial rewards possible. Perelman then added that because of this he had grown up with and had retained till the time of the interview, "the keenest hatred of chickens." Perelman's family was poor, and he had to go to work at an early age. Perelman also had to live through the Great Depression. Although Perelman never wrote about economic theory in general, he was nevertheless obsessed with money and other practical matters throughout his writing career. In fact, a notable feature of Perelman's work is that he never targetted anything really "significant" or "serious." He did not write about the Great Depression as a social phenomenon. He also did not write about the Second World War or the development of the atomic bomb. Instead, he wrote about subjects that are timeless, because they represent the everyday annoyances that have always plagued mankind and will continue to do so. Over his 50 years as a professional humorous author, Perelman wrote more than 500 prose pieces, 440 of which were reprinted in twenty volumes of collected works. He also wrote eleven humorous plays and eleven humorous film scripts.

691. Gale, Steven H. "S. J. Perelman." <u>Dictionary of Literary Biography, Volume 11: American Humorists, 1800-1950</u>. Detroit, MI: Gale, 1982, 382-404.

Indicates that early in his career, Perelman was interested not in becoming a humorous writer but rather a cartoonist. This is one of the reasons that his writing developed the "deceptive simplicity" of cartoons. Perelman's first book, <u>Dawn Ginsbergh's Revenge</u>, contained the somehow appropriate legend, "this book does not stop in Yonkers." It contains mostly selections that were originally written by Perelman for <u>Judge</u>, but ironically, the publishers forgot to include the author's name. In the late 1930s, the Marx Brothers seduced Perelman to move to Hollywood, where he wrote eight screenplays in ten years for MGM and Paramount, but he didn't like working for money and compared his Hollywood work to playing the piano in a whorehouse. Perelman especially detested the Marx brothers, whom he considered to be "capricious, tricky beyond endurance, and altogether unreliable." He said that all of the people he knew who had worked for the Marx Brothers had later said that they would rather be chained to a galley oar and frequently lashed than ever work for them again. Most of Perelman's books were collections of sketches that had originally appeared in such magazines as the <u>New Yorker</u>, <u>New Masses</u>, <u>Broun's Nutmeg</u>, and <u>The Funny Bone</u>. <u>The Dream Department</u>, (1943) was dedicated to Perelman's close friend and brother-in-law, Nathanael West. <u>Acres and Pains</u> (1947) was the first of Perelman's thematic books. A collection of essays that originally appeared in the <u>Saturday Evening Post</u> and <u>Country Book</u>, it recounted Perelman's twelve years of country living. <u>Westward Ho</u>, a collection of <u>Holiday</u> pieces, recounted his travel experiences.

692. Gale, Steven H. "Sydney Joseph Perelman: Twenty Years of American Humor." <u>Bibliography</u> 29.1 (January-March 1972): 10-12.

Documents the Perelman pieces that appeared in major American periodicals between 1940 and 1960, and his books published during that same period. During this period, Perelman wrote mainly for the <u>New Yorker</u>, but he also published articles in <u>Saturday Evening Post</u>, <u>Holiday</u>, <u>Reader's Digest</u>, and <u>Good Housekeeping</u>. His books during this period were <u>Acres and Pains</u> (1947), <u>Crazy Like a Fox</u> (1944), <u>The Dream Department</u> (1943), <u>The Ill-Tempered Clavachord</u> (1952), <u>Keep It Crisp</u> (1946), <u>Listen to the Mocking Bird</u> (1949), <u>Look Who's Talking!</u> (1940), <u>The Most of S. J. Perelman</u> (1958), <u>Perelman's Home Companion</u> (1955), <u>The Road to Miltown; or, Under the Spreading Atrophy</u> (1957), <u>The Swiss Family Perelman</u> (1950), and <u>Westward Ha! Around the World in Eighty Cliches</u> (1948). During this period, Perelman also co-authored two books. With Ogden Nash he wrote <u>One Touch of Venus</u> (1944), and with his wife Laura West Perelman he wrote <u>The Night before Christmas: A Comedy in Three Acts</u> (1942).

693. Hasley, Louis. "The Kangaroo Mind of S. J. Perelman." <u>The South Atlantic Quarterly</u> 72.1 (Winter 1973): 115-21.

Classifies Perelman with Lardner, Benchley, and Thurber as the four best humorists of the twentieth century. Hasley considers Perelman's world to be thoroughly subjective, with his only subject himself. Perelman ridicules sham, naivete, and mechanization without the bitter anger of a Jonathan Swift but also without any hope of things changing for the better. Hasley feels that Perelman borrowed his style from the authors he read. From George Ade he developed his jaunty and sophisticated slanginess. From Ring Lardner he developed his sardonic vision but with less bleakness and disillusioned bitterness. From Robert Benchley and Stephen Leacock he developed his surrealism, and his tendency toward self-mockery. And from James Joyce he developed his "dazzling array of verbal pyrotechnics." Perelman said of Joyce, "James Joyce is the writer I revere more than any other. I think he is the greatest comic writer in English--comic in the deepest sense." Hasley feels that Perelman was one of the first writers of the "reasoned absurd." Perelman always utilized "enough stylistic playfulness to keep the absurd from becoming merely absurd." Hasley admits that Perelman is thin in substance, but regards this as a plus. It allows his readers to enjoy the crazy roll of Perelman's dice without having to worry about the ethics of the management. Perelman's style is effervescent. It is based on gymnastics of sound, verbal punning, and abrupt lexical and logical reversals. This is what gives Perelman his deft sophistication, his novel charm, his kangaroo mind.

694. Pinsker, Sanford. "Jumping on Hollywood's Bones, or How S. J. Perelman and Woody Allen Found It at the Movies." _Midwest Quarterly_ 21.3 (Spring 1980): 371-83.

Compares and contrasts nineteenth-century humorists with twentieth-century humorists. The nineteenth-century humorists occupy a middle ground between a frontier culture that swapped tall tales around an open fire and a sedate New England culture that was fascinated by the wild West and its ring-tailed roarers. The twentieth-century humorists occupy a middle ground between what Hollywood packages as dreams and the gritty disappointments of actual life. People perceive humorists to be living in a lively, energetic, exciting, crowded place, but their world is actually isolated and lonely and introspective. The energy and the excitement are only in the authors' minds, and this irony often surfaces as comic grotesquery or even tragic vision. Perelman's characters are irritated innocents. They are men of rarified taste who are repelled by all of our culture's expectations and its junk. Perelman often complained that Hollywood didn't allow him to write an adult script. He compared writing in Hollywood to herding swine, since both of these occupations lack subtlety and cause the vocabulary to be pungent.

695. Pinsker, Sanford. "Perelman: A Portrait of the Artist as an Aging _New Yorker_ Humorist." _Studies in American Humor_ NS3.1 (Spring 1984): 47-55.

Traces the influence of James Joyce on Perelman from his first book, _Dawn Ginsberg's Revenge_ (1929) where Perelman said he had bartered a cartoon to _Judge_ for the last forty pages of _Ulysses_ to his September 10, 1979 sketch for the _New Yorker_ entitled "Portrait of the Artist as a Young Cat's Paw." Like Joyce, Perelman used forced dictions, both high and low, both foreign and domestic, and like Joyce, Perelman wrote densely packed paragraphs. Unlike Mark Twain, James Thurber, and E. B. White, Perelman and his writing style aged gracefully. Twain's writing became bitter and sophomoric.   During his last days Thurber fell to drinking and haunting the <u>New Yorker</u> offices carrying rejection slips from people he did not even know, while White retired to Maine to pass his old age away from Manhattan's critical view.   In contrast, Perelman's last piece has the grace and style of vintage Perelman.

696. Schmid, Maureen. "The Changing Voices of S. J. Perelman."
       <u>WHIMSY</u> 1 (1983): 74-76.

       Investigates the range of Perelman's writing style but concludes that there are some constants in all of his writing. There are mangled cliches and inappropriate pronoun references. There is the omission of <u>of</u> in genitive constructions. And there is the relative clause with a redundant anaphoric word.   Furthermore, there are constant indications that Perelman is well read and widely traveled, that he has a prodigious vocabulary, a keen ear for language, and an unerring memory. He can remember the good old days when a nickle could buy "a firkin of gherkins," or "a ramekin of fescue," or "a pipkin of halvah," and he appropriately entiled his autobiography <u>The Hindsight Saga</u>. When an interviewer for the <u>Paris Review</u> asked him why he had never written a serious book, Perelman replied that he regarded his comic writing as serious. He then went on to say that in art, the muralist is no more valid than the miniaturist.   Perelman lamented the fact that in America Thomas Wolfe outranks Robert Benchley mainly because of the size of his works, and then adds ironically that he is content to stitch away at his embroidery hoop.

697. Toombs, Sarah. "S. J. Perelman: A Bibliography of Short Essays,
       1932-1979." <u>Studies in American Humor</u> NS3.1 (Spring 1984): 83-
       97.

       Agrees with Douglas Fowler that Perelman basically treats four subjects: The writing of others, show business, home ownership, and travel.   Perelman was obsessed with a number of aspects of these four topics, namely, the evils of advertising, the dangers of nostalgia, the offensiveness of self-aggrandizement, and the vicissitudes of life.   His setting was almost always the prism of life in the country. Perelman carefully balanced his work between play, screenplay, and prose work. During the 1950s and 60s Perelman specialized in lampooning popular culture, especially as reflected in films and in advertising. After this period there was a gradual deceleration in the amount of his production.   Nevertheless, his latest pieces "shine with expert polishing and a subtle mellowness which blunts none of the edge of his satire." Perelman's writing career is in fact quite typical. His early pieces are short and simple. His later pieces are longer and more complex. Still later his pieces become ascerbic, but there is a mellowing in his last and unfinished series, <u>The Hindsight Saga</u>. Toombs' article lists all of Perelman's works from 1932 until 1979 in chronological order and contains brief annotations.

698. Yates, Norris W. "The Sane Psychoses of S. J. Perelman." <u>The
       American Humorist: Conscience of the Twentieth Century</u>. Ames,
       Iowa: Iowa State Univ. Press, 1964, 331-50.

       States that in 1925 Perelman graduated from Brown Univ. and moved to Greenwich Village where he drew cartoons and wrote parodies and burlesques for <u>Judge</u>, <u>College Humor</u>, and <u>Life</u>. His later work for the <u>New Yorker</u> gave his prose its characteristic high compression and crackle. Following the example of Bangs, Cobb, Lardner, Benchley, Parker, and Thurber, Perelman left New York in 1932 and moved to the country. The others had bought land in Bucks County, Pennsylvania, which was called an "exurb" because it was too far from New York to be considered a "suburb." Perelman's move from New York resulted in an "exurb" book entitled <u>Acres and Pains</u>. After World War II, Perelman took several ocean voyages, and these resulted in his <u>Westward Ha!</u> (1948), and <u>The Swiss Family Perelman</u> (1950). In her foreword to <u>The Most of Perelman</u>, Dorothy Parker wrote that Benchley and Lardner are Perelman's only worthy predecessors, and in the foreword to <u>Strictly from Hunger</u>, Benchley wrote that Perelman perfected the "dementia praecos" genre of writing. Like Leacock, Benchley, and Joyce, Perelman had a special talent for parody and monologue. On occasion Perelman employs Jewish dialect humor. An example appears in <u>Dawn Ginsbergh's Revenge</u> where he says, "If you must vex somebody, why don't you go home and vex the floors?"

Isaac Bashevis Singer (1904-1991)

699. Cohen, Sarah Blacher. "The Jewish Folk Drama of Isaac Bashevis Singer." <u>From Hester Street to Hollywood</u>. Bloomington: Indiana Univ. Press, 1986, 197-212.

Considers Singer's <u>Teibele and Her Demon</u> to be a comic reversal of the typical male-female conflict. Teibele is so caught up in her passions that she sees nothing inappropriate about having an affair with Alchonon. The central theme of the novel is the difference of a dream-like appearance and a relationship with vision and the day-to-day boring relationship with an actually living being.

Mary Lasswell (1905-)

700. Bly, Mary. "Feminist Humor in the Novels of Mary Lasswell." <u>WHIMSY</u> 1 (1983): 205.

Discovers a great deal of feminist humor in the novels of Mary Laswell. Before Bly started to read Lasswell's <u>Suds in Your Eye</u>, she expected it to be a typical domestic comedy about washing dishes in the manner of Teresa Bloomingdale and Erma Bombeck. When she got into the novel, however, she discovered that it was about three feisty old ladies who love to carouse, swear, and drink beer. <u>Suds in Your Eye</u> is therefore an allusion to drinking beer rather than to washing dishes, and Lasswell's three old ladies contradict the stereotype of older women as sweet, conservative, and temperate ladies who spend their time puttering around the house except on weekends when they take their cars out for a Sunday drive. When a bartender in Lasswell's novel tells the group that they don't serve ladies, one of them answers, "Who said we was ladies?" When a bar patron refers to one of the ladies as "mother," she responds that she couldn't be his mother; she was married. The women contribute

such aphorisms as "Home is the best place after all the gin mills is
closed," and "You can't make no silk purse out of a souse's ear,"
and "Swearing is the seamy side of prayer." Lasswell's novels
contain much irony along with earthy uninhibited fun.

Phyllis McGinley (1905-1978)

701. Simms, L. Moody, Jr. "Phyllis McGinley." Encyclopedia of
     American Humorists. Ed. Steven H. Gale. New York: Garland,
     1988, 301-303.

     Suggests that McGinley was encouraged by New Yorker editor
Katharine White to inject more humor into her work. The New Yorker
responded so energetically to her light verse that McGinley resigned
her teaching position and moved to New York City. Her first
collection of light verse was entitled On the Contrary (1934). This
was followed by One More Manhattan (1937), and A Pocketful of Wry
(1940). In all three of these collections McGinley playfully
satirizes department stores, shopping, and fashions as well as other
domestic subjects. McGinley uses parody in her Stones from a Glass
House: New Poems (1946). McGinley also wrote many humorous
children's books such as The Horse Who Lived Upstairs (1944). The
Love Letters of Phyllis McGinley won the Edna St. Vincent Millay
Award in 1954. The poems contained in this volume are gentle satire;
they celebrate rather than condemn. The poems in Sixpence in Her
Shoe (1964) range from sarcastic to nostalgic; most critics feel
that the book is written as a rebuttal to Betty Friedan's The
Feminine Mystique. Many of the inspirations for McGinley's prose
and poetry came from newspaper headlines on such topics as war,
poetry, and progressive education. Her prose and poetry is written
from the perspective of a woman, a wife, and a mother. Her tone
varies from lighthearted mirth to biting wit. Simms considers
McGinley to be one of the most prolific and famous writers of light
verse in twentieth-century America.

702. Walker, Nancy. "Phyllis McGinley." Dictionary of Literary
     Biography, Volume 11: American Humorists, 1800-1950. Ed.
     Stanley Trachtenberg. Detroit, MI: Gale, 1982, 317-23.

     Considers McGinley's winning of the Pulitzer Prize in 1961 for
her Times Three: Selected Verse from Three Decades, with Seventy New
Poems to be a milestone, for it was the first time a Pulitzer Prize
had been awarded for a collection of light verse. McGinley was born
and raised on a ranch in Iliff, Colorado, that was so isolated it
prompted McGinley to remark, "I am probably the only person left
living who has read the entire works of Bulwer-Lytton." When
Katharine White accepted McGinley's first poem for the New Yorker
her acceptance letter said, "We are buying your poem, but why do you
sing the same sad songs all lady poets sing." McGinley got the
message and started writing the humorous light verse she has become
so famous for. McGinley had an intimate acquaintance with many of
the top humor writers of her time. Her "Ballade for a Bard" is a
review of Franklin P. Adams' The Melancholy Lute, and her "Evolution
of a Benedick" is a review of Ogden Nash's The Bad Parent's Garden
of Verse; the review employs some forced rhymes a la Nash, like
"nursery" followed by "versery." McGinley was capable of writing

irony. In her "Trinity Place," for example, she contrasts the fat
pompous pigeons with the jobless men in a park. She observes that
it is only the men who go hungry, for the pigeons are regularly fed.
Part of McGinley's success in writing children's verse is her
dimeter and trimeter lines which give the effect of a jog trot
rhythm. McGinley tells the reader of "In Praise of Diversity" to be
thankful that there are only twelve months, nine muses, and two
sexes.

703. Walker, Nancy, and Zita Dresner, eds. Redressing the Balance:
      American Women's Literary Humor from Colonial Times to the
      1980s. Jackson, MS: Univ. Press of Mississippi, 1988, 300-308.

      Considers McGinley to have a wide audience but laments the
fact that critics seldom consider McGinley pieces as part of the
canon of the American humor tradition. Her marriage, her children,
and her move to New York City had two effects on her writing style.
First, she turned to writing children's books. And, second, she
began focusing on suburban family life rather than the urban topics
of her earlier New Yorker poems. By the 1950s McGinley was
publishing most of her material in women's magazines, and during
this time she became classified with the "housewife writers" of the
period, though McGinley resented that classification. McGinley
wrote two books defending women's traditional role in American
society, The Province of the Heart (1959), and Sixpence in Her Shoe
(1964). The humor in Times Three: Selected Verse from Three Decades
ranges from biting to wistful, but it is always insightful and
witty.

Richard Willard Armour (1906-)

704. Bartelt, C. J. "Richard Armour." Encyclopedia of American
      Humorists. Ed. Steven H. Gale. New York: Garland, 1988, 14-18.

      Considers Armour to be one of the most prolific twentieth
century American humorists. Armour's six-thousand humorous essays
and poems have appeared in more than 200 magazines in America and
England. His fifty books include satire, children's literature,
light verse, and nonfiction. Nevertheless, Armour's scholarly
output has been sparse, despite the fact that he taught at a number
of good universities and was Dean of the Faculty at Scripps College.
Armour's first book of satire for university students, It All
Started with Columbus, is a tongue-in-cheek history of America,
written in mock-scholarly format. It contains many puns and
humorous footnotes. Later books would use a similar approach to
deal with such subjects as Shakespeare, Marxism, medicine, art, sex,
sports, warfare, and education. Drug Store Days is Armour's
nostalgic autobiography. As an only child, Armour was never bossed
around or beaten up by older brothers or sisters, and he was never
punished by his parents for bossing around or beating up younger
brothers or sisters. Armour was raised by an eccentric family. He
had a mother who dressed him in lace collars, a grandmother who
sewed sheets for the Ku Klux Klan during the Civil War, and another
grandmother who was both physically and psychologically domineering.

John Betjeman (1906-)

705. Kiley, Frederick, and J. M. Shuttleworth. Satire: From Aesop
     to Buchwald. New York: Macmillan, 1971, 367-68.

     Describes Betjeman's verse as light on the surface but with a
deadly serious satiric underpinning.   In his "In Westminister
Abbey," for example, Betjeman ironically uses an architectural
setting to satirically criticize politics, religion, and society in
general.

Harry Allen Smith (1907-1976)

706. Fackler, Herbert V. "Multiple Myth and Folklore in H. Allen
     Smith's Picaresque Satire Mister Zip." Satire Newsletter 6.6
     (Fall 1968): 35-42.

     Feels that Smith has used the traditions of Don Quixote, of
the American frontier, of Hollywood, and of the Boy Scouts in his
Mister Zip.   The novel is a masterful satire of manners,
concentrating on the twentieth century but drawing heavily from the
sixteenth century Quixote tradition.   The title, "Mr Zip," refers to
Zip LeBaron, a hero of Western movies.   Mr. Zip is naive and
idealistic.   Like Don Quixote, he perceives appearances as reality
and believes in the sharp contrast between good and evil, and like
Don Quixote he sallies forth in search of adventure, taking a
servant with him.   He has a romanticized and idealized notion of
pure womanhood, but his final quest is for Miss Marybob Thomas, a
saloon manager.   Mr. Zip is a picaresque novel in which Zip moves
from one episodic adventure to another, and like Don Quixote, Zip's
interpretations and reactions to these various adventures are
greatly influenced by his reading and his imagination.   Zip's
ambiance is only slightly different from that of Don Quixote, as he
rides off in glorious sunsets to fight exhilarating range wars
against the forces of evil.   At one point, the allusion to Don
Quixote is made even more explicit, as Van Wyck Brownell tells Zip
he is fighting in the tradition of Galahad, of Roland, and even of
Don Quixote of La Mancha.

707. Hayward, Malcolm, "Harry Allen Smith." Encyclopedia of
     American Humorists. Ed. Steven H. Gale. New York: Garland,
     1988, 400-402.

     Traces Smith's humor leanings to the age of fifteen, when
Smith became a proofreader, then a reporter, and finally a column
editor for the Huntington Press in Indiana.   The humorous column
that Smith edited was entitled "Miss Ella Vator," and at the age of
seventeen he wrote an off-color piece entitled, "Stranded on a
Davenport" that was judged to be so lewd, licentious, obscene, and
lascivious that Smith was arrested and convicted of writing obscene
material.   In his To Hell in a Handbasket, Smith objects to being
classified as a humorist.   He prefers to think of himself as "a
reporter with a humorous slant."   He says that he is funny only in
the sense that the world itself is funny.   Smith falls into the
tradition of Mark Twain and H. L. Mencken as reporters with a sense

of irony and cynicism.   Like Twain and Mencken, Smith's style is
clear, direct, straightforward, and colloquial, and he has a good
ear for dialect.   He will be remembered for his anecdotes, yarns,
interviews, and reminiscences.   His humorous observations are
especially well developed in <u>Low Man on a Totem Pole</u>, <u>Life in a
Putty Knife Factory</u>, <u>Lost in the Horse Lattitudes</u>, and <u>The Compleat
Practical Joker</u>.

708. Simms, L. Moody, Jr. "H. Allen Smith." <u>Dictionary of Literary
     Biography, Volume 11: American Humorists, 1800-1950</u>. Detroit,
     MI: Gale, 1982, 452-58.

     Considers Smith to have been an overnight success with the
publication of his <u>Low Man on a Totem Pole</u> in 1941.   Throughout the
1940s Smith published a book a year, and his books were usually on
the best-seller lists.   Between 1941 and 1946 there were about 1.4
million copies of his books sold.   <u>Low Man on a Totem Pole</u> (1941) is
a collection of interviews, autobiographical articles, and general
trivia.   He writes about chorus girls who are barefoot up to their
chins, a man who bounced eggs on a bar, and a storekeeper who liked
to ring up "No Sale" on his cash register and then spit in the penny
compartment.   His tone was light, lively, and funny.   <u>Life in a
Putty Knife Factory</u> (1943) is a collection of interviews and
literary caricatures, frequently dealing with celebrities from radio
or the movies.   Smith's putty knife is a symbol of his incisive wit,
used to expose the underbelly of the "high-class morons of
Hollywood."   <u>Lost in the Horse Latitudes</u> (1944) is an autobiography
written with "impish frankness and the calculated touch of
irreverence."   He said a movie studio was similar to a newspaper
office only on a larger scale, with its mob of eccentric,
capricious, temperamental screwballs.   <u>The Rebel Yell</u> (1954) is a
satire of the South's chauvinistic fondness for the past.   <u>The Pig
in the Barber Shop</u> (1958) is a travel book about Mexico.

709. Simms, L. Moody, Jr. "H. Allen Smith: An Annotated
      Bibliography of His Book-Length Works." <u>American Humor: An
      Interdisciplinary Newsletter</u> 9.1 (Spring 1982): 5-11.

     Agrees with Bergen Evans that Smith is squarely in the long
tradition of American humorists ranging from Davy Crockett through
Mart Twain, Finley Peter Dunne, and George Ade.   Simms agrees with
Gregory Curtis who says that Smith's preference for bawdy yarns with
much cussing and dialect places him in the tradition of the
humorists of the Old Southwest.   And Simms also agrees with Fred
Allen that Smith is "the screwball's Boswell."   The main purpose of
this article, however, is to provide annotations for all of Smith's
thirty-six books, from <u>Robert Gair: A Study</u> (1939) to <u>The Life and
Death of Gene Fowler</u> (1977).

Jesse Hilton Stuart (1907-)

710. Hall, Wade. "'The Truth is Funny': A Study of Jesse Stuart's Humor." Terre Haute, IN: Indiana Council of Teachers of English, 1970, 76 pp.

Suggests that Stuart never intended out to write a humorous piece. Instead he set out to write a story--to tell the truth--and discovered that the pretentions and foibles of the Kentucky hill people were just plain funny. In a story about a man who has been hornswoggled by a boy horse-trader who had told the truth about a plug horse he had traded, Stuart concluded "The truth was funny." Hall feels that humor permeates all of the works of Jesse Stuart-- his novels, short stories, essays, children's books, and poetry but feels that his humor is best in his short stories. One critic said that the humor in Stuart's short stories is "like great comic ballads in prose." Stuart's humor was the result of his knowledge and appreciation of the long and noble tradition of southern American humor. It is based on his accurate portrayal of hill dialect and on his knowledge of hill superstitions and eccentric and colorful characters. Stuart writes about feuds, the land and animals, the coming of age in the hills, politics, and religion. Stuart's most controversial novel, Foretaste of Glory is also the best extended example of Stuart's humor and satire. Stuart once remarked that he couldn't keep the humor out even if he tried. The humor episodes in Stuart's books are as organic and natural as are the seasons to the Kentucky hill people.

Anne Elizabeth Campbell Bard (1908-1958)

711. Walker, Nancy, and Zita Dresner. "Betty MacDonald." Redressing the Balance: American Women's Literary Humor from Colonial Times to the 1980s. Jackson: Univ. Press of Mississippi, 1988, 279-99.

Observes that The Egg and I, published in 1945 under the pen-name of Betty MacDonald, was written to target the back-to-the-land romancing so prevalent at the time. The book uses understatement, overstatement, and irony to humorously attack the "I'll-go-where-you-go-do-what-you-do-be-what-you-are-and-I'll-be-happy" syndrome. The novel does not shy away from the physicality, brutality, crudity, or craziness inherent in farm living. As Clifton Fadiman said in his review of the book, "MacDonald calls a spade a spade, and there were plenty of spades." The book is largely autobiographical, recounting the author's life on a chicken farm in a remote area of the Olympic Mountains in Washington. The book was a best-seller, and in 1947 it became a successful film as well. Even though The Egg and I was Bard's most famous novel, she later wrote similar humorous autobiographical novels such as The Plague and I (1948), Anybody Can Do Anything (1950), and Onions in the Stew (1955), but these later novels were simply less engaging than her first.

Jack Crickard Douglas (1908-)

712. Kollar, Stuart. "Jack Douglas [Jack Crickard]." Encyclopedia
     of American Humorists. Ed. Steven H. Gale. New York: Garland,
     1988, 136-39.

     Contrasts the lack of humor in Douglas' early life with the
abundance of humor in his later life. Douglas was born in Lynbrook,
New York, a place which Douglas described as so boring that the only
fun he had as a kid was watching railroad crossing accidents. In
1940 he became a writer for Bob Hope, who believed in competitive
writing. Hope would pit his writers against each other to see who
could come up with the funniest material. Douglas handled this
pressure-cooker situation well and matured in the process. He later
wrote for Ozzie and Harriet Nelson, Dean Martin and Jerry Lewis,
Jimmy Durante, Jack Carson, Johnny Carson, Phil Harris, Garry Moore,
Danny Thomas, Ed Wynn, Jack Paar and others. He won an Emmy for his
"George Gobel Show," and a second Emmy for a Red Skelton show. His
first book, My Brother Was an Only Child is ninety-six pages long,
containing forty-seven chapters of anecdotes, short jokes, and black
humor. There are portrayals of many zany characters, like "George
the Toilet Seat," "Doctor Murgeon, the Virgin Surgeon," and "Old
John," who in his younger days had been "Young Old John." A year
later, 1960, Douglas wrote Never Trust a Naked Bus Driver, and two
years after that, 1962, he wrote A Funny Thing Happened to Me on the
Way to the Grave. During the 1960s and 1970s Douglas wrote ten
humorous books.

John Kenneth Galbraith (1908-)

713. Baer, John W. "The Great Depression Humor of Galbraith,
     Leacock, and Mencken." Studies in American Humor NS3.2-3
     (Summer-Fall 1984): 220-27.

     Compares and contrasts the ways that Galbraith, Leacock, and
Mencken use humor to deal with a very difficult economic situation.
Galbraith used humororous commentary to demonstrate how stupid we
humans were to get ourselves into such a predicament. But Galbraith
also used humor to understand and explain the cures for the Great
Depression. Leacock didn't see any humor in the Depression itself
but did see humor in the conflicting economic theories that were
intended to explain why the Depression had happened. And Mencken
used the Depression to criticize Hoover's inadequacies in handling
the Depression.

Leonard Calvin Rosten (1908-)

714. Cronin, Gloria L. "Leo[nard Calvin] Rosten." Encyclopedia of
     American Humorists. Ed. Steven H. Gale. New York: Garland,
     1988, 380-83.

     Points out that Rosten was born in Lodz, Poland, and was taken
by his parents to Chicago at the age of three. By 1930 he had

completed his Ph.D and was supporting himself by teaching night-
school English to immigrants. He started writing the Kaplan stories
for the New Yorker in order to help pay some debts incurred through
the illness of his wife, Priscilla Ann Mead. Rosten feels that
humor is the subtlest and most difficult of forms and offers as
supporting evidence the fact that there are "a thousand novelists,
essayists, poets, and journalists for each humorist in American
literature." Rosten's humor depends on comic dialect, the solecism,
the pun, the malapropism, the glib quip, slang, genteelisms,
oxymorons, metathesis, litotes, synecdoche, polyptoton, mimesis,
paranomasia, metonymy, and the "malaprintism," as he develops the
mock heroic situation comedy of his adult ESL students. The
teacher, Mr. Parkhill, is compared to Don Quixote as he attempts to
correct each and every error of usage or pronunciation. Parkhill's
gentleness of spirit, lack of imagination, and verbal niceties are
played against Kaplan's noble spirit, excessive imagination and
limited verbal skills. Charles Rolo calls Kaplan "a Shakespeare of
broken English."

715. Hasley, Louis. "Hyman Kaplan Revisited." Studies in American
      Humor NS3.1 (Spring, 1984): 56-60.

      Considers The Education of Hyman Kaplan and The Return of
Hyman Kaplan to be part one and part two of the same book, even
though they were published twenty-two years apart--1937 and 1959,
respectively. Leo Rosten was working on a doctorate in political
science when he first wrote and published the adventures of Hyman
Kaplan. In order to conceal this non-serious diversion from his
professors, he coined the pen-name of Leonard Q. Ross, a name very
similar to his own. The setting for the Kaplan episodes is the
beginner's class of the American Night Preparatory School for Adults
in New York City. The plot complications are slight, and there is
very little carryover or action from one episode to the next, but
there are recurring themes, such as the ongoing feud between Miss
Rose Mitnick, the best student in the class, and Hyman Kaplan, the
most "remarkable" student in the class. And both Miss Mitnick and
Mr. Kaplan had a small group of supporters. Hyman Kaplan was in his
forties. He was plump and red-faced, with wavy blond hair, and two
fountain pens sticking out of his shirt pocket. And he smiled
continually. The center seat in the front row was Kaplan's chair,
and he wrote his name in large block capital letters with red
crayon, each letter outlined in blue and separated from other
letters with a carefully drawn green star. Kaplan was determined to
establish his own identity.

716. Golub, Ellen. "Leo Rosten." Dictionary of Literary Biography,
      Volume 11: American Humorists, 1800-1950. Detroit, MI: Gale,
      1982, 410-18.

      Notes the ironic stance of Hyman Kaplan who "dismantles the
English language with his misguided passions for it." Kaplan loves
to study American history and literature and exudes pleasure as he
writes about Abraham Lincohen, Valt Viterman, Mocktwain, and Jack
Laundon. Kaplan also writes about Judge Vashington, Tom S.
Jefferson, L. X. Hamilton, Tom Spain, John Edems, and James
Medicine. Kaplan's grammatical innovations are just as creative, as
he gives the plural of "sandwich" as "delicatessen," that of
"blouse" as "blice," and that of "cat" as "katz." His superlatives

move from "good" to "batter" to "high-cless."   His verbs are
conjugated into "fail," "failed," and "bankropt." The opposite of
"new" is "second-hand."   Rosten has a keen eye for incongruity,
pretentiousness, irony, and funniness in his character and plot
development.   Rosten is especially aware of the effects of the
words, the syntax, and the rhythms of language that people use.
Linguistic play permeates both his factual and his fictional
writings. His dialect is not merely an accurate transcription; it
is a new creation that strives more for inventiveness than for
accuracy.

717. Van Gelder, Robert. "A Mr. Malaprop in the Bronx Idiom." The
     New York Times Book Review, 29 August 1937: 11.

     Compares Rosten's Hyman Kaplan with Sheridan's Mrs. Malaprop
in The Rivals. In his very first recitation period, Kaplan shows
off by announcing that the three most famous writers in America are
Jack Laundon, Valt Viterman, and the author of Hawk L. Berry-Feen,
Mocktvain. Kaplan is portrayed as a cutter in a New York dress
factory, who has decided that rather than learning English he will
bluff his way through the English night class with his wit and
energy. Kaplan refers to his teacher as "our lovely Mr. Pockheel"
(Parkhill); he cannot add without the use of dollar signs; and he
appologizes with "I back you podden." Kaplan uses the language, as
he uses everything else, to promote his own purposes, for Kaplan
knows   that   business   comes   before   pleasure.   Rosten's
characterization of Kaplan can be summed up in one succinct Kaplan
sentence: "Is planty mistakes, I s'pose..., but that's because I'm
tryink to give dip ideas."

Nelson Algren (Abraham) (1909-1981)

718. Conroy, Jack. "Nelson Algren--A Tribute." Dictionary of
     Literary Biography Yearbook: 1981. Detroit, MI: Gale, 1982,
     xi-xii.

     Indicates that Holiday magazine decided to publish a special
edition on Chicago, and they commissioned Algren to write the lead
article. It is ironic that when the editors of Holiday read the
article that Algren wrote, they considered it to be so unflattering
that they placed the article on the rear pages of the magazine and
asked Albert Halper to write a more flattering piece about Chicago.
The Algren article formed the basis for Algren's 1951 book entitled
Chicago: City on the Make. In this book, Algren compared Chicago to
loving a woman with a broken nose. "You may find lovelier lovelies.
But never a lovely so real."

719. Cox, Martha Heasley, and Wayne Chatterton. Nelson Algren.
     Boston: Twayne, 1975.

     Points out that in Somebody in Boots (1935) and A Walk on the
Wild Side (1956) Algren developes an interesting device of imagery,
the color compound. This is a noun followed by the past participle
"colored." Thus, instead of describing a man's cap as grey, Algren
would describe it as "pavement colored," and evening as "slander
colored." He began using wild images as early as his Somebody in

Boots (1935): "It was fantasy that had pursued them, every one, all
their lives; they had not pursued it." Cox feels that A Walk on the
Wild Side demonstrates Algren's maturing sense of comedy as he
exploited the ribald, grotesque, surrealistic style that he had by
now developed.

720. Gleason, Ralph J. "Perspectives: Is It out of Control?"
      Rolling Stone 64 (August 6, 1970): 9

      Considers Algren to have been a mature writer by the time he
wrote his 1956 A Walk on the Wild Side. Gleason feels that this
novel should be read by all of the Catch 22 and Cuckoo's Nest freaks
just so they can find out what earlier novel made these later novels
possible. Gleason writes that it was Algren who first developed the
fantasy-reality and the inside-outside paradoxical inversion of the
American dream that Heller and Kesey would later use so effectively.

721. Harden, James. "Nelson Algren." Dictionary of Literary
      Biography Yearbook: 1982. Detroit, MI: Gale, 1983, 121-22.

      Explains the title of Algren's The Devil's Stocking. Harden
indicates that Algren was once told by a prostitute that a "devil's
stocking" is a stocking made inside out. It therefore has no useful
function. The book is, appropriately, about a man who is sentenced
to life in prison. The character is named Ruby Carter, but the
character is based on Ruby Calhoun. The book was originally meant
to be historically accurate but became fiction in order to give more
poetic license to the author. Harden however feels that even after
this transition, the book is still basically a documentary because
all of the figures of the novel had their counterparts in real life.

722. Kinsman, Clare D. Contemporary Authors, Volumes 13-16.
      Detroit, MI: Gale, 1975, 18-19.

      Portrays Algren as a physical writer who relied more on his
stomach than his intellect. In an interview in the Paris Review
Algren is described as good humored and nonchalant. He is both
uniquely American, and from a contemporary point of view, quite un-
American. If he wore a tie, it would be askew, and his syntax, like
his clothing, is slightly eccentric. Algren published The Man with
the Golden Arm in 1949. This is a story about Frankie Majcinek, a
Chicago stud-poker dealer who becomes a dope addict and commits
suicide. As a poker player, Majcinek is the man with a golden arm;
he is a machine, and in the novel, he has the nickname of Frankie
Machine. Sheldon Grebstein says that this novel alternates between
comic and tragic episodes and, furthermore, suggests that this is
the novel's most distinctive structural device. Chester Eisinger
considered Algren to be the poet of the jailhouse and the
whorehouse. He made a close study of cockroaches, drunkards, pimps,
the garbage in the street, and the spittle on the chin.

723. Metzger, Linda, and Deborah A. Straub. "Nelson Algren."
      Contemporary Authors, Volume 20. Detroit, MI: Gale, 19-24.

      Describes Algren's characters as drifters, prostitutes, petty
thieves, con men, drug addicts and call him the "poet of the Chicago
slums." Algren himself, however, prefers to be referred to as the

"tin whistle of American letters." Norman Grebson notes that nowhere in Algren's writings can be found people who are vibrantly healthy, free of guilt, clean, fulfilled, or content.

724. Riley, Carolyn. "Nelson Algren." Contemporary Literary Criticism, Volume 4. Detroit, MI: Gale, 1975, 16-18.

Compares Algren's writing to musical orchestration, where the instruments are reedy winds, one lonesome oboe, and an augmented string section playing slightly off key with some of the strings broken. Saul Maloff describes Algren as a yarn-spinner, a teller of tall tales, whose stories typically outgrow their limits and expand toward legend. Maloff also comments on Algren's colorful characters. Algren is especially skilled in the effective use of street language. Algren reminisces that some of the best lines he ever wrote were not written by him--they were remembered. And ironically although they are now famous in the written literature, they were originally uttered by people who couldn't read or write. But although Algren didn't create these lines, he was intimately associated with the people who did. Algren's characters are failures even at vice. They are the "underdogs of sin." Algren was born in Detroit and raised in a working class section of Chicago. He hitchhiked from Chicago to New Orleans, where he sold coffee and bogus beauty parlor discount certificates door to door. From there he went to Hondo, Texas, to work as a gas-station attendant, and then he hopped a freight train to El Paso where he was thrown in jail for vagrancy and fined five dollars. While in El Paso, he discovered that he could use the typewriters at Alpine Teachers College without detection. It was here he wrote his first short stories, some of which were later published.

725. Williams, J. Kenny, and Bernard Duffey, eds. "Nelson Algren." Chicago's Public Wits: A Chapter in the American Comic Spirit. Baton Rouge: Louisiana State Univ. Press, 1983, 267-74.

Describes Algren's Chicago: City on the Make as a long prose poem that compares Chicago to a tired strumpet desired and fought over by the "promoters" who want to exploit her, the "do-gooders" who want to reform her, and the "poets" who alone respond to and cherish her true nature.

Eudora Welty (1909-)

726. Arnold, St. George Tucker, Jr. "The Conflict Lost before It's Begun: The Reader's Quest for a Truly Perceptive Consciousness in Eudora Welty's Losing Battles." WHIMSY 6 (1988): 7.

Considers Welty's Losing Battles to be a sustained joke on the readers of the novel, who are forced time after time to change their opinions and reevaluate the evidence of the family history or legend as the same events are presented differently by one biased narrator after another. The story is viewed from the perspective of various kin, neighbors, and even unexpected guests such as the district judge, Oscar Moody. The story is told as a comedy in which the reader must sort through the jumble of conflicting details and reassemble these details into a credible account. Arnold describes

the novel as "a sort of mystery story of the heart" and considers
the writing to be engaging, amusing, and touching.

727. Arnold, St. George Tucker, Jr. "Mythic Patterns and Satiric
     Effect in Eudora Welty's 'Petrified Man.'" <u>Studies in</u>
     <u>Contemporary Satire</u> 4 (Spring 1977): 21-27.

Portrays Welty as well informed in archetypal myths, who
employs this knowledge to create ironic contrasts between powerful
ancient heroes and the powerless modern characters which she
created. Arnold further feels that Welty's "Petrified Man" is a
good illustration of Welty's ability to use mythic structure to
achieve satiric effects. Welty investigates the ceremonial and
ritual behavior that occurs in the contemporary religious shrines we
call beauty parlors. These shrines are filled with the incense of
unemptied ashtrays, noxious chemicals that are poured on the
customers' heads, and miscellaneous hair-salon litter. There is a
screaming and gnashing of teeth as the beauticians sink their
scarlet-painted finger nails into the customers' scalps. There are
also certain taboos which must not be violated by anyone who is a
member of this cult. They can attack each other verbally with
impunity; however they may never violate their basic mission--the
proper restraint and discipline of men. Both the beauticians and
the customers are dedicated to the task of keeping their men in
tight check, minimizing their husbands' influence over themselves,
and going through any pains necessary to attain their most powerful
tool--feminine beauty. Arnold investigates the "hair-raising
images" that Welty develops as the customers' heads of hair are
pulled and curled and cooked by beauticians' devices that seem more
designed for torture than for indulgence.

728. Bouson, J. Brooks. "The 'Infinitely Gay and Cruel' World of
     Welty's <u>The Robber Bridegroom</u>." WHIMSY 2 (1984): 36-37.

Views Welty's <u>The Robber Bridegroom</u> as a comic but violent
parody of the fairy-tale genre. The novel contrasts the gaiety with
the cruelty of the world we live in. This darkly humorous novel
contains animal metaphors, tall-tale hyperbole, sly puns, verbal
irony, and other aspects of flamboyant verbal high jinx. Salome,
the wicked stepmother in the novel, is portrayed as an old rabbit
hunched over its catch. Jamie Lockhart, the robber bridegroom, is
both a gentleman and a thief. His transformation from bandit to
merchant is such a natural metamorphosis that it receives very
little notice in the novel. Welty's novel, like the fairy-tale
genre which it parodies, displays a world of superficial happiness
and gaiety, but in both cases, there is animal savagery that lurks
just beneath the surface. Bouson sees the comic-horrific vision
that Welty develops as an extension of the humor of the American
frontier. The novel develops tension, and relieves tension in
turns. It is tragi-comedy in the best sense.

729. Gross, Seymour L. "Eudora Welty's Comic Imagination." <u>The Comic</u>
     <u>Imagination in American Literature</u>. Ed. Louis D. Rubin, Jr.
     New Brunswick, NJ: Rutgers Univ. Press, 1983, 319-28.

Considers Welty to have command over a wide range of tones,
styles, and narrative techniques. Welty has written only four
collections of short stories and five novels; nevertheless, she is

often considered second only to William Faulkner in the quality of her fiction. Almost everything she writes is received enthusiastically and is given critical acclaim. Welty is a very creative writer. She writes the hilarious monologue of a frenzied Southern woman's fight with her family in "Why I Live at the P.O." She writes the haunting passions of a deaf-mute in "First Love." She writes the wild story of a nutty saint in The Ponder Heart. She writes about tragic loneliness in "Death of a Travelling Salesman." She writes surrealistic innuendo in "The Purple Hat." She writes the stark realism of a young man controlled by his past in "Keela, the Outcast Indian Maiden." She writes a blistering attack on how women manipulate men in "Petrified Man." And she writes the screaming vulgarity of Italian Americans in "Going to Naples." Welty's comic writing is filled with energy and magical surprises, as she dazzles the reader with transformed identities and mischievous portrayals of nature, as she investigates the ways in which her characters break free from the bonds which would impede their spontaneity. Welty's comedy tends to be celebrative rather than critical. She is not trying to correct society by exposing its hypocrisies and stupidities. Rather, she belongs to the American transcendentalist comic tradition represented by Emerson, Thoreau, Ellison, and, especially, Whitman.

730. Skaggs, Merrill Maguire. "The Uses of Enchantment in Frontier Humor and The Robber Bridegroom." Studies in American Humor 3.2 (November 1976): 96-102.

Compares Welty's stories to the folk tales of Europe and suggests that American tall tales follow from the traditional elements of these European folk tales. Welty's legendary folk heroes are in the fairy tale tradition and in the tradition of Mike Fink. Welty's The Robber Bridegroom is a historical novel, and Welty herself invites comparisons between her episodes and particular historical events. "The Robber Bridegroom" was originally a fairy tale collected by the Brothers Grimm in which an adolescent girl suspects that the groom her father has chosen for her will rob her of her true life. In the original fairy tale she finds her lover's animal instincts disgusting during the day but very stimulating in bed at night. In her own The Robber Bridegroom, Welty reverses the older plots and uses irony as a device for foreshadowing. In the first sentence of the novel, she uses the term "innocent" to describe the planter, Clement Musgrove, hoping that the reader will allow the word to shine like a flashing light revealing what lies ahead in the novel. Skaggs sees The Robber Bridegroom as representing the tradition of the ringtailed roarer of frontier humor. It is our way of whistling in the dark. The roarer stories, and the fairy tales help us not to worry in times of profound danger and reassure us all that everything will turn out all right in the end.

Peter De Vries (1910-)

731. Ballenger, Grady W. "Peter De Vries." Encyclopedia of American
     Humorists. Ed. Steven H. Gale. New York: Garland, 1988, 126-
     31.

    Considers De Vries' career as a literary humorist to have
begun in April of 1944 when he invited James Thurber to Chicago to
give a benefit lecture for his journal, Poetry.   Thurber later
convinced De Vries to become a writer for the New Yorker. Three of
De Vries' novels have been made into movies--Comfort Me with Apples
(1956), The Mackerel Plaza (1958), and The Tents of Wickedness
(1959).   All three of these novels are witty, satirical portraits of
suburban Connecticut, and all three received positive critical
reviews.   In 1959, De Vries' daughter, Emily, died of leukemia, and
after this time, De Vries' humor becomes noticeably darker.   De
Vries describes himself as "a serious writer of the comic novel."
Kingsley Amis considers De Vries to be the funniest serious writer
on either side of the Atlantic.   De Vries considers himself a
humorist rather than a satirist.   The distinction he makes is that
the satirist shoots to kill, while the humorist tries to bring his
prey back alive.   De Vries' writing is filled with word games,
parodies, paradoxes, bungled allusions, witty retorts, twisted
aphorisms, malapropisms, and sudden switches in style as from slangy
to formal.   The worst characters in his novels are those who take no
pleasure in language or those who compose advertising jingles or in
other ways abuse the language.

732. Davies, Marie-Hélène. "Fools for Christ's Sake: A Study of
     Clerical Figures in De Vries, Updike and Buechner." Thalia:
     Studies in Literary Humor 6.1 (Spring-Summer 1983): 60-72.

    Investigates the ability of three Protestant writers--De
Vries, Updike, and Buechner--to depict ministers not as egocentric
racketeers as Sinclair Lewis had done but as well-meaning fools in
the service of Christianity.   Davies considers their treatment of
ministers favorable rather than hostile.   De Vries' Reverend Andrew
Mackerel is the minister of the "People's Liberal Church," and he is
driven by his congregation's wishes.   After his wife's death, for
example, he has to mourn longer than he has wanted to because of the
devotion that his parishioners have for her memory.   Davies points
out the relevence of the name "Mackerel," which is an allusion to a
spotted fish that scavenges for whatever it can get.   The irony
which pervades The Mackerel Plaza is similar to the irony of
Updike's A Month of Sundays, which is written as a diary of a
minister who has been sent by his bishop to a sanitorium because of
his sexual indiscretions. The protagonist of A Month of Sundays is
named "Reverend Marshfield" because he is in an ideological
marshland between his belief and disbelief, between fidelity and
adultry.   Unlike De Vries and Updike who devoted only a small
portion of their writing to the study of the minister as God's fool,
Buechner has concentrated most of his writing on this subject and
has so far written six novels that deal with the ministry.   De
Vries, Updike, and Buechner are all convinced church-going

Christians. They nevertheless are concerned with the discrepencies between what people know they should do and what they actually do. Their criticism is gentle; their irony is coaxing; their laughter is liberating.

733. Evans, T. Jeff. "Deviance and Conformity in the Novels of Peter De Vries." WHIMSY 2 (1984): 37-39.

Investigates the irony of De Vries' Let Me Count the Ways. Elsie's religious fanaticism causes Stan to become an equally fanatic atheist, as he develops his role of intellectual skeptic to counter her extreme faith and simplicity. On Stan's birthday, Elsie illuminates her simplicity by giving Stan a "Bible Belt," a belt in which scriptural texts have been tooled into the leather. In the same novel Tom gets deathly sick while making a pilgrimage to Lourdes, ironic because Lourdes is supposed to be a place of miraculous cures. There is a double irony, however, as Tom's miraculous illness reunites him with Marion. In The Mackerel Plaza, Reverand Andrew Mackerel preaches from the pulpit of the first split-level church in America. The pulpit consists of a slab of marble lying on four legs of delicate fruitwoods. The fruitwoods are similar enough to symbolize the four Gospels but different enough to symbolize the fact that the four Gospels don't harmonize with each other very well. The ending of Cat's Pajamas is also weirdly ironic. On a cold winter night, Hank Tattersall is trying to get back into the warmth of his house. He freezes to death with his head caught in the camera shutter-like doggie door of his kitchen, with his body projecting outside into the storm. In his fading awareness, his conscience chides him that his end is in sight.

734. Evans, T. Jeff. "Language Control and Humor in Peter De Vries." WHIMSY 1 (1983): 77-79.

Contends that plot, characterization, theme and tone succeed in De Vries' Comfort Me with Apples because of his skillful manipulation of comic language and form. The novel is filled with aphorism, parody, pun, epigram, paradox, burlesque and other devices of language play. Chick Swallow's father writes a newspaper advice column and is named "The Lamplighter." Chick learns to appreciate the epigram from his father, and he makes such pronouncements as "I'll wend my maze." This is later ironically reversed into the legitimate epigram, "I'll mend my ways." Chick inherits his father's column when his father dies "legging out a home run during the annual Fourth of July softball game." The column consists of daily "Pepigrams," epigrams that are inspirational in nature. Now Chick is "The Lamplighter," and his friend Nickie accuses him of selling out to the establishment rather than retaining his pristine state of unemployment. Nickie says that platitudes are important; they are like the lower teeth in a smile. Chick rejoins that epigrams are parasols, while platitudes are umbrellas. It is up to the individual to determine which is of more benefit to mankind.

735. Evans, T. Jeff. "The Madder Music of Peter De Vries." Studies in Contemporary Satire 8 (Spring 1981): 21-29.

Compares the madness of mental patients with the madness of non-mental-patients in the mental institution in De Vries' 1977

novel, <u>Madder Music</u>. In this institution, the doctors perform shock
treatment on the patients by having them sneak glimpses at their
bills.   The novel is written in three parts--The Fugue, The
Principal Themes, and The Resolution. The title alludes to Dowson's
poem of decadence, "Non Sum Qualis Eram Bonae Sub Regno Cynarae,"
which suggests that contemporary man is dancing to a madder music in
the universe. Evans considers this to be De Vries' darkest novel,
as it turns to self-reflexiveness and self-parody. In most of De
Vries' novels, the protagonist, who is under great pressure to
conform to social conventions or to accept communal responsibility,
retreats into a private world. For George Thwing of <u>But Who Wakes
the Bugler?</u> the retreat is to the world of fantasy, like that of
Thurber's Walter Mitty. For Dick, the narrator of <u>Tunnel of Love</u>,
the retreat is to a mythical cabin on the Maine coast that he calls
"Moot Point." For Tom Waltz of <u>Let Me Count the Ways</u> and Chick
Swallow in <u>Tents of Wickedness</u> the retreat is merely from the rigors
of marriage and professional responsibility. For Bob Swerling in
<u>Madder Music</u> the retreat is to another persona, first, Groucho Marx,
and, later, W. C. Fields, comics who do violence to language with
outrageous puns, and syntactic disruptions.

736. Evans, T. Jeff. "Peter De Vries in American Humor." <u>WHIMSY</u> 6
      (1988): 13-15.

      Characterizes De Vries twenty-four novels as dealing with the
rigors not of urban life but of suburban and exurban life.   The
title of his <u>Tents of Wickedness</u> is derived from a quote from Psalms
which says that it would be better to be a doorkeeper for the house
of God than dwell in the tents of wickedness. When De Vries decided
to dwell in the tents of wickedness, there was nothing left for him
to do but satirize it. Ironically, De Vries stance is against both
morality and immorality, and this double vision pervades his novels.
De Vries repressive upbringing in the home of devout Dutch
Calvinists provided him with insight into why people with such
strict beliefs tend to be highly neurotic. The neuroticism that can
be found in all of De Vries' novels follows a long comic tradition
of urban and suburban neuroticism from the henpecked husbands of
James Thurber, to Charlie Chaplin, to Peter Arno's characters in
conflict with technology and mechanization, to Robert Benchley's and
James Thurber's "little men," to Woody Allen's putzes.

737. Evans, T. Jeff. "Peter De Vries: A Retrospective." <u>American
      Humor: An Interdisciplinary Newsletter</u> 7.2 (Fall 1980):13-16.

      Suggests that religion is a constant subject matter and source
of critical inquiry for De Vries because of his childhood in a
strongly Dutch Calvinistic household in Chicago.   In 1944 James
Thurber hired De Vries to write for the <u>New Yorker</u>. It was here
that De Vries refined his craft as a writer of comic novels about
the baffling manners of suburban America.   In 1952 De Vries
published a collection of short sketches entitled <u>No, But I Saw the
Movie</u>. These sketches had originally appeared in the <u>New Yorker</u>.
Generally, De Vries' novels begin with a reaction against marriage
and end with a comic acceptance of this institution. At the end of
De Vries' second book, Chick Swallow tells an old girl friend,
"Thanks just the same..., but I don't want any pleasures interfering
with my happiness." In <u>Tents of Wickedness</u>, each chapter is a tour
de force written in the style of a particular 20th century writer,

ranging from James Joyce to James Jones. Both the style of language
and the development of the plot are aspects of the parody. There is
an evangelical mother and an atheistic father in Let Me Count the
Ways, and they have difficulty deciding how to bring up the child.
Their compromise solution is to bring him up as an agnostic.   De
Vries unites language, style, wit, and theme to create an enduring
comic vision of the way we live.

738. Hasley, Louis. "The Hamlet of Peter De Vries: To Wit or Not to
     Wit." The South Atlantic Quarterly 70.4 (Autumn 1971): 467-76.

     Considers De Vries to be our wittiest contemporary novelist.
Hasley asks how it is possible to assimilate a great deal of humor
into a novel without the humor being a distraction and asks the
related question of whether it is possible to be too witty in a
novel.   Hasley concludes that the humor in De Vries novels is
frequently a distraction, as when De Vries writes, "winter sports
leave me cold"; "she was crazy about mental health"; and "there's no
jack in the pulpit."   Rain is called "Jehovah's wetness"; a
particular church is "so modern they're thinking of making divorce
a sacrament." A woman's slipping on the floor she is waxing is said
to have put her behind in her work.   In a De Vries novel there are
constant puns, parodies, paradoxes, epigrams, repartees, and other
types of "verbal wizardry." De Vries' wit is indeed a distraction.
Even when it comes from the mouth of a character, it sounds like the
author cutting in.   And often the events seem to be manipulated to
showcase De Vries' wit rather than being a natural part of the
story. Hasley notes that the wit has in general decreased from book
to book. In the later works, the reader is not so often jolted by
the interjected wisecrack or puns, and Hasley concludes that De
Vries must have seen the rationing of humor as an effective
fictional technique.

739. Kehl, D. G. "Ring Around the Clerical Collar: Humor of the
     Cloth in Recent American Novels." WHIMSY 4 (1986): 18-19.

     Quotes Don Wanderhope, the protagonist of De Vries' The Blood
of the Lamb as saying, "Nothing proves the validy of the Church so
much as its ability to survive its own representatives." De Vries
has many clerics in his novels.   Kehl compares the Rev. Andrew
Mackerel in De Vries' The Mackerel Plaza with Father Urban of J. F.
Power's Morte D'Urban, and with Rev. Thomas Marshfield of John
Updike's A Month of Sundays, and with Leo Bebb of Frederick
Buechner's The Book of Bebb. Kehl suggests that such satirical
portraits of clerics are based on satirical portraits of clerics in
earlier American novels such as Sinclair Lewis' Elmer Gantry,
Thornton Wilder's Heaven's My Destination, and Erskine Caldwell's
Journeyman.   In the later novels the characters are less
stereotypical and are more fully rounded and complex, but in all of
these novels there is a diversified humor, ranging from basic
slapstick to Black Comedy to parodic wit.   For Kehl, these novels
constitute not only a literary humor of theology but also a theology
of humor.

740. Kehl, D. G. "Thalia Pops Her Girdle: Humor in the Novels of
     Peter De Vries." <u>Studies in American Humor</u> NS1.3 (February
     1983): 181-89.

     Contrasts Thalia, the muse of comedy, with her more
prestigious sister, Melpomene, the muse of tragedy. Kehl suggests
that the Greek concept of "thalia," which means "to burst forth" or
"to flourish," has too long been girdled by authors, critics, and
audiences who prefer her more serious sister. In De Vries' <u>Witch's
Milk</u>, Pete Seltzer tells Tillie Shilepsky, "Want to know something
about yourself? Don't wear a girdle.... Let the merchandise gallop
a little." And De Vries does exactly that. De Vries' humor ranges
from situational to rhetorical to linguistic. The irony ranges from
cogent irony to Horatian satire to Black Humor. A typical example
of De Vries irony involves Joe Sandwich, who impersonates a disc
jockey as he calls people to tell them they have just won a free
trip to a place they have just visited. Throughout his novels, De
Vries gives at least seven explanations of why we laugh,
explanations first postulated by Plato, Aristotle, Bergson, Kant,
Schopenhauer, Freud, and Huxley. De Vries concludes that each
theory gives us nine-tenths of the explanation of why we laugh, but
that all of them omit one-tenth, leaving, "an unaccounted-for
overflow that reminds you of a fat lady trying to pack more into a
girdle than it will legitimately contain." Through the mouth of one
of his characters, De Vries also offers his own explanation for
laughter, suggesting that the joke is a ritual--a ceremony. The
joke, like the prayer, is a device for resolving fear.

741. Potter, Nancy. "The Road to Christian Atheism in <u>Slouching
     Towards Kalamazoo</u>." <u>WHIMSY</u> 3 (1985): 191-93.

     Considers <u>Slouching Towards Kalamazoo</u> to be a classic De Vries
Bildingsroman. It chronicles the slouching pilgrimage of Anthony
Thrasher from his home in Ulalume, North Dakota, to Kalamazoo and
points east. In Ulalume, the greatest public entertainment of Tony
Thrasher's youth had been two public religious debates between his
father and their dermatologist, Dr. Humphrey Mallard. The result of
the debate is that each man converts the other, the atheist becoming
an evangelist, and the evangelist losing his faith and moving to New
York where he founds the church of Christian Atheism. Another irony
of the book is that a fifteen-year-old boy fails eighth grade
because he is reading Joyce and Proust and therefore falling behind
in his geography lessons. When he has an affair with Maggie
Doubloon, his teacher, he is described by his father as "Once an
underachiever, always an underachiever." In class, Maggie Doubloon
refers to <u>The Scarlet Letter</u> as hardcore chastity, and her
precocious student assigns his teacher an A+ for her performance in
bed. And so the novel goes, exhibiting giddy sequences, heaped-up
hyperbole, multiple reversals, extended misunderstanding, and
exaggerations of various types. Potter concludes that in De Vries'
writing, you laugh at things which, if there were just a little bit
more, would be very painful. For De Vries, comedy is tragedy looked
at from just a slightly different perspective.

742. Rodewald, Fred A. "Middle Class Values in the Novels of Peter
     De Vries." WHIMSY 1 (1983): 81-82.

     Maintains that De Vries targets such middle-class concepts as
marriage, the work ethic, and religious faith in his novels. His
tone is therefore appropriately humorous (middlebrow), rather than
witty (highbrow). In The Tents of Wickedness, Chick Swallow returns
to middle-class values when he says that he can't have sex with an
old friend because he doesn't want his pleasures to interfere with
his happiness. In The Mackerel Plaza, the middle-class values are
renounced by the Rev. Andrew Mackerel, minister of the People's
Liberal Church. In his highbrow, urbane concept of God, "It is the
final proof of God's omnipotence that he need not exist in order to
save us." In Angels, the father concludes a debate on the existence
of God by saying that death is neither a question mark nor a semicolon but rather a period. All of this is compatible with the
conclusion of Herman Hesse's Steppenwolf, where humor is described
as always having something of the bourgeois in it, even though the
true bourgeoisie are incapable of understanding it.

Margaret Halsey (1910-)

743. Walker, Nancy, and Zita Dresner. Redressing the Balance:
     American Women's Literary Humor from Colonial Times to the
     1980s. Jackson: Univ. Press of Mississippi, 1988, 326-31.

     Places Margaret Halsey's writing into the tradition of the
American eiron or wise innocent. Halsey uses the power of humor to
engage her readers in moral issues such as racism, McCarthyism,
cultural conformity, and political immorality. She is a moral
positivist with humor as one of her most effective tools. With
Malice Toward Some (1938) was her first book. It is an amusing
account of her travels in Europe and has been compared to Mark
Twain's Innocents Abroad. Halsey wrote Some of My Best Friends Are
Soldiers in 1944 and Color Blind in 1946 after she had observed as
a volunteer at the Stage Door Canteen in New York that Black and
Jewish soldiers were frequently discriminated against. Halsey's
humorous themes, style, and tone have been compared to Marietta
Holley's. She states that pigment of the skin has nothing to do
with intelligence and then adds that if it did, we would all be
stupider whenever we got sunburned. In 1960, Halsey joined the
ranks of such domestic humorists as Phyllis McGinley and Jean Kerr
with the publication of This Demi-Paradise: A Westchester Diary.
Halsey's autobiography was entitled No Laughing Matter: The
Autobiography of a WASP (1977). It is candid, revealing,
insightful, and funny.

Sam Levenson (1911-1980)

744. Simms, L. Moody, Jr. "Sam Levenson." Encyclopedia of American
     Humorists. Ed. Steven H. Gale. New York: Garland, 1988, 277-
     78.

     Describes Levenson as a folk humorist who relies very heavily
on autobiographical material in his writing. Levenson was born into
a poor but happy New York family, the youngest of eight children.
In 1938 Levenson became a teacher in Brooklyn's Samuel J. Tilden
High School, where he taught for eight years. Levenson developed a
reputation as a humorist, and in 1940 he was asked to be the master
of ceremonies for a group of teachers that was meeting in the
Catskill mountains. His routine, consisting mainly of amusing
personal recollections and observations, was good enough to make him
a full-fledged entertainer, appearing not only in night clubs but
also on Ed Sullivan's, Rudy Vallee's, Milton Berle's, and Jack
Benny's TV programs. In 1951 he had his own TV show, full of shrewd
and witty observations. In personal appearances and later in books,
Levenson concentrated on his experiences of growing up in a large
Jewish immigrant family and teaching in Brooklyn. His Meet the
Folks: a Session of American-Jewish Humor (1948) was a compilation
of earlier anecdotes and jokes. His Everything but Money (1966) was
again warm and witty. Sex and the Single Child (1969) is about the
curiosities of growing up. In One Era and Out the Other (1973)
discusses family, freedom, sex education, etc. Other humorous books
include You Can Say That Again, Sam (1975), and You Don't Have to Be
in Who's Who to Know What's What (1979). Levenson reminisces on the
"good old days" with insight, wit, and old-fashioned values.

Ruth McKenney (1911-1972)

745. Johnson, Eric W. "Ruth McKenney." Encyclopedia of American
     Humorists. Ed. Steven H. Gale. New York: Garland, 1988, 305-
     308.

     Says that McKenney began writing stories for the New Yorker in
1936. These stories were about growing up in Ohio and moving to
New York and becoming a working girl. McKenney wrote both humorous
and serious books but even in her serious books, the humor is
constant. Industrial Valley discusses a somber and serious topic,
but McKenney's satiric stance makes the book effective. The three
books in the Eileen trilogy are the core of McKenney's light
writing. They include My Sister Eileen (1938), The McKenneys Carry
On (1940), and All About Eileen (1952). In these books, Eileen is
beautiful, popular, and unconcerned, while Ruth is not so beautiful,
not so popular, and consumed by the important matters of life.
Eileen is also vulnerable, and Ruth is constantly trying to protect
her. The books contain many zany situations, such as when the girls
try to fight off the amorous advances of the Brazilian navy. The
Eileen stories are about two small-town girls trying to be
successful in the big city. The humor is exaggerated, and often
borders on slapstick. The Loud Red Patrick is about McKenney's
maternal grandfather, a Democrat in a Republican neighborhood who
expresses his opinions loudly and gruffly. McKenney's telling of

the incidents is often more hilarious than are the incidents themselves. The Patrick stories would probably be too sentimental and too unbelievable if it were not for McKenney's sense of the ridiculous.

John Cheever (1912-1982)

746. Anfinson, Stacie. "Cheever's Black Humor: Aversion versus Immersion." WHIMSY 6 (1988): 5-6.

Compares and contrasts the black humor of Cheever's "Goodbye, My Brother" with that of his "The Swimmer." Anfinson suggests that the black humor of the first is humor of aversion, while that of the second is humor of immersion. In "Goodbye My Brother," the mother says that she doesn't know if there is an afterlife, but if there is, she knows that she is going to have children who are fabulously rich, witty, and enchanting. This is humor of aversion--not facing the issue but rather making a joke about it. "The Swimmer" is a comedy of manners that pokes fun at the shallow communication in supermarkets, swimming pools, commuter trains, and cocktail parties. This short story is about the day that Neddy Merrill "swam" across the country, and it contains all of the elements that Bruce Friedman feels are necessary for black humor--shallow, one-dimensional characters, a detached, isolated society, a wasteland setting, and an ironic mocking, apocalyptic tone. Cheever's short stories, especially these two, are prototypical examples of black humor with their absurd terror, dark grotesqueness, crass cynicism, and exaggerated effect. In a way these stories are not humorous at all; they are jokes devoid of humor. They are suburban parodies heavily laden with irony and satire. They are some sort of a bridge between the comic and the tragic.

747. Tavernier-Courbin, Jacqueline, and R. G. Collins. "An Interview with John Cheever." Thalia: Studies in Literary Humor 1.2 (1978): 3-9.

Investigate the humor of John Cheever's short stories and how the humor of short stories in general differs from the humor of the novel. Cheever makes the statement that all of the fiction he can think of contains humor except for the Greek dramas. Then Cheever corrects himself to say that on second consideration, the Greek dramas have humor as well. Cheever views fiction as transcendent of both biography and history, and he further views it as a sort of triumphant celebration. He considers fiction to be the triumph of order over chaos. But the short story is different from the novel. The short story is a "burst." But in a novel, a burst destroys the structure. And in a novel, if there is a really successful burst, then readers will want to close the novel and think. They won't want to read any further. Cheever feels that the primary responsibility of the author is aesthetic, and that the primary feature of the aesthetic is interest, and interest is intimately connected with causes and effects. Cheever feels that in order for humor to be aesthetically significant it must be stylish, and he considers Dorothy Parker to have been a stylish humorist. She had the ability to knock one of the legs out from under the table, but

she was not malicious or destructive. Good humor can't be too
amiable. If it is too amiable, it won't get people's attention.

Mary McCarthy (1912-)

748. Martin, Wendy. "The Satire and Moral Vision of Mary
      McCarthy." Comic Relief: Humor in Contemporary American
      Literature. Urbana: Univ. of Illinois Press, 1978, 187-206.

Describes McCarthy's satire as a way of providing perspective
on the tensions between twentieth-century men and women. Her wit is
penetrating and uncompromising as McCarthy uses ridicule to explode
dehumanizing sexual stereotypes. Her humor is often painful, but it
is also effective as a moral corrective. McCarthy feels that the
best satire is based on hatred and repugnance. She considers satire
to be a way that powerless people can gain revenge against the
powerful. Martin compares McCarthy's satire to the eighteenth-
century satire of Jane Austen. In both cases, the satire not only
describes a complex social and economic reality and exposes the
pretentions of men and the illusions of women in a patriarchal
society, but it also makes judgments and expects changes in the
society it is illuminating.

Walt Kelly (1913-1973)

749. Brucker, Carl. "Walt Kelly's Pogo: The Eye of the Whole Man."
      Studies in American Humor NS2.3 (Winter 1983-84): 161-170.

Refers to Arthur Berger's portrayal of Kelly as one of the
most savage satirists in America. Kelly wrote a timely comic strip
that contained such powerful satire that it was frequently switched
to the editorial page. Thomas Dewey was portrayed as a mechanical
doll. Joseph McCarthy became in the strip Simple J. Malarkey, a
lynx who attempted to terrorize the swamp. Spiro Agnew was a hyena
who spouted out alliterative gobbledegook. But Brucker feels that
in the main Kelly's humor should be viewed more as persistent
persuasion rather than savage attack. For Kelly, the real danger
did not reside in the venal politician but rather in the human
susceptibility to fear, ignorance, and conformity. Kelly views the
force of humor not so much as a way of correcting error but rather
as an "inextricable thread in the fabric of life." It is a basic
aspect of humanity, because it is the enemy of regimentation and of
tyranny.

John Berryman (1914-1972)

750. Wallace, Ronald. "John Berryman: Me, Wag." God Be with the
      Clown. Columbia: Univ. of Missouri Press, 1984, 171-201.

Considers Berryman's The Dream Songs a parody of Walt
Whitman's "Song of Myself" with its "barbaric yawp." Whitman begins
his poem with "I, now thirty-seven years old in perfect health

begin,/ Hoping to cease not till death." Berryman begins his parody
with "I, Henry Pussy-cat, being in ill-health / & 900 years old,
begin & cease, / to doubt." Whitman is actually writing about a
symbolic everyman figure, even though he appears to be writing about
himself. Berryman, in his parody, is actually writing about
himself, even though he appears to be writing about a fictional
character. In Dream Songs, Berryman parodies not only Whitman, but
Dickinson, Frost, and Stevens as well. Wallace suggests that
Berryman's combination of the styles and techniques of other poets
helps him to define his own poetry. Berryman's comic stance is a
combination of Yankee wit, self-deprecation, and omnipotent-Kentucky
backwoods boasting. Berryman's humor is mainly autobiographical and
confessional, as it incorporates both sadness and celebration, both
self-deprecation and self-aggrandizement, both evasion and attack.
To these qualities Berryman adds a touch of melancholy to his poetry
resulting in what Wallace calls the minstral voice. The banter,
dance, ego, and flamboyance of Whitman and Stevens are combined with
the sadness, doubt, uncertanty, private pain, and humiliation of
Dickinson and Frost to produce this tone of the Negro minstral show
in Berryman's poetry.

William S. Burroughs (1914-)

751. Palumbo, Donald. "Science Fiction as Allegorical Social
     Satire: William Burroughs and Jonathan Swift." Studies in
     Contemporary Satire 9 (Spring 1982): 1-8.

     Postulates that even though Burroughs' and Swift's styles and
surface textures differ radically, they use similar means and
produce similar effects in their development of an exceptionally
brutal brand of satire. They also target the same types of social
inadequacies--the shortcomings, the folly, and the senseless animal
visciousness of their fellow human beings and the social milieus in
which they opperate. In addition, both Burroughs and Swift present
their satire with the hope of affecting social change. Both
Burroughs and Swift wrote fantasies; both wrote parodies of the
literature popular at the time; and the works of both are comic and
satiric. In his Naked Lunch, The Soft Machine, Nova Express, and
The Ticket That Exploded, Burroughs uses a style that is very
similar to the montage technique frequently used in motion pictures.
Rather than developing plots or characters, he juxtaposes disparate
scenes next to each other to promote emotional associations and
reactions from his readers. Burroughs' juxtapositions occur so
frequently that the feelings of revulsion stimulated by the earlier
images are retained to the later images, reinforcing the readers'
negative attitudes and desires to change society.

Ralph Waldo Ellison (1914-)

752. Schafer, William J. "Irony from Underground: Satiric Elements
     in Invisible Man." Satire Newsletter 7.1 (Fall 1969): 22-29.

     Feels that satiric irony is a major device in Ellison's
Invisible Man, which uses folk humor, Black slang, and the

"underground" viewpoint to present the tragicomic and grotesque Black vision in America during the first half of the twentieth century. Ellison creates his satiric effect through extensive use of heavy irony. Schafer compares Ellison's Invisible Man with Swift's Gulliver's Travels. In both cases an unsophisticated person is being presented by bewildering and deceptive appearances ranging from comfortable misapprehensions to desperate dangers. Both works rely on the reader's sympathy with the protagonist-narrator. Both works use hyperbolic and ironic images to create a symbolism for corruption and deception in a society that is more complex than is the mind of the observer. The difference between the two works is that Swift uses a fantastic voyage as his metaphorical vehicle, while Ellison's work is modern and naturalistic. While Swift uses allegory to veil the targets of his attack, Ellison uses irony. While Swift's images tend to be physical, Ellison's images tend to be psychological. In both Ellison's and Swift's novels, we see the world from the perspective of the victim, but Ellison's novel has us see the world through eyes that are like those of blues singers carefully shaping their double entendres.

Bernard Malamud (1914-1986)

753. Chard-Hutchinson, Martine. "The Functions of Humor in Bernard Malamud's Fiction." HUMOR: International Journal of Humor Research 4.2 (1991): 177-87.

     Contrasts Malamud's use of humor with his use of irony, and suggests that Malamud's writing is more humorous than ironic. For example, Malamud's writing is filled with comic pathos that has something of a cathartic function. Malamud also develops clown figures which gently subvert traditional values. Chard-Hutchinson furthermore feels that Malamud's humor has a "poetic" function. In conclusion, Chard-Hutchinson suggests that the victory of humor over irony in Malamud's fiction clearly asserts his attachment to humanism.

754. Dickson, L. L. "Hit or Myth: Comic Treatments of Baseball in the Contemporary American Novel." WHIMSY 3 (1985): 35-37.

     Compares the ironic treatments of the quest motif, the mythic heroes, and the archetypal symbolic test in Bernard Malamud's The Natural (1952), Robert Coover's The Universal Baseball Association (1968), Philip Roth's The Great American Novel (1973), Paul Hemphill's Long Gone (1979), and Jerome Charyn's The Seventh Babe (1979). Malamud pokes fun at baseball journalism and especially the ubiquitous sports cliches. One reporter writes that Malamud's protagonist Roy Hobbs is a player who can catch "anything that flies." During one game a woman who lives next to the ball park is cleaning her bird cage and the canary escapes and flies toward the diamond. Roy leaps high into the air and bags the canary in his glove, later getting rid of the bloody mess in the clubhouse trash can. Robert Coover's novel is even more playful and more comic than Malamud's, and Philip Roth's novel owes a great deal of its humor to the tradition of the Old Southwest humor, since it abounds in scatology, homely images, vernacular speech, and descriptive exaggeration. Paul Hemphill's novel has a great deal of fun with the relationship of aptonyms to the real world, as when Joe Louis Brown is passed off as a Venezuelan in order to continue to play in a white Class D league in the 1950s South. Jerome Charyn uses this same device with Babe Ragland, who incongruously is a left-handed third baseman. These authors also use baseball concepts to divide up their novels into nine parts (innings), eight parts with a rained-out ninth inning leaving the rest of the game still to be played, three sections (June, July, and August), and "Pre-Game" and "Batter Up," etc.

Thomas "Tennessee" Lavier Williams (1914-1987)

755. Hart, James D. "Tennessee Williams." The Oxford Companion to American Literature. 4th edition. New York: Oxford Univ. Press, 1965. 928-29.

Considers Williams' The Rose Tattoo (1950) Williams' only comedy of sex. The novel is set in a Gulf Coast town and treats a Sicilian woman's eager quest for love.

Saul Bellow (1915-)

756. Cohen, Sarah Blacher. "The Comedy of Urban Low Life: From Saul Bellow to Mordecai Richler." Thalia: Studies in Literary Humor 4.2 (1982): 21-24.

Points out the hypocrisy of such Bellow characters as Herzog, Sammler, and Citrine. These characters deliver public diatribes on the degeneration of the times, saying that in Jewish culture crime is a forbidden activity, for it contradicts the notion of menschlichkeit and edelkeit (humanity and gentility). Yet these characters are closet criminals who are secretly grateful to law breakers for infusing excitement into their dull lives. And ironically, these characters even consider themselves compassionate and virtuous, as they pride themselves in being patient with criminals and psychopaths. There is an ironic disparity between the stated intentions of these characters and their self-deceptions. Cohen points to the similarities between Saul Bellow's characters and those of Mordecai Richler in this regard and says that in both cases the readers are laughing at a kind of playful and pugnacious urban humor.

757. Colbert, Robert E. "Satiric Vision in Herzog." Studies in Contemporary Satire 5 (Spring 1978): 22-33.

Feels that Saul Bellow's satiric style derives from such nineteenth-century satirists as Dickens, Gogol, and Dostoevsky. There is lack of order in Herzog, since most of the characters do not behave as they are expected to behave. Friends and wives betray; lawyers practice against their clients; priests go Hollywood; and business and government leaders do not represent their constituents but act only in their own interests. The novel is presented from an impressionistic point of view. The actions, memories, emotions, speculations, and fantasies are all filtered

through Herzog's mind, and the resulting distortion and slanting is
the device through which the satire is driven.

758. Galloway, David. "The Absurd Man as Picaro." The Absurd Hero in
     American Fiction. Second Revised Edition. Austin: Univ. of
     Texas Press, 1981, 129-203.

     Indicates that in Bellow's first two novels, Dangling Man and
The Victim, Bellow depicts dislocations of metropolitan life by
exposing distortions of contemporary values and victimization by the
urban environment.   The situations in both of these novels can be
described as "absurd."   Galloway compares the absurdity of Bellow's
Dangling Man with that of Camus' The Stranger.   The characters in
these novels (Joseph and Meursault) ultimately are driven to an
absurd stance as the result of an indiscriminate clustering of
circumstances.   These circumstances do not seem to be part of a
higher plan; rather they just happen, and the narrators of the
novels merely observe rather than attempting to explain or evaluate.
Joseph is an insignificant clerk who finds himself dangling between
commitments and value systems.   The monotonous routine of Joseph's
daily life is suddenly interrupted by a draft notice, which leaves
him dangling between his regular job and his induction into the
army.   Both the writings of Bellow and the writings of Camus are
tributes to man's resourceful and perseverance, but they are not
tributes to man's victory--only tributes to his survival.   For both
authors the prevailing metaphor is the myth of Sisyphus.   The
characters in Bellow's and Camus' novels will never prevail, but
they will persist.   They gain power over the absurdities of life by
realizing and accepting the fact that life is absurd.

759. Guttmann, Allen. "Saul Bellow's Humane Comedy." Comic Relief:
     Humor in Contemporary American Literature. Urbana: Univ. of
     Illinois Press, 1978, 127-51.

     Discusses three Bellow novels: The Dangling Man (1944), The
Victim (1947), and The Adventures of Augie March (1953), indicating
that in all three, Bellow has been fascinated by "ideas."   Guttmann
contends that a laughing response to The Dangling Man would be
churlish and perhaps even sadistic.   A laughing response to the
ironies of The Victim would be equally inappropriate.   But The
Adventures of Augie March is a comic novel, to which laughter is the
only appropriate response.   After publication of The Victim, Bellow
started to publish pieces of a comic nature, like "Sermon by Doctor
Pep" and "Address by Gooley MacDowell to the Asbeens Club of
Chicago," because by then he was secure with himself as a writer and
was ready to "indulge himself as an unsurpassed comedian."   Augie
March is a picaresque protagonist who narrates his own story "with
a gusty eloquence far beyond that of Bellow's previous characters."
Augie is forced to choose between complaint and comedy, and he
chooses comedy.   Augie recounts his own misadventures and grins,
because he is the "animal ridense" who is able to laugh at life and
at himself.   For Augie, the laughter is reflective.   Guttman also
discusses the humor and irony in Seize the Day (1956), and Henderson
The Rain King (1959), Mr. Sammler's Planet (1970) and Humboldt's
Gift (1975).

760. Karl, Frederick R. "Bellow's Comic "Last Men." Thalia: Studies
     in Literary Humor 1.1 (Spring 1978): 29-36.

     Considers Bellow's earlier novels to have been picaresque and
episodic in nature. These earlier novels provided Bellow with the
writing skills he would later use in his more mature works such as
Herzog (1964) and Mr. Sammler's Planet (1969), novels which were
more successful and more organic as syntheses. Bellow was concerned
with antithetical notions and with how to bind together disparate
elements into a single unified whole. He used wit and irony to
deal with his tragic awareness, and he created a tension in his
novels between the surface and the truth that lies beneath the
surface. The wit and irony that are on the surface of Bellow's work
create a sense of openness, a sense that anything is possible. But
underneath, there is always the possibilities of chaos and anarchy.
The contrast is between the witty, the ironic, the mocking, the
comic on the top, and the ideas, the ideology, the doctrine, the
homiletics underneath. The pattern was established by the old
rabbis and judges; the treatment is Rabelaisian in its proportions.

761. Kehl, D. G. "The Animal Ridens: Laughter as Metaphor in Modern
     American Literature." WHIMSY 2 (1984): 39-40.

     Contrasts Whitman's "barbaric yawp sounding over the roofs of
the world," and Ginsberg's "howl echoing in the kingdom of Moloch,"
Hawthorne's "sharp, dry cachinnation," and Twain's laughter that can
"blow the colossal humbug to rags and atoms at a blast" with
Bellow's "animal ridens, the laughing creature, forever rising up."
Those primal laughs of the nineteenth century represented loss of
self control, bitterness, scorn, despair, hysteria, insanity,
demonic possession, and dehumanization. But those primal laughs of
the twentieth century are different. Like the primal laughs of the
nineteenth century they represent defiance and mockery of a decadent
socio-political system, but in addition they are used as a weapon of
survival in an absurd world. Consistent with Bellow's view of
animal ridens--the laughing creature is Ken Kesey, whose McMurphy
opposes the system by teaching the inmates of the asylum to be black
humorists; and Sherwood Anderson who discusses the primal laughter
of Blacks; and Vladimir Nabokov, who wrote Laughter in the Dark; and
James Purdy, whose Cabot Wright "relieved himself in laughter;" and
Peter De Vries with his Joe Sandwich; and John Updike, whose
"poisonous laughter distilled all the cruelty and blasphemy in the
world."

762. Opdahl, Keith. "The 'Mental Comedies' of Saul Bellow." From
     Hester Street to Hollywood. Bloomington: Indiana Univ. Press,
     1986, 183-96.

     Establishes the influence that the theatre had on Saul
Bellow's writing. In Dangling Man there is the actor Alf Streidler;
in Herzog there are pervasive allusions to acting; in Humboldt's
Gift, Citrine is a playwright; in The Victim Albee developes a
relationship with a movie actress; and in Seize the Day, Tommy
Wilhelm quits college to become an actor. At times Bellow uses
theatre imagery to represent falseness or pretention, but at other
times he uses it to represent the real and the dramatic.
Nevertheless, Bellow's fiction is largely observation and
meditation; he enjoys describing in detail a scene, an image, or an

emotion, and these are the aspects which a play mainly leaves up to the director and the actors. Bellow's interest in theatre caused him to write five plays, four of which were one-act farces. "A Wen," "Orange Souffle" and "One From Under" were performed as a single entertainment entitled <u>Under the Weather</u>, so named because that is how all the protagonists felt. Bellow's plays were praised in London but failed on Broadway, where Walter Kerr felt they were too frivolous. He wrote that Bellow had written plays more with a sense of "giggle" than with a sense of "accepted obligation." Bellow himself confessed that he wrote plays because they were easier to write than novels. To Bellow, theatre meant freedom. In a play he didn't have to worry so much about moods or details, so the author could come to the point easier. Bellow's farcical plays allowed him to mix the high with the low, the earthy and the sublime, sexy obsessions with metaphysical speculations. For Bellow, the play is swept along by its emotion and energy rather than by careful structure. Opdahl feels that "Bellow has done very well given the essentially untheatrical cast of his imagination."

763. Scheer-Schäzler, Brigitte. "Saul Bellow's Humour and Saul Bellow's Critical Reception." <u>Literary and Linguistic Aspects of Humour</u>. Barcelona, Spain: Univ. of Barcelona English Department, 1984, 73-85.

Points out that Bellow has won the National Book Award for Fiction three times--for <u>The Adventures of Augie March</u> in 1953, for <u>Herzog</u> in 1964, and for <u>Mr. Sammler's Planet</u> in 1970, and that Bellow also won the Nobel Prize for Literature in 1976. Nevertheless, Bellow's critics vary drastically in their evaluations of his work, and the reason for their disagreement is that they have different perceptions of his humor. Some of Bellow's critics consider him to be basically a serious novelist who happens to use humor; other critics consider him to be basically a humorous or comic writer who sometimes says something profound. Even those critics who consider him a humorist are divided in their opinions, with comments ranging from "Bellow is a minor comic novelist" to "Bellow is surely one of the great modern metaphysical comedians." Sheer-Schäzler suggests that these disparate perceptions of Bellow's work result from the dissimilarity between what Bellow is and what he appears to be. She makes the comparison between Bellow and the circus clown who makes a clumsy entrance tripping over his own feet and running into things but who turns out to be a marvelous equestrian and acrobat. Humor has this ability to mystify the differences between appearance and truth.

Henry Kuttner (1915-1958)

764. Robillard, Douglas. "Henry Kuttner." <u>Encyclopedia of American Humorists</u>. Ed. Steven H. Gale. New York: Garland, 1988, 259-63.

Contends that any fiction published under any of Kuttner's pen names during the 1940s and 1950s could be assumed to be written in collaboration with his wife, C. L. Moore. During this period, Kuttner wrote mainly under the pseudonym of Lewis Padgett, and all of the Lewis Padgett stories first appeared in <u>Astounding Science Fiction</u>. The Padgett stories tended to have a certain nightmarish quality. In 1942, for example Kuttner wrote "The Twonky" a device invented by a time traveler to do his chores. But the "twonky" also has a way of taking charge, censoring and changing people's thoughts, and blocking any attempts at individualized thinking. Kuttner is capable of developing interesting time-travel metaphors. After his head clears, the time traveler in "The Twonky" figures out why he has been marooned in the past. In his time travel, he has hit a "temporal snag." For Kuttner, time is a river, and time travelers are like river boats that must be cautious to avoid dangerous snags. In 1944 Kuttner published "Mimsy Were the Borogoves," which is a serious story told with touches of humor. In 1952 his <u>Robots Have No Tails</u> is about Gallegher, a scientist who has to be drunk in order for subconscious inventive genius to be unlocked. The irony of the novel is that while he is drunk he can invent devices that he cannot comprehend while he is sober. Between 1947 and 1949 Kuttner wrote a collection of humorous stories entitled <u>Thrilling Wonder Stories</u>, in which a radioactive plague has given people unusual talents, like longevity, the ability to fly, or be invisible, or read minds. The humor of Kuttner's science fiction is based on the taming of science gone wild.

Arthur C. Miller (1915-)

765. Brater, Enoch. "Ethnics and Ethnicity in the Plays of Arthur Miller." <u>From Hester Street to Hollywood</u>. Ed. Sarah Blacher Cohen. Bloomington: Indiana Univ. Press, 1986, 123-36.

Explains that Miller's drama was about the archetypal Jewish-American family during the depression. The plays illustrate the struggle for survival amidst the petty conditions that are caused by poverty. Clifford Odets' <u>Awake and Sing!</u> had set the stage for Miller by employing raw realism to expose the life of an urban Jew growing up in the thirties. The Millers lived in Brooklyn at this time, and out of pity, Arthur's mother was constantly taking people off the street. She had one man come in for a bowl of soup, and he stayed for twelve years, at which time Arthur's grandfather threw the man out for coming home drunk once too often. Miller's <u>The Creation of the World and Other Business</u> examines the ancient Judaic myths from an ethical rather than from a religious point of view. God is reduced to comic dimensions and is played as an actor on stage, interacting with other actors who portray humans. God is seen as the creator, but he is not seen at the exclusive power above all others. In Miller's play, God and man occupy center stage together. The play begins in a whimsical tone, but by the end of the play, the tone has changed to deadly seriousness.

Leonard Wibberly (1915-)

766. Senese, Joseph C. "Using Humor to Teach the Unthinkable, Or,
     How I Learned to Talk about the Bomb." WHIMSY 4 (1986): 102-
     103.

     Discusses Wibberly's satirical novel, The Mouse that Roared
(1954). The novel takes place in the bucolic mythical kingdom of
Grand Fenwick, nestled picturesquely in the Alps. Because of its
isolation from other countries, Grand Fenwick is still in the
fourteenth century in terms of technology; however, the country does
have enough sophistication to realize that the way to enter the
twentieth century is to declare war on the United States with the
intention of losing. The problem is that Grand Fenwick wins the war
and captures the powerful Q-Bomb, making the smallest country in the
world the most powerful as well. The book is populated by colorful
characters. Tully Bascomb, the leader of the expeditionary forces
disagrees with everyone, including himself. Dr. Kokintz, the
inventor of the Q-Bomb, is an absent-minded professor type who
carries moldy sandwiches in his lab coat because he forgets to eat
them; he triggers the bomb with a hair pin borrowed from his
landlady. The novel catches the sense of paranoia that was rampant
in the 50s. The satire is biting, and the wit is sometimes mordant;
however, the fairy-tale world, and the lovable characters give the
reader a measure of security.

John Ciardi (1916-)

767. Hart, James D. "John Ciardi." The Oxford Companion to American
     Literature. Fourth Edition. New York: Oxford Univ. Press,
     1965, 157.

     Indicates that Ciardi's poetry is often marked by vernacular
diction and homely wit. This poetry is published in such
collections as Homeward to America (1940), Other Skies (1947), Live
Another Day (1949), From Time to Time (1951), As If, Poems New and
Selected (1955), I Marry You (1958), I Met a Man (1960), and In Fact
(1963). Hart describes I Marry You as a collection of love poems
and I Met a Man as nonsense verses for children.

Felicia Lamport (1916-)

768. Walker, Nancy, and Zita Dresner. Redressing the Balance:
     American Women's Literary Humor from Colonial Times to the
     1980s. Jackson: Univ. Press of Mississippi, 1988, 353-56.

     Compares the playfulness of Lamport's light verse to that of
Ogden Nash. Lamport's writing, like that of Nash, abounds in puns,
word inventions, and unlikely rhymes. But Lamport's subjects are
very different from those of Nash. Lamport writes about the tyranny
of fashion, dieting, women's political power, and domestic issues.
Like Phoebe Cary and Carolyn Wells, Lamport is also an excellent
parodist. One of her most successful parodies is entitled "The Love

Song of R. Milhous Nixon, 1973," which appeared in <u>Light Metres</u> (1982). It is a parody of T. S. Eliot's "The Love Song of J. Alfred Prufrock," and its theme is the Watergate scandal. In the Eliot poem, Prufrock measured his life in coffee spoons. In the Lamport parody, Nixon measured his life in reels of tape. Lamport forms a nice pun on the "peach" in the Eliot poem that Prufrock doesn't dare eat. In the Lamport parody, this word appears embedded into the word "impeach." Lamport wrote for <u>Harper's</u>, <u>The Atlantic</u>, <u>The New Yorker</u>, <u>Life</u>, and the <u>Saturday Evening Post</u>. Her collections of light verse include <u>Mink on Weekdays</u> (1950), <u>Scrap Irony</u> (1961), and <u>Cultural Slag</u> (1966).

Gwendolyn Brooks (1917-)

769.   Walker, Nancy, and Zita Dresner. "Gwendolyn Brooks." <u>Redressing the Balance: American Women's Literary Humor from Colonial Times to the 1980s</u>. Jackson: Univ. Press of Mississippi, 1988, 309-11.

Asserts that Brooks' first collection of poems entitled <u>A Street in Bronzeville</u> (1945) was highly praised and won for Brooks two Guggenheim fellowships. Brooks' second collection of poems, <u>Annie Allen</u> (1949) was the basis for Brooks' 1950 Pulitzer Prize for poetry, the first to be given to a Black American. In <u>Maud Martha</u> (1955), Brooks employs a sardonic tone and an ironic contrast to point out contradictions between the ways in which women perceive themselves in contrast to how they are perceived by their own families, lovers, class, race, and white American society as a whole.

James Farl Powers (1917-)

770. Kiley, Frederick, and J. M. Shuttleworth. <u>Satire from Aesop to Buchwald</u>. New York: Macmillan, 1971, 391-400.

Presents Powers' story "The Valiant Woman" in its entirety, indicating that it is a witty story about the relationship between a domineering housekeeper and a long suffering Catholic priest. Powers' use of the imagery of a mosquito is effective. This mosquito appears in the middle of the story and has a devilish reemergence at the end of the story.

Glendon Swarthout (1918-)

771. Vanderwerken, David L. "Of Steaks, Compliments, and Death in Glendon Swarthout's <u>Cactus League</u>." <u>Studies in American Humor</u> NS5.2-3 (Summer and Fall 1986): 99-105.

Examines Swarthout's story "The Ball Really Carries in the Cactus League Because the Air Is Dry" as belonging to the tradition of athletes (including gunfighters) whose best days are behind them. Al, the protagonist, hits with great power during the spring practice but loses his power during the regular season. Al's theory is that spring practice is in Arizona, where the air is so dry that it is easy to hit the long ball, but the air of Al's franchise's home city is too muggy to allow him to hit very many home runs. On one day when Al does hit a home run, the Chamber of Commerce gives him a number of gifts, including a steak dinner for two at the OK Steak Corral. On his way out of the park he signs a program for an old geezer who seems to be the only one in the crowd who remembers Al's grand past. He says he remembers Al when he used to catch with Detroit. Al responds, "Detroit? I was never with Detroit." Al drives a good old American car, a Chevrolet. His rival, the bonus catcher, drives a Ferrari. Al considers this to be very unpatriotic. Al feels that if you play the great American game, you should also drive an American car.

Marion Hargrove (1919-)

772. Goldstein, Kalman. "Marion Hargrove." Encyclopedia of American Humorists. Ed. Steven H. Gale. New York: Garland, 1988, 191-94.

    Traces Hargrove's humorous writing to 1941 when he became the feature editor fo the Charlotte News. There he contributed a column named, "In the Army Now." The columns that he wrote for the Charlotte News became the basis for See Here, Private Hargrove (1942). During his service in the Army, Hargrove was transferred to New York to become editor for the magazine Yank and promoted to Corporal. As a result of his wide audience, Hargrove became an official spokesman for the American soldier, writing articles for the New York Times Magazine about G.I. problems, behavior, and morale. George Baker and Barrie Stavis had Hargrove write prefaces for The Sad Sack and Chain of Command, respectively. In 1948 Hargrove published Something's Got to Give, and during the 1950s and early 1960s Hargrove was especially productive. In 1956 he published his third novel, The Girl He Left Behind. Since Hargrove concentrated on the irritations of training for war rather than on the grim realities of war itself, it was reassuring to both soldiers and their relatives and friends. Hargrove and his soldier buddies went through a series of sophomoric hazings, short-sheeting beds and frustrating sergeants. Their dialogue is very similar to that of college freshmen. The soldiers are portrayed as young men away from their homes for the first time, trying to adjust to a radically different environment. They are not willfully disobedient or inherently inept; they are just inexperienced. Even those critics who claim that Hargrove's work is thin or glib and who argue that all his characters are the same still praise his breezy tone, his skill at writing credible dialogue, and his characterization of lovable rogues.

773. Secor, Robert. "Marion Hargrove." Dictionary of Literary Biography, Volume 11: American Humorists, 1800-1950. Ed. Stanley Trachtenberg. Detroit, MI: Gale, 1982, 176-79.

    Considers much of Hargrove's work autobiographical. A soldier in Fort Bragg, North Carolina, described Hargrove as a six-foot scarecrow. Hargrove saluted non-commissioned officers, tripped over his own feet during calisthenics, and spent most of his time requesting furloughs. This tone is consistent with that of See Here, Private Hargrove, a comic best-seller published in 1942 recounting Hargrove's transition from civilian to army life. Toward the end of the 1950s Hargrove published two more novels on the same theme. All of them depict the confrontation between the career soldiers, who want to make their charges into men, and the charges, who are not especially interested in becoming men. When Hargrove is issued his uniform, he says that he wears a size nine. The supply sergeant replies, "The expression is, 'I wore a size nine'." When Hargove is told to paint some white garbage cans with black lettering, Hargrove chooses instead pastel colors. More than two million copies of Hargrove's books were sold, and they were read so widely that many army terms entered the civilian vocabulary, "GI," "PX," "over the hill," "chow," "goldbricking," and more. In 1948 Hargrove wrote Something's Got to Give, a satire of the era's radio programs and the values they represented. Hargrove had learned in the army that the best thing to be is a corporal in order to avoid the dirty work of the privates and the responsibility of the sergeants. He explains that that's also what he's trying to be in civilian life--a corporal.

Shirley Jackson (1919-1965)

774. Downing, Janay. "Much Ado about Nothing: Narrative Strategies in Shirley Jackson and Teresa Bloomingdale." WHIMSY 1 (1982): 206-208.

Suggests that Shirley Jackson's books set the stage for such later writers as Jean Kerr, Peg Bracken, Phyllis Diller, Ann Toland Serb, Joan Wester Anderson, Phyllis Naylor, Terry Hekker, Prudence MacKintosh, Shirley Leuth, and Teresa Bloomingdale. The novels of all of these authors have a number of elements in common. They are all set in the home, and all communicate a sense of enclosure and confinement. Furthermore, they all employ a narrative technique which Downing calls the "Drop the Handkerchief Pattern." The allusion is to a game where the "it" child moves around the outside of a circle of other players and then drops the handkerchief. At this point everyone changes places with everyone else in a somewhat random order, and the person who doesn't find a place is "it" for the next turn. The game is played until everybody gets tired of playing. Downing noticed that the novels of all of the authors mentioned follow the same development as the child's game. Shirley Jackson's Life Among the Savages for example tells about "The Great Grippe Mystery," whereby the Jackson family (two adults, three children, and a dog) exchange beds with each other, bringing with them pillows, books, armless dolls, cardboard suitcases, glasses of fruit juice, blankets, glasses of brandy, cigarettes, matches, and other miscellaneous items. By morning, everybody is in the wrong bed with a random array of partners and items. There is no plot and no climax. It is what Downing calls much ado about nothing in a world where physical objects take on a life of their own. Downing researched twenty-two books by thirteen different female humorists and suggests that this is a newly developed genre for women authors.

775. LeCroy, Anne. "The Different Humor of Shirley Jackson: <u>Life among the Savages</u> and <u>Raising Demons</u>." <u>Studies in American Humor</u> NS4.1-2 (Spring-Summer 1985): 62-73.

Notes that most libraries place Jackson's two family biofictions, <u>Life among the Savages</u> and <u>Raising Demons</u>, either on the nonfiction or the biography shelves rather than categorize them appropriately as fiction. Almost all reviews of <u>Life among the Savages</u> (1953) have been favorable; however no reviews point to any special excellence in this work. <u>Raising Demons</u> (1957) has met a similar fate, with one reviewer saying that the book is "a shrewd and witty social document as well as a beguiling family chronicle." Shirley Jackson's comic family novels have gained a wide readership, because Jackson has a gift for the casual telling of humorous stories and for giving the stories credibility, whether the events actually happened or not. Some readers of Jackson's works see the gothic tradition, whereby her novels and stories concentrate on psychological and occult phenomena. They tend to lose sight of Jackson's persistent humor or see it as dark and macabre. LeCroy feels, however, that humor has pervaded Jackson's work from the very beginning and has always been an intrinsic aspect of her style. Her tone is frequently light and warm. She often recounts funny episodes and gives a witty and wry presentation of human nature even in the foreboding ambiance of Hill House and the violent underpinnings of <u>We Have Always Lived in the Castle</u> or "The Lottery." But Jackson's stories are longer and more interlinked than are the stories of Erma Bombeck, Judith Viorst, or Nancy Stahl. The flavor of Bombeck, Viorst, or Stahl humor can be communicated in short excerpts, while an appreciation of Jackson humor is possible only by reading the complete work.

776. Walker, Nancy A. "Shirley Jackson." <u>A Very Serious Thing: Women's Humor and American Culture</u>. Minneapolis: Univ. of Minnesota Press, 1988, 33 and 48.

Feels that Jackson's <u>Life Among the Savages</u> demonstrates her mastery as a humorous writer, and contributes to what Walker calls "post-World War II Domestic Humor." This humor uses techniques of slapstick comedy to deal with the myriad details connected with motherhood and housekeeping and shows a housewife's lot to be repetitive and demeaning. Walker compares the hyperbolic and slapstick tone of this genre to the tall tale, only the setting is the home or the neighborhood since the authors who employ this genre are typically women.

777. Walker, Nancy, and Zita Dresner. "Shirley Jackson." <u>Redressing the Balance: American Women's Literary Humor from Colonial Times to the 1980s</u>. Jackson: Univ. Press of Mississippi, 1988, 315-25.

Refers to the ambiance of Jackson's <u>Life Among the Savages</u> (1953) and <u>Raising Demons</u> (1957) as "domestic chaos." These novels are largely autobiographical in nature, and the daily trials and problems of child-rearing and homemaking in Jackson's books set the stage for Jean Kerr's future books. Jackson bases her novels on realistic detail of actual experiences as she uses deadpan humor to develop the persona of a harried housewife faced with conflicting demands of her husband, her children, and literary agent. Her humorous tone allows her to be somewhat detached and bemused. There is much situational irony in Jackson's novels as her protagonist tries to be all things to all people. At the time of her death, Jackson was working on what she considered to be her first comic novel. The title was to have been Come Along with Me.

Andy Aitken Rooney (1919-)

778. Jones, Veda. "Andrew Aitken [Andy] Rooney." Encyclopedia of American Humorists. Ed. Steven H. Gale. New York: Garland, 1988, 376-80.

   Believes that Rooney is being a humorist when he says that he does not consider himself a humorist. Rooney's tongue-in-cheek delivery, his wry wit, his folksy philosophy all point to the fact that he has a dry sense of humor. Rooney ruminates over the ordinary things of life; he "approaches a subject, turns it inside out, flips it over and back again, gives it a couple of twists, puts it back together and presents an essay on it from a fresh perspective." In his audience Rooney is searching for the grunt of recognition that people make when they are struck by a homely truth. Rooney got his training as a journalist by writing for the Stars and Stripes. With "Bud" Hutton he later wrote The Story of the Stars and Stripes (1946), which consisted of lively anecdotes about aspects of war that were not reported in the newspapers. These two authors went on to write Conqueror's Peace: A Report to the American Stockholders (1947). Rooney was a ghost writer for Arthur Godfrey, Garry Moore, and other humorous celebrities. He also wrote straight news for 60 Minutes until 1978 when he was the summer replacement for the "Point-Counterpoint" segment of 60 Minutes. He was an immediate success, and many of his three-minute pieces have been collected into such books as A Few Minutes with Andy Rooney (1981), And More by Andy Rooney (1982), Pieces of My Mind (1984), and Word for Word (1986). He polishes his TV commentaries considerably before publishing them as sketches in book form.

Jerome David Salinger (1919-)

779. Galloway, David. "The Love Ethic." The Absurd Hero in American Fiction: Updike, Styron, Bellow, Salinger. Austin: Univ. of Texas Press, 1981, 204-27.

   Proposes that Salinger's Holden Caulfield is responsible for as much devotion, imitation, and controversy as any other character in contemporary literature. To Holden Caulfield the world is fragmented, distorted, and absurd; he himself uses the word "phony." Galloway describes Holden as being "often childishly ingenuous" and describes his language as "frequently comic." Holden is like Camus' absurd man, for both are trying to apply ethical standards to an indifferent and nihilistic world. Holden is attempting to find truth and unity and coherence in a phony world, and he succeeds in finding them only in New York's Museum of Natural History, because only here is everything so carefully catalogued and coordinated. Here was a place he could count on to be constant and unchanged.

Every time you went there the Eskimo had just finished catching two
fish, and the birds were on their way South, and the deer would be
drinking out of their water hole, and the squaw with the naked bosom
would still be weaving the same blanket.   He could count on
everything being exactly where it should be.   It was the only place
in New York that was not absurd.

780. Workman, Brooke. "Parody: A Student's Response to J. D.
      Salinger." English Journal 70.1 (January 1981): 53-54.

       Presents Salinger as an author who is very accessible to high
school students. Workman takes a chronological approach, beginning
his course by having his students first read such early Salinger
stories as "The Young Folks" and then the 1945 story that introduced
Holden Caulfield, "I'm Crazy," and the 1948 story that introduced
the Glass family, "A Perfect Day for Bananafish."   From here his
students move on to the books that fleshed out these characters, The
Catcher in the Rye (1951), Franny and Zooey (1961), and finally on
to a Salinger story written in 1963.   Workman constantly reminds
students of how the characters developed from the time of their
first introductions until they finally emerged as fully developed
characters.   Workman also discusses Salinger's prose style, and
talks about characteristic Salinger trademarks like his immediate
contact with the reader, his confusing story lines, his italizing
words for stress, his colloquial language often too strong for those
who want to censor or ban his books, the symbolic names of his
characters and the titles of his stories, the Zen images, and the
depiction of honest feelings by such characters as Holden, Seymour,
Franny, or Buddy, who are all looking for meaning in a crazy world.
Workman has his students write parodies of Salinger style to see if
they are able to write as he does.   Many of Workman's students
succeed very well in this task.

Max Shulman (1919-)

781. Hodgins, Francis. "Max Shulman." Dictionary of Literary
      Biography: Volume 11: American Humorists 1800-1950.   Ed.
      Stanley Trachtenberg. Detroit, MI: Gale, 1982, 439-47.

       Gives Shulman's reason for becoming a humorous writer--simply
that life was bitter and Shulman was not.   Hodgins feels that
Shulman chooses not to face issues straight on.   He usually writes
farces, where unpleasant social conditions are acknowledged but not
dealt with or satires that are so mild that they fall short of being
seriously critical.   The laughter that results from reading Shulman
is somewhat visceral.   Nevertheless, Shulman is a successful writer
of humorous pieces in a number of different genres--novels, short
stories, plays, screenplays, television scripts, and a syndicated
column for college newspapers.   His first book, Barefoot Boy with
Cheek, published in 1943, established Shulman as a legitimate
humorous author. His next two novels, The Feather Merchants and The
Zebra Derby were written on Sundays, at night and during furloughs
while Shulman was serving in the army.   In 1955 he published Max
Shulman's Guided Tour of Campus Humor.   His books have always been
popular among college undergraduates.   The Many Lives of Dobie
Gillis was published in 1951, basically a collection of earlier

magazine stories.   This later became a popular TV series, running
from 1959 to 1963. Shulman's most prominent writing style is farce.
He develops the farce through skillful use of exaggeration,
caricature, broad verbal play, gags, and ludicrous situations.
There is little plot or character development but rather digression
after digression amusingly presented.   The expression "But I
digress" is not an apology for straying but rather a joke, for there
is nothing but digression.

782. Rowe, Pearl. "The Humor of Deprivation: Max Shulman." Los
     Angeles Times, 28 April 1978, 22-23.

     Quotes Shulman as having said, "I believe every humorist is a
deprived person." Shulman notes that humorists generally look like
Phyllis Diller, Woody Allen, or Mel Brooks.   They don't look like
Robert Redford or Candy Bergen.   Shulman wrote his first seller,
Barefoot Boy with Cheek when he was twenty-two. When he brought the
book home to show his mother, she exclaimed, "Oh, a printer."
Shulman says that writing has never come easy for him, adding that
it is like the old speak-easy door.   You knock and knock and the
door doesn't open.   And then sometimes a small window slides open
and you try to get a glimpse and sometimes you see what you want and
sometimes not.   Shulman indicates that from early on he was accused
of imitating Perelman.   When Shulman met Perelman he mentioned this
fact, and Perelman said that people had accused him [Perelman] of
imitating Ring Lardner and told him of Robert Louis Stevenson's
advice to writers--"Copy until you find out who you are."   In the
mid-1970s Shulman had success with his House Calls, and he signed
with Pan Arts to adapt Mixed Singles by Douglass Wallop for
television. However, Shulman's latest novel, Potatoes Are Cheaper,
did not make the best-seller lists.

Isaac Asimov (1920-)

783. Evory, Ann. "Isaac Asimov." Contemporary Authors. New Revision
     Series, Volume 2. Detroit, MI: Gale, 1981, 27-32.

Indicates that Asimov usually wrote his humor and satire under
the pseudonym of Dr. A.   In the category of Asimov's humor and
satire, Evory includes The Sensuous Dirty Old Man (1971), Isaac
Asimov's Treasury of Humor (1971), Lecherous Limericks (1975), More
Lecherous Limericks (1976), Still More Lecherous Limericks (1977),
and a book coauthored with John Ciardi entitled Limericks: Too Gross
(1978).   Evory depicts Asimov, who often writes under the pen name
of Paul French, as a prolific author of more than two hundred books
and   innumerable   short   stories   and   nonfiction   articles.   She
indicates that he has over fourteen million words in print, and that
over the past thirty years he has written on the average of one book
every six weeks.   He writes in such widely divergent fields as
science   fiction,   mysteries,   biology,   science,   chemistry,
biochemistry, mathematics, astronomy, history, earth science, and
literary studies, just to mention a few.

Peg Bracken (1920-)

784. Fisher, Martha A. "Peg Bracken." Encyclopedia of American
     Humorists. Ed. Steven H. Gale. New York: Garland, 1988, 57-59.

Portrays Bracken as the champion of the rebellious modern
housewife.   In 1960 her I Hate to Cook Book was an immediate
success.   This was followed by The I Hate to Housekeep Book (1962),
I Try to Behave Myself (1964), Peg Bracken's Appendix to the I Hate
to Cook Book (1966), and I Didn't Come Here to Argue (1969).   In
this last book, Bracken commented on important omissions from the
original Ten Commandments like pulling wings off robins or dumping
all of Boston's garbage into Walden Pond (as long as it's not done
on Sunday).   Bracken's humor is gentle and bemused.   She says that
she considers herself to be an essayist, a humorist, and a satirist
rather than a militant housewife.   Early in life her Aunt Liz Noah
encouraged her to develop her abilities in word play, and she has
also been influenced by such writers as Mark Twain, James Thurber,
E. B. White, Katherine Mansfield, and Phyllis McGinley.   Bracken's
allusions are as divergent as are her influences--George Washington,
Plautus, the New Testament, and Leroy "Satchel" Page, to name a few.
Bracken's writing tends to be less slapstick than that of Bombeck.
Unlike Bombeck, who has "explosive forays" into the world of the
female, Bracken has "quiet meanderings."   Like Teresa Bloomingdale,
Bracken rejects the feminist movement, preferring to keep the
advantages in society that are already afforded to women rather than
starting from scratch in competition with men.

785. Walker, Nancy, and Zita Dresner. "Peg Bracken." <u>Redressing the</u>
     <u>Balance: American Women's Literary Humor from Colonial Times</u>
     <u>to the 1980s</u>. Jackson, MS: Univ. Press of Mississippi, 1988,
     332-39.

     Groups Peg Bracken with Jean Kerr and Erma Bombeck in that all
three authors attempt to undermine the seriousness demanded of women
in their role as homemakers after World War II. Bracken began as a
humorist by writing the humor column of her high school paper. At
Antioch College, she became the editor of <u>The Antiochan</u>. After
graduation, Bracken became a freelance writer in Cleveland, Ohio,
and Portland, Oregon, and started publishing her light verse and
short humorous pieces in such magazines as <u>The Saturday Evening</u>
<u>Post</u>. One of her more successful pieces was entitled, "If I Were My
Husband I'd Fire Me." The success of this article turned her into
the direction of devoting her full time to writing humorous
housewife pieces. Her first best seller was published in 1960 and
was entitled <u>The I Hate to Cook Book</u>. This was followed in 1962 by
<u>I Hate to Do Housework Book</u>. In the meantime Bracken was writing
pieces for <u>Ladies' Home Journal</u>, <u>Cosmopolitan</u>, and <u>McCall's</u>, and
many of these pieces were later published in such collections as <u>I</u>
<u>Try to Behave Myself</u> (1964), <u>I Didn't Come Here to Argue</u> (1969), <u>But</u>
<u>I Wouldn't Have Missed It for the World</u> (1970), <u>A Window Over the</u>
<u>Sink</u> (1981), and <u>The Compleat I Hate to Cook Book</u> (1986). Bracken
once described a humorist as a person who is able to find the snail
beneath the prettiest leaf.

Alice Childress (1920-)

786. Walker, Nancy, and Zita Dresner. "Alice Childress." <u>Redressing</u>
     <u>the Balance: American Women's Literary Humor from Colonial</u>
     <u>Times to the 1980s</u>. Jackson, MS: Univ. Press of Mississippi,
     1988, 312-14.

     Characterizes the importance of Childress' writing as her
ability to explode the stereotypical attitudes regarding Blacks,
especially Black women. Childress portrays Black women as gutsy,
funny, and strong, and her women characters will not be subservient
and docile. Mildred, the narrator of <u>Like One of the Family</u>, for
example, is a Black domestic who protests at being condescendingly
called "one of the family." Childress is the granddaughter of a
slave and was born into a South Carolina family whose only option
for employment was domestic service. Childress and her grandmother
moved to Harlem when she was five, and she did not graduate from
high school. But she nevertheless went on to write some powerful
novels, such as <u>A Hero Ain't Nothin' but a Sandwich</u> (1973), about an
adolescent drug addict. Childress is not afraid to deal with
controversial subjects with realism and candor and without
sensationalism.

Philip Klass (1920-)

787.   Robillard,   Douglas.   "William   Tenn   (Philip   Klass)."
       Encyclopedia of American Humorists. Ed. Steven H. Gale. New
       York: Garland, 1988, 428-30.

       Classifies the stories in Tenn's _The Wooden Star_ (1968) as
social satires, even though they are written in the form of science
fiction. As social satires, these stories have been misunderstood,
but as social satires some of them have also effected social change.
Tenn's stories are in fact parodies of science fiction, and they run
the full range of humor from wit through satire to slapstick and
farce, as when an official of the Temporal Embassy enters a drop of
water only to find that it is filled with intestinal amoebae. His
attacking them with his sword gives the reader the image of an
infinitesimal Conan the Magnificent. Much of Tenn's satire is
directed at political targets. In his 1958 "Eastward Ho," history
is reversed, and the Indians have regained control of all of America
except for a thin strip of land containing parts of New Jersey and
New York. Tenn published two novels in 1968. _A Lamp for Medusa_ is
"brief and light weight" but _Of Men and Monsters_ is more
significant. The story line deals with an invasion of our planet by
aliens and contains a number of ironic inversions.

William Gaddis (1922-)

788. Hénault, Marie. "The Darwinian Struggle as a Metaphor in
      Gaddis's _Recognitions_. WHIMSY 2 (1984): 41-43.

      Discusses the allusions to Darwin and to Darwin's work that
appear in Gaddis' _Recognitions_. One of the chapters in _Recognitions_
begins with the words "We will now discuss in a little more detail
the struggle for existence"--from Darwin's _Origin of Species_.
Gaddis also alludes to Darwin's title "Origin of Species" and uses
many other Darwinian phrases, such as "laws of survival,"
"reptilian,"   "evolutionary,"   "jungle   floor,"   "Paleozoic,"
"prehistoric,"   "mutations,"   "species,"   "earth's   crust,"
"pleiosaurus," "pterodactyl," and "jawless progenitors." In fact,
Henault considers the Darwinian struggle for existence to be Gaddis'
underlying metaphor in _Recognitions_, especially in the chapter that
is devoted to a cocktail party, in which one guest says, "I feel
like we've been here for ages," and another responds, "I feel like
I was born here." In this Darwinian cocktail party, the same laws
of survival are in effect as in the larger natural world.

789. Hénault, Marie. "Linguistic Humor in William Gaddis's _The
      Recognitions_." WHIMSY 1 (1983): 85-87.

      Considers the full range of word play in Gaddis' _The
Recognitions_. The incorrect spellings of "Sendy Claus," and "Yom
Kippur" bring to mind the "send" that is associated with Christmas
and "kipper," which is also associated with the holiday season.
Gaddis also gives a phonetic spelling of the title of Mozart's
opera, "Cosi fan tutte" as "cozy," "fan," and "tooty," which is
strangely appropriate to the original, which means, "Something for

everyone."   There are also appropriate character names in The
Recognitions, from the ribald "Recktall Brown," the name of a devil
figure, to "Agnes Deigh," a strayed lamb of God, to "Mr. Inononu"
and "Sinisterra" (later to become "Mr. Yàk). Appropriately enough,
"Mr. Farisy" has been scientifically investigating the early methods
of crucifixion.   During the cocktail party, there are some strange
verbal exchanges which include phrases like "a latent heterosexual,"
"a three-time psychoanaloser," and a "positive negativist." And in
response to someone who says he has just bought a Renault, a guest
responds, "Oh yes, I do love them. An original?" When Carruthers
is said to have run off with a horse, and one guest asks whether it
was a stallion or a mare, another guest responds, "A mare of course.
Nothing queer about Carruthers."   Another linguistic feat which
Gaddis accomplishes in The Recognitions is the translation of the
"Our Father" into street jargon, which as a result contains phrases
like "Daddy-noster," who is "up in thy way-out pad," and continues,
"Thy joint be right, thy squares be swung," and ends with "For thine
is the horse, the hash, and the junk."

790. Safer, Elaine B. "The Allusive Mode, The Absurd and Black Humor
     in William Gaddis's The Recognitions." Studies in American
     Humor NS1.2 (October 1982): 103-118.

     Compares William Gaddis' The Recognitions to the novels of
John Barth and Thomas Pynchon in that all three of these authors
employ ironic allusions to traditional sources in their long
narratives. The allusive mode has a long tradition in literature.
Virgil made extensive allusions to The Odyssey and to The Iliad in
The Aeneid. Milton made extensive allusions not only to the Bible
but also to the writings of Homer and Virgil in Paradise Lost.
Cotton Mather made extensive allusions to Paradise Lost in Magnalia.
Milton's Paradise Lost can be considered the prototype for a
discussion of the traditional allusive mode, since it both
frequently alludes and is frequently alluded to. T. S. Eliot also
made extensive use of the allusive mode, and he described the common
themes and common treatments in the earlier and later texts as
providing what he called "simultaneous existence" or "simultaneous
order" for the whole of literature. But the allusions of Gaddis,
Barth, and Pynchon are not traditional allusions. Rather, they are
comic or ironic allusions.   Barth first constructs and then
collapses various references to the Bible and to Christ in Giles
Goat-Boy or the Revised New Syllabus.   In this novel, the
protagonist is born of a virgin mother who has been impregnated by
a computer. In Gravity's Rainbow, Pynchon juxtaposes Puritan order
with contemporary randomness as he divides society into the "elect"
and the "preterite."

791. Safer, Elaine B. "Ironic Allusiveness and Satire in William
     Gaddis's The Recognitions." The Contemporary American Comic
     Epic: The Novels of Barth, Pynchon, Gaddis, and Kesey.
     Detroit, MI: Wayne State Univ. Press, 1988, 111-37.

     Feels that both William Gaddis and Nikolai Gogol use black
humor and the comic grotesque to develop their comic epic novels.
They both lampoon a society where appearances rather than substance
enable men to become leaders, a society whose members are constantly
on the move but without meaningful direction or goals.   Gaddis'
Carpenter's Gothic (1985), for example, satirizes the power that

resides in society's religious, political, and business institutions. Safer contends that Gaddis' major tool for exposing the shallow, materialistic inclinations of American society is ironic allusion. Gaddis alludes to earlier literature in order to depict the traditional beliefs of earlier society and to contrast this structured society with the chaotic superficialities of twentieth-century America. In JR Gaddis alludes to The Recognitions, and contrasts the banal and arrogant comments of some of his critics with the book itself. He fictionalizes the reviews by saying that they are reviews of seven different novels, but, in fact, all seven of these novels have names that are anagrams of The Recognitions. Gaddis suggests that the Bible in twentieth-century America is commercialism. According to Gaddis, our culture has changed from a concentration on "things worth being" to a concentration on "things worth having."

Mark Harris (1922-)

792. Hart, James D. "Mark Harris." The Oxford Companion to American Literature. 4th Edition. New York: Oxford Univ. Press, 1965, 351-52.

Examines Harris' epistolary Wake Up, Stupid (1959), a humorous novel about a month in the life of a professor who is also a novelist.

Charlotte MacLeod (1922-)

793. Bakerman, Jane S. "Bloody Balaclava: Charlotte MacLeod's Campus Comedy Mysteries." WHIMSY 1 (1983): 88.

Describes the three subjects of MacLeod's The Luck Runs Out as being the armed robbery of a silver-crafting establishment, the murder of Flackley, the Farrier, and the pignapping of Belinda of Balaclava. But Bakerman warns readers not to take this last event too lightly. Belinda was not just an ordinary sow. Rather, she was the vital link in a long chain of genetic experiments in the college's animal husbandry department that had been conducted over a period of almost thirty years on the subject of efficient pig breeding. And Belinda was about to farrow. The Luck Runs Out is a humorous novel about campus protests and activism and the "Vigilant Vegetarians," who by perpetrating the above crimes were attempting to sabotage their college's experiments dealing with the use of farm animals as food. They wanted the research with pigs to lead in other directions, like training pigs to be potato diggers, security guards, or seeing-eye guides, experiments where the natural talents and sagacity of the pigs could be utilized on a continuing basis rather than only once on the American table.

Charles M. Shulz (1922-)

794. Berger, Arthur Asa. "Peanuts: The Americanization of
Augustine." Humor in America. Ed. Enid Veron. New York:
Harcourt, Brace, Jovanovich, 1976, 298-304.

        Argues for the literary and philosophical merit and
significance of the Charles Schulz comic strips. In Berger's view,
Schulz has a "positively amazing command of the techniques of
humor." He mixes graphic, verbal, and ideational humor in
innovative ways. His characters are monomaniacs who pursue their
destinies with zany abandon reminiscent of divinely inspired
zealots. He does not portray children as sweet innocents but rather
presents them "in all their Augustinian corruptness."   The name
"Peanuts" is symbolic because it refers to a tiny and insignificant
person. But although Schulz's characters are peanuts in terms of
size, they are giants in terms of their own egos.   Schultz's
characters are innocents; they are prepubescent and asexual. They
are nevertheless susceptible to passions and whims, and they are
motivated by greed or love. And they never change. The qualities
of Schultz's children are the qualities of people in general. The
children show pride, and stupidity and gullibility and many of the
other characteristics of mankind that are frequent targets of
satire. Nevertheless, Schultz accepts humans with all their faults,
for what they are, not for what they claim to be. "Schulz relieves
us of the awesome burden of innocence, and we are all grateful."

Kurt Vonnegut, Jr. (1922-)

795. Harris, Charles B. "Illusions and Absurdity: The Novels of Kurt
Vonnegut, Jr." Contemporary American Novelists of the Absurd.
New Haven, CT: College and Univ. Press, 1971, 51-75.

        Suggests that the variety of novels that Vonnegut has written
is responsible for his being classified as a writer of science
fiction, a black humorist, and a satirist. His first two novels,
Player Piano (1952) and The Sirens of Titan (1959), are science
fiction. Mother Night (1961) is an extended comic metaphor about a
purposeless universe. It targets the social attitudes that result
in war and its atrocities.   Vonnegut's last three novels, Cat's
Cradle (1963), God Bless You, Mr. Rosewater, or Pearls Before Swine
(1965), and Slaughterhouse-Five, or the Children's Crusade (1969),
use absurdist themes and absurdist techniques to explain an absurd
universe. Of the four absurdist novelists considered in Harris'
study (Heller, Vonnegut, Pynchon, and Barth), Vonnegut enjoys the
largest audience for his novels; however, Vonnegut has received
little attention from the critics. As late as 1969, only two
studies devoted exclusively to Vonnegut's works had appeared, and
one of these was in Italian. Leslie Fiedler suggests that one
reason that critics have ignored Vonnegut is that science fiction,
like the western, the comic strip and pornography, is considered
sub-literature, written to exploit the masses. There is a resultant
inverse relationship between a wide readership and critical aclaim.
Harris feels that Vonnegut's craft and theme make him an artist to
be taken seriously. In his progression from the satiric to the

absurd vision, there has been an increasing intensity. But from
beginning to end, Vonnegut's novels have always been comic.

796. Keough, William. "Kurt Vonnegut, Jr." Punchlines: The Violence
    of American Humor. New York: Paragon House, 1990, 101-24.

    Places Vonnegut with Twain, Bierce, and Lardner as midwestern
humorists. Vonnegut named his first son "Mark" after "Mark Twain,"
and like Twain, Vonnegut was a court jester. Like Bierce, Vonnegut
was more of a satirist than a humorist. The distinction Keough
makes between the humorist and the satirist is that the humorist is
attempting to please his readers and make them feel relaxed, while
the satirst is attempting to provoke his readers and make them feel
uncomfortable. Vonnegut wields his penknife to "lance the boils of
the body politic." The boils which Vonnegut lances through his
satire are the sacred cows of capitalism and Christianity, and as a
result, his books are often banned by librarians and school
committees. Vonnegut says that his goal is to write short books
with simple messages that can be understood by anybody--even Richard
Nixon. Vonnegut's audience is large and it is growing, because the
pacificism and anti-machismo attitudes he espouses are becoming more
and more popular. Some of Vonnegut's critics say that his works are
too anti-establishment. Some of his other critics say that he is
not anti-establishment enough, because his writing does not have the
venom of a Jonathan Swift or a Philip Wylie. But Vonnegut is
attempting to keep from becoming a misanthrope, and that is what
makes his works appealing, even though some critics consider them
sentimental and adolescent. Keough feels that Vonnegut's view is
that our world is heading toward total annihilation but that
Vonnegut is too intelligent to feign hope and too honorable to lie.
So he jokes.

797. Schulz, Max F. "The Unsensing of the Self; and, the Unconfirmed
    Thesis of Kurt Vonnegut." Black Humor Fiction of the Sixties:
    A Pluralistic Definition of Man and His World. Athens: Ohio
    Univ. Press, 1973, 43-65.

    Proposes that a superficial viewing of Vonnegut's novels
suggests that they are artless, especially in their pluralistic
handling of form and theme. Both readers and critics are often put
off by these characteristics and feel that his novels may not
deserve much serious attention. But Schulz further proposes that
Vonnegut's readers and critics are learning how to read his stories.
God Bless You, Mr. Rosewater continues the Christian ethic that
people should love each other. The fact that we are now overwhelmed
by technology that renders humans obsolete and substitutes efficient
machines for defective humans makes that love all the more
important. In Vonnegut's novel, Eliot Rosewater is a millionaire
philanthropist in America's new Eden. He is the modern reenactment
of the Christ-like commitment to spiritual rather than materialistic
values. But the novel questions its own moral stance as it
describes its Indiana utopia. The imagery, the symbolism, the tone
and the structure of the novel are clues that the novel is a parody
of the views it proclaims. God Bless You, Mr. Rosewater, like other
black humor novels, is determined to resist the tendency to confirm
its own thesis or formulate easy answers. In Cat's Cradle and God
Bless You, Mr. Rosewater, Vonnegut courageously allows the problems

to remain unresolved. In this sense they are like Pynchon's V̲ and
can be described as honest novels.

Paddy Chayefsky (1923-)

798. Field, Leslie, "Paddy Chayefsky's Jews and Jewish Dialogues."
     From Hester Street to Hollywood: The Jewish-American Stage and
     Screen. Ed. Sarah Blacher Cohen. Bloomington: Indiana Univ.
     Press, 1986, 137-51.

     Establishes "dialogue" as Chayefsky's most powerful rhetorical
device. This dialogue is not between one character and another or
even between a character and the author, narrator, or audience.
Rather, it is a dialogue between the character and God, whereby the
protagonist either asks God a crucial Jewish question like "Why have
you chosen us" or probes a traditional folkloric Jewish motif of the
"dybbuk." The dialogue always concerns the theological and ethical
parameters of being Jewish. Chayefsky's most successful dramas are
Marty (1956), which explores Chayefsky's poignant concern with
loneliness, The Hospital (1971), a Kafkaesque view of bureaucracy,
and Network (1976), which explores how major institutions block our
freedom to know and commercialize and trivialize the information
they give to us in a way that almost parallels the situation in Nazi
Germany. Chayefsky's Holiday Song continues this dialogue with God,
and although God may be both Jewish and non-Jewish at the same time,
the dialogue with God is specifically Jewish. And the dialogue
concerns the burden of Jewish history, the Holocaust, pogroms,
Jewish customs, and the marginality of Jews in a predominantly non-
Jewish society. The effect of this dialogue technique is a humorous
situation where God and man are equals in trying to solve the
world's problems.

Bob Elliott (1923-)

799. Dickson, Larry L. "The Sports Humor of Bob Elliott and Ray
     Goulding." WHIMSY 5 (1987): 191-93.

     Proposes that sports humor is a prominent element in all three
Bob and Ray collections--Write if You Get Work (1975), From
Approximately Coast to Coast... (1985), and The New! Improved! Bob
and Ray (1985). They follow the tradition of Thurber, Benchley, and
Perelman in writing understated humor based on exaggerated premises,
but they break with this tradition in their predominant topic--games
and sports, which Americans, as part of their puritan heritage, are
obsessed with and take very seriously. Dickson lists three
categories of Bob-and-Ray sports humor--1). the overspecialization
of professional athletes, 2). the ubiquitous sports clichés and 3).
the athlete-hero who is able to talk a much better game than he can
play. As a solution to the overspecialization of athletes, Bob and
Ray suggest making the ball much larger and softer in major league
baseball, so that everybody looks good playing the game. Then Rod
Carew, who would look like everyone else, couldn't ask for more than
a couple hundred dollars in contract negotiations. Bob and Ray's
play-by-play announcer, Biff Burns, is a master of the sports

cliche. Bob and Ray have also invented a new sport called "low jumping." Rather than starting in a low place and seeing how high you can jump, the athlete would stand in a high place and see how low he could jump. The sport has strict rules, like "if you get killed, the jump doesn't count." Garrison Keillor, Andy Rooney, and Kurt Vonnegut have all praised Bob-and-Ray characters, who never let the readers know that there is anything funny about what they're saying.

Joseph Heller (1923-)

800. Fetrow, Fred M. "Joseph Heller's Use of Names in Catch-22." Studies in Contemporary Satire 1.2 (Spring 1975): 28-38.

Suggests that few novels have such diverse characters as are found in Catch-22. Heller's treatment of such a wide range of characters on the surface seems incomplete and chaotic unless the reader has some sense of the structure of character development in this novel. There are basically four types of characters in the novel. First, there are the minor characters who are insignificant in their own right, as their significance resides totally in what they symbolize. These characters have no names at all, only descriptions, like "the soldier in white." Second, there are the somewhat minor characters who have only tag-names like "Dori Duz" (who does what the name suggests), "Sheisskopf," and "P. P. Peckam" (who are what the name suggests). These names efficiently describe their behavior patterns or their plot roles. Third, there are the non-characters who are merely names and nothing more; these characters are two dimensional and lack real presence in the novel. An example is "Appleby" a character who is as traditionally American as is "apple pie" itself. Fourth, there are the symbolic characters who Heller uses to develop his thematic concerns and whose names suggest their symbolic and thematic significance. An example of this fourth type of character is "Major Major," who has lost his individuality by becoming a cog in the huge military machine. Another example is Milo Minderbinder who is the epitome of the capitalistic system. He founds and manages M and M Enterprises, which contracts to bomb his own base because it is good business.

801. Fletcher, M. D. "Heller's Catch-22: Satiric Political Apalogue. Contemporary Political Satire: Narrative Strategies in the Post-Modern Context. New York: Lanham, 1987, 59-82.

Contrasts the satire of Heller's Catch-22 with that of Voinovich's Private Chonkin. Even though both novels were begun in the late 1950s and appeared in the 1960s, the two novels use quite different approaches to satiric exposé, thereby giving their treatments of particular episodes a quite different hue. More specifically, Catch-22 is in the absurdist tradition, while Private Chonkin is in the didactic. Furthermore, Catch-22 is apologetic, while Private Chonkin is suggestive. Heller uses linguistic relativism to demonstrate moral relativism. Thus, he discredits the language at the same time as he discredits society, but by discrediting the language, he is also discrediting himself, and that is the genius of his work, because Heller is writing in the absurdist tradition. From Heller's perspective, there are confusion, slogans, lack of logic. Heller's irony and satire tend to absorb, while Voinovich's irony and satire tend to delete. Heller's Catch-22 is an apologue that uses satiric techniques to expose the relevant political and military targets, so that these targets are not obviously culpable in a conventional sense. And that is what accounts for the differing tones of these two novels. Heller uses caricature to develop Yossarian as a protagonist, and the result is macabre rather than grotesque (as in the case of Private Chonkin). Heller merely exposes and ridicules the system he is observing. Heller's writing therefore remains humorous in tone although serious in intent. Voinovich's satire goes one step further to suggest a possible solution.

802. Gillen, Francis P. "Joseph Heller." Encyclopedia of American Humorists. Ed. Steven H. Gale. New York: Garland, 1988, 213-20.

Explains that Heller actually did serve in the U. S. Air Force in 1941, did achieve the rank of first lieutenant, and did fly sixty missions as a B-25 wing bombardier stationed in Corsica. In the first part of Catch-22 Heller makes his readers laugh, but by the end of the novel he has shown readers the sinister implications of what at first appeared to be comic, and they are made to feel ashamed for having laughed. Milo Minderbinder is an entrepreneur who buys commodities, controls the market, and resells to himself, appearing to take a loss. He gives everyone a share of the profits so that they will all support his enterprise out of self-interest. He makes money by contracting with the Germans to bomb his own airfield and defends the strafing because it's in the contract. He siphons military goods from one country to another, always making a profit, and bribes the American government to buy his useless Egyptian cotton. Milo's claim that anything that is good for M & M Enterprises is good for the country echoes Colonel Cathcart's claim that anything that is good for him is good for his men. Milo represents anybody who makes a profit on war. He is symbolic of the fact that greed can transcend national boundaries. The reader sees war through the eyes of Yossarian. Both Yossarian and the reader laugh in the novel, only to be horrified a page or two later by what they are laughing at. We identify with Milo until he starts bombing his own troops--for a profit. Heller feels that to be human we must feel pain and loss as well as laughter, love and joy; they are inseparable.

803. Harris, Charles B. "Catch-22: A Radical Protest against Absurdity." Contemporary American Novelists of the Absurd. New Haven, CT: College and Univ. Press, 1971, 33-50.

Characterizes the early criticism of Heller's Catch-22 as quite negative. Richard Stern called the novel repetitive and monotonous. Whitney Balliett refused to call it a novel at all, saying that it doesn't appear to have been written but rather gives the impression of having been shouted onto paper. Even Heller admirers were careful not to give too much support. Robert Brustein said that the novel was bitterly funny but then admitted that it was as formless as any picaresque epic. Harris suggests that these early reviewers were confusing Heller's abandonment of conventional novelist techniques with the abandonment of craft or form. But Harris contends that in Catch-22 the structure is carefully

controlled and that the theme of military absurdity is reinforced by
the absurd language and organization. Heller introduced a new
pattern of literary expression that would later become not only
acceptable but would in fact become the standard for novel writing
in the 1960s. This was the tradition of the radical protest novel
written in the style of absurdist black humor. Heller's satire
attacked the new images of power, the interlocking bureaucracies of
industry, the military, and the political administration. Heller
feels that the absurdity that he writes about in his novel is a by-
product of this interrelationship which provides the prevailing
metaphor of modern American culture. Catch-22 is a burlesque. The
chaotic structure of the book reinforces the denial of logical order
that is already present in our society as a result of the military-
industrial-political bureaucracy.

804. Kiley, Frederick, and Walter McDonald. A "Catch-22" Casebook.
     New York: Thomas Y. Crowell, 1973, x + 403 pp.

     Feels that although Catch-22 is set against the background of
World War II, it is not a novel about that war. Rather it is about
America and the American people, now as much as then. It is
Rabelaisian, Swiftian, and Faulknerian both in its satiric style and
in its scope. It is, in Kiley and McDonald's opinion, a
masterpiece. The hollow laughter that is elicited early in the
novel turns to chilling awareness in the later chapters. It is a
tragicomedy based on the American metaphor. You have to be sick to
be a soldier, and Yossarian is sick. He has a liver condition,
again, an appropriate metaphor. Both physically and
psychologically, Yossarian is not too sick; he is just sick enough
to be a soldier. This casebook is divided into eight sections: Book
Reviews, Criticism, Theme, Structure, Absurdity, Interviews, Other
Works by Joseph Heller, and Catch-22 the Film.

805. Mechling, Jay. "Play and Madness in Joseph Heller's Catch-22.
     Play and Culture 1.3 (August 1988): 226-38.

     Applies Gregory Bateson's idea about communication, play, and
the double bind to Heller's Catch-22. Heller's choice of the
military during wartime as his subject provides an excellent setting
for the development of "pragmatic paradoxes." Different people
react to the double bind in different ways. People can become
schizophrenic, paranoid, hebephrenic, catatonic, etc. Yossarian
chooses to develop the craziness aspect of his personality as a
creative solution to his double bind. It is uncanny how similar the
thinking of Bateson is to the thinking of Heller in reference to the
double bind. Bateson sees the double bind theory as a way of
explaining how people learn schizophrenic and related behavioral
patterns such as humor, art, poetry, and play. Bateson's double-
bind theory does not distinguish between these various behaviors by
indicating which are good and which are bad. Bateson's theory
merely suggests that placed in a double bind situation, a person
could become a clown, a poet, a schizophrenic, or some combination
of these. Mechling considers the most important metaphor of the
novel to be "Snowden's secret." When Snowden is shot Yossarian
tries to patch up his superficial wounds, not knowing that his blood
and entrails will soon spill out all over the messy floor.
Snowden's secret is that man is matter. Polluted by Snowden's blood
and flesh, Yossarian throws away his clothing and, naked watches

Snowden's funeral from a tree.   He was still naked at the ceremony
where he was to receive his medal for bravery over Avignon.
Heller's novel doesn't make a judgment about these actions.   There
is no clear statement in the novel as to who is sane and who is mad.

806. Nagel, James. <u>Critical Essays on "Catch-22.</u>" Encino, CA:
      Dickenson, 1974, 179 pp.

     Describes the mixed early responses by critics of Heller's
<u>Catch-22</u>. The novel was described as "monotonous," "disappointing,"
"needing craft and sensibility," and "an emotional hodge podge."
Roger Smith said the novel was "worthless," because it had no
characters and no story.   Smith felt the novel was filled with
stereotypes and bad style and it was furthermore pretentious,
destructive, and immoral.   But other reviewers called it an
"explosive, bitter, subversive, brilliant book" or "the best
American novel that has come out of anywhere in years."   They
considered it to be "serious" and "well constructed."   One reviewer
described it as a "surrealist <u>Iliad</u>," and another said it was a
"book of enormous richness and art, of deep thought and brilliant
writing."   Present-day readers and critics tend to be more in accord
with the favorable responses cited above.   The book has now sold
more than eight million copies in more than a dozen different
languages, this despite the fact that Simon and Schuster printed
only four thousand copies in their first printing.   The novel is a
mock epic in which the disorderly style reflects the psychological
and moral disorder in the world.   The book is a serious one, and
throughout its existence there has been a standing debate among
critics as to whether the humor contributes to or weakens the
serious implications of the events.

807. Pletcher, Robert C. "Overcoming the 'Catch 22' of Institutional
      Satire: Joseph Heller's 'Surrealistic' Characters." <u>Studies in</u>
      <u>Contemporary Satire</u> 15 (1988): 20-26.

     Explains some of the problems inherent in institutional satire
in general and <u>Catch-22</u> in particular. American society is diverse
and heterogeneous.   Many people reading institutional satire will
therefore not give the satire its appropriate weight.   When their
behavior or values are being attacked, they will have difficulty
seeing the attack as satiric; rather, they will see it as hostile,
absurd, or amusing.   If the satirist further exaggerates the actions
of the characters to expose folly or vice, they will still fail to
see the satire but will now change their characterization of the
writing to "grotesque" or "absurd."   For these reasons, Heller
develops his satire gradually.   Each succeeding dialogue in the
presentation of a character reveals more and more about the
villain's feelings and motives.   Heller uses dialogue to dramatize
the inner states of the villain's mind, as he gradually unmasks the
villain exposing him to be not comic, but tragic.   Pletcher feels
that this technique of gradual exposure of character motives and
feelings through the use of dialogue is an ingenious device Heller
has developed to allow his implications to be understood and applied
by readers of widely diverse backgrounds and belief systems.

<u>Lucille Kallen (c1923-)</u>

808. Bakerman, Jane S. "C. B. Greenfield: The Metaphor Is the
Man." <u>WHIMSY</u> 2 (1984): 46-48.

Perceives Kallen's protagonist in <u>Tanglewood</u>, C. B.
Greenfield, as conservative and childish, as he equates the familiar
and established with goodness and quality. In good conscience,
Greenfield can only use Palmolive soap and Parker 51 pens. When
Betty Crocker's Date Bar Mix cannot be found on grocers' shelves for
a year, Greenfield is despondent. He becomes especially depressed
when he can't find a bottle of Cutter's, his favorite insect
repellent. When he does find some Cutter's, he buys twelve bottles,
remarking that it's possible that the factory will stop
manufacturing it. Reader's can see a little bit of themselves in
Greenfield's simplistic adherence to tradition, and it makes them
laugh. Kallen is skilled in the use of irony, antithesis, and
gentle satire. She amuses the reader at the same time that she is
criticizing society and exposing the dark underside of the "frontier
mentality."

<u>Jean Collins Kerr (1923-)</u>

809. Johnson, Eric W. "[Bridget] Jean [Collins] Kerr." <u>Encyclopedia
of American Humorists</u>. Ed. Steven H. Gale. New York: Garland,
1988, 253-56.

Places Kerr into the tradition of Betty MacDonald and Ruth
McKenney in that all three authors wrote humorous sketches about
women's attempts to juggle household, husband, children, and career.
Kerr uses her sharp wit to expose the lunacy of such mundane events
as writing letters of complaint, buying a house, traveling and
dieting. Her humor is gentle and evokes nods of understanding from
her readers. The constant sequence of catastrophes in Kerr's world
never dulls her sense of humor. Kerr's style is not harsh or
threatening; rather, it is simple, friendly, even conversational.
She usually has memorable women characters in her plays. However,
Johnson feels that except for the heroine protagonist the characters
in <u>Goldilocks</u> (1958) are not fully developed. Johnson furthermore
feels that the relationships between the main characters in this
novel need more fleshing out. Kerr's <u>Mary, Mary</u> (1961) had many
laughs and pleased both critics--and audiences. It is about a
recently divorced woman and her successful attempt to mend her
marriage. Kerr's next play is a romantic comedy, <u>Poor Richard</u>
(1964) about a poet who lives in the fast lane and feels guilty
about it. <u>Finishing Touches</u> (1973) is a comedy about the sexual
revolution in which Katy Cooper, the protagonist, is married to a
professor who has fallen in love with one of his students, but this
is only part of the problem. Her teenage son has also brought home
his live-in girl friend, and Katy's next-door neighbor wants to have
an affair with her (Katy). By the end of the play, all of the
problems have been neatly resolved. Kerr's 1980 <u>Lunch Hour</u> is a
brittle romantic comedy written in a darker tone.

810. Walker, Nancy, and Zita Dresner. "Jean Kerr." Redressing the
     Balance: American Women's Literary Humor from Colonial Times
     to the 1980s. Jackson: Univ. Press of Mississippi, 1988, 340-
     50.

     Categorizes Kerr with Betty MacDonald, Cornelia Otis Skinner,
and Shirley Jackson as humorous women writers who write from their
own personal experiences. Kerr's three autobiographical books are
Please Don't Eat the Daisies (1957), The Snake Has All the Lines
(1960), and Penny Candy (1970). Walker and Dresner compare these
three novels to the novels of Cornelia Otis Skinner in being
collections of short pieces that originally appeared in various
magazines. The pieces are related to each other only in the sense
that they all represent facets of Kerr's life and personality.
Walker and Dresner describe Kerr as a playwright, a parodist, a
clever satirist of popular fads and fashions, and wife of drama
critic Walter Kerr. The pattern that emerges from such a background
is not a narrow domestic life, but rather the harried life of a
capable woman trying to juggle the demands of homemaking with her
literary talents. Her humor is warm and good-natured. It concerns
housewife chores, the raising of children, weight control, and
physical attractiveness. She encourages women to be themselves by
allowing them to laugh at what society tells them is the norm.

Norman Mailer (1923-)

811. Trouard, Dawn. "Norman Mailer's Deadly Sin: Metaphor and the
     Ironies of the Appropriated Self." WHIMSY 2 (1984): 44-46.

     Portrays Norman Mailer as the author that everybody loves to
hate. Mailer marched on the Pentagon, hated Richard Nixon, stabbed
his fourth wife, was in debt to the IRS, and smoked marijuana, but
during the 1960s the establishment took control of him and he has
never been the same since. All of Mailer's books have a number of
charactistics in common. There is always the problem with generic
identities; all are well conceived and commercially successful; they
all deal with Mailer's fascination with tragic karmas; they all deal
with cult personalities; they help to satisfy his own longings for
cult status. Although Mailer never met Marilyn Monroe personally,
he was obsessed with her, as can be seen in his Marilyn (1973) and
Of Women and Their Elegance (1981). Marilyn was the model for Lulu
Myers in The Deer Park, and he wrote a play about her called
Strawhead. The theme of Mailer's Marilyn is simply excess. The
style is overwrought. The metaphors create a tone of euphoria. It
begins with an extravagant description of Marilyn as blonde and
beautiful with her "sweet little rinky-dink of a voice."   He
considered her "our angel, the SWEET angel of sex."   She was
"gorgeous, forgiving, humorous, compliant and tender." She was the
female Napoleon; she was Madame Bovary, Delilah and Joan of Arc in
one, but she was also an addict, an invalid, and a fatherless child.
She was the "Stradivarius of sex." He considered Marilyn to have a
sense of humor like his own, what Mailer refers to as "a jock sense
of humor." Her sense of herself was almost ironic.

Thomas Berger (1924-)

812. Shaw, Patrick W. "The American West as Satiric Territory: Kesey's <u>One Flew Over the Cuckoo's Nest</u> and Berger's <u>Little Big Man</u>. <u>Studies in Contemporary Satire</u> 10 (1983): 1-8.

Contrasts Kesey's strategy of accepting legends as the basis for correct action with Berger's attacking legends as fabricated from pure lies, believable only by the most naive. Berger considers the Wyatt Earps, the George Custers, the Bill Hickoks, and the Calamity Janes of the world to be a tawdry assortment of pathetic crazy people who enjoyed shooting, clubbing, stabbing, stampeding raping, and other old-time horrors. Although Kesey's characters act very much like Berger's characters, the difference is that Kesey approved of their actions, while Berger did not. The result is that Berger's work is much more filled with tragicomic irony than is Kesey's. Kesey begins his novel by portraying McMurphy as an antihero, but during the progression of the novel he is converted into a traditional hero. In <u>Little Big Man</u>, by way of contrast, the protagonist is just as reprehensible at the end of the novel as he was at the beginning. There is no evidence that Berger considers heroes to be possible, let alone desirable. It is ironic that Berger and Kesey are both advocating personal freedom, for only Berger seems to be aware of the futility of such a quest, while Kesey looks for super personalities that Berger doubts ever existed in the real world.

813. Sheraw, C. Darrel. "Thomas Berger's <u>Regiment of Women</u>: Beyond Lysistrata." <u>Studies in Contemporary Satire</u> 1.2 (Spring 1975): 1-3.

Considers Berger's satiric <u>Regiment of Women</u> to be a utopia of sexual inversion based on the "gimmick" of little men, big women, and a total inversion of sex roles. In this novel, timid men move coyly through a jungle of sex-crazed women and ecological traumas. The power is still to be found in the establishment, but the politicians, psychoanalysts, jailers, and masters of this establishment are cigar-smoking women in pin-striped suits. Sheraw compares Berger's utopia with Capek's <u>R.U.R.</u>, Orwell's <u>1984</u>, Huxley's <u>Brave New World</u>, and Lucas' <u>THX 1138</u>. In all of these utopias, the way out of the chaotic system and into the utopian Eden is love and sex--the old fashioned kind. Berger, like these other writers of utopian literature, writes from the perspective of the future but has a nostalgia for the present as he does so.

814. Trachtenberg, Stanley. "Berger and Barth: The Comedy of Decomposition." <u>Comic Relief: Humor in Contemporary American Literature</u>. Ed. Sarah Blacher Cohen. Urbana: Univ. of Illinois Press, 1978, 45-69.

Suggests that in <u>Little Big Man</u>, Berger relies on the technique of mythic parody in developing the comedy of the novel. Berger is not writing so much about the American West as he is writing about the myth that has grown up about the American West. The novel presents the American West through the eyes of Jack Crabb, a 111-year-old white survivor of the Battle of Little Big Horn. However, Crabb's "remembrances" do not coincide with the depictions

of the frontier West by Owen Wister or Zane Grey.   Crabb wears
elevator shoes; he cheats at cards; and he runs away when the odds
are against him.   In Crabb's account, Wild Bill Hickock kills his
enemies from ambush, and George Armstrong Custer is almost bald.
The Indians in Little Big Man are presented as superstitious
children.   Rather than being a nobel savage, Old Lodge Skins wears
a plug hat and is preoccupied with keeping his blanket from falling
off.   For both Thomas Berger and John Barth, reality is decomposed
into a number of splintered versions, all equally true and all
equally false.   This decomposition does not infer nor conclude.   It
accepts no particular frame of reference.   It does not construct
reality but rather displaces reality. Random situations replace the
connected plot.   The focus is on the manner of telling.   The voice
is filled with ambiguities and lexical tensions.   Memory,
association, nostalgia, legend and myth become impediments to rather
than advantages of the textual development.

815. Weber, Brom. "Special Issue Honoring Thomas Berger: Part II."
     Studies in American Humor NS2.2 (Fall 1983): 83-152.

     Contains the following articles: "Thomas Berger: His World of
Words, and Stereoscopes of Style" by Max F. Schulz, "The World
According to Carl Reinhart: Thomas Berger's Comic Vision" by Sanford
Pinsker, "The Voice of Our Culture: Thomas Berger's Reinhart in
Love" by Ronald R. Janssen, "The Kraft of Fiction: Nomenclatural
Vandalism in Who is Teddy Villanova?" by Philip Kuberski, "The
Renegade Mood in Thomas Berger's Fiction," by David W. Madden, and
"Works By and About Thomas Berger" by James Bense.   Berger has
published twelve novels, ten short stories, twelve pieces classified
as "Other Fiction," nine articles, and twenty-five reviews.   There
are at least thirty-eight articles written about him and at least
112 reviews of his various books.

Truman Capote (1924-1984)

816. Dickson, Larry L. "Truman Capote's Wild Women: The Ironical
     Humor of Music for Chameleons." WHIMSY 1 (1983): 89-90.

     Proposes that there are basically three patterns in Capote's
humor.   There are the amusing single-sentence descriptions,
providing vivid images with maximum economy.   There are the ironic
narrative situations, tottering tantalizingly between the believable
and the ridiculous.   Finally, there are the jokes themselves, which
most directly establish Capote's comic tone.   Music for Chameleons
is filled with strong sexual imagery and caustic wit as it focuses
on the rollicking good spirits of Mary Sanchez who gives Capote some
marijuana.   After taking the marijuana, Capote is seized and
embraced by a "delicious demon."   This demon tickles Capote's toes,
scratches his itchy head, kisses him hotly with its red sugary lips,
and shoves its fiery tongue down his throat.   There are many other
humorous vivid details Junebug Johnson's hair turns white because of
being sexually compromised; she had been a virgin--almost.   Pearl
Bailey is described as a star surrounded by giddy, chattering
gaudily dressed chorus boys.   Marilyn Monroe closes her eyes to get
a mental picture of Los Angeles, and what she sees is a large
varicose vein.   Capote tells about a prominent minister who comes

across as a country bumpkin wearing expensive suits; he calls him "Billy Grahamcrackers." In conclusion, Dickson feels that Capote's humor entertains his readers with "bubbles and good spirit."

817. Riedell, Karyn. "The Gothic Parody of Truman Capote." WHIMSY 1 (1983): 90-93.

    Suggests that Capote's Other Voices, Other Rooms is a parody of the Gothic novel genre. It contains all of the elements of the traditional Gothic novel--a haunted castle, violent action, supernatural activity, a passive heroine, and the brave rescuing hero. Capote's haunted castle is called "Skully's Landing." It is located in the swamps and surrounded by giant tiger lilies with blooms "the size of a man's head" and green logs that "shine like drowned corpses." The chivalric theme of traditional Gothic novels is reversed in Capote's novel, for Joel plays the role of a passive heroine, and Idabel is the dashing hero who comes to Joel's rescue. Joel is described as "too pretty, too delicate and fair-skinned." Idabel, on the other hand has a "boy-husky" voice, and she swaggers as she walks. All of the other characters at Skull's Landing are freaks. Jesus Fever is described as a "pygmy figure," a "gnomish little Negro," and a "sad, little brokeback dwarf." His daughter, Zoo, is "a human giraffe" who still wears the scar of a slashed throat. Joel's new family, Amy and Randolph, are fused together like Siamese twins. The ghosts in Voices are very human. Cousin Randolph is the ghost who has a sense of humor; he dresses up in drag and haunts the top floor. No reader should be frightened while reading Voices, as the ominous atmosphere of the Gothic novel is reduced to impotent absurdity as a result of the parodic tone.

Russell Wayne Baker (1925-)

818. Gaston, Georg. "Russell Baker's Political Satire: The '76 Presidential Election." Studies in Contemporary Satire 7 (Spring 1980): 17-21.

    Suggests that the reason Baker's favorite target is the American Presidency is that he views the President as Everyman in this intensely political age. Baker changes his rhetorical methods and patterns to portray the variety of masks that the President can wear. Many of Baker's pieces begin with conventional dignity but turn into outrageous burlesques as the parody develops. As the intensity of political campaigning increases, so does Baker's satire. One piece he wrote is a bestiary which features the "Fordopatamus," an animal which not only does not like to move but is uncomfortable when anything else moves either. In this bestiary there is also the Jimcat which has "blue eyes, a gentle smile, and fuzzy issues." Baker's satire is playful, restless, and experimental. Baker seldom becomes self-indulgent or patronizing. Baker is not a cynic; he is a hard-edged skeptic, designed not to make us sniff with contempt at the corruption around us but rather to see the truth clearly and objectively. Baker is in the tradition of satirists going back to John Trumbull of the Connecticut Wits and to Benjamin Franklin before him. Baker's satire is like Franklin's in being a playful, wry blend of reason and irony.

819. Heflin, Woodford A. "Russell Wayne Baker." American Humor. Ed.
   O. M. Brack. Scottsdale, AZ: Arete, 1977, 153-69.

   Describes Baker as the writer of the sharp and witty
commentary in the "Observer" column for the New York Times and
places him in the tradition of such newspaper humorists as H. L.
Mencken, Irvin S. Cobb, and Will Rogers. Heflin considers Baker's
humor to be built on subtle incongruities, unstrained, and carefully
interwoven into his regular reporting. Although Baker's humor is
topical, Heflin nevertheless feels that Baker will have his place in
the tradition of American humor. Heflin feels that the
effectiveness of Baker's humor and his reporting techniques make
Baker one of the best reporters in America today.

820. Skow, John. "The Good Humor Man: To Columnist Russell Baker,
   Laughter Is Serious Business." Time, 4 June 1979, 48-55.

   Points out that over a seventeen-year period Baker has written
the "Observer" humor column in the New York Times and that this
column has also appeared in the 475 newspapers which subscribe to
the Times News Service. Baker won the Pulitzer Prize for his
column, the first time a humorist has received the commentary award
since it was established as a separate Pulitzer category in 1970.
His column is a blend of light humor and substantive comment.
Baker's humorous tone is usually what carries his columns; however,
his writing can also exhibit a haunting melancholy or delight and
exuberance. Baker is cynical about Big Business, Big Government,
and Big Labor. Baker has managed to be sharp and fresh 150 times a
year for seventeen straight years. S. J. Perelman praised Baker for
the honesty of his humor and for his ability to make his column both
serious and humorous even when he's angry about a subject.

821. Stewart, E. Kate. "Russell Wayne Baker." Encyclopedia of
   American Humorists. Ed. Steven H. Gale. New York: Garland,
   1988, 21-23.

   Describes Baker's humor in An American in Washington (1961),
No Cause for Panic (1964), Poor Russell's Almanac (1972), So This Is
Depravity (1980), Growing Up (1982), and The Rescue of Miss Yaskell
and Other Pipe Dreams (1983) as being satiric and wry, designed more
to entertain than to instruct as he gently chides the reader into
seeing the foibles of present-day American society. His informal
essays are about the worries of everyday life. Baker writes about
life and politics in the nation's capital with good humor and mild
reproof that is reminiscent of a milder version of H. L. Mencken.
He uses his sarcastic and sardonic wit to expose such universal
experiences as eccentric relatives and politicians, taxes,
hometowns, and daily irritations. Baker's wordplay is easily
accesible and it works. His Poor Russell's Almanac is a parody of
Benjamin Franklin's Poor Richard's Almanac. Baker's writing style
is often compared to that of Franklin.

Lenny Bruce (1925-1966)

822. Pinsker, Sanford. "Lenny Bruce: Shpritzing the Goyim/Shocking
     the Jews." Jewish Wry: Essays on Jewish Humor. Ed. Sarah
     Blacher Cohen. Bloomington: Indiana Univ. Press, 1987, 89-104.

     Disagrees with Lenny Bruce's characterization of himself as a
"neologist." Pinsker says that a neologist either invents new words
or uses old words in new ways, and he contends that Bruce did
neither. What Bruce did was to use words to shpritz and to shock.
Bruce was very interested in words, and he turned words loose on his
audiences: "Words, showers of them, unleashed, sprayed, machine-
gunned at the audience." In other words, he shpritzed his audiences
with a torrent of vivid images and weird associations. Bruce's
shpritz was designed as overkill. It was confrontational and
painfully public. Bruce used words as if they were drumsticks,
constantly bam-bam-bamming his audiences with a rapid-fire rhythm
that contrasted with the slow and deliberate rhythms of other comics
of his day like George Burns and Jack Benny. It also contrasted
with the shtetl humorists, who were fascinated with words but who
were also more thoughtful, more private, more cautious, and more
Yiddish.

823. Schwartz, Richard Alan. "Lenny Bruce." Encyclopedia of
     American Humorists. Ed. Steven H. Gale. New York: Garland,
     1988, 62-65.

     Portrays Bruce as fascinated by the power of words. He
studied their sound qualities, their connotations and denotations,
and their uses and abuses in society. He knew they were powerful,
and he used them to their full potential. He realized that language
not only shapes our view of the world but that it cannot be
separated from the world in people's minds. He pointed out that
saying an obscene thing is not the same thing as doing an obscene
thing. In 1964 Bruce published How to Talk Dirty and Influence
People and Stamp Help Out. In 1967 he published The Essential Lenny
Bruce, and in 1984 his The Almost Unpublished Lenny Bruce was
published posthumously. In his comedy routines and in his books, he
concentrated on irony, incongruity and social taboo. Bruce used
words to shock his audiences, but the shock value of his words was
reduced by their constant repetition, as he criticized society's
tendency to "condemn the language while condoning the activity." He
points out, for example, that society is very careful to use polite
language to refer to minority groups even while their underlying
attitudes and behaviors fail to accord them genuine respect.
Bruce's writing was influenced by his contemporaries Eugene Ionesco,
Thomas Pynchon, Kurt Vonnegut, and Garry Trudeau.

Art Buchwald (1925-)

824. Adair, Bill. "Comic Writer Claims No Sense about Humor." WHIMSY
     1 (1983): 94-95.

     Describes Buchwald's talk to humor scholars at Arizona State
University as cautionary. Buchwald warns that the trick of being

funny is trying _not_ to figure out why something is funny. Buchwald describes a small group of people who want to know the DNA of humor and claims that that's a deadly quest. Buchwald states that humorists themselves don't know what makes people laugh and states further that he's afraid that if they did know, they wouldn't be funny anymore. But despite this confession that humorists are in the dark about humor, Buchwald nevertheless feels that humorists provide an important function in society. Nobody else has been able to solve the world's problems, and Buchwald says that it's time we gave humorists a shot. Buchwald describes humor as the most socially acceptable form of hostility--and it doesn't kill people, though it _may_ occasionally break them up.

825. DeMuth, James. "The Political Humor of Art Buchwald." WHIMSY 3
     (1985): 16-17.

     Considers Buchwald's humor to be impudent and sarcastic. Buchwald takes on the mannerisms of a wiseguy who can quickly cut through sentimentality and obfuscation to reveal simple truths and human motives. Most of Buchwald's writing is some sort of parody. He tells us to beware of the "Washington Triangle"--that area between the White House, the Capitol and the Jefferson Memorial. He says that in the last ten years we have lost thirty-four hundred trial balloons, 200 congressional reforms, 433 executive mandates, 230 tax cuts and one ship of state; they lost their moral compass. DeMuth describes Buchwald as frequently being embarrassingly frank. Buchwald says, for example, that the Reagan administration was having great difficulty finding a "qualified" black person to appoint to an important governmental position. By "qualified," Reagan means a black person who is against busing, job-training programs, welfare, food stamps, government-subsidized housing, and equal-opportunity legislation. Buchwald writes in the tradition of Poor Richard, Jack Downing, Mr. Dooley, and Will Rogers, as he uses brashness and ironic impudence to expose social failures. The colloquial language, candor, and lack of subtlety in the humor comes across as honesty as Buchwald scolds and mocks. Son of the Great Society depicts Buchwald as Peck's Bad Boy in short pants; Down the Seine and Up the Potomac puts Buchwald into the uniform of a Revolutionary War officer; and Laid Back in Washington has him wearing a ten-gallon cowboy hat and a sequined white vest.

826. Linneman, William R. "Art Buchwald: A Political Cartoonist in
     Words." WHIMSY 3 (1985): 17-19.

     Suggests that Buchwald uses the same tools in his trade as does the political cartoonist--symbolism, exaggeration, and reinforcement. Buchwald's visual imagery portrays Jimmy Carter as a Southerner from Georgia, Lyndon Johnson as a Westerner from Texas, and Richard Nixon as an image maker from California. Buchwald places Lyndon Johnson into the setting of poker players in the Great Society Saloon as he explains Johnson's Vietnam policies. The picture is filled out by Johnson's Western language diet. Nixon is skilled in the use of superlatives. Nixon promises that there won't be a nuclear attack, but if there _were_ a nuclear attack, it would be the greatest nuclear attack in the history of mankind. Buchwald dug up an old quote where Nixon had criticized Truman's salty language and then points out that Nixon was probably the cussingest President in recent history and further suggests that these cuss words were actually code words that the Russians would not be able to decipher properly. Buchwald considered Nixon to be a perfect president from a humorist's point of view, because there is so much inconsistency between the word and the deed that very little exaggeration is required. Like the political cartoonist, Buchwald keeps his characters stable and their traits easily recognizable. He is truly a "cartoonist in words."

827. Nilsen, Don L. F. "Art Buchwald." Encyclopedia of American Humorists. Ed. Steven H. Gale. New York: Garland, 1988, 65-67.

Considers Buchwald a master of parody. His parody is based on developing an incongruity between the frame of a piece and the actual subject. In "Win One for Hoffa," for example, the subject is football, but the semantic framework is union negotiations; when asked why he dropped a pass, Walnicki responds that he has caught his quota for the half and that if he caught another pass he would be accused of speeding up the game. Buchwald has a very wide readership because he is able to make shrewd and perceptive observations, and he can write pieces which seem to be sensible even though he is dealing with highly incongruent subject matters. His mastery of this technique makes him an important social critic. Buchwald feels that it is ironic that he has become an honored member of the establishment by criticizing the establishment. Buchwald writes about such economic indicators as Alka-Seltzer and Rolaid sales and points out that when the economy is in trouble the system has fewer irritants. When the economy is doing well people are constantly digging up the streets and drilling steel pilings into the ground early in the morning. Also, when the economy is doing well, people have less time for personal contacts or for relaxation, so Buchwald concludes that "The price of a good economy is a breakdown in services that the economy provides." Buchwald is the most widely syndicated political satirist in America, being read in 550 newspapers. Between 1953 and 1984 he wrote twenty-nine books of political satire for major publishers.

John Hawkes (1925-)

828. Boyer, Jay. "Point of View and Comic Distance in John Hawkes's The Blood Oranges." WHIMSY 1 (1983): 93-94.

Considers Hawkes' most obvious comic rhetorical devices to be paradox, contradiction, non sequitur, and oxymoron of the type that are frequently encountered in the Irish bull. Hawkes' character Skipper tells us in a few words that he is not a man of few words but is rather something of a windbag. Hawkes is fascinated by the timbre and lilt of language. One passage in Blood Oranges seems to be a parody of a parody as he develops images that outdo some of the scenes in Fielding's Tom Jones. Two lovers are at the dinner table, and Cyril tells Rosella that they must eat the entire birds, the heads, the beaks, and all, to achieve the full effect. They are eating a sparrow casserole, and the entrails and heads are still intact. The reader can experience Cyril's total revulsion as he watches Rosella take her first bite and the butter drip from her lips. After they have eaten a couple of birds, Cyril turns his attention to the erotic implications of the meal, explaining that according to the rules there is to be no touching of knees, no kissing of sticky lips, no removal of shoes or sandals, no meeting of bare feet, no slipping down the dress, or licking. The total eroticism here is achieved through litotes, whereby the language negates what is actually being communicated--passion and seduction. This rhetorical device places the meaning of each expression at comic odds with its tone.

829. Wallace, Ronald. "The Rarer Action: John Hawkes's _Second Skin_." _The Last Laugh: Form and Affirmation in the Contemporary American Comic Novel_. Columbia: Univ. of Missouri Press, 1979, 45-64.

Considers Hawkes' writing to be misunderstood by many critics, who concentrate on the terror and violence of his novels without recognizing adequately the underlying comic form and vision. In an interview, Hawkes explains that he attempted to write _Second Skin_ in such a way that it could not be mistaken for anything other than what it is--a comic novel. Hawkes' comic method is to create sympathy and compassion while at the same time judging human failings as severely as possible. Hawkes contends that the most difficult aspect of writing comedy is to maintain the ambivalence necessary in the comic hero. Skipper is both comic and heroic. He is comic in his innocence, his limited perception, and inability to understand a situation, but he is heroic in his exposure of his comic society. Like the child victims of Dickens (Pip), James (Maisie), and Joyce (young Stephen), he is the comic innocent, the fool, the buffoon, who seems to be almost immune from knowledge. Skipper responds to the world as a child would. He is comically rotund in shape, and the hard sharp things of the world are constantly pricking his sensitive skin. The comedy is reinforced by the incongruity between Skipper's childish mind and his immense body, his naval background, and his age. Skipper has had too many experiences to still be an innocent--yet he is one.

Flannery O'Connor (1925-1964)

830. Archer, Jane Elizabeth. "'This is my Place': The Short Films Made from Flannery O'Connor's Short Fiction." _Studies in American Humor_ NS1.1 (June 1982): 52-65.

Indicates that O'Connor's early critics classified her as a Gothic writer who exaggerates her characters into symbols of narcissistic love that causes the characters' families to disintegrate; however, more recent critics consider her to be in the Grotesque rather than the Gothic tradition, since an important feature of O'Connor's style is the blending of humor and horror in her development of secular characters in naturalistic environments. These later critics suggest that O'Connor is especially indebted to the Southwest Humorists, and to Nathanael West. O'Connor is also in the tradition of Southern novelists best exemplified by William Faulkner. Five of O'Connor's short stories have been produced as films, each one running an hour or less. These are "The Life You Save May Be Your Own," "The Comforts of Home," "A Circle in the Fire," "Good Country People," and "The Displaced Person." Typically, O'Connor's stories begin in a calm and pastoral Southern setting; then the rapid development of conflict and strong visual imagery culminates in a violent clash of characters, setting, symbolism, and theme. This clash usually highlights the conflicts that result from male-female struggles but with the added complication of an outsider who provides a sexual challenge. The resulting confrontations are often comic in tone.

831. Becker, Isidore H. "Flannery O'Connor's Satiric Humor." Selected Essays: International Conference on Wit and Humor Ed. Dorothy M. Joiner. Carrollton, GA: West Georgia College, 1988, 9-13.

Considers O'Connor's fiction to be permeated with comic insights developed by O'Connor's effective use of wit, satire, and irony. The two O'Connor short stories which best exemplify this comic spirit are "Greenleaf" and "Temple of the Holy Ghost." Mrs. May in "Greenleaf" is a self-righteous, egotistical neighbor of the Greenleafs. When the Greenleaf's bull starts chewing on Mrs. May's hedge, she rises against the Greenleafs in righteous indignation because she considers the beauty of her hedge to be a symbol of her righteous living. The real reason for Mrs. May's attack, however is that the Greenleafs are prospering and Mrs. May is not, even though Mrs. May considers herself to be a much better person than they are. This satire attacks the pride, prejudice, folly, ignorance, and hypocrisy of the supercilious Mrs. May. The second short story discussed in this article, "Temple of the Holy Ghost," satirizes such targets as the romantic illusions of teenage girls, sibling rivalry, education, individual follies and the blatant opportunism of people who exploit the handicapped or the unfortunate. O'Connor develops the satire by allowing the reader to see the world through the eyes of a child. This is an effective device, since the child blurts out whatever she thinks. There are no pretensions or constraints as the child expresses her emotions as she feels them. This lack of pretension also contrasts markedly with the pretensions and constraints of the other characters of the short story.

832. Gosset, Thomas F. "Flannery O'Connor's Humor with a Serious Purpose." Studies in American Humor 3.3 (January 1977): 174-80.

Proposes that the humor of O'Connor's fiction ranges from introspective and ironic to extroverted and uproarious. Hulga Hopewell in "Good Country People" is a Ph.D. with a wooden leg. She entices a Bible salesman up into the hay loft for a roll in the hay with the added titilation in her mind that she is seducing a religious and innocent gentleman. Hulga's mother had told her how fine this Bible salesman was; he was admired as being in the class of "good country people." Hulga on the other hand is an existentialist, who says that she believes in nothing. But during the seduction, Hulga is surprised to discover that the Bible salesman is more worldly than she had thought. And he also wasn't all that religious, as he exclaims, "You ain't so smart. I been believing in nothing ever since I was born!" O'Connor is playing on the irony that an intelligent Ph.D. is so ignorant in this particular situation. O'Connor is a firm believer in the Christian faith, and much of her fiction exposes the follies and misunderstandings of very intelligent and educated people, as she considered these follies to be highly ironic. There are many twentieth century American authors who concentrate on wit, satire,

and irony in their writings.   Unlike most of these other writers,
however, O'Connor's humor comes not from her skepticism but from her
faith.

Jean Shepherd (c1925-)

833. Scholl, Peter A. "Jean Shepherd: The Survivor of Hammond." The
     Great Lakes Review: A Journal of Midwest Culture   5.1 (Summer
     1978): 7-18.

        Describes Shepherd as four-time winner of the Playboy
humor/satire award. Shepherd wrote humorous stories for Playboy and
for Car and Driver, and many of these stories have gotten into high-
school and college anthologies. Shepherd has published three
collections of his own writings and one edited volume entitled, The
America of George Ade (1961). In God We Trust: All Others Pay Cash
(1966) is a collection of short stories held together by common
characters, a common setting, and a narrative frame device.   The
narrator is Ralph Parker, who has returned to his home town of
Hohman, Indiana. Hohman is a milltown and has the same general feel
of Shepherd's own home town, Hammond.   Ralph Parker presents the
views of Jean Shepherd in the same way that Huckleberry Finn
presented the views of Samuel Clemens, from an author-centered
perspective. The frame device allows Shepherd to tell an oral tale
in written prose. Wanda Hickey's Night of Golden Memories and Other
Disasters (1971) is again set in Hohman, and The Ferrari in the
Bedroom (1972) is a disparate collection of essays and short stories
on various topics.   The totality of Shepherd's writings show that
"you can't go home again." Shepherd says that the Kiwanis Club just
doesn't provide an adequately fulfilling life anymore.   Scholl
compares Shepherd's writing to that of Mark Twain, indicating that
both Twain and Shepherd left their hometowns in the Midwest to
become successful and famous. Twain's Hannibal was frontier, and
Shepherd's Hammond was depressed, and these towns provided the
materials for both Twain's and Shepherd's best stories.   It is
appropriate that Shepherd won the International Platform
Association's "Mark Twain Award" in 1976.

834. Simms, L. Moody, Jr. "Jean Shepherd." Encyclopedia of American
     Humorists. Ed. Steven H. Gale. New York: Garland, 1988, 391-
     93.

        Describes Shepherd as a storyteller with a keen imagination,
a maverick wit, and an eye for authentic detail.   His fables are
partially drawn from his earlier life in Middle America and present
something of an anti-nostalgic perspective of the 1930s and 1940s in
a tough industrial Midwestern town.   Ralph Parker, the narrator,
goes on blind dates, cleans fish on the back porch, undergoes the
trauma of a prom and listens to radio programs like Little Orphan
Annie with his secret decoder ring close at hand. Shepherd can spot
the absurdities and idiocies in his home town. In A Fistful of Fig
Newtons (1981), Shepherd uses mental flashbacks to contrast the
present urban ambiance with his unstructured musings of earlier
days. Shepherd has a clear affection for his subjects, as he
needles, fondles, and reminisces about the quirky habits and
embarrassing events connected with growing up.   Simms feels that

Shepherd is "addicted to America," as he compares him to a piece of fly paper on which the dust and crud of his surroundings have been collecting for years.

William Styron (1925-)

835. Galloway, David. "The Absurd Man as Tragic Hero." The Absurd Hero in American Fiction: Updike, Styron, Bellow, Salinger. 2nd edition. Austin: Univ. of Texas Press, 1981, 81-128.

Considers the time compression of Lie Down in Darkness to have been influenced by Joyce's interior monologues and Faulkner's experimentation with time. The novel deals only with a few hours (from the time that Milton Loftis meets the train that is carrying the disfigured dead body of his daughter until the funeral itself); however, the book also deals with all of the events which bring Loftis, his daughter, his estranged wife, and his mistress together for the funeral. The novel is concerned with the chaos of the past, and how this chaos is able to resolve itself somewhat in calmness and objectivity. The tragedy of the novel is so strong that the reader feels relief that nothing more bad can happen. It is an absurdist novel and, in a very dark sense, a tragi-comic novel as well.

Gore Vidal (1925-)

836. Fletcher, M. D. "Vidal's Duluth as "Post-Modern" Political Satire." Thalia: Studies in Literary Humor 9.1 (Spring-Summer 1986): 10-21.

Claims that the satire of Duluth exposes the fact that violent means are used to achieve peaceful ends in our society. Hypocrisy is one of Vidal's targets. Mayor Herridge is a corrupt cigar-smoking politician out of range of the TV cameras, but on camera he is nice, and he never smokes his cigar. The corrupt cigar-smoking politician is a stereotype in our culture. Vidal also exposes other stereotypes. The Mexicans are all named Gonzales, even though they are not related to each other. And they are taken in by blond gringas who all look like Darlene. The Mexican women have "age-old Aztec faces" and are busy ironing tacos, folding enchiladas, and doing their other domestic chores by the light of a single kerosene lamp. The markets and the dresses are always "colourful," even when the dresses are simple and black. The Blacks are fun loving and preoccupied with sex, as they sit around listening to their transistor radios. The parody nature of the stereotyping is achieved in soap-opera fashion through the use of gushiness, repetitions, and cliché, and role reversal. Vidal mocks his own style by excessive repetition and by foregrounding the clichés of the satiric tradition, as he imitates the techniques of post-modernism, transposing his characters from one "fiction" to another in willie-nillie fasion to show that they are interchangeable.

837. Fletcher, M. D. "Vidal's <u>Duluth</u>: Post-Modern Political Satire."
<u>Contemporary Political Satire: Narrative Strategies in the</u>
<u>Post-Modern Context</u>. New York: Univ. Press of America, 1987,
137-54.

Contrasts <u>Duluth</u> to Vidal's earlier novels, <u>Myra Breckinridge</u>,
<u>Myron</u>, and <u>Kalki</u>. While the satire of the earlier works is
incidental, the satire of <u>Duluth</u> is what gives it its coherence.
While the earlier works deal with sex and politics, these themes are
much more fully integrated in <u>Duluth</u>. And <u>Duluth</u> is much more
successful than are the earlier novels in adopting devices from
post-modern literature. <u>Duluth</u> has a double focus. It focuses
generally on the Duluth police as they come into direct contact with
the Hispanic and Black American sub-cultures, and more specifically
on Darlene Ecks, the blond, blue-eyed sexy policewoman who takes
delight in strip-searching the Hispanics. And it examines the
Duluth upper crust. The novel's satire targets not only the police
and their treatment of minorities but also corrupt politicians
(including many identified by their real names in the novel), the
shallowness of pulp fiction and the media, and post-modern
literature. The satiric exposure is achieved through the actions
and behaviors of the characters through parody and through direct
statement. By portraying the mayor's election as depending on Bill
Toomey's violent schemes and by showing the violent actions of the
police, Vidal exposes "the violent origins of established processes
and institutions." But at another level, satire itself is
satirized, for there is no "sympathetic" central protagonist, and
there is no suggestion given as to how societies processes and
institutions <u>should be</u> established. The satire of satire is also
established by using post-modern techniques in a parody fashion.

<u>Carl Frederick Buechner (1926-)</u>

838. Davies, Marie-Hélène. "Fools for Christ's Sake: A Study of
Clerical Figures in DeVries, Updike and Buechner." <u>Thalia:</u>
<u>Studies in Literary Humor</u> 6.1 (Spring-Summer 1983): 60-72.

Contrasts the writing of DeVries, Updike, and Buechner with
that of Sinclair Lewis in that the former three writers portray the
minister in a favorable but comic light. They consider the minister
to be a "fool for Christ's sake," because of his devotion and self-
sacrifice in serving the Christian cause. Buechner has written six
novels that deal with the ministry. Four of these novels are
contained under the single title, <u>The Book of Bebb</u>, a novel that
centers not on one but several ministers. These ministers are
depicted as picaresque heroes in the tradition of Don Quixote.
Buechner's ministers are grotesque. They are no better than their
fellow men and no wiser, except that they know that man's actions
are of little significance. The comic tone is achieved through the
use of language. Like Twain, Buechner uses idiosyncratic language
to emphasize the follies of human beings. It is because DeVries,
Updike, and Buechner are devout church-going Christians that they
present their ministers, who never quite succeed in emulating their
Master as sympathetic characters--honest and well meaning and doing
the best they can in their clown-like fashion. The criticism by

these three authors is gentle. The irony is used to coax. The
light tone is liberating rather than hostile or confining.

Forest Carter (1926-1979)

839. Clayton, Lawrence. "Satiric Humor in Carter's The Education of
Little Tree." WHIMSY 1 (1983): 95-96.

Explains the satire in Carter's The Education of Little Tree
as being based in Native American values and traditions. Little
Tree decides to give a frog to Willow John during church. But
unlike non-Indians who would merely hand something to someone,
Indians have a tradition of indirect giving whereby they merely
leave the object close by so that it will be discovered by the
recipient. So John is unaware that he has been given a frog until
it lets out a loud bullfrog croak just when the preacher is calling
on the Lord to speak. The congregation is, of course, startled and
amazed by this event, and they jump and run out of the church
hollering "God almighty!" and "praise the Lord!" One of the targets
of much Native American humor is the white man. Carter explains why
Indians say "How." Every time a white man met an Indian he would
ask, "How are you feeling?" or "How are your people?" or "How are
you getting along?" The Indians came to believe that the white
man's favorite subject was "How," and so the Indian decided that
whenever he met a white man he would just say "How" and then the
white man could decide which particular "how" he wanted to talk
about. So when the white man laughs at the Indian who says "How,"
he is merely laughing at an Indian who is trying to be polite and
considerate.

James Patrick Donleavy (1926-)

840. Masinton, Charles G. J. P. Donleavy: The Style of His Sadness
and Humor. Bowling Green, OH: Bowling Green Univ. Popular
Press, 1975, vi + 75 pp.

Suggests that the protagonists of Donleavy's The Ginger Man
(1955), A Singular Man (1963), The Saddest Summer of Samuel S
(1966), The Beastly Beatitudes of Balthazar B (1968), The Onion
Eaters (1971), and A Fairy Tale of New York (1973) are all motivated
by their feelings and desires. Sebastian Dangerfield in The Ginger
Man, for example, is mischievous, energetic, and driven by the
pleasure principle, and these qualities make him a vital and
interesting and original comic character. But in each succeeding
book the other characters become more and more dull and lifeless.
Masinton considers Donleavy's skill at comic writing to be his chief
skill as a writer. The Ginger Man is filled with bawdy humor and
Dangerfield's speech contains much sly and evasive irony. The vigor
that results from the bawdy humor and the sly irony is what makes
this novel "one of the most entertaining works of fiction in the
last quarter-century or so." It may be true that Dangerfield
suffers from much anxiety and depression, but his ironic humor and
his will to live allow him not only to survive but to triumph.
George Smith in A Singular Man is a clever businessman and witty

letter writer, and Samuel S is wise to the fact that he has reached
middle age without accomplishing anything significant; however, the
spirit of vigor and confidence that is present in The Ginger Man is
replaced by a tone of gloominess in Donleavy's later novels.

841. Moseley, Merritt. "James Patrick Donleavy." Encyclopedia of
    American Humorists. Ed. Steven H. Gale. New York: Gale, 1988,
    131-36.

    Traces the history of The Ginger Man back to the time when it
was an underground classic read mainly by the young but praised by
other writers. Sebastian Dangerfield had a powerful attraction for
many readers and even provided the stage name for one of America's
most popular entertainers--Rodney Dangerfield. Sebastian is
charming and energetic. It is true that he is a rogue and a picaro,
a sponger, a lazy day-dreamer and a bad husband and father, and a
lousy student who cheats on exams. The only time he doesn't neglect
his wife is when he abuses her, wheedling money from her, beating
her when she is pregnant. He neglects his child so badly that she
has rickets. He spends the milk money and pawns the child's pram
for drinking money. He destroys his house's plumbing and showers
his family with excrement. But in spite of all of this, Dangerfield
is a sympathetic character, because he is funny and resourceful and
vital and sometimes charitable and also because he is a victim. The
title of the novel, The Ginger Man, suggests a man running from his
death, is Sebastian's situation. The books which follow The Ginger
Man are not of the same quality. The protagonists are improbable,
riotous, ribald, and adventurous. These novels, which are usually
set in Dublin, Ireland, tend to be both funny and sad. Donleavy's
The Destinies of Darcy Dancer, Gentleman (1977) recaptures some of
the vitality and humor of The Ginger Man. Donleavy has written nine
novels and a nonfiction book entitled The Unexpurgated Code: A
Complete Manual of Survival and Manners (1975). This book is a
tongue-in-cheek "manual for social climbers." It explains "how to
achieve undeserved social status." Moseley considers Donleavy a
cross between Henry Miller and Franz Kafka.

842. Shaw, Patrick W. "The Satire of J. P. Donleavy's Ginger Man.
    Studies in Contemporary Satire 1.2 (Spring 1975): 9-16.

    Considers Donleavy's Ginger Man one of a group of novels
published in America after World War II that re-established the
picaresque tradition. For many years after Twain's Huckleberry Finn
the picaresque tradition had been largely absent from American
literature. But then came Donleavy's Ginger Man along with other
novels like Bellow's Augie March, Ellison's Invisible Man, Kerouac's
On the Road, and Berger's Little Big Man. The picaro was able to
roam at will, and the picaresque tradition therefore has a natural
relationship to humor and satire. But the wild humor of the
picaresque tradition is often not so funny as it first appears.
Ginger Man, for example, is a picaresque ironic parody of the
Christian myths, which have been inverted for satiric effect.
Throughout the novel, Sebastian is on a quest for enjoyment--or
survival. He is a modern Everyman. In the novel, the Virgin Mary
is portrayed by Mary the nymphomaniac, who wants Sebastian to give
her his body on Christmas Day. The resurrected Christ is depicted
by Percy Clocklan, who fakes suicide and is later "reborn" as
Sebastian recognizes his "round face flowering angelically" on a

trip to England. These are only a couple of the characters in
Ginger Man with Christian counterparts, and the parody of Christian
values is further supported by expressions like "Why can't we all be
little friends. Friends in Jesus."

843. Shaw, Patrick W. "The Satire of J. P. Donleavy's _Ginger Man_."
     Studies in Contemporary Satire 12 (1985): 22-26.

     Presents much the same information as did an earlier article
with the same title in _Studies in Contemporary Satire_. Shaw
considers _Ginger Man_ to be succinct and poignant. He suggests that
Donleavy clearly establishes the targets of his satire (the church,
blatant sexuality, materialism, inappropriate idealism), and attacks
these targets quite straightforwardly. But although Donleavy
demonstrates that the old values are dead, he offers nothing to
replace them. Donleavy tells stories with many humorous, bawdy, and
wild episodes. But his satiric tone tells us that the fun is
superficial and that the more we think about it, the less funny the
humor becomes.

Allen Ginsberg (1926-)

844. Géfin, Laszo K. "This Invisible Humor: The Black Comedy of
     Ginsberg's 'Howl.'" _WHIMSY_ 1 (1983): 96-99.

     Uses two performances of Ginsberg's "Howl" to support Henri
Bergson's thesis that as participants turn into spectators, drama
turns into comedy. Bergson considered detachment to be the friend
of comedy but the enemy of drama and seriousness. Ginsberg's 1959
presentation of "Howl" was charged with outrage and lament and
anger. But during his 1981 presentation the audience broke into
spontaneous laughter, for Ginsberg presented the poem to his 1981
audience as a travesty. Géfin describes the humor of "Howl," which
had remained hidden between 1959 and 1981 as "invisible humor." The
poem had not been written as a humorous poem; the humor, which was
not intended in the original writing was nevertheless coaxed out by
the author in the 1981 reading. And the humor in the second reading
is possible only due to the fact that the audience is now confronted
by a baffling text. The laughter is nervous laughter, almost the
laughter of embarrassment. "Howl" changes from an anti-war poem to
a travesty, a parody. Gèfin compares Ginsberg's "Howl" to Whitman's
"Song of Myself," except that what is heroic and grandiose in
Whitman is mockheroic and grotesque in Ginsberg. What Whitman only
implies, Ginsberg treats openly, and this places "Howl" clearly
within John Jump's definition of travesty. Géfin then tells a
relevant story about a Jewish soldier serving in the Austro-
Hungarian army during World War I. He wanders around lost,
disoriented, and hungry. When he finally finds his unit the guard
shouts, "Halt or I'll shoot!" He responds, "Shoot?.... Can't you
see that this here is a human being?"

Murray Joseph Schisgal (1926-)

845. Holladay, LuAnne Clark. "Murray Joseph Schisgal." Encyclopedia
     of American Humorists. Ed. Steven H. Gale. New York: Garland,
     1988, 388-91.

     Proposes that the humor and satire of Schisgal's Luv (1964)
are more incisive and effective than that of his earlier The Typists
(1960) or The Tiger (1960). All three pieces are the result of
Schisgal's continuing fascination with the comedic relationships
between men and women. Luv describes all of the strange
entanglements possible for its three protagonists, Harry, Milt, and
Ellen. They end up by trying to top each other with stories of
their deprived childhoods and unhappy marriages. All Over Town
(1975) continues this theme as a prolonged joke, as the protagonist,
Louie Lucas, is able to father nine illegitimate children. This
novel contains mistaken identies, unfaithful spouses, inept
burglars, and a great deal of sexual innuendo, as the author
skillfully intertwines verbal comedy, slapstick comedy and careful
parody. Tootsie (1980) exhibits this same intertwining of puns,
slapstick, and parody. A Need for Brussels Sprouts (1982) again
exploits the battle-of-the-sexes theme, as the protagonists, Leon
and Margaret, attempt to communicate with each other in their
various humorously hostile encounters. Schisgal is satirizing the
American need for emotional crutches and panaceas for emotional
inadequacies. His comedy is both physical and farsical, as he
parodies the existential posturing of the 1950s and 1960s.

Erma Bombeck (1927-)

846. Cruse, Irma R. "Erma Bombeck." Encyclopedia of American
     Humorists. Ed. Steven H. Gale. New York: Garland, 1988, 54-56.

     Points to the humor of the titles of Bombeck's books: At Wit's
End (1967), Just Wait Until You Have Children of Your Own (1971), I
Lost Everything in Post-Natal Depression (1973), The Grass Is Always
Greener over the Septic Tank (1976), If Life Is a Bowl of Cherries,
What Am I Doing in the Pits? (1978), Aunt Erma's Cope Book (1979)
and Motherhood, the Second Oldest Profession (1983). All of
Bombeck's books present routine domestic drudgery that readers can
easily relate to. Her housewife experiences are larger than life.
Describing herself as a "nonviolent mother of three unplanned
children," she writes about subjects that are very close to her--her
children and her husband. Bombeck has always defended the domestic
role of women, though she at first resented being excluded from the
women's movement. She has later supported the women's movement,
while at the same time insisting that women be given recognition for
their talents and abilities not only in the workplace but in the
home as well. One of Bombeck's major inspirations is Jean Kerr,
especially Kerr's Please Don't Eat the Daisies. She feels that
Kerr's writings enabled and encouraged her to present her own
unorthodox and funny perspective of domestic life.

847. Dresner, Zita. "Delineating the Norm: Allies and Enemies in the Humor of Judith Viorst and Erma Bombeck." Thalia: Studies in Literary Humor 7.1 (Spring-Summer 1984): 28-34.

Laments the fact that many contemporary feminists have criticized domestic humorists like Viorst and Bombeck for their perpetuating of negative persona--the overwhelmed housewives who are unable to cope, whose minds are obsessed by minutia, and whose bodies are controlled by the needs of their husbands and children. Dresner suggests that while these domestic humorists are not using their satire to attack the chores of the housewife herself, they are using their satire to attack the social and cultural institutions and values that have placed women into this double-bind situation. Bombeck writes mainly for working-class women, who tend to marry young, have children early, and devote their lives to living in the suburbs and being good wives and mothers with middle-class comforts, modern appliances, matching furniture and new cars, because these are the people Bombeck knew when she was young. She may not challenge these values or offer any alternatives, but she does challenge the suggestion that being a housewife should be a satisfying,   full-time,   life-long   goal.   Bombeck   especially challenges the media's portrayal of female domesticity by focusing on real rather than idealized domestic behavior. And she views the housewife as a victim of "bad press."

848. Walker, Nancy, and Zita Dresner. "Erma Bombeck." Redressing the Balance: American Women's Literary Humor from Colonial Times to the 1980s. Jackson: Univ. Press of Mississippi, 1988, 357-72.

Explains that Bombeck first wrote humor columns for the Dayton Journal Herald and that these columns became so popular that by 1985 she was syndicated in more than 900 newspapers. She has written eight books, and all of them have been highly successful. Her two most recent books are Motherhood: The Second Oldest Profession (1984), and Family Ties that Bind...and Gag! (1987). In all of her books, the housewife is the victim of bad press, greedy advertisers, and "experts who have never washed a dish or changed a diaper." She points out the incongruities between domestic reality and the myths of motherhood promoted by popular culture. She pokes fun at the idealized concept of the suburbs and the absurd image the mass media presents of the ideal homemaker. Bombeck hopes to free her readers from the guilt, depression, and frustration that come from people like Betty Friedan. Her writing contains many concrete descriptive details, as she is a local- color realist. But her writing also contains wild exaggerations, and examples of parody and burlesque as she attempts to debunk the images of superwomen and supermoms.

M. E. Kerr (1927-)

849. Nilsen, Alleen Pace. "Kerr's Light Touch." Presenting M. E. Kerr. Boston, MA: Twayne, 1986, 88-97.

Describes Kerr's writing style as digging out the little inconsistencies of life, exaggerating them to the point of ridiculousness and sprinkling them throughout her books, where they serve not only to amuse but to inform as well. In Is That You, Miss Blue? Mr. Diblee tells a story about an Episcopalian minister whom many people take to be a Catholic priest. The punchline of the story is "He's no Father; he's got four kids," but the real message is that we shouldn't take religion too seriously. Kerr also uses humor to reveal her characters. When Carolyn Cardmaker says that you can find "The Rich" in libraries, in drawing rooms, in Rolls Royces, in stock markets, in costume balls overlooking a canal of Venice, or returning from a Safari, she is revealing as much about herself as about "The Rich." Many of the jokes in Dinky Hocker Shoots Smack! evoke not a loud guffaw but rather a quiet smile. Kerr's writing is also filled with such ironies as the tyranny of dieting. Kerr is also adept at the selection of humorous names that effectively describe the characters they belong to. One character in Little Little is named Opportunity Knox because he is constantly scheming to get something extra for himself. Kerr also uses alliteration in such names as Little Little, Belle La Belle, Carolyn Cardmaker, Wallace Witherspoon and $uzy $lade. In the Twin Orphans' Home, there is Wheels Potter who has no legs, and Bighead Langhorn, who is hydrocephalic, and Cloud, a one-armed albino with wavy white hair, and Pill, who was born with flippers rather than arms because of pills his mother took during pregnancy. Finally there is "Sara Lee," which stands for "Similar and Regular and Like Everyone Else"

Mort Sahl (1927-)

850. Prinsky, Norm. "Abstract of Mort Sahl and the Comedy of Consciousness." WHIMSY 3 (1985): 162-63.

     Suggests that the essence of Sahl's comedy is the merging of abstract concepts like politics, medicine, business, relationships between the sexes, religion, actors, education and the military with detailed events from his own personal life. Sahl has recorded nine albums, as follows: The Future Lies Ahead, Mort Sahl 1960--Or Look Forward in Anger, A Way of Life, Mort Sahl at the hungry i, The Next President: Mort Sahl, The New Frontier, On Relationships and Anyway... Apocryphal of Lie. In all of these, Sahl imposes his current autobiography onto the themes of his comedy, thus making the treatment more concrete and more immediate than it would otherwise be. Discussing "medicine," for example, Sahl says that the entertainment industry is so aware of his battle with mononucleosis that it has become known as "Sahl's Disease." Discussing "religion," he indicates that his attending a Billy Graham rally was sort of a "consumer's test" on behalf of his audience. Prinsky proposes that the distinctive trademark of Sahl's comedy is his chronic digressions. Sahl's word games are attempts to win the battle of "mind over matter," and Prinsky is referring to two senses of "matter" in this suggestion, the matter of his own material and the matter of the material world.

Neil Simon (1927-)

851. Lang, William. "Why You Laugh in the Theatre: An Analysis of
     Neil Simon's Odd Couple." WHIMSY 4 (1986): 19-20.

     Considers Simon's humor in The Odd Couple to be the humor of
recognition.   Lang also considers Simon's humor to be highly
structured, each joke beginning with a "preparation" phase, being
enhanced by the "anticipation" phase, and ending with a "pay off"
phase. The preparation phase is set into operation mainly through
characterization.   The main conflict that determines the words,
associations, events, characters, and general situation is between
neatness and the saving of money as opposed to sloppiness and the
spending of money. The compulsive Felix proclaims that he cooks and
cleans and takes care of the house and saves lots of money, and then
adds "don't I?" This is the "anticipation" phase, and of course
Oscar's response is never what Felix wants. In this case, Oscar
responds, "Yeah, but then you keep me up all night counting it."
This is the "pay off." The pay off is never what either Felix or
the audience expected, but it nevertheless is perfectly logical
within the context of the play, because Oscar has already been
established as a wise guy who is extremely irritated at Felix's
compulsive order. Lang suggests that the audience needs to be in
a moderate state of tension to enjoy the play. The audience needs
to know about divorce, cooking, cleaning, and saving money. But on
the other hand, they can't be going through a traumatic divorce, for
then they will understand all of the issues entirely too well, and
they will be too much associated with the characters to be a part of
the laughing audience.

852. Walden, Daniel. "Neil Simon's Jewish-Style Comedies." Ed. Sarah
     Blacher Cohen. Bloomington: Indiana Univ. Press, 1986, 152-66.

     Considers Simon's characters to exhibit Jewish features but
only superficially, because they tend to be upwardly mobile lower-
to middle-class Jews, aware of their Jewish heritage but not
religious. They are politically and socially liberal. But Simon's
humor nevertheless has its roots in the humor of the Jewish ghettoes
of Eastern Europe (the shtetls), and like that humor, it is based on
the recognition of the helplessness of the Jews and the power of the
surrounding community. And like shtetl humor it blends sentiment
with irony and self-deprecating satire with earthiness. Simon
writes with the same mixed feelings about his Jewish heritage as do
Saul Bellow, Bernard Malamud, and many other Jewish-American
writers.   It is the tradition of smiling through tears,   the
tradition with a strong sense of comic strife, of Jewish irony, of
the "shlemiel" or "sainted fool." Simon writes about people and
about situations, and he's funniest when the situation is at its
worst. In an interview with Edythe McGovern, Simon said that life
is both sad and funny, and that he couldn't think of a humorous
situation that did not involve some pain. He also said that he used
to look for funny situations, but now he looks for sad situations
and figures out how to tell them humorously.

Edward Franklin Albee (1928-)

853. Brown, Daniel R. "Albee's Targets." Satire Newsletter 6.2
     (Spring 1969): 46-52.

        Comments on Albee's effective use of understatement. Jerry in
The Zoo Story describes the landlady as "a fat, ugly, mean, stupid,
unwashed, misanthropic, cheap, drunken bag of garbage" and then
explains that he doesn't use profanity, so he can't describe her as
well as he might. Brown uses understatement himself in his critique
of Albee's targets, as he describes Jerry as "not a pleasant
person." Brown feels that Jerry's invective (stated above) is
typical of Albee's unsympathetic depiction of the smug and glib
middle class. Claire in A Delicate Balance makes sarcastic comments
about Julia's four marriages, the marital problems of Tobias and
Agnes, and John's marriages which fail because his mother, Agnes,
"wants her daughter to remain a daughter rather than a wife." The
nurse in The Death of Bessie Smith is also effective in her use of
strong language. She doesn't like this "hot, stupid, fly-ridden
world." She hates her desk, her uniform, other people, the smell of
Lysol, everything about her environment. She concludes her
invective by saying that she is even sick and tired of her own skin.
She wants out. The invective in most of Albee's plays is
incidental, however, while the invective of Who's Afraid of Virginia
Woolf? is an integral part of the entire play, as George and Martha
impale each other and their guests in a tour de force about
"civilized savagery." Their insults and their drinking are
gargantuan in their proportions. Brown compares them to freakish
reflections in a carnival's house of mirrors. Albee's main target
is the status quo as he fires his barbs at motherhood, marriage, and
middle-class values in general.

854. Brustein, Robert. "Self-Parody and Self-Murder." The New
     Republic 182.10 (March 8, 1980): 26-7.

        Worries about how the royalties of Albee's works should be
distributed in view of the fact that Albee borrowed so heavily from
August Strindberg, Eugene O'Neill, and T. S. Eliot. Albee even
borrowed from living authors, like Samuel Beckett, Eugene Ionesco,
and Harold Pinter. He borrowed their plots, their characters, and
their styles. Brustein suggests that in The Lady from Dubuque Albee
has borrowed from an unusual source for him. He has finally started
to borrow from himself, and Brustein suggests that "Albee faking
Albee is better than Albee faking Eliot." Brustein does not suggest
that all of this borrowing is a bad thing; rather he suggests that
it is a form of parody and, as such, is a very effective rhetorical
device.

855. Evory, Ann, and Linda Metzger, Eds. "Edward Albee."
     Contemporary Authors. Volume NR 8. Detroit, Michigan: Gale,
     1983, 17-23.

        Considers the main theme of Who's Afraid of Virginia Woolf to
be "the chasm between people, and their inability to connect except
through pain." Albee seems to be saying through the voices of his
characters that despite our constant bickering and fierce hostility,
we all need each other. Critics have been highly divergent on the

significance of Edward Albee's work and his evolution (or de-
evolution) as a playwright. C. W. Bigsby wrote that "few
playwrights have been so frequently and mischievously misunderstood,
misrepresented, overpraised, denigrated, and precipitatedly
dismissed." After the tremendous success of The Zoo Story and Who's
Afraid of Virginia Woolf, Albee found himself billed both as
"America's most promising playwright" and as "a 'one-hit' writer."
"The progress was essentially that suggested by George in [Albee's]
Who's Afraid of Virginia Woolf?, 'better, best, bested.'"   In an
interview with Contemporary Authors Albee was told that his plays
were going to be reissued. Albee responded that the reissue of all
of his plays into a four- or five-volume set would be much better
than having various editions all over the place, because that would
make them easier for burning. When Contemporary Authors told Albee
not to be a cynic, he responded that he wasn't a cynic; he was an
optimist. Then he continued that he would rather have his books
burned than unread.

856. Kalem, T. E. "Primordial Slime." Time, 10 February 1975, 57.

    Submits that Albee's work started out great but that it
deteriorated after Who's Afraid of Virginia Woolf?. He considers
Virginia Woolf to be a work of permanence and suggests that
expressions like "a Virginia Woolf couple" or a "Virginia Woolf
marriage" have become common allusions in the language of educated
Americans. Kalem says that the seven plays that Albee wrote after
Virginia Woolf if considered as a single bunch have had "the
cumulative magnetic impact of a shelf of dead batteries." In
reviewing Seascape, one of Albee's latest plays, Kalem said, "It is
not a hateful play; it is bland and innocuous, a two-hour sleeping
pill of aimless chatter." Kalem says that the reason for the
decline was three-fold. First, Albee was not good at plot
construction, and yet his later plays stress plot construction.
Furthermore, his later plays were basically adaptions of works by
Carson McCullers, James Purdy, and others. Finally, Albee was good
at "vituperatively explosive dialogue and bitchy humor." This he
abandoned in his later work.

857. MacNichols, John. Ed. "Edward Albee." Twentieth-Century
     American Dramatists Part I: A-J. Detroit, Michian: Gale, 1981,
     3-23.

    Suggests that Albee's writing style is affected by the fact
that he was given up by his natural parents to be raised by Reed and
Frances Albee. Albee has been prohibited by law from discovering
either the true identities of his natural parents or his true place
of birth. He therefore has felt since his childhood an intense loss
of true parental understanding and direction. In The Death of
Bessie Smith (1960) the black protagonist is injured in an
automobile accident and is denied admittance to an all-white
hospital in Memphis, Tennessee. In the play, the nurse jokes about
the mayor's hemorrhoids, while another man is nearby with his guts
falling out of his abdomen. Somehow, the mayor is more important
because he made it possible for the hospital to be built. "The seat
of government is now in Room 206." In both The Sandbox (1960) and
The American Dream (1961), Grandma is the foil. Both plays attack
the trite insincere chatter, and both play on Grandma's acute and
funny perceptions. In The Sandbox, Grandma is left on the beach to

die. There is strong visual imagery as Grandma tries to bury
herself in the sand with a toy shovel. When she dies, Mommy says,
"She looks so happy. It pays to do things well." In both The
American Dream and in Who's Afraid of Virginia Woolf there is an
imaginary child. In The American Dream the parents purchase "bumble
of joy," a toy doll which loses its eyes, heart, sexual organs, and
hands, and then finally "dies." They demand their money back
because the product did not give them satisfaction. In Virginia
Woolf, George and Martha supposedly have a twenty-year-old child.
It is ironic that the visitors, Nick and Honey, are only a little
older than George and Martha's child--28 and 26, respectively.

858. Quinn, James P. "Myth and Romance in Albee's Who's Afraid of
     Virginia Woolf?" Arizona Quarterly, Autumn 1974: 197-204.

     Proposes that the third act of Who's Afraid of Virginia Woolf?
is a parody of the romantic myth. This act is entitled, "The
Exorcism" and deals with the telegram that George receives that
their fantasy son has died. After he reads the telegram about his
imaginary son's death, George symbolically "eats the telegram."
Quinn feels that the entire play inverts the romantic form in order
to parody the ideals of western civilization. In this parody,
romantic love, marriage, sex, the family, status, competition, and
power are all attacked as illusions that men have erected to make
everybody the same. Martha and George take turns at being the hero
and the villain, and when playing the role of villain, they have the
features of typical villains--moral confusion, darkness,
destruction, and sterility. The setting is New Carthage, which
brings to mind Old Carthage, a city founded by a woman ruler, Dido,
who later committed suicide because of a failed romance. The
prototype of Who's Afraid of Virginia Woolf? is Shakespeare's The
Taming of the Shrew. In both of these plays there is much verbal
and emotional violence, and in both there is a loving bond between
the protagonists.

859. Schneider, Howard. "Has the Tarantula Escaped?" Authors in the
     News. Vol 1. Ed. Barbara Nykoruk. Detroit, Michigan: Gale,
     1976, 7-8.

     Considers Albee's plays to be political in the same sense that
Arthur Miller's plays are sociological and O'Neill's plays are
psychological. In Who's Afraid of Virginia Woolf?, for example, the
protagonists, George and Martha are the namesakes of George and
Martha Washington. Their fabricated child symbolizes the failure of
the founding fathers to carry on the tradition of the American
Revolution. So the politics in Albee is far ranging rather than
topical.

Gene Hill (1928-)

860. Tanner, Stephen L. "Gene Hill and Outdoor Humor." Thalia:
     Studies in Literary Humor 9.2 (Fall-Winter 1987): 49-55.

     Considers the humor that Gene Hill wrote for Field and Stream
to be a continuation of the Southwest Humor tradition. Twain says
that there are five features of Southwestern humor and Hill's

writing exhibits all five: 1). dead-pan delivery, 2). tall-tale
exaggeration, 3). homely and fantastic comic similes, 4).
understatement and 5). juxtaposition of comically incongruous
elements. Hill's humor is like the humor of the Old Southwest in
that it derives mostly from the way the stories are told. Another
important similarity is that in both cases the humor is masculine,
and it takes place out of doors. In Gene Hill's case, it is the
humor of hunting, fishing, camping, and dog training. It is also
self-effacing, nostalgic, and sentimental. For example, a companion
of Hill's describes his follow-through on a skeet shoot as being
like "a blind man trying to hit a mouse with a broom handle," and on
a particularly cold and miserable goose hunt a friend of his said
that he looked "like death chewing on a dry cracker." Hill
describes animals as if they were humans. "The mallard, for
instance is a Republican, because he enjoys conventions and good
stories, and he likes to brag and show off in front of the ladies."
Hill describes wives as bewildered by their husbands' devotion to
the out-of-doors. Hill's humor is collected in four books, A
Hunter's Fireside Book (1972), Mostly Tailfeathers (1975), Hill
Country (1978) and Tears and Laughter (1981). His humor is about
Americans' desire to return to rural frontier values while at the
same time accepting urban and technological values, as outdoorsmen
purchase all of the conveniences possible to take with them on their
adventures into the wilderness.

Tom Lehrer (1928-)

861. Baker, Margaret. "The Pun-Gent, Tom Lehrer." WHIMSY 3 (1985):
     37-39.

     Discusses the black humor of Lehrer's "Irish Ballad" in which
a girl murders each member of her family. "She sets her sister's
hair on fire, and dances around the funeral pyre," all the time
playing her violin. "She cuts her baby brother in two and serves
him up as Irish stew," after which she invites the neighbors in to
share in the merriment. The police finally arrive, and the girl
does not deny committing any of the murders because lying is a sin.
Lehrer presents similar ironic humor in "So Long, Mom, I'm off to
Drop the Bomb," and in "Pollution," which advises foreign tourists
that it's OK for them to visit America as long as they don't drink
the water or breathe the air. Lehrer's puns were often subtle and
sophisticated, as in "Whatever became of Hubert," where he makes a
musical allusion in the phrase, "Take me to your lieder." Lehrer's
works contain many allusions to history and to literature as well as
to classical and popular music. Lehrer's parodies are effective
because the sweetness of the music contrasts so violently with the
bitterness of the message. His "Love Song" plays on the "-ility"
suffix as he describes old age as "an awful debility, a lessened
utility; a loss of mobility is a strong possibility," and continues
in this vein discussing "virility," "fertility," "desirability,"
"liability," "sterility" "futility" and more. Baker considers
Lehrer to be one of the best twentieth-century American satirists.

862. Bernstein, Jeremy. "Tom Lehrer: Having Fun." The American
     Scholar, Summer 1984: 295-302.

       Presents an intimate account of Lehrer's life. Bernstein
first met Lehrer at Harvard where he [Bernstein] was in charge of
the entertainment for his senior dinner. He engaged Al Capp and Tom
Lehrer, and Capp was so impressed by Lehrer's songs that he hired
him immediately for a television spot on a satire program that Capp
was then doing in Boston. Although it was considered bad form for
anyone to spend more than four years in Harvard graduate school,
Lehrer was able to spend ten years there (not to mention an
additional year at Columbia). During that time, he wrote the
Harvard fight song, entitled "Fight Fiercely, Harvard," which
admonished Harvard to "Demonstrate to them our skill." The lyrics
conceded that the opponents may possess the "might," but that
Harvard has the "will." Bernstein indicates that An Evening Wasted
with Tom Lehrer sold more that 200,000 copies and that Tomfoolery
and Side by Side by Sondheim were equally successful. Cameron
Mackintosh co-produced both of these shows.

863. Willis, Lonnie L. "Tom Lehrer." Encyclopedia of American
     Humorists Ed. Steven H. Gale. New York: Garland, 1988, 274-76.

       Proposes that Songs by Tom Lehrer established Lehrer's
sardonic writing style of providing black humor framed in parodies
of popular song styles. Lehrer considers his own writing to be a
"form of permissible idiocy..., complete with a simple story line
and inane refrain." With tongue in cheek, he says that his "The
Irish Ballad" is not like the ancient ballads primarily because it
was written in 1950. "The Irish Ballad" has a wry and macabre tone
as it discusses how Lizzie Bordon killed her mother, father, sister,
and brother. "She weighted her brother down with stones / and sent
him off to Davy Jones. / All they ever found were some bones / and
occasional pieces of skin." Lehrer also wrote about how the poor
folks hate the rich folks, and how the rich folks hate the poor
folks. "All of my folks hate all of your folks, / It's American as
apple pie."

Terry Southern (1928-)

864. McKeen, William. "Terry Southern." Encyclopedia of American
     Humorists. Ed. Steven H. Gale. New York: Garland, 1988, 411-
     14.

       Considers Southern to be the "hippest" of the black humorists
of the 1960s with his shy, retiring, almost courtly manners. In
introducing Terry Southern to an audience at Clemson Univ., Raymond
Merlock explained the profound influence that Southern had had on
his personal life. Candy had taught him how to laugh about sex; Dr.
Strangelove had taught him how to laugh about nuclear war, and The
Loved One had taught him how to laugh about death. Merlock
continues that when he saw Barbarella he fell in love with Jane
Fonda, and when he saw Easy Rider he sold his motorcycle.
Southern's The Magic Christian received mixed reviews when it
appeared in 1960. The Times Literary Supplement said that it
displayed the "worst possible taste," and that Southern had failed

to provide the basic sanity and decent values on which any satire must be based. Nelson Algren, in <u>The Nation</u>, however, considered the same novel to be a "profoundly satiric and wildly comic account of our life and times." Tom Wolfe points to <u>Red-Dirt Marijuana and Other Tastes</u>, as he suggests that Southern is the real father of Gonzo Journalism. McKeen feels that few writers of the 1960s could match Southern's humor. Southern accurately documented America's "obsessiveness and obsessions" during this period.

Jules Feiffer (1929-)

865. Estrin, Mark W. "Jules Feiffer." <u>Encyclopedia of American Humorists</u>. Ed. Steven H. Gale. New York: Garland, 1988, 147-49.

Describes Feiffer's world of perpetual adolescence as a place where sex and friendship are mutually exclusive. This is especially well illustrated in <u>Carnal Knowledge</u> (1971). Estrin considers <u>Little Murders</u> (1966) and <u>Grown Ups</u> (1981) to exhibit Feiffer's best writing. In <u>Little Murders</u> he uses outrageous satire, and absurdist overstatement to make the point that the violence that is so ubiquitous in society can't help but affect the daily lives of ordinary Americans. He illustrates this with the Newquist Family which finally decides that if you can't beat 'em, you might as well join 'em, and so they happily fire their guns at passing targets from the New York apartment where they have been imprisoned by the terrorism of the city below. The play concludes with the "general merriment" that is felt by the protagonists as they delight in the increasing accuracy of their aim, and the prospect that after dinner Mom too will take a turn with the rifle. Estrin considers <u>Grown Ups</u> to be Feiffer's "funniest, most mature, and complex play." It draws on the tradition of family violence present in the works of Eugene O'Neill, Tennessee Williams, and Arthur Miller. Feiffer's cartoons, plays, novels, and screenplays all exhibit a satiric view of urban America with its neurotic citizens attempting meaningful relationships in their daily struggle for survival. Feiffer cynically exposes the relationships between the powerful government and corporate structures and the personal sexual politics of private citizens. Feiffer's satire seems to offer the possibilities of changing society for the better while at the same time suggesting that the human impulse will resist change at all cost.

866. Whitfield, Stephen J. "Jules Feiffer and the Comedy of Disenchantment." <u>From Hester Street to Hollywood</u>. Ed. Sarah Blacher Cohen. Bloomington: Indiana Univ. Press, 1986, 167-82.

Suggests that satire is Feiffer's specialty in his role as a cartoonist, a novelist, a movie script writer, or a dramatist. Feiffer concentrates on the disintegration of minority culture as ethnic creativity becomes absorbed into mass American culture. Whitfield considers Feiffer to be a minimalist, who writes very economically. He has a limited number of characters in a landscape without detail. But even though the physical environment of Feiffer's writing is bare, the psychological environment is rich, as his characters attempt to communicate and make contact with each other. His plays are not ambitious in what they attempt, but they

are nevertheless brilliant in what they achieve. Whitfield applies
to Feiffer's work the same accolade that was once given to
Hemingway's work. It is "merely perfect." Feiffer writes in the
tradition of the theatre of the absurd. With the exception of the
various voices of Joan of Arc in <u>Knock Knock</u>, all of the characters
of Feiffer's plays are contemporary Americans. Feiffer decided to
write <u>Little Murders</u> after a series of violent events had transpired
in the 1960s. Between 1963 and 1971, a President and his brother,
Medger Evers, Martin Luther King, and Malcolm X had all been
assassinated, the last one during National Brotherhood Week. These
murders were reinforced in Feiffer's mind by Truman Capote's 1967
account of the murder of a Kansas family and Charles Whitman's
murdering of fourteen people from a tower at the University of
Texas. Whitman was the product of an "age of anxiety." He had
taken several guns, snack food, and a can of spray deodorant with
him to the top of the Texas tower.

John Barth 1930-)

867. Bedetti, Gabriella. "Women's Senses of the Ludicrous in John
    Barth's 'Dunyazadiad.'" Studies in American Humor NS 4.1-2
    (Spring-Summer 1985): 74-81.

    Characterizes Barth's "Dunyazadiad" as a retelling of the
difficulties of Scheherazade. In "Dunyazadiad" Barth adopts the
voice of the Genie from Maryland who finds himself in the company of
Scheherazade and her sister Dunyazade. The voice is the voice of a
man who speaks as a woman. It is a "ludicrous" or "playing" voice
that finds life amusing and absurd. The masculine Genie tells his
stories to the feminine Scheherazade, but the stories are taken from
1001 Nights and Scheherazade therefore already knows the stories.
In this way the roles and the genders that accompany the roles are
immediately reversed. This reversal allows woman to take control of
the situation without man losing his sense of maleness. Like the
tale of Scheherazade, "Dunyazadiad" is a story that breaks down the
opposition between the sexes. Woman uses humor to break down man-
made predicaments and to initiate change. The humor challenges
man's need for control and reinforces woman's need for displacement.
The "Dunyazadiad" illustrates how women can participate in men's
vicious masculine world through playful linguistic and psychological
interaction. Bedetti feels that in this story woman has "diverted,
distracted, faked, deflected, digressed," and "turned aside" man's
oppositional thinking and has therefore changed the rules in the
battle of the sexes.

868. Harris, Charles B. "Paradigms of Absurdity: The Absurdist
    Novels of John Barth." Contemporary American Novelists of the
    Absurd. New Haven, CT: College and Univ. Press, 1971, 100-20.

    Describes the difficulties critics have had in trying to
classify Barth's The Sot-Weed Factor. Richard Kostelanetz says that
it is written in the tradition of the anti-realistic romances; Earl
Rovit calls it a "shallow parody.". Other critics have called it a
"genuinely serious comedy" or a "ludicrous mock-heroic adventure" or
simply a "traditional mock-epic." Some of the categories that the
novel have been placed into have been contradictory. One critic
called it a "historical novel"; another called it an "anti-
historical novel," and a third called it a "mock historical novel."
Because of the absurdity, black humor, and lack of stance of
contemporary American novels, some critics in recent years have
predicted that the genre of the novel is doomed, but Harris
disagrees with this prediction. Harris suggests that Barth
skillfully manipulates imitation and farce. He weaves language,
incident, and form into an ironic metaphorical fabric. His
absurdist vision of a decadent society has allowed him to invert
paradigms and themes in order to create a new and original and vital
literature that insures the survival of the novel for many years to
come.

869. Safer, Elaine B. "Comic Retrospection in John Barth's The Sot-
     Weed Factor and Giles Goat-Boy." The Contemporary American
     Comic Epic: The Novels of Barth, Pynchon, Gaddis, and Kesey.
     Detroit: Wayne State Univ. Press, 1988, 50-78.

     Describes the constant historical precedent in the novels that
Barth published after 1958.   Barth's The Sot-Weed Factor (1960) is
based on a poem written by Ebenezer Cook in 1708 entitled "The Sot-
Weed Factor." Barth's novel is set in seventeenth- and eighteenth-
century America but has a twentieth-century sensitivity.   Cook's
poem is incorporated into Barth's novel, as Barth satirically
depicts Cook, the poet laureate of Maryland, as a British emigré and
a foolish greenhorn poet named Eben.   Barth also satirically
fictionalizes history in Giles Goat-Boy (1966).   This is a comic
epic novel that has fun with the notion that America is the new Eden
and the hero is the new Adam.   In this mock epic, Barth parodies the
lives of the saints by putting them into a modern context.   In
Chimera (1972) Barth reinvigorates the myths of Scheherazade,
Perseus, and Bellerophon, and Letters (1979) in the form of an
eighteenth-century epistolary novel and continues some of the
characters of his earlier fiction while at the same time introducing
a new character, Germaine G. Pitt. Barth's Sabbatical was published
in 1982 and satirically treats contemporary targets ranging from the
CIA to academe.   In all of his writings, Barth adapts old forms to
new purposes.   Safer considers Barth's humor to be Rabelaisian in
its proportions and full of rollicking good fun.

870. Schulz, Max F. "The Metaphysics of Multiplicity; and, the
     Thousand and One Masks of John Barth." Black Humor Fiction of
     the Sixties: A Plurastic Definition of Man and His World.
     Athens: Ohio Univ. Press, 1973, 17-42.

     Contrasts the view of the satirist with that of the black
humorist.   To the satirist reality can be viewed as either good or
bad, but to the black humorist all perceptions of reality are the
result of mental constructs.   The satirist views life in terms of
unity and conclusiveness while the black humorist views life as a
maze that is variable and endless.   From his detached perspective,
the black humorist confronts as many combinations as he can in the
kaleidoscope of shapes, actions and possibilities, and cultivates an
"indiscriminative appetite" that enjoys equally the bizarre and the
mundane.   By these criteria, John Barth is a black humorist rather
than a satirist, and The Sot Weed Factor luxuriates in the political
venality of colonial America.   And the stories in Lost in the
Funhouse alternate between the realistic and the mythical.   Barth
considers love to be an important source of anarchy and chaos from
the time of the Trojan War through colonial America and to the
present as it is rendered onto computer tape at West Campus.   Life
does not provide answers for Barth.   What provides answers is our
ability to parody. Dealing with multiplicity of perspectives in the
Great Labyrinth that is both human and cosmic is too much for the
human to bear and that is not only why black humor evolved but why
it had to evolve.

871. Trachtenberg, Stanley. "Berger and Barth: The Comedy of
     Decomposition." Comic Relief: Humor in Contemporary American
     Literature. Urbana: Univ. of Illinois Press, 1978, 45-69.

     Presents the stories of Barth's Lost in the Funhouse as
parodies of conventional literary forms. These stories attempt to
establish a link between the randomness of life's events and the
human desire to give meaningful significance to these events. We
are all "lost in the funhouse" because we are trapped by our
consciousness. And it is our struggle to deal with this situation
that provides much of the comic tension of modern times. Typical in
Barth's novels is the antithetical relationship between an
"innocent" character who is searching for a single interpretation of
experience and an "amorphous" character whose role is determined by
the situation. In End of the Road the contrast is between Joe
Morgan and Jake Horner on the one hand and an unnamed Negro doctor
on the other. In The Sot-Weed Factor the contrast is between
Ebenezer Cooke and Henry Burlingame. In Giles Goat-Boy it is
between Giles and Harold Bray. Trachtenberg makes the point that
even though these pairs of characters are antithetical and play off
each other as opposites, they are also different aspects of a single
identity, sort of a Dr. Jekyll and Mr. Hyde in two different bodies.

872. Wallace, Ronald. "Dwarfed into Dignity: John Barth's The
     Floating Opera." The Last Laugh: Form and Affirmation in the
     Contemporary American Comic Novel. Columbia: Univ. of Missouri
     Press, 1979, 26-44.

     Contrasts the two different endings which Barth wrote for The
Floating Opera. Barth's editor to the 1956 edition of his book
evidently required him to to make the ending more "happy," however,
a second edition of Barth's novel that appeared in 1967 contained
the original, less happy, ending. In both versions Todd fails to
commit suicide, but in the 1956 version he accepts the viability of
relative values, while in the 1967 version he feels no emotion and
affirms no values at all. Therefore readers of the 1956 version
tend to view Todd positively while readers of the 1967 version tend
to view him negatively. Most critics classify both versions of The
Floating Opera as a comic novel, and Barth himself considered it to
be a "nihilistic comedy." Todd Andrews is both an "eiron" and an
"alazon." The Floating Opera is a novel within a novel, a comic
novel about a man writing a comic novel dealing with his own past.
Todd Andrews, the narrator, humorously criticizes his own ridiculous
society with an eye toward understanding it and improving it. Since
he is a beginning novelist and has no talent, he decides to tell his
story as simply and clearly as possible, "making no effort to
confuse or mystify." Todd establishes a friendly relationship with
the reader. In Chapter 20 Todd confesses his ignorance of stylistic
tricks while at the same time exposing a stylistic trick he has just
done--beginning the novel with two parallel and simultaneous
introductions. Thus, in Chapter 20 Todd changes from "alazon," the
insecure self-deprecating narrator to "eiron" the narrator who knows
much more than he pretends. As the name implies, the whole novel is
based on the "Floating Opera" metaphor.

Teresa Bloomingdale (1930-)

873. Fisher, Martha A. "Teresa Bloomingdale." Encyclopedia of
      American Humorists. Ed. Steven H. Gale. New York: Garland,
      1988, 48-49.

      Describes the humor of Bloomingdale's first four books as
being about her life as a wife and mother. These books are entitled
I Should Have Seen It Coming When the Rabbit Died (1979), Up a
Family Tree (1981) and Murphy Must Have Been a Mother (1982). She
claims that her fourth book, Life Is What Happens When You're Making
Other Plans (1984) is about her experiences as an author, columnist,
lecturer, and talk show guest; however, here as well her family is
her main concern, and the book is dedicated to her children. Her
fourth book has greater range than did the first three, as she
discusses her pet peeves (like video games and grocery coupons),
etiquette for career women, advice to aspiring authors, and her
thirties vocabulary for young Americans, which includes such words
as "going steady," "being pinned," "chaperone," and "boogie-woogie."
This book also contains a number of letters that should have been
written--to childhood enemies, benefactors, authorities, and one
letter to Paul Newman, who is advised that he should pass the letter
on to Robert Redford if he's not interested. Bloomingdale believes
in a strict separation of roles for men and women and indicates that
God intended man to clean the garage, adding that it says so in the
Bible. Bloomingdale's writing has been influenced by that of Aloise
Buckley Heath, also a mother of ten children, and by such recent
authors as Jean Kerr. She is often classified with Erma Bombeck and
Peg Bracken; however, these latter authors "range more widely and
prod more sharply" than does Bloomingdale. Bloomingdale treats her
subjects with great affection. Her voice is soft; her words are
simple and charming.

Gregory Corso (1930-)

874. Hart, James D. "Gregory Corso." The Oxford Companion to
      American Literature. 4th edition. New York: Oxford Univ.
      Press, 1965, 186.

      Suggests that the tone of Gregory Corso's poetry has changed
over time. The poems in The Vestal Lady of Brattle (1955), Gasoline
(1958), Bomb (1958), The Happy Birthday of Death (1960), and Long
Live Man (1963) were originally written as poems of protest, but as
read by contemporary readers, the tone changes to amusing
irreverence.

Stanley Elkin (1930-)

875. Charney, Maurice. "Stanley Elkin and Jewish Black Humor."
     Jewish Wry: Essays on Jewish Humor Ed. Sarah Blacher Cohen.
     Bloomington: Indiana Univ. Press, 1987, 178-95.

Indicates that Elkin does not like to be classified as a
Jewish writer. Nevertheless, he resents it if he sees an anthology
of Jewish writers from which he is excluded. Charney feels that
Elkin's Jewishness and his black humor intertwine, because being
Jewish develops an ironic self-consciousness that is basically
comic. Jewish writers are alien observers of a scene they only
partly belong to, and this is why they tend to be comically detached
and ironically indulgent. This is also why their writing tends to
be quite absurd and grotesque. Elkin's world is the world of
existential absurdity, the sardonic, mocking, unstable, treacherous
world where there is no alternative reality--basically, the Jewish
condition. Suffering is never heroic; it is always trivialized.
Tragedy turns to dark comedy. Even though there is little Jewish
detail or local color in Elkin's works, the world he creates is
nevertheless unmistakably Jewish--Jewish in its spontaneous
assumptions, its suggestion that triumph has to be mixed with
catastrophe, its manic depiction of the little man, its use of
cunning, slyness, and whimsy to conquer the world. Elkin's
protagonists are prophets, but they are tinged with neurotic
inadequacies. There is a pervasive irony that undercuts all
pretensions in favor of fancy, self-aggrandizement, and wish
fulfillment. Charney compares Elkin's characters with Saint
Sebastian who was bound, powerless, and pierced with arrows. When
asked if it hurt, he is said to have responded, "Only when I laugh."

876. Raff, Melvin. "Wyndham Lewis and Stanley Elkin: Salvation,
     Satire, and Hell." Studies in Contemporary Satire 8 (Spring,
     1981): 1-8.

Quotes Elkin as having said, "I'm not a satirist. I don't
enjoy satire myself and certainly do not aspire to it." But Raff
nevertheless considers Elkin's fifth novel, The Living End, to be
squarely in the tradition of Menippean satire. The novel contains
all of the important features of Menippean satire--monologue curses,
bathos, non-sequitur, and encyclopedic knowledge. There is the
coupling of high and low language and the overturning of convention.
There is the "inconvenient data" of second phase-satire and the
"attack on common sense" of third phase satire. Not only is it an
example of Menippean satire, but it is an excellent example of this
type of satire. The obsessiveness of Elkin's characters is
remarkable, invigorating, and energetic. But the message of The
Living End is more ironic than satiric. The message is that there
is no message. The world is the chaotic world of third-phase
satire. Since there is no message, we are left only with the
language, but that is enough, for the language has energy and
creativity and is in itself something positive. But we should not
lose sight of the fact that life itself also has meaning. But the
meaning of life is not determined by the achievement of goals and
rewards. The meaning of life is in the struggle, the energy, the
experience. It is process, not product.

Bruce Jay Friedman (1930-)

877. Moseley, Merritt. "Bruce Jay Friedman." Encyclopedia of
     American Humorists. Ed. Steven H. Gale. New York: Garland,
     1988, 164-69.

     Describes the characters of Friedman's early novels as "funny
ha-ha." Their mordant outlook on life and their focus on
disturbance, mutilation and embarrassment causes the reader to
"laugh out loud." Moseley considers Stern, Friedman's first book,
to be his best with its subtle blend of humor and horror. It is the
story of a middle-class Jew who believes that moving to the suburbs
will be eutopian but discovers instead that it is a nightmare.
Stern is unsure of himself as a worker, as a father, and as a
husband, and his worry and paranoia come through on every page. The
success of Stern's comedy (and also of Friedman's other best work)
is the result of his rich use of detail, his ability to create
convincing but strange characters, and his "vivid, nervous,
excessive style, full of vigorous verbs and heightened figures of
speech." Far from the City of Class and Black Angels are Friedman's
two other major works of the early sixties. Moseley considers The
Dick to be less successful than the other novels mentioned here.
About Harry Towns is a "hip story" about a man who is disjointed but
nevertheless happy. And The Lonely Guy's Book of Life is a funny
compendium of advice for lonely guys. Friedman's novels, short
stories, plays, and screen plays tend to mix comedy, despair,
realism, and fantasy in a uniquely Friedmanesque fashion. His
edited non-fiction book entitled Black Humor is often cited as the
prototype of the black-humor movement. It suggests that black
humorists write about resilient outsiders in conditions of despair.
Black humorists are able to expose the comic elements in situations
that are basically terrible, uncertain, or sick.

878. Schulz. Max F. "The Aesthetics of Anxiety; and, the Corformist
     Heroes of Bruce Jay Friedman and Charles Wright." Black Humor
     Fiction of the Sixties: A Plurastic Definition of Man and His
     World. Athens: Ohio Univ. Press, 1973, 91-123.

     Characterizes Friedman's novels as chaotic. Time and space
are indefinite. The future is not viewed as being tightly linked to
the present or the past. And there are many chance meetings and
leave-takings. In Stern and A Mother's Kisses, for example,
uniformity and sequence are replaced by discontinuity and
simultaneity. In Stern's novels there is no clear sense of places,
names, or family histories. For example, the reader is never told
what Stern's first name is, nor is the last name of either Joseph or
Joseph's father known. The nervousness of Friedman's writing and
the high number of active verbs also suggest a kind of violence.
Schulz suggests that while Henry James' characters "swim into
rooms," Friedman's characters "fly through them." There is much
violence connected with the character of Stern, even though this is
mental violence more than physical violence. Schulz explains the
black humor of Friedman's novels as deriving out of the pluralistic
world that his characters live in. Schulz believes that our present
technology leaves people too impersonal and too faceless to elicit
a tragic or a heroic impulse. Contemporary characters, therefore,
cast off their heroic and tragic trappings and become comic instead,

but this new comedy is filled with the angst that is appropriate and
even necessary for facing a frightening electronic culture.

879. Seed, David. "Bruce Jay Friedman's Fiction: Black Humour and
     After." Thalia: Studies in Literary Humor 10.1 (Spring-Summer
     1988): 14-22.

Traces the origins of the black-humor genre back to Friedman's
1965 anthology entitled Black Humor.   This anthology brought
together a very disparate collection of writings by Thomas Pynchon,
Joseph Heller, Terry Southern, and others.   The introduction to
Black Humor suggests that during the 1960s the territory of the
novelist was invaded by the newspaper reporter.   "American reality
had virtually overcome the novelist's imagination."   This invasion
by reporters forced novelists to search for new territory. As they
sailed into darker and darker waters, they finally discovered the
area of "black humor."   Friedman's Stern (1962) is a parody of the
notion that there is such a thing as "social progress."   The suburbs
are supposed to be perfect, and when Stern moves to the suburbs, a
neighbor knocks down Stern's wife and calls her a "kike,"
challenging in a single word both his manhood and his ethnic pride.
Stern tries to down play some of his Jewishness in order to fit
better into his new environment; however, this makes him feel
guilty.   The novel deals with the anxiety, isolation, and
uncertainty about the meaning of life that is so much a part of the
thinking of the 1950s, as Friedman exaggerates every detail to its
incredibly shrill climax.   The novel is consistent with Friedman's
contention that "there is a fading line between fantasy and
reality."   Note that this fading line was also being exploited by
newspaper journalists.   Friedman's writing style consists of
developing a false sense of security both for his characters and for
his readers by presenting what appears to be a realistic and idyllic
scenario and then pulling the rug out from under his characters' and
readers' feet by presenting the extraordinary, absurd, and violent
dimensions of the situation.

Elaine Lobl Konigsburg (1930-)

880. McNamara, Shelley G. "Saying One Thing and Meaning Another:
     Sarcasm in the Contemporary Novels of E. L. Konigsburg."
     WHIMSY 6 (1988): 66.

Portrays Konigsburg as a creator of humorous up-to-the-minute
realistic mystery novels that blend together the bizarre, the zany,
the unpredictable, the ridiculous, the slapstick, and the incoherent
in order to allow young readers to see that there are alternative
coping devices for various tense situations.   Her writing style is
to provide asides, puns, and other linguistic clues to show the
reader that the novel is ironic, satiric, and often sarcastic.

Donald Barthelme (1931-)

881. Dixon, Wheeler. "Donald Barthelme." Encyclopedia of American
     Humorists. Ed. Steven H. Gale. New York: Garland, 1988, 28-32.

     Points to 33 critical articles about Barthelme's work and
suggests that he is a major contemporary American writer. Although
Barthelme is not considered basically a humorous writer by most
critics, these critics nevertheless continually mention that humor
is a major element of his writing. Dixon describes Barthelme's
humor as dark, brooding, convoluted, deeply personal, anguished, and
often sardonic and bitter. Barthelme is a satirist who writes
parody fables. His characters are grounded in nursery tales and
other fables. Barthelme reconsiders the myths of the past by
dressing them in the garb of the present. In Snow White the message
is presented in a mordantly ironic and moralistic tone that almost
becomes Calvinistic in its fervor. Barthelme's short stories are
playful and are filled with sly puns and allusions, but they are at
the same time deadly serious commentaries on contemporary society.
It is obvious that Barthelme enjoys himself during the composition
process, as he considers humor to be a salvation and mediating
force. Snow White is a pastiche that displays Barthelme's
"quicksilver approach to his material." Dixon considers Barthelme
to be "one of the twentieth century's most enterprising and
entertaining word-smiths." His style is an amalgam of shifting
locations, pop imagery, and rejuvenated myths and fairy tales. The
narrative voice often intrudes into the story and parodies the
narrative style of most humorous writing. Dixon considers Barthelme
not only to be one of the twentieth century's best humorists but
also a humorist who has received renown as a serious writer.

882. Olson, Lance. "Linguistic Pratfalls in Barthelme." South
     Atlantic Review 51.4 (November 1986): 69-78.

     Proposes that nothing much happens in Barthelme's works. In
"Game" two characters sit in an underground missile silo and watch
each other. In "Alice" a doctor spins on a piano stool while
mentally seducing his best friend's wife. In "Nothing: A
Preliminary Account" a lyrical philosopher humorously considers
Sartre and his concept of absence. All in all, the events in
Barthelme's work are mislocated and understated. Barthelme's
dialogues are disjointed and ungrounded as they are devoid of the
traditional clues that let the reader know who is speaking and where
and why. For Barthelme, such matters are unimportant, for it is not
the situations or the plots or the characters that Barthelme is
interested in developing. He is interested in developing the
concepts, and he uses absurdity, parody, irony, burlesque, farce,
satire, and other linguistic devices to do this. Barthelme is a
post-modern writer, and his writing is therefore self-reflexive,
artificial, and often absurd. He is not merely interested in the
fiction he is creating; rather he is interested in the
interrelationships between this fiction and himself and his
audience. Like a poet, he is interested in the words and the
linguistic games they play in the text. Olsen cites Kant,
Schopenhauer, Freud, Bergson, and others who feel that dislocation
is at the heart of comedy, but Olsen further suggests that for most
writers of comedy there is a dislocation of events, while for

Barthelme there is a dislocation of discourse. "His language wears outrageously ill-fitting words that bump and thump over themselves..., careening off cliffs of significance into ridiculousness." Olsen calls these words "verbal banana peels" and says that they undermine the tidy syntax of earlier writing.

883. Schmitz, Neil. "Donald Barthelme and the Emergence of Modern Satire." The Minnesota Review NRP1 (Fall 1971): 109-18.

Suggests that the best way to describe Barthelme's writing is as a collage. His language is rich, ironic, and idiomatic. His words, which come both from the language of contemporary literary criticism and the socio-political jargon of the mass media, spill and tumble through his prose. Barthelme cares more for the situations he is describing than he does for the points of views of his characters. His characters often have whimsical and cryptic names, often consisting merely of simple letters, so that the characters remain anonymous and ephemeral. They exhibit themselves not so much from their behavior as from their language, as they speak their "urbanized post-baccalaureate jargon." Barthelme's transitions are abrupt as they record random movements and banal talk of various characters. Barthelme's sentences are without beginnings and without ends. The sentences merely "aim for the bottom" of the page, or is it the next page, or the next? The sentences merely proceed. They simply are. For Barthelme, the sentence becomes the focus, the object he is constructing, the message.

Toni Morrison (1931-)

884. Begnal, Kate. "Women in Morrison's Sula and Tar Baby: Mother, Companion or Artist?" WHIMSY 4 (1986): 13-14.

Contrasts the maternal with the non-maternal female characters in Morrison's Sula and Tar Baby. She says the maternal characters have a "family-love" or "mother love," while the non-maternal characters have a "man-love" or a "self-love." Morrison feels that both kinds of love are important. Tar Baby best illustrates maternal love; Nel is the nurturer. Sula best illustrates self love; Sula is the free spirit. Begnal suggests that these two types of love are reconcilable and that the two novels support the need for women to develop both of these kinds of love in order to be whole. Sula is a would-be artist, but she has no vision. Jadine is also a would-be artist, but she is a critic and a connoisseur with an eye for beauty. Begnal feels that for Morrison the complete woman has an aesthetic consciousness of herself and of other people as well. She is, in Begnal's terms, "supremely the artist."

885. Geuder, Patricia A. "The Bluest Eye: Black, Black Humor in Toni Morrison's Novel." WHIMSY 1 (1983): 100-101.

Discusses the various senses of Blackness in Morrison's The Bluest Eye. The novel is Black in its ethnicity; the author is Black, and the humor is black, relying on "wounding sarcasm," "pointed repartees," and "speared malapropisms." The novel is about a pubescent Black girl named Pecola Breedlove, who perceives herself as ugly because she is not as popular as the white girls. She prays for a miracle--she wants to have blue eyes. Pecola Breedlove feels bad every time she thinks about Maureen Peal, a bright child with lovely clothing and long brown braided hair. It is obvious to everyone that Maureen gets preferential treatment: the teachers smile at her; the boys don't trip her or throw rocks at her; and the girls are her friends. Pecola hopes that Maureen has some flaws and finally discovers two. Maureen has a dog tooth, and she was born with six fingers on each hand. So Pecola and her group delight in calling her "six-finger-dog-tooth meringue pie" but only behind her back. But Pecola, who is brutalized by her mother and impregnated by her father, still wants to have blue eyes, and she implores the reverend from Soaphead Church to have God perform a miracle and grant her blue eyes. He convinces her that she now has blue eyes, at the same time writing a letter to God explaining that Pecola had kept asking God for blue eyes and he hadn't complied, so he had just gone ahead and given her the blue eyes that she wanted. "I looked at that ugly little black girl, and I loved her. I played you. And it was a very good show!"

886. Geuder, Patricia A. "Deviant Similes." WHIMSY 2 (1984): 50-52.

Discusses the far-fetched character of the similes in Morrison's The Bluest Eye. The years are folded up like handkerchiefs. A voice is like a headache in the brain. A brain curls up like wilted leaves. Insults are little nuisances of life, like lice. The relationship between a woman and her husband and children is like a crown of thorns and a cross. Morrison uses hyphenation to get the exact expressive tone she wants for many of her similes. Thus, Pecola wants her eyes to be morning-glory-blue, Alice-and-Jerry blue, blue-like Mrs. Forrest's blue-blouse eyes. The characters in The Bluest Eye have strong emotions. Claudia hates white dolls, so in trying to find out what makes them loveable to other people, she breaks off the tiny fingers, bends the flat feet, loosens the hair, and twists the head around. The doll has a single sound, the plaintive cry of "Mama," but Claudia gives a less generous interpretation of the sound, for to her it sounds like the bleat of a dying lamb or the screech of the icebox door opening on rusty hinges in July. At one point in the novel Morrison describes what Geuder calls the "antiseptic Black woman." During sexual intercourse, this woman wonders why the private parts of the human body aren't located in more convenient places, like the armpit or the palm of the hand. Places where we could get to them more easily and quickly and without undressing. In summary, Begnal explains eight functions of deviant similes in Morrison's writing. They are used to correct, convert, isolate, extend, complement, exemplify, exclude, and squint. They underscore the ethnic points being made in the novel as they discuss the deviation from the American myth of blond beauty.

887. Omitted.

888. Omitted.

Robert Coover (1932-)

889. Adams, Charles S. "The Idea of the Game: Baseball, Robert
     Coover, and the Imaginative Act." Play and Culture 3.1
     (February 1990): 44-50.

     Compares and contrasts the baseball game invented by J. Henry
Waugh in Coover's The Universal Baseball Association, Inc., J. Henry
Waugh, Prop with the actual game of baseball, noting that the game
in the novel is one step further removed from reality than the real
baseball game. Henry Waugh sees games and gaming as substitutes for
experience and for life itself. His games are much more satisfying
than life, and baseball is the ultimate game, the ultimate diversion
from reality.   Coover sees it as both ordered and unordered and
containing all of the possibilities of the world without presenting
any of the significant problems. Waugh invents a baseball game that
is played with dice and based on the laws of probability.   Unlike
real baseball, and unlike other dice games that are based on
baseball, Waugh's invention is truly based on laws of probability.
Waugh quotes Ed Purcell, Nobel laureate in physics and baseball fan,
who says that "The longest runs of wins or losses are as long as
they should be, and occur about as often as they ought to," but to
people who are engaged in the game, such runs of wins or losses or
such sequences of throws of the dice seem to be beyond the laws of
probability.   Coover seems to be making fun of baseball fans, but
what he's really doing is examining the relationships between
fantasy and reality and suggesting that by improving our abilities
at fantasy we will all be able to lead much more imaginative lives.

890. Estes, David C. "Robert Coover's The Public Burning: Literature
     and Folk Humor in the American Grain." WHIMSY 3 (1985): 39-41.

     Examines the gallows humor of Coover's The Public Burning.
The central theme of the novel is the electrocution of the
Rosenbergs in Times Square amidst great celebration.   Before the
"public burning" Uncle Sam hosts a gala variety show presenting all
of the great events of American history. Great crowds have poured
into New York to witness the spectacle of Kate Smith singing "God
Bless America," a sermon by a woman evangelist, a re-enactment of an
important battle of the Revolutionary War, a parade of American
Presidents and other national heroes. There are skits and songs and
chorus lines acting out the building of our nation.   There is also
an "epistolary contest" during which famous entertainers like Jack
Benny, Edgar Bergen, Charlie McCarthy, and the Marx Brothers compete
with each other in humorous skits based on the letters the
Rosenbergs sent to each other while they were imprisoned.   In the
audience are U. S. Senators, Supreme Court Justices, and members of
the executive branch all with their wives. Betty Crocker functions
as the mistress of ceremonies. For Coover, the essence of America
is our humor and our frontier spirit. Coover's Uncle Sam is saying
that "fighting" is the basis of American freedom. Anyone who wants
to enjoy the blessings of a true democracy must earn the right by
"twistin' noses and scrougin' eyeballs and ribbrakin' and
masacreein.'"   In Coover's view, the events leading up to the
electrocution of the Rosenbergs indicates the true spirit of the Old
Frontier West that continues to be played out over and over again on
new stages.

891. Schultz, Max F. "The Politics of Parody; and, the Comic
     Apocalypses of Jorge Luis Borges, Thomas Berger, Thomas
     Pynchon, and Robert Coover." Black Humor Fiction of the
     Sixties: A Plurastic Definition of Man and His World. Athens:
     Ohio University Press, 1973, 66-90.

     Suggests that the black humorists of Coover's decade display
an inventiveness that earlier black humorists like Malamud, Bellow,
and Mailer don't have. The attention that Coover and his American
contemporaries pay to plot, setting, narrative pace, and psychology
places them instead with such British authors of the same period as
Kingsley Amis, John Osborne, John Braine and Angus Wilson. Coover
is like Borges, Barth, Nabokov, Pynchon, Berger, Grass and Cohen in
his ability to invent his own histories and pass them off as real,
so long as they are not used to displace the real histories
altogether. In other words, they are not absolutists, and they
furthermore feel that people and events happen over and over again.

892. Wallace, Ronald. "The Great American Game: Robert Coover's The
     Universal Baseball Association, Inc. J. Henry Waugh, Prop."
     Columbia: Univ. of Missouri Press, 1979, 115-36.

     Considers The Universal Baseball Association... to be Coover
at his best. In true philosophical fashion, the novel discusses
human creativity, good and evil, the role of the artist, the
deterioration of society, the comedy of history, the origins of
belief, and the nature of reality. Coover's own philosophical
stance as writer of this novel is that tragedy is an adolescent
response to the universe and that the comic response is a more
mature response. Coover's protagonist, J. Henry Waugh, has invented
many games, but he has not yet invented the ultimate game. He
therefore decides to reinvent baseball as his "final great project."
Henry finds the real game of baseball boring and his own game
exciting. His own game is played with three dice, a bunch of
complex charts that account for the different abilities of the
players, and other statistics relating to the baseball league that
he has invented. The novel is based on the cliche that baseball is
"the Great American Game." It parodies America's tendency to deify
its sports heroes and investigates the extent to which baseball has
intruded into every American's life, as we comment that a person
"has two strikes against him," is "way off base," "has something on
the ball," "throws someone a curve," "pinch hits," or "goes to bat"
for a friend. In life there are "close calls" and sometimes we
"make a hit," while other times we feel "out of our league."
Henry's invented game of baseball is a balance between the folk
aspects of baseball (expressions and religious and superstitious
beliefs) and the scientific aspects (statistics and historical
facts). The novel is a parody of every aspect of baseball from its
beginnings to the present day.

Paul Krassner (1932-)

893. Galligan, Edward L. Satire Newsletter 2.2 (Spring 1965): 82-
     90.

     Traces Krassner's underground magazine The Realist back to its
beginnings in the summer of 1958. It billed itself as "an angry
young magazine" and featured social, political, and religious
criticism and satire. The magazine takes pride in the fact that it
is in bad taste and boasts that every reader will be able to find
something offensive somewhere in the magazine. If the scatology or
the mocking of religion and patriotism doesn't offend the reader,
the sexual frankness and mocking of liberal pieties might. When
asked why he included four-letter words in the magazine, Krassner
replied that everything in the magazine offended somebody and he
could see no reason for making a special case for four-letter words.
Even though most little magazines devoted to criticism and satire do
not last, The Realist has not only endured but has actually thrived
and perhaps even prevailed. It began with only six hundred
subscribers and has increased its subscription list to forty
thousand, with probably more than a hundred thousand readers.
Krassner was not only the founder of The Realist, he is also the
editor and major contributor. He also suggests many of the ideas
for articles and cartoons prepared by other authors and functions as
business and production manager as well. He gives The Realist its
unique point of view, a sort of off-Broadway existentialism. In
order to preserve the tone, the magazine does not accept
advertisements. Newsweek described the magazine as "a sometimes
sophomoric, often significant, frequently funny satirical magazine."
It almost never comes out on time; the October issue is much more
likely to appear in November or December or even September than it
is to appear in October. There are usually but not always ten
issues per year.

Thomas Edward Meehan (1932-)

894. Kiley, Frederick, and J. M. Shuttleworth. "Thomas Meehan."
     Satire from Aesop to Buchwald. New York: Odyssey/Bobbs-
     Merrill, 1971, 427-30.

     Suggests that there are two types of satire at work in
Meehan's "Early Morning of a Motion-Picture Executive"--the
character satire of the movie executive and the satire of what
happens to important novels like James Joyce's Ulysses when they are
turned into financially successful movies by Hollywood moguls. This
piece is a stream-of-consciousness parody of Joyce which culminates
in a stream of "yes's" that echo the final speech of Molly Bloom in
Ulysses.

Sylvia Plath (1932-1963)

895. Van der Wal, Linda. "Comedy in 'Lady Lazarus.'" WHIMSY 4
     (1986): 171-73.

     Considers Plath's poem "Lady Lazarus" to be comical. It uses
common language to describe someone's triumph and mutes all
disorderly forces. Furthermore, "Lady Lazarus" contains vivid
imagery, multilevel symbolism, and an energetic tone. Van der Wal
sees "Lady Lazarus" as a grotesque entertainment with repulsive
imagery for the reader who is interested in vicarious thrills. In
the poem, rebirth is seen as a striptease act in front of a shoving,
peanut-crunching crowd. The poem is written in colloquial speech
and employs short sentences using the dash as a major mark of
punctuation. The sounds in Plath's poem add to the humorous effect:
"the grave cave ate" causes the mouth to open up and simulate the
actual act of eating. In this poem, Plath maintains an irreverent
tone to help the reader accept the comedy of Lady Lazarus' "happy
ending."

Edwin A. Roberts, Jr. (1932-)

896. Kiley, Frederick, and J. M. Shuttleworth. "Edwin A. Roberts,
     Jr." Satire from Aesop to Buchwald. New York: Odyssey/Bobbs-
     Merrill, 1971, 456-59.

     Believes that Roberts' "If the Spirit of Rebellion Runs its
Course," which originally appeared in The National Observer,
achieves its satiric effect by employing exaggerated contemporaneous
insanities to their illogical limits. The story concerns a protest
by the Pine Crest Elementary School. The third graders were
picketing the principal's office, and no one, including the
kindergarteners, would cross the picket lines. The picketers were
carrying signs that read, "We Demand Longer Recesses," "Homework Is
Oppression," "Compulsory Education Violates Our Civil Rights," "Nuts
to Show-and-Tell," "End Testing Now," and "Equal Marks for All."

Mike Royko (1932-)

897. McKeen, William. "Mike Royko." Encyclopedia of American
     Humorists. Ed. Steven H. Gale. New York: Garland, 1988, 383-
     84.

     Suggests that Royko has been a successful newspaper columnist
from the time of his first column for The Chicago Daily News in the
1960s though his column for the Chicago Sun Times in the 1970s to
his present column for The Chicago Tribune. His various columns
have resulted in four best sellers, Up Against It (1967), I May Be
Wrong, But I Doubt It (1968), Slats Grobnick and Some Other Friends
(1973), and Sez Who? Sez Me! (1983). In 1972 Royko won the Pulitzer
Prize for commentary. Many critics feel that Mike Royko's
presentation of Chicago to the world is similar to Damon Runyon's of
New York. Royko manages to find the humor in everyday events, and

the stories he tells are essentially true. <u>Harper's</u> places Royko into the school of "beer-and-a-shot journalism." Royko's characters are humorous, credible, and tough-talking, and this refers not only to the characters in his fiction but in his non-fiction as well. <u>Boss</u> is a book about Chicago's Mayor Richard J. Daly and illustrates well how Royko used humor to rise to the top of his profession as a writer

898. Williams, Kenny J., and Bernard Duffey. "Mike Royko." <u>Chicago's</u>
      <u>Public Wits: A Chapter in the American Comic Spirit</u>. Baton
      Rouge: Louisiana State Univ. Press, 1983, 274-89.

      Consider Royko's writing an unpredictable mixture of the tough and the sympathetic. Royko views the texture of Chicago living from very close range. His wit is replete with irony, and it is sometimes directed at the meanness he finds in most city dwellers, sometimes in the downtrodden masses but often in the places of power and authority. Royko constantly attacks the pretensions of hypocrisy, status and power. His writing is sometimes arrogant and impatient, and he often uses shock but it is not shock for the sake of shock, but rather shock to increase the reader's perceptions and understanding. Royko wants the reader to take the city on its own terms, even though these terms are often hard and cruel. Royko's sharp wit penetrates the hustling, turbulent, often irrational daily life in Chicago.

<u>Mark Russell (1932-)</u>

899. Goodman, Joel. "Mark Russell Live!" <u>Laughing Matters</u> 5.2
      (1988): 47-59.

      Mentions a half-dozen or so topical musical parodies that Mark Russell presents each year as PBS Specials. To <u>The Washington Post</u> Russell is considered to be "a national monument." Ted Kennedy says that he can prick at pomposity and arrogance of power while at the same time bringing tears to the listener's eyes and warmth to the listener's heart. <u>The New York Times</u> suggests that Russell's humor is based on the assumption that America does not take its politicians as seriously as they take themselves. Bob Hope considers Russell to be the funniest man in Washington if you don't count the men in Congress. Russell himself feels that most Americans have a healthy cynicism, that they look at government with a jaundiced eye, which is why his irreverent tone is so well received. Russell's musical parodies owe a great debt to those of Tom Lehrer.

<u>John Hoyer Updike (1932-)</u>

900. Davies, Marie-Hélène. "Fools for Christ's Sake: A Study of
      Clerical Figures in De Vries, Updike and Buechner." <u>Thalia:</u>
      <u>Studies in Literary Humor</u> 6.1 (Spring-Summer 1983): 60-72.

      Indicates that Updike is investigating the doubts and beliefs that most Christians have in his <u>A Month of Sundays</u>. The novel

takes the form of a diary written by Reverend Marshfield, who has
been sent by his bishop to a sanitorium because of his sexual
deviations and other matters. The title of the novel is based on
Marshfield's dilemma of belief as he vascilates in the wasteland of
belief vs. disbelief and fidelity vs. adultery. Although the
conflict between the sacred and the profane is the main subject of
Updike's novel, the book also criticizes the literary ideas of the
period. Updike sees a similarity between the preacher and the
writer, for they both live by "the word"--they are "both limited and
defined by the alphabet." In its treatment of religion, sex, and
art, the novel revolves around one basic image, the letter "O," or
more properly, the Greek letter "Omega." This is symbolic of "a
woman's sex, the Jungian mandala and the importance of Christ the
judge at the Grand Assize when history ends." Even the asylum is
shaped in the form of an Omega, and the swimming pool rests at its
center. Davies suggests that Updike has two purposes in the novel--
to restore his own belief system and to seduce the ideal reader--
Mrs. Prynne. Updike feels that it used to be easier to be a
Christian because now there is not a single Christian theology but
rather a profusion of them. Christianity used to soothe sick souls,
but now it gives headaches to anyone who is trying to understand and
believe.

901. Galloway, David. "The Absurd Man as Saint." The Absurd Hero in
     American Fiction: Updike, Styron, Bellow, Salinger. Second
     Revised Edition. Austin: Univ. of Texas Press, 1981, 17-80.

     Discusses Updike's first novel, The Poorhouse Fair, as a
criticism of the failure of contemporary systems to fulfill our
spiritual needs. He attacks the humanistic welfare state, which
attempts to provide security, coherence, and meaning to human life
but fails in all three attempts, because the welfare state only
makes life more precarious, obtrusive, and sterile. Updike focuses
on "the poorhouse" and on Mr. Conner, the "humanist" who is the CEO
of that agency. The central ironic theme of Updike's novel is that
Conner and the people like him are prolonging life at the same time
that they are stifling living. Updike sees present-day America as
a country of superlatives. We drive our super cars on our
superhighways to the supermarket, where we park in a superlot and go
in to buy some Super Suds. Updike considers such hyperbolic
adjectives to be self-defeating.

902. Greiner, Donald J. "Updike's Witches." Selected Essays:
     International Conference on Wit and Humor. Carrollton,
     Georgia: West Georgia College, 1988, 20-25.

     Discusses the black humor of Updike's The Witches of Eastwick,
saying that the tone is closer to Hawkes' Second Skin than it is to
his own Rabbit, Run. Updike remarks that in the past he has been
criticized for making his women characters subsidiary to his men
characters and answers that the charge is well founded, because it
is normal for a male to view women as "something other." In The
Witches of Eastwick, Updike is investigating the notion that for
women "husbandlessness brings power." The novel is about "witchy
women." He feels that there is a sinister reminder of the old myths
in women who are obsessed with being liberated and developing raised
consciousness. "He smells the odor of sulfur in the current power
struggle between the sexes," and the novel gives gossip and faintly-

heard human voices a great force and power. Updike believes that
the insatiable lust for gossip is by no means trivial and even
suggests that "we write and read novels to satisfy it." Greiner
indicates that Updike has been committed to comedy from the
beginnings of his writing career. His first book, The Carpentered
Hen and Other Tame Creatures (1958), is a collection of comic poems.
He has since published many delightful essays on humor and parody,
such as "Beerbohm and Others" (1961), which discusses the role of
subversion in humor. Updike uses humor to gently undercut militant
feminism. In a 1964 essay on the humor of light verse he noted that
order is comic while chaos is tragic. He wrote The Witches of
Eastwick as a comic novel, as can be seen by his ending, which
reestablishes the order of the family and thus gives a comic tone to
what might have otherwise been considered a tragic story.

Charles Stevenson Wright (1932-)

903. Schulz, Max F. "The Aesthetics of Anxiety; And, The Conformist
     Heroes of Bruce Jay Friedman and Charles Wright." Black Humor
     Fiction of the Sixties: A Pluralistic Definition of Man and
     His World. Athens: Ohio Univ. Press, 1973, 91-123.

     Portrays the mind of Wright's protagonist Lester in The Wig as
a grab bag of commercial slogans. For Lester, Harlem is what Harlem
sells. His silky-smooth hair, referred to by Wright as "the wig,"
is symbolic of Lester's product-oriented and medium-controlled
world. Lester's life has no purpose and no coherence. It is
fragmented by one-minute television commercials. For Lester, there
is no history and therefore no lasting significance. Most of the
advice he receives comes from the labels of various products that
tell how the products are to be used. Lester lives the life of a
twentieth-century American consumer. Lester is not a single
character; rather, he is many characters, constantly being
influenced by the commercial world around him. He is an Uncle Tom,
a militant, a terrified hermit, a self-hating Negro, a white
American who happens to have a black face. He is the Negro everyman
as he flits from role to role. He represents the pluralistic world
of the American Black and the pluralistic world of the Black
Humorist as well.

904. Sedlock, Robert P. "Jousting with Rats: Charles Wright's The
     Wig." Satire Newsletter 7.1 (Fall 1969): 37-39.

     Describes Wright's protagonist Lester Jefferson as a
picaresque hero. Although he is Black, Lester tries to adopt the
standards of white society, and the major symbol of this novel is
therefore Lester's use of a product named "Silky Smooth." This is
a hair bleach and hair straightener that gives Lester's hair a
burnished-red-gold appearance commonly referred to in Black slang as
"a wig." The irony of the novel is that Lester is a failure in
trying to be a white man, but his attempt to do so has caused him to
lose his integrity as a Black man. The picaresque nature of Lester
Jefferson can be seen in the mock-heroic tale in which Lester
attempts to get one hundred rat skins to make a fine fur coat for
"The Deb." Wright uses many military images to describe the battle
between Lester and the rats. The rats halted; they formed a V-

formation; one rat broke ranks; their strategy was to sneak up from the left flank; they retreat; some rats were described as deserters. There were also athletic images as Lester flung his Dizzy-Dean arms, made a Jesse Owens leap, and lunged like Johnny Unitas. The encounter is comically chaotic as Lester falls on three rats and traps two others in the wastebasket. In typical mock-heroic fashion, Wright's most important rhetorical device is overstatement as he describes the combatants, the speeches, the challenges, the defiances, the boasts, and the elaborate battle scene in hyperbolic detail.

Vine Deloria (1933-)

905. Childers, Yolanda Elaine. "American Indian Humor and Non-Indian 'Indian' Humor." WHIMSY 1 (1983): 109-12.

Notes that Vine Deloria and many other Native Americans are disappointed that history has failed to present the humorous side of Indian life. Rather, Indians are presented as granite-faced, grunting redskins. But Deloria suggests that the Indian people are exactly the opposite of this stereotype and that Indians have found a humorous side to nearly all of their problems. When one Indian was asked what the biggest joke in Indian country was he responded, "The Bureau of Indian Affairs." Another Indian was asked by an anthropologist what this land was called before the white man came, and he responded simply, "Ours." Deloria feels that laughter encompasses the soul of the Native American, who uses humor to define his existence and irony and satire to get keener insights into the group's collective psyche and values.

906. Thompson, William R. "The American Indians' Attempt to Get the Last Laugh." WHIMSY 5 (1987): 53-55.

Compares the Indian humor of Deloria's Custer Died for Your Sins with the Indian humor of Don Bibeau, Joseph Cash, Robert Easton, David Edmunds, Robert Freeman, W. W. Hill, Nancy Lurie, Charles Trimble, Shirley Witt, and Stan Steiner. Deloria's book contains a twenty-two-page chapter entitled "Indian Humor," in which he tells a number of humorous Indian stories. He tells about a survey that was taken among Indians during the Vietnam War that asked whether Americans should get-out of Viet Nam. Fifteen percent of the Indians thought that the Americans should get out of Vietnam, and eighty-five percent thought they should get out of America. Indians from all tribes also tell many Columbus stories, even though none of these tribes actually had anything to do with Columbus. These stories provide a strong unifying sense of purpose and show that all tribes share a common attitude. One story is that when Columbus landed, one Indian turned to another Indian and said, "Well, there goes the neighborhood." But a subject that is even more popular among Indians than is Columbus is the subject of Custer's last stand. Deloria suggests that there are probably more jokes about the relationship between Custer and the Indians than there were Indians who actually participated in the battle. All of the Indian jokes have a common theme--Custer got what was coming to him.

Philip Milton Roth (1933-)

907. Bender, Eileen T. "Philip Roth: The Clown in the Garden."
     Studies in Contemporary Satire 3 (Spring 1976): 17-30.

     Alludes to the Garden of Eden, saying that Roth writes about
the inhospitable modern garden not the utopian original garden.   In
Roth's contemporary garden, nature is quixotic and leaves mankind
dangling without firm support.   Roth's Our Gang, which was reissued
in a special "Watergate" edition, satirically attacks the body
politic in Swiftian fashion.   Roth uses the pastoral setting to
present man as half wistful and half-hostile, dealing with one
absurd dilemma after another.   There is a mocking tone in Roth's
portrayal of urban protagonist Neil Klugman in Goodbye, Columbus.
He is overwhelmed by the beauty of American suburbia, with its long
lawns that seem to be twirling water on themselves.   Suburbia seems
to place Klugman nearer to heaven; even the sun seems to be bigger,
rounder, and closer.   On the surface Goodbye, Columbus, has a
pastoral setting, but this new Garden of Eden has many terrors, and
Roth dons the guise of a clown and develops a tone of self-parody to
restore nature to its proper order.

908, Bier, Jesse. "In Defense of Roth." Etudes Anglaises. Paris:
     Didier, 1973, 49-53.

     Suggests that the basic tone of Roth's Portnoy's Complaint is
comically extravagant but with a serious purpose.   The novel's
sexual busy-ness is devoid of affection and connection.   There is
much one-line, self-centered, anecdotal humor in the novel.   Roth's
protagonist, Portnoy, is a sort of stand-up comedian delivering a
self-deprecating comic monologue, always at center stage giving a
solo performance in front of an audience that may be just slightly
alienated by his narcissism.   The "complaint" is the "kvetch" of
neurotic whining, but it is lament and lamentation as well.   It is
a schizoid complaint filled with both love and hate, with both
protective comedy and sharp fury. .It is filled with despair as well
as with slapstick.   The novel deals with issues that are both
repugnant and laughable, but Bier cautions the reader to look beyond
the surface drives and cheap actions to the subtler and even
poignant human cry that is the basic undertone that makes the novel
significant.

909. Cooper, Alan. "The Jewish Sit-Down Comedy of Philip Roth."
     Jewish Wry: Essays on Jewish Humor. Ed. Sarah Blacher Cohen.
     Bloomington: Indiana Univ. Press, 1987, 158-77.

     Believes that Portnoy's Complaint is grounded in stand-up
comedy.   Various critics have compared Alex Portnoy with Lenny
Bruce, Sam Levenson, Myron Cohen, Milton Berle, Sid Ceaser, Mort
Sahl, Buddy Hackett, Alan King, Woody Allen, and Jackie Mason in the
way he delivers his material.   But Alan suggests that the novel is
also like the "sit-down comedy" of Franz Kafka.   The features of
stand-up comedy that can be seen in Portnoy's Complaint include
shtick, set pieces, one liners, shpritzes, rapid changes, and
juxtapositions of disparate subjects.   The features of sit-down
comedy in the novel include the extended monologue, the idea that
guilt is somehow a comic subject, the idea that the protagonist is

the butt of some huge cosmic joke, the basic absurdity of life, the satiric criticism of authority, the ironic reversals, and the sustained absorbing narrative giving shape to the material. Cooper points to the "demonic giggle" in some of Kafka's grimmest stories that can also be seen not only in Portnoy's Complaint but in The Breast, My Life as a Man, The Professor of Desire, and the Zuckerman trilogy.   In addition, Kafka is frequently alluded to in these various works. Cooper suggests that there are three different ways to read a Roth novel, and three different resultant reactions to the novel.   Those readers who believe that serious writing must be accompanied by a frown will be disappointed by Roth. Those readers who respond to Roth in the same way that they would respond to stand-up comedy will perceive Roth as being lightweight. But those readers who read Roth as a "sit-down comic" and who therefore read Roth in the same way that they would read Kafka will get the true message of the novels.

910. English, James F. "'Mental Flypaper': The Joke of Perfect Memory in Philip Roth's Zuckerman Unbound."WHIMSY 5 (1987): 29-31.

Portrays Alvin Pepler of Zuckerman Unbound, the middle novel in the Zuckerman trilogy, as an ex-quiz-show wizard from Zuckerman's hometown of Newark, New Jersey. Pepler has a photographic memory, and this is a problem because he remembers everything he encounters. In the novel he is described as "glue," as "mental flypaper." He, "can't forget a thing. All the interfering static, he collects." Pepler's conversation is very boring, because he is able to produce endless dialogues about pop songs beginning with "You're," or things that happen with the number 98 in them, or the literary history of Newark. Pepler's specialty is "Americana," and he can provide any information requested on sports, old-time radio, slang, proverbs, commercials, famous ships, the Constitution, great battles, and longitudes and latitudes. Pepler does not display knowledge but a kind of travesty of knowledge--machine knowledge, knowledge without warmth or personality. English suggests that there is something inherently funny about a character like Pepler, whose monologues have an effect similar to computer-written poems. They are divorced from what Bergson calls the elan vital, the vital spirit of mankind. Zuckerman views Pepler as someone who is still studying for his final exams. Even an ordinary mind has vast amounts of unnecessary short-term information like the sort of thing that is put down as answers to exam questions--old phone numbers, bad song lyrics, and random dreck from an old newspaper. Pepler has a "photographic memory," a term that suggests a machine-like process and recalls Bergson's definition of the comic as "something mechanical encrusted on the living, the momentary transformation of a person into a thing."

911. Grebstein, Sheldon. "The Comic Anatomy of Portnoy's Complaint." Comic Relief: Humor in Contemporary American Literature. Ed. Sarah Blacher Cohen. Urbana: Univ. of Illinois Press, 1978, 152-71.

Compares Alex Portnoy with Lenny Bruce in terms of antithetical emotions. They are both attractive and repulsive, brilliant and neurotic, awful and hilarious, aggressive and self-destructive. Grebstein further indicates that the first few pages of Lenny Bruce's autobiography, <u>How to Talk Dirty and Influence</u> <u>People</u> is similar to <u>Portnoy's Complaint</u> both in the kind of material presented, and in the method of presentation. Grebstein feels that <u>Portnoy's Complaint</u> is written with "brutal candor and comic genius," as it treats such topics as Jewish sexuality, Jewish family life, and Jewish self-hatred. <u>Portnoy's Complaint</u> in Grebstein's eyes is part of the "Yiddishization of American humor" that was being promoted as well by other famous humorists like Sam Levenson, Myron Cohen, Milton Berle, Henny Youngman, Sid Caesar, Woody Allen, Shelly Berman, Jack Carter, Jan Murray, Jackie Miles, Buddy Hackett, Jack E. Leonard, Mort Sahl, Mike Nichols, Elaine May, Alan King, Jackie Mason, and others. Unlike previous Jewish comedians, these comedians both asserted and abused their Jewish identity. Rather than using the ethnic sentimentality and and dialect comedy of earlier entertainers like Al Jolson, Fanny Brice, and Eddie Cantor, these comics used sharp satire. And for Sheldon Grebstein, Alexander Portnoy was a stand-up comedian in this new tradition. Portnoy's humor is grounded in embarrassment, but it is not innocent. It is needling and often abrasive. It is spontaneous satire which may start innocently enough, but it gathers momentum and its energy carries it along to the point of exhilarating anarchy and total freedom from inhibition.

912. Mintz, Lawrence E. "Devil and Angel: Philip Roth's Humor." <u>Studies in American Jewish Literature</u> 8.2 (1989): 154-67.

Links Roth's style to that of the earliest manifestations of American comedy and places Roth in the tradition of comic novelists that includes Bellow, Malamud, Updike, Barth, Reed, Coover, and others. Roth's comic rhetorical devices run the full gamut from playful language and description to ironic assessment to scathing ridicule, to anger disguised as humor. In Roth's writings it is easy to find samples of parody, burlesque, slapstick, ridicule, insult, invective, lampoon, wisecrack, nonsense, levity, and other types of verbal play. Roth's protagonists are anti-heroes who are uncomfortable in the world as it is and uncertain about the world as it might be. They seemed to be trapped in a Jewish joke. They desperately seek commitment--marriage, fatherhood, a job--while at the same time evading commitment. They are narcissistic and insatiable. They have enormous desires but at the same time are intelligent enough to see that everything they use to satisfy their desires is flawed. Roth's characters are similar to other "little men" of American humor in that they refuse to be overwhelmed by the pressures in their lives. Because of their sense of humor, which is at the very core of their existence, they are good at pretending that reality is kinder than it is. Roth's constant theme is that human life is fundamentally incongruous. Mintz places Roth in the tradition of "sitdown comics" that includes such other authors as Kafka, Rabelais, Swift, Mann, and Flaubert, and such artists as Hogarth and Daumier. Roth feels that "serious comedy" is <u>not</u> an oxymoron, for he feels that "sheer playfulness" and "deadly seriousness" are both his closest of friends.

913. Rice, Julian C. "Philip Roth's <u>The Breast</u>: Cutting the Freudian Cord." <u>Studies in Contemporary Satire</u> 3 (Spring 1976): 9-16.

Considers Roth's <u>The Breast</u> to be a glimpse into the uninhibited Freudian aspects of the human mind. It is a surrealistic blend of sanity and reality and alludes in various places to the grotesque satire of Kafka, Gogol, and Swift. Rice feels that Roth may be opening himself to the charge of flattery by self-comparison, but that he should not be thus criticized, for the basic theme of his writing is modern man's inability to take himself seriously in a world of psychological determinism. The Breast is a parody of a parable as it tells about the re-creation of human identity by placing his re-creation into a sexual and therefore realistic (for Roth) perspective. Roth feels that Freudian "sanity" can drive a person crazy. Roth's narrator, Kepesh, who learns about his infantile self by undergoing psychoanalysis, tries to become something more than merely a passive recipient. Kepesh is dependent on Claire, his doctor, and Claire's books as a psychological crutch, and he knows he must change his life. But in his attempt to change his life, he unwittingly repeats the patterns of his former life, seeking such sources of comfort as parents, sex, psychoanalysis, literary criticism, fame and money. David's rebirth as a breast satirizes Freud's theories of infantile pleasure and sexuality.

914. Rugoff, Kathy. "Humor and the Muse in Philip Roth's The Ghost Writer." Studies in American Humor NS4.4 (Winter 1986): 242-48.

Points out that many critics condemned Portnoy's Complaint for presenting the Jew in a not totally favorable light, as they point to Alex's sexual obsessions and complaints about his mother. They said that Roth is vulgarizing Jewish culture. Irving Howe says that Roth's writings encourage younger Jews to let go of their heritage and perhaps to let go of themselves as well. As a result of this criticism, Roth wrote The Ghost Writer (1979), which Rugoff describes as a brilliant and witty book about the assimilation of the Jew in America, but Roth's critics feel that his light and sometimes irreverent and humorous treatment of Jews is encouraging the ever-present threat of anti-Semitism. Nevertheless, Rugoff views the book as an honest portrayal of Roth's personal reaction to the Holocaust and to his own reception as an author. Roth has been just as influenced by the Holocaust as his critics have, but unlike his critics, Roth does not allow the Holocaust to dictate what is or is not appropriate for discussion, and this is because Roth uses his sense of humor to get distance and perspective from his subject. In The Ghost Writer, all the characters take themselves too seriously, and this even includes Nathan, the ghost writer himself. The basic message of the novel is that while the Holocaust should be recognized as significant, it should not become the burden of Jewish culture, tradition, or history. Roth addresses Anne Frank, the central symbol of the Holocaust, to show that he is concerned, but at the same time he throws darts at the self-righteousness of his critics. Roth uses humor to defend his own humor.

Gloria Steinem (1934-)

915. Walker, Nancy, and Zita Dresner. Redressing the Balance:
      American Women's Literary Humor from Colonial Times to the
      1980s. Jackson: Univ. Press of Mississippi, 1988, 428-32.

      Compares Gloria Steinem with Black feminist activist Flo
Kennedy, both of whom have said that a revolution without humor is
as senseless as is a revolution without music.   In 1972 Steinem
became the first editor of and frequent contributor to Ms. magazine.
She has also published articles in The Ladies' Home Journal,
Seventeen, Esquire, Vogue and Cosmopolitan.   Steinem was concerned
with subtle sexual messages that occured in such magazines and once
said that it was difficult to persuade advertisers that women should
be able to look at shampoo ads without accompanying articles on how
to wash their hair. Walker and Dressner suggest that humor has been
an important part of Steinem's writing since the mid-1960s when she
wrote for the satiric television series "That Was the Week that
Was." Steinem later contributed satiric photo captions to Help!, a
spin-off from Mad magazine.   Steinem's humor was influenced by
Dorothy Parker, a close personal friend.   Steinem's commonsense
exposure of the absurdities of sexism also places her in the company
of Nora Ephron, Marietta Holly, Alice Duer Miller, and other women
who have satirized men's assumed superiority.   Steinem writes on
taboo subjects, and she is assertive about it. A female taxi driver
once told her that if men got pregnant, abortion would be a
sacrament.   Later Steinem wrote an article on a very similar topic
entitled, "If Men Could Menstruate."

Gerald Robert Vizenor (1934-)

916. Owens, Louis. "Coyote Humor in the Fiction of Gerald Vizenor."
      WHIMSY 3 (1985): 55.

      Considers Vizenor's Darkness in Saint Louis Bearhert to be a
disturbing, often shocking novel.   Behind the dark and bitter
absurdist comedy directed at both whites and Indians lies Coyote,
the American Indian trickster. Vizenor, a Chippewa poet, novelist,
editor, and teacher, makes readers uncomfortable by overturning
stereotypes and challenging traditions. Darkness is a novel of chaos
and disorder where social conventions are being circled by Vizenor's
"clown crows."   The novel provides a cathartic release through
laughter and demonstrates the necessity of order by depicting a
world of chaos.

Woody Allen (Allen Stewart Konigsburg) (1935-)

917. Lewis, Paul. "The Collapse of Humor in Woody Allen's Stardust
      Memories." WHIMSY 2 (1984): 28-29.

      Compares the blend of humor and pain and nausea and horror and
grief in Woody Allen's Stardust Memories with that in William
Shakespeare's King Lear.   Critics have attacked Stardust Memories on

two fronts. They say that the film is indulgent and narcissistic, and they feel that the mingling of jokes with images of suffering is in bad taste. The title of Stardust Memories is an allusion to the scriptural message that humans start as dust and return to dust, but it is also an allusion to our present state since we are all "stardust," with memories that glisten and then evaporate. Lewis suggests that Allen's laughter is not obscene and that jokes about genocide and murder and war are not in poor taste, for such humor is merely reflecting our mangled world. Allen's humor is not inappropriate; it is only dark, very dark, as in his house party that is attended by rape- and heart-attack victims. Allen's character is able to bring hope into this situation by observing that if he had been born in Poland, he'd be a lampshade by now. But he wasn't, and he isn't.

918. Mast, Gerald. "Woody Allen: The Neurotic Jew as American Clown." Jewish Wry: Essays on Jewish Humor. Ed. Sarah Blacher Cohen. Bloomington: Indiana Univ. Press, 1987, 125-40.

Considers Woody Allen a transitional humorist. Before Allen started writing, ethnic humor was mostly based on negative stereotypical traits. The Irish were constantly brawling; the Germans were drinking beer and eating Limberger cheese; the Blacks were fainting every time they saw a white sheet move; and the Jews were counting their shekels. The stereotypical humor was written to appeal to a largely immigrant, working-class audience. Before Allen, no Jewish writer or performer wanted to appear too Jewish. Annie Hall (1977) contrasted the lifestyles of Jews and Gentiles, their preoccupations and conversations, and the cramped, dark, noisy interiors of New York City with the expansive, light, pastoral exteriors of rural America. Mast feels that Annie Hall is Allen's "most sincere, most personal, and most richly comic statement about both his life and his art." Allen associates sunlight, nature, tasteful shades, fancy furniture and clothing, and objets d'art with goyim, but he also considers goyim to be cold, unpredictable, frivolous, faddish, flippant, and suicidal. Mast describes the quiet at the Halls' table to be "gracious but deadly," while the noise at the Singer table is "tacky but vital." Life with the Halls would be lovely and lifeless; life with the Singers would be a noisy ride on a rollercoaster. It would be loud and bumpy, but it would move--up and then down and then up again.

919. Rapf, Joanna E. "Woody Allen [Allen Stewart Konigsberg]." Encyclopedia of American Humorists. Ed. Steven H. Gale. New York: Garland, 1988, 8-14.

Lists the twenty-two films, six plays, and three books that Woody Allen has written as well as the eight books and at least fourteen articles that have been written about Woody Allen's works. Allen's first play, Don't Drink the Water (1966) is about a New Jersey caterer, his wife, and daughter who are touring in a country behind the Iron Curtain and taken to be spies when they snap a photo of something that turns out to be a top secret Communist military installation. The family is forced to take refuge in the American Embassy. Allen's next play, Play It Again, Sam (1969) was based on his second divorce. In his fantasies he turns to Humphrey Bogart for advice about women. Allen's only other full-length play is The Floating Lightbulb (1981), but he has also written some one-act

plays--"Death Knocks" (1971), a mock-heroic depiction of the
Christian allegory in which darkly robed Death appears on the scene
to play chess for the life of a man. A companion piece to "Death
Knocks" is "Death" (1976), in which a salesman named Kleinman is
searching for a killer only to discover that this killer is Death
himself. From the late 1960s on, Allen has been contributing comic
essays and short stories to such national magazines as Life,
Esquire, The New Yorker, and Playboy. Many of these pieces were
later published as collections in Getting Even (1971), Without
Feathers (1975), and Side Effects (1980).

920. Pinsker, Sanford. "Woody Allen's Lovably Anxious Schlemeils."
     Studies in American Humor NS5.2-3 (Summer-Fall 1986): 177-89.

     Considers Allen's anxious and bespectacled "punin" to be a
national icon, a "beautiful loser par excellence." Allen's "Little
Man" is firmly in the tradition of Charlie Chaplin (the Little
Tramp) as well as the tradition of the "Little Man" of Robert
Benchley, James Thurber, S. J. Perelman, and other New Yorker
writers. He is a 98-pound weaking who suffers many physical and
psychological indignities. Allen was raised in Brooklyn where
people didn't talk; they shouted and waved their hands, and they
ended their sentences with exclamation marks rather than periods.
It was an environment of combative warmth. And this early lifestyle
affected Allen's writing. His style places airy ideas and gritty
urban detail into the same paragraphs, "often on opposing sides of
a semicolon." Allen allows us to accept and enjoy our nihilism. In
Getting Even (1971), Allen challenges arrogant and brainy
professorial types. Stardust Memories (1980) is also an exercise in
biting the hands that have fed him--his adoring fans, his reviewers,
and especially those who subject his work to intense critical
scrutiny. Allen is like Benchley, Thurber, and Perelman in
remembering tragic events as if they were comic, but Allen has an
advantage over these other authors in that he is writing for a more
sophisticated audience. Woody Allen's Little Man is fully
developed. He is a bumbling Jewish neurotic with thick eyeglasses
and a sad expression on his face. He has obsessive worries and
guilts, a tentative voice, and various physical mannerisms like
shrugs, quivers, and hesitant pauses. Woody Allen in character says
that when he played softball, he'd steal second, and then feel
guilty and give it back.

921. Schechner, Mark. "Woody Allen: The Failure of the Therapeutic."
     From Hester Street to Hollywood: The Jewish-American Stage and
     Screen. Ed. Sarah Blacher Cohen. Bloomington: Indiana Univ.
     Press, 1986, 231-44.

     Proclaims that Allen shares with other comedians the problem
of being stuck in place with the desire for but not the realization
of upward mobility. Such comedians would like to become true
satirists, true social critics, true novelists, even "auteurs," but
they have a problem. Nevertheless, Schechner feels that Allen has
become an "auteur" in four films, Annie Hall, Interiors, Manhattan,
and Stardust Memories. Allen's earlier works are filled more with
jokes than with sustained humor, and these jokes would start out as
regular statements and then end with a twist. He says that his
parents were old-world people whose values were God and carpeting.
He says that he has an intense desire to return to the womb--

anybody's. Getting Even is a clever parody of a Sam-Spade type
detective story. Kaiser Lupowitz, Allen's protagonist, is asked to
investigate the death of God. "God," a one-act play in Without
Feathers is also based on the death of God. The play is a modern
rendition of a Greek tragedy that gets out of control of both the
playwright and the actors. Zeus comes down from Mount Olympus to
set things right but is accidentally strangled by the machinery on
the set. Schechner feels that Allen's writing becomes less
significant and less entertaining as he strives for more order and
control, more maturity and responsibility. Schechner feels further
that what made Allen's earlier works better was their surreal
quality bordering on chaos, their extraordinary imagination, and
their nervous energy. They were good because they were out of
control. In his later films the id is suppressed, and the ego has
taken over. Schechner laments the passing of a rare and gifted
child.

Richard Brautigan (1935-1984)

922. Begnal, Kate. "Dreaming of Babylon as a Laughing Matter."
      WHIMSY 2 (1984): 53-55.

        Quotes C. Card, the private detective in Dreaming of Babylon,
as saying, "this could be very funny if it was a laughing matter."
Begnal discusses the humor of the novel, the one-line jokes, the
wisecracks, the obscene insults, the physical humor, the
literalizations of clichés, the diatribes with ironic twists, and
the various overturnings of reader expectations. In most detective
stories there is the super detective who can solve all mysteries,
beat all opponents, attract all desirable women, and impose his
definitions on justice and society at large. But C. Card has none
of these qualities. The novel begins with a standard joke: "January
2, 1941 had some good news and some bad news." The good news is
that Card has been declared 4F and will therefore not be drafted
into the Second World War. The bad news is that he is a detective
with a case, but he does not have any bullets for his gun. Card's
mother blames him for having killed his father when he was four
years old. Card's father was killed when he was hit by a car trying
to retrieve his son's ball. So Card's mother says that he made her
a widow, and she calls him a "bastard after the fact for losing his
father so early." At the end of the case, Card does not get the
money and an office and a pretty secretary to make love to. Rather
he finds a dead whore in his refrigerator. The parody in Dreaming
of Babylon comes from Brautigan's setting up his readers to expect
a typical hard-boiled detective novels, but then Brautigan violates
their expectations by giving them something different. "Babylon" in
the title of the novel is Card's fantasy world, where he runs to
whenever life gets too difficult.

923. Kolin, Philip C. "Food for Thought in Richard Brautigan's Trout
      Fishing in America." Studies in Contemporary Satire 8 (Spring
      1981): 9-20.

        Discusses the food images in Trout Fishing in America. The
novel satirically evaluates America by examining America's food
fetishes. It discusses America's food supply and eating habits as

well as the description, preparation, and spoilage of food. Food images are throughout the novel, from the first chapter where the poor are given a sandwich of spinach leaves to the last word of the novel, "mayonnaise." There is even a chapter which contains a recipe on how to prepare a compote of apples and ketchup. The picaro narrator of the novel travels through the Northwest and California and makes judgments about people's morals based on what they eat and drink. One of Brautigan's creeks is described as being like a beer belly, and there are place names like Mushroom Springs and Salt Creek. Trout Fishing in America is a novel of the absurd in which American values are turned upside down. In the novel, inedible objects become food, and trout becomes waste symbolizing our perverted traditional values. American industrialization and bureaucracy and loss of emotional ties is jeopardizing American values; the trout has become one of the endangered species, and fruits and seeds have become sour and infertile. Kolin believes that Trout Fishing in America provides readers with much "food for thought" about the problems plaguing America.

Ken Kesey (1935-)

924. Safer, Elaine B. "The Absurd Quest and Black Humor in Ken Kesey's Sometimes a Great Notion." The Contemporary American Comic Epic: The Novels of Barth, Pynchon, Gaddis, and Kesey. Detroit: Wayne State Univ. Press, 1988, 138-55.

Places Sometimes a Great Notion into the same category as other postmodern novels in having black humor, encyclopedic and epic scope, and an absurdist and farcical perspective. Our traditional heroes--Hercules, Ulysses and Aeneas--are replaced by comicstrip heroes--Captain Marvel, Superman, Plasticman, and the Flash--thereby making our heroes one dimensional and easier to contemplate. Safer notes that during his heyday as a cult hero Kesey would often attend psychedelyic events dressed in a white cape and leotards, playing the role of one of his superheroes. Kesey uses the comic book style both in Sometimes a Great Notion and in One Flew Over the Cuckoo's Nest, thereby reducing complex and multifaceted issues to simple issues of good versus evil. Kesey is a caricaturist who presents the individualistic Stamper clan as an uncompromising never-give-an-inch family in conflict with the evil labor union which requires conformity of all its members. There is a similar depiction of good versus evil in One Flew Over the Cuckoo's Nest, where the liberating hero is placed into conflict with the stultifying rules of the hospital. Terry Sherwood describes the protagonist as "an exemplary he-man versus a machine-tooled, castrating matriarch."

925. Shaw, Patrick W. "The American West as Satiric Territory: Kesey's One Flew Over the Cuckoo's Nest and Berger's Little Big Man. Studies in Contemporary Satire 10 (1983): 1-8.

Agrees with Terry Sherwood that Ken Kesey's philosophy is not based on religion or history but rather comes from comic books, radio serials, and Saturday matinees. Shaw sees R. P. Murphy as the sidekick of every American boy who buckles on his cap pistols and rides off on his stick horse only to be squelched by the omnipresent matriarchial society trying to make him "civilized." Kesey's satiric messages come through clearly and unambiguously; he advocates laughter, sensuality, and camaraderie. Kesey's heroes are like the legendary heroes of frontier America fighting for their individual freedoms. In One Flew Over the Cuckoo's Nest, Kesey expects the reader to embrace the laughing male and reject the dour female. Big Nurse is a mad controller of her world, but although the reader identitifies with McMurphy the reader still realizes that turning control over to the McMurphys of the world would be no improvement. But Shaw notes that this is an irony which is unintentional in the novel and which Kesey may not even himself see, for Kesey views McMurphy as the Lone Ranger or Mighty Mouse and Nurse Ratched as the evil enemy. Shaw views the main problem of the novel to be Kesey's inability to divorce himself from McMurphy. He attempted to do this by making Chief Bromden the narrator of the novel; however McMurphy dominates the stage, making Chief Bromden merely the "conveyer of the Word" about McMurphy. So the result is that Chief Bromden provides a more subjective view of McMurphy rather than a more objective view, and the shift in the point of view that results from having Chief Bromden as the narrator also weakens the satiric effect of the novel.

926. Wallace, Ronald. "What Laughter Can Do: Ken Kesey's One Flew Over the Cuckoo's Nest." The Last Laugh: Form and Affirmation in the Contemporary American Comic Novel. Columbia: Univ. of Missouri Press, 1979, 90-114.

Presents the mixed reactions that One Flew Over the Cuckoo's Nest has motivated. Even though the novel has been widely read and highly successful and has become a popular school textbook, an off-Broadway play, and a celebrated film, it has been criticized as "macho" and "sexist," portraying women as dangerous "ball-cutters." The novel also portrays Blacks as ugly caricatures of evil. Thus the novel seems to accept and reinforce the worst attitudes prevelant in our society. But Wallace suggests that many critics are incorrect in their evaluations of the novel because they are reading it as a romance rather than as a comedy. A romance should be read in terms of various antithetical concepts--the self versus the society, the human versus the mechanical, the emotional versus the reasonable, the primitive versus the civilized, freedom versus control, in sum, heart versus mind. But Wallace suggests that the novel should not be read as a romance. It is clear that McMurphy's life style--fighting, fucking, violence and sex--is just as manipulative as is Big Nurse's shock therapy and lobotomies. And ironically, the dictums of "enjoy" and "be free" can be just as repressive and constricting as the dictum of conformity. There is also a comic reversal of expectations and inversion of values. In real life it is males who are usually oppressive and domineering, but in the novel the male and female roles have been reversed, so that in the asylum weak, ineffectual men are being controlled by strong, domineering women.

Fred Chappell (1936-)

927. Niessen de Abruna, Laura. "Fred Chappell." Encyclopedia of
     American Humorists. Ed. Steven H. Gale. New York: Garland,
     1988, 75-81.

     Describes Chappell as a social critic, a humorist, a
philosopher and a poet with a talent for strong vernacular dialogue
and expressive natural imagery. Chappell writes about the rural
mountain country of western North Carolina, and his writing
sometimes takes on a Dantean perspective as Chappell attempts to
classify all world events as either good or evil. Chappell's
characters react to the absurdity of their situations in detached
and humorless ways, and this reaction accounts for much of the
humor. Niessen de Abruna considers humor a major force in
Chappell's most recent work, I Am One of You Forever, a collection
of short stories. His tetralogy, Midquest is a verse novel evoking
laughter through eccentric characters like Virgil Campbell, a
backwoods ringtail roarer. He exaggerates and he boasts as he tells
his story to the incredulous and amused J. T. and Fred. Virgil
Campbell gets his values and his imagery from the natural world.
Chappell is very accurate in portraying the language and the values
of the mountain folk of western North Carolina. He captures their
voice, their images, and their hatred of pretension and hypocrisy.

928. Niesen de Abruna, Laura. "Fred Chappell and Southern Humor in
     Midquest and I Am One of You Forever." WHIMSY 6 (1989): 23-25.

     Considers Virgil Campbell in Midquest to be the major source
of amusement in the tetralogy. There is a poem devoted to Campbell
in each of the volumes. In River it is "Dead Soldiers"; in
Bloodfire it is "Firewater"; in Wind Mountain it is "Three Sheets in
the Wind"; and in Earthsleep it is "At the Grave of Virgil
Campbell." "Dead Soldiers" is about the 1946 flood that threatened
to destroy Fiberville bridge. Rather than being overwhelmed by the
disaster Virgil fights back by shooting at the whiskey jars (dead
soldiers) that float out of his basement. "Firewater" is a tall
tale about a moonshiner named Big Mama who gets to parade down Main
Street with her model still. The mule walking behind her float gets
staggeringly drunk just from the fumes. "Three Sheets in the Wind"
has Campbell telling J. T. about the time he was caught with a
"frolic girl." They are caught in her bedroom, and Virgil escapes
naked and covers himself with a sheet hung out to dry. Elsie sews
him into the sheet and beats him with a curtain rod while Virgil
believes that he has died and gone to Hell. "At the Grave of Virgil
Campbell" is more elegaic than humorous. All of Midquest presents
life through comic and optimistic eyes. Chappell lightens the tone
of the novels by presenting Virgil Campbell as an eccentric,
independent, hard-drinking preacher-cussing mountain shopkeeper.
Virgil's vernacular stories and tall tales, his exaggerations, hard
drinking, boasting, and independence are firmly in the tradition of
nineteenth-century southern humor. Niesen de Abruna considers
Campbell to be Huck Finn, only a little older and less naive.

929. Ragan, David Paul. "At the Grave of Sut Lovingood: Virgil
     Campbell in the Work of Fred Chappell." The Mississippi
     Quarterly 37.1 (Winter 1984): 21-30.

     Suggests that Chappell's Midquest is a "semi-autobiographical
verse novel" that owes a great debt to the oral traditions of yarn
spinning in the Old Southwest in general and the Southern
Appalachians in particular. Chappell has acknowledged his debt to
Augustus Baldwin Longstreet and to Mark Twain; however Ragan
believes that Chappell is even more indebted to George Washington
Harris. Even though Virgil Campbell is grounded in the twentieth
century and has a greater distance from the land, he is similar to
Sut Lovingood in many respects. Virgil has Sut's prejudices, his
brutality, his cowardice, his sensuality, his coarseness, and his
vulgarity. Like Sut Lovingood, Virgil Campbell extolls truth and
freedom and hates hypocrisy. Furthermore, Virgil's father, J. T.,
has the same function in Virgil's poems as does George in Sut's
yarns. He is an outsider, a genteel observer who serves as a foil
for the narrator of outrageous tales. Both Sut Lovingood and Virgil
Campbell represent freedom and independence. They both experience
life directly and unashamedly, not bound by rigid codes of thinking
and behavior. It may be true that both Sut and Virgil tell lies,
but these lies contain higher truths--truths which are not bound to
a particular time or place.

Florence King (1936-)

930. Van Spackeren, Kathryn. "Pop Anthropology as Humor: The Works
     of Florence King." Kennesaw Review 1.2 (Spring 1988): 50-58.

     Compares King's taxonomy of types--WASPs, American men,
Southerners, etc.--with the taxonomies of the French encyclopedists
and of the structural anthropologists. In Confessions of a Failed
Southern Lady (1985), King tells how she became a writer. She was
in the University of Mississippi library writing a grant application
so that she could continue work on her M.A. degree when she ran
across Writer's Market. There she discovered that she could get
five cents a word writing for True Confessions, which seemed a safer
bet than applying for a grant, so she started writing for True
Confessions. Her first article was entitled, "I Committed Adultery
in a Diabetic Coma." Between 1964 and 1967 King was a feature
writer for the Raleigh News and Observer. Between 1968 and 1972 she
wrote thirty-seven pornographic novels under various pseudonyms,
novels like Moby's Dick, but then she stopped, finding formulaic
writing tedious. Since 1975 she has published five books under her
own name, all of them deft, witty, and provocative. The first is
entitled Southern Ladies and Gentlemen (1975), and sets the tone for
the other four novels to follow. King's tone is brisk and jokey as
she investigates a number of psychological issues. King suggests
that Southern women are expected to be frigid but passionate, sweet
but bitchy, and, above all, scatterbrained. King feels that one of
the Southern woman's many difficulties is that she succeeds in
matching the stereotype. King has also written a number of other
humorous novels, such as WASP, Where Is Thy Sting? (1977), He: An
Irreverent Look at the American Male (1978), and When Sisterhood Was
in Flower (1982).

Larry McMurtry (1936-)

931 Kehl, D. G. "Thalia's "Sock" and the Cowhide Boot: Humor of the
    New Southwest in the Fiction of Larry McMurtry." Southwestern
    American Literature 14.2 (Spring 1989): 20-33.

Affirms the appropriateness of Thalia as the name of the small
Texas town in four of Larry McMurtry's earliest novels. Since
Thalia is the Greek muse of comedy, this name sets the ambivalent
and mock-heroic tone of these novels. But ambivalence and a mock-
heroic tone are qualities of McMurtry's other seven novels as well,
especially Lonesome Dove. Kehl suggests that the frontier spirit of
both the Old Southwest and the New Southwest have made an indelible
impression on the American psyche. The dominance of the Old
Southwest (Georgia, the Carolinas, Alabama, Tennessee, Arkansas, and
Louisiana) lasted only about twenty-six years (1835-1861), yet the
humor of the Old Southwest is the most consistent and sustained
humor genre in America. Likewise, the dominance of the New
Southwest (Texas, New Mexico, Arizona, Nevada, and Southern
California) with its cattle drives and cowboy-Indian confrontations
lasted only about twenty years, but nevertheless had an exaggerated
influence on the American imagination in the Western novels, pulp
magazines, movies, and television programs it stimulated. In
addition to this, Kehl notes that over half of the twenty subjects
and themes that Henig Cohen and William Dillingham listed as
characteristics of Old Southwestern humor can also be found, with
some variation, in the fiction of Larry McMurtry. "Games, horse
races, and other contests" become the rodeo in Moving On and The
Last Picture Show. "The hunt" becomes the cattle drive in Lonesome
Dove, and it becomes the picaresque search for antique junk in
Cadillac Jack. The "riverboat" becomes the horse or the pickup
truck.

Judith Viorst (1936-)

932. Dresner, Zita. "Delineating the Norm: Allies and Enemies in the
     Humor of Judith Viorst and Erma Bombeck." Thalia: Studies in
     Literary Humor 7.1 (Spring-Summer 1984): 28-34.

Relates Viorst's writing to her upbringing. She was raised by
upper-middle class, urban upwardly bound parents in a New Jersey
suburb of New York City. Through hard work, Viorst's parents had
risen out of their working-class heritage, so Viorst's parents
encouraged her to strive for social and economic success and develop
her intellectual and creative talents. At the same time, however,
they discouraged her from pursuing a career. Viorst was thus raised
as something of an anachronism. She had received a liberal
education from a good college and developed a liberal social
conscience, and she had a strong romantic desire to be something
other than a middle-class housewife. Viorst's solution was to
become a writer and to write about the ironies of this double-bind
situation to an audience that found itself in the same types of
double-bind situations. In "Nice Baby," for example, Viorst
contrasts last year, when she talked about black humor, the

flamenco, and the impact of the common market on the European economy, with this year, when, because she has a baby, she must talk about nursing versus bottle-feeding and the problems of finding a baby sitter. Viorst's audience laughs at Viorst's persona, but more importantly they laugh at the problems that obsess and disturb her. Viorst's poems are not so much about a particular protagonist who appears ridiculous as they are about all of us who, no matter who we are, want to be something else. In "Anti-Heroine" she says she dreamt of being Heathcliff's Cathy, Lady Brett, or Scarlett O'Hara, but in real life she became an expert on buying Fritos and cleaning the cat box.

933. Walker, Nancy, and Zita Dresner. "Judith Viorst." Redressing the Balance: American Women's Literary Humor from Colonial Times to the 1980s. Jackson: Univ. Press of Mississippi, 1988, 373-80.

    Describes Viorst's humor as resulting from the conflict between what women are and what they want to or think they ought to be. Her first volume of verse is entitled The Village Square (1965) and is based on her life in Greenwich Village. This book establishes the persona and issues which will be further explored in later volumes, It's Hard to Be Hip over Thirty (1968), People and Other Aggravations (1971), and How Did I get to be Forty and Other Atrocities (1976). Viorst describes her own verse as "aggravation recollected in tranquillity," as she plays the woman's role of trying to be all things to all people. Viorst's poetry can be described as obsessively self-critical.

Gail Godwin (1937-)

934. Riedell, Karen. "Gail Godwin's Comic-Gothic Novels." WHIMSY 6 (1988): 145-47.

    Considers Gail Godwin's The Odd Woman, Violet Clay, and A Mother and Two Daughters feminist comedies in the Gothic tradition. The Gothic features in these three novels are distorted, however, and the result is somewhat ironic. In her modern rendition of the Gothic tradition, Godwin blends the natural with the supernatural and the weird. Like authors of straightforward Gothic novels, Godwin is concerned with terrors, but she confronts the terrors, thereby exorcising them. Like Jane Austen and Charlotte Bronte before her, Godwin has transformed the Gothic form to her own purposes. In the traditional Gothic novel, imagination is often the source for fear, but in Godwin's novels the imagination can also be a way of overcoming fear and assuming control. At the beginning of The Odd Woman, Jane Clifford, the protagonist, hears a loud noise outside of her bedroom window and assumes that it is "the Enema Bandit," who attacks women and gives them enemas. This is a parody of the Gothic hero-villain antithesis that arose out of the chivalric tradition whereby women were denigrated by people who were pretending to serve and honor them. The protagonist in Violet Clay has Gothic-style dreams. In one such dream she is approached by two masked figures. One of them makes her part her legs while the other one brandishes a poker. "Relax," says one of the figures. "We've only come to clean out your fireplace." Consistent with the Gothic

tradition, Godwin's supernatural forces are ambiguous, allowing
either natural or supernatural explanations. Riedell feels that the
humorous Gothic tradition is appropriate for exploring the
transitional state of today's women.

Cyra McFadden (1937-)

935. Walker, Nancy, and Zita Dresner. "Cyra McFadden." Redressing
     the Balance: American Women's Literary Humor from Colonial
     Times to the 1980s. Jackson: Univ. Press of Mississippi, 1988,
     416-22.

     Notes McFadden's ambivalent feelings toward her father. In
her memoir entitled Rain or Shine (1986), she credits her "silver-
tongued" charismatic father for her love for language even though he
lived hand to mouth and was an alcoholic. McFadden's 1977 novel,
The Serial, became a best seller. It is a tongue-in-cheek
documentary soap opera about a year in the life of Marin County,
California, during the 1970s. The novel exposes the fads, the
languages, and the habits of the women who have little else to do
than worry about other women's waistlines and husbands. McFadden
has also been a regular contributor to the New York Times, McCall's,
The Nation, and Smithsonian.

Thomas Pynchon (1937-)

936. Fletcher, M. D. "Pynchon's The Crying of Lot 49: Post-Modern
     Apologue." Contemporary Political Satire: Narrative Strategies
     in the Post-Modern Context. New York: Lanham, 1987, 113-36.

     Contrasts Lot 49, an apologue which presents the world as an
"either-or" dilemma with Gravity's Rainbow, a contemporary jeremiad.
Fletcher presents Pynchon's argument in Lot 49 in terms of a number
of logical cause-effect relations. The basic assumption is that
reality is not understandable, but a paradoxical corollary
assumption is that interpretion is unavoidable. As a result, we
find patterns whether the patterns exist or not, and furthermore,
these patterns present themselves as binary and exclusive
(either/or), and since our lives must be structured and patterned,
these patterns tend to become ossified and institutionalized. And
in terms of syllogistic reasoning, this leads to the "excluded
middle," but it also leads to the appearance of a legitimate logical
argument, and the results are therefore resistent to criticism or
change. Pynchon feels that political solutions are especially prone
to this binary conceptualization and institutionalization. This
explains not only the tenacity with which people hold onto their
systems but the American Pentagon's paranoid insistence on seeing
conspiracies everywhere, for these conspiracies threaten the
Pentagon's system of belief. Pynchon's Lot 49 is studded with
Pentagon acronyms like W.A.S.T.E. (We Await Silent Tristeros
Empire), which is darkly humorous in that it is placed on rubbish-
bin-like mail boxes, and also in that it echoes the Vietnam War
euphemism of "to waste" meaning "to kill," and thus blends the

mundane with the menacing. Character names have this same quality--
Oedipa Maas, Genghis Cohen, Dr. Hilarius, and Manny Di Presso.

937. Harris, Charles B. "Death and Absurdity: Thomas Pynchon and the
     Entropic Vision." Contemporary American Novelists of the
     Absurd. New Haven, Connecticut: College and Univ. Press, 1971,
     76-99.

        Suggests that the main contributing factor to a sense of the
absurd is a feeling of meaninglessness, anxiety, and imminent death.
But Pynchon's concern is not just with the death of individuals; it
is with cosmic decay and the resultant death of the universe. And
the cause of this death is entropy. The second law of
thermodynamics states that there must be a gradual leveling of the
energy in the universe. This leveling or loss of energy can be seen
in steam engines and in human beings, and it applies equally well to
cultures or to galaxies. In all of these, time is moving
irreversibly towards death or towards chaos, which is the same
thing. In his novels, Pynchon looks at the process of entropy as it
relates to social systems. Man like his universe is in a constant
state of decay. There are accidents and natural disasters and wars,
crises and riots. There are dehumanizing processes where a
mechanized society transforms man into an animal or into a machine.
Pynchon has written a short story entitled "Entropy" about Callistro
a fifty-five-year-old student of thermodynamics who is obsessed with
the prospect of "heat-death." Callistro converts his apartment into
a hothouse filled with birds, plants, and art objects that is immune
from the deterioration that is going on outside. Pynchon's V is
also concerned with human and social disintegration, as again,
entropy is the central metaphor. Here involuted chronology, comic
chapter headings, and two-dimensional characters with funny names
are all absurd ways of dealing with an inevitable process of
deterioration. Pynchon's absurdity is based not only on the concept
of entropy, but on Werner Heisenberg's "uncertainty principle" as
well.

938. Henkle, Roger B. "The Morning and the Evening Funnies: Comedy
     in Gravity's Rainbow. Approaches to Gravity's Rainbow." Ed.
     Charles Clerc. Columbus: Ohio State Univ. Press, 1983, 273-90.

        Discusses Pirate Prentice's outrageous banana breakfast which
consists of banana omelets, mashed bananas molded in the shape of a
British lion rampant, banana croissants, banana mead, and banana
flambé. The banana is a parody of the rocket; both are phallic
symbols, and both play prominently as symbols in Gravity's Rainbow.
Rocket imagery even invades Pynchon's candy concoctions. He talks
about an English bonbon that is in the shape of a six-ton earthquake
bomb which detonates in Slothrop's mouth like an explosive charge,
deadening his nerves and sending "freezing frosty-grape alveolar
clusters" into his lungs and giving him a temporary floating
sensation very much like a sexual climax. Henkle describes the
central purpose of the novel to be the "metaphorical reduction of
the fearful into the playful." In Pynchon's universe seriousness is
not acceptable, as only characters like Roger Mexico and Tyrone
Slothrop, characters who are able to laugh at themselves, are able
to escape their obsessions and survive. Pointsman lacks a sense of
humor and is doomed to live within his obsessions until they "grow
surrealistically supernatural and devour him." The comedy of

Gravity's Rainbow occurs in four stages. At first, it is there to
vent the anxieties and the pressures of the outside world. Later it
is used to deal with life in the Zone, "penetrating deep into its
own perverse shadows." Then it becomes an uninhibited, frenetic
improvisation to cope with the problems of randomness. And finally,
it leads us to a mastery of an emerging new comic vision.

939. Price, Penelope. "The Komical Kamikazes: Dying of Laughter in
     Gravity's Rainbow." WHIMSY 1 (1983): 101-102.

     Concentrates on the subtitle of Pynchon's Gravity's Rainbow,
which is "A Moment of Fun with Takeshi and Ichio, the Komical
Kamikazes."   As the subtitle suggests, these characters are
ridiculous and cartoonlike in their proportions, forcing us to
develop an attitude of aloofness. The "Komical Kamikazes" are
stationed on a remote island during World War II, and they are not
informed that the war is over. They are committed to dying for the
war, but every morning when they go to the radar shack manned by Old
Kenosho to find out when they can die they are informed that it is
not yet time. So on moonless nights they cover themselves with
dried Cypridinae, which makes them glow in the dark, and run around
giggling under the palm trees. It is ironic that dead fish is the
source of their light. The novel is so filled with outlandish
images--the giant adenoid, the banana breakfast, Gregori the
Octupus--that it becomes surreal. Old Kenoshi is struck by the
humor of the fact that the Komical Kamikazes are unable to die for
their noble cause, so he writes a haiku about the occasion: "The
lover leaps into the volcano! / It's ten feet deep, And inactive--."

940. Safer, Elaine B. "Pynchon's World and Its Legendary Past: Humor
     and the Absurd in a Twentieth-Century Vineland." Critique:
     Studies in Contemporary Fiction 32.2 (1990): 107-25.

     Considers Zoyd Wheeler of Vineland to be a schlemiel figure
who is continually frustrated in his attempts to be reunited with
his wife, Frenesi. Prairie, their daughter, tries to get closer to
her mother by piecing together secrets from her mother's past. As
the title suggests, Vineland is about contemporary California
society, and about the ludicrous, extravagant, and destructive
behavior of many Californians. These Californians are interested in
all of the new fads such as Zen, the martial arts, and the New Age
movement. The fact that the novel begins in 1984 suggests a
connection with George Orwell, and this connection is reinforced by
the characters' obsessions with the television screen.   The
difference is that Pynchon's characters view the TV screen
voluntarily, but their viewing isn't truly voluntary, because many
of them are addicted. Pynchon calls those who are addicted to TV
Thanatoids, and Pynchon names the addiction center to which
Thanatoids are sent the Tubaldetox Institution. Pynchon's writing
is compelling, as he moves swiftly between high and low style, and
between farce and horror. His writing is also filled with
slapstick, incongruity, verbal play, and puns.

941. Safer, Elaine B. "The Tall Tale, the Absurd, and Black Humor in Thomas Pynchon's V. and Gravity's Rainbow." The Contemporary American Comic Epic: The Novels of Barth, Pynchon, Gaddis, and Kesey. Detroit: Wayne State Univ. Press, 1988, 79-110.

Proposes that Pynchon's V. (1963) satirizes man's quest for meaning in a world which has no meaning. Our world is absurd because of the discrepancy between the human mind which desires and the world which disappoints. Pynchon, like Barth and other black humorists, intentionally disorients the reader by shifting quickly between horror and farce. Pynchon uses methods of the tall-tale teller in developing episodes that appear fantastic, but then he brings the problem into a modern perspective by involving the reader emotionally in the tension of the story. In the end, he will point out the work's artifice. Pynchon uses slapstick, incongruity, verbal play, and puns to accomplish his task. Safer portrays Pynchon's Benny Profane as a character who sometimes represents a "comedy of errors" and sometimes "a comedy of terrors." The tall tales present heroes whose accomplishments are larger than life; the tall tales in V. conform to this pattern. However, the characters in V. tend to be fearful and paranoid rather than bragging and confident. They are schlemiels who exaggerate and fantasize, but the result tends to be grotesque, farcical and horrible, because the black-humor tone of Pynchon merges distress with laughter and horror with farce.

942. Schulz, Max F. "The Politics of Parody; and, the Comic Apocalypses of Jorge Luis Borges, Thomas Berger, Thomas Pynchon, and Robert Coover." Black Humor Fiction of the Sixties: A Plurastic Definition of Man and His World. Athens: Ohio Univ. Press, 1973, 66-90.

Considers Pynchon's V. to be a baroque parody of the obsession of humans to find patterns in events. It is a parody of the spy tale, the romance, the political novel, the Oedipus quest, and the documentary. It echoes the symbolic texture of Conrad, the complex dreams of Freud, the social commentary of Dos Passos, the aesthetic decadence of Nabokov, the wasteland mythography of Eliot and the moral vision of Faulkner. It also parodies more general themes, like the technological apprehension of science fiction, the empty heroics of comic opera and the utopianism of Lost Horizon. V. also parodies the U.S. state department that finds patterns of conspiracy in unrelated incidents, conspiracies which displace the actual events and give them new significances. The title V. is a bilingual pun, based on the German word "Wie" meaning "how." Since German "Wie" is a question word, the title "V." is not meant as an answer; it is meant as a question. The world of V. is multifacted and pluralistic. It represents unlimited perspectives, and reality is to emerge out of some reconciliation of the diverse points of view.

943. Tylee, Claire. "Metaphor in the Early Fiction of Thomas Pynchon: A Study of Entropy." Literary and Linguistic Aspects of Humor: Actas del VII AEDEAN Congreso. Ed. Patricia Shaw. Madrid, Spain: Universidad Complutense, 1983, 219-25.

Explains that Pynchon wrote four important comic short stories before he wrote the three comic novels for which he is famous. "The Small Rain" was published in The Cornell Writer (1959); "Mortality

and Mercy in Vienna" was published in Epoch (1959); "Lowlands" was
published in New World Writing (1960), and "Entropy" was published
in Kenyon Review (1960). Both "Entropy" and "Mortality and Mercy in
Vienna" involve bureaucrats, and both are set in Washington during
the McCarthy era. The McCarthy era lasted the seven years from 1950
to 1957. "Entropy" is set in 1957 and is about middle-aged
Callistro, who has spent the last seven years creating his
hermetically sealed hothouse jungle that is designed to insulate him
and his lover, Aubade, from the city's chaos, its weather, its
politics, and its civil disorder. On a different floor of the same
house where Callistro's hothouse apartment is located Meatball
Mulligan is in his fortieth hour of an uninhibited lease-breaking
party. Meatball's raucous anarchic party below is meant to contrast
contrapunctally with Callistro's hothouse above. Tylee feels that
Pynchon never intended his stories to have definitive readings, for
they are richly allusive like a poem or a myth or a musical fugue.
Tylee further suggests that Pynchon's endings tend to be ambivalent.
"Lowlands" ends with Flange agreeing to stay underground "for a
while at least." In "The Small Rain" the reader is uncertain if
Levine has returned to his starting position, as Levine says, "Back?
Oh, yeah, I guess so." "Entropy" ends as Callistro and Aubade sit
waiting for Meatball's fugue to end.

Hunter S. Thompson (1937-)

944. Caron, James E. "The High White Sound: Hunter S. Thompson's The
    Curse of Lono as Contemporary Tall Tale." WHIMSY 3 (1985): 41-
    43.

    Refers to the tension of The Curse of Lono as "the high white
sound," an expression which Thompson himself also used. This
metaphor identifies the tension as modern, suggesting as it does
electronic distortion. Caron traces The Curse of Lono to the
nineteenth-century American backwoodsmen who told tall tales either
about fumbling a chance to shoot a bear or about successfully
shooting a bear in an extraordinary and unbelievable manner
involving great luck. The characters in such stories are either
slow witted or clever only in narrow, mean or petty ways that are
usually manifest in various types of practical jokes. Caron
suggests that this tradition continues in the cartoon violence
involving Tom and Jerry, Sylvester and Tweety Pie, or Wile E. Coyote
and the Roadrunner. These characters are like Sut Lovingood and
Hunter S. Thompson in never being in any real danger. The reader
laughs at Thompson because he is out of control and because he has
self-destructive impulses and acts mechanically just like Tom,
Sylvester, or Wile E. Coyote.

945. Caron, James E. "Hunter S. Thompson's "Gonzo" Journalism and
    the Tall Tale Tradition in America." Studies in Popular
    Culture 8.1 (1985): 1-16.

    Compares Hunter S. Thompson's "gonzo" journalism to that of
Mark Twain. Both of these journalists were "spit-polished, copper-
bottomed, double-boiler yarnspinners" for which "facts are just so
much cord-wood fuel for the imagination." Caron traces gonzo
journalism to the long history of yarn spinning and suggests that

Thompson's The Curse of Lono is best understood if read as a tall
tale. The basic assumption of gonzo journalism is that reporting
should have a certain aesthetic dimension, best achieved by applying
techniques and devices that are usually associated with novels and
short stories. Tom Wolfe suggests that applying such techniques to
the writing of lively and interesting non-fiction does not sacrifice
accuracy. In fact, such writing requires the reporter to spend days
or even weeks on assignment in intimate subjective and emotional
interactions in order to absorb the details and become able to think
like the subjects. This will provide an equal footing between the
observer and the observed. Thus Thompson can become the protagonist
of his own stories, and furthermore imagination can replace memory
as a guide to reporting people's thoughts and feelings. Caron feels
that both Fear and Loathing in Las Vegas and The Curse of Lono
represent the far end of gonzo journalism's ability to metamorphose
itself from non-fiction to fiction. America's frontier yarnspinners
told tall tales to react to the fact that life was brutish and
uncertain. Caron feels that Thompson's gonzo yarns, based on truth,
and prone to drifting into violent and sometimes self-destructive
behavior echo America's antebellum comic writing.

946. Steinbrink, Jeffrey. "Mark Twain and Hunter Thompson:
      Continuity and Change in American 'Outlaw Journalism.'"
      Studies in American Humor NS2.3 (Winter 1984): 221-35.

      Compares Mark Twain and Hunter Thompson in their reporting
techniques.   Both of these reporters were able to distance
themselves from the material and add their own idiosyncratic writing
talents to their stories, which contrasts drastically with the
traditional, eastern, or "straight" journalism that prevails. Gonzo
journalism is "aggressive, subjective, intensely imaginative,
determinedly iconoclastic and unremittingly literary." It is mostly
picaresque, and mainly follows a comic central character, often the
author, through a series of episodes and (mis)adventures. The basic
assumption of gonzo journalism is that traditional journalism is
rooted in a lie. Thompson says, "With the possible exception of
things like box scores, race results, and stock market tabulations,
there is no such thing as Objective Journalism.   The phase is a
pompous contradiction of terms." Thompson and Twain are observing
a truth that transcends mere facts and documentary. This truth
conforms to William Faulkner's notion that the best fiction is far
more true than is any kind of journalism.   Gonzo journalism frees
the writer from the narrow confines of facts and allows him to
discover and reveal the larger, seminal truths.   Steinbrink feels
that Thompson's shadow does not fill that cast by Twain, but he
feels that the two shadows have a dark and foreboding intersection
in their "orneriness, heterodoxy, profanity and brooding
seriousness."

John Kennedy Toole (1937-1969)

947. McKeen, William. "John Kennedy Toole." Encyclopedia of American
     Humorists. Ed. Steven H. Gale. New York: Garland, 1988, 451-
     53.

      Recounts the tragic story of Toole's life and death. Toole
wrote a massive and rich comedy entitled A Confederacy of Dunces but
had difficulty finding a publisher for the novel.   One publisher
showed interest and requested a number of revisions but then decided
against publication. Toole was depressed over the rejection of his
book, and in Biloxi, Mississippi, he committed suicide in March of
1969. John's mother convinced Walker Percy to read John's novel and
Percy was so impressed that he convinced Louisiana State University
Press to publish John's novel. It was published and received the
Pulitzer Prize for fiction in 1981. The front page of the 1981
edition states: "POSTHUMOUS PULITZER GIVEN TO WRITER WHO COULDN'T
GET NOVEL PUBLISHED."   The novel tells the hilarious story of
Ignatius J. Reilly as he confronts the modern age. McKeen feels
that except for Toole's suicide, the timing of the novel was
excellent, because John Irving published The World According to Garp
in 1978, and this set the stage for Toole's A Confederacy of Dunces.
Irving's book was hugely successful, and Toole's book had the same
wild and colorful characters and bizarre occurrences.

948. Ruppersburg, Hugh. "The South and John Kennedy Toole's A
     Confederacy of Dunces." Studies in American Humor NS5.2-3
     (Summer-Fall 1986): 118-26.

      Considers A Confederacy of Dunces to be firmly grounded in the
southern literary tradition while at the same time representing the
urban alienation literature that flourished during the 1950s and
1960s by J. D. Salinger, Philip Roth, Saul Bellow, Joseph Heller,
and others. Even though Confederacy is set in an urban environment,
Ruppersburg views it as a Southern novel. Ignatius J. Reilly
believes in traditions, morality, and human dignity, and he believes
in trying to punish those who do not have these values.   Like
Faulkner's V. K. Ratliff and Harris' Sut Lovingood, Ignatius is a
fool killer, but unlike Ratliff and Lovingood, Ignatius believes
that he himself is morally superior, and therefore his pranks that
are designed to expose the hypocrisy of his victims only confirm his
own foolishness. Confederacy is linked to the tradition of southern
literature not only in the attitudes of the protagonist but also in
the local color presented. The novel is rich in dialect, vivid
descriptions of setting, and development of a variety of colorful
ethnic characters. But part of Toole's local color relates to the
lower middle-class Catholic urban atmosphere of New Orleans, the
setting for the novel. Many of the streets and places talked about
in the novel actually exist; thus Ruppersburg considers New Orleans
to be a necessary aspect of the story.   Ignatius is a quasi-
intellectual adult man who lives with his mother in New Orleans. He
despises farm land, stimulates dissension among factory workers, and
is saddened by the country's improper understanding of geometry and
theology. He is a southern protagonist but not a typical one.

949. Stewart, Penny. "Ignatius J. Reilly and the Peter Pan Syndrome." WHIMSY 4 (1986): 26-27.

Considers Toole's protagonist to exhibit the "Peter Pan Syndrome" discussed by Dr. Dan Kiley. He has all of the symptoms--narcissism, chauvinism, irresponsibility, anxiety, loneliness, and difficulty determining appropriate sexual behavior. Reiley considers himself to be a genius in conflict with a world of dummies. He is against anything modern and feels that he should not be required to work. He dislikes everybody and leaves New Orleans in search of a better place with better people. Myrna Minkoff is his sometime-girlfriend, but Myrna also is his "mother" in the Never-Never Land Ignatius lives in.

950. Tadie, Andrew. "John Kennedy Toole's Confederacy of Dunces. WHIMSY 3 (1985): 66-68.

Discusses the humor of Toole's 1981-Pulitzer-Prize winning novel. Ignatious J. Reilly sells Paradise hot dogs on the streets of New Orleans. His sign reads, "Twelve inches of Paradise." Tadie describes Ignatius as a brazen irreverent gargantuan oaf with a Master's Degree, who is convinced that the world is corrupt because it is not medieval. Ignatius tells everyone he meets that the modern world is too materialistic with people tripping over themselves trying to get the latest gadgets, while the medieval world was superior in its theology, geometry, taste, and decency. As he peddles his hot dogs, he wears an outlandish pirate's costume and meets a kaleidoscope of characters such as Dorean Greene, the homosexual who runs a home for homosexuals. Boethius' Consolation of Philosophy almost becomes a character in the novel in terms of its significance to the story line. In the last quarter of the novel, Ignatius lends his copy of The Consolation of Philosophy to Officer Mancuso. The book is taken from Mancuso during an abortive arrest and changes hands several times before Ignatious gets it back. And toward the end of the book Ignatius reveals himself as a fraud as he refers to the fortunae rota in the book, describing Fortuna of the wheel of fortune as an uncaring, inconstant woman who elevates or crushes men at her pleasure. There are many levels of humor in the novel but especially the humor of characterizations and the humor of improbable or coincidental events. Tadie suggests that the novel is, in the end, a medieval novel.

Ishmael Reed (1938-)

951. Uruburu, Paula. "Ishmael Reed." Encyclopedia of American Humorists. Ed. Steven H. Gale. New York: Garland, 1988, 359-62.

Describes the voice in Ishmael Reed's seven novels and four volumes of poetry, two collections of essays, and numerous articles as usually sardonic and deeply based in the aesthetic of what Reed calls "Neo-Hoo-Dooism." Reed's biting social satire and high comedy have been influenced by such Afro-American writers as Rudolph Fisher, George Schuyler, Wallace Thurman, and Zora Neale Hurston in the immediate past and to such writers as Juvenal and Jonathan Swift in the more distant past. To Reed, life is at the same time mysterious, holy, profound, exciting, serious, and fun. His satire is biting, but his tone is positive, affirming, and humble. His work doesn't take itself too seriously, and the conventions of comic literature are frequently the targets of his own comic literature. Reed ridicules past traditions and present authority. He exposes stereotypical attitudes and overly sentimental emotions. Much of Reed's inspiration comes from American folklore, popular culture, and history as seen through Afro-American eyes. Uruburu considers Reed to be at the forefront of the post-modern Black-American movement. Reed was described in The Nation as "the brightest contribution to American Satire since Mark Twain." In 1973 he won a Pulitzer Prize in poetry.

Paula Gunn Allen (1939-)

952, Walker, Nancy A. and Zita Dresner. "Paula Gunn Allen." Redressing the Balance: American Women's Literary Humor from Colonial Times to the 1980s. Jackson: Univ. Press of Mississippi, 1988, 443-45.

Describes Paula Gunn Allen as a poet, a critic, and a Sioux who is very conscious both of her Native-American and her female heritage. Her mother was a Laguna Sioux, and her father was Lebanese-American. Her first book of poetry was The Blind Lion (1974). She has since published several other books of poetry, plus a novel entitled The Woman Who Owned the Shadows (1983). Allen's "Taking a Visitor to See the Ruins" appeared in Open Places magazine in 1985. It contains several different types of humor as it is based on both a practical joke and a pun. It also humorously juxtaposes traditional pueblo dwellings with high-rise apartment buildings. Walker and Dresner feel that a sense of irony permeates Allen's work, a sense of irony that results in Allen's attempt to mediate between the mythology and heritage of her own Sioux background and contemporary Anglo-American culture.

Toni Cade Bambara (1939-)

953. Walker, Nancy A., and Zita Dresner. "Toni Cade Bambara." Redressing the Balance: American Women's Literary Humor from Colonial Times to the 1980s. Jackson: Univ. Press of Mississippi, 1988, 400-406.

Refers to Bambara's "deft use of irony" in her two collections of short stories (Gorilla, My Love [1982] and The Sea Birds Are Still Alive [1977]), and in her novel (The Salt Eaters [1981]) which won the American Book Award in 1981. Bambara's use of street dialect is a celebration of Black pride. She writes with warmth and wit, and her characters are well drawn. She specializes in adolescents, elderly people, and females of all ages and types. Her most common theme is the conflict between mothers who hold onto traditional values and daughters who have new ideas and are a bit militant in their ideals. Walker and Dresner point out that this is a theme that runs through the works of Black women writers from Zora

Neale Hurston to Dorothy West to Lorraine Hansberry and Paule
Marshall.

Thomas Francis McGuane III (1939-)

954. Carter, Albert Howard, III. "McGuane's First Three Novels:
Games, Fun, Nemesis." Critique: Studies in Modern Fiction.
17.1 (August 1975): 91-103.

Suggests that games structure the interplay between humor and
pathos in McGuane's three novels, The Sporting Club (1969), The
Bushwhacked Piano (1971), and Ninety-Two in the Shade (1973). Games
serve as a satiric criticism of the inflexible structures of our
society, and provide a nemesis-type of competitive opposition for
non-game reality. For McGuane, games include sports, hunting,
jokes, parties, art forms, con games, and mock duels, and they are
both physical and psychological in nature. Typically, McGuane
matches a protagonist like Quinn, Payne, or Skelton against an
antagonist like Stanton, Codd, or Dance, and then, to make the game
more interesting he throws a girl-into the competition like Janey,
Ann, or Miranda. Joyce Carol Oates praised The Sporting Club for
the light, fashionably cool tone, adding that McGuane has a good ear
for dialect and a good eye for the absurd. She also liked the crazy
pranks and jokes and the vigor and enthusiasm of the writing. The
Bushwhacked Piano has a different tone. There is still violence and
drama, and even more modulated humor than The Sporting Club, but it
"sprawls self-indulgently over time and space." The main image of
the novel, which is alluded to in the title, involves a child named
Nicholas, who is sitting in a tree shooting at a piano in his
neighbor's living room with his small-caliber rifle.   Carter
considers Ninety-Two in the Shade to be a spare, taut, and tragic
novel with both hilarity and satire throughout.

955. Moseley, Merritt. "Thomas Francis McGuane, III." Encyclopedia
of American Humorists. Ed. Steven H. Gale. New York: Garland,
1988, 303-305.

Considers The Bushwhacked Piano, McGuane's second novel, to be
his funniest and best. It is the unsettling and picaresque story of
Nicholas Payne, who devotes his life to travel. Nicholas starts in
Michigan, then goes to Montana, and finally ends up in Florida. He
aimlessly travels from place to place until he confronts C. J.
Clovis, a builder of bat towers, who sells these towers to farmers
for insect control. Much of the characterization of Nicholas is
achieved through contrast with a buttoned-down junior executive
named George Russell. The ending of the book is not a happy one.
The bat-tower business collapses; C. J. Clovis dies; Nicholas is
mutilated in a botched hemorrhoid operation; and Ann has left
Nicholas to be George's lover. But Nicholas has an indomitable
spirit, and the novel ends in triumph as Nicholas insists that he is
still at large. There are two types of humor in the novel: wit and
the involvement of characters in outlandish events. The tone of the
novel is manic and sometimes mordant as man plots against man and
nature in a never-ending struggle that often results in outrageous
self-expression and wild humor.

Maxine Hong Kingston (1940-)

956. Lightfoot, Marjorie J. "Kingston's Whimsy in China Men."
WHIMSY 4 (1986): 20-23.

Considers Kingston's humor to lie in juxtaposition.
Kingston's China Men contains eighteen sections, each section
autonomous and displaying a particular type of humor, but the humor
of witty juxtapositions of disparate materials forces the reader to
make critical comparisons and see analogies that point to universal
truths. Kingston also relies on the humor of role reversal. Her
short story entitled "On Discovery" is about a traveling man who is
accosted by ladies in the "Women's Land" and forced to undergo foot
binding and hair plucking to make him more attractive, sensual, and
passive. While he's serving a meal at the queen's court, the women
of the court make such comments as "She's pretty, don't you agree?"
The role reversals are intended to suggest that Chinese men would
not like to undergo the painful sexist treatment that is accorded to
Chinese women. A short story entitled "On Fathers" expresses the
humor of outward appearances as the narrator and her brothers and
sisters run to greet their father and ask for treats only to find
that they have startled a total stranger. "On Mortality Again" is
a short story about the Polynesian demi-god Maui the Trickster, who
tries to steal immortality from Hina by diving into her vagina at
night to steal her heart. He emerges from the vagina feet first, as
if from an unnatural childbirth, and a bird laughs so hard at the
event that Hina is awakened and closes her legs together and kills
Maui. His search for immortality has caused his death. China Men
displays paradoxical and ironic truths and uses analogies to teach
readers about life's many logical inconsistencies.

John Nichols (1940-)

957. Pellow, Ken. "From Humor to Comedy in the Novels of John
Nichols." WHIMSY 5 (1987): 33-35.

Contrasts the humor of John Nichols' first two novels with the
humor of his later New Mexico trilogy. Pookie and Jerry are the
characters most responsible for the humor in Sterile Cuckoo, and
Wendall Oler is the "comedian" in The Wizard of Loneliness. Pookie
especially is a masterful comic invention, as she has a fanciful way
of thinking about ordinary events. In explaining why her parents
had stayed married for so long, she says that for them the fear of
freedom kept them together as if this fear were some sort of a
nuclear deterrent. Her comparisons are also amusing. She describes
innocence as "the powdered sugar on a doughnut," and she says that
life is like an artichoke in that you have to nibble through many
tasteless leaves to get to the tasty part, and then it's too small
anyway. In these earlier novels, the humor is zany, kooky, bizarre,
and sometimes macabre or grotesque. In the later New Mexico
trilogy, the comedy has become more ethnic, regional, and bilingual
in nature, though it is still bizarre and sometimes macabre. In

these later novels, some of the best humor relates to Hispanic legends, myths, and miracles, as the Hispanic characters satirize the goals, methods and life styles of the Anglo characters. A characteristic of Nichols' novels is the almost Faulknerian ability of his characters to endure. In The Milagro Beanfield War, Amarante Cordova is ninety-two years old, and has been "playing seven card stud with death since 1980, winning every hand." His son, Jorgé, came home from Australia three different times because his father was dying, but Amarante always lived.

James Welch (1940-)

958. Owens, Louis. "The Absurd Indian: Humor in the Novels of James Welch." WHIMSY 1 (1983): 140-42.

Describes the humor of Welch's comic novel Winter in the Blood (1974) as not only bitter and ironic but absurdist as well. In writing the novel, Welch relied not only on his having read much that was surreal and darkly humorous in contemporary literature but also on his heritage as a Montana Blackfoot poet. Welch's characters are separated from their Indian heritage, thereby losing the history and the meaningful order of their lives and becoming tragically absurd figures in an absurd non-Indian environment. The narrator's father is a clown as is the narrator; his name is "First Raise," and he enjoys going to town to make the white ranchers laugh at his funny stories. On his way home one time he freezes to death in a ditch beside the road. His wife said that he was on his way home, as that was the way he was pointed. It is ironic that he froze to death on his way home from making the white men laugh. Another example of Welch's humor can be found in Lame Bull's eulogy for his grandmother. "Here lies a woman who devoted herself to...rocking." She could "take it and dish it out," and she "never gave anybody any crap." After describing what all of the people wore to the funeral, the narrator went on to say, "the old lady wore a shiny orange coffin with flecks of black ingrained just beneath the surface." Lame Bull then has to jump on the coffin to get it into a hole which he had dug too short. Owens feels that there is a close relationship between the absurd humor and the pathos of Welch's writing. When Loney's father asks why he is weeping, he replies that he is not weeping; he is laughing. But he's really not sure.

Max Isaac Apple (1941-)

959. Locher, Francis Carol. "Max Apple." Contemporary Authors. Detroit, MI: Gale, 1979. 81-84.

Considers Apple's primary asset to be his startling imagination. Apple is witty and original, and he writes deftly and economically. He is able to transform our cultural clichés into "glistening artifacts." He has a versatile range of voices and a talent for punning that places him into the "wonderful realm of linguistic high jinks and buffoonery." Apple "uses a feather, not

a blowtorch" on his characters in the development of his mildly
satiric style.

960. Marowski, Daniel G., and Jean C. Stine. "Max Apple."
     Contemporary Literary Criticism. Detroit, MI: Gale, 1985, 33.

     Describes Ira Goldstein, the protagonist of Zip: A Novel of
the Left and the Right (1978) as a person without drive, a person
who derives his energy and ambition from the other people he latches
onto. The novel uses the sport of boxing to satirize religion and
politics. Apple's fictional characters have archaic names like
Jesus, Solomon, and Moses or contemporary names like Fidel Castro,
Jane Fonda, and J. Edgar Hoover. Terence Winch feels that Zip
should be read as a parody on Christianity, as Jesus (pronounced as
a Spanish name) is presented as a middleweight (not a heavyweight).
Jesus' last name is Goldstein, a mixed metaphor where the
spirituality of the first name is counterbalanced by the material
connotations of the last name. In the novel, Solomon is smart but
not wise, and the crucifixion becomes a boxing match in Cuba.

961. Metzger, Linda. "Max Apple." Contemporary Authors. Detroit,
     MI: Gale, 1987, 19.

     Notes Apple's fascination with the English language. Apple
himself once said that the endless suggestiveness of English had
carried him through many plots and entertained him when nothing else
could. Apple's humor is a blend of fantastic and airy humor and shy
nudges to share a laugh at someone else's expense. But it is never
malicious or aggressive, as he uses the jargon of both postmodern
literary criticism and Washington lobbying and comes up grinning.

962. Nilsen, Don L. F. "Max Isaac Apple: Surrealistic 'Satirical'
     Punster." Indiana English 13.2 (Winter 1989): 17-21.

     Considers Apple's The Oranging of America to be a funny and
moving account of how the Howard Johnson rooftops dappled more and
more of America. Newsweek feels that this novel is written by an
affectionate ironist, a satirist without scorn, who has filled the
novel with wit, slapstick humor, and farcical situations. The title
of Apple's Zip, A Novel of the Left and the Right is a pun, but in
the main it does not refer to the "left" and "right" of boxing.
Nicholas Delbanco feels that Apple frequently uses puns in his
titles, but he also feels that usually "his books are better than
their names." John Leonard also comments on Apple's gimmicks,
saying that the novel Zip is less a novel than it is "a box of toys,
epigrams, firecrackers, political pot shots, Talmudic maunderings,
whistles and screams."

963. Vannatta, Dennis. "Satiric Gestures in Max Apple's The
     Oranging of America." Studies in Contemporary Satire 7 (Spring
     1980): 1-7.

     Classifies Apple's The Oranging of America as comic, or
romantic, but not satiric, because for Vannatta satire must be
critical, and even a little bit hostile. Vannatta feels that Apple
was unable to write genuine satire because he liked people too much.
Although Apple is exposing folly, foibles, vices, and pretentions,

he does not censure these attributes as vices but rather accepts
them and in fact enjoys them as sources of fun and entertainment.
It is true that The Oranging of America criticizes the pollution
that results from technology, but it is also true that readers
develop a kind of fondness for the major polluter of the novel,
Howard Johnson.

Roy Blount, Jr. (1941-)

964. Ballenger, Grady W. "Roy Blount, Jr." Encyclopedia of American
     Humorists. Ed. Steven H. Gale. NY: Garland, 1988, 49-53.

     Describes Blount as a "self-styled crackro-American humorist,
a humorist with a love of language which Blount feels is typically
Southern." Blount feels that Southerners derive the same type of
energy from lively figures of speech as plants derive from
photosynthesis. In 1974 Blount published his Three Bricks Shy of a
Load, a highly irregular account of the year the Pittsburgh Steelers
were "super but missed the bowl." This novel fulfills Blount's
childhood dream of "making it in the NFL," but he didn't make it as
a football player; rather, he made it as a "scribe," a sports
journalist. Blount's Crackers (1982) presents a view of the Carter
administration that is both Georgian (Blount was born and raised in
Georgia) and not Georgian (Blount left Georgia early in life). The
book highlights the significant events of the Carter administration
from the attack by a rabbit to the Playboy interview to the failed
raid to free the hostages in Iran. Blount describes Southerners as
"the chosen people whose duty it is to be out of whack. It is the
duty of Georgians to provide "rip-roaring red-blooded embarrassment
to the nation." One Fell Soup (1984) is a collection of essays and
light verse on social issues, language and letters, sports, and sex.
Blount's What Men Don't Tell Women (1985) provides scraps of
testimony which he labels "blue yodels" about men who can't decide
whether high heels are sexy or tools of bondage, whether the toilet
seat should be left up or down, and about whether Male Empowerment
Workshops are of any value. Not Exactly What I Had in Mind (1985)
presents Blount as philosopher, and in Organic Gardening, Blount
described his writing as dealing with the compost pile of life.

Nora Ephron (1941-)

965. Walker, Nancy, and Zita Dresner. "Nora Ephron." Redressing the
     Balance: American Women's Literary Humor from Colonial Times
     to the 1980s. Jackson, MS: Univ. Press of Mississippi, 1988,
     381-87.

     Considers Ephron a social critic who uses wit to cut through
pretense and to expose the exploitation of women. Ephron wrote for
the New York Post, New Yorker, Cosmopolitan, and Esquire, and
published her first collection of essays in 1970 under the title of
Wallflower at the Orgy. This was followed in 1975 by Crazy Salad:
Some Things about Women, and in 1978 by Scribble Scribble: Notes on
the Media. Her 1983 film Silkwood dealt with the ways that
Americans allow themselves to be manipulated by fads and the media.

Walker and Dresner feel that Ephron's voice has certain similarities
with that of Marietta Holley's Samantha Allen, since both authors
describe the pitfalls of consciousness-raising groups and expose the
conscious exploitation of women by manufacturers of feminine hygiene
products. Crazy Salad portrays the confusion of the early days of
the women's movement, when feminists considered participating in the
Pillsbury Bake-Off or wearing makeup to be subversive to the
movement. In 1972 Ephron published "On Never Having Been a Prom
Queen" in which she says that the various divisions within the
women's movement make the American Communist Party of the 1930s look
like a monolith.

Veronica Geng (1941-)

966. Moseley, Merritt. "Veronica Geng." Encyclopedia of American
Humorists. Ed. Steven H. Gale. NY: Garland, 1988, 169-71.

Indicates that Geng published several humorous pieces in the
New Yorker in 1976 and shortly thereafter she became the fiction
editor, contributing a number of humorous "casuals" to the journal
during her tenure from 1977 to 1982. These "casuals" were aimed at
deflating pomposity, solemnity and dishonesty with their satiric
edge, their parody, and their absurdity. Geng wrote for a
sophisticated and highly literate audience. Geng's Partners
contains many incongruous and funny parodies. Ron Givens gave it a
strongly positive review entitled "Truly Tasteful Humor" in Newsweek
in September of 1984. Moseley considers Geng to be a prolific and
highly accomplished writer. Her parodies are consistently well
written and are accurate and amusing. Her technique is to parody a
particular style of writing while at the same time focusing on a
wildly incongruous story line. Geng falls not only into the
tradition of major nineteenth-century magazine and newspaper
humorists but into the twentieth-century tradition of writers like
Ring Lardner, S. J. Perelman, and Robert Benchley as well.

967. Walker, Nancy, and Zita Dresner. "Veronica Geng." Redressing
the Balance: American Women's Literary Humor from Colonial
Times to the 1980s. Jackson, MS: Univ. Press of Mississippi,
1988, 436-42.

Traces Geng's interest in humor back to 1969 when she edited
In a Fit of Laughter: An Anthology of Modern Humor. Geng's Partners
(1984) received much praise from critics for the cleverness of
Geng's satiric essays, many of which had originally appeared in The
New Yorker. Geng's parodies are incisive and display an excellent
talent for mimicry. She parodies the jargon of contemporary
rhetoric and enjoys the loony incongruity of a writing style that
parodies an author in which the content deals with a subject the
writer would never have addressed. Her parodying of the style of
Henry James to satirize a group of radicals of the 1960s is an
example. Geng's wit exposes the absurdity and potential
perniciousness of things which on the surface appear to be merely
innocuous. Walker and Dresner compare Geng to Judith Sargent
Murray, to Carolyn Wells, and to Jean Kerr. Like these other
authors, Geng had an excellent ear for idioms and verbal styles and
could distinguish the various voices of American culture. Like them

Geng also had a sense of the absurd and the incongruous, and a wide-ranging intelligence that enables her to select a vulnerable subject, find its soft spot, and attack it with her lethal wit.

Ellen Goodman (1941-)

968. Walker, Nancy, and Zita Dresner. "Ellen Goodman." <u>Redressing the Balance: American Women's Literary Humor from Colonial Times to the 1980s</u>." Jackson, MS: Univ. Press of Mississippi, 1988, 433-35.

Traces Goodman's writing career to 1964 when she was a researcher and reporter for <u>Newsweek</u> magazine. From there she went to the <u>Detroit Free Press</u>, where she wrote feature stories from 1965 to 1967. In 1970 she began writing her "At Large" column for the <u>Boston Globe</u>. This column was so popular that it became syndicated in 1976 by the <u>Washington Post</u> Writers Group and was published in more than 250 papers throughout the country. In 1979 Goodman published her first book, <u>Turning Points</u>, in which she interviews men and women to discover how they have been affected by the women's movement. In 1979 she also published her first collection of newspaper columns as a book entitled <u>Close to Home</u>; this won for her the Pulitzer Prize for distinguished commentary. She published her second collection, <u>At Large</u>, in 1981. Goodman writes about child rearing, the changing attitudes relating to marriage and divorce, abortion, equal rights for women, and basic moral and ethical issues, and other subjects she considers to be more significant than are the various "political" subjects which men pass off as important. Goodman writes with wit and humor and exposes the ironic and incongruous ways that people act in professional, social, and personal situations. Walker and Dresner compare Goodman's writing style to that of Erma Bombeck and Nora Ephron, although Goodman's range is wider; her tone is more serious; and her point of view is less subjective than theirs. Walker and Dresner conclude that Goodman's style is both sensible and humorous.

John Irving (1942-)

969. Craven, Jackie. "The World According to the Amsterdam Ladies' Book Discussion Club: Eight Women Look at John Irving." <u>WHIMSY</u> 6 (1988): 9-11.

Illustrates the mixed reviews that Irving's <u>The World According to Garp</u> has received by concentrating on the responses of an eight-lady book discussion group. Reactions to this 1976 novel have ranged from hilarity to horror. It has inspired laughter and amusement, but it has also inspired comments such as "vulgar," "pathetic," "godless," and "gross." The non-laughing members of the book discussion group were repelled by recurring themes of disfigurement and emasculation and were outraged by Irving's farcical portrayal of stutterers, stammerers, and mutes. These readers were further repelled by Irving's description of Garp's unorthodox conception and his wacky sexual adventures. Craven compares these non-laughing readers to Garp's mother, Jenny, who is

a no-nonsense nurse who "took no joy in peter jokes." She had seen
the troubles that peters could get a person into, babies not being
the worst of it. The laughing readers of the book club laughed at
Garp's biting the ear off from the dog that had just bitten his own
ear off, and they saw the poetic justice of the gelding of Helen's
arrogant lover. Craven suggests that those passages where the non-
laughers saw horror, the laughers saw whimsical suitability. The
laughers found no villainy in the narrator's droll telling of Garp's
biography; rather they found the narrator to be a foolish figure, a
crusty, self-important scholar who elevated the trivial and wallowed
in inane understatement and irrelevance. For the non-laughers,
however, Garp's biographer was shrewdly and accurately recording the
world as it is, and the resulting image was frightening.

970. Horton, Andrew. "Comic Triumph in George Roy Hill's Adaptation
     of John Irving's The World According to Garp." Studies in
     American Humor NS4.3 (Fall 1985): 173-82.

     Considers The World According to Garp to be more melancholic,
sad, and cynical than ludicrous. It is nevertheless playful and
comic in many individual scenes. Horton considers Hill's adaptation
of Irving's novel to preserve the spirit and major themes of the
original novel while at the same time developing an even more
genuinely comic sense of triumph than was to be found in the
original. Steve Tesich was the screenwriter, and his approach was
to keep the original womb-to-tomb sweep of the novel while
eliminating certain details and concentrating on the three loves of
Garp's life--wrestling, being a family man, and writing. Tesich
concentrated on the celebration of the simple pleasures of life and
the chaos, violence, greed, and lust that threaten constantly to
destroy them. The ending of the film presents an outside shot of a
helicopter in flight and then cuts to the baby Garp floating into
the frame. The viewer is clued to Garp's impending death off
camera, and Garp's smiling sense of triumph at the moment of death
is caused by his floating sensation, as he says to himself "I am
flying!" But the baby-Garp we see at the end of the movie is not
the same baby-Garp we had seen at the beginning for there is no
longer the happy innocence. The film ends with the triumph of the
human spirit as Garp is able to tell the woman he loves that he has
finally realized his lifelong dream to fly as his father had done.
But the viewers are able to recognize the bitter irony of Garp's
triumph, as his spirit floats away.

971. Lounsberry, Barbara. "The Terrible Under Toad: Violence as
     Excessive Imagination in The World According to Garp." Thalia:
     Studies in Literary Humor 5.2 (Fall-Winter 1983): 30-35.

     Recounts the excessive physical and psychological violence of
The World According to Garp. The novel contains three rapes, two
assassinations, two accidental deaths, the loss of an eye, the loss
of two ears, the loss of an arm, the loss of a penis, and a whole
society of women with amputated tongues. The World According to
Garp satirizes excesses and extremes of all sorts. Irving uses his
satire to expose excesses of the imagination by both males and
females. Jenny Fields is killed by an extremist male--a macho
chauvinist, and Garp is killed by an extremist female, an Ellen
Jamesian. The novel is set at the Steering Academy, a long time
bastion of all-male education, and Dong's Head Harbor, a bastion for

wounded women. And the protagonist Garp jogs back and forth between
these two settings. Male sexual excesses, particularly rape, are
exposed and denounced by the satire of the novel but so are the
excesses of the women's movement. The women of the Ellen Jamesian
Society do violence to themselves out of extremist devotion to their
cause of anti-violence. As Garp says in the novel, such "radical
self-damage gives feminism a bad name." The sexual drive is an
important motif of the novel, and one of Irving's favorite lines in
the novel is "human sexuality makes farcical our most serious
intentions." Much of the novel deals with the comic and tragic
implications of sexual excess. There is one moderating image in the
novel, however, and that is the image of Roberta Muldoon who unites
the warring sexes from her transexual stance. In her androgynous
state, she seems to be the only character in the novel who is able
to find the middle ground.

972. Skaggs, Merril L. M. "Garp's World, Irving's Laughter."
Studies in American Humor NS 1.3 (February, 1983): 163-72.

Portrays Garp's world as a world of painful comedy. The
reader must gasp with Garp, grieve with him, suffer with, and then
laugh with him. Garp's philosophy can be summed up by one of his
statements: "I have nothing but sympathy for how people behave--and
nothing but laughter to console them with.... Laughter is my
religion." Laughter, like other forms of religion, allows people a
means short of suicide to confront a world so hostile that it can
otherwise produce only despair. Garp lives in a world where there
are no absolute values. His world contains many negative facts--
confusion, rape, fury, lust, despair, and death, but the world
according to Garp also contains many positive facts as well--faith
(though it may be naive faith), hope (though it may be childlike
hope), love (though it may be misdirected love), and laughter. And
Skaggs feels that for Irving, and for Garp, the greatest of these is
laughter.

Erica Jong (1942-)

973. Friedman, Edward H. "Girltalk: Narrative Discourse in the
Feminine Picaresque Novel and Erica Jong's Fanny." WHIMSY 2
(1984): 55-57.

Classifies Jong's novel Fanny as picaresque. Fanny's
philosophy is that neither sex should have dominion over the other.
Rather, they "must fit together, like lock and key, both
indispensable, both precisely made and well-oil'd." Fanny's balance
of picaresque and social consciousness places the novel into the
middle ground between its literary precedents and modern women's
liberation. The irony of its discourse looks backward while
pointing forward. The novel is written in a neo-Augustan style
which unites archaic discourse with an antisocial stance. Jong
gives three advantages of dressing like a boy. First, a person so
dressed is left in peace (except from robbers, who prey on both
sexes almost equally). Second, a person so dressed can dine
anywhere without being presumed to be a trollop. Third, a person so
dressed can move freely through the world without the pain of
restraints of stays, petticoats, hoops, and the like. The message

behind the message of <u>Fanny</u> is that her sister outsiders should rise in the picaresque tradition and fight in the grand struggle. One of the sisters who will hear her call to arms is Fanny's daughter, Belinda, who at the end of the novel is about to embark on a trip to America--a land of free men and unliberated women.

974. Walker, Nancy, and Zita Dresner. "Erica Jong." <u>Redressing the Balance: American Women's Literary Humor from Colonial Times to the 1980s</u>. Jackson, MS: Univ. Press of Mississippi, 1988, 386-90.

Considers Jong's semiautobiographical <u>Fear of Flying</u> to have been not only one of the most financially successful but also one of the most sensational novels of the 1970s. The novel has evoked both praise and damnation for its sexual frankness and raunchy language. It deals with female ambivalence about love versus career and the need for security, which undercuts the desire for independence. It also deals with the conflict between male and female expectations about women's nature, roles, and experiences. The novel is packed with rollicking humor that exposes the discrepancies between accepted ideas of female and male sexuality and the actual thoughts and actions of Isadora Wing. Isadora is a picaresque heroine whose character is developed satirically through comments on the foibles and pretensions of the educated and affluent class in both America and Europe. But unlike the conventional rogue, Isadora wryly scrutinizes herself and candidly exposes her comic eccentricities. <u>How to Save Your Own Life</u> (1977) is the sequel to <u>Fear of Flying</u>. It continues the first-person confessions of Isadora, who is now a famous writer. Her later novels include <u>Fanny</u> (1980), a parody of eighteenth-century novels (purporting to be what Fanny Hill might have said if she had written the novel herself), and <u>Parachutes and Kisses</u> (1984) which continues the story of Isadora Wing. Jong is also an accomplished poet. Her <u>Fruits and Vegetables</u> (1971) is full of rich, earthy images. Her later <u>Half-Lives</u> (1973), <u>Loveroot</u> (1975), <u>At the Edge of the Body</u> (1979), and <u>Ordinary Miracles</u> (1983) are written in energetic language and are rich in ironic humor.

<u>Garrison Keillor (1942-)</u>

975. Cooney, Barney. "Garrison Keillor." <u>Encyclopedia of American Humorists</u>. Ed. Steven H. Gale. NY: Garland, 1988, 251-53.

Traces Keillor's contributions to <u>The New Yorker</u> back to 1970. Keillor's <u>Happy to Be Here</u> (1982), a collection of his stories from <u>The New Yorker</u>, are mostly satires on fads, movements, passing fancies, and lunatic causes championed by various segments of the American people. His second book, <u>Lake Wobegon Days</u>, is a series of monologues from his radio show, "Prairie Home Companion." The stories take place in Lake Wobegon, "the town that time forgot...where all the women are strong and all the men are good-looking and all the children are above average." The residents of Lake Wobegon are Norwegian Lutherans and German Catholics, and their town motto is "Sumus quod sumus" (we are what we are). Although some reviewers for religious journals have praised Keillor as preaching their gospel of Christian fellowship to an audience that regular priests and pastors seldom reach, it must also be recognized that Keillor is a sharp critic of the pretensions and postures of organized religion.   Nevertheless, Keillor writes nostalgically about a romanticized rustic paradise.   His midwestern small-town America is reminiscent of the past but with all of the bad parts of the past filtered out.   Keillor is able to evoke vivid images of his own childhood and of the childhoods of most other Americans as well. Keillor says that he grew up among storytellers, and he is doing little more than carrying on their traditions.

976. Fedo, Michael. **The Man from Lake Wobegon**. New York: St. Martin's Press, 1987.

Capitalizes on Keillor's refusal to cooperate by boasting on the dustjacket that this is "an unauthorized biography of Garrison Keillor." When Keillor is asked about this biography he proclaims, "unauthorized isn't really the word for it. Unresearched would be more the word." A year after the book's appearance Keillor had gained some artistic distance and was able to write a parody piece entitled "My Life in Prison," in which he exaggerated some of the criticisms of himself and then added "But people are afraid to talk, otherwise there'd be a lot more that'd come out that you wouldn't believe." In a 1986 review of Fedo's book in Studies in American Humor, Peter Scholl describes Fedo's book as resembling the fable of the ugly duckling that became a swan. In Keillor's case, "a lonely boy from a working-class, fundamentalist family becomes a thinking person's hero, a shy celebrity who could be safely idolized by people with advanced degrees." But then Scholl adds, "But Fedo's swan apparently hisses and occasionally bites." Both Scholl and Fedo believe that Keillor's genius lies in his ability to reach various audiences with diametrically opposed attitudes and have all of these audiences say, "Yes, that's right." Keillor does not scoff at fundamentalists or their faith, yet he treats deadly serious theological points in a humorous manner. While certain members of his audience may be left a bit aghast, others interpret his message as evangelical, and still others read his stories as gentle satires of the faithful and their faith.

977. Riley, Kathryn. "Garrison Keillor's **Happy To Be Here**." **American Humor** 9.1 (Spring 1982): 11-12.

Considers the twenty-nine essay-stories of Happy To Be Here to range from satirical to humorous to reflective. Riley considers the volume diverse and uneven in quality, with Keillor's strengths being his imagination and his ability to portray the endearing and eccentric details of everyday life while not losing sight of his narrative line. Riley feels that Keillor writes effective parody. Keillor relies on much local color, and therefore much of his material becomes quickly dated, so that some of his pieces that were originally written for their satiric effects become instead nostalgia pieces, with the cutting bite being greatly dulled by the passage of time. Keillor's weaknesses are that his narrative line sometimes rambles, and that his pieces sometimes lack a consistent context and tone. Riley also feels that there is a lack of a controlling vision that would unify the volume. Riley compares Keillor's selection of topics and his writing style to the writings of Art Buchwald and Fran Lebowitz. But Keillor's stance seems to Riley to be unpredictable and inconsistent. She says that she sometimes has the impression she is reading something written by

Will Rogers in collaboration with Woody Allen. In attempting to offer variety, Keillor sometimes disorients the reader, who, when he turns the page, is not sure whether he will find parody, satire, or an introspective piece. Nevertheless, Keillor has a genuine comic gift and a fertile imagination.

978. Scholl, Peter A. "Garrison Keillor." Dictionary of Literary Biography Yearbook. Detroit: Gale, 1988, 326-38.

    Singles out Keillor's Aunt Ruth Blumer and Great Uncle Lew Powell as storytellers who were able to hold family gatherings spellbound with their long and meandering tales. While listening to them, Keillor made up his mind that the most wonderful thing he could do in the world would be to become a storyteller. Keillor's family believed that television was a bad influence like movies or smoking or playing cards. But Keillor was allowed to listen to the radio and later used that medium for his story telling skills. Deloyd Hochstetter, one of Keillor's boyhood friends remembers Garrison as a tall, thin kid who sat in the back of the room and never contributed to class discussions. But Hochstetter then goes on to say that one day Keillor changed. One day he wrote a laid-back satire about what was in the files in the principal's office. And when he read it, everyone was rolling in the aisles, but for Keillor, everything had to be written out, because he was too shy and introverted to rely on his spontaniety. Keillor's heroes were Thurber, Liebling, Perelman, and White, all writers for The New Yorker. He always cheered for them as they "took the field against the big mazumbos of American Literature." Keillor was in Nashville, Tennessee, listening to the Grand Ol' Opry when he first thought of starting up a similar-type show in Minnesota. Keillor says that from the beginning, his radio show has been at heart a gospel show. Keillor's show was Keillor's show. He wrote and delivered the monologue, "The News from Lake Wobegon." He prepared the "rube jokes" and the commercials for Jack's Auto Repair and other Lake Wobegon businesses. In the early years he wrote almost all of the spoken material and was assisted in delivering sketches and commercials by regulars like "Jim-Ed Poole" (Tom Keith).

979. Scholl, Peter. "Garrison Keillor and the News from Lake Wobegon." Studies in American Humor NS4.4 (Winter 1985-86): 217-28.

    Describes Keillor's Prairie Home Show as having the second largest radio audience currently running in the United States, second only to NPR's news magazine, All Things Considered. Keillor's Lake Wobegon monologues followed the crackerbarrel philosopher traditions of Mark Twain with their local-color narrative stories of life in the Upper Midwest. They are filled with sentimentality and nostalgia. But Keillor is actually two people--a wandering storyteller from Lake Wobegon and an urbane wit who writes for The New Yorker. When he is on stage his aphoristic wisdom told with a Minnesota accent is frequently charged with irony or satire, and even when he sounds perfectly sincere, his "double presence" keeps his stories from being excessively pious or sentimental. During one of his Powdermilk commercials, Keillor describes himself as "just a biscuit." "God coulda made me a croissant, but he made me a biscuit instead." But Keillor is not just a biscuit. He is at the same time a biscuit from Lake Wobegon

and a croissant from the Big City, and this double presence serves
a function very similar to that of the frame tale of nineteenth-
century American literature whereby a cultured and educated narrator
tells a story about an uneducated and free spirited protagonist.
Scholl says that the success of Keillor's story telling draws on his
keen eye for local color, his ability as a nostalgic realist, his
charming rustic ambiance, and his brilliance as a vernacular yarn-
spinner. Keillor's humor comes from his awareness of death and pain
and his further awareness of humor and laughter as a way of
vanquishing the death and pain at exactly the right comic moment.

Nikki Giovanni (1943-)

980. Walker, Nancy, and Zita Dresner. "Nikki Giovanni." Redressing
the Balance: American Women's Literary Humor from Colonial
Times to the 1980s Jackson: Univ. Press of Mississippi, 1988,
407-409.

Characterizes Giovanni's prose and poetry as filled with tough
wit and irreverence. Giovanni is an outspoken and controversial
Black female writer who takes pride in being both Black and female.
Giovanni has written two books of poetry, Black Feeling, Black Talk
(1967) and Black Judgement (1968). Many critics felt that
Giovanni's autobiography, Gemini: An Extended Autobiographical
Statement on My First Twenty-Five Years of Being a Black Poet was a
bit arrogant in being written before the author was thirty years
old, however, Giovanni's writing is consistently good. Her most
recent books of poetry are The Women and the Men (1975) and Cotton
Candy on a Rainy Day (1978). Such poems as "Woman" (in the former),
and "Housecleaning" (in the latter) use a self-assured voice to
describe women's difficult relationships with men. The ironic
endings of these poems are reminiscent of Dorothy Parker's poetic
style.

Sam Shepard (1943-)

981. Siegel, Mark. "The Sound of One Lip Laughing: The Nature of
Comedy in the Plays of Sam Shepard." WHIMSY 1 (1983): 103-105.

Believes that Shepard's novels pay homage not to the
historical West but to the mythical West, as he exploits the great
communication gap that used to exist between the stolid,
intellectual East and the wide-open mysterious West. The Jessie
James of Shepard's Mad Dog Blues, his Cowboy Mouth, and his The
Unseen Hand are grounded in myth and religion rather than in
reality. Almost as a kind of parody, Shepard employs stereotypical
western names like Slim, Waco, Hoss, Cody, and Pop. Siegel
summarizes The Unseen Hand by saying that a 120 year-old gunslinger
is hired by someone in outer space to free his enslaved people. In
La Tourista, dysentary becomes a symbolic metaphor for American
Colonialism. In The Mad Dog Blues a rock and roll singer and a
junkie join up with Paul Bunyon, Mae West, Jessie James, and others
looking for wealth, meaning, and a true home. Again and again in
Shepard's plays characters use outmoded social and psychological

tools to confront a disintegrating society.   Again and again we
laugh nervously at the disfunctional behavior of the characters.
And the laughter becomes more and more uncomfortable as the
characters become more and more grotesque.   "We are no longer
staring at Yorrick's belled cap, but at his bald skull." Shepard's
Suicide in Bb presents a comic nation, a comic household, and comic
personalities in a futile attempt to make order out of disorder.
Pablo drags his partner's body around the room trying to align him
with the chalked outline of the victim.   This doesn't work, so they
try falling onto the marks.   Then, in something that resembles a
Laurel and Hardy routine, they bicker over various ways the crime
might have been committed.

Lisa Alther (1944-)

982. Avant, John Alfred. "Bildungsroman Times Five." The Nation
     232.16 (April 25, 1981): 506-07.

     Considers Original Sins to be five times better than Kinflicks
because Alther has provided five protagonists rather than just one,
and the result is five different points of view.   Alther's title,
"Original Sins," alludes to the fact that "everyone's condition is
inadequate and that being Southern is a particular handicap, sort of
the "original sin."   Alther pummels the reader with glaring image
after glaring image.   "The fury drained away quickly, like air out
of a bicycle tire." The characters had sex, and "afterward they lay
in each other's arms and watched the long pale fingers of dawn
gently stroke the night sky until the grey became engorged with
crimson."

983. Bakerman, Jane S. "You Might as Well Laugh: Lisa Alther's
     Funny, Befuddled, Courageous Heroes." WHIMSY 5 (April 1986):
     35-36.

     Believes characterization to be one of Alther's strongpoints
as a writer.   Alther's flawed characters may irritate or annoy us,
but they also make us laugh, because their less pleasant moods and
attitudes are described with a graceful and skillful use of humor.
Alther's characters can and do laugh at themselves, and they laugh
at the messes they have made of their lives.   Their lack of
bitterness earns the readers' respect and allows the reader to share
with them common attributes.   Once the characters decide that they
might as well laugh, they are ready to live, and in fact live
happily ever after in a flawed but funny world.   Bakerman feels that
Lisa Alther is one of the feminist writers who expose the canard
that feminist writers are never funny or self-mocking and are
seldom, as a consequence, interesting.

984. Cantwell, Mary. "Serious When Once She Was Funny." New York
     Times Book Review, May 3, 1981: 9, 38.

     Describes Lisa Alther's alternation between Ginny Babcock's
point of view and that of her mother as "an almost flawless balance
of light and dark, the skittery and the sad."   In fact, she feels
that Kinflicks is a much better novel than Original Sins.   In
Kinflicks, Alther doesn't telegraph her punches, and the denouements

are therefore a continual surprise. This is not true of Original
Sins. Cantwell feels that part of the reason that Alther's second
novel is not successful is that her first novel was successful, and
Cantwell makes the observation that "the parody, it seems, was
published before its target."

985. Gray, Paul. "Being the Sophomore Jinx." Time 117.17 (April 27,
     1981): 71.

     Describes a sexual encounter between Jed and Sally. Amidst
much comic fumbling and steamy negotiating, Jed finally takes
Sally's virginity. In the Southern tradition of the 1960s, she
responds by clinging to his hand as assurance that he still
respected her and would protect her reputation and would eventually
marry her and love her forever. That didn't seem like too much to
ask. Gray has a mixed reaction to Original Sins. He praises Alther
for taking a risk as an author but points out that she did not
always succeed by doing so. She often sacrificed plausibility for
comic effect. There are places where the plot development seems
more dictated than inevitable. But Gray considers such lapses to be
more than offset by the novel's verve and intelligence.

986. Harris, L. Joe. "Kinflicks: Sad Laughter and Satire." WHIMSY
     3 (April 1985): 43-45.

     Points out that since Ginny Babcock doesn't know who she is,
she tries to discover herself through reminiscences. The title of
the novel, Kinflicks is an allusion to home movies ("flicks") about
various relatives ("kin"), and the humor of the novel is mainly to
be found in the flashbacks--the kinflicks--but Alther's flashbacks
are not G-rated. They are X-rated; they emerge as thematic
clusters; and they are very funny. The thematic clusters even have
names. The link between Ginny's sexual dilemmas and puritanical
religion is appropriately entitled, "Walking the Knife's Edge, or
Blue Balls in Bibleland." Although Harris considers Kinflicks to be
both human and hilarious, he nevertheless sees three basic flaws in
the novel. First, the humor sometimes degenerates into cuteness;
second, the strong shift in the point of view is somewhat
disruptive; and third, the development of the heroine produces
expectations in the reader that are not fulfilled by the end of the
novel. When Ginny's mother finally dies, Ginny decides that she
herself must commit suicide, but she is as much a failure in death
as she is in sex. When she attempts to drown herself by tying a
large rock to her ankle and heaving the rock into a pond, the rock
makes her fall into a rowboat. When she puts a gun barrel to her
mouth to practice shooting herself and pulls the trigger with her
toe, everything works fine, but then she discovers that the
ammunition she has doesn't fit the gun. When she attempts to stab
herself with a bowie knife, she is both fascinated and chagrined
when her blood clots before her eyes.

987. Kaplan, Carey. "Female Stereotypes as Satiric Metaphors in
     Lisa Alther's Kinflicks." WHIMSY 2 (April 1984): 57-58.

     Considers there to be a "daring shift in point of view" in
Lisa Alther's Kinflicks, as the novel see-saws between subjective
and objective narration, between burlesque and realism, between
youth and old age, between past and present, between mother and

daughter, between sex and death. This dualism and the resultant contradictory metaphors are symbolic of women's situation in modern society.

988. Leonard, John. "Kinflicks." The New York Times Book
     Review, March 14, 1976: 4

Describes Kinflicks as a novel about men who don't understand women and women who don't understand themselves any better. Leonard feels that Ginny Babcock's voice is often heard in American fiction. He feels that Ginny is the female counterpart of J. D. Salinger's Holden Caulfield, and of Saul Bellow's Augie March, and even of Mark Twain's Huckleberry Finn. Leonard describes Kinflicks as a very funny book about very serious matters.

989. Metzger, Linda. "Lisa Alther." Contemporary Authors. Volume
     12. Detroit, MI: Gale, 1984,

Contrasts the viewpoint of twenty-seven-year-old Ginny Babcock with that of her dying mother in Kinflicks. Ginny's story is told from the first-person perspective and is grounded in the past. Her mother's story is told in third person and is grounded in the present. Ginny's story is intimate, irreverent, and at times burlesque, while her mother's story is detached and serious. Metzger suggests that Ginny is a female Holden Caulfield. Alther graphically describes Ginny's Tennessee teens, her flight north, and her later return south to her mother's deathbed. Like Holden, Ginny is an adolescent who has learned how to survive.

990. Schechner, Mark. "A Novel of the New South." The New Republic
     184.24 (June 13, 1981): 34-36.

Compares Alther's Ginny Babcock with Charlie Chaplin. Ginny's social and sexual calamities are Chaplinesque pratfalls, and after each such pratfall, she gets up, brushes off her baggy pants, straightens her bowler, and struts off in search of her next calamity. Schechner considers the novel to be alternately ironic and rueful with its brilliant detail. The comic imagination of the novel is based on disillusionment and seems eager to suffer the calamities just for the sheer fun of them.

991. Sternhell, Carol. "At Last, a Cure for Politics." The Village
     Voice 29.51 (December 18, 1984): 71.

Describes Other Women (1984) as a novel told from two antithetical perspectives, that of Caroline Kelly, who confuses the world's suffering with her own, and that of Hannah Burke, her psychologist. Caroline is suffering from "cosmic depression," and when Hannah asks what is causing this depression Caroline responds, "the Jonestown thing, I guess." Other Women is written in alternating chapters from the viewpoint of the patient and the psychologist. Sternhell's evaluation of the book is quite negative, saying that the novel specializes in therapeutic platitudes. The central insight of the novel is that each of us is responsible for our own moods, and Sternhell suggests that such an insight might just as well be stated as a Leo Buscaglia pop sermon, one of Cosmo's "How Well Do You Know Yourself?" quizzes, or a fortune cookie.

992. Woods, William C. "Projection of Things Past." Book World--The
Washington Post, March 28, 1976: H1.

Considers the dual perspective of Kinflicks to be a delicate
balance of Ginny Babcock's rebellion and her mother's tragic sense
that she has lost her life in living for her children. Ginny's
mother is dying because her blood won't clot, and at one point,
Ginny describes her hemorrhaging mother as an "overripe tomato."

Rita Mae Brown (1944-)

993. Walker, Nancy, and Zita Dresner. Redressing the Balance:
American Women's Literary Humor from Colonial Times to the
1980s. Jackson, MS: Univ. Press of Mississippi, 1988, 391-99.

Describes Brown's collections of poetry, The Hand that Cradles
the Rock (1971) and Songs to a Handsome Woman (1973) as having
limited appeal. Brown's first novel, Rubyfruit Jungle (1973),
however is exuberant, picaresque, and semiautobiographical and has
a much broader appeal. The paperback edition of this novel was
published in 1977 and has sold more than a million copies. The
novel's heroine, Molly Bolt, has been described as a kind of a
lesbian Huck Finn. The humor of the novel ranges from broad and
ribald to subtly ironic, as Molly uses her wit and resilience to
triumph over adversity. Brown's second novel, Six of One (1978) is
another commercial success that has been praised for its humor.
Based on personal experiences, it is a comic history of a
Pennsylvania-Maryland bordertown from 1909 to 1980 from the point of
view of three generations of colorful, chatty, and homey women.
Brown is effective in presenting positive images of women that
counter the distorted traditional notions. In fact, Brown uses
humor to attack offensive stereotypes of all kinds.

Alice Walker (1944-)

994. Geuder, Patricia A. "The Butcher, the Baker, and the
Candlestick Maker." WHIMSY 1 (1985): 45-47.

Notes that The Color Purple won both the Pulitzer Prize and
the American Book Award in 1982. This novel contains letters
written by two black sisters during their thirty-year separation.
Most of Celie's letters were written to God, but many were written
to her sister Nettie, a missionary in Africa. The letters describe
local events and local characters like Shug Avery, christened
"Lillie" but called "Shug" because she is so sweet. Shug never
takes any man seriously; she nevertheless admits that some men can
be lots of fun. Shug's Albert and Grady were two such men. But
Grady's ability to amuse was short lived. "Grady so dull, Jesus.
And when you finish talking about women and reefer you finish
Grady." Shug tries to figure out who tried to teach him about sex;
judging from his technique, it must have been a furniture salesman.
Shug's last fling was with a nineteen-year-old flute player named
Germaine. She said he was little, he was cute, and he had nice
buns. In Germaine, her third lover, Shug had found a man who was "a

third her age, a third her size, and a third her color." Shug's topics of conversation are not those of most women--hair and health and how many babies are living or dead and which of them have teeth. She is liberated, and she sleeps alternately with Albert and Celie for a while and then alternates between Grady and Celie. Shug's unorthodox relationships with men and women carry over to her unorthodox relationship with God--when she found out that God was white, and a man, she invented her own God--"God is everything.... It pisses God off if you walk by the color purple in a field somewhere and don't notice."

995. Lightfoot, Marjorie J. "Purple--with Laughter." WHIMSY 5
     (1987): 180-83.

     Suggests that Walker's light tone should not be misinterpreted as indicating that Walker's characters are not in pain. The characters' light tone and comic perspective are their ways of dealing with the enormous pain that women, especially poor black women, have to endure. The light tone is set before the novel even begins, as Walker dedicates the novel to "...the Spirit, without whose assistance neither this book, nor I, would have been written." The incongruities and the reversals of expectations in the novel are sources of laughter. Fourteen-year-old Celie is raped by her stepfather, who has warned her, "You better not tell nobody but God." So if Celie is going to be able to tell her troubles to anybody, she must tell them to God, but once she has written her letters to God, she doesn't know where to mail them. Her writing of letters that cannot be mailed is symbolic not only of Celie's wit but of her desperation. Celie's stepfather doesn't want Celie to become educated, so Celie must educate herself, but she doesn't always get it right. She remembers the Nina, the Pinta, and the Santa Maria, for example as the "Neater, the Peter, and the Santomareater." Celie is proud of her stepson's wife, Sophie, for not being dominated by her [Sophie's] husband, Harpo. Harpo puts on some weight to become Sophie's equal, but this makes him look pregnant not fierce. Celie's stepfather, Albert, is referred to as "Mr." Celie remarks that nobody cares when he leaves home, because when he stays home he never does any work around the place anyway; so nobody misses him. The novel has a fairytale ending in which the sisters are reunited, and Celie's grown children meet their real mother. Walker thanks everybody for reading the book and signs off as "A.W., author and medium."

David Carkeet (1946-)

996. Bjarkman, Peter C. "David Carkeet and the Absurdist Theater of
     the Diamond: Black Humor and the American Baseball Novel."
     WHIMSY 6 (1988): 7-8.

     Considers baseball to be America's national game because it is the sport of nostalgia. It is a national ritual celebration of an older and simpler rural America. And it is the only game that has become a literary archetype and symbol of our mythical past. It is also the only game to sustain a body of serious literature--novels, essays, poems, movies, stories of all kinds which are not so much about baseball as they are about our rural and comic natural spirit.

Important comic baseball novels include Bernard Malamud's The
Natural, Mark Harris' Bang the Drum Slowly, Philip Roth's The Great
American Novel, Robert Coover's The Universal Baseball Association,
W. P. Kinsella's Shoeless Joe, and finally David Carkeet's raunchy
and raucous novel entitled The Greatest Slump of All Time, which
describes the ultimate slapstick team. The team is a pennant
contender which is able to knock the cover off the baseball and
which seems as well to have an air-tight defense. But the team
consists of oddballs, eccentrics, and athletic misfits like a
catcher who fantasizes about a pitchout so that he can jump free
from his claustrophia-causing equipment and eight team mates who
suffer from every psychological malady imaginable. Bjarkman
considers The Greatest Slump to be an outrageous satire of both the
intricate details of baseball and of America's neurotic craze for
the game. It is a seminal work of baseball humor that investigates
the comic-serious hold that baseball has on the American
consciousness, a hold that a contemporary European reader could not
possibly understand.

Octavia Butler (1947-)

997. Shinn, Thelma. "Science Fiction as Metaphor: Octavia Butler's
     Ironic Transformations." WHIMSY 2 (1984): 58-60.

      Explains that Butler set her first two novels, Patternmaster
(1976), and Mind of My Mind (1977) in California. Patternmaster
describes a new society in which all people without telepathic
abilities are called "Mutes." These Mutes seem to be wielders of
great worldly power, but everything they do is determined by the
Patternmasters, who control their minds.   The irony of their
domination is that they do not realize they are being dominated.
Butler's Mary in Mind of My Mind is a combination of Eve, Madonna,
and Satan. Mary is a new kind of female character both in science
fiction and in Afro-American fiction, a strong female character who
can be described either as a witch or as an Earthmother. Mary is
protectress of the Earth and ecology. She represents the force that
opposes the assumption that man has the right to dominate women and
Nature. In Mind of My Mind Anyanwu has learned how to change her
body; she can be older or younger; she can be a hunting leopard or
a swimming dolphin. Butler is saying that in order to survive in a
patriarchical society, women must learn how to shape shift.   By
blending into their environments, women can make themselves
invisible and therefore not vulnerable to attack. The scene of
Butler's next novel, Survivor, shifts from earth to another planet,
a planet conscious of color differences among the inhabitants.
There are the Garkohn, who are predominately green, and the Tehkohn,
who are predominately blue, but the aristocracy of the planet are
the Hao, who are the darkest blue. Shinn says that these blue
bloods (blue furs) are respected and feared. She also says that the
novel contains a satiric message about judging the quality of a
person by skin/fur color.

Douglas C. Kenney (1947-1980)

998. Kiley, Frederick, and J. M. Shuttleworth. "Bored of the
     Rings." Satire from Aesop to Buchwald. NY: Odyssey Press,
     1971, 460-66.

Includes "Bored of the Rings" plus commentary about the author
and about the piece in their anthology. This is a full-length
parody of Tolkien's trilogy and was first published by the Harvard
Lampoon in 1969. Kiley and Shuttleworth consider this witty take-
off to be a good test of the reader's response to satire. Because
some readers may consider the original trilogy to be sacred, they
may be more irritated than entertained by Kenney's parody. But
other readers will enjoy the parody and will see it as a criticism
of the faddish, cultish worship of a delightful but not messianic
piece of literature.

Stephen King (1947-)

999. Egan, James. "Sacral Parody in the Fiction of Stephen King."
     Journal of Popular Culture 23.3 (Winter 1989): 125-42.

Considers King's novels to be parodies of the Gothic novel
genre, and the Gothic novel genre itself is something of a parody of
both the romance and the realistic fiction of its day. Egan
suggests that the Gothic world is a world of constant change and
unresolved chaos, a surrealistic world filled with monstrous and
grotesque shadows. The Gothic world is also filled with religious
images. Shelley's Frankenstein plays on ironic variations of the
creation, the resurrection, and the Adam motifs. Stoker's Dracula
uses Christian ritual to defeat the vampire. Lovecraft has a
pantheon of dark gods. In this same tradition, Stephen King
develops powerful images relating to science, materialism, and
religion. Tony Magistrale has argued that King's satires attack the
very foundations and values upon which society is built--societal
bonds, science, and religion. King portrays both organized
government and organized religion as spiritually bankrupt and
condemns religious extremists. King uses the strategems of satire--
caricature, ironic inversion, the grotesque, the burlesque, and
satiric juxtapositions-- to expose his targets. He bonds himself to
the target and then mocks it both literally and allegorically.
King's humor is a way of intensifying the sacral parody, a way to
define the Gothic ambiance more fully, and a way to question
conventional religious beliefs of the regular world, and, of course,
one of King's major targets in his sacral parodies is fundamentalist
obsessions. He targets ministers, priests, sacraments, rapture,
communion with the Godhead, formal rites, rituals, divine
providence, mysticism, and the suprarational point of view. And he
uses dark humor to do so.

Ntosake Shange (1948-)

1000. Walker, Nancy, and Zita Dresner. "Ntosake Shange." Redressing
    the Balance: American Women's Literary Humor from Colonial
    Times to the 1980s. Jackson, MS: Univ. Press of Mississippi,
    1988, 410-15.

    Indicates that Ntosake Shange was born Paulette Williams but
adopted her Zulu name in 1971 in protest at America's racist
attitudes and as a show of independence as a Black woman in a
society that discriminates against Blacks and women. Her For
Colored Girls Who Have Considered Suicide...When the Rainbow Is Enuf
(1975) is a collection of performance pieces, or what Walker and
Dresner call a "choreopoem." Jack Kroll, Edith Oliver, and other
New York critics praised the work for its dramatic power, its poetic
beauty, its strong passion, and its social irony. In Black
communities it soon became a focus of controversy because of its
feminist stance and its negative depiction of the relationship
between Black men and Black women. But the work can also be read on
another apolitical level because of the effective use of humor,
street idiom, vernacular poetry, and realistic detail to tell about
both the joys and the horrors that a Black woman must endure in
order to grow up, come of age, and confront the dual obstacles of
sex and race. These issues are also treated in Shange's play Spell
7 (1979), in her novels, Sassafras, Cypress, and Indigo (1982),
and Betsy Brown (1986), and in her nonfiction See No Evil: Prefaces,
Essays, and Accounts, 1976-1983 (1984). What these various works
have in common is verbal energy, humor, vivid characterization and
settings, and emotional responses which unite rather than divide.
Shange is able to establish many links between African, Afro-
American, and some other Third World American women's cultures,
styles, and rhythms.

Leslie Marmon Silko (1948-)

1001. Evasdaughter, Elizabeth Neely. "Leslie Marmon Silko's
    Ceremony: Healing Ethnic Hatred by Mixed-Breed Laughter."
    WHIMSY 6 (1988): 33-45.

    Suggests that because Silko grew up as a Native American but
also read widely (Steinbeck, Faulkner, Poe, Borges, Flannery
O'Conner, and others), her humor blends affectionate feelings about
her Pueblo culture with the black humor of twentieth century
American white culture. Silko herself is a mixed blood, and she is
able to describe the clowning and joking experiences of mixed bloods
especially well. Betonie is a mixed blood medicine man who is able
to aid victims "tainted by Christianity or liquor." Emo, another
character in Ceremony is an evil clown, who jokes at the expense of
others. But Tayo, another clown figure, is passive, and he loses
control by weeping and vomiting. Tayo is a sad clown who does not
even realize that he is funny. Silko teases her white readers by
having the head of an Indian family say to his grown daughter,
"Church...Ah, Thelma, do you have to go there again?" Silko likes
to present the stereotypes of whites, and then, after the reader has
formed opinions, Silko suggests that the facts should have been

interpreted quite differently. This is a way of teasing whites
about their presumption of certainty. But Silko chides her Indian
readers as well. Evasdaughter notes that much of the Indian humor
in Ceremony is overlooked or misinterpreted by white readers; they
tend to take light and humorous passages as solemn and tense. But
then, Tayo himself takes everything too seriously and is sad that
whites monopolize the world. But Bertonie responds by telling Tayo
about a witches' contest in which the evilest action award is won by
a witch who invents white people with nuclear capabilities.
Bertonie presents Tayo's message but with humor.

Garry B. Trudeau (1948-)

1002. Blair, Walter, and Hamlin Hill. "Cinema, Cartoon, and Stand-up
      Comic." America's Humor from Poor Richard to Doonesbury. NY:
      Oxford Univ. Press, 1978, 507-19.

      Refers to Art Buchwald's introduction to a collection of
Trudeau's cartoons entitled Still a Few Bugs in the System (1972) in
which he predicted that "As with all anti-Establishment figures, Mr.
Trudeau will soon be an honored member of the Establishment." In
1975 President Gerald Ford remarked that there are three major ways
that a person can be kept informed in Washington--"the electronic
media, the print media, and Doonesbury...not necessarily in that
order." In May of that same year, Doonesbury became the first comic
strip to win the Pulitzer Prize, at which point Holt, Rinehart, and
Winston, the publisher of Doonesbury, took out a large ad in the New
York Times Book Review extending condolences to Trudeau's cast of
characters. "It was nice to be honored," they said, "but it's quite
another thing when the Establishment clutches all of the Walden
Commune to its bosom." Yale University is the setting for the
Doonesbury characters, but it might as well be Haight-Ashbury in San
Francisco, Telegraphy Avenue in Berkeley, the plaza in Taos, or
Greenwich Village. Mark Slackmeyer is the campus radical; Calvin is
the black activist; and Joanie Caucus is the women's libber. All of
Trudeau's characters are in constant frustration. When Mark's
mother asks him how he feels about material wealth and private
ownership he replies that he agrees with Marx, Gandhi, and Christ
that it is the curse of mankind. "I'm glad you feel that way," his
mother responds, "I just backed over your motorcycle."

1003. Diot, Rolande. "Humor for Intellectuals: Can it be Exported
      and Translated? The Case of Garry Trudeau's In Search of
      Reagan's Brain." WHIMSY 4 (1986): 185-88.

      Separates translatable humor from nontranslatable humor in In
Search of Reagan's Brain. Allusions, references, and cultural
idiosyncracies are translatable, but the rest of the content and
form of the humor is not translatable. Diot contends that although
both Woody Allen and Garry Trudeau write for intellectuals, Allen's
writings are much easier to translate because Allen's humor is
largely derived from parody of Jewish attitudes and Jewish humor in
general. Diot claims that intellectuals are the same around the
world. Whatever faction is in power, the intellectuals take on the
point of view of the opposition. Intellectuals also have a neurotic
guilt complex for all of the troubles they see in the world,

something which Sartre used to call "the petty bourgeois syndrome." Trudeau is no exception, as he attacks the Evil King, the Father Figure, the President. In Search of Reagan's Brain is presented in a setting of science and discovery, as a case of biological exploration. On the expedition, there are the media--the TV and pressmen, the well-known Washington papers, TV stars, etc. This fantastic journey is being reported by Roland Hadley, dressed as a speleologist who leads the expedition and the readers into the fascinating recesses of Ronald Reagan's brain. The voyage is surrealistic, as they wade waist-deep in some unidentified fluid, evidently the moist substance of cerebral matter. The brain's circumvolutions look like lascivious nudes lying on soft cushions, and they seem to have their buttocks sprawled on Oriental carpets. But because the foreign reader misses many of the cultural allusions, the piece comes across more as satire than as humor.

Frances Ann Lebowitz (1950-)

1004. Merman, Patrick William. "Fran[ces Ann] Lebowitz." Encyclopedia of American Humorists. Ed. Steven H. Gale. NY: Garland, 1988, 271-74.

Considers Lebowitz to be an efficient and succinct writer in the tradition of Dorothy Parker and Oscar Wilde. Although Lebowitz was addicted to reading, she was expelled from her private school; she did, however, later pass the GED certificate examination. Reviewers liked the bite of her "hard-boiled, down-to-earth, aphoristic sentences" in her 1978 Metropolitan Life, which satirizes not only her own field of journalism but also such treasures as Arthur Conan Doyle's stories. Merman feels that her satirization of style is worthy of the New York Times or American Speech. Merman compares the ironic plot twists at the ends of many of Lebowitz's stories with those of O'Henry. Her wide range of satiric targets make Lebowitz popular with both middle-class and lower-class readers, who can identify with landlords who are able to provide 4,000 roaches per tenant. Merman feels that what makes Lebowitz's style so appealing is a mean-spirited tone coupled with her clever epigrammatic punch lines. In Social Studies, for example, the reader learns that "polite conversation is rarely either" and that "great people talk about ideas, average people talk about things and small people talk about wine." The central message of Social Studies is that social standing and wealth are not good indicators of personal worth. Lebowitz never rises to true political satire. She never poses as an intellectual. Instead she writes about quiet joys and "leisure unencumbered by pretension." In short, she writes excellent urban satire.

1005. Walker, Nancy, and Zita Dresner. "Fran Lebowitz." Redressing the Balance: American Women's Literary Humor from Colonial Times to the 1980s. Jackson, MS: Univ. Press of Mississippi, 1988, 423-27.

Suggests that the fact that Fran Lebowitz is a New Yorker might invite comparison of her writing with that of Dorothy Parker. But Walker and Dresner feel that Parker's work has more pathos and is more compassionate than Lebowitz's, and they would rather compare

her writing to that of Oscar Wilde. Cathleen Schine in <u>Vogue</u> said
that Lebowitz "writes pedagogical satire, tapping her pointer at the
blackboard, waiting stoically for her slackjawed students to catch
on." Her aggressive humor does not contain awe, and it has no
constraints in terms of targets. Lebowitz's <u>Metropolitan Life</u>
(1978) and <u>Social Studies</u> (1981) were both best sellers, and
Lebowitz became an instant celebrity, enjoying this honor, and
saying that she considered autographing books to be "the ultimate
human activity." Lebowitz writes about subjects that are staples of
women's humor, such as dieting and children, and she writes from the
point of view of a tough-minded, opinionated, single New Yorker who
wants dramatic changes in women's lives. But she says flatly that
she is not part of the "feminist cause." And her tone is that of a
person more bemused than beleaguered by her situation.

Gail Sausser (1952-)

1006. Walker, Nancy, and Zita Dresner. "Gail Sausser." <u>Redressing
       the Balance: American Women's Literary Humor from Colonial
       Times to the 1980s</u>. Jackson, MS: Univ. Press of Mississippi,
       1988, 446-48.

       Indicates that for three years Sausser wrote articles for
<u>Lights</u>, <u>Washington Cascade Voice</u>, and <u>Seattle Gay News</u> that were
later collected into her 1986 book entitled <u>Lesbian Etiquette</u>, in
which Sausser's humorous essays are accompanied by Alice Muhlback
cartoons. Walker and Dresner compare Sausser's wit and subject
matter to that of lesbian-feminist stand-up comic Kate Clinton. In
both cases, the topics typically deal with the personal and
professional behavior of gay women. Sausser specializes in the
great differences that exist between people's expectations of gay
behavior and the actual gay behavior. <u>Lesbian Etiquette</u> is a
humorous book for gays and for non-gays alike, as it allows both
gays and non-gays to identify with the situations and find the humor
in them. Sausser is an admirer of the humanistic humor of Bill
Cosby, Lily Tomlin, and Bette Midler, and her writing reflects this
admiration. Sausser has a wry sense of the absurd, and she would
rather gently poke fun in a good-natured way than use malicious or
hostile humor.

Chapter 5
Black or Gallows Humor

1007. Davis, Douglas M., ed. The World of Black Humor. New York: E.
P. Dutton, 1967. 350 pp.

Considers some of the best examples of contemporary American
black humor. In Terry Southern's The Magic Christian, Guy Grand
buys a huge newspaper and converts it entirely to readers' opinions.
In John Hawkes' The Cannibal, Leevey takes over all of West Germany
in the name of America. In William Gaddis' The Recognitions,
Recktall Brown helps in the production of fake works of art. In
Cabot Wright Begins, the protagonist commits over 300 rapes out of
boredom; one of the victims sues her mother for being a friend of
the rapist. In Warren Miller's The Siege of Harlem, Harlem secedes
from the union and petitions the United Nations for recognition as
an independent country. Davis considers "Black Humor" to be that
humor which "laughs at the absurd tragedy which has trapped us all,
man, woman, child, self." Davis likes the term "Black Humor" better
than "Yankee Existentialism," or "the American Absurd Novel" for
this genre, because he sees a parallel between "Black Humor" and
"Black Power." In both cases there is a special tension created by
the enigmatic ambivalence of joy and hate. "Black Humor" is part of
a broader American movement that includes "Neo-Dada," "Pop Art,"
"The Happening," "Electronic Poetry," and "Computer Music." They
all say that science and technology has gone too far and must fail.

1008. Friedman, Bruce J., ed. Black Humor. NY: Bantam, 1965, xi +
174 pp.

Discusses the black humor of Thomas Pynchon, Bruce J.
Friedman, Joseph Heller, J. P. Donleavy, Vladimir Nabokov, Charles
Simmons, John Rechy, Edward Albee, John Barth, Terry Southern, James
Purdy, Conrad Knickerbocker, and Louis-Ferdinand Celine. Friedman
admits that these thirteen authors are very different from each
other. Each has a private and unique vision. They don't interact
with each other as a group. But there are certain similarities as
well. They are all continuing the strong tradition of storytelling
in America. They all play with the "fading line between fantasy and
reality." For all of them there is a nervousness, an upbeat tempo,
a near-hysteria or frenzy. And what is happening in the literature
is also happening in music, and in talk, and in films, and in the
theatre. Friedman feels that this frenzy comes down to The New York
Times, which he describes as "the source and fountain and bible of
black humor." Black humor, like the satires of Jules Feiffer, Paul
Krassner, and Lenny Bruce, is not so different from actual newspaper
accounts. The TV asks Mrs. Malcolm X, "How does it feel" when her

husband is assassinated. Mrs. Luzzo is killed by a bullet through her brain, and it is reported that "her civil rights have been violated." One of our Vietnam poison gases is described as "fragrant-smelling."

1009. Heller, Terry. "Notes on Technique in Black Humor." Thalia: Studies in Literary Humor 2.3 (Winter 1979-80): 15-21.

Agrees with Matthew Winston that black humor has a tone which is at the same time frightening or threatening and farcical or amusing. This "violent combination of opposing extremes" knocks us off balance so that we become disoriented and confused. We are no longer certain of moral or social values, and we no longer have a secure norm. Heller divides "black humor" into two categories, the "absurd" and the "grotesque," explaining that the former provokes laughter while the latter provokes a more serious response. In a typical black-humor novel, the reader is suspended between the horror (the grotesque) and the humor (the absurd), sometimes pulled in the one direction, sometimes in the other.

1010. Hill, Hamlin. "Black Humor and the Mass Audience." American Humor. Ed. O. M. Brack, Jr. Scottsdale, Arizona: Arrete Press, 1977, 1-11.

Looks at early twentieth-century humor and contrasts "high-culture humor," which tends to be "satiric, fantastic, intellectual, and defeatist," with "mass-culture humor," which is "realistic, optimistic, common sensical, and unsatiric almost to the point of self-censorship." Hill concedes that as many critics have suggested, American black humor is "a phenomenon limited to the 1960s"; nevertheless, he feels that the 60s have left a legacy of black humor that continues dramatically to the present day.

1012. Janoff, Bruce. "Black Humor, Existentialism, and Absurdity: A Generic Confusion." The Arizona Quarterly 30.4 (Winter 1974): 293-304.

Doesn't like "black humor" to be lumped together with "the existential novel," "novel of the absurd," "the anti-novel," "Yankee existentialism," "nightmare fiction," or "the comic apocalyptic school" because "black humor" stresses the darkness of the writing, while the other labels stress the existential attitudes of the characters. Janoff feels that such writers as Jean-Paul Sartre and Albert Camus write existential novels but not black-humor novels. Although the existential novel is heavily ironic, it is not consistently wry or comic in perspective as is black humor. The writings of Sartre and Camus are sombre; they stress an existential sense of loss and alienation, and the development of the novels is serious and technically controlled prose, with rare plays for laughs. Both genres stress a fascination with horror, but in black humor the horror is made darker by intermingling comedy with despair. Sartre's Antoine Roquentin becomes physically nauseated in confronting the existential "void," and Camus' Dr. Rieux fights invincible forces of a plague with fervid determination. But Heller's Yossarian protests the brutality of war by sitting naked in a tree, and Barth's Todd Andrews works out a puzzle involving three million dollars and 129 pickle jars filled with excrement as he contemplates his own suicide.

1013. Keough, William. <u>Punchlines: The Violence of American Humor</u>.
      New York: Paragon House, 1990, xxiv + 279 pp.

      Suggests that American humor is typically violent. It tends
to be sexist, racist, brutal, and disgusting as well. The
suggestion that Columbus discovered America in 1492 is the first
American joke, for when Columbus came to America, the Arawaks and
Caribs were already here. The second American joke was Columbus'
insistence that he had landed in the West Indies and his naming of
the inhabitants Indians. The third joke is that America was named
after Amerigo Vespucci, a pickle-dealer in Seville who never saw
America and whose lies convinced the world that the discovery should
be named after him. The English used the early American colonies as
a dumping ground for convicts, disgruntled Irishmen, and dissident
religious sects like the Puritans. So in America there has been a
long tradition of claiming more than is really there, and this is a
kind of dark humor. In 1642, Thomas Morton set up a commune which
he called "Merry Mount," where people could live together and get
drunk and frolic around Morton's May Pole. The Puritans frowned on
this spectacle and resented his getting rich from the merriment.
When Thomas Morton ridiculed the Puritans, they had him expelled.
Three centuries later when Dick Gregory, Richard Pryor, and Lenny
Bruce ridiculed the establishment, they lost bookings and sometimes
were jailed. In America there has always been a quarrel to
determine what is funny and what is not.

1014. Lindberg, Stanley W. "One Alternative to Black Humor: The
      Satire of Jack Matthews." <u>Studies in Contemporary Satire</u> 1.1
      (Spring 1974): 17-36.

      Suggests that such modern American writers as Kurt Vonnegut,
John Barth, Joseph Heller, Thomas Pynchon, etc., don't write genuine
satire so much as they write "black humor" "ironic humor," or
perhaps "absurdist" humor. The humor of this genre simply rails out
against fate and does not attempt in any way to reform society.
Rather than releasing tensions, this genre tends to dwell on
absurdity and to intensify the tensions. In contrast, Jack Matthews
is an American writer who writes satire in the classical sense.
Matthews' satire is in the tradition of Fielding, Sterne, and Samuel
Johnson in that he humanizes the satire by clearly identifying and
empathizing with the targets of his satire. Unlike Vonnegut, Barth,
Heller, and Pynchon, Matthews criticizes as he entertains.

1015. Lubow, Arthur. "Screw You Humor: The Comedian as Oppressor."
      <u>The New Republic</u> 179.17 (October 21, 1978): 18-22.

      Traces lampoon humor from the <u>Harvard Lampoon</u> to the <u>National
Lampoon</u> and <u>Saturday Night Live</u> and <u>Animal House</u> and Fran Lebowitz'
<u>Metropolitan Life</u>, which lampoons New York, and Cyra McFadden's <u>The
Serial</u>, which lampoons Marin County, California. Lampoon humor
probably originated with Oscar Wilde and continued with Dorothy
Parker and Lenny Bruce, but Wilde, Bruce, and Parker were cultural
elitists and political leftists, while lampoon humor picks the
easiest targets whether they are elite or plebian, left or right.
Lampoon humor targets women, blacks, or homosexuals; "It victimizes
society's victims." David McClelland was a cartoonist for the
<u>Harvard Lampoon</u> and the <u>National Lampoon</u>. On September 9, 1976 he
arrived at a friend's apartment in a Manhattan high-rise, shook

hands, walked through the living room, continued through the plate-
glass window, and fell to his death on the pavement below. Jokes
followed: "What's the difference between David McClelland and a
pizza?" "You don't have to watch out for broken glass in a pizza."
"Where are they keeping David McClelland?" "The International House
of Pancakes." Lampoon humor is sharp; it's viscious; and it's
ubiquitous. The original Harvard lampoons were arrogant, male,
Catholic, and "Crimson." McFadden and Lebowitz are not male,
Catholic, or "Crimson," but they retain the same arrogance.

1016. Mandia, Patricia M. "Chimerical Realities: Black Humor in The
      Mysterious Stranger," Studies in American Humor NS5.2-3
      (Summer-Fall 1986): 106-17.

      Proposes that Mark Twain's The Mysterious Stranger was an
important precursor to the American contemporary black-humor genre.
Like contemporary black humor, The Mysterious Stranger dealt with
horrible events in a humorous and absurd manner. There is an
intermingling of cruelty and death with humor in a deterministic
universe, and it is presented in a kind of satire that does not
attempt in any way to reform. The Mysterious Stranger is a
nihilistic and solipsistic novel in which life is presented as a bad
dream. Just as contemporary American black humor was the result of
the Holocaust, the Atomic Bomb, and the development of
impersonalizing technology, The Mysterious Stranger was the result
of Twain's losing the $200,000 he invested in the Paige typesetting
machine, the bankruptcy of his publishing firm, and the death of his
daughter, Susy. The rambling plot of The Mysterious Stranger is
consistent with the contention of black humorists that life lacks
relevance and coherence. Like contemporary black humorists, Twain
also distances himself from his characters and his subject. The
novel takes place in a distant locale (Austria) at a distant time
(1590), and Twain's humor provides an emotional distance between the
reader and the characters, allowing the reader to laugh at their
sad, even tragic, situations.

1017. Olsen, Lance. Circus of the Mind in Motion: Postmodernism and
      the Comic Vision. Detroit, MI: Wayne State Univ. Press, 1990,
      163 pp.

      Gives evidence that many of the techniques of deconstruc-
tionism and black humor have been around for a very long time.
Olsen alludes, for example, to the wacky graffiti on the walls of
Rome and to the dark jokes in English monasteries. But the
difference between these earlier forms and those of postmodernism is
the proliferation, the intensity, and the easy access to the media
of the dominant culture. Olsen describes the post-modern writer as
an "aesthetic and metaphysical terrorist," who believes that no one
text has more validity than any other text. The postmodern writer
employs the bitter and cynical stance of the absurdist black
humorist. The resulting text is ironic, acidic, biting, and
unstable. The goal is to decompose and dismember, but in addition
to this negative function, there is also a positive function, for
the gaps that result from the terrorist activity need to be filled
and can be filled in an infinity of ways. So while we may have
deconstruction as the result of this process, we also have potential
construction, or what Olsen calls the promise of "a radical freedom"
that results from creative and humorous free play. And in this

view, it is process, not product, that is emphasized. In <u>Gravity's Rainbow</u>, Pynchon tells a joke about a boy who is born with a golden screw in his navel. He devotes his life to talking with specialists trying to find someone who will help him get rid of his golden screw. He finally consults a voodoo doctor who gives him a potion that sends him into a wild dream, and when he wakes up the golden screw is gone. In ecstasy, he jumps out of bed... and his ass falls off. The deconstructionist moral of the story is that we should not be looking for neat solutions that don't exist.

1018. Olsen, Lance. "Making Stew with What you Got: Postmodern Humor in Barth, Nabokov, and Everybody Else." <u>Thalia: Studies in Literary Humor</u> 10.1 (1988): 23-29.

Describes postmodernism as a form of radical democracy in which every form, every medium, and every structure is just as good and just as bad as every other form, medium, or structure. Gilbert Sorrentino refers to this fusing of forms, media, and narratives as "Mulligan Stew." In earlier times literature, art, and music did not allow things to be put together unless they were compatible, but during the period of postmodernism, everything is intermixable, and the resultant incongruity produces a special kind of humor. In earlier times, culture and even the universe had a single and unified significance, but postmodernism attacks this assumption, suggesting instead a perspective of "plurisignification" that is in direct conflict with any particular perspective of unification. This multiplicity of perspective can be seen in the many colors of Pynchon's <u>Gravity's Rainbow</u>. Olsen suggests that realism, romanticism, expressionism, and even surrealism all suggest a norm. The realist sees a near perfect correlation between life and art. The romanticist adds the contraries of innocence and experience. The expressionist deals with emotions. And the surrealist brings the dream-mind into the process to provide an even deeper and richer texture and tone. But the deconstructionist perspective of postmodernism is truly transcendental, for it assumes no norm at all. It is based on radical skepticism and is nonjudgmental. The postmodernist sees a universe without fault, without truth, and without origin--a universe that is neither good nor bad but just there.

1019. Pinsker, Sanford. "The Graying of Black Humor." <u>Studies in the 20th Century</u> 9 (1972): 15-33.

Feels that it was Bruce Friedman's <u>Black Humor</u>, published by Bantam in 1965, which legitimatized the genre of black humor. Pinsker agrees with Friedman that "black humor" is not so much a "school" as it is a "sensibility," and actually, it's more "protean" than both. In 1965 Friedman had written that he could not define "black humor." "I think I would have more luck defining an elbow or a corned-beef sandwich." No black humorist of the 1960s was like any other black humorist of that period; furthermore, if a critic scratches beneath the surface of any major writer of the fiction during this period he will find a "black humorist." Pinsker feels that "black humor" provided an angle of vision for some authors and a comic technique for others. But black humorists are separate writers with separate concerns who "are certainly not going to attend any bi-monthly meetings to discuss policy and blackball new members." 1965 was the epitome of the black-humor movement;

since then the movement has become considerably "grayed." Heller hasn't finished his promised second novel. The Washington, D.C., of today is pretty much the same as the Washington, D.C., of 1965. Kesey has abandoned fiction altogether. "And those clouds which do remain look gray, very gray indeed."

1020. Schulz, Max F. Black Humor Fiction of the Sixties. Athens, Ohio: Ohio Univ. Press, 1973: xiv + 156 pp.

Portrays the black-humor movement as a group of guerrillas who charge the exposed flanks of an absurdly uncoordinated enemy. Bruce Jay Friedman is the field commander not only because of his writings but also because in 1965 he published a book for Bantam entitled Black Humor. This book contained pieces by Southern, Rechy, Donleavy, Albee, Simmons, Celine, Purdy, Heller, Pynchon, Nabokov, Knickerbocker, and Barth, authors whose novels have very little in common except that they are "black." Schulz' anthology contains writings by Barth, Vonnegut, Borges, Berger, Pynchon, Coover, Friedman, and Wright, but he feels that his own anthology has defined "black humor" a little bit more precisely, for he has distinguished between the contemporary novel and some earlier novels that had been classed as "black humor." He also distinguished between means (plot, character, thought, and diction) and the end (effect on the reader, such as laughter, tears, etc.). Schulz in fact defined "black humor" to exclude all but a very few European writers, saying that it is mainly an American literary movement of the 1960s, developing ironically out of cultural pluralism on the one hand and a need to conform on the other.

1021. Schulz, Max F. "Toward a Definition of Black Humor." Comic Relief: Humor in Contemporary American Literature. Ed. Sarah Blacher Cohen. Urbana: Univ. of Illinois Press, 1978, 14-27.

Considers "black humor" a vague term that does not distinguish among various genres. It doesn't differentiate contemporary from past expression, nor does it identify the means (plot, character, thought or diction) or the effect on the reader (laughter, tears, etc.). Schulz maintains that for a term to useful it must not only determine what it includes but what it excludes. The term "black humor" does neither. For example, Bruce Jay Friedman's Black Humor brought together authors that differed greatly in their philosophies, their styles, their effects, and their tones. Schulz considers Friedman's term "tense comedy" to be better than "black humor" but still not good enough. Schulz feels that the feature that what most differentiates "black humor" from other genres is the non-judgmental perspective. The black humorist is not so much concerned with how to deal with life as he is concerned with how to tolerate it. He challenges the basic hysterias of society but only to expose them, not to change them for the better. He takes a comic stance to deal both with tragic fact and with moralistic certitude in order to survive, but he is not so naive as to think that his writing will have any important effect on the world, and this attitude is reflected constantly in his writing.

1022. Weber, Brom. "The Mode of 'Black Humor'" The Comic Imagination
in American Literature. Ed. Louis D. Rubin, Jr. New Brunswick,
NJ: Rutgers Univ. Press, 1983, 361-71.

Begins with Edmund Wilson's 1954 criticism of George
Washington Harris' Sut Lovingood sketches charging that the sketches
were "unadulterated poison."   By 1964 (a decade after Wilson's
criticism), a number of important black-humor novels had appeared,
including, Nabokov's Lolita, Gaddis' Recognitions, Berger's Crazy in
Berlin, Purdy's Malcolm, Burroughs' The Naked Lunch, Donleavy's The
Ginger Man, and Southern's The Magic Christian.   By another decade
there were some even darker novels, such as Heller's Catch-22,
Kesey's One Flew Over the Cuckoo's Nest, Pynchon's V., Percy's The
Moviegoer, Barth's The Sot-Weed Factor, Hawkes' The Lime-Twig, and
Friedman's Stern. These black humorists are now regarded by many as
some of the most significant of contemporary American novelists, but
Wilson and other people who are critical of black humor feel that
humor should be "light-hearted, funny, amusing, [and] laughter
arousing...good natured, trivial, and kindly." They are bothered by
black humor, which seems to be hostile and sadistic and which
appears to have little respect for their values and behavior.   They
see black humor's disruptive influences rather than its ability to
correct wrongs and to help people cope with a very complex society.

Chapter 6
Children's and Adolescent Literature

1023. Anderson, Celia Catlett. "The Comedians of Oz." Studies in
American Humor NS 5.4 (Winter 1986-87): 229-242.

Compares the writings of L. Frank Baum to those of Lewis
Carroll and Edward Lear both in terms of quantity and quality. All
three writers specialized in reversals, incongruities, and word
play. But in addition to these qualities, Baum's writings had a
touch of drama that resulted from Baum's early training in
vaudeville. Baum was also an excellent parodist. There are
unmistakable similarities between Dorothy's adventures adrift in a
chicken coop and the adventures in Stephen Crane's "The Open Boat."
The mechanically run, glass-domed city in Glinda of Oz is very
similar to Edward Bellamy's futuristic city in Looking Backward.
And the centrally fortified city of Oz with its surrounding farms is
very similar to the pre-Raphaelite views of William Morris. The
many automations and contraptions of Oz may indeed be a parody of
the entire science-fiction genre of that period, and the phrase
"Well met, Brothers!" seems to echo Rudyard Kipling's Jungle Books.
The comic heroes that Dorothy meets on her journey to Oz and other
Baum characters as well resemble circus clowns in their dress, their
bearing, and their speech; And Baum's comic villains (witches, angry
kings, and spinster queens) are similarly comic characters. The
Wicked Witch of the West condemns Dorothy to a life of household
drudgery and is herself ironically destroyed by a bucket full of mop
water.

1024. Apseloff, Marilyn Fain. "The Big, Bad Wolf: New Approaches to
an Old Folk Tale." Children's Literary Association Quarterly
15.3 (Fall 1990): 135-37.

Discusses two satires based on the folk story of the "The
Three Little Pigs." Jon Scieszka's The True Story of the 3 Little
Pigs (1989) was written under the penname of Alexander Wolf, which
is shortened to "A. Wolf." A. Wolf is telling the "true story" of
the three little pigs to the book's author, Jon Scieszka. Wolf
claims that it's not his fault that wolves eat cute little animals
like bunnies, sheep, and pigs. The language is similar to, but also
sufficiently different from, the original story to produce an
effective parody-type satire. An example of this is "Go away wolf.
You can't come in. I'm shaving the hairs on my chinny chin chin";
another example is "I huffed and I snuffed." Apseloff suggests that
children are able to handle the subtleties and sophistication of
this satire as it is developed through size and role reversals,
exaggerations, irreverence, and scatology. Children enjoy and
understand the juxtaposition of the formal-old with the slangy-

contemporary speech. Jane Yolen's fantasy tale about the big bad
wolf is entitled "Happy Dens or a Day in the Old Wolves' Home."
Yolen's wordplay is excellent, and she does a good job in reversing
allegiences by presenting the story through the eyes of Wolfgang and
Oliver Wolf and others in the Old Wolves' Home, who suggest that
wolves have received bad press and go about correcting the stories
of "The Three Little Pigs," "Little Red Riding Hood," "The Lone
Wolf," and "Peter and the Wolf." Although younger children will
miss some of the parody and satire, they will nevertheless enjoy and
laugh at these satires because of their familiarity with the
original traditional tales.

1025. Bugniazet, Judith. "Ellen Conford: Biography and Books." The
      ALAN Review 14.1 (Fall 1986): 23-24.

    Explains that Conford "wrote her first book when her son was
four years old and she couldn't find a book in the library for him.
She decided that she could write something better than what was
available, and out of that Impossible Possum was born." In order to
provide a good alternative to television, Conford writes humorous
novels. "She writes to entertain." "Most of her protagonists are
girls between the ages of eleven and sixteen who are average in
every way, except one. They are witty and adept at sarcasm and one-
liners. They sound almost like stand-up comics and, in fact, the
protagonist in Strictly for Laughs is one." In this book, Joey
Merino handles every problem by joking, and it's hard for her to let
Peter know how she really feels. Instead, he wonders "what has
happened to change her personality from funny to sarcastic.... Joey
has to learn that there some things you don't joke about." In If
This Is Love, I'll Take Spaghetti the protagonist decides that love
takes a tremendous effort, so she'd rather just eat. In The Alfred
G. Graebner Memorial High School Handbook of Rules and Regulations
the protagonist's first disaster is her schedule. Other disasters
treated with humor include sex education, gym, skipping school, the
school store, and student government. The book is both humorous and
realistic; it describes high school as it really is."

1026. Bugniazet, Judith. "Jerry Spinelli: Biography and Books." The
      ALAN Review 14.1 (Fall 1986): 20.

    Says that to have lived closely with seven teenagers and still
be able to write about them with humor is admirable. Bugniazet
feels that this is probably why Spinelli's writing is so realistic.
All the fighting that siblings normally do and the things they fight
about are humorously detailed in Spinelli's writing. Who Put That
Hair in My Toothbrush?, for example, is about Megin and Greg, a
brother and sister who were constantly fighting. This book takes a
close look at a brother-sister relationship providing two points of
view that are both funny and heartwarming.

1027. Bugniazet, Judith. "Paul Zindel: Biography and Books." The
      ALAN Review 14.1 (Fall 1986): 8-12.

    Describes Zindel's books as usually being told in first-person
narrative style. His plots are fast paced, and his chapters are
short. Because he writes for teenagers and he gives them what they
want in a book rather than what adults think they should read.
Zindel shows teenagers that life may be fun, but despite its

difficulties.   Although   Zindel   is   a   very   popular   author   of
adolescent   novels,   he   considers   himself   to   be   primarily   a
playwright.   He especially likes to write plays about women because
he likes to write about "what's happening" and "women are what's
happening today."   Many of Zindel's titles are humorous, including,
Confessions of a Teenage Baboon, The Effect of Gamma Rays on Man-in-
the-Moon-Marigolds, Harry and Hortense at Hormone High, My Darling,
My Hamburger, Pardon Me, You're Stepping on My Eyeball, and The
Undertaker's Gone Bananas.

1028. Cline, Ruth, and Elizabeth Poe. "Now that You Asked...." The
       ALAN Review 14.1 (Fall 1986): 74.

       Links the sense of humor developed in order to appreciate the
personal relationships of adolescent literature to the sense of
humor that can contribute to a long life, happy marriage and
balanced perspective.   The humor in adolescent novels can be found
in the language, characters and situations and can be developed by
building on vernacular experiences with jokes, funny stories or
witty remarks.   Cline feels that by examining clever uses of
language, students will be able to increase their appreciation of
humor in children's and young adult literature, as well as build a
foundation   for   appreciation   of   humor   in   more   sophisticated
literature.

1029. Conford, Ellen. "I Want to Make Them Laugh." The ALAN Review
       14.1 (Fall 1986): 21-23.

       Recounts an incident when a woman asked if there are any
subjects that can't treat be humorously.   Conford replied that is
difficult to joke about cancer and abortion, but that except for
these two topics jokes can be told about virtually anything.
Conford considers growing up to be very difficult and she feels that
this is why it is important for the child to have some amusement,
some distraction, and some distance from the immediate concerns of
everyday life.   Adolescents have to deal with acceptance, self-
esteem,   the   opposite   sex,   parental   expectations,   friendship,
teachers, classes and glands.   Humor helps them deal with these
difficulties.   Humorous books are ideal for kids with school weary
heads and TV-shortened attention spans.   Much of what is funny
depends on brevity, the soul of wit.   Even the words associated with
humor tend to be short and to the point: gag, joke, quip, and punch
line.   Conford considers puns one-word jokes.   She says that in an
effectively funny book the reader knows that he or she is going to
get the payoff, the laugh, on almost every page.   In a humorous
story, the reader isn't merely entertained; he or she is motivated
to continue reading.   Conford feels that in their spare time, kids
have two basic entertainment options.   They can watch TV or they can
read a book.   A reader once indicated what made a book good for
adolescents.   This reader had three rules: "Don't bore me.   Don't
make it stupid.   And don't treat me like a child."   Conford tries to
abide by these rules.

1030. Donelson, Kenneth. "Humor." Literature for Today's Young
       Adults. 2nd Edition. Auths. Alleen Nilsen, and Ken Donelson.
       Glenview, IL: Scott Foresman, 1985, 335-59.

       Refines the four stages of humor interests of children and
young adults presented by Lance Gentile and Merna McMillen in their
"Humor and the Reading Program." STAGE I--Ages 10-11: "Literal
humor and slapstick..., accidents..., misbehavior"; STAGE II--Ages
12-13: "Practical jokes, teasing, goofs, sarcasm, joke-riddles, sick
jokes, elephant jokes, grape jokes, tongue twisters, knock-knock
jokes, moron jokes, TV bloopers"; STAGE III--Ages 14-15: "More lewd
jokes..., humor aimed at schools and parents and adults in
authority"; STAGE IV--Ages 16-up--"More subtle humor, satire and
parody..., witticisms..., Adult humor is increasingly part of their
repertoire, partly because they are anxious to appear sophisticated,
partly because they are growing up." Lewdness and grossness appear
in increasing frequency and intensity in the first three stages.
Examples and discussion of literature representing these stages are
given in sections on films, television, children's books, YA novels,
poetry, gentle humor, gentle satire, more sophisticated satire,
black humor, wacky British humor and parodies, the humor of death,
and the "ultimate" in teenagers' humor--Seuss, Keillor, M. E. Kerr,
Bob and Ray, Frank Sullivan, Judie Angell, Douglas Adams, Benjamin
Lee, and especially P. G. Wodehouse.

1031. Hanks, D. Thomas Jr. "The Wit of E. L. Konigsburg: To 'One Dog
       Squatting' from the Metropolitan Museum of Art." Studies in
       American Humor NS 5.4 (Winter 1986-87): 243-254.

       Explains that Konigsburg's narrator, Bo, in Journey to an 800
Number, received his name according to an old Indian custom. Bo's
father, Woody, had promised Bo's mother to name him in honor of the
first thing he saw after Bo was born. What he saw when he left the
hospital was a rainbow, and that accounts for Bo's name. Bo is
thankful that things worked out as they did, for he just missed
being named "One Dog Squatting." This juxtaposition of a celestial
image--the rainbow--with an earthy image--one dog squatting--
typifies Konigsburg's characteristic wit of joining together
concepts that are highly disparate. This same quality can be seen
in some of her titles: Jennifer, Hecate, Macbeth, William McKinley,
and Me, Elizabeth (Newbury Second Prize), and From the Mixed-up
Files of Mrs. Basil E. Frankweiler (Newbury Award, 1968).
Konigsburg's plots are as incongruous as are her titles. About the
B-Nai Bagels features a Jewish mother managing a Little League
baseball team; The Dragon in the Ghetto Caper is about a dragon in
two ghettos, one poor and black, the other a wealthy suburb;
Father's Arcane Daughter is about a kidnapped daughter who was never
kidnapped, George is about Ben and the little man who lives inside
him; Journey to an 800 Number is about a camel and a camel-driving
father and his preppie son, and Up from Jericho Tel is about a boy
and a girl interacting with the ghost of Tallulah Bankhead.

1032. Hartvigsen, M. Kip, and Christen Borg Hartvigsen. "The
       Terrible Hilarity of Adolescence in Dinky Hocker Shoots
       Smack!" The ALAN Review 14.1 (Fall 1986): 25-29.

       Alludes in the title to Dale Carlson's statement that
adolescent literature helps the adolescent ponder "the terrible

hilarity of adolescence." Kip and Christen Hartvigsen say that
adolescence is "like a house on moving day--everything is in a
temporary mess," and they claim that "few writers of young adult
literature have so skillfully shown humor embedded in oftentimes
serious adolescent quandaries as M. E. Kerr." Kerr has written
"dialogue with verve," and she has "created believable characters,
observed life accurately, and most notably used humor to make
serious points." In Dinky Hocker Shoots Smack, words are not used
in their ordinary meanings, since the protagonist is neither "dinky"
(at 165 pounds) nor a shooter of smack. The novel also exhibits
other comic aspects common to many adolescent novels. There is the
"comedy of adolescent manners" where characters are caught up in
"the intricacies of prescribed dress, speech, conduct, and even
humor." There is the "comedy of initiation" where characters have
bittersweet first experiences--"the first date, the first shaft...,
the first realization that parents are not perfect." And there is
the "comedy of getting along with authority figures--the challenge
of living with and understanding, and pleasing adults, most notably
parents."

1033. Huse, Nancy L., and Janice M. Alberghene. "Children's Humor:
Subversion or Socialization?" Children's Literary Association
Quarterly 15.3 (Fall 1990): 114-37.

Traces the major trends in the humor written for American
children from the latter half of the eighteenth century to the
present day. There are articles about the humor of Roald Dahl, Mark
Twain, E. B. White, Louise Fitzhugh, Joe Scieszka, Jane Yolen, L.
Frank Baum, Astrid Lindgrin, Maggie Browne, William Makepeace
Thackeray, Sarah Chauncey Woolsey, Elizabeth Stuart Phelps, Louisa
May Alcott, and others. Some papers suggest that the understanding
of the humor of these authors not only brings a sense of history but
also brings about a recognition of differences, divisions,
disjunctions, and dominances in American culture. The basic trend
has been away from the assumption of innocence on the part of the
child reader and away from a didactic dichotomy that assumes that
some themes are appropriate for girls while others are appropriate
for boys. Nevertheless, renegade comedy has been present since the
nineteenth century, both for boys (e.g., Huck Finn and Tom Sawyer)
and for girls (e.g., Jo in Little Women). One of the themes of this
special issue of Children's Literature Association Quarterly is that
optimism is the basis for comedy. Another is that deviant behavior
is rooted in failures to adapt to the "unrelenting reality of a
social order that remains constant." A third theme is that
children's humor is very different from adult humor, both in the
nature of the protagonists and in the extremes and extravagances of
their adventures. This collection is designed to give readers
glimpses and insights into children's humor viewed from a literary-
criticism point of view. The analysis of the various works is
intended to be both pleasant and insightful.

1034. MacDonald, Ruth. "The Weirdness of Shel Silverstein." Studies
in American Humor NS 5.4 (Winter 1986-87): 267-79.

Considers Silverstein to have been a significant member of the
group of American poets who broke with the tradition that the main
reason for writing children's poetry was to provide lessons to
children in manners and values (mainly Protestant and puritanical).

Silverstein is a leading twentieth-century children's poet who invites the child into the poetry rather than using the poetry to speak condescendingly to the child. Silverstein's A Light in the Attic and Where the Sidewalk Ends are both best sellers because they contain qualities of poetry that children love--identifiable rhythm, rhyme and sound patterns, a light, inviting tone, and most importantly, humor. Silverstein is aware of language, rhyme, meter, and stanzaic formulas, but MacDonald feels that he is a "less-than-perfect craftsman" in these matters. But where Silverstein excells is in his use of humor. His tone is uproarious, zany, and delightful, and it appeals both to adult buyers and to child readers. Silverstein has an appreciative audience of children in the late twentieth-century United States, and when these children grow up they will read Silverstein books to their own children.

1035. McNamara, Shelley G. "Saying One Thing and Meaning Another: Linguistic Devices in the Young Adult Novels of E. L. Konigsburg and Avi." WHIMSY 2 (1984): 48-49.

Suggests that although Konigsburg and Avi write for children, their writing is nevertheless sophisticated and mature. They use satire to attack established cultural beliefs, institutions, and traditions. They tend to use short, unvaried sentence patterns as well as obscenities and other vernacular expressions that are often associated with street talk. Their underground and violent themes often discuss issues that previously had been relegated only to adult literature, issues like contemporary cosmopolitan living, anti-establishment attitudes, and a diversity of values and ethics. Their satire is both contemporary and timeless as they deal with universal issues of life and living.

1036. Metcalf, Eva-Maria. "Tall Tale and Spectacle in Pippi Longstocking." Children's Literature Association Quarterly 15.3 (Fall 1990): 130-35.

Evaluates Astrid Lindgren's Pippi-Longstocking novels--Pippi Longstocking (1945), Pippi Longstocking Goes on Board (1945) and Pippi in the South Seas (1948). Pippi's real name is Pippilotta Delicatessa Windowshade Mackrelmint Efraimsdaughter Longstocking, which illustrates the basic rhetorical technique of Lindgren's novels--extravagance and excess. These books are much more enjoyable to children than they are to adults, and in addition, as Lindgren herself has noted, children and adults don't laugh in the same places. The books treat subjects and attitudes that most adults have outgrown and forgotten, but Lindgren has been able to retain her childhood memories and feelings. Lindgren's techniques for achieving humor in the series are varied. She uses humorous expressions; she inverts letters; she has clever puns; she also develops some gallows humor, and writes quite sophisticated self-parody. Pippi's chief characteristic is her drive to be strong, clever, and independent, and she succeeds. As Pippi says, "It's surely best for little children to live an orderly life, especially if they can order it themselves." One of the reasons for Lindgren's success is her reliance on the forms and techniques of the oral storytelling tradition. Each of the three Pippi books can be viewed as a tall tale, containing a great deal of comic expression from nonsense to boisterous exhuberance to self-parody to delicate irony.

1037. Nilsen, Alleen Pace. "Chapter 3: The Writer." Presenting M. E.
     Kerr. Boston: Twayne, 1986, x + 142 pp.

     Suggests that Kerr's ability to treat such serious subjects as
sex, drugs, racial differences, physical and mental disabilities,
troublesome family relationships, political problems, and feelings
of worthlessness and despair "and leave her audience smiling is her
biggest strength." "Kerr uses fresh metaphors both to create vivid
pictures and to develop characterization," as when Sabra St. Amour's
brassy, New York stage mother in I'll Love You When You're More Like
Me tells Sabra, "You're not just another salami decorating the deli
ceiling--you're special." In Is That You, Miss Blue?, when Flanders
goes for dinner with the family of her newly rich roommate, a cousin
tells Flanders that her eyes are going to pop right out of her head
if she orders a steak because "they come big as toilet seats." When
young readers comment on Kerr's books, the compliment they usually
give is that "she is a funny writer." "Kerr digs out life's little
incongruities, exaggerates them to the point of ridiculousness, and
then sprinkles them through her books, where they serve various
purposes." For example, in Little Little, the scheming protagonist
is named "Opportunity Knox" and at Miss Lake's (the residents called
it Mistakes) orphanage the deformed Sydney Cinnamon and his disabled
roommates referred to outsiders as Sara Lees--Similar and Regular
and Like Everyone Else.

1038. Nilsen, Alleen Pace. "Panel on Humor in Literature for Young
     Readers." WHIMSY 1 (April 1, 1983): 177-87.

     Quotes excerpts from various authors of children's books who
attended the 1982 conference of the World Humor and Irony Movement.
Tomie de Paola said that his Watch Out for the Chicken Feet in Your
Soup was done in celebration of his Italian grandma. And when his
Italian relatives saw the book, they didn't laugh at first, they
cried, "'Oh Nana would have loved it that you wrote a book about
her, Tomie.' And then we all laughed." Jack Prelutsky said he plays
with the language. When he hears a pun he keeps a notebook and
writes down every idea because every idea is valuable. "That's idea
A. But idea A leads to idea B and B prime.... The only thing that
sets us really above the animal kingdom is the ability to
extrapolate indefinitely. It just keeps going, so idea B leads to
idea C and C prime and C double prime." Ann Bishop talked about her
new book, Hello, Mr. Chips. Her visual aid was a MacIntosh apple
with a miniature keyboard mounted on it. She said it was the "only
real Apple Computer in the world." Alvin Schwartz talked about the
word play in Flapdoodle, and Tomfoolery. Mike Thaler, the riddle
king, talked about Plastic Man, whose "special power was that he
could change his shape. He could bend and twist and flatten
himself. He could slip under doors and through keyholes, and he
always snapped back to his original shape. A riddle is the plastic
man of the English language."

1039. Nilsen, Don L. F. "Dr. Seuss as Grammar Consultant." Language
     Arts, May 1977: 567-72.

     Analyzes the humorous grammatical deviation in the thirty-four
Dr. Seuss books written between 1937 and 1973. Theodore Seuss
Geisel violates phonological rules when he rhymes "number" and
"Cucumber" with the month of "Septumber" or when "myself" becomes

"mysolf" to rhyme with "golf." In the same way, "shouldsters," "eyses," "fastly" and "eaches" are coined to rhyme with "oldsters," "surprises," "gastly," and "beaches." respectively. Seuss also stretches children's minds with illogical cause-effect relations, as in <u>Because a Little Bug went Kachoo</u>, where a bug's sneezing caused a seed to drop, hitting a worm, making it kick a tree, causing a coconut to fall and so on. Dr. Seuss coins such verbs as "gleap," "zum," "slupp," "snargle," "snuffle," and "whuff," and he also makes his verbs do extra duty, as, for example, in <u>The Lorax</u> where he writes "I biggered my factory. I biggered my roads. I biggered my wagons. I biggered the loads." Dr. Seuss's nouns are especially imaginative. He has invented such vehicles as the "One Wheeler Wubble," the "Skeegle-mobile," the "Bumble Boat," and the "Abrasian-Contusion." Dr. Seuss is even able to give the sound of two goldfish kissing--"pip."

1040. Nilsen, Don L. F. "Dr. Zeus: The Creator." <u>Arizona English Bulletin</u> 20.1 (October 1977): 58-62.

Explores the techniques Theodore Seuss Geisel uses in order to get his creative humor-juices flowing. Even though Dr. Seuss is a prolific writer of children's books, he doesn't have any children of his own. When he is writing his first drafts, Dr. Seuss doesn't even have children in mind. In order to give the story some spontaniety, he will swear and use dirty words and end up with a piece of very adult writing on a child's topic. He then goes back and cleans up the manuscript, but even then he tries to remain as uninhibited as possible. When he has trouble getting an idea, he puts on his thinking cap, and like Bartholemew Cubbins, he has about 500 of them, including a shako made of rock-wallaby fur and an Ecuadorian fireman's helmet. When he is in his creative frame of mind, Dr. Seuss writes about impossible animals, machines, and situations, and his drawings are as fantastic as are the concepts they illustrate. Almost all of Dr. Seuss's writing employs the anapestic tetrameter rhythm pattern, the same pattern that is used in "The Star Spangled Banner," and "T'was the Night Before Christmas." This pattern can be demonstrated by quoting the ending of <u>The Lorax</u>: "And all that the Lorax left here in this mess / was a small pile of rocks, with the one word 'UNLESS'." Dr. Seuss's creativity lies not only in his writing and illustrations but even more significantly in his interaction with his readers.

1041. Nilsen, Don L. F., and Alleen Pace Nilsen. "Parenting Creative Children: The Role and Evolution of Humor. <u>The Creative Child and Adult Quarterly</u> 12.1 (Spring 1987): 53-61.

Explains about how the humor of George Carlin, Tomie de Paola, Lillian Morrison, and Carl Withers relates to various ages of children. In <u>Strega Nona</u> by Tomie de Paola, for example, when older children read the book they roar with laughter, but younger children react very differently. They "don't laugh. Their eyes get big. It's real and serious, as if he's telling them about nuclear war. Life is very serious for younger children. When Big Anthony made the pasta pot work when he wasn't supposed to, they knew that he would be punished. In their own fear of being punished, they identified with the wrong-doer." Older children feel more of a distance from the story. For them, there is much less personal involvement.

1042. Nilsen, Don L. F., and Alleen Pace Nilsen. "An Exploration and Defense of the Humor in Young Adult Literature." Journal of Reading, October 1982: 58-65.

Proposes that humor draws teenagers to such sophisticated writers as Kurt Vonnegut, Richard Brautigan, Philip Roth, John Irving, and Joseph Heller, and further suggests that perhaps the general lack of humor in Robert Cormier's writing is why it isn't as popular as the less skillful but funnier writing of Paul Zindel, Richard Peck, Paula Danziger, Shel Silverstein, Judy Blume, Jean Shepherd, and M. E. Kerr. Humor forces teenagers to be active instead of passive readers. As they mentally stretch, they are training themselves to become expert in the subtle manipulation of an amazing set of symbols.

1043. Pollack, Pamela, ed. The Random House Book of Humor for Children. New York: Random House, 1988, 311.

Anthologizes the best chapters and short stories in twentieth century American children's literature, with a few samples from earlier authors like Rudyard Kipling and Mark Twain. The book contains excerpts of adventure stories (e.g., Shirley Jackson's "Life Among the Savages," Louise Fitzhugh's "Harriet the Spy," and Mark Twain's "Tom Sawyer"), animal stories (e.g., "Betsy Byars' "The Midnight Fox," Rudyard Kipling's "The Elephant's Child," James Thurber's "The Moth and the Star," and Patrick McManus' "The Skunk Ladder"), family life (e.g., Frank Gilbreth and Ernestine Carey's "Cheaper by the Dozen" and Garrison Keillor's "Lake Wobegon Days"), growing up (e.g., Judy Blume's "Tales of a Fourth Grade Nothing," Barbara Robinson's "The Best Christmas Pageant Ever," and Thomas Rockwell's "How to Eat Fried Worms"), and the supernatural (e.g., Richard Peck's "Ghosts I Have Been," Betty MacDonald's "Mrs. Piggle-Wiggle's Magic," Norton Juster's "The Phantom Tollbooth," and Natalie Babbitt's "The Harps of Heaven"). There are a few British authors represented such as Roald Dahl and Rudyard Kipling.

1044. Reynolds, Clay. "The Book That Scarry Built: Being in Part a Discourse on the Importance of the Role of Children in Children's Literature." Studies in American Humor NS 5.4 (Winter 1986-87): 280-286.

Considers Scarry's books to contain idiotic, vacuous characters involved in "a bedlam of moronic activities while wearing stupid smiles on their wide, lunatic, animal faces." He feels that Scarry's books are insidiously designed to "drive parental readers insane with insipid inanity and irritating irrelevancy." Before he had ever heard of Richard Scarry, Reynolds had envisioned himself as a parent, snuggly wrapped in wollen nightclothes reading Mother Goose, Aesop's Fables, or Winnie the Pooh to the child snuggled in his lap with eyes all aglow with fascination, but instead, every evening his child is able to find a new book by Richard Scarry about cats, dogs, pigs, chickens, mice, rabbits, worms, monkeys, hippos and rhinos dressed in humanoid clothing, and while the story is being read the child pummels him with questions like "What kind of animal is that, daddy," about forty times per page. Scarry's animals are unimaginably stupid, and they are always doing inane, usually irrelevant tasks. The plots are insipid--a pig mistakes a steam shovel for the family car, or a rabbit gets stuck in hot,

sticky tar on a new roadway. The child being read to always asks,
"Why did he do that, daddy?" The "surprise" endings of Scarry books
are obvious from the first page, and Scarry builds tension by asking
"Why do you suppose he did that?" But although Reynolds <u>hates</u>
Scarry's books, his children <u>love</u> them, and Reynolds begrudgingly
admits that children themselves are the best judges of children's
books. Scarry's genius, wit, and sense of human comedy are <u>perfect</u>
for the very young readers they are designed for.

1045. Richardson, Alan. "Nineteenth-Century Children's Satire and
      the Ambivalent Reader." <u>Children's Literature Association
      Quarterly</u> 15.3 (Fall 1990): 122-26.

      Suggests that the reason for the development of the children's
book industry during the latter half of the eighteenth century was
primarily to draw the child into the adult world and frame the child
according to adult desires. The books assumed that children were
innocent and simple. The books taught lessons and abided by the
"norm of closure." Originally, the books were all very much the
same, and the characters were very much stereotyped. But then,
Lewis Carroll started writing ambivalent messages for children in
England, and this type of writing soon came to America in the
writings of Maggie Browne and William Makepeace Thackeray. Browne's
<u>Wanted--A King, or How Merle Set the Nursery Rhymes to Rights</u> (1890)
considers children to be enthusiastic and ready to grow from their
nursery rhyme experiences. It taught them that subversion is OK,
that they should challenge adult attempts at control. Likewise,
Thackeray's <u>The Rose and the Ring</u> (1855) parodies the literary
conventions of children's fairy tales to make the child less naive.
Thackeray has many allusions to Shakespeare, as he expects his young
readers to be sophisticated adolescents with some knowledge of
Shakespeare. In comparing the writings of Carroll, Browne, and
Thackeray, Richardson suggests that all three work against the
mainstream of official children's literature not only by questioning
the assumption of childhood innocence but by subverting the
didacticism in forcing children to abide by adult values.

1046. Russell, David L. "The Comic Spirit and Cosmic Order in
      Children's Literature." <u>Children's Literature Association
      Quarterly</u> 15.3 (Fall 1990): 117-19.

      Contends that L. Frank Baum's <u>The Wizard of Oz</u> is more
sophisticated than most critics give it credit for being. Baum is
using great irony, understatement, and satire when his Scarecrow
says, "I cannot understand why you should wish to leave this
beautiful country and go back to the dry, gray place you call
Kansas," and when Dorothy responds, "That is because you have no
brains," and then continues, "No matter how dreary and gray our
homes are, we people of flesh and blood would rather live there than
in any other country, be it ever so beautiful. There is no place
like home." Russell suggests that the full breadth of this humor
may be lost on most children but that for adults it is "splendid
irony." And furthermore, Dorothy's message is not only comedy, it
is the essence of comedy, for as Russell suggests, "the comic spirit
is the denial of human limitations." In contrasting tragedy with
comedy, Russell says that tragedy envolves a confrontation with the
world as it is, while comedy seeks a way to make the world better
than it is. It is this comic vision that gives children their

relentless spirit and their optimism. They see limitations as challenges to be overcome rather than as inevitabilities to be endured. Russell gives an insightful example of the comic spirit in action. His daughter drew an amusing picture of a man with a top hat, a beard, and a long black coat. She explained that she had started to draw a picture of a Christmas Tree, but it wasn't turning out right, so she drew a picture of President Lincoln instead. This is the essence of the comic spirit; and it is the essence of childhood as well.

1047. Schmidt, Gary D. "A Merger of Traditions: Sources of Comedy in Robert McCloskey's Homer Price Stories." Studies in American Humor NS 5.4 (Winter 1986-87): 287-98.

Consider's McCloskey's Centerburg Tales not to be "stories" so much as they are "stories about stories." These are tales about how stories are supposed to be retold, how they gain new life on each telling. All of the children in the story watch Grandpa Herc very closely, and they know that when he starts stroking his chin he is about to tell another story. McClosky's Homer Price books are the only books which McClosky intended to be humorous. The stories in these books are gleaned from the stock of epic stories passed down through history. The stories come from American tall tales, from European folk literature, even from The Odyssey. They continue the tradition of exaggeration and of presenting characters and events in a larger-than-life perspective. But the significance of the stories is their setting and the details of the new retelling. Centerburg, Ohio is a place where "the pace is slow, the work is honest, the people are virguous, if sometimes silly," a place where, in a phrase, nothing ever happens. The irony is in the contrast between the town, which is very non-dramatic, and the stories, which are very dramatic. Schmidt furthermore feels that the exaggeration is not exaggeration at all. The events are seen from the viewpoint of a young naive child, and the exaggerated world is how this child actually sees the world--everything is meant to be perfectly literal. Schmidt compares this exaggerated perspective of the child in the Homer Price stories with the exaggerated perspective of the mallard family in Make Way for Ducklings. In both cases, the tone is quite serious but amusing to adults, nevertheless.

1048. Schuman, Samuel. "Comic Mythos and Children's Literature--Or, Out of the Fryeing Pan and into the Pyre." It's a Funny Thing, Humour. Eds. Antony J. Chapman, and Hugh C. Foot. New York: Pergamon, 1977, 119-21.

Applies the methodologies of Carl Jung and Northrop Frye to three classics of children's literature--Jack and the Beanstock, Hansel and Gretel, and The Wizard of Oz, the first two collected by the Brothers Grimm and the last one written by American author, L. Frank Baum. Schuman also compares the regenerative patterns of The Wizard of Oz to the regenerative patterns in some of Shakespeare's "adult comedy." And he compares the beginning of The Wizard of Oz to T. S. Eliot's The Wasteland. "When Dorothy stood in the doorway and looked around, she could see nothing but the gray prairie on every side. Not a tree nor a house broke the broad sweep of the flat country that reached the sky in all directions" appears near the beginning of The Wizard of Oz. "A heap of broken images, where the sun beats, and the dead tree gives no shelter, the cricket no relief and the dry stone no sound of water" appears near the beginning of The Wasteland.

1049. Spinelli, Jerry. "Before the Immaculate Cuticles." The ALAN Review 14.1 (Fall 1986): 15-18.

Explains that he wrote his first book as an adult novel, but since the protagonist was a thirteen-year-old boy, it wound up in the children's department of his publisher's office. At first he regretted this placement; however since then he has taken a more deliberate look at kids "just hitting double-digits, the pubescent, the metamorphic creature who's showing just enough leg to shed the name of tadpole, but who is still hauling around too much tail to qualify for full froghood." Spinelli suggests that there are two major qualities needed to be a good writer of adolescent novels-- memory and attention. "Isn't it a magical, wonderful thing that our childhoods are not irretrievably lost to us..., and that without moving so much as an eyelash we can call back Buddy Brathwaite's bare, rat-proof feet, or Ginny Sukoloski's dungaree-nipping pet duck, or Joey Lapella's green teeth? Our school graduations from year to year are never really total. Something of each of us is "left back" in every grade we pass. We carry attic treasures in our heads." In reference to "paying attention," he says, "Start with a single kid. Pick one out. Any one. Get to know him. All his colors and shadings, all his moments. Because each kid is a population unto himself, a walking cross-section, a demographic grab bag, and a child's bedroom is as much a window to the universe as a scientist's lab or a philosopher's study."

1050. Stahl, J. D. "Satire and the Evolution of Perspective in Children's Literature: Mark Twain, E. B. White, and Louise Fitzhugh." Children's Literature Association Quarterly 15.3 (Fall 1990): 119-22.

Proposes that throughout its history children's satire has been different from adult satire, because children see themselves as the center of their "mythopoetic" universes. For children, the real world is "infinitely signifying," and for children it is therefore a small step from the world of reality to the world of fantasy. Nevertheless, children's satire has changed over the years. Twain has a narrator who is a naive reporter of an adult world, interpreting the world on the basis of limited experiences, he is unable to comprehend the world fully. Twain satirizes the evils of Southern society by creating inner contradictions in Huck's value system. E. B. White presents a pig who talks like an adult but thinks like a child. White's satire is gentle and urbane and highly ironic. The adults in Charlotte's Web are just as absurd and potentially dangerous as are those in Huckleberry Finn. Louise Fitzhugh's Harriet takes adult forms of literacy and transforms them to fit her own purposes. The satire of Fitzhugh's Harriet the Spy is often more blunt and brutal in its caustic attacks on adults. Mrs. Plumber, for example, feels she must lie in bed all day long in order to discover the true meaning of life, until her doctor tells her she must lie in bed, at which time she starts wishing that she could do anything at all rather than being forced to stay in bed. All three of these authors present the world through children's eyes, and all three satirize the world of the adult, thereby legitimatizing the world of the child.

1051. Strong, Emily. "Juvenile Literary Rape In America: A Post-Coital Study of the Writings of Dr. Seuss." Studies in Contemporary Satire 4 (Spring 1977): 34-39.

Offers a tongue-in cheek analysis of the prose and poetry of Dr. Seuss, suggesting that his writing and illustrations are responsible for our "exponentially rising promiscuity rates." Stong notes that Dr. Seuss's books are floridly illustrated in "rapturous reds, pubescent purples, and burlesque blues" and that these erotic colors have been playing with the erogenous zones of our nation, resulting in an entire population of perversions. In order to make her point, Stong looks in detail at a number of Dr. Seuss books. She describes Hop on Pop, for example, as developing an "oedipal-electra parent image" for children.

1052. Taylor, Mary-Agnes. "Humor in Children's Literature" Special Issue of Studies in American Humor NS 5.4 (Winter 1986-87): 233-298.

Elucidates the wide variety of humor used by such important American authors of children's literature as L. Frank Baum (1856-1919), E. L. Konigsburg (1930-), Robert McCloskey (1914-), Richard Scarry (1919-), and Shel Silverstein (1932-). Celia Anderson discusses the low humor and psychological implications of Baum's cast of comic characters. Tom Hanks discusses Konigsburg's wit of joining together disparate concepts in an ingeniously humorous manner. Ruth MacDonald shows how twentieth century authors of books for children have broken with the tradition of moralism and preachy didacticism that has been in effect since the days of Isaac Watts. She presents Silverstein as something of an adult basher and questionable craftsman but enormously popular author from the child's perspective. Gary Schmidt points out that the value of Robert McCloskey's books lies in the way they are retold rather than in the content, which tends to be taken from earlier sources. Elvin Holt discusses the racist drawings found in Edward Windsor Kemble's A Coon Alphabet and contrasts this book with contemporary alphabet books like Adam's ABC by Dale Fife (illustrated by Don Robertson), where each gentle scene demonstrates that Black is beautiful. E. W. Kemble, by the way, is the illustrator of Mark Twain's Huckleberry Finn, and his attitudes were typical of his time.

1053. Vallone, Lynne M. "Laughing with the Boys and Learning with the Girls: Humor in Nineteenth-Century American Juvenile Fiction." Children's Literature Association Quarterly 15.3 (Fall 1990): 127-30.

Contrasts the nineteenth-century subject matter of boys' books--adventure, school days and practical jokes--with the subject matter of girls' books--home, family and romance. The most popular nineteenth-century American book for boys was Mark Twain's Adventures of Tom Sawyer (1876), and the most popular nineteenth-century American book for girls was Louisa May Alcott's Little Women (1868). Almost everything was funny in the boyish world of Tom Sawyer--the wry tone of the narrator, the stock characters, Tom's superstitions, and especially Tom's capers. But in Little Women, the girls had very little to do with humor--except for Jo, and she was a tomboy, which was further proof that humor was for boys and not for girls. Vallone suggests that the humor in Tom Sawyer is to

help us laugh at the boy that is in each of us, while the humor of
Little Women is to help us exorcise the evil in ourselves. Jo is
presented as a bad example. Her humor illustrates that she is not
properly playing her role as a selfless "little" woman.

1054. Van Dyk, Howard. "Embrace the Comic." English Journal 70.6
      (October 1981): 48-49.

     Demonstrates that comic or humorous writers should be an
important part of the high-school English curriculum. Van Dyk deals
with contemporary main-stream humorous writers such as Dorothy
Parker, Terry Southern, Max Shulman, Thomas Heggen, E. B. White,
George Kaufman, Moss Hart, Bernard Malamud, Ogden Nash, Ambrose
Bierce, Samuel Hoffenstein, Robert Benchley, Donald Barthelme,
Richard Armour, Ring Lardner, Frank Sullivan, Jean Kerr, Joseph
Heller, and Will Rogers; popular contemporary humorous writers such
as Art Buchwald, Steve Allen, Woody Allen, Steve Martin, Erma
Bombeck, Garry Trudeau, and Lawrence Peter; and earlier writers such
as Mark Twain, Washington Irving, Petroleum Nasby.

1055. West, Mark I. "The Grotesque and the Taboo in Roald Dahl's
      Humorous Writings for Children." Children's Literature
      Association Quarterly 15.3 (Fall 1990): 115-16.

     Contrasts adults' reactions with children's reactions to
Dahl's The Twits. Adults consider the stories, situations and jokes
tasteless and immature, while children consider them great fun.
This is because the adults and the children are in different stages
of physical and psychological development. Much of the humor in The
Twits relates to cleanliness, body functions, scatology, and other
forms of grossness. The children who like this book have just gone
through a period of bladder and bowel training and have just learned
that adults seem to be very concerned about exactly when and where
these bowel and bladder movements occur and become very upset when
they happen in the wrong place or at the wrong time. The children
are anxious about such matters, and one way of dealing with their
anxiety is through humor. So children at this age are very
concerned with the concept of grossness. And everyone admits that
The Twits contains much gross humor, including the maggoty green
cheese and the moldy old cornflakes and the slimey tail of a sardine
that are found in Mr. Twit's whiskers and the time when Mrs. Twit
takes out her glass eye and places it into Mr. Twit's beer mug and
he nearly swallows it or the time when Mr. Twit puts a slimey frog
in Mrs. Twit's bed and convinces her that it is a deadly monster.
The Twits not only deals with the anxieties of toilet training, but
it also pokes fun at the moral authority that adults have over
children and that children naturally resent.

1056. Zindel, Paul. "Of Fiction and Madness." The ALAN Review 14.1
      (Fall 1986): 1-8.

     Quotes one of his readers as having written to say "your
writing is a lot of senseless junk." Then, this reader continues,
"My real name is Louise Walker and I think your senseless junk is
the best senseless junk I've ever read. I particularly like The
Undertaker's Gone Bananas and The Effect of Gamma Rays on Man-In-The
Moon Marigolds." Zindel says that his newest book Harry and
Hortense at Hormone High is anecdotal. "My fiction comes out of my

life." "I was in my own male menopause or climacteric. Adolescents seem to be in perpetual menopause." This article was originally presented as a speech and Zindel had two whistles. TWEET (like a sweet little canary) was used if he was talking about the fictional areas of the book and HONK (like a loud duck) was used if he was back into REALITY of his adventures. The TWEET and HONK are retained in the written version.

Chapter 7
Ethnicity

1057. Barksdale, Richard K. "Black America and the Mask of Comedy."
The Comic Imagination in American Literature. Ed. Louis D.
Rubin, Jr. New Brunswick, NJ: Rutgers Univ. Press, 1983, 349-
60.

Considers comic ridicule to have been an effective device that
Blacks used during slavery to counterbalance the powerful white
landowners. Barksdale suggests that there was Black laughter hidden
in ballads, in songs, and in stories, and he feels that Joel
Chandler Harris was especially effective in the use of comic
ridicule. "Brer Rabbit, symbolizing the powerless slave, always
outtricked Buh Bear and the other animals who represented the white
power structure." Barksdale also discusses the use of comic
ridicule by contemporary Black writers--James Baldwin, Ralph
Ellison, and Douglas Turner Ward. Barksdale notes that comic
ridicule may not cause radical changes in the power relationships
that exist between Blacks and whites, but it is an important device
nevertheless because it may not be not as destructive as other
coping devices such as marches and civil disobedience and because it
provides an opportunity for "therapeutic laughter that can help to
heal the long-festering wound of racism."

1058. Cohen, Sarah Blacher. "The Jewish Literary Comediennes." Comic
Relief: Humor in Contemporary American Literature. Ed. Sarah
Blacher Cohen. Urbana: Univ. of Illinois Press, 1978, 172-86.

Contrasts the Jewish writer before World War II with the
Jewish writer afterward. Before World War II, Jewish writers did
not stress the Jewishness of their Jewish characters. Arthur
Miller's Willie Loman is Jewish, and Miller portrayed him as a
schlemiel-salesman. But he was not specifically Jewish; he was a
secular everyman. After World War II, people felt sympathy for the
Jews because of their losses during the Holocaust and admiration
because of their creating the State of Israel from a barren desert.
Now Jewish-American comedians such as Lenny Bruce, Shelley Berman,
Mel Brooks, Milton Berle, and Woody Allen not only showed pride in
their Jewishness but, in fact, made it a significant part of their
writing. They exposed the "schmaltz," the "schmutz," and the
"meschuggas" of their heritage. Jewish-American novelists like Saul
Bellow, Bernard Malamud, Philip Roth, Herbert Gold, Bruce Jay
Friedman, and Stanley Elkin could now accurately portray Jewish
manners, folkways, values, and language. They could mock the Jews
not only for their minor lapses but for their major offenses. For
centuries Jewish women had been even more constrained than were
Jewish men. During Talmudic times women were more prized for their

frailty than for their virtue. They were considered too trivial to
study the Torah and were denied exposure to the wit of biblical
commentary and the sharp exchanges of Yeshiva students. But the
East European "shtetl" woman developed independence in the
nineteenth and twentieth centuries. She became regarded as a shrewd
businesswoman who learned her language skills in the marketplace,
and contemporary Jewish-American authors have further refined these
skills.

1959. Cohen, Sarah Blacher. Jewish Wry: Essays on Jewish Humor.
Bloomington: Indiana Univ. Press, 1987, x + 244 pp.

Discusses the non-kosher tone of such Jewish authors as Lenny
Bruce, Sophie Tucker, and Joan Rivers and contrasts this tone with
the schlemiel tone of Woody Allen, and the guilty tone of Philip
Roth and Stanley Elkin. Lenny Bruce's humor is hostile. He divides
the world into Jews and Gentiles, and then he attacks both groups.
He uses humor and irony and satire to criticize the vindictiveness,
the venality, the racism (especially anti-Semitism), the prudery,
and the lechery of the gentile. But Bruce also felt a need to shock
the Jews, to go public with their most private secrets. Bruce's
autobiography is appropriately entitled, How to Talk Dirty and
Influence People. Sophie Tucker, Belle Barth, Totie Fields, and
Joan Rivers continued the tradition of the unkosher comedians;
however, now they were even more unkosher, because their uproarious
brazen voices violated the code of gentility observed by respectable
Jewish women. Woody Allen, the opposite of the tough, unkosher
comediennes and the super macho Lenny Bruce, portrays himself as the
schlemiel figure. Cohen considers the writings of Philip Roth and
Stanley Elkin to come from a different Jewish tradition, that of the
stand-up comic and the Borscht Belt. Like the stand-up comics who
influenced them, their writing contains dualities of the trivial and
the tragic, the parodic and the painful. Cohen considers Roth's
Portnoy's Complaint to combine the stand-up comedy of a Henny
Youngman with the sit-down comedy of a Franz Kafka. Stanley Elkin
writes Jewish black humor and adds the dimension of the grotesque.
His characters are disfigured and malformed either physically,
mentally, or both. He calls them "human lemons," and said that if
they had been made in Detroit, they would have been recalled.

1060. Garrett, George. "Ladies in Boston Have Their Hats: Notes on
WASP Humor." Comic Relief: Humor in Contemporary American
Literature. Ed. Sarah Blacher Cohen. Urbana: Univ. of Illinois
Press, 1978, 207-37.

Believes that WASP humor, like WASP culture, is contradictory
in nature. WASPs believe in democracy, but they also believe in
faith and in conformity. Their faith is basically heretical,
individualistic, and anarchic, but it is nevertheless necessary.
They also believe in fair play--or at least the appearance of fair
play. It is difficult for WASPs to comprehend that racial groups
have been discriminated against for so long that they are
disadvantaged by the rules of fair play which keeps them at a
disadvantage. So "fair play" becomes "unfair play" when people
don't begin the race from the same starting line. This sense of
fair play can be seen in the WASP's most famous game, the Civil War.
There is nothing in modern history to match the brutality and
savagery of this war. By the end of the war, one-tenth of all

military-age Northerners and one-fourth of all military-age
Southerners were dead or disabled. Yet when the war ended the
Northerners and the Southerners became somewhat amiable. The war
had been merely a game, devised to see who would win and who would
lose. It was a game that stressed conformity to the ideals of the
group rather than those of the individual. Even today, the WASP is
amused at the black runningback who does a little dance when he
scores a touchdown, for the WASP knows that he didn't score the
touchdown at all. It was the whole team.

1061. Guttman, Allen. "Jewish Humor." The Comic Imagination in
      American Literature. Ed. Louis D. Rubin, Jr. New Brunswick,
      NJ: Rutgers Univ. Press, 1983, 329-38.

      Feels that there is no such thing as "Jewish humor" because it
cannot be traced to Judaism as a religion nor can it be traced to
the experiences of Biblical Jews. He feels that "Jewish humor" is
rather the result of a people having left their own country and
having to maintain "a precarious existence within the larger culture
of Christendom." Guttman then goes on to discuss the "Jewishness"
of such writers as Isaac Bashevis Singer, Abraham Cahan, Montague
Glass, Bernard Malamud, Saul Bellow, and Philip Roth.

1062. Hurd, Myles. "Uncle Tom as Smirking Muse: Ward's Happy Ending
      and Day of Absence." Studies in Contemporary Satire 11 (1984):
      1-9.

      Indicates that Douglas Turner Ward's best two plays (Happy
Ending, and Day of Absence) are both satires that offer a balance
between laughter and venom. Ward relies mainly on Juvenalian satire
to attack the ways of white folks. Both plays are intended for
Black audiences, and both use humor that exposes the white community
as insipid and stupid, unconsciously manipulated by a Black world
they hold in contempt. Ward uses an ironic reversal of the Uncle
Tom stereotype to indicate the unitedness of Blacks in the Black
cause. Ward's detachment and humor have allowed him to clarify the
true worth of Black people.

1063. Jackson, Blyden. "The Harlem Renaissance." The Comic
      Imagination in American Literature. Ed. Louis D. Rubin, Jr.
      New Brunswick, NJ: Rutgers Univ. Press, 1983, 295-303.

      Suggests that such Black writers as James Weldon Johnson, Jean
Toomer, Langston Hughes, Rudolph Fisher, Wallace Thurman, Claude
McKay, Countee Cullen, and George Schuyler are Renaissance authors
and furthermore suggests that Jean Toomer and Langston Hughes "set
the limits of the comic spirit" for this Renaissance. "If no writer
of the Renaissance matched Toomer as a metaphysician of the human
condition, none other, in great probability, was quite as free of
gall and gloom, quite as much the true, disinterested comedian, even
with his penchant for irony, as Hughes."

1064. Jackson, Blyden. "The Minstrel Mode." The Comic Imagination in
      American Literature. Ed. Louis D. Rubin, Jr. New Brunswick,
      NJ: Rutgers Univ. Press, 1983, 149-56.

      Credits James Weldon Johnson with having said that every
plantation in the South had a band of minstrels that could tell

Black jokes, play the banjo and the bones, and sing and dance.
Johnson said that whenever the wealthy plantation owner wanted to
have a party he would usually call for his troupe of Black
minstrels. Jackson, however, sugests that it was the everyday non-
party relationships between the Blacks and the whites that developed
the first Black humorists.   The Black minstrels were actually
satiric characters, and "each comic figure added a dimension of
social nuance, a humanizing influence, to an often otherwise
brutelike existence." The first significant white impersonation of
Blacks took place on an American stage in 1769. The impersonator
was Thomas Dartmouth Rice, and he established a long and mocking
tradition that lasted until 1928. The Black reaction to white
impersonation of Blacks on stage can be seen in Langston Hughes'
novel, Not Without Laughter, where Hughes' Negro vagrant, Jim-boy,
is used to show contempt for "the conventional American minstrel
mode."

1065. Nichols, Charles H. "Comic Modes in Black America (A Ramble
       through Afro-American Humor)." Comic Relief: Humor in
       Contemporary American Literature. Ed. Sarah Blacher Cohen.
       Urbana: Univ. of Illinois Press, 1978, 105-26.

       Suggests that Blacks have been forced to observe American
society from the outside. They have been verbally scorned and
physically attacked and have learned to express a rich variety of
idea and feeling to reflect the ironies, paradoxes, and
contradictions of their everyday lives. They have especially
developed the comic modes of colloquial speech and imaginative
writing, not only of irony and paradox, but of exaggeration,
innuendo, sarcasm, word play, and role-playing--what Nichols
describes as "the whole arsenal of satire." The Black writers'
perspective is the precipice from which they can see a bottomless
abyss and total chaos and destruction. This accounts for their
heightened consciousness and the wild joy in their writing. Their
art is their only real freedom, and their mastery of the ridiculous
is their way of coping as well as their way of being effective
writers. The black man was defined by the white man. The foolish-
but-comic darky is portrayed in the works of such prominent American
authors as James Fenimore Cooper, Mark Twain, Irwin Russell, Joel
Chandler Harris, and Harriet Beecher Stowe. But there has always
been an in-group black humor, and since 1945 the rise of independent
states in Africa and the rise of Black Power in the United States
has allowed Blacks to determine their own identity and create their
own images.

1066. Nilsen, Alleen. "We Should Laugh So Long? The Influence of
       Jewish Humor on Contemporary Books for Young Readers." School
       Library Journal, November 1986: 30-34.

       Concentrates on the humor of Judy Blume, Paula Danziger, Norma
Klein, Robert Lipsyte, Harry and Norma Fox Mazer, E. L. Konigsburg,
and Mary Rodgers--Jewish authors of YA books--who helped to
establish the flip, irreverent, and dynamic tone that characterizes
much of the realistic contemporary literature for young adults. M.
E. Kerr is not Jewish. Nevertheless, many of her YA novels include
Jewish humor. She is a pivotal illustration of an author who has
been influenced by Jewish writers and colleagues and, in turn, has
influenced both young readers and the adult publishing world to be

receptive to Jewish humor. Jewish authors of humorous YA novels present a wide range of beliefs and approaches: Some are religious and some are not. Some cling closely to Jewish family and friends and some have become assimilated into the larger American community. At a minimum they reflect the Jewish upbringing alluded to in Milton Meltzer's entry in Something about the Author: Autobiography Series. Meltzer says that his parents were not observant, that they rarely if ever went to synagogue. They didn't talk about being Jewish. Nevertheless, their behavior, the way they moved, walked, laughed, cried, and talked, and their attitudes made an imprint that exposed the social history they brought with them.

1067. Stora-Sandor, Judith. L'Humour Juif dans la Litterature de Job a Woody Allen. Paris: Presses Universitaires de France, 1984, 349 pp.

Evaluates the influence of such Jewish American authors as Woody Allen, Saul Bellow, Leslie Fiedler, Joseph Heller, Erica Jong, Bernard Malamud, Sylvia Plath, Leo Rosten, Phillip Roth, and Constance Rourke and suggests that the great popularity of Jewish humor in France was originally the result of the effective Woody Allen films that were transported there. Stora-Sandor notes that Jewish humor is also popular in Germany, in Austria, and in Eastern European countries not only because of Jewish films but also from reading Jewish authors. This article suggests that there has not yet been a thorough study of Jewish humor in literary works and says that the present book is an attempt to do that. It describes the characteristic traits of Jewish humor and outlines the principal steps in its development.

1068. Wisse, Ruth R. The Schlemiel as Modern Hero. Chicago: Univ. of Chicago Press, 1971, xi + 134 pp.

Contends that extremist survivalist Jews so bitterly remember the Holocaust that they lose historical perspective by reading death into every event, thereby denying Yiddish Jews important creative achievements. Wisse makes the analogy to her son who doesn't allow her to read him "Little Red Riding Hood" without numerous nervous inquiries about the wolf. In both cases, "they are too anxious about the villainy to appreciate the tale." Yiddish humor cuts; it is more a humor of harshness than of merriment. The schlemiel is vulnerable and inept. He is not saintly nor pure, just weak. But he is highly symbolic of Jewish culture. The Jew, like the schlemiel, has traditionally not been in a position of strength but has allowed humor to turn his weakness into strength. How else could either survive? There is a story of a Jew who went to visit the city of Krotoshin. There he was publicly humiliated by the Krotoshin Chief of Police, and when he returned home his neighbor taunted him with that fact. The Jew shrugged his shoulders, and responded, "Krotoshin. Some place." The shlemiel became a significant recurring figure in America during the 1950s. He started in popular culture, and made his way into good fiction where, "his success was so great as almost to defeat his claim to failure."

Chapter 8
Geography

<u>America</u>

1069. Blair, Walter, and Raven I. McDavid, Jr., eds. <u>The Mirth of a Nation: America's Great Dialect Humor</u>. Minneapolis: Univ. of Minnesota Press, 1983, xxvii + 303 pp.

Divides the nineteenth century American humor into five categories--Rustic Yankees, Frontier Storytellers, Phunny Phellows, Local Colorists, and Mark Twain. <u>Rustic Yankee humor</u> demonstrated that "inhabitants from different parts of the country were quite unlike one another." These regional differences would later result in the Civil War. The down-to-earth, wide-ranging yarns of the <u>frontier storytellers</u> "drew upon popular lore about frontier ring-tailed roarers." They represented a strange mixture of fact and legend and like the <u>phunny phellows</u> to follow, they published mostly in newspapers, almanacs, and books sold door to door. The humor of <u>phunny phellows</u> tended to be political in nature, and they often would have "a clownish yarn spinner traitorously collaborate with the faction that his creator opposed and tell about what happened in such a way as to show up the enemy." The <u>local colorists</u> "fostered national unity...by playing up regional backgrounds, characters, and mores." They demonstrated "an emotional involvement with their characters that was largely absent from the earlier comic writings." Furthermore, their work was published mostly in "highly respected literary magazines." Finally, the transitional Mark Twain, "the greatest American humorist," required a special section of his own.

1070. Cracroft, Richard H. "'Against the Assault of Laughter...Nothing': Humor as the Means of Solving 'The Mormon Question.'" WHIMSY 2 (1984): 222-24.

Illustrates how humor was used in nineteenth century America as a way of dealing with people who had socially divergent views. At the conclusion of <u>The Mysterious Stranger</u> Mark Twain wrote that "Against the assault of laughter, nothing can stand." Cracroft applies this to his article by saying, "Nor could polygamy." Twain tells about the prophet's famous seven foot by ninety-six-foot bedstead that failed because of its overuse and says that the prophet told him not to encumber himself with a large family, adding that ten or eleven wives is all that he will ever need. Artemus Ward said that while he was in Utah seventeen young widows, all the wives of a particular deceased Mormon--offered him their hands in marriage. He refused, telling them it was "on account of the muchness" that he had to decline. In developing this concept of "muchness" Ward discussed the problem of multiple mothers-in-law, saying that one mother-in-law is enough to have in a family "unless you're very fond of excitement." Bill Nye attacked "polygamy, bigamy, trigamy, and pigamy." Max Adeler tells about Bishop Potts, whose family was sealed to the bishop while he was on a trip. And in Marietta Holley's novel, Samantha's particular problem is that Elder Judas Wart has convinced her husband that he should add the Widder Bump to the Allen household.

1071. Inge, M. Thomas. <u>The Frontier Humorists</u>. Hamden, CT: Archon, 1975, x + 331 pp.

Points to three factors which were prerequisite to the emergence of Southwestern frontier humor: The development of America as a legitimate and respected entity as opposed to England, the westward expansion of the frontier, and the development of the frontier as a legitimate and respected entity as opposed to New England and the development of the American newspaper as an important contributing factor for the development of both America in general and the American frontier in particular. It was the presence of the frontier that allowed Americans to turn their eyes away from Europe and to see something that was uniquely their own. The work on the American frontier was difficult and demanding. The frontier newspapers provided relief from these hardships--relief in the form of humorous sketches. The frontier newspaper developed out of the tradition of sitting around a campfire and spinning yarns after a hard day's work, and most of the frontier humorists got their start as reporters for these yarn-spinning newspapers.

1072. Kronenberger, Louis. "The American Sense of Humor." <u>Humor in America</u>. Ed. Enid Veron. New York: Harcourt, Brace, Jovanovich, 1976, 266-71.

Suggests that Americans lack wit precisely because Americans have suffered so little. All Americans are secure, and all Americans are convinced not only that they themselves have a good sense of humor but that America has a long and dynamic tradition of humor and that contemporary American humor is presently of high quality. They point to the tradition of overstatement, the tall tale, the wooly yarn, and the gigantism of the American frontier. But Kronenberger suggests that this is humor of release not humor of reflectiveness. It is the fizz not the fine Champagne. He suggests that in American humor there is little that is wise, little that is even melancholy, and certainly little of what could be called rueful. Kronenberger suggests that Americans have not grown and matured by having to struggle against overwhelming odds. We have not yet learned how to be a serious people, and because of this, we cannot, in the best sense, be a humorous one.

1073. Macrae, David. "American Humor." <u>National Humor</u>. New York: Frederick A. Stokes, 305-57 pp.

Contrasts Scottish, Highland, English, Cockney, Welsh, and Irish humor with American humor. American humor is described as exaggerated and boastful. Every state has something to boast about. Boston boasts about its big organ; New York boasts about Central Park; Chicago boasts about its elevators and its pig-killing machines. In the South, where they have no big organs, fancy parks,

elevators, or pig-killing machines, they boast about their river
steamers. "They sail faster, and they blow up oftener, and shoot
men higher, than any other steamers in the country. P. T. Barnum
both capitalized on and contributed to American exaggeration and
boasting. His circus was advertised as "the biggest show on earth."
One year, when a bright comet appeared in the heavens and became an
important part of the national news, Barnum proudly announced that
he had specially arranged for the comet. American humor also
exhibits a spirit of freedom and independence. When an American
woman was remonstrated for doing something improper, she responded
in defiance, "If I choose to do it, it becomes proper."

1074. Nilsen, Don L. F., and Alleen Pace Nilsen. "Humor in the
     United States." National Styles of Humor. Ed. Avner Ziv.
     Westport, CT: Greenwood, 1988, 157-88.

     Traces literary humor in America from the 1500s to the
present. The first theatrical performance given in America was a
Spanish comedy about an expedition of soldiers. It was performed on
April 30, 1598. In 1647 Nathaniel Ward published The Simple Cobbler
of Aggawam., and in 1666 New Englanders were shocked by George
Alsop's humorous A Character of the Province of Maryland, with such
statements as "Herds of deer are as numerous in this province of
Maryland as cukolds can be in London, only their horns are not so
well dressed and tipped with silver." In 1714 Robert Hunter,
governor of New York published Androboros, the first play written in
the colonies. It was a political satire lampooning the senate and
Hunter's lieutenant governor. In 1725 Nathaniel Ames, a
Massachusetts physician published the Astronomical Diary and
Almanack. It served as a model for the later almanacs that Benjamin
Franklin published between 1732 and 1757. There were two major
trends in humorous literature of the 1800s. First was the
exaggeration of heroes. While most other countries focused on "the
little people" (dwarves, elves, fairies), Americans were doing big
jobs and wanted big heroes. The second trend was vernacular--in
almanacs, newspapers, and magazines. The twentieth century brought
cynical, dark, and absurd humor.

1075. Rourke, Constance. American Humor: A Study of the National
     Character. Tallahassee: Florida State Univ. Press, 1939, xli
     + 334 pp.

     Alleges that humor is related to virtually every aspect of the
American character. It affects literature, not only as an
occasional touch, but as a major force determining large patterns
and intentions. As a lawless element, it is full of surprises. It
is appealing, vigorous and absorbing. Rourke suggests that the most
salient feature of the American character and, therefore, of
American humor is a quarrel that Americans have with their own
country. Rourke refuses to enter the quarrel, saying that a person
might as well try to dispute some established feature in the natural
landscape. In the Introduction, W. T. Lhamon, Jr., says that
American Humor has become a classic text of American scholarship,
important to the literary critic, the folklorist, the theater
historian, and the American studies scholar. He suggests that the
book is the first theory of American culture as such, for it shifts
emphasis from simple historical questions to a fully dimensioned
process with adequate complexity. He further goes further, to say

that where literary historians have limited themselves to questions
of when and where, Rourke also wondered about what, why, how, and
what for.

1076. Rubin, Louis D., Jr. "The Great American Joke." Humor in
       America. Ed. Enid Veron. New York: Harcourt, Brace,
       Jovanovich, 1976, 255-65.

Contends that from the beginning, the American literary
imagination has been at least as comic as it has been tragic, but at
the same time Americans have tended to equate gravity with
importance. The best thing we can say about a comic writer is that
he makes a "serious" contribution. Rubin feels that in an effective
democracy, the capacity for self-criticism is crucial, and that an
important function of comedy is to amend human follies by exposing
them. And much of the comic criticism should be self focused. H.
L. Mencken was a journalist; nevertheless, some of his sharpest
criticisms were aimed at journalists. Robert Penn Warren points to
the irony of the great promise that is given to everyone in America
in our "Declaration of Independence." Warren suggests that in
America we are guaranteed our independence just as long as we make
money, and get ahead, and open world markets, and raise our
children, and do all of the other things we have to do.

1077. Shalit, Gene, ed. Laughing Matters: A Celebration of American
       Humor. Garden City, New York: Doubleday, 1987, xxix + 622 pp.

Recalls when he was seventeen years old and ill enough to be
told to miss his high-school graduation and spend the following
summer in bed. "One dusk it actually happened: I fell out of bed
laughing. It was Frank Sullivan's 'A Garland of Ibids' that pushed
me over the edge." Shalit selects excerpts from such classics as
Benchley, Perelman, Sullivan, and Hoffenstein, but he also selects
a number of pieces from more modern authors. He says, "Not a single
piece [was] included for posterity's sake.... There is hardly
anything sadder than humor past its prime. A lot of it ought to be
stamped with a date, like a carton of milk." Shalit defends the
inclusion of ethnic humor in the anthology. "Good hearted ethnic
humor in America has largely vanished. Too bad for America.
Millions were once made merry (and millions more ought now to be) by
Mr. Dooley and Mrs. Nussbaum, by Bella Gross and Hyman Kaplan, by
the rural Lum and Abner, the urban Amos and Andy, by Dixie's Senator
Claghorn, by Mr. Kitzel and Rochester, and Billy Gilbert's sneezing
Greek. The finest dialect humor has a kindness about it," and that
is the kind of humor included in Shalit's anthology. The humor
pokes and ridicules and lampoons, but it does so in a friendly way.
"What we do not want is cruelty, and you will find none in the good
things I have chosen."

England

1078. Rees, John O. "Some Echoes of English Literature in Frontier
      Vernacular Humor." Studies in American Humor. NS 1.3 (February
      1983): 153-62.

      Investigates the influence of Charles Dickens and especially
Sam Weller in the Pickwick Papers on various American frontier
humorists. Rees suggests that Charles Dickens and Augustus Baldwin
Longstreet had a common source of inspiration in Samuel Beazley's
play, The Boarding House, which was first performed in London in
1811, but Bret Harte was more directly influenced by Dickens, from
his earliest writings to his last. His masterful mixing of pathos
and humor would probably not have been possible had he not read
Dickens, and this is true as well for the local color he was able to
create. Dickens' influence on Harte even went so far as to provide
specific oddities of some of Harte's characters, and the linguistic
quirks of his blacksmith Joe Gargery. One stylistic device that
Dickens used constantly was also picked up by many American frontier
writers; this was the "which" clause. Bret Harte used it
frequently, as did Alfred Henry Lewis in the tales about Wolfville,
Arizona. Damon Runyan also used it. Rees refers to this
construction as "mock-elegant" and concludes that its frequent use
by American frontier humorists showed a significant influence by
Charles Dickens.

France

1079. Austin, James C. American Humor in France: Two Centuries of
      French Criticism of the Comic Spirit in American Literature.
      Ames: Iowa State Univ. Press, 1978, x + 177 pp.

      Presents a sampling of French criticism of American humor from
the seventeenth century to the present and suggests that the French
do not view American humor in the same way that Americans do. One
French critic has said that American humor is no longer American,
but international. Furthermore, even today, it sometimes takes a
French critic to show us the pervasive humor in Whitman, Poe, James,
or Hawthorne. Austin and other Americans (such as Daniel Royot and
Judith Stora-Sandor) are studying the reception of American humor in
France not only to provide insights into the French way of thinking
but also to learn more about ourselves and our literature. Austin
is interested both in what the French critics saw and in what they
thought they saw and also what they failed to see. After
establishing a point of view and an approach, the book is arranged
in chronological order from Franklin to Cooper and Irving, to Twain,
to the first half of the twentieth century, and finally to today.

1080. Gribben, Alan. "Review of <u>American Humor in France: Two Centuries of French Criticism of the Comic Spirit in American Literature</u> by James C. Austin." <u>Resources for American Literary Study</u> 9.1 (Spring 1979): 113-14.

Concentrates on the favorable responses of prominent French critics to American literature, such as M. Grouvelle's praise for Benjamin Franklin and Regis Michaud's affection for Mark Twain's writing. Austin's book does a good job of discussing the secondary sources as well as the original works themselves. Austin is not all positive. For example, he discusses Madame Th. Bentzon's negative reaction to Mark Twain's "Jumping Frog" story. However, it had been Madam Bentzon's awkward translation of Twain's story that Twain translated back into highly Frenchified English. Madame Bentzon was not amused at his parody and was, in fact, generally miffed.

Germany

1081. Blair, Walter. "A German Connection: Raspe's Baron Munchausen." <u>Critical Essays on American Humor</u>. Eds. William Bedford Clark and W. Craig Turner. Boston: G. K. Hall, 1984, 123-39.

Proposes that the eighteenth century German author by the name of Rudolf Erich Raspe was a major influence on the plots, motifs, and techniques of the American tall tale even though he never visited the United States. Blair feels that Raspe's Baron Munchausen was a predecessor of such American comic characters as Sam Slick, Thimblerig, Simon Suggs, Petroleum V. Nasby, Col. Sellers, the Gentle Grafter, Egbert Souse, and other con-man characters. Blair notes that books about Baron Munchausen's exploits were well circulated and read in the United States. Blair further points out that from the 1830s on, a large number of "Munchausen expressions" entered the language--for example "New York Munchausens" to describe local lying champions. There were also "Vermont Munchausens," "Texas Munchausens," and "Munchausen's Syndrome," an expression that medical doctors use to describe patients who tend to exaggerate their misfortunes. This was a time in American history when folk heroes were generated by both oral and written yarn spinning. The Munchausen stories were very popular, and Baron Munchausen was a folk hero to many Americans.

Midwest

1082. Andrews, Clarence A. "The Comic Element in Iowa Literature." <u>American Humor</u>. Ed. O. M. Brack. Scottsdale, Arizona: Arete, 1977, 119-37.

Agrees with Paul Engle, an Iowa descendent of nineteenth century settlers, that Iowa is the state of "poets and pigs." Andrews discusses the cacography and tongue-in-cheek seriousness of Captain Eugene Fitch Ware's doggerel poetry. Ware wrote for the <u>Hawkeye</u> and was the Poet Laureate of Kansas. Robert Jones Burdette also wrote doggerel poetry for the <u>Hawkeye</u>, and his reputation as a

humorist won him such friends as Mark Twain and James Whitcomb
Riley. In Hamlin Garland's comic story entitled "Some Village
Cronies," the dialogue and the local color helped establish the
image of the Iowa country "hick." Ellis Parker Butler wrote comic
sketches about a character named Mike Flannery for <u>American
Magazine</u>. His "Pigs Is Pigs" "became an overnight sensation." This
poem is entitled "To Iowa" and ends with the following motto: "Three
millions yearly for manure, but not one cent for literature."
Andrews also discusses the comic contributions of other Iowa
authors, such as Bess Streeter Aldrich, Arthur Davidson Ficke,
Witter Bynner, Carl Van Vechten, Surrajer Fewkes, Jay G. Sigmund,
James Stevens, Phil Stong, Richard Bissell, James Hearst, and
Meredith Wilson.

1083. Conroy, Jack, ed. <u>Midland Humor: A Harvest of Fun and
        Folklore</u>. New York: Current/Wyn, 1947, xviii + 446 pp.

        Discusses the early humor of Davey Crockett, Caroline
Kirkland, John S. Robb; the later humor of Finley Peter Dunne,
Eugene Field, Julia Moore, Petroleum V. Nasby, Peck, M. Quad, Opie
Read, James Whitcomb Riley, Mark Twain, Artemus Ward, and Ten Eyck
White; and the modern humor of George Ade, Nelson Algren, Jack
Conroy, Peter De Vries, Sydney J. Harris, Ernest Hemingway, Kin
Hubbard, Ring Lardner, Ruth McKenney, Vance Randolph, Carl Sandburg,
Max Shulman, Booth Tarkington, James Thurber, and others.
Throughout this period the colonial writers of the Atlantic Coast
smugly laughed at the frontiersmen, and the frontiersmen in return
raucously laughed at the Easterners. The Easterners tended to keep
a constant and direct contact with England in terms of books, music,
art, and other cultural manifestations. Nothing seemed more
incongruous to the midwestern frontiersman than an eastern dandy
with his books, music, art, and refinement sitting squarely in the
middle of an untamed wilderness, where the skills needed were
physical courage, knowledge of woodcraft and plant and animal life,
and skill with fire arms and a hunting knife. "Book larnin'" and
"smug pride in material possessions soon became targets of ridicule
for midwestern humorists.

1084. DeMuth, James. <u>Small Town Chicago: The Comic Perspective of
        Finley Peter Dunne, George Ade and Ring Lardner</u>. Port
        Washington, NY: Kennikat, 1980, 122 pp.

        Points out that this book about Chicago was written by an
author living in Minneapolis and teaching in Wisconsin. DeMuth
feels that Dunne, Ade, and Lardner were the first strong writers of
American urban humor. The were all Chicago journalists whose major
works appeared during the turn of the century (between 1890 and
1920). They all communicated the speech, mannerisms, and attitudes
of various types of Chicagoans. Mr. Dooley" was a Chicago saloon-
keeper who explained that politics "ain't no bean bag." Artie
Blanchard was a brash young office clerk from the South Side of
Chicago who called his boss the "main squeeze." Jack Keefe was a
rookie pitcher for the Chicago White Sox who complained that it was
"the rotten support" he got that beat him. In 1890 Chicago was a
frontier boomtown. Between the year of the Chicago fire (1871) and
the Chicago's World's Columbian Exposition (1893) Chicago grew from
368 thousand to 1.3 million. Chicago was seen as the city of
opportunity. It was the hub of the United States where the buyers

met the sellers--where the East met the West.   It was roughshod,
belligerent, uncultured, and rude.   It had sprung from the grandiose
traditions of Davy Crockett and Mike Fink, and it had become the
cosmopolitan of speculators--Irish, German, Bohemian, Polish,
Scandinavian, and more.

1085. Duffey, Bernard. "Humor, Chicago Style." The Comic Imagination
      in American Literature. Ed. Louis D. Rubin, Jr. New Brunswick,
      NJ: Rutgers Univ. Press, 1983, 207-16.

Suggests that there was very little humor published in Chicago
between 1830s and 1880, when the city was preoccupied with
diversity, growth, and wealth, but that from the mid 1880s to the
1920s there was an increase in both the quantity and the quality of
Chicago's humor, mainly from Chicago's newspapers.   At this time,
Chicago humor was witty and sophisticated, but it was also highly
topical and very much limited in time and space.   The acceleration
started with Eugene Field's column, "Sharps and Flats," in the Daily
News in 1883, and continued through Peter Finley Dunne's
contributions to the Chicago Evening Post, and later contributions
to the Daily News and the Tribune by George Ade, Ring Lardner, and
Keith Preston.

1086. Holman, C. Hugh. "Anodyne for the Village Virus." The Comic
      Imagination in American Literature. Ed. Louis D. Rubin, Jr.
      New Brunswick, NJ: Rutgers Univ. Press, 1983, 247-58.

Discusses how the humor of the Midwest (especially that of the
Great Plains) can be soothing and calming.   This midwestern humor is
considered to be based on romantic idealization and self-mocking and
sardonic laughter.   The liberating mechanism which is freed by humor
can elevate the lonely man into a forceful, and energetic
individual.   Freedom is coupled with laughter as a way for the
little man threatened by a vast and frightning wilderness to cope.
Midwestern humor has borrowed less from the exuberance, wildness and
high-spirited extravagance of the Southwest, than from the subtle,
understated humor of New England.

1087. Pogel, Nancy. "Midwest." Dictionary of Literary Biography,
      Volume 11: American Humorists, 1800-1950. Detroit, MI: Gale,
      1982, 603-18.

Feels that the dominant trend in midwestern humor is cracker-
barrel humor--the triumph of the wise fool over more sophisticated
strangers.   Midwestern humorists not only continued the tradition of
this genre, but they also changed the environs of the cracker-barrel
philosopher from a rural to an urban setting.   Authors discussed in
this article include David Ross Locke, Robert Jones Burdett, Finley
Peter Dunne, Charles B. Lewis, Frank McKinney (Kin) Hubbard, George
Ade, John T. McCutcheon, and Ring Lardner.   The tradition of
Midwestern (heartland) humor continues with such talk-show hosts as
Garroway, Allen, Paar, and Carson, and of course, their guests.
Johnny Carson also dons the comic personae of Aunt Blabby and Floyd
E. Turbo.   Carson says that his best guests are the uninhibited
people.   "They know who they are, and don't try to prove they're
something else."   Herb Shriner, Jack Benny, Max Shulman, Mike Royko,
and Cliff Arquette (Charlie Weaver) continue the tradition.

1088. Williams, Kenny J., and Bernard Duffey, eds. <u>Chicago's Public Wits: A Chapter in the American Comic Spirit</u>. Baton Rouge: Louisiana State Univ. Press, 1983, xxii + 289 pp.

Alleges that newspapers and magazines were the foundation of Chicago's humor as opposed to lecture circuits that were more common in other parts of the United States during the late nineteenth century. Chicago's satirists saw a world trying to establish itself, and they felt that no one should be excempt as a target--not the high or the low, not the immigrant nor the native, not the Democrats nor the Whigs. Williams and Duffey feel that there has been so much analysis of the nineteenth-century frontier humor of the Southwest that the urban humor of the Middle West has been overlooked. Chicago humor is based on wit. It is humor filled with a sense of discovery. But Chicago humor is also like all American humor in providing an interplay between "the cultural ideal and the everday fact."

<u>New England</u>

1089. Briggs, Peter M. "English Satire and Connecticut Wit." <u>American Quarterly</u> 37.1 (Spring 1985): 13-29.

Portrays early American humor as ambivalent, since the earliest humorous authors sought the proper balance of old ("European-ness") and new ("American-ness") values. Briggs' evidence comes from the writings of the Connecticut Wits--John Trumbull, Timothy Dwight, Joel Barlow, David Humphreys, and Lemuel Hopkins. Briggs also says that early American humor was "belated humor," since the humor "had to wait until people had the time, detachment, and inclination to write it down, along with the expectation of an audience to share it." Briggs says this new American humor was like a boistrous child--"energetic, brash, familiar and plain-spoken, irreverent, insistently uninhibited," and he suggests that this "boistrous child" grew up to become Mark Twain, who had more historical distance from the European tradition than the Connecticut Wits but who nevertheless dealt with English characters, social institutions, modes of expression and behavior in order to poke fun at them. Briggs says that Twain appeared to be "running up to twist the lion's tail one more time, just to make sure that the lion was <u>still</u> dead."

1090. Drennan, Robert E., ed. <u>The Algonquin Wits</u>. Secaucus, New Jersey: Citadel Press, 1983, 176 pp.

Discusses the humor of Franklin Pierce Adams, Robert Benchley, Heywood Broun, George S. Kaufman, Ring Lardner, Dorothy Parker, Alexander Woollcott and other "Algonquin Wits." The term "Algonquin Wits" designates the humorists who got together regularly for lunch at their favorite restaurant, the Algonquin Hotel, in New York City. These Algonquin wits had come from many places; Lardner came from Niles, Michigan; Connelly from Keesport, Pennsylvania; Benchley from Worcester, Massachusetts; and Murdock and Brock Pemberton from Emporia, Kansas. In 1920, Frank Case, owner of the Algonquin Hotel, installed a huge round table in the Rose Room for the gathering of literati. The lunches recall a gay, lawless, prosperous time in

American history, exhibiting the urbanity, sophistication, literacy, taste, and fashion that are replacing the old frontier spirit. Murdock Pemberton set up the first Algonquin lunch in mock honor of Alexander Woollcott and arranged to have banners flying varying the spelling of his name in every way imaginable. After the lunches the group would stay together in a pack all day, ending up at somebody's house for supper, word games, and poker. Their barbs were sharp. Broun, for example, referred to Alexander Woollcott as "the smartest of Alecs."

1091. Eby, Cecil D. "Yankee Humor." The Comic Imagination in American Humor. Ed. Louis D. Rubin, Jr. New Brunswick, NJ: Rutgers Univ. Press, 1983, 77-84.

Describes the early antagonism that held between the British and the Americans as one of the contributing factors to the uniqueness of Yankee humor. The word "Yankee" is a flippant and pejorative term.   Many etymologists suggest that the term was originally an Anglicized corruption of the Dutch expression "Jan Kees," or "John Cheese." This expression is also associated with the verb "to yank," which describes the British perception of what America was doing from England--wrenching violently, or pulling away. A British surgeon first wrote the satirical song, "Yankee Doodle," and this was later adapted by Americans as their theme song, their battle hymn, and even a sort of national anthem, with hundreds of stanzas added by the Americans themselves. This was the setting for Thoreau's serious Civil Disobedience, Seba Smith's humorous Downing Sketches, and Lowell's more biting Biglow Papers. It also established an ambience necessary for Sarah Orne Jewett, Mary Wilkins Freeman, George Savary Wasson, and other pre-Revolutionary-War Yankee writers. Calvin Coolidge, the last Yankee President, nicely illustrated the Yankee mentality when he was seated next to a lady at an official dinner who told him someone had bet her that she couldn't make him say three words. Major Jack Downing would have been pleased by Coolidge's response: "You lose."

1092. Franklin, Benjamin V. The Poetry of the Minor Connecticut Wits. Gainesville, FL: Scholars' Facsimiles and Reprints, 1970, xvi + 968 pp.

Contrasts the four "Major Connecticut Wits" (John Trumbull, Timothy Dwight, David Humphreys, and Joel Barlow) with the five "Minor Connecticut Wits" (Richard Alsop, Mason Fitch Cogswell, Theodore Dwight, Lemuel Hopkins, and Elihu Hubbard Smith). The "Major Connecticut Wits" "dominated the American literary scene in the last two decades of the eighteenth and the first decade of the nineteenth century. These poets, all born between 1750 and 1754 and all graduated from Yale College, wrote poetry that, for the most part, praised the history and the society of our new nation." Although the Minor Connecticut Wits tended to hold the same cultural beliefs as the major group, the average age of the Minors was ten years younger than the Majors, and some of them held honorary degrees from Yale rather than earned degrees. In addition, the Major Wits were prolific to the extent of tedium, while, the Minor Wits were much less prolific. The Major Wits have been published widely and have received a great deal more critical attention than the Minor Wits. Franklin's book attempts to help redress that imbalance.

1093. Franklin, Benjamin, V. <u>The Prose of the Minor Connecticut Wits</u>. Delmar, NY: Scholars' Facsimiles and Reprints, 1974, xviii + 231 pp.

Discusses straightforwardly the prose of Richard Alsop (1761-1815), Theodore Dwight (1764-1846), and Elihu Hubbard Smith (1771-1798). Mason Fitch Cogswell (1761-1830), and Lemuel Hopkins (1750-1801) are also considered "Minor Connecticut Wits;" however, they are excluded from Franklin's treatment because they did not write prose. The Minor Connecticut Wits must be read with close reference to their conservative geography (Connecticut) and the politics of their day (the decline of Federalism which they still embraced with vigor). The Minor Connecticut Wits were not very talented or popular, and their artistic abilities can be better seen in their poetry than their prose. Their significance lies mainly in the fact that they are the first group of important authors that America produced.

1094. Gribben, Alan. "Review of <u>The Literary Humor of the Urban Northeast</u> by David E. E. Sloane." <u>American Literary Realism</u> 16 (Autumn 1983): 307-10.

Describes the focus of Sloane's book as temporal (beginning in 1830), as well as geographical (Northeast), and cultural (urban). These three focuses are related in that 1830 was the date when industrialization began to change the character of the Northeast from farming country to a basically urban environment. Twenty authors are discussed, including Joseph C. Neal, Thomas C. Haliburton, Mirtomer N. Thompson, Charles G. Leland, John W. DeForest, and Marietta Holley. The book charges that prior to its publication, humor scholars had been preoccupied with humorists of the American Southwest, depicting country ruffians speaking in regional dialects and expressing frontier viewpoints. Sloane felt that a new direction in humor studies was needed and wrote this book to help change that direction.

1095. Holliday, Carl. "The Hartford Wits." <u>The Wit and Humor of Colonial Days</u>. Williamstown, Massachusetts: Corner House, 1975, 228-44.

Explains that the reason for the organization of a group of Yale men into a group named the "Hartford Wits" was that Yale men (especially Timothy Dwight, who later became president of Yale) considered Harvard men dangerously unorthodox. These Yale scholars pointed out that some Harvard scholars had boldly asserted that there wasn't an ounce of brimstone in all of hell and that other Harvard scholars had even been so bold as to have doubted the very existence of that place. There were three major organized contributions of the Hartford wits. The first was a series of satirical prose and poetry, <u>The Anarchiad</u>, which dealt with the ruffian element in the lower classes and the enemies of the union in the upper classes. There were twenty-four installments of <u>The Anarchiad</u>, all published in <u>The New Haven Gazette</u>. <u>The Anarchiad</u> was said to have been dug up from extremely ancient ruins of an Indian fort and made detailed prophecies about "the future." The second contribution was a series of poems published in the <u>American Mercury</u> from 1791 until 1796 that mocked or "echoed" the bombast of the day. It was entitled <u>The Echo</u> and was written almost entirely

by Richard Alsop and Theodore Dwight. The third contribution, The
Political Green House (1799), mainly attacked Jefferson and all
Jacobins.

1096. Parrington, Vernon Louis. The Connecticut Wits. New York:
      Harcourt, Brace, and Co., 1926, lvii + 514 pp.

      Discusses and illustrates the work of Joel Barlow, Timothy
Dwight, Lemuel Hopkins, David Humphreys, and John Trumbull.
Parrington feels that Joel Barlow was the most interesting and
original of the Connecticut Wits but history has not treated him
kindly, since Barlow is mainly remembered for a few lines from Hasty
Pudding. And this neglect is because of Barlow's "defection from
Connecticut respectability." Ironically, much of the work of the
other Connecticut Wits has also remained inaccessable to history but
for the opposite reason--it is too conservative. Modern readers
view their verse as "stilted and barren, and their robust prejudices
hopelessly old-fashioned." The Connecticut or Hartford Wits were
intellectual and spiritual children of Yale, a tenaciously
conservative university in a very conservative state. "In no other
New England State did the ruling hierarchy maintain so glacial grip
on society." Nevertheless, these Connecticut Wits are "annually
recalled by a considerable number of undergraduates on the eve of an
examination." Parrington feels that the writing of the Connecticut
Wits was worthy of a twentieth century audience. He also feels this
material is historically significant for giving insights into
"provincial New England in the acrid years of the 1790s, when
America was angrily debating what path to follow...."

1097. Sloane, David E. E. "The Humor of the Old Northeast: Barnum,
      Burnham, and the Hen Fever." Studies in American Humor NS6
      (1988): 154-62.

      Suggests that entrepreneuralism and materialism are the two
features which best characterize the humor of the Old Northeast.
Sloane provides what he considers to be a prototypical story in this
tradition. An old farmer takes his brandy bottle and goes fishing
in a mill stream, but cannot catch any fish, though he doesn't get
discouraged because he takes a nip of brandy from time to time.
After a while the farmer sees a pike jump up out of the water and
grab a frog from a lily pad. The farmer decides to try to catch a
frog for himself but he is too slow to be successful. Finally, he
sees a blacksnake swimming ashore with a frog in its mouth, and he
catches the blacksnake and forces the snake's mouth open and forces
some brandy into the snake's mouth as he wrenches the frog away.
The snake swims off, and the farmer is baiting up his hook when he
feels a tug on his pants leg. He looks down to see the blacksnake
returning with another frog.

1098. Trachtenberg, Stanley. "East and Northeast." Dictionary of
      Literary Biography, Volume 11: American Humorists, 1800-1950.
      Detroit, MI: Gale, 1982, 587-97.

      Considers eastern humor to be associated with urban centers
both in terms of imagination and local color. Eastern and
northeastern humor tends to be sophisticated, understated, self-
deprecatory, ironic, and knowledgeable. Part of the vitality of
eastern and northeastern humor is related to Jewish culture and the

Yiddish language. Jewish humor is the humor of helplessness rather than of heroism; It represents the merging of Jewish culture into mainstream culture. Yiddish "calls attention to its own pretensions." Yiddish has had an important effect on American spoken language. Saul Bellow considers Yiddish to be "full of the grandest historical, mythological, and religious allusions [which] may get into the discussion of an egg, a clothesline, or a pair of pants." Authors discussed in this article include not only Saul Bellow, but also Woody Allen, S. J. Perelman, James Thurber, Robert Benchley, Dorothy Parker, Alexander Woollcott, Heywood Broun, Marc Connelly, Franklin P. Adams, Edna Ferber, George S. Kaufman, Robert Sherwood, Lynn Fontanne, Alfred Lunt, Frank Crowninshield, Frank Case, Joseph C. Neal, Charles Farrar Brown, Thomas Chandler Haliburton, James Russell Lowell, Henry Wheeler Shaw, and David Ross Locke.

1099. Weales, Gerald. "Not for the Old Lady in Dubuque." The Comic Imagination in American Literature. Ed. Louis D. Rubin, Jr. New Brunswick, NJ: Rutgers Univ. Press, 1983, 231-46.

Discusses the literary humor that has appeared in the New Yorker over the years. Harold Ross, editor of the New Yorker, once said that the magazine was concerned with the minutiae of New York City, was written with a metropolitan audience in mind, and that it was not appropriate for "the little old lady in Dubuque." E. B. White, James Thurber, Robert Benchley, Dorothy Parker, John O'Hara, Frank Sullivan, Elmer Davis, and Gilbert Seldes were all frequent contributors to the New Yorker. Ernest Hemingway, Upton Sinclair, F. Scott Fitzgerald, Frank Harris, and Peter De Vries also wrote comic pieces for the New Yorker.

1100. Wilson, James Grant. Bryant and His Friends: Some Reminiscences of the Knickerbocker Writers. New York: Fords, Howard, and Hulbert, 1886, 443 pp.

Attempts to avoid the natural tendency among biographers to contract "the disease of admiration" and to portray Bryant and his Knickerbocker friends in a more realistic light. Wilson hopes that the unlearned will thank him for informing them about the Knickerbocker writers, and he hopes that the learned will forgive him for reminding them of the interesting writings of these Knickerbockers. The writers discussed in this book include William Cullen Bryant (1794-1878), James Kirk Paulding (1778-1860), Washington Irving (1783-1859), Richard Henry Dana (1787-1879), James Fenimore Cooper (1789-1851), Fitz-Greene Halleck (1790-1867), Joseph Rodman Drake (1795-1820), Nathaniel Parker Willis (1806-1867), Edgar Allan Poe (1809-1849), and Bayard Taylor (1825-1878).

South

1101. Budd, Louis J. "Gentlemanly Humorists of the Old South."
       Southern Folklore Quarterly 17 (December 1953): 232-40;
       reprinted in Critical Essays on American Humor. Eds. William
       Bedford Clark and W. Craig Turner. Boston: G. K. Hall, 1984,
       76-84.

       Criticizes critics who glibly state that American humor was
the result of democracy-loving pioneers who used humor to promote
individualism, equality, and self-reliance. Such a statement fails
to adequately distinguish between far western humor, Yankee humor,
and southern humor.   Such powerful southern antebellum humorous
writers as Augustus Baldwin Longstreet, Joseph Glover Baldwin,
William Tappan Thompson, Johnson J. Hooper, and George Washington
Harris were first and foremost Southerners and only secondarily
Americans or frontiersmen.   Their writing was dominated by
provincial prejudices and loyalties.   Only the southern writers
placed a barrier between the author and the unlettered folk. While
Yankee humor developed the crackerbarrel philosopher who relied on
mother wit to comment intelligently on both private and public
affairs in a kind of aphoristic monologue, the southern humor
tradition was based on literary grace and urbane provincialism.

1102. Cohen, Sandy. "South and Southwest." Dictionary of Literary
       Biography, Volume 11: American Humorists, 1800-1950. Detroit,
       MI: Gale, 1982, 597-603.

       Considers southern and southwestern humor to be deeply rooted
in southern folklore and tradition and to reflect the prejudices and
idiosyncracies of the area.   Much of the local color of southern
writing relates to violence, dirty streets, rough-hewn yellow pine
floors, and Baptist meeting halls.   Newspapers became more chatty,
and editors became more individualistic as Jacksonian democracy
emerged. Newspapers developed the humor of mirthful exaggeration.
They were designed to portray the South as a Garden of Eden with a
sense of humor.   Throughout their history, southern newspapers
reflected the values and attitudes of their southern readers.
Authors discussed in this article include Mason Locke Weems, James
Kirke Paulding, Augustus Baldwin Longstreet, Johnson Jones Hooper,
Wiliam Tappan Thompson, George Washington Harris, Thomas Bange
Thorpe, Joseph Glover Baldwin, Charles Henry Smith, Henry Clay
Lewis, Joel Chandler Harris, Mark Twain, and William Faulkner.
Cohen feels that Southern humor has come full circle in the recent
rise of the oral folk story as represented by Andy Griffith and
Tennessee Ernie Ford.   Contemporary tellers of tall-tale satire
include Brother Dave Gardner, and Moms Mabley.   And Jerry Clower
continues the tradition of the "phunny phellows."

1103. Duke, Maurice. "John Wilford Overall's Southern Punch: Humor
       in the Rebel Capital." Ed. O. M. Brack, Jr. Scottsdale,
       Arizona: Arete, 1977, 43-58.

       Suggests that Overall had exactly the right characteristics to
edit Southern Punch, "the only illustrated humor publication of the
South" during its short but influential tenure from 1863 to 1865.
Overall was trained in law, journalism, and politics. He also had

an intimate knowledge of and respect for Southern culture that
allowed him to produce a "plucky little weekly" that would find a
large sympathetic audience in the heart of the Confederacy.
However, the major strength of <u>Southern Punch</u> was also its major
weakness, for in the end the Southern bias became too pronounced.
Humor requires some distance and objectivity, and Overall lost this.
When he began to react too emotionally, his satire lost its humor.
Irony and even invective took the place of the humor, and this
accounted for the fact that <u>Southern Punch</u> had such a short tenure.

1104. Hall, Wade H. <u>Reflections of the Civil War in Southern Humor</u>.
      Gainesville: Univ. of Florida Press, 1962, viii + 84 pp.

      Considers a study of people's humor to reveal as much about
them as an investigation of the more somber historical records. And
besides that, the time spent reading humor is more enjoyable. Hall
feels that the Southerner's sense of humor helped him fight a war he
believed honorable and accept the bitter defeat which ended it.
Without the escape valve of humor, many a 'rebel' would have been
overtaken by despair. The Southerner survived because he read
humorists like Bill Arp, who once wrote comically but seriously too
that the South was "conquered but not convinced."

1105. Hall, Wade. <u>The Smiling Phoenix: Southern Humor from 1865 to
      1914</u>. Gainesville: Univ. of Florida Press, 1965.

      Considers the period of 1865 to 1914 one of great change in
the South, which went from a feudal society uprooted by the Civil
War to a more democratic society represented by Reconstruction. The
South during this period is compared to the mythical phoenix which
arises reborn from its own ashes. But unlike the phoenix, the South
arose smiling. Southerners laughed about politics, religion,
education, economics, commerce and industry, and folklore during
their greatest period of turmoil and change. It was the
Southerners' sense of humor that helped them to fight a war they
believed to be honorable against overwhelming odds. Bill Arp said
that the South was "conquered but not convinced."

1106. Holman, C. Hugh. "Detached Laughter in the South." <u>Comic
      Relief: Humor in Contemporary American Literature</u>. Ed. Sarah
      Blacher Cohen. Urbana: Univ. of Illinois Press, 1978, 87-104.

      Traces contemporary Southern humor to the humor tradition of
the Old Southwest. In both cases, the humor is ribald, triumphant,
and vigorous. The early Southern humorist belonged to a social
class quite superior to the characters he wrote about. Each
narrator affected a cool, detached, tolerant, amused, and often
sardonic tone as he described the extravagant and exuberant wild
frontier for his urbane and educated readers, many of them living in
the East. In tracing contemporary Southern humor to its nineteenth
century roots, Holman contrasts two types of contemporary Southern
humor. There is the polished, charming and witty humor of James
Branch Cabell, Robert Molloy, and Josephine Pinckney characteristic
of the Virginia Tidewater and Carolina Low Country. The best
example of this tradition is the Queenborough trilogy by Ellen
Glasgow, consisting of <u>The Romantic Comedians</u> (1926), <u>They Stooped
to Folly</u> (1929), and <u>The Sheltered Life</u> (1932). The other type of
contemporary Southern humor is raucous, ribald, and extravagant.

William Faulkner wrote in both of these traditions. <u>Sanctuary</u> is
filled with Gothic horrors and extravagances; <u>Absalom Absalom</u> is a
historical novel; <u>The Unvanquished</u> is an idealized and sentimental
view of the Civil War; <u>Light in August</u> and <u>The Sound and the Fury</u>
contain both naturalism and symbolism; <u>The Hamlet</u>, <u>The Town</u>, and <u>The
Mansion</u> could be described as realistic comedy. Although Faulkner
worked in the tradition of frontier comedy, his work was also
polished and refined.

1107. Hudson, Arthur Palmer, ed. <u>Humor of the Old Deep South</u>. Port
      Washington, New York: Kennikat, 1936, xxiv + 276 pp.

Discusses the humor of the Old Deep South, which is defined as
between the Tennessee River bend on the North, the Mexican Gulf on
the South, the Mississippi River on the West, and the Tombigbee-
Black Warrior-Alabama River system on the East. The period covered
is the sixteenth, seventeenth, and eighteenth centuries (the time of
De Soto, Bienville, D'Iberville, and La Salle) but specializes in
the eighteenth century and "doesn't begin to talk loudly till the
late thirties and the roaring forties." The humor of this time and
period is described as "comedie humaine," and the region is
described as geographically unified, naturally homogeneous,
historically one storied, and inhabited by people of the same racial
and social background, irritated by the same outside influences and
committed to the same destiny. The targets of the humor included
preachers; politicians; lawyers; duelists; outlaws, rogues and
bullies; flatboatmen; steamboatmen; soldiers; editors;
schoolmasters; barkeepers; play-actors; doctors; poets; darkies;
sundry ladies; and others.

1108. Jones, Horace Perry. "Southern Editorial Humor and the Crimean
      War." <u>Studies in American Humor</u> NS2.3 (Winter 1983-84): 171-
      84.

Proposes that America's South was vitally interested in the
Crimean war because of the effects it could have on Southern
economics--America's rights to the open seas, because of its effect
on the South's desire to acquire Cuba and the religious battle
between the Cross and the Crescent. As a result of this
preoccupation much southern humor during the mid-nineteenth century
alluded to the Crimean war. Because of his desire to acquire new
lands, the Russian Czar was accused of "Poly Gamy," because he had
taken possession of Bess Arabia, was holding Moll Davia, and was
stretching one arm over Behring's Straights and toward Miss Issippi
and Miss Souri. A number of southern editors pointed out the
similarities between Turkey, the nation, and Turkey, the animal.
When General "Nlepokoitcpyzky" took command of a Russian army
division it was noted that if he were to beat the Turks, they
wouldn't be able to tell what hit them. In the South, many Russian
names were invented like "Somanosoff," "Blowmanosoff,"
"Kutmanosoff," "Polmanosoff," and "Nozbegan." "Malakoff" became the
name of a new southern lady's hat, and "Sebastopol" was a kind of
cloak she could buy. It was called "Sebastopol" because "what is
inside of it can't or won't be taken."

1109. Oehlschlaeger, Fritz. "A Bibliography of Frontier Humor in the
      St. Louis Daily Reveille, 1844-1846." Studies in American
      Humor NS 3.4 (Winter 1984-85): 267-89.

     Contends that the New Orleans Picayune and the St. Louis Daily
Reveille were the two most important publishers of frontier humor of
the Old Southwest. The Daily Reveille was published between May 14,
1844 and October 6, 1850. It was inspired greatly by New York's
Spirit of the Times, edited by William T. Porter, and contained many
sketches by four of the most significant humorists of the time,
Joseph M. Field, (who wrote under the names of "Straws" and
"Everpoint"), Matt Field (who used the pen name of "Phazma"), John
S. Robb (better known as "Solitaire"), and Sol Smith (who used his
own name). The name for the journal, Daily Reveille, was selected
in a rather strange way. The editors went to great pains studying
lexicography in search for an appropriate title. Finally, in a
state of despair, they decided that although they had not found a
good name they were at least in agreement that the worst name that
had presented itself was Reveille. At this point they unanimously
decided to choose Reveille as their title. The subjects of the
humor usually related to the frontier--hunting, marrying,
electioneering, gambling, swindling, and drinking. The Reveille
especially liked to publish stories about life on the Mississippi
and its riverboats and about the theater. The authors employed such
devices as the mythic narrative, the tall tale, the bragging
anecdote, the comic epistle and the mock sermon, and, of course, the
frame narrative was very much in evidence. Any kind of pretense of
the time became the target of the satire.

1110. Oehlschlaeger, Fritz. "A Bibliography of Frontier Humor in the
      St. Louis Daily Reveille, 1847-1850." Studies in American
      Humor NS 4.4 (Winter 1985-86): 262-83.

     Presents this bibliography as a companion piece to an earlier
article on the humor of the Daily Reveille from 1844 to 1846. The
period between May 13 and May 31, 1850, is missing, because
Oehlschlaeger could find no extant issues. The annotations attempt
to keep the flavor of the original sketches. In addition to the
many unsigned articles annotated, there are also articles signed
"Solitaire," "Linton," "John Robb," "Dr. Quid, of Bates,"
"Everpoint," "Sol Smith," "John Brown," Carondelet," "Ned," "One of
'Em," "Hunt," "An Old Ranger," "Wakeful Peabody," "Stahl," "Jerry
Nobs," "Bon Soir," "Oak Hey," "Maniensis," "Rudder," "Major Joseph
Jones," "Little 'Un," "Percussion," and "Plume" (evidently that was
his "Nom de Plume").

1111. Phillips, Robert L. Jr. The Novel and the Romance in Middle
      Georgia Humor and Local Color: A Study of Narrative Method in
      the Works of Augustus Baldwin Longstreet, William Tappan
      Thompson, Richard Malcolm Johnston and Joel Chandler Harris.
      Ph.D. dissertation. Chapel Hill: Univ. of North Carolina,
      1971, 503 pp.

     Discusses the work of two antebellum Georgia humorists
(Longstreet and Thompson) and two postwar local colorists (Johnston
and Harris) in terms of the relationship of their fictional accounts
to actual Middle Georgia life. Phillips concludes that when the

narrators represented by these authors deal objectively with their
material, the resultant stories take on the appearance of a "novel."
When they interpret for the readers, the resultant stories take on
more the appearance of a "romance." Longstreet, Thompson, and
Harris were newspaper editors. Johnston was a schoolmaster. But
all four authors chose to accept Middle Georgia values rather than
rebel against them in their writings.

1112. Piacentino, Edward J. "Confederate Disciples of Momus: The
      Bugle-Horn of Liberty and Southern Punch. Studies in American
      Humor NS 4.4 (Winter 1985-86): 249-61.

      Considers the summer of 1863 to have been a very bad period
for the South. This is the year that General Grant took Vicksburg,
Virginia, giving the North control of the Mississippi River and
basically separating the upper southern states from the lower ones.
The South was also defeated at Gettysburg in 1863, ending any hope
for a successful invasion of the North. There was a northern
blockade of the Atlantic coast, and as a result essential foods were
in short supply. Even Richmond, the Confederate capital, had
shortages of basic necessities, and extortioners and profiteers
plagued the southern economy. But during this period of darkest
despair, two humor magazines arose from the southern ashes--The
Bugle-Horn of Liberty and Southern Punch. Both had a light and
humorous tone. Both presented the world from a southern
perspective. Both helped to boost the sagging morale of the
downtrodden South. These two southern journals were also
significant in providing literature for Southerners, because the
northern blockade of the Atlantic seaboard had also cut off the
supply of books and periodicals to the South. But most importantly,
these two magazines helped the South to promote its own culture and
maintain its own identity.

1113. Stewart, Randall. "Tidewater and Frontier Humor." Georgia
      Review 13 (Fall 1959): 296-307.

      Contrasts the Tidewater humor of the Virginians (Ellen Glasgow
and James Branch Cabell), the Tennesseeans (John Crowe Ransom and
Allen Tate), the Mississippians (Stark Young and Eudora Welty) with
the frontier humor of Augustus Baldwin Longstreet, Davey Crockett,
George Washington Harris, Johnson Jones Hooper, Joseph Glover
Baldwin, and Thomas Bangs Thorpe. Tidewater humor is described as
courtly, sophisticated, intellectual, and witty. It is ironic and
elitist. Authors in this tradition practice restraint, dignity, and
a sense of form; they are classicists. Frontier humor, on the other
hand, was lively, spontaneous, and unconstrained. Frontier humor
continues today in the writings of Erskine Caldwell and Jesse
Stuart, while the writings of Faulkner and Warren exhibit qualities
of both Tidewater and frontier humor.

1114. Stoneback, H. R. "Southern Humor" A Special Issue of Thalia:
      Studies in Literary Humor 6.2 (Winter 1983): 1-64.

      Presents as a special issue of Thalia the following articles:
"The Modes and Functions of Humor in Faulkner" by Ruel E. Foster,
"Southern Humor: The Light and the Dark" by Robert J. Higgs, "Joseph
B. Cobb and the Evangelicals in the Old South" by Robert L.
Phillips, "Johnson Jones Hooper and the American Picaresque" by

James L. Treadway, "Baldwin's Patrician Humor" by Mary Ann Wimsatt, "A Nat'ral Born Durn'd Fool" by Thomas Daniel Young, "Faulkner's Humor and Some Chinese Writers" by Tao Jie, and "Long Long Ago: A Romantic History of Catchup Country" by Jim Wayne Miller.

1115. Sullivan, Walter. "Southerners in the City: Flannery O'Connor and Walker Percy." The Comic Imagination in American Literature. Ed. Louis D. Rubin, Jr. New Brunswick, NJ: Rutgers Univ. Press, 1983, 339-48.

Demonstrates that Percy and O'Connor have a lot of common features. They were both born and raised as Roman Catholics in southern regions that were mainly Protestant, and both wrote about "the alienation of contemporary man." But there are also ways in which Percy and O'Connor differ. Percy is very serious as he writes about alienation, doubt, and loneliness, but at the same time he can "find life amusing and hopeful in spite of contemporary agonies and doubts." His voice "is amusing and comforting and extremely gifted." In contrast, Sullivan feels that O'Connor had more of a gift for comedy and that she was better able to use it as a tool for reconciliation.

1116. Thorp, Willard. "Suggs and Sut in Modern Dress: The Latest Chapter in Southern Humor." Mississippi Quarterly 13 (1960): 169-75.

Contends that there has been a renaissance of Southern humor in twentieth-century southern literature. Many of the humor conventions of modern southern humor can be traced directly to conventions of the old southern humor. Modern southern humor varies all the way from Faulkner's rogue stories about the Snopes clan and Erskine Caldwell's comic treatment of the Lester family and the characters in God's Little Acre to the fantastic humor of Truman Capote and the grotesque humor of Flannery O'Connor. This variation can also be seen in older southern humor traditions. Furthermore, in both traditions the major characters move outside of conventional, well-behaved, hard-working, God-fearing society. In the old humor they are the rogues, brawlers, con-men, gamblers, hunters, and natural-born durned fools. In the new humor they are the Snopeses, the Ty Ty Waldens, the un-educated, and the religious fanatics, all with child-like qualities. There is also a more direct relationship between the old and the new traditions in southern humor and that is that many of the modern writers are avid readers of the older writers. Carson McCullers, for example, loved to read Henry Junius Nott and Johnson J. Hooper. Flannery O'Conner treasured her copies of George Washington Harris' Sut Lovingood Yarns. And these are only two of many examples.

1117. Turner, Arlin. "Realism and Fantasy in Southern Humor." Georgia Review 12 (Winter 1958): 451-57; reprinted in Critical Essays on American Humor. Eds. William Bedford Clark and W. Craig Turner. Boston: G. K. Hall, 1984, 85-90.

Contends that the most significant American humor had its roots in the South or, more particularly, the Old Southwest. This humor had its roots in eighteenth century British authors like Joseph Addison and Alexander Pope and was based on the strict observance of a caste system, on Greek-columned mansions, the code of the duel, and other attributes of the southern gentleman. Nevertheless, this early humor was extravagant, unlettered, irreverant, raucous, and frequently in bad or at least questionable taste, exploiting the differences between the various classes of Southerners.

1118. Wade, John Donald. "Southern Humor." Culture in the South. Ed. W. T. Couch. Chapel Hill: Univ. of North Carolina Press, 1934.

Considers the two strands of early southern humor to have been satire and irony. Conscious southern humor that was written to correct social ills was satire. Unconscious southern humor that was written for amusement was irony. This article traces Southern humor from its earliest author, William Byrd, through the horse swappings and eye gougings of Longstreet and the tobacco spitting of Thompson and others. R. M. Johnston, Sidney Lanier, Bill Arp Smith, and Joel Chandler Harris wrote of Georgia. Hooper and Baldwin wrote of Alabama; Crockett and G. W. Harris of Tennessee; Prentice of Kentucky; Thorpe, Opie Reed, and Mark Twain of Mississippi; Dr. Bagby of Virginia; and Simms and Mrs. Gilman of South Carolina. In a literary form reminiscent of Addison's essays, they wrote about unsophisticated country folk. They wrote of the foibles of men and women who had hearts of gold beneath their superficial crudities. But these southerners used vernacular rural dialect and spelling unlike Addison.

1119. West, James L. W., III. Gyascutus: Studies in Antebellum Southern Humorous and Sporting Writing. Atlantic Highlands, NJ: Humanities Press, 1978, 240 pp.

Describes the Gyascutus as a relative of both the Wang-Doodle and the Snipe. Its color changed seasonally, ranging from dark, lush green to bright, glowing orange. It could have two legs, three, four, or even five legs. At the ends of these legs there might be three toes, five toes, or even cloven hooves. Some Gyascutuses were furry; others had scales; and one mutant variety had a whistle on the end of its tail. Living at the same time as the Gyascutus was a "mutant" group of humorists--Augustus Baldwin Longstreet, William Tappan Thompson, Thomas Bangs Thorpe, Johnson Jones Hooper, Henry Clay Lewis, George Washington Harris, and a few others. Gyascutus was not only contemporary in time and space with these authors but also symbolized their favorite genre--the tall tale. These authors collectively were seen as a kind of mutant group--unique from humorists of other times and places. They were called "Southwest Humorists" and represented "The Big Bear School of Humor." West, however, feels that this group was not so unique as other critics have claimed. He feels that they are part of a humor tradition stretching back to the eighteenth century in both English and American literature and forward to the late nineteenth-century local colorists and even twentieth-century authors like Faulkner and Lytle.

Southwest

1120. Arnold, S. G. Tucker, Jr. "The Animal in Man--Man in the Animal: Anthropomorphism and Animalization in the Works of Twain and Other Southwest Humorists." Spectrum of the Fantastic. Ed. Donald Palumbo. Westport, CT: Greenwood, 1988, 87-94.

Suggests that Twain was following a well-established Southwestern tradition by depicting humans as animals and animals as humans and further suggests that this reveals a great deal about the nature of fantasy as it relates to American frontier humor, because in frontier society, men and beasts were "perilously close to being in a state of equality." Southwestern humorists compared their characters to sheep, geese, and other critters. George Washington Harris' Sut Lovingood had a father who decides to replace the recently deceased plowhorse personally because he is too poor to buy a new horse. Johnson Jones Hooper has Simon Suggs run for office, and Suggs admits that he may not be a strong enough candidate to win but nevertheless vows that he "will allers be found sticking thar like a tick onder a sow's belly." Mark Twain provides his creatures with "a blend of naturalistic precision, caricature, comedy, and pathos." Arnold suggests that Walt Disney and his fellow artists borrowed this same tradition of animal depiction from the nineteenth-century Southwestern humorists they frequently read.

1121. Blair, Walter. "Humor of the Old Southwest." Native American Humor (1800-1900). New York: American Book Company, 1937.

Discusses the comedy of background, custom, and character of the Old Southwest--Tennessee, Georgia, Alabama, Louisiana, Mississippi, Arkansas, and Missouri. Augustus Longstreet was a lawyer, legislator, judge, and editor; Madison Tensas was a medical student, printer, cotton-picker, ploughboy, cabin boy, cook, and runaway; Johnson Hooper was a lawyer, politician, and newspaper editor; Sol Smith was an editor, actor-manager, preacher, and lawyer; Thomas Bangs Thorpe was a painter, soldier, and newspaper editor; William T. Thompson was a soldier, printer, law student, and journalist; Joseph M. Field was an actor-manager and journalist; John S. Robb was a journeyman printer and editor; Joseph G. Baldwin was a young frontier lawyer, and George W. Harris was a jeweler's apprentice, river boat captain, silversmith, political writer, postmaster, hunter, and inventor. Before they became authors, all of these individuals knocked around from job to job, involved in the teeming life that they would later write about. They were lawyers who wrote stories between swings on the circuit, journalists who scratched out their yarns on their desks in newspaper offices, and soldiers and doctors who jotted down tales during lulls in their strenuous daily activities. And they were all writing for eastern publishers and eastern readers.

1122. Cohen, Hennig, and William B. Dillingham, eds. Humor of the Old Southwest. 2nd edition. Athens: Univ. of Georgia Press, 1975, xviii + 427 pp.

Treats mainly Southern frontier humor during the first half of the nineteenth century. It contrasts the genteel literature which was being enjoyed by protected young ladies in New England drawing rooms with the masculine humor to be found in the Spirit of the Times. It submits that the wide use of pseudonyms during this period suggests the extent to which basic materials were common property, an aspect of the folk heritage of the region. The typical southwestern humorist smiled easily but was not a clown. He was typically a Whig, who felt deeply and spoke with conviction. He was keenly angered by the North, which seemed to have very little compassion for the South and its institutions. He defended slavery and, when the time came, secession. Seldom has a literary movement or school of writers reflected more unanimity in background, temperament, literary productions, aims, and beliefs. The traditions of southwestern humor have remained alive from Mark Twain on into the twentieth century. Southwestern humor has remained alive in such writers as Erskine Caldwell, Robert Penn Warren, and more recently, William Price Fox. In the work of William Faulkner, who read Southwest humor with great pleasure, it shows signs of continuing for a very long time.

1123. Cox, James M. "Humor of the Old Southwest." The Comic Imagination in American Literature. Ed. Louis D. Rubin, Jr. New Brunswick, NJ: Rutgers Univ. Press, 1983, 101-12.

Argues that the South's position below the North on all maps contributes to the Northern attitude that Southerners are "a little more poor, more ignorant, more lazy, more lawless, more violent, and more sensual than the Northerner," because they are from the "lower regions." Another geographical reason for the South's inferiority complex is that what used to be the Southwest is now the Southeast, because the original frontier was in reference to New England, but then the frontier became the land West of the Mississippi. Cox suggests that this is why the Old Southwest did not produce any important serious writers (except for Poe), and it is also why the Old Southwest dominated the humor genre (except for Irving). "Aside from Irving, the greatest of the Northern humorists was Seba Smith." Cox suggests that a major differences between Northern humor and Southern humor is that Southern humor is not so closely linked to morality. Cox discusses such Southern writers as Augustus Baldwin Longstreet, Johson Jones Hooper, Joseph Glover Baldwin, Thomas Bangs Thorpe, Henry Clay Lewis, and George Washington Harris, who tended to be professional men and politically conservative. Furthermore, unlike Northern writers, they considered themselves "gentlemen first and writers second."

1124. Fienberg, Lorne. "Laughter as a Strategy of Containment in Southwestern Humor." Studies in American Humor NS3.2-3 (Summer-Fall 1984): 107-22.

Suggests that the depression of the late 1830s was especially felt in the plantation aristocracy of the American South because the Southerners had had such a glorious past and because they lacked the ability to adapt to a changing economic environment. The humor of Joseph Glover Baldwin, for example, showed that he aligned himself with the planter aristocracy, but at the same time he criticized Southerners for trying to hold onto a lifestyle that was clearly destined to fail. The plantation owners had invested virtually all of their financial resources in property, and in 1837 when they couldn't liquidate their finances they were forced to sell their

lands to the banks, which began to call in their loans. Many of the
humorous sketches written during this period were about the fiscal
and moral weaknesses of southern gentlemen and the emergence of
backwoods characters who, in contrast to the plantation owners, were
able to succeed through their pragmaticism and free spirit. The
economic depression that began in 1837 brought about the downfall of
many members of the leisure class and their sporting pastimes, such
as turf racing. Such magazines as William T. Porter's _Spirit of the
Times_ which had been devoted to racing and other sporting news now
had to broaden their appeal, so they turned to publishing humorous
sketches. Joseph G. Baldwin's _The Flush Times of Alabama and
Mississippi_ looked back at the good old southern planatation days
with longing and nostalgia.

1125. Keller, Mark A. "Reputable Writers, Phony Names: Identifying
      Pseudonyms in the _Spirit of the Times_." _The Papers of the
      Bibliographical Society of America_ Volume 75, Second Quarter
      (1981): 198-209.

      Contends that _The Spirit of the Times_ was a significant
vehicle for making many writers of the early Southwest famous such
as A. B. Longstreet, William Tappan Thompson, Thomas Bangs Thorpe,
George Washington Harris, Johnson Jones Hooper, Henry Clay Lewis,
Joseph M. Field, Sol Smith, and John S.Robb. But many other good
writers who wrote for the _Spirit of the Times_ have not become
famous, for one reason, because they wrote under pseudonyms. The
pseudonyms were necessary at the time because the prevailing
Protestant ethic regarded sporting events and sporting literature as
reprehensible forms of entertainment, and the positions and
reputations of these writers would have been impugned if their real
names had been disclosed. An extreme example of tortured anonymity
is Thomas Kirkman of Alabama who had his letters copied by a friend
and then had the letters transported five hundred miles from his
home before mailing them to the _Spirit_. But now the audience is
more tolerant of humorous writing, so we are now discovering the
real names of "Sam Spray" who wrote a poem entitled "Sea Weed," and
"Puff" who wrote "The Pleasures of Smoking," and "Sunshine" who
wrote chatty letters about life in California, and many others.

1126. Meine, Franklin J. ed. _Tall Tales of the Southwest_. New York:
      Alfred A. Knopf, 1946, xxxii + 456 pp.

      Claims the Civil War was responsible for cutting us off from
much literature of the past, including antebellum Southern humor.
During the 1840s and 1850s a number of important southern and
southwestern humorists flourished. They were not professional
humorists but rather "lawyers, newspaper editors, country gentlemen
of family and fortune, doctors, army officers, travellers, actors--
who wrote for amusement rather than for gain." Meine feels that the
early humor of America's South had no counterpart in any other
section of America. It was anecdotal, provincial, and thoroughly
local, and it produced such comic figures as "Ned Brace, the
practical Georgia joker; Major Joseph Jones, Esq., of Pineville,
Georgia, famous lover and traveller; Captain Simon Suggs, of the
'Tallapoosy Vollantares'; Ovid Bolus, Esq., of the flush times in
Alabama and Mississippi; Sut Lovingood, 'ornary' hell-raising
mountaineer of the Great Smokies; and the Rev. Hezekiah Bradley, who
discoursed on the 'Harp of a Thousand Strings'." Meine feels that

the cornerstone of this literature was Augustus Baldwin Longstreet's
Georgia Scenes (1835).   The sketches originally appeared in
newspapers and periodicals and dealt with such topics as local
customs, courtships and weddings, law circuits and political life,
hunting, oddities in character, travel, frontier medicine, gambling,
religion, and fights.

1127. Rickels, Milton. "Elements of Folk Humor in the Literature of
      the Old Southwest." Thalia: Studies in Literary Humor 4.1
      (Spring-Summer, 1981): 5-9.

      Suggests that the vernacular perspective of the humor of the
Old Southwest represented not only the language of the rustic
backwoods characters but their ethical and aesthetic values as well.
The diction the humorists used contrasted violently with what was,
at the time, considered appropriate for literature.   However, the
values described contrasted even more violently, and the writing of
the southwest humorists was considered by many of their contemporary
critics to be not only crude and vulgar but irreverent as well.   The
comic literature tended to be skeptical of official dogmatism,
mysticism, and piety.   It offered freedom and escape from the social
and legal rules of the day.   The messages were ambiguous and
ambivalent, and the gay, triumphant, and mocking tone was considered
by many to be subversive.   In the past, much of the criticism
relating to the southwest humorists has dealt with the vernacular
language, because the colloquial tone is its most obvious feature.
However, Rickels suggests that more attention should be directed at
analyzing the folk values in the humorous literature of the Old
Southwest.

1128. Rickels, Milton. "The Grotesque Body of Southwestern Humor."
      Critical Essays on American Humor. Eds. William Bedford Clark
      and W. Craig Turner. Boston: G. K. Hall, 1984, 155-66.

      Considers   language   to   be   the   most   salient   aesthetic
achievement of the humor of the Old Southwest.   This included not
only the rhythm, sounds, and diction but the imagery as well, and
much of the humorous imagery of the Old Southwest was quite
grotesque.   Bodies were especially grotesque--too fat or too thin,
too short or too tall.   Simon Suggs had a head that was too large
and was thinly covered with coarse silver white hair.   His eyes
twinkled in such a way that an aqueous substance formed at the
corners.   Sut Lovingood was long-legged but short-bodied, and his
head was small.   Old Thorp was described as being like a crane, and
when he walked his head hung down as if his mother had weaned him
too early.   Harden Taliaferro tells the reader about cripples, and
Mark Twain describes Miss Wagner, who was a physical mess and had to
borrow Miss Jefferson's glass eye to receive company in.   Sut
Lovingood's dad was certainly grotesque as he drops to his hands and
knees and kicks high in the air and begins plowing the field.   These
grotesque body images of southwestern humor may be celebratory, but
they also have dark and negative implications as well.

1129. Rickels, Milton. "Inexpressibles in Southwestern Humor."
      Studies in American Humor 3.2 (October 1976): 76-83.

      Uses Mikhail Bakhtin's study of Rabelais to develop a
methodology   for   studying   southwestern   humor.   Bakhtin   had

established three major categories for Rabelaisian vocabulary: 1) abusive and insulting language, 2) profanities and oaths, and 3) obscenities or indecent expressions. Rickels contends that the vocabulary of the humorists of the Old Southwest written between 1830 and 1860 fits very nicely into these same categories. The humor was effective because it violated the strong taboos of the day against obscenities and profanities. The strong language gave the writing credility, for it suggested that the character was speaking from the heart without social constraint. The characters were calling things by their real names rather than mouthing the official views of society. The language also celebrated the energy and vitality of backwoods America. Rickels concludes that these abuses, curses, profanities and improprieties were "by no means gratuitous." Rickels feels that they represent a "cultivated stylistic form," displaying both vigor and literary merit.

West

1130. Adams, Ramon F. The Cowboy and His Humor. Austin, TX: Encino Press, 1968, 73 pp.

Considers one of the outstanding traits of the American cowboy to be his quick wit and his love of humor and of rough pranks. The cowboy's life was hard and dangerous, and humor was one of his few sources of relaxation and amusement. It provided a release from the strain and pressure of their lives. Because there was little recreation available to cowboys, they were continually playing practical jokes on each other, joshing each other, and telling funny stories--some true, and some not. Cowboys also used wild figures of speech. One old timer was named "flannel mouth" and was described as "wrinkled as a burnt boot." Another "orates as how he's got more troubles than a rat-tailed hoss tied short in fly-time." The cowboy's humor was picturesque, full flavored, fertile, and vigorous, and the practical jokes, rough horseplay, and tall tales were centered around the campfire after a hard day's work. The cowboy storyteller had a lot of time for close observation and for refining the story in his mind to improve it. The cowboys' sense of humor often eased tensions and kept them from getting trigger-happy, for a good sense of humor was often the best solution for many range problems.

1131. Boatright, Mody C. Folk Laughter on the American Frontier. New York: Macmillan, 1949, vi + 182 pp.

Believes that much of the crudeness, roughness, and exaggeration of western humor is in books written about the West by outsiders. These books both reflected and created the myth and gave it a wide dissemination. To these outsiders, the frontier West was seen as uncouth, provincial, and crude, and so the western writers decided to go along with the myth and exaggerate it even more. In 1850, the following poem was published in the Galveston Weekly Journal: "They fit and fit / And gouged and bit, / And struggled in the mud / Until the ground / For miles around / Was kivered with their blood / And a pile of noses, ears, and eyes, / Large and massive reached the skies."

1132. Kesterson, David B. "West." <u>Dictionary of Literary Biography,
      Volume 11: American Humorists, 1800-1950</u>. Detroit, MI: Gale,
      1982, 619-22.

    Feels that American western humor shares certain
characteristics with the humor of other frontiers, the result of
extreme weather, harsh living conditions, and strange people in
strange occupations. Frederick Jackson Turner considered western
humor to be "the meeting point between savagery and civilization."
Turner continues, "The landscape, the climate, living and working
conditions, the types of people and occupations, and a definite
personal and cultural image deriving from place are all key
ingredients of Western humor." The article considers such Western
humorous authors as Mark Twain, Bill Nye, and Will Rogers. Since no
part of America still has a genuine frontier mind set, most of the
raw and untamed humor of the frontier West is dying out. Our nation
has become urbanized, with mass transit and mass communication and
a more mobile and better-educated population, and American humor has
been influenced accordingly. There are nevertheless a few surviving
traces, such as the "Jackalope" picture postcards and the
everything's-bigger-in-Texas frame of mind.

1133. Reynolds, R. C. "Humor, Dreams and the Human Condition in
      Preston Jones's 'A Texas Trilogy.'" <u>The Southern Quarterly</u>
      24.3 (Spring 1986): 14-24.

    Considers Texas to be America's last frontier. It is the land
of the television program, "Dallas," and of the play <u>The Best Little
Whorehouse in Texas</u>. It is aptly named "the Lone Star state."
Preston Jones captures this concept in <u>The Last Meeting of the
Knights of the White Magnolia</u>, <u>The Oldest Living Graduate</u>, and <u>Lu
Ann Hampton Laverly Oberlander</u>. These three novels form "The Texas
Trilogy," and they are linked both by character and by location, a
fictional West Texas town named Bradleyville. The trilogy is a
hilarious romp through Bradleyville with its strange cast of
residents. Events cause both amusement and insight into some
stirring and perhaps disturbing truths about the human condition.
The characters' speech is also entertaining and insightful. It is
often profane, sometimes obscene, and frequently bigotted,
xenophobic, and intolerant of anyone who has not "paid his dues" to
the bitter life of West Texas. It is real language from real
people; it is language that comes from the heart. Jones's
characters are western archetypes, whose idea of great art is a
mural of a cattle stampede and whose idea of great music is a
televised program by the Country Jubilee singers.

1134. Rourke, Constance. "The Tall Tale." <u>Humor in America</u>. Ed. Enid
      Veron. New York: Harcourt, Brace, Jovanovich, 1976, 272-80.

    Discusses the legends of Davy Crockett, the backwoods hunter
and frontiersman, and Mike Fink, whose feats of strength and
marksmanship are equalled only by his frolics and pranks. Such
characters provide the stimulation for endless storytelling. Mike
Fink stories were frequently cruel, but readers claimed that such
cruelty is necessary on the frontier and that Mike Fink is actually
a kind person. Rourke claims that the real importance of the Mike
Fink legend is not that he was a pioneer and a frontiersman but that
he was a conservative, a holdout. When the steamboats came, their

efficiency and luxury quickly made the flat boats obsolete.   But
Mike Fink was a symbol of the previous era. As the steamboats would
pass, Mike Fink could be heard to shout, "What's the use of
improvements? Where's the fun, the frolicking, the fighting?" The
Mike Fink legends were an important part of America's oral culture.
Rourke feels that if he had lived in ancient Greece, Mike Fink could
have rivaled the feats of Jason. If he had lived among the ancient
Scandinavians he would have been a river god--in fact, he was a
river god, a god on the river Mississippi.

1135. Sonnichsen, C. L., ed. The Laughing West: Humorous Western
       Fiction Past and Present: An Anthology. Athens: Ohio Univ.
       Press, 1988, xi + 300 pp.

       Presents various themes of American Western humor. There are
pieces by Frank Applegate, Bill Gulick, and Dan Cushman in "Red
Man's West: The Transformation of the Indian"; Ross Santee, Max
Evans, and Glendon Swarthout contributed to "On the Range: The
Unromantic Cowboy"; Dorothy Pillsbury, Richard Bradford, and John
Nichols to "Blood of Spain: A Humorous Image for the Mexican-
American"; Thomas Berger, David Markson, and Will Henry to "New
Times, New Faces: Humor in Contemporary Western Fiction"; Robert
Lewis Taylor, David Wagoner, and George MacDonald Fraser to
"Pilgrims: Humor of the West on the Move"; Don Imus, Larry King, and
Edward Abbey to "Crusaders: The Humor of Real and Imitation
Reformers"; and H. Allen Smith, Dan Jenkins, and William Brinkley
to "Humor of the Towns and Cities." Sonnichsen's book also contains
a seventeen-page introduction on "The Humorous West" and a
postscript on humorous western writers on the horizon. The authors
need not be western to be included, but the settings and the
characters need to be. All of the authors included have a humorous
perspective, yet they all make a serious point as well. There is a
short introduction to each subdivision and a brief note introducing
each writer.

Pre-Sixteenth Century

1136. Bradley, Sculley. "Our Native Humor." North American Review
242.2 (Winter, 1936-37): 351-62; reprinted in Critical Essays
on American Humor. Eds. William Bedford Clark and W. Craig
Turner. Boston, MA: G. K. Hall, 1984, 62-69.

Contrasts British humor with American humor and concludes that
humor is deeper and more fertile in America than in most other
countries and is an important key to our national character. Both
England and America are founded in Anglo-Saxon, moralistic humor
that is first and foremost corrective. But there is an important
difference. British humor is satiric, while American humor is
ironic. The British laugh at something because it is ridiculous.
The Americans laugh at something because it is not what it should be
or what they expect it to be. British humor is based on ridicule;
American humor is a blend of awe and irony. British humor is
defensive, while American humor is offensive. The British like to
display wit under fire; the Americans like to play jokes on the
unwary. American humor is in the vernacular; it is homely and
homespun and has a blunt directness. It is the humor of courage and
necessity resulting from the crossing of prairies, the conquering of
forests, the building of cities. It is the humor learned as a
result of looking through gunsights. American humor lacks
refinement or finish according to British standards. For the
British, American humor tends to be a bit too undisciplined--a bit
too boisterous.

1137. Clark, William Bedford, and W. Craig Turner, eds. Critical
Essays on American Humor. Boston, MA: G. K. Hall, 1984, viii
+ 232 pp.

Traces the history of American humor from pre-colonial days to
1984 and observes that a study of American humor is a valuable tool
in the understanding of the American character. Clark and Turner
agree with H. R. Haweis (an author in this anthology) that American
humor has had three main roots. The first basis of humor was the
result of the tensions arising out of the clash between American
pragmaticism and materialism on the one hand and religion on the
other. The second arose from the juxtaposition of Europeans who
came to America with the Native Americans who were already here.
And the third arose from the vastness of North America, which
resulted in a tendency toward hyperbole.

1138. Ferguson, J. DeLancey. "The Roots of American Humor." American
      Scholar 4 (Winter 1934-35): 41-49; reprinted in Critical
      Essays on American Humor. Eds. William Bedford Clark and W.
      Craig Turner. Boston, MA: G. K. Hall, 1984, 51-58.

      Points out that many critics have claimed that American
humorous folk literature and especially the tall tale are indigenous
to the United States and contrast with the more formal humor of
Europe. Ferguson, however, feels that American humor is not a new
creation but rather has a literary heritage as old as our country
itself. History and literature both suffer from an aristocratic
bias, so that the history and literature of the common folk do not
receive the same prominance as the history and literature of kings,
courts, and aristocracy. America was not settled by aristocracy but
rather settled by the working class, providing the foundation for a
more informal--a more humorous--kind of literary tradition.
Ferguson notes, however, that this folk humor tradition was already
well established in Scottish, Scotch-Irish, and North of England
stock-ballads long before America was settled. He says that the
plain ordinary people of early Great Britain were well trained in
exaggeration, far-fetched metaphor, and tall stories. These were
aspects of their daily speech. The more one reads the Celtic
legends, the more one discovers the roots of American folk humor.
Almost the entire range of American comic stereotypes can be found
in earlier British folk literature--only the labels have changed.

1139. Rourke, Constance. "Examining the Roots of American Humor."
      American Scholar 4 (Spring, 1935): 249-53; reprinted in
      Critical Essays on American Humor. Eds. William Bedford Clark
      and W. Craig Turner. Boston, MA: G. K. Hall, 1984, 58-62.

      Emphasizes the uniqueness of American humor, and disagrees
with J. Delancey Ferguson when he says that American humor has its
roots in European humor. Rourke asks, if American humor is so
similar to British humor, then why are the British so puzzled by our
comedians (and conversely, why are we so puzzled by theirs)? Rourke
concedes that there are parallels between the Davy Crockett myths
and the Gaelic myths. She also concedes that early Americans
frequently culled jokes from English joke books (such as Joe
Miller's). But Rourke feels that the borrowing was gradually
superseded by American invention, American twists, American local
color, and, in fact, an entirely new humor tradition.

Sixteenth Century

1140. Holliday, Carl. The Wit and Humor of Colonial Days.
      Williamstown, MA: Corner House, 1975. 320 pp.

      Traces American humor from the days of the first settlement to
the beginning of the nineteenth century. Humor is perhaps the only
genre where American literature excels that of the European.
American humor is "as old as the nation. The colonists had scarcely
landed in Virginia before witty letters telling of ludicrous sights
and mishaps in the raw settlement began to go back to England."
American humor is remarkable evidence of the sturdiness of the Early
American people, who faced the terrors of the wilderness and the

difficulties of tyrannical misrule. "There were blue laws, witch burnings, and Indian massacres; but in spite of these and the sorrows, superstitions, and unbending theologies" Americans had a sense of humor. Early American humor ridiculed foes, encouraged defenders, and turned hardships of war into merriment. In New England there developed "a taunting satire like that of the Hebrew prophets of old." Holliday dispels the notion of colonial somberness, by providing examples of colonial humor written by Alsop (George and Richard), Ames, Barlow, Brackenridge, Burgoyne, Byles, Byrd, Cook, Douglas, Dwight, Dunlap, Franklin, Freneau, Green, Hopkins, Hopkinson, Humphreys, Morton, Odell, Paine, Stansbury, Trumbull, Tyler, Ward, and Witherspoon.

1141. Micklus, Robert. "Colonial Humor: Beginning with the Butt." _Critical Essays on American Humor_. Eds. William Bedford Clark and W. Craig Turner. Boston, MA: G. K. Hall, 1984, 139-54.

Points out that Constance Rourke's _American Humor_ and Walter Blair's _Native American Humor_ are indispensable works on American literary humor but they have promoted a prominent bias in American humor scholarship--that colonial humor is bad humor because it is not "American." Micklus feels that we should accept early American humor for what it is. For these earliest American humorists the butt of the joke was always whatever was "out there." It may have been the British, the Indians, or even some country bumpkin, but before Benjamin Franklin's time there was little humor at the expense of the author himself or at his persona. Most colonial humor seems immature today not because it is derivative of British humor conventions or is in some other way not American but rather because it is so defensive. The colonial Americans lived in insecure times. Colonial humorists struck a superior pose and ridiculed the people and customs that ran counter to their own way of life. By laughing at other people, who did not meet their standards, they were able to convince themselves that their standards were appropriate and valid.

Seventeenth Century

1142. Blair, Walter, and Hamlin Hill, eds. _America's Humor: From Poor Richard to Doonesbury_. New York: Oxford Univ. Press, 1978, xvi + 381 pp.

Traces American humor from colonial times to the present in its various representations--"high-falutin and low-falutin; rustic, frontier and urban; white, black, blue and parti-colored." This anthology includes even humor which is "unfunny," provided it was "influential, typical, or widely enjoyed." The assumption is that American humor "reveals a great deal about America's history," and that "much of it, whether forgotten or still admired, is fine enough as literature to justify critical analysis," therefore, the pieces selected are viewed as artistic achievements, as historical documents, or both. Most of the pieces are reactions to events-- "the exploration and settlement of the New World, the Revolution and subsequent wars, the westering of the frontier, widening education, expanding suffrage, the aftermaths of the Civil War, urbanization, scientific developments, the new psychologies, the proliferation of

mass media, and the growth of the counterculture." Relevance was
considered the primary determinant for inclusion, whether the
relevance was demonstrated through resemblances or through
incongruities. In some cases, two selections were placed side by
side to show "significantly different versions of the same comic
story."

1143. Dodge, Robert K. Early American Almanac Humor. Bowling Green,
OH: Popular Press, 1987, viii + 163 pp.

Points out that in the early days of colonial America very
little humor was written down or published. William Byrd, Thomas
Merton of Merrymount and Stephen Burroughs were probably the only
significant writers of humor during this period.
But in 1639, Stephen Daye published America's first almanac, and for
the next two and a half centuries almanacs were to be a significant
part of American life. In order to increase almanac sales,
Nathaniel Ames and James Franklin started to include short
paragraphs on current topics and on morality. James Franklin even
invented the character of Poor Robin and his "sayings." James'
brother, Benjamin, continued the tradition of almanacs and the
tradition of humorous sayings, but the sayings of Poor Robin became
the sayings of Poor Richard in Benjamin's case. Poor Richard's
Almanack soon set sales records, and other almanacs began adding
humor and trivia to boost their sales and to provide material for
larger editions. Between 1776 and 1800 more than 2,000 comic items
were included in basically serious almanacs much the way The
Reader's Digest inserts comic filler today, and this became the
first important source of written popular humor. More and more
humor was added to the almanacs until by the nineteenth century the
humor had become the most significant feature of many almanacs.
Dodge points out that much of this humor has been overlooked by
today's critics because it is scattered through more than a thousand
sources, each of which has to be examined page by page to dig out
the humorous items. A careful gleaning, however, reveals the extent
of the humor and provides an insightful glimpse into the nature of
the early American republic.

1144. Leacock, Stephen, ed. The Greatest Pages of American Humor.
New York: Doubleday, 1936, x + 293 pp.

Discusses the humor of the Indians and the Puritans as the
origins of American humor. Leacock traces American humor from
Benjamin Franklin to Will Rogers in this anthology. He has chapters
devoted to Benjamin Franklin, Washington Irving, Nathaniel
Hawthorne, David Crockett, Josh Billings, Artemus Ward, Bret Harte,
Mark Twain, Max Adeler, Joel Chandler Harris, Oliver Wendell Holmes,
Finley Peter Dunne, John Kendrick Bangs, Wallace Irwin, George Ade,
O. Henry, Robert Benchley, Irvin S. Cobb, Ring Lardner, and Will
Rogers.

1145. Lemay, J. A. Leo. The Frontiersman from Lout to Hero: Notes on
the Significance of the Comparative Method and the Stage
Theory in Early American Literature and Culture. Worcester,
MA: American Antiquarian Society, 1979, 223 pp.

Contends that the seventeenth-century view of the frontiersman
as a shiftless outcast, a lazy villain, a stupid and vulgar lout

changed in the nineteenth century to a pathfinder, pioneer, trailblazing hero. This transformation came about as a belief in degeneration shifted to a belief in progress. Seventeenth-century Americans looked backward--toward history; nineteenth-century Americans looked forward--to the future. This is reflected as the perception of the settler changed from the seventeenth-century "backwoodsman" "backsettler, "bushman," "bushwackers," to become the nineteenth-century "frontiersman." "pathfinder," "pioneer," or "trailblazer." LeMay contends that in this transformation the orientation changed from "back" to "front."

1146. Pogel, Nancy, and Paul P. Somers, Jr. "Literary Humor." Humor in America: A Research Guide to Genres and Topics. Ed. Lawrence Mintz. Westport, CT: Greenwood, 1988, 1-34.

Traces the history of humor in American literature by following Louis D. Rubin's contention that humor arises "out of the gap between the cultural ideal and the everyday fact." The article suggests that the tall tale was the first American art form. A second important genre was the almanac, and this was followed by the development of many comic personae. The article discusses Yankee humor, and Southwestern humor as well as the misspellers, the "phunny phellows," the literary comedians, and the "wise fool." The ten-year period 1895 to 1905 was described as the turbulent decade, since it saw the change from the old, primarily agricultural America to the new, industrial America. In the 1960s black humor became the dominant genre, and since the 1960s much of American literatary humor has turned from black to "dark grey." Pogel and Somers describe the major characteristics of contemporary American literary humor to be "self-parody, parody, irony, reflexivity, metafiction, and intertextuality"; however, they are quick to point out that these characteristics are not confined to contemporary humor. An important point presented in this article is that many writers are bigger than life because we-the-readers have made them so, and Pogel and Somers agree with Louis Budd that Mark Twain is actually "our creation" to some extent.

1147. Royot, Daniel. L'Humour Américain, Des Puritains aux Yankees. Lyon, France: Presses Universitaires de Lyon, 1980, 384 pp.

Translates American humor into French, trying to retain the flavor the original American humor, and provides the French perspective on American humor, especially New England or Yankee humor and southern humor. Royot feels that Mark Twain contributed to Yankee humor as well as to southern humor. He also feels that reading Ben Jonson or Robert Burton will show that American theoreticians do not always distinguish "comedy" from "humor." Royot presents a number of statements from French critics which have bearing on the analysis of American humor--Twain, Baudelaire, Rabelais, Diderot, Bergson, etc., and concludes that for some, humor wears a mask that protects and thus covers up a complex reality. But for others, it provides a distance that corresponds to an attitude of clear-headed disengagement from the world and from one's self. In contrasting puritan humor and Yankee humor, Royot provides characteristics of these two opposing types of humor. In doing this, the book discusses humor and religion from a Puritan point of view and Puritan and Yankee aspects of wisdom, the comic, the picaresque, political satire, pastoralism, provincialism, New Englandism, and other cultural movements in the United States.

1148. Royot, Daniel. "The Grinning of America: Native Humor: The Giggle for Life." Revue Française d'Etudes Américaines 4 (October 1977): 5-11.

Maintains that since colonial days Americans have tried to import humor to Europe in the form of crude hoaxes, homespun metaphors, madcap antics, and hyperbolic perceptions. Seventeenth century American humor contained "comic elegies rapturously describing decaying bodies"; This was the Puritan humor of dying men making fun of departing from this world and getting ready for the joyful next world. Eighteenth century American humor was used to exorcise the terrors of the frontier wilderness with cocky braggadocio. During the Civil War, humor became the mask of the picaro in the form of Sam Slick, Haliburton's Yankee peddler, and Sut Lovingood, George Washington Harris's rogue, also allowed readers to deal with the perverse nature of mankind. Europe was not interested in importing any of these types of humor. However, in the 1920s Will Rogers brought a more amiable vision to American humor. Europeans finally related to the grass-roots philosophy of a humorist who was wary of intellectual systems and the spread of dehumanizing technology and who defended rural values over the chaos of the urban rat race. It was then that Europeans finally started to vigorously consume American humor both in movies and novels.

1149. Thorp, Willard. American Humorists. Minneapolis: Univ. of Minnesota Press, 1964, 48 pp.

Feels that no American writers in the seventeenth or eighteenth century used it exclusively, although a great many of them used humor to some extent because of the incongruities and ridiculous frustrations of frontier life. When Sarah Kemble Knight journeyed from Boston to New York in 1704 her tribulations were lightened by the odd people she met along the way, so she recorded their quaint speech and manners in her journal. Like Sarah Kemble Knight, William Byrd, the Virginian, also had an eye for the riduculous. Ben Franklin's humor was intended to entertain and instruct in Poor Richard's Almanack and the Silence Dogood letters respectively. John Trumbull and the other Connecticut Wits used humor and satire as weapons in the colonial arsenal during the Revolution. Francis Hopkinson, a signer of the Declaration of Independence, wrote satires of the British as did Philip Freneau, the poet of the Revolution. The English wanted to export their goods to America, and when the English reported that there was not enough wool produced in the colonies in a year to make a pair of stockings, Franklin responded that American sheep were so laden with wool that each had to pull a little wagon behind to keep their wooly tails from dragging on the ground. The book goes on through the humor of Washington Irving, Edgar Allan Poe, Seba Smith, Ring Lardner, James Thurber, S. J. Perelman, Saul Bellow, Will Rogers, William Faulkner, and others.

1150. Veron, Enid. "Brief History of Humor in American Literature." *Humor in America*. Ed. Enid Veron. New York: Harcourt, Brace, Jovanovich, 1976, 326-32.

Contends that there was very little written humor among the first colonists because they were preoccupied with taming the wilderness. They wrote mostly diaries, travel accounts, religious tracts, and sermons. Humor began to emerge in seventeenth-century America, however, due to a growing interest in ballads, jest books, and picaresque and satiric narratives. Many funny stories were told about such legendary figures as Miles Standish, and there developed certain targets for humor such as women and New England preachers, both of whom tended to be more concerned with the fashions and manners of the day than with Puritan ethics. By the eighteenth century, satire was flourishing throughout America. Ebenezer Cook burlesqued Marylanders in "The Sot-Weed Factor" (1708). William Byrd II satirized North Carolinians in *History of the Dividing Line* (1728). Sarah Kemble Knight satirized travel chronicles in her description of a journey from Boston to New Haven (1704). By the nineteenth century, an indigenous American humor had emerged with the letters of Major Jack Downing of Downingville, who developed his democratic leanings by becoming a close friend of President Andrew Jackson; these letters were actually written by Seba Smith. During this period there was also Sam Slick, the itinerant Yankee peddler, a character developed by Thomas Chandler Haliburton. During this same period humor was also developing special characteristics in the South, marked by dialect, violence, and gusto.

1151. Weiss, Helen S., and M. Jerry Weiss, eds. *The American Way of Laughing: A Collection of Humor from Benjamin Franklin to Woody Allen*. New York: Bantam, 1977, xii + 244 pp.

Suggests that much early American humor was oral. In discussing the trek westward, for example, the authors say that jokes and anecdotes were exchanged around campfires. These jokes and anecdotes were then retold around pot-bellied stoves in general stores and trading posts. "Over the years, the stories were expanded, exaggerated. In a comparatively short time, they grew into tall tales and legends." Nineteenth century humor is characterized as "rustic, homespun humor." Cracker-barrel philosophers used their wit to expose inconsistencies in politics, religion and human nature. Anecdotes, sketches, letters and almanacs are the main sources of humor during this period, abounding with dialect spellings and malapropisms. Mark Twain was pivotal, because he "saw a radical change in America from an agrarian to an industrial society." Finally, the twentieth century humor dealt with the problems of the "pressure cooker" society. Much of this humor "censures the plight of the individual, drowning in a sea of complications." Interestingly, many American humorists began as newspaper and magazine reporters, columnists, editors and/or publishers. The list includes Franklin, Holmes, Billings, Twain, Dunne, Rogers, Thurber, Parker, Hughes, Nash, White, and Buchwald.

1152. Wright, Louis B. "Human Comedy in Early America." <u>The Comic
      Imagination in American Literature</u>. Ed. Louis D. Rubin, Jr.
      New Brunswick, NJ: Rutgers Univ. Press, 1983, 17-31.

      Considers satire to have been a very practical form of writing
for early American authors. The literature of colonial America did
not contain much humor. The early settlers were serious as they
struggled to establish themselves in the wilderness. They didn't
have time for polite letters, literature, or other types of
entertainment. However, satire for them was not considered
entertainment. Satire was a very practical way of "poking fun at
pretentiousness, pomposity, and vainglory." It was "an instrument
of reform" used to point out some of the shortcomings of society.
Much of the earliest American humor appeared in very practical books
called "almanacs." Benjamin Franklin began publishing humorous
didactic aphorisms in <u>Poor Richard's Almanac</u>. Many of the aphorisms
were already part of the folk literature of the day even though we
lack the evidence for this today. Benjamin Franklin's aphorisms
were preserved because, "Franklin merely made a better selection
than his predecessors."

Eighteenth Century

1153. Bier, Jesse. <u>The Rise and Fall of American Humor</u>. New York:
      Holt, Rinehart and Winston, 1968, xii + 506 pp.

      Finds authentic American humor to be caustic, wild, and
savage. Our comic expression may be placed along a continuum from
irreverence to outright shock. Some examples of our humor hold our
society together, while other examples enrich the society or oppose
fanaticism by encouraging dissent and perhaps even attack. American
humor tells the whole truth, and this explains why there is so much
cruelty in our humor. Our humor is <u>antithetical</u>. It is the humor
of <u>simplification</u>--cliches, shibboleths, proverbs, slogans, and
formulas--but it is also the humor of <u>complication</u>--the Rube
Goldberg cartoon, etc. It is possible to conclude that overt
American humor is filled with more complication than the humor of
other nations. Some humor is typically American. It may be <u>obvious</u>
as when the suds of the overflowing dishwasher advance into the
living room. It may be <u>exaggerated</u>, as in cowboy humor. It may use
<u>non-sequiturs</u> such as Artemus Ward's "I knew a man from Oregon once
who didn't have a tooth in his head, and that man could play the
drums better than anyone I ever met." American humor can also
exemplify comic momentum, as when Groucho Marx is trying to sell a
hat for $15. The customer wants to pay $6.00. In their bargaining,
they cross each other's prices, and Groucho's final price is $5.00.

1154. Cox, S. S. <u>Why We Laugh</u>. New York: Harper, 1876; excerpted in
      <u>Critical Essays on American Humor</u>. Eds. William Bedford Clark
      and W. Craig Turner. Boston, MA: G. K. Hall, 1984, 22-29.

      Discusses the humor of Franklin, Ward, Billings, Nasby,
Adeler, Twain, Harte, Breitmann, Newell, and other eighteenth- and
nineteenth-Century American humorists and concludes that there is
more humor in America than in most other countries precisely because
there is more individuality in America than in most other countries.

Americans follow their own bent and take both pleasure and pride in demonstrating it.

1155. Dudden, Arthur Power. "American Humor." American Quarterly. 37.1 (Spring 1985): 7-12.

Says that by 1840 a number of American humorists had begun to earn money by lecturing and writing. Shortly thereafter, Artemus Ward, Josh Billings, and Petroleum Vesuvias Nasby established celebrity status as humorists, and Mark Twain established American literary humor as a permanent tradition with his treatises on politics, ethnicity, and sexuality. In 1888 Mark Twain, William Dean Howells, and Charles Hopkins Clark got together to publish Mark Twain's Library of Humor to establish the tradition even more firmly.

1156. Granger, Bruce Ingraham. Political Satire in the American Revolution, 1763-1783. Ithaca, NY: Cornell Univ. Press, 1960, xi + 314 pp.

Considers this to be the first detailed treatment of the satirical record of the American Revolution, even though literary and social historians have long recognized that personalities, issues, and events of the Revolution were frequently held up to ridicule at the time. Most of the satires contained in this volume were written by Americans for Americans with a focus on the two-decade period from 1763 to 1783. The 530 satires that were collected from this period came from American newspapers, magazines, broadsides, pamphlets, and manuscripts. Two rich sources were Scots Magazine and Gentleman's Magazine. During the eighteenth century satire was regarded as a method of changing behavior. The satirist was regarded as a Censor Morum, and he served the cause of virtue by ridiculing irrationality and error.

1157. Hansen, Arlen J. "Magnificent Liars: Exaggeration on American Humour." It's a Funny Thing, Humour. Eds. Antony J. Chapman and Hugh C. Foot. New York: Pergamon. 1977, 181-84.

Considers the work of such humorous American authors as Mark Twain, Thomas Bangs Thorpe, David Crockett, Arlo Guthrie, Joseph Heller, and Lennie Bruce. What these authors write are not merely exaggerations and magnificent lies; they are dreams and fantasies and jokes as well. He quotes William Dean Howells as having said about Mark Twain's Roughing It, "The grotesque exaggeration and broad irony with which the life is described are conjecturably the truest colors that could have been used, for all existence there (in Nevada) must have looked like an extravagant joke."

1158. Haweis, H. R. American Humorists. New York: Funk and Wagnalls, 1882; excerpted in Critical Essays on American Humor. Eds. William Bedford Clark and W. Craig Turner. Boston, MA: G. K. Hall, 1984, 29-31.

Suggests that American wit has three main roots. The first root is the clash between business and religion. The second root is the clash between the Yankee and the American Indian whom he supplanted. The third root is the clash of the vastness of the

American frontier wilderness with the smallness and insignificance
of man.

1159. Holliday, Carl. "Ebenezer Cook." The Wit and Humor of Colonial
Days. Williamstown, MA: Corner House, 1975, 38-42.

Explains that in the eighteenth century the title of a book
was a good day's work for the author. The title of Cook's book was
as follows: The Sot Weed Factor; or a Voyage to Maryland--a satire
in which is described the laws, government, courts, and
constitutions of the country, and also the buildings, feasts,
frolics, entertainments, and drunken humors of the inhabitants in
that part of America. The term "Sot-weed" was a seventeenth- and
eighteenth-century term for tobacco. Cook's poetry is normally
considered to be mere doggerel by modern standards, but it is
humorous, slam-bang doggerel in which the author laughed loudly and
unrestrainedly. Cook's writing again illustrates that the Puritans
had the irreverent tendency to poke fun at all things, no matter how
dignified or how honored. In other words, the founders of the
Commonwealth could enjoy the ridiculous.

1160. Jessup, Emily. "Teaching and Preaching While Doing Neither:
Artemus Ward, Mark Twain, and Garrison Keillor." WHIMSY 3
(1985): 23-25.

Agrees with Twain that the longevity of humorous work depends
upon its ability to operate on different levels. In Autobiography
of Mark Twain, Twain said, "Humor must neither teach nor preach yet
it must do both if it is to last forever. By forever I mean thirty
years." In a sketch entitled, "Reverend Henry Ward Beecher's Farm,"
Twain satirizes the overdependence on books for solving practical
problems. Even though Beecher was "morally certain that the hay
ought to be cut, the hay book could not be found, and before it was
found it was too late, and the hay was all spoiled." Under the
pseudonym of Artemus Ward, Charles Brown would try to explode the
mind by developing a mind-set and then following it with an
incongruity. "My farm is located in the interior of Maine....
Eleven miles is quite a distance to haul immense quantities of
wheat, corn, rye and oats; but as I haven't any to haul, I do not,
afterall, suffer much on that account." Garrison Keillor also
stresses incongruity, as he tells about a city dude who has a
tendency to think while he is showering, and who speaks in a "sneaky
city prose style." One day while driving to town he shouts to a
farmer, "That's certainly doing well," but then he suddenly realizes
that he doesn't know what "that" is. "Also it looked burnt."

1161. Simpson, Lewis P. "The Satiric Mode: The Early National Wits."
The Comic Imagination in American Literature. Ed. Louis D.
Rubin, Jr. New Brunswick, NJ: Rutgers Univ. Press, 1983, 49-
61.

Contrasts satires expressing two opposing attitudes toward
American history--the millennial view, and the doomsday view--and
explains how both of these views account for the flavor and tone of
early American humor. Both of these views "decry the rule of kings
and praise the rule of the people"; however the overthrow of kings
has a utopian ending in the millennial view but a dystopian ending
in the doomsday view. From this point of view, Simpson discusses

the works of Philip Freneau, John Trumbull, Joel Barlow, Timothy
Dwight, and Hugh Brackenridge.

1162. Sloane, David E. E. "Humor in Periodicals." Humor in America:
      A Research Guide to Genres and Topics. Ed. Lawrence E. Mintz.
      Westport, CT: Greenwood, 1988, 49-65.

     Indicates that burlesque was an early American genre that
allowed slang, neologisms, and vernacular language. The article
contrasts the American literary magazines that did not have long
lives with the more general-purpose magazines that did: Vanity Fair,
Saturday Evening Post, Colliers, Look, Life, Esquire, and The New
Yorker. These have all published important humorous literary pieces
during their tenure, but there was a balance between humor and
seriousness. The article traces American literary magazines from
1765 to 1985 and declares that the most important eras seem to "lie
in the 1800-1820, Civil War, Mauve Decade, and post-World War I
eras." Sloane considers the first American literary magazine to
have been The Bee. It was first published in Philadelphia in 1765
by "William Honeycomb" and became very involved in Pennsylvania
politics. Many early satiric magazines had stinging (or at least
touching) titles. In addition to The Bee, there was The Wasp, The
Tickler, Pepper, and Thistle, not to mention National Lampoon.
Perhaps the sting was too great; the famous Zenger case (1733-1734)
held that "the greater the truth the greater the libel," and many
literary magazines had to print retractions. This legal literalism
was in force for American satirists for a century or more.

1163. Trent, W. P. "A Retrospect of American Humor." Century
      Magazine 63 (November 1901): 45-64; reprinted in Critical
      Essays on American Humor. Eds. William Bedford Clark and W.
      Craig Turner. Boston, MA: G. K. Hall, 1984, 32-46.

     Contrasts Benjamin Franklin's early humor with his late humor.
At first his humor was dependent on the changing demographics from
rural life to the slowly evolving urban life. The rise of democracy
under President Jackson and the assumption of leadership by people
who had previously only been led culminated in the "Biglow Papers."
Unique stereotypes emerged in early American humor such as the
Mormons, the Pike County men, the Mississippi boatmen. During the
eighteenth and nineteenth centuries, there was only a limited amount
of humorous and satiric verse in America produced by such writers as
Hopkinson, Freneau, Trumbull, Drake, and Halleck. These humorous
verse writers contrasted with the academic humorists, and the socio-
political humorists. Trent feels that in addition to James Russell
Lowell, there are basically five significant political humorists
during the period from 1830-1870--Seba Smith, Charles Augustus
Davis, Robert Henry Newell, Charles Henry Smith, and David R. Locke.

Nineteenth Century

1164. Batts. John Stuart. "American Humor: A Late Victorian View."
      WHIMSY 5 (1987): 26-18.

      Describes   nineteenth-century   American   narrative   as
exaggerated, often told by a self-deprecating speaker in colorful,
slangy, idiom, while exposing strange ways of looking at otherwise
serious experiences. Thomas Chandler Haliburton wrote a series of
books that feature Sam Slick, in which Sam Slick created a number of
colorful expressions that are very much in use in today's English,
such as "quick as a wink," "stick in the mud," "upper crust," "as
large as life and twice as natural," and "six of one and half-a-
dozen of the other." Halliburton is also responsible for a number
of amusing aphorisms like, "Nothing is so heavy to carry as
gratitude." Batts also shows some interesting parallels between the
work of the British humorist Jerome K. Jerome and American humorist
Mark Twain.   Batts feels that Jerome's The Three Men in a Boat--To
Say Nothing of the Dog relies heavily on Twain's Innocents Abroad,
and Roughing It. It may even be a parody of Twain's earlier books.
Jerome tells about three tenderfoots who attempt a holiday afloat on
the Thames. The three "innocents abroad" are frequently forced to
"rough it" in their adventures with weather, locks, the need to row
upstream, and so forth.

1165. Blackbeard, Bill. "Humorous Book Illustration." Dictionary of
      Literary Biography, Volume 11: American Humorists, 1800-1950.
      Ed. Stanley Trachtenberg. Detroit, MI: Gale, 1982, 625-39.

      Points out that because there was no effective international
copyright protection in the United States before 1890, many early
American publishers used illustrations by such British cartoonists
as George Cruikshank, Hablot Knight Browne (Phiz), and John Leech.
This not only created the lack of a market for good American
illustrators, but it also created the illusion that all of the good
comic art was to be found in England or Europe. After the Civil
War, however, American illustrators such as Thomas Nast, Fred Opper,
and Edward W. Kemble rose to fame and were used frequently with by-
line recognition and decent pay. This article discusses the comic
illustration not only of Thomas Nast (illustrator for Rufus E.
Shapley), Fred Opper, and Edward W. Kemble (illustrator for Finley
Peter Dunne) but of F. O. C. Darley (illustrator for Washington
Irving), Mullen (illustrator for George Washington Harris), Gean
Smith (illustrator for George W. Peck), R. W. Wallis (illustrator
for Robert J. Burdette), John T. McCutcheon (illustrator for George
Ade), Kin Hubbard (illustrator for Abe Martin), Bill Breck
(illustrator for Edward Streeter), Fontaine Fox (illustrator for
Ring Lardner), George Herriman (illustrator for Don Marquis), Miguel
Covarrubias, and Frank Sullivan (illustrators for Corey Ford),
Gluyas Williams (illustrator for Robert Benchley), Ralph Burton
(illustrator for Anita Loos), O. Soglow (illustrator for George S.
Chappell), Charles Addams (illustrator for Peter De Vries), Syd Hoff
(illustrator for Arthur Kober), and Al Hirschfeld (illustrator for
S. J. Perelman).

1166. Blackbeard, Bill. "Newspaper Syndication of American Humor."
Dictionary of Literary Biography, Volume 11: American
Humorists, 1800-1950. Ed. Stanley Trachtenberg. Detroit, MI:
Gale, 1982, 642-52.

   Feels that the widespread syndication of humorous prose and
cartoon work in America is the result of the huge size of the United
States and the great distances between urban centers in America. In
nineteenth-century England and Europe the tradition was to buy a
local paper (Birmingham or Edinburgh) for the local news and a
London paper for the national and international news. That
tradition remains in England and Europe. In America, however,
syndication is much more highly developed, and local papers,
therefore, contain much non-local material, much of it humorous.
Syndicated humorous writers in America include Mark Twain, Ambrose
Bierce, Finley Peter Dunne, George Ade, Joel Chandler Harris, Ring
Lardner, John Kendrick Bangs, Damon Runyon, Gelett Burgess, Montague
Glass, and Will Rogers.

1167. Blair, Walter, Ed. Native American Humor (1800-1900). New
York: American Book Company, 1937, xv + 569 pp.

   Suggests that early American humor had an amateur exhuberance
that was lost when America's humor began to be more
professionalized.   American humor had a number of distinct
qualities. It was basically oral; it was sharply individual, it was
decidedly poetic, even fantastic; it developed its own imagery, its
own accent, its own patterns of thought, but most of all it required
the sound of the human voice. [This book was reviewed by Bernard
DeVoto in Saturday Review of Literature (25 September, 1937).]

1168. Caron, James E. "Laughter, Politics, and the Yankee Doodle
Legacy in America's Comic Tradition." Thalia: Studies in
Literary Humor 10.1 (Spring-Summer 1988): 3-13.

   Suggests that there are two traditions of comic characters in
antebellum American writing. There are reputable characters who are
part of a moral and predictable universe, and there are the
irreputable characters or subversives who flaunt the law, decency
and modesty and have no clear sense of right and wrong. And there
seems to be a geographical correlation to these two comic
traditions.   The reputable characters are associated with New
England, and the irreputable characters are associated with the Old
Southwest. But it is not as simple as this, for many characters are
rogues in respectable clothing. Sam Slick dresses reputably and
speaks reputably and dispenses homespun wisdom, but he sells clocks
of dubious value. Jim Doggett in "The Big Bear of Arkansas" has the
reputable quality of being a sage, but he is nevertheless a ring-
tailed roarer. Caron suggests that there are many characters in
America's comic tradition who in some sense are subversive while
they are in some other sense reputable and suggests that many comic
characters throughout American history need to be reexamined with
this ambivalence in mind.

1169. Cohen, Hennig. "A Comic Mode of the Romantic Imagination: Poe, Hawthorne, Melville." The Comic Imagination in American Literature. Ed. Louis D. Rubin, Jr. New Brunswick, NJ: Rutgers Univ. Press, 1983, 85-99.

Considers the major works of Poe, Hawthorne, and Melville to be pessimistic, egocentric, guilt ridden, and admitting to a profound sense of human limitations. These are the qualities in Poe's tales of terror and madness, Hawthorne's The Scarlet Letter, and Melville's Moby-Dick, all written in the tragic mode. But Cohen feels that these same characteristics also led these three authors in the direction of comedy to provide a sense of balance, a sense of sanity, and a sense of hope to their works. The more tragic the insights of these works, the more there is a need for the countervaling comic perspective. Poe, Hawthorne, and Melville wrote in the tradition of the comic satire. They satirized manners, politics, literature, business, technology, and self-deception. All three authors enjoyed word play, wit, and joking. Cohen feels that all three of them enjoyed toying with their readers, pushing them around, sometimes not very gently, often making the readers the butts of their jokes.

1170. Crandell, George W. "Emperors and Little Empires: The Schoolmaster in Nineteenth-Century American Literature." Studies in American Humor 5.1 (Spring 1986): 51-61.

Depicts the schoolmaster of nineteenth-century American fiction as an emperor wielding a hickory scepter over the heads of his pupil-subjects in his small empire--his one-room schoolhouse. This is the situation in Walt Whitman's "Death in the School-Room (a Fact)" (1841), Richard Malcolm Johnston's "The Goosepond School" (1864), Edward Eggleston's The Hoosier School Master (1871), Mark Twain's The Adventures of Tom Sawyer (1876), William Dean Howells' A Boy's Town (1890), and Booth Tarkington's Penrod (1914), and Washington Irving was in this same mindset when he wrote "The Legend of Sleepy Hollow." When Ichabod Crane was teaching, he was the Emperor, and the classroom was his Empire. "In his hand he swayed a ferule, that sceptre of despotic power; the birch of justice reposed on three nails, behind the throne, a constant terror to evil doers." In his classroom he was so constantly plagued by the problems of discipline that he became physically strong but intellectually weak. When Crane left his classroom and ventured out into society, he was no longer an emperor. he assumed an "idle gentleman like personage," and became both gentle and ingratiating and vulnerable. He was not an Emperor when he arrived at the party at the Van Tassel estate on his broken-down plough horse ironically named Gunpowder. Outside of his classroom, Crane was variously compared to a grasshopper, a water-fowl, an anaconda, and a weather cock. His whole frame was described as a scarecrow eloping from a cornfield. His name was somehow very appropriate--Ichabod Crane.

1171. Habegger, Alfred. "Nineteenth-Century American Humor: Easygoing Males, Anxious Ladies, and Penelope Lapham." PMLA 91 (October 1976): 884-99.

Considers American humor of the nineteenth century to have been masculine. There were no women Southwestern humorists before the Civil War--no women literary comedians of the 1860s--no women

comedians in the silent movies. The jokes were male, and the places
where they were circulated were also male--saloons, smoking cars,
and barber shops. During American humor's classic period--the 1860s
to the 1880s--humor, like politics, had only male participants.
This was largely because of traditional roles expected of boys and
girls during this period. Typical boys' books included The Story of
a Bad Boy (1870), Tom Sawyer (1876), and Peck's Bad Boy and His Pa
(1883). The boys joked and the kind motherly women--Aunt Polly, or
Aunt Sally, or Mrs. Partington--were the victims of the jokes. It
was good to be a bad boy, because the bad boy was expressing an
enterprising spirit that would later bring success in business.
During this period there was no corresponding series of girls'
books. Little Women (1868) was written for girls, but in this book
the practical joker is a boy, Laurie, who victimizes a girl, Meg.
It is true that one of the girl characters, Jo, has a sense of
humor, but she's not a typical girl. She also whistles and uses
slang, cuts her hair, runs a race with Laurie, and goes by a boy's
name, Jo. Penelope Lapham in Howells' The Rise of Silas Lapham,
like Jo in Little Women, is the exception that proves the role.
"Penelope is a female humorist who marches to a different drum."
She is the first humorous heroine of an American novel. Penelope is
sane, shrewd, unfashionable, and plain. She is self-reliant with a
lot of horse sense and an odd and active sense of humor.

1172. Haliburton, Thomas Chandler, ed. Traits of American Humour, by
      Native Authors. 3 Volumes. London: Colburn, 1852, xxiii + 310
      pp; v + 313 pp; v + 332 pp.

      Traces the roots of New England, Western, and Midland humor to
Scotland, Ireland, and England, respectively. New England humor,
like that of Scotland, is sly, cold, quaint, practical, and
sarcastic. Western humor, like that of Ireland, is extravagant,
reckless, rollicking, and strong hearted. And Midland humor, like
that of England, is manly and hearty, embellished by fancy but not
exaggeration. Haliburton breaks down the humor stereotypes still
more. There are the Hoosiers of Indiana, the Suckers of Illinois,
the pukes of Missouri, the buck-eyes of Ohio, the red-horses of
Kentucky, the mud-heads of Tennessee, the wolverines of Michigan,
the eels of New England, and the corn-crackers of Virginia.

1173. Hollis, C. Carroll. "Rural Humor of the Late Nineteenth
      Century." The Comic Imagination in American Literature. Ed.
      Louis D. Rubin, Jr. New Brunswick, NJ: Rutgers Univ. Press,
      1983, 165-77.

      Presents evidence that humor was the form of cultural
communication of greatest popularity during the last quarter of the
nineteenth century. Hollis contends that during this period, more
people read or listened to humorists than read or listened to
"historical romancers, oral or printed sermons, sentimental tales,
western stories, drama, domestic novels, local color stories, or
Horatio Alger's dime novels." Hollis furthermore contends that it
is rural humor which is pervasive in American culture. For most of
the nineteenth century, America was basically an agricultural
nation. By the final decades of the nineteenth century, most of the
city dwellers had moved to the cities from farms or from small
towns. From the beginning, farmers' almanacs had dominated American
literature, and Will Rogers was only one link in a long progression

of down-home humor that tended to be folksy, anonymous, pervasive, and indigenous to its region. The fact that the writers of this tradition wrote for money rather than for fame does not detract from their contribution; it only means we must look at them as professionals. Their contribution was more journalistic than literary, and they did a great deal to enhance the literacy rate of a basically rural nation.

1174. Kesterson, David B. "The Literary Comedians and the Language of Humor." Studies in American Humor 1.1 (June, 1982): 44-51.

Considers Samuel Clemens, George Horatio Derby, Charles H. Smith, Henry Wheeler Shaw, Charles Farrar Browne, Edgar Wilson Nye, David Ross Locke, and Robert H. Newell to have broadened their audiences by appearing as "wise fools." On the comedy circuit, Mark Twain wore a white suit, smoked an unlit cigar, and shuffled back and forth across the stage. Artemus Ward was a portly "genial showman." Charles Farrar Browne's stage presence was dapper and deadpan. Bill Nye was a tall lanky figure with a shiny bald head and a blank expression. And Josh Billings had shaggy hair, a formal black suit with no necktie, and a pitcher of milk in front of him on the lecture table. The "wise fool" image is reinforced by their pen names. "Mark Twain" (Samuel Clemens), connotes river lore; "Petroleum Vesuvius Nasby" (David Ross Locke) implies an erupting volcano. "Orpheus C. Kerr" (Robert H. Newell) is a political pun (Office Seeker). To these we can add the crackerbarrel-philosopher names of Artemus Ward (Charles Farrar Browne), Bill Arp (Charles H. Smith), Josh Billings (Henry Wheeler Shaw, and Squibob (George Horatio Derby). These literary comedians used puns, understatements, anticlimax, antiproverbialism, homely and colorful imagery, intentional misspellings, and distorted syntax to appeal to the broader audience.

1175. Kesterson, David B. "Those Literary Comedians." Critical Essays on American Humor. Eds. William Bedford Clark and W. Craig Turner. Boston, MA: G. K. Hall, 1984, 167-184.

Indicates that the literary comedians characteristically struck a non-literary pose in order to camouflage their substantial literary backgrounds. This tradition was started by Mark Twain, and continued to other literary comedians such as Charles Farrar Browne, Henry Wheeler Shaw, George Horatio Derby, David Ross Locke, Robert H. Newell, Charles Henry Smith, James M. Bailey, Edgar Wilson Nye, and, finally, Finley Peter Dunne. These literary comedians hid behind personae who were far removed from learning--personae like Huckleberry Finn, Artemus Ward, Josh Billings, Squibob, Petroleum Vesuvius Nasby, Orpheus C. Kerr, Bill Arp, the Danbury News Man, Bill Nye, and Mr. Dooley, respectively.

1176. Landon, Melville D. Wit and Humor of the Age. Chicago: Star Publishing Co., 1883, 774 pp.

Contrasts humor and wit by saying that humorous writings are "true descriptions of scenes and incidents that actually occur," while witty writings are "fanciful descriptions of scenes and incidents that occur only in the minds of the authors." Bret Harte's "Luck of Roaring Camp" is pure humor, because it is absolutely true. Irony, satire, and ridicule are all species of

wit, because they are all untrue. To illustrate the distinction
between humor and wit, Mark Twain wrote a chapter on building
tunnels out in Nevada. His description was pure humor for four or
five pages, but then it blossomed into wit. The experts told the
miner that he had better stop his tunnel when he got through the
hill, but the miner said that it was his tunnel and he would take it
as far as he wanted to. So he continued his tunnel on over the
valley and into the next hill. He managed this by building a
trestlework to hold the hole up in the sky between the two
mountains. Landon says that readers don't laugh at pure humor.
They enjoy it. They say how faithfully the author has described a
particular scene. But they do not laugh. But when the wit comes
out, with the exaggerations and the fantasy added to the truth, then
the reader laughs outright. Landon feels that it is an easy matter
to separate the humorists from the wits. Nasby is a satirist, and
therefore a wit. Josh Billings, Mark Twain, Artemus Ward, Orpheus
Kerr, and John Phoenix are sometimes humorists and sometimes wits.
Max Adler and Bill Nye are both Baron-Munchausen liars, or wits.
Max Adler's exaggeration is wit.

1177. Lenz, William E. **Fast Talk and Flush Times: The Confidence Man
     as a Literary Convention**. Columbia: Univ. of Missouri Press,
     1985, 237 pp.

     Considers the confidence man to be a distinctly American
version of the archetypal trickster, arising from the historical
boom-or-bust conditions of the frontier West. Wherever in America
there are "flush times," there you will find the confidence man as
well. The American con-man represents disorder, transition, and
unrest. He shares with Odysseus, Satan, and Till Eulenspiegel the
ability to change his appearance. Like the stereotypical peddler,
the Yankee, and the rustic Jonathan, the confidence man is the
direct result of the ambiguities faced in the New World. He uses
shifty language partly in the interest of fun, but his cardinal
motive is always profit. The confidence man disdains the triviality
of mere jokes and pranks; he avoids eastern cities and criminal
partners; he shuns all of the tools of other criminals except for
his own sweet tongue. His pattern is to win the confidence of
everybody he meets and then to betray that confidence for his own
advantage.

1178. McKay, Douglas R. "The Puissant Procreator: Comic Ridicule of
     Brigham Young." WHIMSY 1 (1983): 128-29.

     Agrees with Henri Bergson's claim that "derisive humor is the
universal corrective for deviancy in the social order." McKay's
example is the conflict between Mormons and Gentiles over the
polygamy issue in the second half of the nineteenth century. Mark
Twain, Artemus Ward, and many other writers of the time joined in on
the taunting criticism of polygamy. Brigham Young was called
"Bigamy Young, King Brigham, The Tycoon of Utah, the Sultan of the
Wasatch, the Great Marrier, the Mormon Bull, the Incestuous Saint,
the Salt Lake Sodomite, and the Puissant Procreator." Artemus ward
said, "The pretty girls in Utah mostly marry Young," "Brigham's
religion is singular and his wives are plural," "Out in Utah they
practice Bigamy, Trigamy, and Brighamy." There was a common saying
of the day that read like a scriptural aphorism: "The first

principle of Mormonism is, that women are a good thing; and the second principle is, that you can't have too much of a good thing."

1179. Marschall, Richard, and Carol J. Wilson. "Selected Humorous Magazines (1820-1950)." Dictionary of Literary Biography: Volume 11: American Humorists, 1800-1950. Ed. Stanley Trachtenberg. Detroit, MI: Gale, 1982, 655-78.

Considers the earliest American literary humor magazines to have been Salmagundi, edited by Washington and William Irving and James Kirke Paulding. In 1876 Joseph Keppler founded Puck in New York, and it was successful for more than forty years. Puck's first important rivals were Wild Oats and The Judge. Writers for Judge included Heywood Broun, Donald Stewart, James Metcalfe, Benjamin deCasseres, Richard Le Gallienne, Gelett Burgess, Ellis Parker Butler, George Jean Nathan, and Walter Prichard Eaton. Life began publishing in 1883, and from the beginning it was interested in American humor; its readers were cultivated, involved in social causes, and familiar with society's fancies. The New Yorker was founded in 1925 and was soon changed from a humor magazine into a magazine of more general interest for a sophisticated metropolitan reader. Its writers have included such notables as Ring Lardner, George S. Kaufman, Alexander Woollcott, Franklin P. Adams, Fairfax Downey, Arthur H. Folwell, James Thurber, S. J. Perelman, Robert Benchley, Robert E. Sherwood, Frank Sullivan, Clarence Day, Ogden Nash, Nunnally Johnson, Phyllis McGinley, Margaret Fishback, and E. B. White. In 1931 Norman Anthony founded Ballyhoo, a nihilistic magazine of advertising spoofs, parodies, sight gags, puns, and irreverent satire. In the 1980s The American Bystander, and Vanity Fair appeared, showing a renewed interest in humorous American literary magazines.

1180. Masson, Thomas L. Our American Humorists. Freeport, New York: Books for Libraries Press, 1966, xx + 448 pp.

States that no country other than America has "an actual race of professional humorists." Masson then criticizes his own term "professional," because it suggests planning and premeditation. Masson suggests that humor must appear spontaneous, even though it must in fact be carefully planned. For twenty-eight years, Mason was literary and managing editor of Life, and in that capacity "all of the humorists of the day, incipient or otherwise, passed before me in review." This is the basis for Masson's decision to publish works by Ade, Adams, Bangs, Benchley, Burgess, Butler, Cobb, Croy, Dunne, Folwell, Ford, Gillilan, Glass, Herford, Hubbard, Irwin, Johnson, Lardner, Leacock, Lewis, McCardell, Marquis, Morley, Parker, Shute, Streeter, Townsend, Waldron, Wilson, and Wells. Masson also has chapters on "The Columnists," "The Younger Set," "The Comic Poets," "Our Comic Artists," and "Our American Humorists Since the War."

1181. Mintz, Lawrence E. "American Humor and the Spirit of the Times." It's a Funny Thing, Humour. New York: Pergamon, 1977, 17-21.

Considers democracy to have been the thrust of pre-twentieth-century American humor, with the central figure being the "wise fool." Although the "wise fool" has earlier origins, occurring in

Old Testament, medieval, Shakespearean, and many tribal texts, his
development in nineteenth century American humor is especially
revealing. "He is the vehicle by which the norms, values, opinions
and attitudes toward democracy, progress, and social goals can be
expressed; an archetypal hero articulating the core of America's
self-definition." The name of the "wise fool" in the nineteenth
century was "Jonathan," and his tradition has carried into the
twentieth century as the "solid citizen." But the twentieth century
"solid citizen" is a little more pompous, cliched, and naive than
his nineteenth-century counterpart. He may even be something of a
trickster and is sometimes the butt rather than the vehicle of the
humor. Furthermore, much absurdist or black humor of the twentieth
century is not democratic humor. In fact, it can become "anti-
democratic, anti-optimistic, anti-progressive humour." Samuel
Beckett describes this as "the bitter laugh," "the laugh laughing at
the laugh," "the risus purus," and Mintz mentions some of the
writings of Bartholeme, Pynchon, Donleavy, and Friedman as
illustrating "the risus purus."

1182. Nilsen, Don L. F. "The Earliest Nineteenth-Century Humorists:
Brackenridge, Trumbull, Dwight, Tyler, Weems, and Tenney."
Montana English Journal 13.2 (Spring 1990): 34-42.

Admits that Brackenridge, Trumbull, Dwight, Tyler, Weems, and
Tenney are minor nineteenth-century humorous authors but suggests
that they are nevertheless very important because they illustrate
the transition from the relatively unproductive pre-nineteenth
century to the productive nineteenth and twentieth centuries. Hugh
Brackenridge's Modern Chivalry anticipated frontier humor and local
tales. John Trumbull, the unofficial leader of the Connecticut Wits
developed the genre of the mock epic in The Anarchiad. Timothy
Dwight, another Connecticut Wit, wrote heroic couplets that
specialized in light thrusting caricatures. Royall Tyler's Jonathan
Ploughboy in The Contrast was the first well-developed "Yankee"
character in American literature. Tabitha Gilman Tenney's Female
Quixotism is a parody of Cervantes' Don Quixote. It is, in fact,
the story of Don Quixote told from a woman's perspective.

1183. Nilsen, Don L. F. "Mike Fink, James Kirk Paulding, and David
Crockett: the Legends vs. the Men." The Journal of the
Mississippi Council of Teachers of English 12.1 (1990): 21-32.

Investigates the role that historical facts play in the making
of nineteenth-century legendary heroes. Mike Fink had Scotch-Irish
ancestry and participated in the fight against the Indians and
against the British during Revolutionary War times. He explored the
Mississippi River and its tributaries, where he was a boatman, and
the wilderness frontier, where he was a hunter and a trapper. David
Crockett the man and Davy Crockett the legend were so intertwined
that when people came to a train station to meet Davy Crockett and
found a respectable, tidy man, dressed decently and with his hair
neatly combed, they were confused and disappointed. Crockett's
motto of "Be always sure you are right. Then go ahead" is the stuff
legends are made of. Although James Kirke Paulding claimed that his
character Nimrod Wildfire was not based on the legend of Davy
Crockett, everybody knew that, in fact, he was. In The Lion of the
West, Colonel Nimrod Wildfire was a Kentucky frontiersman who called
himself "half horse and half alligator." The Lion of the West was

transformed into a play, and when this play opened in Washington,
Davy Crockett was sitting in the front row. James Hackett, the
actor who played Nimrod Wildfire, came onto the stage and bowed
ostentatiously to Crockett. Crocket arose from his seat, returned
the bow, and the play commenced.

1184. Porte, Joel. "Transcendental Antics." Harvard English Studies
      3 (1972): 167-83.

      Quotes Emerson as having said, "Transcendentalism is the
Saturnalia or excess of Faith." Porte also shares Constance
Rourke's opinion that many cults that resulted from
transcendentalism had humorous names--Shakers, Groaners, Come
Outers, New Lights, Hard Shell Baptists, and Muggletonians. Rourke
goes on to say that sometimes these names were provided by the
movement, sometimes from outsiders. "Frequently it was hard to tell
when burlesque was involved, when fakery, when a serious intention."
The basic movement was romantic, but it often crested into an
uninhibited gaiety that went well beyond the romantic. It was a
comic extravagance in American-- revivalism. Porte sees the
transcendental movement as an American Renaissance and Reformation
of the spirit, in which the silly and solemn merge into a sensible
congruence. Henry James called it "a kind of Puritan carnival
[that] produced no fruit." Porte feels that the comedy of the
movement arises from "the tensions of a deeply serious human
debate."

1185. Tandy, Jennette. Crackerbox Philosophers in American Humor and
      Satire. New York: Columbia Univ. Press, 1925. xi + 181 pp.;
      reprinted in Critical Essays on American Humor. Eds. William
      Bedford Clark and W. Craig Turner. Boston, MA: G. K. Hall,
      1984, 50-51

      Discusses the succession of comic stereotype caricatures from
1830 to 1867. Although all of these personages could be classed as
"unlettered philosophers," there were a great many subtypes, such as
the boor, the clown, the peasant, the small bourgeois, the homely
American, the Yankee, the Southerner, the Jewish clothing merchant.
These stereotypes provided local color and picaresque adventure.
They contributed wise saws, rustic anecdotes, and deliberately cruel
innuendo.

1186. Turner, Arlin. "Comedy and Reality in Local Color Fiction,
      1865-1900." The Comic Imagination in American Literature. Ed.
      Louis D. Rubin, Jr. New Brunswick, NJ: Rutgers Univ. Press,
      1983, 157-164.

      Alludes to the introduction of Joel Chandler Harris' anthology
entitled, The World's Wit and Humor (1904), where Harris claims that
every day in the history of America has been either trimmed with
humor or charged with humor. Turner especially discusses the humor
of Nathaniel Hawthorne, William Gilmore Simms, and Edgar Allan Poe.
Turner indicates that the 1840s and 1850s were especially rich
periods, since these two decades saw the development of the earthy,
extravagant humor of Henry Clay Lewis' Louisiana Swamp Doctor,
Johnson Jones Hooper's Simon Suggs, and George Washington Harris'
Sut Lovingood. Turner feels that American antebellum humor is

sophisticated and cites as evidence the local color of A. B. Longstreet's humor about rural Georgia and Seba Smith's Down-East humor about Maine. Turner says that American humor is not merely the humor of waggery and wit. It displayed a rich variety of forms as it dealt with the picturesque incongruities in the New World--the Puritans, the Indians, the cavaliers, the Dutch, and the Blacks and other immigrants. The humor dealt with makeshift inventions that were necessary on the frontier and the vastness and richness of the newly claimed land, the leveling effects of democracy, freedom, and independence. Much of American local-color fiction laughs at rather than with the distinctive characters of the American frontier, and therefore most readers of this fiction are more pleased with the accounts of their ancestors than with the accounts of themselves.

1187. Weber, Brom. "The Misspellers." The Comic Imagination in American Literature. Ed. Louis D. Rubin, Jr. New Brunswick, NJ: Rutgers Univ. Press, 1983, 127-37.

Contends that Charles Farrar Browne (a mid-nineteenth-century humorist who used the pen name of "Artemus Ward") was "the first American writer to earn a truly national reputation during his lifetime." Weber also suggests that Browne was the first humorous writer to popularize misspellings, bad grammar, and dialect as effective literary devices. Weber indicates that Emerson, Whitman, Longfellow, Holmes, Melville, Lowell, Whittier, and Hawthorne were all contemporaries of Ward. "Nevertheless, it was Ward, rather than any of these men, who was read enthusiastically from the Atlantic to the Pacific, who attracted large audiences in a Western village or an Eastern city when he appeared on the lecture platform..., who wrote so perceptively and freshly about national life that he became an acknowledged favorite of war-time President Abraham Lincoln." Weber suggests that Ward and the other Civil War misspellers were "uniquely individual writers." Although they have frequently been grouped together by critics as "The Misspellers," in reality, each of them treated spelling, grammar, dialect and other "linguistic shenanigans" in a way that was different from all of the others.

Twentieth Century

1188. Cerf, Bennett, ed. An Encyclopedia of Modern American Humor. Garden City, New York: Doubleday, 1954, xvi + 688 pp.

Feels that since 1941 a brand-new bunch of first-rate humorists have appeared on the horizon including Thomas Heggen, Max Shulman, Russell Lynes, Cleveland Amory, H. Allen Smith, John Crosby, Art Buchwald, Mac Hyman and others. Cerf's book is confined to modern or contemporary humor and is organized geographically with sections on writers from New England, New York, the South, the Midwest, the Southwest, and the Far West. There are also two genre sections--parodies and humorous poetry. Cerf indicates that the long tradition of good humorous materials coming out of the Deep South is still continuing; however, he was astonished to discover how much of our contemporary humor centers around New York City. Cerf's inclusion of a section on light verse is based on the impression he has that this is a humor genre in which American authors truly excel. He observes that twentieth-century American

prose is also of high quality and cites as an example the writings
of James Thurber, E. B. White, Frank Sullivan, S. J. Perelman,
Clarence Day, Wolcott Gibbs, and Robert Benchley, whose major
contributions all came in a single twenty-year period.

1189. Clark, John R., and Anna Lydia Motto. "Running Down and
       Dropping Out: Entropy in Modern Literature." Studies in
       Contemporary Satire 10 (1983): 9-22.

Proposes that the second law of thermodynamics, which states
that the universal dissipation of energy is constant and
irreversible, is as true in literature as it is in physics. This is
consistent with T. S. Eliot's suggestion that the world will end
"with ridiculous and lumpish inertness--not with a 'bang' but with
a 'whimper.'" Clark and Motto point out that the dada movement, and
other contemporary artistic movements that stress randomness and
chaos are further evidence of this proposal.   Tony Tanner has noted
that the word "entropy" occurs with great frequency in critiques of
American literature, especially in conjunction with the works of
Norman Mailer, Saul Bellow, John Updike, John Barth, Walker Percy,
Stanley Elkin, Donald Barthelme, and Thomas Pynchon. Tanner feels
that this frequent repetition of "entropy" by contemporary critics
in reference to works by contemporary authors may be an indication
of where we are in the history of ideas. However, Clark and Motto
suggest that the advancement of entropy is not only a sign that
satire is alive and well, but that we have now enriched our satire
by adding a new ingredient--entropy. This allows our authors to be
critical of society in a new and creative manner.

1190. Cohen, Sarah Blacher, ed. Comic Relief: Humor in Contemporary
       American Literature. Urbana: Univ. of Illinois Press, 1978, x
       + 339 pp.

Provides evidence that the periods of American history that
have produced the most humor are also the most tragic periods. One
of these periods extends from the Civil War until 1900, a time when
Jacksonian democracy was developing in the United States. Another
period was during the 1930s during the Great Depression. Cohen also
notes that during these periods most people are too demoralized and
too involved in mere survival to originate much humor.   Comic
artists always seem to emerge who speak for the masses, many of them
with deadpan deliveries, grammatical infelicities, and caustic
vernacular wit designed to expose skullduggery.   There are many
problems in the twentieth century--race riots, civil rights
violence, rampant crime, disaffection, increased automation, not
enough education for the good jobs, and not enough jobs for the
undereducated. We need the Lenny Bruces and the Mort Sahls to deal
with the McCarthys of the world and to gleefully mention the
unmentionables like drug abuse, sexual perversion, bigotry, and
gratuitous violence. Such humorists joked about H-bomb fallout,
neo-Nazism, increased Russian-American tensions, Vatican corruption,
and political self-interest. Lenny Bruce's creed seemed to be that
everything is rotten, including mother, God, and the flag. And he
used rotten language in order to reinforce this message. Donald
Barthelme and Stanley Elkin need to expose the dreck in our lives.
Edward Albee, Arthur Kopit, John Guare, Rochelle Owens, Sam Shepard,

Megan Terry, and Ed Bullins need to expose the many excesses of "camp," and they do it with a form of verbal flagellation.

1191. Coyle, William. "From Scatology to Social History: Captain Billy's Whizbang." Studies in American Humor 3.3 (January 1977): 135-41.

Suggests that much of the present-day audience of The Music Man will not understand Harold Hill's question, "Is your son memorizing jokes out of Captain Billy's Whizbang?" This was an extremely popular humor magazine of the 1920s and early 1930s, published and edited by Captain Wilford H. Fawcett after he was honorably discharged from the army. The title "Whiz Bang" was an allusion to a World War I artillery shell. Early issues carried the statement, "This magazine is edited by a Spanish-American and World War I veteran and is dedicated to the Fighting Forces of the United States and Canada." The magazine contained cartoons (e.g., by John Held, Jr.), jokes, journalistic bloopers (e.g., by Mencken), parody questions and answers, and poetry like "Casey at the Bat" and "The Shooting of Dan McGrew." Much of the humor is based on situations and character types that would not be recognized by a modern audience. Elitist critics felt that the editor was using low art to drive out high art. The magazine was so successful that its profits were used to subsidize True Confessions and Peanuts. Ironically, in the end the magazine supported both low art and high art, for Captain Billy's Whizbang also became the base for Fawcett Publications, one of the most successful and prestigious paperback houses--publisher of such distinguished authors as John Updike, Joyce Carol Oates, and Isaac Bashevis Singer.

1192. Godshalk, W. L. "Cabell and Barth: Our Comic Athletes." The Comic Imagination in American Literature. Ed. Louis D. Rubin, Jr. New Brunswick, NJ: Rutgers Univ. Press, 1983, 275-83.

Describes Cabell's writing as "resolute frivolity," and Barth's writing as "cheerful nihilism," but what these two writers have in common is their comic athleticism. Godshalk contends that after all of the facets of an art form have been exhausted the writer must do one of two things. He must turn to another art form, or he must turn the art form he is developing on itself and play with it as a new kind of game with entirely new rules. Both Cabell and Barth had this ability. One of Cabell's characters says, "I can play with words rather nicely." Barth played with the conventions of the eighteenth-century novel in the same way that Cabell had played with the pseudo-medieval romance. Both authors weave the fictional into the real and present something to the reader that they pretend is "reality." Both authors mock man's conception of his own importance in the universe. Both mock man's myths and his "history." But there is a basic difference between the two. While both of them use irony in an attempt to explode the myths, Cabell sees the possibility that myths have some validity and some value. Barth, on the other hand, cannot see the possibility of positive effects resulting from the acceptance of illusions.

1193. Harris, Charles B. <u>Contemporary American Novelists of the Absurd</u>. New Haven, CT: College and Univ. Press, 1971, 159 pp.

Considers the dominant themes of contemporary American literature to be the absurdity, the chaos, and the meaninglessness of the universe. Contemporary authors do not adopt an anti-style. Rather they use the techniques and devices of the conventional novelists but without the same beliefs and goals. The result is a burlesque, a parody, an ironic and farcical inversion of the conventional novel. Contemporary novelists present the conventional novel as obsolete by mocking it, and so they use the traditional rhetorical devices in vitally new ways. The absurd vision of the contemporary novel invades not only the themes but also the incidents, the characterizations, and the language. They fuse form and content to form a new kind of ironic metaphor. Harris considers Joseph Heller, Kurt Vonnegut, Jr., Thomas Pynchon, and John Barth to be the most significant contemporary American authors of the absurd novel. Although the four authors vary widely in date of birth (1922, 1923, 1930, 1937), all of their important novels were published during the 1960s. Heller, Pynchon and Barth have received an inordinate amount of critical attention; their writings are responsible for more than fifty major critical articles in professional journals, not to mention chapters in books, and hundreds of review articles written about them. Although Vonnegut has not received the same amount of critical attention as the other authors mentioned here, he has by far the largest audience.

1194. Hassan, Ihab. "Echoes of Dark Laughter: The Comic Sense in Contemporary American Fiction." <u>Humor in America</u>. Ed. Enid Veron. New York: Harcourt, Brace, Jovanovich, 1976, 316-21.

Presents the 1950s as the period when black humor first came into vogue. The movie <u>Dr. Strangelove</u> was subtitled, <u>How I Learned to Stop Worrying and Love the Bomb</u>. There were also many off-Broadway plays and experimental novels that appeared during this time that can be characterized as "dancing under the gallows." A list of the best novels of the period from 1949 to 1962 would have to include John Hawkes' <u>The Cannibal</u> (1949), Carson McCullers' <u>The Ballad of the Sad Cafe</u> (1951), J. D. Salinger's <u>The Catcher in the Rye</u> (1951), Ralph Ellison's <u>Invisible Man</u> (1952), Flannery O'Connor's <u>Wise Blood</u> (1952), Vladimir Nabokov's <u>Lolita</u> (1955), J. P. Donleavy's <u>The Ginger Man</u> (1955), John Cheever's <u>The Wapshot Chronicle</u> (1957), John Barth's <u>The End of the Road</u> (1958), Saul Bellow's <u>Henderson the Rain King</u> (1959), James Purdy's <u>Malcolm</u> (1959), William Burroughs' <u>Naked Lunch</u> (1959), John Updike's <u>Rabbit Run</u> (1960), Joseph Heller's <u>Catch-22</u> (1961), and Thomas Berger's <u>Reinhart in Love</u> (1962). These novels not only express a deep sadness, madness, and mortality but are also comic or ironic in tone. They are both intelligent and celebrant and show a kind of inward heroism not in excelling, but in surviving. They recognize human limitations not in terms of broken pride nor in terms of saintly humility but rather in terms of ironic acceptance. These postwar novelists cultivate the picaresque and fantastic modes. They avoid neat formulations. They are tolerant of loose ends and broken links and surprises and reversals. They realize that the truth is overwhelming, and they do not pretend to subdue it with a flourish and a symbol.

1195. Hassler, Donald M. Comic Tones in Science Fiction: The Art of Compromise with Nature. Westport, CT: Greenwood, 1982, xiv + 145 pp.

Posits that humor in twentieth-century science fiction is frequently understated. One type of humor in this genre comes from chance encounters or various types of serendipity. There is a constant awareness of the indeterminacy of science and even of the possibility of an alternate universe. Science fiction humor is pioneering humor, but at the same time that the space explorers are making new and exciting discoveries (the wanderlust), there is a constant nostalgia, and yearning to regain what has been lost (the Earthlust). This tension is responsible for most of the humor and irony in contemporary science fiction.

1196. Hauck, Richard Boyd. A Cheerful Nihilism: Confidence and 'The Absurd' in American Humorous Fiction. Bloomington: Indiana Univ. Press, xiv + 269 pp.

Feels that the con-man protagonists of Herman Melville, Mark Twain, William Faulkner, and John Barth have a kind of cheerful nihilism. The world is absurd, and so their reaction to it is also absurd--but it is at the same time cheerful. Hauck feels that the roots of contemporary absurd fiction in America can be traced back to Benjamin Franklin, then to the frontier humorists, who developed a kind of dark realistic humor. Mark Twain achieved a perfect balance between nihilism and laughter-eliciting humor. Herman Melville developed the relationship between the absurd world and the confidence man accurately. William Faulkner was a moralist and a humorist who progressed because of a kind of fluid relativism. John Barth displays the interplay between the absurd and the confidence man most consistently as it is the subject of his books and the source of his comic technique. There are various possible reactions to absurdity. Camus dealt with it seriously. Twain dealt with it humorously. Hauck feels that the concept of "America" is sort of an absurd concept, and he furthermore feels that laughter is a typical American response to virtually any stimulus. But the humor that results from the marriage of humor and nihilism is a grim sort of humor.

1197. Henkle, Roger B. "The Social Dynamics of Comedy." Sewanee Review 90 (Spring 1982): 200-16.

Believes that twentieth-century comedy is generally more radical than that of earlier centuries. Henkle notes that some critics believe that humor is basically conservative and reformative while other critics believe that humor is basically irrational and anarchic. He further notes that the liberal critics believe that humor is conservative (critics like Henri Bergson, George Meredith, and Northrop Frye), while the conservative critics believe that humor is irrational and chaotic (critics like Suzanne Langer, George Santayana, and (with certain qualifications) Sigmund Freud).

1198. Hill, Hamlin. "The Future of American Humor: Through a Glass
      Eye, Darkly." Critical Essays on American Humor. Eds. William
      Bedford Clark and W. Craig Turner. Boston, MA: G. K. Hall,
      1984, 219-225.

      Suggests that since 1980 the study of American humor has
reached full maturity. Hill notes that although there are still
some scholars who are skeptical about the academic respectability of
humor scholarship, such scholars are finding themselves in a smaller
and smaller minority.   Important presses publish books on the
subject without hesitation.   There are numerous conferences,
workshops, and seminars on the subject.   Studies of Mark Twain's
humor are especially prevalent, but there are increasing numbers of
studies relating to eighteenth-, nineteenth-, and twentieth-century
humorists. Hill feels that comic poetry is the only field lagging
behind, and there is even important research in this field--such as
Ronald Wallace's book.

1199. Inge, M. Thomas. "American Literary Humor: A Bibliographic
      Guide." Choice, June 1989: 1641-49.

      Provides an excellent annotated listing of secondary sources
in American literary humor. Inge laments the fact that in the past
critics have felt that humor was somehow less important than tragedy
for serious philosophical discussions. Inge regrets that humor is so
hard to define and that, until recently, critical studies relating
to humorous literature have been very sparce. He feels, however,
that in recent decades this imbalance is being redressed.   Inge's
categories include REFERENCE WORKS, such as Trachtenberg's American
Humorists, and Gale's The Encyclopedia of American Humorists;
JOURNALS such as Studies in American Humor, and HUMOR: International
Journal of Humor Research; CRITICAL ANTHOLOGIES, such as Weber's An
Anthology of American Humor, and Veron's Humor in America: An
Anthology; and CRITICAL WORKS, such as Rourke's American Humor: A
Study of the National Character, and Bier's The Rise and Fall of
American Humor.

1200. Middleton, David. "Humorous American Literature and the Film:
      A Bibliography." Studies in American Humor NS4.3 (Fall 1985):
      183-91.

      Contains a summary of the reviews of films of important
American novels. The novels that are treated include Edward Albee's
Who's Afraid of Virginia Woolf?, John Barth's The End of the Road,
L. Frank Baum's The Wizard of Oz, Nathaniel Benchley's The Off
Islanders, The Russians are Coming, and Sail a Crooked Ship, Thomas
Berger's Little Big Man, Paddy Chayefsky's TV Plays, Samuel Clemens'
Adventures of Huckleberry Finn, Man with a Million, The Prince and
the Pauper, and Adventures of Tom Sawyer, William Faulkner's
Intruder in the Dust and Pylon (The Tarnished Angels), Jules
Feiffer's Little Murders, Joseph Heller's Catch-22, Chester Himes'
Cotton Comes to Harlem, Robert Hooker's M*A*S*H, John Irving's The
World According to Garp, Ken Kesey's One Flew Over the Cuckoo's
Nest, Flannery O'Connor's Wise Blood, Philip Roth's Goodbye,
Columbus, Neil Simon's Barefoot in the Park and Prisoner of Second
Avenue, Terry Southern's Candy, Kurt Vonnegut's Slaughterhouse Five,
and Charles Webb's The Graduate.

1201. Pinsker, Sanford. "On or About December 1910: When Human
      Character--and American Humor--Changed." Critical Essays on
      American Humor. Eds. William Bedford Clark and W. Craig
      Turner. Boston, MA: G. K. Hall, 1984, 184-199.

      Holds that 1910 was a transitional year in American humor.
Virginia Woolf wrote "On or about December 1910, Mr. Bennett and
Mrs. Brown, human character changed." Woolf was referring to the
death of Edward VII on May 6, 1910 and to the post-Impressionist
exhibition of Cezanne, Van Gogh, Picasso, and Matisse in London on
November 5, 1910, and to other events that marked the chasm between
the traditional past and the shaken present. 1910 was also the year
in which Mark Twain died. Twain had exploited the full potential of
nineteenth-century writing and made it very clear that nineteenth-
century literary aesthetics could no longer suffice. James Thurber
and the other writers for the New Yorker established the groundwork
for a more sophisticated and urbane humor tradition in America. On
or about December of 1910, Thurber, The New Yorker, and America
crossed into modernism and closed the gap between High Culture and
Low.

1202. Safer, Elaine B. The Contemporary American Comic Epic: The
      Novels of Barth, Pynchon, Gaddis, and Kesey. Detroit: Wayne
      State Univ. Press, 1988, 216 pp.

      Demonstrates the similarities and differences between the
contemporary comic novels of Barth, Pynchon, Gaddis, and Kesey and
the traditional epic novel. Both use such devices as epithets,
similes, catalogues, and multiple cross references. They both
incorporate the same themes, myths, and structural patterns. One
basic difference between these two traditions of the epic novel,
however, is that the traditional epic celebrates national or
religious values, while the contemporary epic tends to ridicule such
values. Another difference is that the protagonist of the new epic
is involved in an ironic quest instead of a holy mission. A final
difference can be found in the serious and logical tone of the
earlier epic writing as contrasted with the humorous and absurd tone
of the later epic writing. Glimpses of the earlier epic vision can
often be seen in the later epic novels but when this happens the
effect is more parody than imitation.

1203. Schwartz, Richard Alan. "The Fantastic in Contemporary
      Fiction." The Scope of the Fantastic. Eds. Robert A. Collins
      and Howard D. Pearce. Westport, CT: Greenwood Press, 1985, 27-
      32.

      Discusses the fantastic element in twentiety-century American
novels by such authors as Joseph Heller, Thomas Pynchon, William
Faulkner, John Barth, Donald Barthelme, and Robert Coover. Donald
Barthelme, for example, has his character struggle up a glass
mountain in New York, using plumbers' friends as hand grips. He was
seeking "a symbol" and was disappointed when he merely found an
enchanted princess at the top of the mountain. Robert Coover
presented the execution of Julius and Ethel Rosenberg as public
entertainment in the middle of New York's Times Square.

1204. Wallace, Ronald. The Last Laugh: Form and Affirmation in the
      Contemporary American Comic Novel. Columbia: Univ. of Missouri
      Press, 1979, viii + 159 pp.

      Discusses the humor of John Barth's The Floating Opera, John
Hawkes's Second Skin, Vladimir Nabokov's Lolita, Ken Kesey's One
Flew Over the Cuckoo's Nest, and Robert Coover's The Universal
Baseball Association, Inc. J. Henry Waugh, Prop. The lead article
for Wallace's anthology is entitled, "Never Mind that the Nag's a
Pile of Bones: The Contemporary American Comic Novel and the Comic
Tradition." Wallace contends that during the twentieth century we
tend to define ourselves in terms of war, violence, sickness,
despair, loss, guilt, and social and political fragmentation. Humor
in twentieth-century novels tends to create a hollow, cynical kind
of laughter. Comedy has become the most typical form of the
contemporary American novel--a kind of dark comedy that is a blend
of violence and chaos. Barth, Hawkes, Nabokov, Kesey, and Coover
use laughter as a weapon against the grotesque, the trivial, and the
preposterous. It allows them to conquer defeat and despair. The
contemporary humorous novel lacks the didacticism of earlier
periods, but it is firm in its belief that a comic perspective is a
viable perspective.

1205. Wilde, Alan. Horizons of Assent: Modernism, Postmodernism, and
      the Ironic Imagination. Philadelphia: Univ. of Pennsylvania
      Press, 1986, xvi + 209 pp.

      Uses "irony" as a heuristic tool to examine twentieth-century
literature. It is an effective tool not only because irony is a
necessary aspect of satire, but also because in the past hundred
years or more it has developed an autonomy of its own and has
provided a special way of apprehending a world that seems to lack
unity and cohesion. Twentieth-century American fiction is marked by
its "fabulation." It has been classified as "post-contemporary,"
"post-realistic," and "surfiction" by various critics, but in all
critical analyses, the concept of irony seems to be preeminent.
Wilde feels, in fact, that to many critics the term "ironic" is
almost synonymous with "contemporary" in terms of fiction.

1206. Wodehouse, P. G., and Scott Meredith, eds. A Carnival of
      Modern Humor. New York: Delacorte, 1967, 240 pp.

      Feels that in the 1920s American humor led the world in both
quantity and quality. The 20s may have been gray times, but the
humor was ubiquitous. Wodehouse and Meredith point to the excellent
quality of the humor of George Ade, Robert Benchley, Will Cuppy,
Clarence Day, Will Rogers, Frank Sullivan, Oliver Herford, Ring
Lardner, Don Marquis, F. P. Adams, Irvin Cobb, Harry Leon Wilson,
Thorne Smith, and many more. And they conclude with the enigmatic
statement that "audiences want comedy, but dramatists won't let them
have it." That's something to think about.

1207. Wodehouse, P. G., and Scott Meredith, eds. The Week-End Book
      of Humor. New York: Washburn, 1952, 251 pp.

      Points to the decline in American humor between 1904 and 1952.
In 1904 (when Wodehouse first came to America), everyone was
lighthearted and funny. The twenty or so major American papers all

with morning and evening editions each had a team of humorists daily turning out prose and poetry. The Saturday Evening Post had two funny short stories and a comic article in every issue. More publishers were publishing humorous books. Wodehouse considers this to have been the golden age of humor and feels that that age needs to be brought back. The problem as Wodehouse and Meredith see it is that humor implies criticism. The humorist has to see the world out of focus, and this disturbs those people who want to see the world straight. People look askance at the authors of light writing. Wodehouse and Meredith contend, tongue in cheek, that in some localities it is legal to hunt these writers with dogs, and that even in more humane societies they are scorned and sneered. Americans need to relax a little, so that they can increase their tolerance and enjoyment of humor.

1208. Yates, Norris W. The American Humorist: Conscience of the Twentieth Century. Ames, Iowa: Iowa State Univ. Press, 1964, 409 pp.

Considers this book to be the first full-length study of humorous twentieth-century American authors. There are chapters entitled, "Genteel Humor and Some History," "Crackerbarrel Survivals," "'Sophisticated' Skeptics," and "Creators of the Little Man." Authors who are highlighted include John Kendrick Bangs, George Ade, Finley Peter Dunne, Kin Hubbard, Will Rogers, Irvin S. Cobb, H. L. Mencken, Ring Lardner, Don Marquis, Clarence Day, Jr., Robert Benchley, Dorothy Parker, James Thurber, E. B. White, Will Cuppy, and S. J. Perelman. Yates presents humor, satire, and critical discussion designed to show what early twentieth-century humorists believed about "man, society, and the cosmos." It is also designed to determine the norms and standards of American humor and satire between 1900 and 1950.

Chapter 10
Oral Literature

1209. Blair, Walter. Horse Sense in American Humor From Benjamin
Franklin to Ogden Nash. New York: Russell and Russell, 1942,
xi + 341 pp.

Defines "horse sense" as "common sense, homespun philosophy,
pawkiness, cracker-box philosophy, gumption, or mother-wit." "Horse
sense" is generally considered to be the kind of practical knowledge
that is better developed among the uneducated classes than it is
among the educated classes. This book traces the history of oral or
colloquial American humor from its beginnings (Benjamin Franklin) to
the present time (Ogden Nash). It deals with a racy and home-grown
laughter, and "our almost religious faith in mother-wit." The book
shows how "horse sense" in some ways remained the same over this
period of time, and how in other ways the "horse sense" changed from
period to period. The book also shows the fine artistry of
colloquial humor which "some pedantic scholars have sniffed at" and
establishes this humor as part of America's body of important
literature.

1210. Brown, Carolyn S. The Tall Tale in American Folklore and
Literature. Knoxville: Univ. of Tennessee Press, 1987, ix +
170 pp.

Treats the tall tale as "a specific mode of performance which
can be adapted and translated into literature." Brown explains the
parameters of the tall tale as an oral genre, explains its raisons
d'etre, its modes of performance, its sources, its uses and its
functions, and tells how it is incorporated into larger non-oral
literary genres. She considers the tall tale a literary genre
rather than a tale type. The book discusses the intertwining of
oral and printed tales, the distinction between sketches, anecdotes,
hoaxes, and frame tales, and the nature of the "colloquial style."
There are special treatments of Sut Lovingood, Mark Twain, and
Garrison Keillor. Concerning Keillor, for example she says that
although Lake Wobegon may be narrow, rigid, backward, and stifling,
it nevertheless contains a richness of heritage that is just as
valuable as that found in more progressive parts of the world.
Brown characterizes Keillor's writing as "a profusion of detail and
a haze of nostalgia [that] make its dullness picturesque."

1211. Caron, James E. "The Violence and Language of Swapping
       Lies: Towards a Definition of the American Tall Tale." Studies
       in American Humor 5.1 (Spring 1986): 27-35.

       Considers Creath S. Thorne's definition of the tall tale in
"The Crockett Almanac: What Makes the Tall Tale?" to be too
restrictive. Thorne says that through the tall tale, fantastic
elements are used with two objects in mind--1) to dupe the greenhorn
(thus producing a horse laugh), and 2) to show admiration for the
heroic frontier spirit (thus producing a comic grin). In
contrasting the tall tale with other genres that employ fantasy,
such as the folk tale, the legend, and the myth, Thorne classifies
the tall tale as a sub-species of myth. Caron would place it as a
sub-species of hoax, a genre which only in the case of the tall tale
employs the fantastic. Caron quotes Neil Schmitz to say that "the
tall tale is never innocent." Caron relates the tall tale to two
other important oral traditions of the nineteenth century--the
practical joker and the con man--and adds that "swapping lies, like
swapping horses, represents the commerce between people along the
frontier." The language and violence of the tall tale, like that of
its neighbor genres, acknowledges the brutality and harsh effect of
the wilderness and uses comic relief to help mitigate that effect.

1212. Cox, James M. "Toward Vernacular Humor." Virginia
       Quarterly Review 46 (Spring 1970): 311-30; reprinted in
       Critical Essays on American Humor. Eds. William Bedford Clark
       and W. Craig Turner. Boston: G. K. Hall, 1984, 105-20.

       Feels that in general critics think that humor must be serious
to be good, and by forcing humor to be serious, critics are allowed
to make a moral judgment rather than an aesthetic judgment. Because
of this, and because comic forms are generally regarded as less
important than tragic (or at least serious forms), critics feel
obliged to tease serious themes out of humorous pieces. They look,
for example, very hard to find satirical or black elements, because
satire has built-in moral judgments and dark humor has a serious
rather than a light-hearted tone. Often critics use the expression
"just humorous" in a rather patronizing tone, making their own moral
judgments if the writing fails to do so. Cox disagrees with those
critics who feel that humor is a form of digression. When children
develop a genuine sense of humor, they are not functioning as
children but are in fact becoming adults--losing their childhood.
Cox concludes, "There is no sense of humor in childhood."

1213. Crowell, Doug. "Why Is Andy Kaufman Funny?" Thalia: Studies in
       Literary Humor 7.1 (Spring/Summer 1984): 35-44.

       Compares the disconcerting humor of Andy Kaufman with that of
Samuel Beckett, James Joyce, Donald Barthelme, William Gass, and,
especially, Gertrude Stein. Like many of our contemporary authors,
Kaufman was not afraid to take risks.

1214. Hill, Hamlin. "Modern American Humor: The Janus Laugh."
       College English 25 (December 1963): 170-76. Reprinted in
       Critical Essays on American Humor. Eds. William Bedford Clark
       and W. Craig Turner. Boston: G. K. Hall, 1984, 91-99.

       Disagrees with those humor critics who believe that twentieth-
century American authors have lost the full-blooded, masculine,
vigorous style that prevailed among nineteenth-century authors.
Hill feels that the influence of The New Yorker from the 1920s on
has made our humor more urbane, sophisticated, and witty with a
tinge of insanity. He feels however that the macho tradition still
remains if our definition of literature is expanded somewhat to
include the radio, the television, the phonograph record, the comic
strip, the cartoon, and other "sub-literary" writing. Dialect humor
finds its modern parallel in Runyon, Caldwell, Milt Gross, the Hyman
Kaplan stories, and the "Lil Abner" comic strip as well as in the
"Ma and Pa Kettle" series. Burlesque and parody survive in Frank
Sullivan's histories, Will Cuppy's almanacs, Don Marquis' columns
about Archy as well as in "Fearless Fosdick" and in Sid Caesar's
versions of silent movies.   Andy Griffith's country-yokel
description of "Romeo and Juliet" is part of a long tradition of
vernacular interpretation of great works, and examples of homespun
philosophers in the tradition of Mr. Dooley and Josh Billings are
easy to find.

1215. Kehl, D. G. "The Graffitist and the Belletrist. The CEA
       Critic 40.4 (May 1978): 31-34.

       Demonstrates that many of the rhetorical devices of the
belletrist are also employed by the graffitist.   Kehl also
demonstrates that the belletrist is also consciously aware of
popular culture in general and the graffitist in particular.
William Faulkner once said in an interview, for example, that the
writer is constantly aware of mortality--aware that he must pass
through that "wall of oblivion," and "he wants to leave a scratch on
that wall." In her essay, "The Place of Fiction," Eudora Welty also
refers to the graffitist in explaining the importance of "location"
and reminding authors that they are not the first to have been
there. "Kilroy at least has been there, and left his name." Welty
feels that writing is not just leaving our names on a wall but is,
more important, seeing that the wall exists and trying to discover
what is on the other side of the wall. Kehl shows that Welty's
distinction is indeed what differentiates the graffitist from the
belletrist.

1216. Kehl, D. G. "Roman Hands Gave Us the Verbal Finger:
       Graffiti and Literary Form" Maledicta I (May 1978): 283-92.

       Quotes Norman Mailer as having said that the graffito
represents "a quintessential marriage of cool and style." Kehl
feels that the genre of graffito is closely related to the genre of
the epigram, one of our oldest literary genres, dating back at least
to classical Greece and Rome. Other members of the graffito-epigram
are "the sententia, apothegm, aphorism, maxim (motto, saw), adage,
proverb, distich, clerihew, and gnome." Griffiti are also part of
the "laconic, earthy folk joke" used by such notable authors
throughout history as Martial, Chaucer, and Steinbeck.

1217. Kullman, Colby H. "Exquisite Madness: The Madhoust Motif in Popular Culture Humor." Studies in Contemporary Satire 12 (1985): 1-5.

Investigates the "madness" motif in American literature, art, music, comic strips, and political cartoons. Mark Twain said that if we all remember we are mad, "mysteries will disappear and life will remain explained." Ken Kesey explores this theme in his One Flew Over the Cuckoo's Nest, where he shows that the insane-asylum setting can be used to explore the sanity of insane people and the insanity of the sane. The chronics in Kesey's novel are described as the "Walkers," the "Wheelers," and the "Vegetables." But these chronics (termed by Kullman as "modern Quixotes") frequently have a sense of humor and a sense of the absurd (though perhaps somewhat distorted), and, ironically, they have relatively sane and practical solutions for many of the strange and unnatural (insane?) problems that are imposed upon them. Kullman uses Twain and Kesey as the base to explore the "madness" theme in various American popular culture genres (especially art, music, comic strips, and political cartoons).

1218. Rubin, Louis D., Jr. "The Great American Joke." The Comic Imagination in American Literature. Ed. Louis D. Rubin, Jr. New Brunswick, NJ: Rutgers Univ. Press, 1983, 3-15.

Contrasts literary and poetic language with "vernacular fact and colloquial speech" and considers Faulkner's The Hamlet an example of the latter, saying that it is like Byrd's Dividing Line, Baldwin's Flush Times, Irving's Knickerbocker History, Longstreet's George Scenes, Clemens' Connecticut Yankee, Hemingway's Torrents of Spring, and Barth's Sot-Weed Factor in this regard. These are all examples of "vernacular fact and colloquial speech" because in all of them there is the "interplay of the ornamental and the elemental, the language of culture and the language of sweat, the democratic ideal and the mulishness of fallen human nature--the Great American Joke."

1219. Tandy, Jenette. Crackerbox Philosophers. New York: Columbia Univ. Press, 1925, xi + 181 pp.

Points out that there are many satirical portraits of the common American in American literary history. Tandy investigates the nature of humorous caricature as it relates specifically to American folk heroes, what she calls "the homely American." She suggests that "Hosea Biglow, Josh Billings, Bill Arp, Mr. Dooley, Abe Martin, are [all] successive incarnations of Uncle Sam, the unlettered philosopher." She is fascinated that at the present time, in our books, in our newspapers, and in real life, Americans are constantly surrounded by "advisers and observers from the lower ranks of life," and she is fascinated by the fact that this situation has been generally true throughout the history of America. Tandy deals with the comic Yankee as he was developed between 1787 and 1830 with the Yankee philosophers of the thirties (Smith, Davis, and Haliburton), with the characters in Lowell's Biglow Papers, with the development of Southern humor, with Civil War and Reconstruction authors like Bill Arp and Petroleum V. Nasby, with what she calls "the funny men"--Artemus Ward and Josh Billings, and with philosophers of "the present day"--Mr. Dooley, Abe Martin, Potash, and Perlmutter. She concludes with a discussion of the works of Kin Hubbard and Montague Glass.

1220. Wells, Carolyn, ed. A Nonsense Anthology. New York: Charles Scribner's Sons, 1915, xxxiii + 279 pp.

Considers the analysis of nonsense literature to be a neglected area of criticism. For example, Hazlitt's "Studies in Jocular Literature" mentions six divisions of "jest," and completely omits "nonsense." Wells suggests that most of the literate world does not appreciate real nonsense because in general readers don't have the ability to distinguish between nonsense of merit and simple chaff. Wells furthermore claims that a person can have a well-developed sense of humor but still be totally lacking in a "sense of nonsense." "Absence of sense is not necessarily nonsense, any more than absence of justice is injustice." The word "nonsense" has two quite different senses. It can refer to "words without meaning," or it can refer to "words conveying absurd or ridiculous ideas." It is this second definition that Wells uses in A Nonsense Anthology.

1221. Wells, Carolyn. A Whimsey Anthology. New York: Dover, 1963, 221 pp.

Considers "whimsey" to be the result of a whim, which is further the result of a freak or capricious notion. Verbal whimseys display ingenuity, and they command a certain admiration because they are spontaneous on the one hand and yet require a certain patience of labor on the other. In A Whimsey Anthology, Wells distinguishes between whimseys of manner (the odd way we have of expressing things) and whimseys of matter (the odd world). A Whimsey Anthology is devoted to whimseys of manner, the linguistic whimseys, or whimseys of expression. In discussing which authors are included and which are not in her anthology, she notes that our earlier authors are more adept at whimsey than are our later authors.

1222. Wilde, Larry. How the Great Comedy Writers Create Laughter. Chicago, Illinois: Nelson-Hall, 1976, ix + 285 pp.

Deals with the writing styles of Goodman Ace, Mel Brooks, Art Buchwald, Abe Burrows, Bill Dana, Selma Diamond, Jack Douglas, Hal Kanter, Norman Lear, Carl Reiner, and Neil Simon. Wilde's book is basically a series of interviews with contemporary comedy writers and covers the range from journalists who write humorous newspaper columns, to screenwriters who write sitcoms or stage plays, and to gag writers who write for stand-up comedians. Goodman Ace talks about composition and phrasing; Mel Brooks talks about "truth" and grounding in reality; Bill Dana talks about the importance of local color; Carl Reiner talks about concentration and observation; Neil Simon talks about opposition and antithesis. Wilde concludes that all of the writers he interviewed are "hypersensitive, indulgent, indefatigable, disciplined, sentimental, highly intelligent, and well educated individuals."

Chapter 11
Parody

1223. **Falk, Robert P., ed.** American Literature in Parody, A
Collection of Parody, Satire, and Literary Burlesque of
American Writers Past and Present. New York: Twayne, 1955.

Suggests that "of all the American classic writers, probably
Longfellow and Poe have been the targets of the greatest number of
parodies with Whitman a close third." Falk illustrates with such
examples as a Demer Cape parody of Poe's "Bells," entitled "Pills,"
as contrasted with a Barry Pain parody of the same poem, entitled
"Tea." Falk also contrasts a C. F. Loomis parody of Poe's "Annabel
Lee" with a parody by Tom Hood, Jr, and another parody by Barbara
Angell. Loomis' parody is entitled "A Poe-'em of Passion"; Hood's
is about a "Cannibal Flea," and Angell's is entitled, "Ulabel Lume."
Although the surface structures of these three parodies are
extremely dissimilar, all three successfully catch the flavor of
Poe's original poem, and all are successful parodies. On the event
of Poe's death, Thomas Holly Chivers published a very dark parody
entitled "Humpty-Dumpty: A La Poe." The parody suggests that Poe
had stolen "The Raven" and other poetic ideas from him [Chivers],
and in fact "The Raven" is uncannily similar to Chivers' earlier
poem, "Isadore." Falk requires a good parody to have "a quiet
explosion of mirth" as one of its features.

1224. **Graff, Gerald, and Barbara Heldt, eds.** W. B. Scott: Parodies,
Etcetera and So Forth. Evanston, Illinois: Northwestern Univ.
Press, 1978, xi + 166 pp.

Classifies W. B. Scott's parodies with the best of literary
parodies, because Scott achieved a blend of "sympathetic mimicry and
critical distance, admiration and irony." Scott had an intimacy
with his subjects that had come from years not only of reading the
various authors but of transporting himself into the times and
places that the authors were writing. Like other parodies, Scott's
parodies have an "edge" to them. Graff and Heldt quote Mizener as
having said, "If it isn't pedantic to say so, these essays are not
just entertaining; they are serious literary criticism" (back
cover). In his preface, Graff supports this opinion by saying,
"writing like this is not only literary criticism of the most acute
kind, but literature in its own right, whatever you take
'literature' to be."

1225. Lowrey, Burling, ed. <u>Twentieth Century Parody: American and British.</u> New York: Harcourt, 1960, xv + 304 pp.

Contrasts Aldous Huxley's statement that "parodies are the most penetrating form of criticism" with Oscar Wilde's statement that parodies "are the tribute that mediocrity pays to genius" and suggests that this "leaves us with a pretty good idea as to who had been burned and who hadn't." Parody is a powerful weapon. Many writers who have no difficulty dealing with ordinary criticism react savagely when they are criticized through parody, which is very difficult for them to do, because they have to pretend to be laughing off the parody at the same time. Wolcott Gibbs said that parody is the most difficult form of creative writing there is, because it is written in a style that is not comfortable for the author and in an exaggerated way. And it must hold the interest of readers who may or may not have read the original. And it must entertain at the same time that it criticizes. Gibbs concludes that the only thing that would make it more difficult would be if it had to be written in Cantonese. There are many different types of parodies in this anthology including parodies of parodists. There is an actress who parodies a playwright (Patricia Collinge on Lillian Hellman); there is a humorist who parodies another humorist (Alex Atkinson on James Thurber); and there are all sorts of other strange combinations.

1226. MacDonald, Dwight, ed. <u>Parodies: An Anthology from Chaucer to Beerbohm--And After</u>. New York: Random House, 1960, xxiii + 575 pp.

Tells how parody functions as criticism by saying that it is a "shorthand for what 'serious' critics must write out at length." Furthermore, "It is method acting, since a successful parodist must live himself, imaginatively, into his parody. It is jujitsu, using the impetus of the opponent to defeat him, although 'opponent' and 'defeat' are hardly the words. Most parodies are written out of admiration rather than contempt. It is hard to make the mimetic effort unless one has enough sympathy to 'identify' with the parody." MacDonald then goes on to explain an even more important function of parody--in-bonding. Parody asks the question, "Do you read the same things I read, and if so, can you recognize these things in disguised form?" MacDonald does not like parodies to be too broad, for he feels that such parodies are not parodies so much as they are burlesques. Before 1900 American parodies tended to be broad while English parodies tended to be narrow. Since 1900, however, the situation has reversed, and English parodies, in the tradition of <u>Punch</u> have become broad, while American parodies, in the tradition of <u>The New Yorker</u> have become delightfully specific. MacDonald likes parodies because they have a bookish flavor and because he loves books. He considers parody to be a kind of literary shop talk.

1227. Nilsen, Don L. F. "Parodies of Poe: A Study in the Nature of Grounding." <u>Massachusetts English Teacher</u>, May 1989: 5-7.

Discusses the distinction between sound-parody and sense-parody and concludes that sense-parody can result in "imitation" rather than parody. Discusses Thomas Holly Chivers' parody of Poe's

"The Raven," entitled "Humpty-Dumpty: A La Poe." This is very dark
humor, because Chivers' parody is actually an accusation that Poe
had originally stolen the poem from him [Chivers].

1228. Rice, Scott, ed. **Bride of Dark and Stormy**. New York: Penguin,
      1988, xiv + 137 pp.

      Presents the winners of the 1986 and 1987 Bulwer-Lytton
Fiction Contest, which challenges writers to compose the first
sentence to "the worst of all possible novels." The contest is
named after Edward George Bulwer-Lytton, a Victorian novelist whose
first line of <u>Paul Clifford</u> (1830) was, "It was a dark and stormy
night." Rice contends that it is not easy to write bad fiction on
purpose, and in this book he offers advice on how to be a
"successful" writer of the kind of writing that is submitted to the
contest judges. This is a "how-to" book, "full of rotten advice and
worse examples" (back cover).

1229. Rice, Scott, ed. **It Was a Dark and Stormy Night**. New York:
      Penguin, 1984, xii + 145 pp.

      Presents the winners of the 1982 and 1983 Bulwer-Lytton
Fiction Contests, which annually attract thousands of entries from
throughout the United States and from many foreign countries. To
Victorian readers, Bulwer-Lytton was second in popularity only to
Charles Dickens, and he has inspired thousands of untalented
writers, the most famous of which is Snoopy in the <u>Peanuts</u> comic
strip, who begins his "Great American Novel" with "It was a dark and
stormy night." Rice says that the contest does not encourage <u>bad</u>
bad writing, but <u>good</u> bad writing, "writing so deliberately rotten
that it both entertains and instructs." Rice feels that "Bad is
only bad when it thinks it is good." The winner of the 1984 contest
received a word processor. The runner-up received the complete
works of Bulwer-Lytton, "a gift calculated to make the nights long,
if not dark and stormy."

1230. Rice, Scott, ed. **Son of "It Was a Dark and Stormy Night."** New
      York: Penguin, 1986, xiv + 127 pp.

      Presents the winners of the 1984 and 1985 Bulwer-Lytton
Fiction Contests. Rice describes the entrants as "reformers,
composing trenchant commentaries on the state of modern literacy."
They are "literary vigilantes prowling the subways of fiction." In
their work, "each sentence is a distilled work of literary
criticism, a lampoon of various species of literary malpractice."

1231. Safer, Elaine B. "Twentieth-Century Comic Epic Novels and
      Cotton Mather's **Magnalia**." **The Contemporary American Comic**
      Epic: The Novels of Barth, Pynchon, Gaddis, and Kesey. Ed.
      Elaine B. Safer. Detroit: Wayne State Univ. Press, 1988, 25-
      38.

      Explains why the study of Mather's <u>Magnalia Christi Americana</u>
(1702) is important for understanding contemporary American comic
epic novels in general and the novels of Barth, Pynchon, Gaddis, and
Kesey in particular. Mather's novel is an early example of the
American epic novel parodied in the later ironic counterparts.
Mather's novel treats America as a new Garden of Eden, as a new

Canaan, and as "the high point of the westward advancement of
culture, the arts, and empire"; such sentiments were mocked in the
later novels.   Mather's novel also develops such genres as the
chronicle, the saints' lives, the jeremiad sermon, and the epic
itself, which are parodied in the later novels.   The twentieth-
century novels that best exemplify the twentieth century parodies of
Mather's <u>Magnalia</u> include Barth's <u>The Sot-Weed Factor</u>, in which the
John Smith-Pocahontas legend is burlesqued, Gaddis's <u>The</u>
<u>Recognitions</u>, where Wyatt Gwyon wants to reverse the journey and
send his New England ancestors back to Europe, and Ken Kesey's
<u>Sometimes a Great Notion</u>, where Kesey portrays early members of the
Stamper family not as strong devout pioneers but as a "clan of
skinny men [involved in] foolish roaming."

1232. Schulz, Max F. "The Politics of Parody; and, the Comic
      Apocalypses of Jorge Luis Borges, Thomas Berger, Thomas
      Pynchon, and Robert Coover." <u>Black Humor Fiction of the</u>
      <u>Sixties: A Plurastic Definition of Man and His World</u>. Athens:
      Ohio Univ. Press, 1973, 66-90.

       Points out that throughout history man has been intent on
looking at the chaos of experience through the perspective of some
value system able to change the chaos into order.   Contemporary
black humorists cast doubt on the resultant apparent objectivity and
absoluteness by parodying these various frames of reference or what
Schulz calls "categorical imperatives." Art is no longer viewed as
a method of resolving, reconciling, ordering, beautifying, or
correcting nature.   Rather, it becomes simply another form of
nature, and is therefore itself as chaotic as is the nature it
attempts to explain. Schulz feels that parody should be expected in
a world that offers endless alternatives for explaining nature.
These endless equivalences that are designed to resolve the chaos
ironically become chaotic themselves when viewed en masse, and this
is the stuff that parody is made of.

1233. Smith, Ron. "In Search of America's Most Successful Literary
      Parodies and Burlesques." <u>WHIMSY</u> 5 (April 1, 1987): 173-74.

       Suggests that Edgar Allan Poe's style, manner and strategy
account for his popularity as a poet <u>and</u> as a tempting target for
parody.   His work is filled with repetitions and highly personal
words such as "Nevermore."   His writing replete with parallelisms,
awsome rhythms, and persistent internal rhymes, some of them
stretched almost to the point of self-parodying.   Smith says of
Whitman that his "free verse, his unmistakable exuberance and brash
ego" make <u>him</u> also a frequent target of the parodist.   Smith
discusses some of the favorite ploys of parody writers and then
demonstrates with a C. L. Edson parody of Poe's "The Raven," a
George A. Strong parody of Longfellow's <u>The Song of Hiawatha</u>, a
Charles Battell Loomis parody of Whitman's <u>Leaves of Grass</u>, and a
Dan Greenburg parody of Salinger's <u>Catcher in the Rye</u>, and others.
He concludes that "What we have in the case of [Greenburg's] "Catch
Her in the Oatmeal" is a good example of 'burlesque,' a sister form
to parody, where the writer puts into a familiar literary work what
is alien to it."

1234. Wells, Carolyn, ed. A Parody Anthology. New York: Scribner,
      1904, xxx + 397 pp.

      Contributes to parody research by suggesting that there should
be three classes of parodies, although the casual critic of parodies
usually divides them into only two classes, parodies of sound and
parodies of sense. Wells' three divisions may be called "word
rendering," "form rendering," and "sense rendering. For Wells,
word-rendering is simply an imitation of the original and depends
entirely upon the substitution of a trivial or commonplace motive
for a lofty one; it follows as closely as possible the original
words. "Form rendering" on the other hand is the imitation of the
style of an author, and is most effective for authors who have
particularly recognizable mannerisms or affectations. For Wells,
"sense-rendering," is the most meritorious, and utilizes not only
the original writer's diction and style, but his train of thought
precisely and basic premises as well. Wells's example of a sense-
rendering parody, which she considers excellent is John Bennett's
parody of "The Raven," which begins, "Could Poe walk again tomorrow, heavy with dyspeptic sorrow, While the darkness seemed to
borrow/darkness from the night before...."

1235. Workman, Brooke. "Parody: A Student's Response to J. D.
      Salinger." English Journal 70.1 (January 1981): 53-54.

      Suggests that having students write parodies is an excellent
way of getting them to recognize the style and rhetorical devices of
a particular author. The students enjoyed the assignment and
afterwards, they were able not only to enjoy reading Salinger more
but to understand better the writing and creative processes.

Chapter 12
Poetry

1236. Bishop, Morris. "Light Verse in America." The Comic
Imagination in American Literature. Ed. Louis D. Rubin, Jr.
New Brunswick, NJ: Rutgers Univ. Press, 1983, 259-73.

Believes that light verse should "promote misunderstanding"
but further believes that there is a kind of understanding in
misunderstanding. Light verse is the casual verse of the evening
when we cast off our clothes. It is the kind of verse that sneaks
around truth from the rear and uncovers the beauty of the hinder
parts. Light verse developed in America during the early nineteenth
century as the result of the spreading of culture and literary
awareness. It was practiced by a wide range of people, not only by
authors such as James Russell Lowell, Oliver Wendell Holmes, John
Godfrey Saxe, Eugene Field, Ben King, Carl Sandburg, Vachel Lindsay,
Robert Frost, and Edwin Arlington Robinson but also by the sixth
President of the United States, John Quincy Adams. Authors who
became famous for their light verse included Franklin P. Adams,
Dorothy Parker, E. B. White, and Ogden Nash. Light verse in its
early days was acceptable only during times of diversion--an after-
dinner speech or the leisure time after a hard day's work. Morris
Bishop feels that there is little light verse remaining today. We
are too sad and apprehensive to enjoy it. Our satire has become
bitterly angry, and our comedy has become cruel and obscene. The
light verse of the past is frequently viewed as over-simple and
puerile.

1237. Coursen, Herbert R. Jr. "The Ghost of Christmas Past:
'Stopping by Woods on a Snowy Evening'" The Overwrought Urn.
Ed. Charles Kaplan. New York: Pegasus, 1969, 86-88.

Satirically suggests that Robert Frost's "Stopping by Woods on
a Snowy Evening" is about Christmas. As evidence, Courson points
out that "the darkest evening of the year" in New England would be
December 21st, just before Christmas. The poet would not have
wanted to use the exact date (December 25), as that would have
"given it all away." As further evidence, Courson ask who it is who
has "promises to keep" at about this time of year. Coursen feels
that the phrase "fill up with snow" is an allusion to his filling up
of countless children's stockings hung above countless fireplaces.
The "harness bells" is really an allusion to sleigh bells. And the
"little horse" is actually a veiled allusion to Santa Claus's
reindeer.

1238. Franklin, Benjamin, V, ed. The Poetry of the Minor Connecticut
Wits. Gainesville, FL: Scholars' Facsimiles and Reprints,
1970, xv + 968 pp.

Contrasts the major Connecticut Wits (Trumbull, Timothy
Dwight, Humphreys, and Barlow) with the minor Connecticut Wits
(Richard Alsop, Mason Fitch Cogswell, Theodore Dwight, Lemuel
Hopkins, and Elihu Hubbard Smith) and indicates that both the Major
and the Minor Wits were politically, socially, and religiously
conservative. The Connecticut wits were the first Americans to
speak out against the free thinking of what they considered to be
the ignorant masses. The minor Connecticut Wits were "minor" in a
number of senses. First, they were not as old, the average age of
the Minors being ten years younger than that of the Majors. Second,
they were less educated. While all of the Major Wits had degrees
from Yale, only Cogswell and Smith from the Minor wits had earned
degrees from Yale, while Alsop, Theodore Dwight, and Hopkins held
only honorary Yale degrees. Third, the quantity of their work was
less than and the quality was inferior to that of the Major Wits.
The Minor Wits emulated the poetic style of English neoclassicism in
particular and of Pope in particular. Their rhetorical devices
included logical patterns of parallel comparison and contrast,
metaphoric meanings, puns, diction, and heroic couplets. Most of
the fame of the Minor Wits relates to a single collection, The Echo;
With Other Poems.

1239. Hayden, Bradley. "In Memoriam Humor: Julia Moore and the
Western Michigan Poets." English Journal 72.5 (September
1983): 22-28.

Includes Dr. William Fuller, S. H. Ewell, J. B. Smiley, Fred
Yapple, Howard Dwight Smiley, Howard Heber Clark, and the clergy
city singers with Julia Moore as the "Western Michigan Poets."
Grand Rapids, which was the center of this poetic oasis, was at the
time the northernmost outpost of civilization in the United States.
The poets were concerned with death and other hardships of the
frontier. Their verse was severe, full of sentimentality, and
totally lacking in aesthetics or good taste, but they had a large
following, and their poems are even now fun to read. Julia Moore
wrote obituary poems to everyone who died around Grand Rapids in the
late 1800s, but she specialized in writing poems to dead children.
Hayden feels that Moore's poetry was more representative of frontier
literature than many would care to admit.

1240. Lewis, D. B. Wyndham, and Charles Lee, eds. The Stuffed Owl:
An Anthology of Bad Verse. London: J. M. Dent and Sons, 1948,
xxiv + 264 pp.

Makes a distinction between bad Bad Verse and good Bad Verse
and includes only what is considered to be good Bad verse in this
anthology, because "the field of bad Bad Verse is vast, and
confusing in its tropical luxuriance." Good Bad Verse "has an
eerie, supernal beauty comparable in its accidents with the beauty
of Good Verse." The placement of poems into this anthology means
that they will automatically be read with an intention different
from what the authors originally planned, for "with two or three
exceptions, all the poets represented in these pages are men and

women to whom Almighty God in His inscrutable providence has seen
fit to <u>deny</u> a sense of humor." [underlining mine].

1241. Nilsen, Don L. F. "Dithyrambs: The Humor of Folk Poetry."
<u>Mississippi Folklore Register</u> 17.2 (Fall 1983): 95-107.

Analyzes the doggerel elements in the poetry of T. A. Daly,
Ogden Nash, James Whitcomb Riley, John Hollander, Leo Rosten, Pat
Egan Dexter, Julia Moore, J. B. Smiley, and Mark Twain. The reason
that a "dithyramb" can be translated is that "since it has little
meaning in the first place, no meaning is lost in translation."
Dithyrambs have four basic values: First, they are a form of
regression; second, they are used to poke fun at people who are
pompous and prejudgmental; third, they have shallow themes but
perfect rhyme and scansion, so they easily enter into long-term
memory (too easily in many cases), and fourth, they define the
limits of poetry. They are what linguists would call starred or
ungrammatical forms. Dithyrambs also tend to have a great deal of
rhetorical density--alliteration, assonance, allusion,
personification, onomatopoeia, chiasmas, oxymoron, etc. So we
should lighten up on our criticism of dithyramb poets. Julia Moore,
the archetypal dithyramb poet wrote:
      And now kind friends, what I have wrote,
       I hope you will pass o'er,
      And not criticize as some have done,
        Hitherto herebefore.

1242. Tanner, James T. F. "Humor in American Poetry." <u>Studies in
American Humor</u> NS6 (1988): 1-104.

Contains articles on humor in American poetry by Jerry
Bradley, Allene Cooper, Maria Damon, Donald E. Hardy, Judith Yaross
Lee, William R. Linneman, Don L. F. Nilsen, Constance J. Post, and
James T. F. Tanner. The poetry treated ranges across time, space,
and politics in subject and across parody, surrealism, satire,
sarcasm, jest, and absurdity in style. The authors' purposes range
from description to explanation and evaluation.

1243. Vernon, John. "Fresh Air: Humor in Contemporary American
Poetry." <u>Comic Relief: Humor in Contemporary American
Literature</u>. Urbana: Univ. of Illinois Press, 1978, 304-323.

Explains that many contemporary American poets are humorous
because they are following Ezra Pound's dictum, "make it new," and
because in order to "make it new," poets are forced to resort to
humorous images. Vernon contends that the influence of French
surrealism has also resulted in wierd and often humorous images for
contemporary American poets. Vernon feels that there are two
schools of humor among contemporary poets. The New York school
includes such poets as Kenneth Koch, John Ashbery, and James Tate,
and could be said also to include such beat poets as Allen Ginsberg
and Gregory Corso. This school refuses to respect traditional
meanings, and the result is a surrealistic skepticism. The poetry
of the second school is assymetrical and unstable; it has the effect
of throwing the reader off balance. Since the poets in this school
are interested in discovery, their poetry tends to zig-zag from
subject to subject. A. R. Ammons and John Berryman, Bill Knott,
Russell Edson, David Ignatow, Jack Spicer, and Edward Dorn are poets

who represent this school.   The tone is that of speculative
bewilderment with pauses and slips and occasional epiphanies.
Vernon feels that what makes contemporary poets funny is their
eclectic ability to allow the world they describe to take on various
shapes.

1244. Wallace, Ronald. <u>God Be with the Clown: Humor in American
      Poetry</u>. Columbia, MO: Univ. of Missouri Press, 1984, ix + 325
      pp.

      Believes that humor has been one of the defining elements of
American poetry, and that it is an important element in the poetry
of Walt Whitman, Robert Frost, Wallace Stevens, John Berryman, David
Wagoner, Maxine Kumin, and Emily Dickinson. He feels that for these
authors, "comedy has informed their style, their characteristic
methods, their themes, and their general assumptions about art and
modern life."   Dickinson's humor is witty and intellectual;
Whitman's is celebrating and affirming; Stevens's consists of
antics; Frost's is Yankee humor and dark laughter; Berryman's is
self-ridicule, but all of their humor questions atrophied beliefs,
criticizes the defects of society, and exposes our pretensions while
at the same time providing laughter as a weapon against chaos and
despair in a world that seems increasingly absurd. "When people or
institutions get too far up, comedy pulls them down; when they get
too far down, comedy pulls them up." The humor in this book ranges
through wit, satire, irony, parody, farce, burlesque, and play.
There is throughout the book, however, constant attention to the
farcical, the bizarre, the incongruous, the lively, the surprising,
and the comic.

Chapter 13
Politics

1245. Adler, Bill, ed. <u>Presidential Wit, from Washington to Johnson</u>.
New York: Trident Press, 1966, x + 241 pp.

Believes that each American president had a specific and
somewhat unique sense of humor. Abraham Lincoln and Lyndon Johnson
enjoyed telling stories from their earlier lives in Illinois and
Texas. John F. Kennedy delighted in sharp witticisms or penetrating
quips. Franklin Delano Roosevelt enjoyed political wit and humor
aimed at his opponents. Woodrow Wilson was amused by good humorous
limericks. Lincoln, Roosevelt, Wilson, and Kennedy were the
wittiest presidents, but even Calvin Coolidge and Thomas Jefferson
had a sense of humor. The humor selections presented here were
taken from presidential speeches, press conferences, letters, off-
the-record remarks, personal diaries, election campaigns, and
interviews.

1246. Caron, James E. "Laughter, Politics, and the Yankee Doodle
Legacy in America's Comic Tradition." <u>Thalia: Studies in
Literary Humor</u> 10.1 (Spring-Summer 1988): 3-13.

Discusses the development of political humor in characters
like Jack Downing, Mike Fink, and Davy Crockett, and other comic
figures from 1830 onward. From 1830 on, the characters were
developed either as reputable social beings who represent "a moral
and predictable universe," or they were developed as subversives,
who flaunt the social order, including the laws, the decency, and
the modesty of a well-ordered society. Most of the characters in
early New England humor were "reputable," while most of the rogues
came out of the Old Southwest; nevertheless, in New England there
developed the character of "Yankee Doodle," which was used by the
British and the Loyalists as a symbol of aristocratic derision,
while the rebels used it as a badge of democratic honor. The Yankee
was laughed at because of his country bumpkin origin; but he was
also admired for his native shrewdness and independence of spirit.
Thus the Yankee Doodle character came to be viewed as having a
richly ambiguous nature.

1247. Dudden, Arthur Power. "The Record of Political Humor."
<u>American Quarterly</u> 37.1 (Spring 1985): 50-70.

Discusses and analyzes the political humor of Seba Smith,
Charles Farrar Browne, David Ross Locke, Petroleum Vesuvius Nasby,
Samuel Clemens, Finley Peter Dunne, Artemus Ward, James Russell
Lowell, Henry W. Shaw, Robert Henry Newell, and Edgar Wilson Nye and
compares this political humor to that of such later writers as Will

Rogers, Ambrose Bierce, H. L. Mencken, James Thurber, Malcolm Muggeridge, and Garry Trudeau. Muggeridge wrote "The enemy of humor is fear," because fear draws people together into a herd, and requires total conformity. Laughter, on the other hand, separates people, and encourages them to be individuals. "In a conformist society, there is no place for the jester. He strikes a discordant note, and therefore must be put down."

1248. Fletcher, M. D. <u>Contemporary Political Satire: Narrative Strategies in the Post-Modern Context</u>. New York: Univ. Press of America, 1987, xvi + 185.

Discusses the work of such contemporary political satirists as Voinovich, Heller, Llosa, Rushdie, Pynchon, and Vidal and suggests that modern satire is not like earlier satire. In earlier satire there are always implied norms against which a target is caricatured and exposed as ridiculous. In earlier satire there was always a shared set of values between the satirist and the audience. However the modern satirist cannot make such an assumption as he is now writing in a culturally diverse world. The earlier satirist could demonstrate an absolute priority of one set of values over another, but the modern satirist cannot do this. And that is why modern satire tends to be "cosmic satire" and tends to stress black humor and irony and absurdities and tends to divide the audience rather than pulling it together.

1249. Gibson, William M. <u>Theodore Roosevelt Among the Humorists: W. D. Howells, Mark Twain, and Mr. Dooley</u>. Knoxville: Univ. of Tennessee Press, 1980, xii + 83 pp.

Concentrates on the political humor of Howells, Twain, and Dunne because Gibson considers these three to have been the best American satirists during the Theodore Roosevelt years as President and because they all three took great interest in "the politics of the gilded age." Dunne wrote very flatteringly of Teddy Roosevelt and was therefore much sought after by that administration. Both Howells and Twain were divided. They liked Teddy Roosevelt the man, but they didn't like his politics. All three humorists were "fascinated by Teddy Roosevelt's fabulous energy and attracted by his friendliness to letters." They also communicated both in public and in private that they felt that Teddy Roosevelt was a skillful politician. One of the reasons that these three humorists were all so concerned about politics and became such effective political satirists is that all three of them had had long careers in journalism, and all three had developed skill in writing commentaries and editorials for their various newspapers.

1250. Granger, Bruce Ingham. <u>Political Satire in the American Revolution, 1763-1783</u>. Ithaca, New York: Cornell Univ. Press, 1960, xiv + 314 pp.

Contains 530 satires gleaned from American newspapers, magazines, broadsides, and pamphlets. These satires were written about America, by Americans, for American readers. The book considers satire to be a "literary mode" and therefore sets out to define it, to set these satires into their proper literary environment, and to examine their range. It also attempts to evaluate the various pieces which "possess distinct literary merit" and provide special background information for the more important pieces. The present study is important because at the time these satires were being written (1763-1783), less was known about the genre of satire, and less was also known about the effects that the various events of the Revolution would have on history.

1251. Carlisle, Henry C., ed. <u>American Satire in Prose and Verse</u>.
New York: Random House, 1962, xxv + 465 pp.

Laments the fact that American history has not recorded in
books much of the rich satiric humor that so well reflected the
character of early Americans. This satiric humor was cocky and
critical and of high quality, but it was also largely oral in its
expression. Carlisle points out that his volume contains no satires
against Communism. While it could be contended that communism isn't
funny, this contention could be countered with the observation that
Ben Franklin didn't think that mercantilism was funny either, but if
he had not been able to effectively ridicule mercantilism, we might
still be paying the Stamp Tax. Carlisle suggests that one of the
basic differences between satire and plain humor is the fury of
satire. "Satire is not respectable; humor is." Satire is clever,
irreverent, and insinuating, but it has to be more than this; it has
to be critical as well. The satirist does not accept life the way
it is but considers normal things to be abnormal, proper things to
be odd, ridiculous, and even at times evil. Furthermore, satire is
both fictional and true. It is also irresistible, and the
irresistibility of American satire is that it contains invective,
paradox, wit, and appeal to the intellect. In other countries it is
the criticism that has become the most salient feature of satire,
but in America, the satire is softer. It tends to be humorous,
disarming, friendly, familiar, and possibly a bit ingratiating.

1252. Clark, John R., and Anna Lydia Motto. "Anthologies of Satire
in Print (1979): A Critical Bibliography." <u>Studies in
Contemporary Satire</u> 5 (Spring 1979): 35-52.

Provides a critical bibliography and also the names and
addresses of publishers of anthologies of satire in print in 1979.
There are five items in the section on "General Anthologies of
Satire," seventeen items in "Special Anthologies of Satire," twelve
items in "Parody," and thirteen items in "Related Topics." This
last section includes satiric poetry, epigrams and epitaphs, sick
verse, aphorisms, graffiti, etc.

1253. Clark, John R., and Priscilla Van Zandt. "Neglected Authors:
The Martyrs and Relics of Satire." <u>Studies in Contemporary
Satire</u> 12 (1985): 6-21.

Describes the human targets of satire as filled with
unwarranted or excessive pride. The satirist shows no mercy in
attacking the person who pretends to be witty, cultured, or learned,

the person who pretends to be superior to other people because of
his intellect, education, or writings. "The satirist has only scorn
for those who believe that they are unlike other men." The satirist
devalues the writings of such authors by pointing out their
insignificance and ephemerality. In Breakfast of Champions, Kurt
Vonnegut satirically suggests that the glut of writing has become so
huge that the words must be destroyed to that the pages on which
they are printed can be recycled to make room for more writing.
This theme is similar to that in Ray Bradbury's Fahrenheit 451 in
which Firemen cleanse the State with their flame throwers, burning
not only all of the books but all of the readers of books as well.

1254. FitzGerald, Gregory. "The Satiric Use of Setting." Studies in
       Contemporary Satire 13 (1986): 2-4.

       Suggests that not only people and institutions can be
satirized but settings as well--both historical and geographical.
In A Connecticut Yankee in King Arthur's Court Mark Twain satirizes
the nostalgia that we have for the romanticized Middle Ages by
discussing the problems of medieval sanitation facilities or the
difficulties of dealing with a swarm of bees trapped inside a suit
of knightly armor. Flannery O'Connor's "Good Country People" [A
Good Man is Hard to Find] may be based on the running joke about a
travelling salesman. This joke (and O'Connor's story) is tightly
linked to the rural setting. E. B. White's "The Hour of Letdown"
[The Second Tree from the Corner] is also based on a running joke,
and again both are tied closely to setting. In White's story, a man
comes into a bar carrying a big ugly machine and places it on the
bar. He then orders two rye-and-waters. Clearly, one of the drinks
is for the machine--just as clearly as in earlier jokes when the
customer had walked in with whiskey-drinking mice, dogs, cats, and
other animals. Setting is an important component in the satire of
the writers of the Old Southwest as it is in the Georgia satire of
Flannery O'Connor or the Yoknapatawpha County satire of William
Faulkner.

1255. Johnson, Edgar. A Treasury of Satire. New York: Simon and
       Schuster, 1945, xxiv + 772 pp.

       Contrasts the opinion that it is the duty of satirists to be
the censors of society, chipping away angrily at bad manners and
corrupt morals with a mood of censure, sadness, and misanthropy. It
is the duty of the satirist to laugh away the absurdities of mankind
by blowing them to bits in a peal of ridicule. Satire can reflect
a wide range of mood. In King Lear, the fool tells bitter and
foreboding jokes. This is satire "from the teeth out," the tragic
satire of a hostile snarl. There is also the high-spirited satire
of mockery, the satire, for example of comparing men to apes at a
zoo where it is difficult to distinguish who is in the cage and who
is out. This is the satire of Thomas Love Peacock, of Clarence Day,
and of George Bernard Shaw. Some critics say that satire without
humor is invective, but Johnson says that invective is indeed a form
of satire. In fact, the only ingredient which Johnson sees in the
wide range of rhetorical techniques that have all been called satire
is criticism. But clearly, even though all satire is critical, not
all criticism is satire.

1256. Kernan, Alvin B. <u>Modern Satire</u>. New York: Harcourt, Brace and
    World, 1962, vi + 234 pp.

    Contrasts "satire" with "comedy" and "tragedy" and indicates
that of the three, "satire" is the least forgiving.   "Comedy"
exhibits a kindly tolerance for the imperfections of mankind.
"Tragedy" exhibits a profound sympathy for the imperfections of
mankind. But "satire" tells man that his failings are his own fault
and his own doing, and he should make things right. Kernan feels
that satire has had a revival in the twentieth century in the works
of Evelyn Waugh, Nathanael West, Aldous Huxley, George Orwell,
Wyston Hugh Auden, and Wyndham Lewis. But Kernan questions whether
such satire can be classified as "great satire," because "Great
satire is usually written, we are told, in periods when there is
general agreement on morals." All of the satires in Kernan's book
attack the modern belief that somehow all human institutions, and in
fact all of mankind, have evolved in our morals, our social
institutions, our technology, and our wisdom to a state of near
perfection.   Yet this belief is held in the face of total war,
concentration camps, overpopulation, nuclear bombs, brainwashing,
dishonest advertising, overproduction, and persistent and widespread
anxiety. The satires in Kernan's book question whether such a world
is actually the result of evolution and progress or the opposite.

1257. Kiley, Frederick, and J. M. Shuttleworth, eds. <u>Satire: From
    Aesop to Buchwald</u>. New York: Macmillan, 1971, xii + 484 pp.

    Considers satire to be a conservative genre, for it tends to
value the traditions that have been developed through centuries of
bloodshed, disaster, and discouragement, it venerates moderation,
and it values the general welfare and the public good.   Satire
exposes corruption, idiosyncrasy, ignorance, and especially pride
and hypocrisy, because these are the things which threaten to
destroy valued institutions and traditions.   Art Buchwald can use
satire to attack the pomposities of the bureaucracy, but Al Capp can
also use satire to attack the irresponsible protest groups that are
also attacking the pomposities of bureaucracy. Both writers are
using traditional satire.   Satire is not a gentle genre.   It
frequently uses shock and exaggeration to make its point. Satire
generally assumes a reasonably intelligent, educated, and rational
audience.   Burlesque is one form of satire, and burlesque can be
categorized as high (where a low or frivolous subject is treated in
a dignified way), or low (where a lofty or serious subject is
treated with derision).

1258. Linneman, William R. <u>Satires of American Realism, 1880-1900</u>.
    <u>American Literature</u> 34.1 (1962): 80-93.

    Characterizes humorous authors of 1880-1900 as realistic in
manner but romantic in material.   Their ideal novel was something
between the dime novel and realistic fiction. They liked colloquial
dialogue and characters depicting real life, but they didn't like
realistic plots.   Rather they preferred entertainment and
excitement. The charge most frequently brought against the realists
such as Henry James was their excessive use of detail.   In realism
there were so many facts that "the significant was buried under the
irrelevant."   Another fault of realism is the excessive use of
analysis.   Realists are constantly explaining behavior and

suggesting motives. The resultant writing tends to be dull and
uninsightful. A third fault of realism is that it is amoral. It
fails to distinguish right from wrong. At the heart of the clash
between the realists and the humorists is how the imagination
functions. The realists want the imagination to be restrained,
while the humorists want the imagination to be unfettered to allow
more interesting writing. Although there are many disagreements
between the humorists and the realists, the humorists are actually
more realistic than the realists in one important respect. The
language they use is _real_ language. The rhythm and vocabulary and
salty dialogue of humorous prose are actually more true to life than
the stilted prose of the realists.

1259. Nilsen, Don L. F. "Satire--The Necessary and Sufficient
      Conditions--Some Preliminary Observations." Studies in
      Contemporary Satire 15 (1988): 1-9.

     States that satire is always grounded in reality, always
distorted, and always an attack on society. In addition, American
satire is usually humorous, usually ironic, usually written for a
very specific audience, and usually negative in tone. This article
contrasts such concepts as "humor," "wit," "satire," "sarcasm,"
"invective," "irony," "cynicism," and "the sardonic," indicating
that humor, wit, and irony are typical features of satire and that
invective, cynicism, sardonicness, and sarcasm are types of satire.
The motive, province, method, and audience are also contrasted for
these various features and types of satire.

1260. Nilsen, Don L. F. "A Survey of Satire Publications." Studies
      in Contemporary Satire 14 (1987): 16-22.

     Lists and annotates American and international satiric
magazines and newsletters. In America, there are the following
magazines: Cracked, Mad Magazine, National Lampoon, Pangloss Papers,
The Realist, Spy, and Sting for the general public, International
Journal of Creature Communication for the field of speech
communication, Journal of Irreproducible Results for science,
Journal of Polymorphous Perversity for psychology, Lingua Pranca for
linguistics, Purlock Society Journal, Satire Newsletter, Scholia
Satyrica, and Studies in Contemporary Satire for literature, and The
Upstart Crow for Shakespeare studies. International satire
magazines like the following often include American satires:
Bulgaria's A Propos for the fine arts, Canada's The Best of
International Humor and Satire for politics, and France's Canard
Enchaine, Turkey's Karakare, Russia's Krokodil, and England's Punch
for various aspects of international culture.

1261. Russell, John, and Ashley Brown. Satire: A Critical Anthology.
      New York: World, 1967, xxxiv + 421 pp.

     Alludes to Aristotle who believed that there were only two
ways of viewing man's activities--in a mood of awe and celebration
or in a mood of disgust and denunciation. Also, since the time of
Homer, the epics have been written in dactylic hexameter, while the
lampoons have been iambic pentameter--the most colloquial of all
poetic measures. Russell and Brown point out that "attack" and
"humor" are two features that are characteristically associated with
satire. They also point out, however, that there are many satirical

works that are so playful and whimsical that there is very little sting in the barbs, and that other satirical works are so ponderous and serious that they could be said to be totally lacking in humor. Furthermore, if reform were the true aim of the satirist, satirists would be considered almost entirely unsuccessful, for satire very seldom accomplishes any real reform. Targets of satire tend to continue to behave in ridiculous ways, even though their actions and motives may have been exposed by satire. Satire is sophisticated because it upgrades and compliments the audience. Satire is a conspiracy between the author and the audience against the target. The author uses wit and irony, and the reader must grasp the implications of what the satirist has implied, in a private-joke close-circle-of-friends sort of relationship. It uses literary conventions to overturn social conventions.

1262. Wells, Carolyn, ed. A Satire Anthology. New York: Charles Scribner's, 1905, xvi + 369 pp.

Contrasts "satire" with "sarcasm," "irony," "ridicule," and "burlesque." Satire is defined largely in terms of the motives of the writer and also in terms of the relationship that holds between the writer and the reader. Satire can be divided into two broad categories: Horatian and Juvenalian. Horace's followers stressed the humor and tolerance aspects of satire, while Juvenal's followers stressed the bitter invective aspects. James Russell Lowell was one of the most important American satirists. The most highly developed type of satire that has developed in America is political satire. This clever and ingenious tradition began in earnest in the early part of the nineteenth century and has continued to the present day.

Chapter 15
Sex Roles

1263. Barreca, Regina, ed. Last Laughs: Perspectives on Women and Comedy. New York: Gordon and Breach, 1988, 321 pp.

Contains the following articles: Catherine Gallagher's "Who Was That Masked Woman? The Prostitute and the Playwright in the Comedies of Aphra Behn," Janet Todd's "Life after Sex: The Fictional Autobiography of Delariver Manley," Rachel M. Brownstein's "Jane Austen: Irony and Authority," Patricia Meyer Spacks' "Austen's Laughter," Kay Rogers' "Deflation of Male Pretensions in Fanny Burney's Celia," Nicole Hollander's "Sylvia," Linda A. Morris' "Frances Miriam Whitcher: Social Satire in the Age of Gentility," Carol Hanbery MacKay's "Hate and Humor as Empathetic Whimsy in Anne Thackeray Ritchie," Regenia Gagnier's "Between Women: A Cross-Class Analysis of Status and Anarchic Humor," Denise Marshall's "Slaying the Angel and the Patriarch: The Grinning Woolf," Judy Little's "(En)gendering Laughter: Woolf's Orlando as Contraband in the Age of Joyce," Mary Ann Rorison Caws' "Truth-Telling: The Self and Fictions of Humor," Nancy Walker's "Ironic Autobiography: From The Waterfall to The Handmaid's Tale," John Glavin's "Muriel Spark's Unknowing Fiction," Regina Barreca's "Metaphor-into-Narrative: Being Very Careful with Words," Esther Cohen's "Uncommon Woman: An Interview with Wendy Wasserstein," Lisa Merrill's "Feminist Humor: Rebellious and Self-Affirming," Jan Marcus' "Daughters of Anger/Material Girls: Con/Textualizing Feminist Criticism," and Fay Weldon's Towards a Humorous View of the Universe."

1264. Bruere, Martha Bensley, and Mary Ritter Beard, eds. Laughing Their Way: Women's Humor in America. New York: Macmillan, 1934, viii + 295 pp.

Regrets that America's view of humor is a "partial view--i.e., masculine view." Native American humor is equated with men's humor. This anthology projects a woman's "angle of vision," "the angle of vision from which women see a lack of balance, wrong proportions, disharmonies, and incongruities in life [as] a thing of their world as it must be--a world always a little apart."

1265. Bryan, Joseph III, ed. Merry Gentlemen (and One Lady). New York: Atheneum, 1985, xiv + 324 pp.

Contains selections and commentary relating to the works of Arthur Samuels, Robert Benchley, Marc Connelly, Frank Sullivan, Dorothy Parker, Fred Allen, Donald Ogden Stewart, Nunnally Johnson, John Steinbeck, Corey Ford, S. J. Perelman, Finis Farr, Hugh Troy, and George Bond, all of whom were born between 1888 and 1909. The editor asks what these fourteen authors have in common and then responds that "two of them never married; the other twelve were

married a total of twenty-one times (Dottie Parker married the same
man twice).... Fred Allen didn't drink; Art Samuels, Marc Connelly,
and Sid Perelman drank moderately; the rest fairly lapped up the
stuff" and continues discussing the various differences of these
fourteen authors. The editor then concludes, "The whole fourteen
have two things in common: All were wonderful company; and all--all,
alas! are dead.   God rest their merry souls."   It was Dorothy
Parker, the one lady represented in this collection, who contrasted
wisecracking with wit.   She considered wisecracking to be
"calisthenics with words," but she considered wit to be grounded in
truth. In the foreword to this book, Caskie Stinnett said that by
this contrasting definition, Merry Gentlemen (and One Lady) is a
collection of wit.

1266. Curry, Jane, ed. Samantha Rastles the Woman Question. Auth.
      Marietta Holley. Urbana: Univ. of Illinois Press, 1983, xvi +
      235 pp.

Deals with women's concerns of the late nineteenth century--
suffrage, temperance, entry into the professions, and equal pay for
equal work. Holley reverses traditional expectations by depicting
Samantha as physically much larger than her husband, Josiah. Josiah
is also portrayed as weaker, less rational, more susceptible to fads
and fashions, and more dependent than Samantha. As a result of this
physical and psychological inferiority, Josiah's arguments against
women's rights are also seen as weak and irrational.

1267. Donovan, Josephine. New England Local Color Literature: A
      Women's Tradition. New York: Continuum/Ungar, 1988, x + 158
      pp.

Describes the Atlantic Monthly tradition of celebrating the
seventieth birthdays of their major authors by bringing together
literary notables for a birthday breakfast. Boston's literary elite
gathered in 1879 for Oliver Wendell Holmes' seventieth birthday.
Guests included Whittier, Emerson, Longfellow, Clemens, Howells, and
others.   In 1882 there was a similar breakfast in honor of the
seventieth birthday of Harriet Beecher Stowe, and this time women
were much better represented--Rose Terry Cooke, Elizabeth Stuart
Phelps, Sarah Orne Jewett, and Annie Adam Fields.   Donovan's
anthology contains the work of these women, plus one other, Mary E.
Wilkins Freeman, who had not been invited to the breakfast because
her works had not yet begun to appear. These authors represent the
women's side of the New England local color movement, a movement in
contrast to the sentimental and domestic convention that dominated
American women's writing through most of the nineteenth century.
The women's local color literature during this period concentrates
on women who are (or should be) in the ascendancy. This realistic
genre authentically depicted regional dialect, local characters,
geographical settings, local customs, and local dress in detail.

1268. Dresner, Zita. "Herodite Humor: Alice Duer Miller and Florence
      Guy Seabury." Journal of American Culture 10.3 (1987): 33-38.

Describes Greenwich Village's Heterodoxy Club as a support
group for unorthodox women. The two most salient features of the
members of the club are their eloquence in expressing pro-woman
sentiment and their ability to use humor, wit, and satire. Alice

Miller and Florence Seabury were especially effective in this last regard. They both took advantage of their times--a period when urban populations were growing, rural populations were declining, and many new humor publications were being introduced that addressed more cosmopolitan concerns, including the concerns of the "new woman." Miller's satiric verse was collected in two volumes, Are Women People? (1915), and Women Are People! (1917). Miller would present a quotation about woman's role, image, nature, or rights that had recently appeared in a newspaper, magazine, article, book, or pamphlet, and this would be followed by a witty poem that ridiculed the argument of the original quotation. Florence Seabury's The Delicatessen Husband (1926) was also effective in countering the anti-woman sentiments of the time. Seabury used dry wit and ironic understatement to explore relationships between the sexes in a period of changing ideas about sex roles, morals, and manners.

1269. Dresner, Zita Zatkin. "Twentieth Century American Women Humorists." Ph.D. Dissertation: Univ. of Maryland, 1982, 351 pp.

Focuses on humor by American women since 1920 and attempts to account for the popularity of this humor in terms of achievement and special function in a society undergoing fundamental changes in the status of women. This dissertation concentrates on the style, characterization, and attitudes of such authors as Mae West, Anita Loos, Dorothy Parker, Betty MacDonald, Jean Kerr, Shirley Jackson, Phyllis McGinley, Erma Bombeck, Judith Viorst, and Erica Jong.

1270. Habegger, Alfred. "Male and Female Humor." Gender, Fantasy, and Realism in American Literature. New York: Columbia Univ. Press, 1982, 115-98.

Includes chapters entitled, "Easygoing Men and Dressy Ladies," "Taking Down the Big One: From Frontier Boaster to Deadpan Loser to Boy," "Petticoat Humor," "Funny Women," "Funny Tomboys," and "Penelope Lapham in The Rise of Silas Lapham." In nineteenth-century American literature, women were portrayed as dedicated, humorless, and uptight. In fiction, folklore, and real life, there were three stereotypes for female characters during this time--the odd or original girl, the wise old woman, and the bright lady. In terms of humor, the first two stereotypes were more often considered funny-peculiar than funny-ha ha. But the humor of the third type-- the witty lady--represented only funny-ha ha, for the humor here was in her putting down of snobs, boors, and other uncivilized men. But the witty woman was not playing her traditional role in society; she was something of a tomboy, a burlesque actress representing a gaudy and euphoric breakthrough. Habegger considers Penelope Lapham (1885) to be the first romantic female lead in a novel written by an American male--W. D. Howells. Howells' The Rise of Silas Lapham presented a most sympathetic treatment of the tomboy, Penelope Lapham. Penelope is such a tease and family entertainer that she frequently gets into trouble by not acting the way a lady is supposed to act.

1271. Hoople, Sally C. "The Spanish, English, and American Quixotes." _Separate de "Anales Cervantinos"_ Volume 22. Madrid: Prudencio Ibanez Campos, 1984.

Discusses Tabitha Tenney's _Female Quixotism_ (1801), and Charlotte Lennox's _The Female Quixote_ (1792), and other novels published during this period that investigate female Quixotism. Tabitha Tenney's heroine, Dorcasina, and Charlotte Lennox's heroine, Arabella, both go mad as a result of their obsessive reading of sentimental fantasy novels rather than mundane literature more grounded in trustworthy reality.

1272. Inge, M. Thomas. "American Sexual Humor." Special issue of _Studies in American Humor_ 4.1-2 (Spring-Summer, 1985): 1-125 pp.

Helps to establish not only the fact that women do indeed have a sense of humor but also the fact that they have a _special_ sense of humor that is unique to their sex. While masculine humor tends to satirize the people who violate the social norms, feminine humor tends to attack the norms themselves. Some of the articles in this special issue are about well-known authors; others are about not well known, or even obscure authors. Authors and the titles of their articles include Zita Dresner's "Sentiment and Humor: A Double-Pronged Attack on Women's Place in Nineteenth Century America," Benjamin Franklin Fisher IV's "Mary Noailles Murfree's 'Special' Sense of Humor," Lucinda MacKethan's "Mother Wit: Humor in Afro-American Women's Autobiography," Anne LeCroy's "The Different Humor of Shirley Jackson," Gabriella Bedetti's "Woman's Sense of the Ludicrous in John Barth's "Dunyazadiad," Suzanne Bunkers' "The Power and Politics of Women's Humor" and Nancy Walker's "_Agelaste_ or Eiron: American Women Writers and the Sense of Humor."

1273. Jankofsky, Klaus P. "Food and Sex in Berger's _Rex_." _Studies in American Humor_ NS6 (1988): 105-114.

Classifies Thomas Berger's _Arthur Rex_ as an ironic fantasy, or a parody of the courtly love tradition and its accompanying chivalric mentality. Berger uses comedy and humor to investigate the discrepancy between the ideal and the real. The sexual encounters of Berger's novel are interesting modifications of the traditional elements to be found Arthur's courtship of Margawse, Launcelot's courtship of Guinevere, and Tristan's courtship of Isolde. Berger tells these stories with vulgar joking and coarse language. Berger also treats the legend of Sir Gawain and the Green Knight with "merry lechery." Berger intends no sacrilege; he has read and loved the Arthurian tales since he was seven. His purpose in _Arthur Rex_ is merely to tell a story that he himself can be amused by. Berger's _Arthur Rex_ celebrates the virtues of honor, bravery, nobility, and chivalry, but it celebrates these virtues within a comic vision that combines humor, and irony with a mastery of his subject to present the King Arthur material from yet another perspective.

1274. **Levy, Barbara.** "Wit as Control: A Technique in Novels by Austen, Drabble, Ephron." WHIMSY 6 (1988): 301-303.

Compares the humor of Austen's Emma, Drabble's Kate, and Ephron's Rachel as they use their wit as a controlling mechanism. When Austen's Harriet expresses surprise to find Emma so charming but still not married, Emma responds that her being charming is not at issue. The reason she has not married is that she has not found other people charming. But Austen had a double consciousness at the end of Emma, for Emma's repentence is placed next to Emma's laughter, and Emma's wit does not lead to any direct control of her life; in fact, Emma is punished for her wit. Gilbert and Gubar say that Emma had a brilliant and assertive playfulness that made her an interesting character, but her wit is criticized as being self-deluding. Austen was a product of her times, but she nevertheless allowed as much of Emma's wit to survive in the novel as she dared. Drabble's Kate is about forty in The Middle Ground. Before this time, Kate had been a fierce, solitary, and angry child, but her personality changed when she learned that people were more acceptable of her if she made them laugh. From this point on, Kate's life seems charmed. Earlier, Kate had thought people were taking advantage of her; later she said that so many people were leaning on her from different directions that if any of them stopped leaning, she would fall over. The situation was the same, but her attitude had changed dramatically. Throughout Heartburn, Ephron's Rachel's verbal wit, humor, and timing remind the reader of a comedian working her audience. Levy feels that if Heartburn were not a witty book it would be a heartbreaking book, for it is a thinly disguised account of Ephron's breakup with Carl Bernstein of Watergate fame. All three characters use wit to empower themselves in a male-dominated society.

1275. **Nilsen, Alleen Pace.** "Women's Wit: How We Control Each Other's Sexuality." WHIMSY 1 (1983): 214-16.

Discusses the wit and humor of Judy Blume's Are You There God? It's Me, Margaret. Margaret is Blume's twelve-year-old protagonist, and Margaret and her pre-teen friends are going through certain sexual transformations. The girls sneak glimpses into Playboy and wonder if they will look like the Playboy centerfolds in a few years. Margaret thinks that the centerfold "looks out of proportion." Throughout the novel, the girls are cruel to Laura Danker because Laura has been wearing a bra since the fourth grade. But ironically, at the same time that they are deriding her and referring to her as "the blonde with the big you-know-whats," they themselves are exercising to the chant of "I must--I must--I must increase my bust." Nilsen also talks about the sexual humor of Dorothy Parker, who said, "Men never make passes at girls who wear glasses," and "You can lead a horticulture, but you can't make her think." Nilsen's basic claim is that women use wit and humor to control each other's sexuality, noting that there is a correlation between being female and being "catty" or "bitchy." Nilsen suggests that this correlation is a result of society's assigning women the task of communicating and enforcing sexual norms. Women are not in power to make unambiguous demands, so they must instead rely on their wit and humor to communicate their attitudes.

1276. Sheppard, Alice. "From Kate Sanborn to Feminist Psychology: The Social Context of Women's Humor, 1885-1985." Psychology of Women Quarterly 10 (1986): 155-70.

Considers Kate Sanborn to have been one of the earliest in a long line of women who promoted humor by and about women. Her important 200-page anthology on The Wit of Women appeared as early as 1885 and laid the groundwork for such later anthologies as Bruere and Beard's Laughing Their Way: Women's Humor in America (1934), Stillman and Beatts' Titters: The First Collection of Humor by Women (1976), and Kaufman and Blakely's Pulling Our Own Strings. As the result of these and other anthologies on women's humor, it became obvious that men's and women's humor was distinct, because men's and women's interests and spheres of activity were distinct. Masculine humor concentrated on violence, power, and adventure--all spheres that were unavailable to nineteenth-century women. Women's humor concentrated on social etiquette, true womanhood, and sentimentality.

1277. Stillman, Deanne, and Anne Beatts, eds. Titters: The First Collection of Humor by Women. New York: Collier, 1976, 192 pp.

Assumes this anthology to be the "first collection of humor by women" even though there were other collections before this one. Nevertheless, this is a legitimate assumption since the earlier anthologies had gone out of print long before Titters was published and since the works of female humorists were generally unavailable to the public at the time this anthology was published.This anthology elevates the domestic sphere of wife, mother, home and society and denigrates the humor of "jock straps, beer, trains, mothers-in-law, dumb blondes, cars, boxing, the Navy..., and poker."

1278. Templin, Charlotte. "Self-Assertive Humor in Recent Women's Comedy." WHIMSY 6 (1988): 311-12.

Considers Isadora Wing, the protagonist of Erica Jong's Fear of Flying to have a gift of joy and a zest for life that is sometimes thwarted but never conquered by the confining nature of the society in which she lives. Her internal conscience keeps urging her in the direction of "zipless fucks," speeding cars, endless wet kisses, and stimulating danger. For Isadora Wing, nothing is taboo and nothing is shameful as she describes in detail menstruation and lovemaking and includes the fat and the farts in doing so. Isadora finds herself glowing after fucking two men in twenty-four hours. She is a little bit appalled at her own promiscuity but then concludes that she was now truly happy and felt truly appreciated for the first time, and then ponders, "Do two men perhaps add up to one whole person?" Ginny Babcock, the protagonist of Lisa Alther's Kinflicks also struggles with her drive for independence in a society that doesn't seem to allow it. Ginny recalls the various roles she has tried out between the ages of thirteen and twenty-seven and concludes that the important lesson she has learned is that women often lead their lives through men. Her epiphany happened when her mother made her give up football after her first period, at which time she was transformed from left tackle into a flag swinger. Molly Bolt is the protagonist in Rita Mae Brown's Rubyfruit Jungle. Molly's approach to life is to move unrelentingly forward like a steam engine or a tank. For Molly, boys are something that girls have to wear to certain school functions like a bra, but she believes that boys should not influence what girls think. Alther, Jong, and Brown all present unliberated women with liberated instincts. They have an appetite for experience and don't engage in self-pity.

1279. Toth, Emily. "A Laughter of Their Own: Women's Humor in the United States." Critical Essays on American Humor. Eds. William Bedford Clark and W. Craig Turner. Boston: G. K. Hall, 1984, 199-215.

Traces the history of women's humor in American literature from Anne Bradstreet to Anna Howard Shaw. Special mention is given to Marietta Holley and her making comic points through role reversal, Sarah Kemble Knight's diary as a compendium of social criticism, Mercy Otis Warren's satiric political poems, and on to Caroline Kirkland, Frances Berry Whitcher, and Fanny Fern (Sara Willis Parton), who use humor to mock people who make the wrong choices and to support better living conditions, sensible conversation, clean air, and other domestic issues. Toth concludes that all of these women humorists were in some way angry--about their limited roles in society, about pious platitudes droned at them to keep them in their place, and about lies made about "women's nature." They attack patriarchal norms, hypocrisy, and irresponsibility. Toth says the first stage of women's humor is the imitation of men's humor. The second stage attacks traditional humor through parody and role reversal. She says women's humor is now in the third stage--using humor to create new norms and new cultures.

1280. Van Spanckeren, Kathryn. "A Funny Thing Happened on the Way to the Apocalypse: Laurie Anderson and Humor in Women's Performance Art." Studies in American Humor NS 1.2 (Spring-Summer 1989): 94-104.

Traces the history of women in performing arts back to the colonial period with writers like Sarah Kemble Knight. The tradition continues during the nineteenth century with writers such as Frances Berry Whitcher, Caroline Kirkland, and Mary Abigail Dodge. The tradition continues with the works of Margaret Atwood, Barbara Charlesworth Gelpi, and others. During this entire history the literature is rich in voice, local color, and dialect, and until recently the humor has been confined to domestic subjects and very light social criticism from the female perspective. Women's performance art originated in European Dadaism, Surrealism, and Futurism in all fields--poetry, dance, painting, sculpture, music, mime, and video. The performance art of Lauri Anderson is the culmination of this history. Her art exhibits what Margaret Atwood and Margaret Charlesworth Gelpi have called "stage four" consciousness, characterized by its "creative non-victimhood." In order to arrive at this stage, the presenter must pass through three earlier stages, as follows: 1) denial, 2) realization of oppression but submission to the status quo, and 3) anger. Only in the fourth stage can people be free to express their full creative energies.

1281. Walker, Nancy A. "'Fragile and Dumb': The 'Little Woman' in
      Women's Humor, 1900-1940." Thalia: Studies in Literary Humor
      5.2 (1983): 24-29.

Discusses James Thurber's "Little Man" as developed in My Life
and Hard Times. For Thurber, the "Little Man" is a humorist, who
sits "on the edge of the chair of Literature." This figure of the
"Little Man" was pervasive in the humor of the first half of the
twentieth century. The twentieth-century "Little Man" is passive.
Instead of being self-made, self-employed and self-reliant, as he
was in the nineteenth century, he is a consumer of both goods and
propaganda. The prime example is Thurber's Walter Mitty, the
henpecked husband who develops a rich fantasy life to compensate for
his humdrum existence. The "Little Man" in American literature is
not equivalent to either the nineteenth-century, or the twentieth-
century "Little Man." The "Little Woman" is herself a victim. Like
the twentieth-century "Little Man" she is insecure, ineffectual, and
bewildered, however there are some differences. The male figure is
at the mercy of indeterminate cosmic forces, while the female figure
is at the mercy of specific societal expectations. The male figure
is bothered at the perception that there are no rules, the female by
the perception that there are too many rules. For the male it is
the world that seems to be absurd; for the female it is she herself.
The differences all relate to locus of control.

1282. Walker, Nancy A. "Humor and Gender Roles: The Funny Feminism
      of the Post-World War II Suburbs." American Quarterly 37.1
      (Spring 1985): 98-113.

Considers women writers of humorous prose and light verse
during the late 1940s and the 1950s--Phyllis McGinley, Jean Kerr,
Margaret Halsey, Betty MacDonald, and Shirley Jackson. She feels
that there is at least a paradox and perhaps even a duplicity in the
fact that these writers often presented themselves as "typical
American housewives of the postwar period," even though "their
successful careers as writers make them by definition atypical."
Walker notes that Betty Friedan also criticizes these authors for
developing their personae as housewives rather than as individuals,
and Walker and Friedan agree that in doing this, these authors are
misleading "real" housewives. Walker suggests that these writers
had excellent models at their disposal in Jane Austen and Emily
Dickinson, whose writing is noted for its "sly, witty social
satire," but McGinley, Jackson, and Kerr failed to be adequately
influenced by these models. About domestic humor, Walker says that
there are three stages--recognition, sympathy, and assent. Walker
also says that there is hostility in women's domestic humor, even
though it tends to be muted, and in fact, Walker goes even further,
to say that women's domestic humor exhibits "increasing hostility
against societal expectations," and can be viewed, therefore, as
subversive, even though it may not be consciously so.

1283. Walker, Nancy A. The Tradition of Women's Humor in America.
      Huntington Beach, California: American Studies Publishing
      Company, 1984, 34 pp.

Contrasts men's humor with women's humor. For example, Walker
says that nineteenth-century male humorists tended to write about
corrupt politicians or frontier braggarts, while female humorists of

the same period were more likely to write about "the gossipy women
at a church social, or the husband-hunting spinster who kept the
neighborhood bachelors on their toes." Walker's point is that
humorists tend to write about their own personal experiences,
whatever they are, and that is why there are two separate traditions
in American humor--one male and the other female. Walker's
monograph traces these two traditions from the nineteenth century,
explaining the various differences between men's and women's humor
and examining in detail the humor of such American women writers as
Dorothy Parker, Kate Sanborn, Frances Whicher, Gail Hamilton, Alice
Duer Miller, Charlotte Perkins Gilman, Mary Roberts Rinehart,
Phyllis McGinley, Jean Kerr, Judith Viorst, June Jordan, Erma
Bombeck, Carolina Kirkland, Phoebe Cary, Betty MacDonald, Marietta
Holley, Helen Rowland, Anne Warner French, Cornelia Otis Skinner,
Margaret Halsey, Shirley Jackson, Nora Ephron, and Wanda Coleman.

1284. Walker, Nancy A. **A Very Serious Thing: Women's Humor and**
American Culture. Minneapolis: Univ. of Minnesota Press, 1988,
230 pp.

Remarks that in the past women's humor has not been taken
seriously enough. Male authors have lamented the fact that women
don't have a sense of humor. Female authors have also acknowledged
that they weren't supposed to have a sense of humor, but then they
have frequently gone on to write very funny material. Women tend to
be "story tellers" rather than "joke tellers." Although some women
authors, like Dorothy Parker, concentrate on pithy and quotable one-
liners, other women authors, like Mary Roberts Rinehart and Ann
Warner French, write stories that are "long and droll." For women,
humor functions "more as a means of communication than as a means of
self-preservation, a sharing of experience rather than a
demonstration of cleverness." Women authors are "almost never
purely comic or absurd."

1285. Walker, Nancy, and Zita Dresner. Redressing the Balance:
American Women's Literary Humor from Colonial Times to the
1980s. Jackson: Univ. Press of Miss., 1988, xxxiii + 454 pp.

Speculates that as long as men's humor is held to be superior
to women's humor, not only is the sense of superiority of male-humor
reinforced, but the outgroup (women and minorities) and its humor
are also disparaged and trivialized. This anthology traces the
development of American women's literary humor from Anne Bradstreet
(1617-1672) to Gail Sausser (1952-). Women's humor is normally not
taken seriously because it is generally associated with private
spheres like food and nurturance. The expression "redressing the
balance" functions in two ways. First, it makes humor by women
available to a large reading public, to help equalize the humor by
men that has been available for a long time. Second, it considers
women's subjects to be important enough for serious (and humorous)
consideration. Women's humor is "more gentle and genteel than
men's, more concerned with wit than derision, more interested in
sympathy than ridicule, more focused on private than on public
issues." Women's humor relies more on understatement, irony, and
self-deprecation, and other such verbal devices than does men's
humor. Laughing at one's shortcoming can diminish their importance
and can "cleanse them of pejorative connotations imposed by the
dominant culture."

Chapter 16
Humor Theory

1286. Eastman, Max. <u>Enjoyment of Laughter</u>. New York: Simon and Schuster, 1936, xviii + 367 pp.

Realizes that nothing kills a laugh quicker than the explanation of a joke. Eastman says that he intends to explain all jokes, and the result will be not only that the reader will not laugh now, but that he will never laugh again. Eastman clarifies the distinction between the good joke and the bad joke, but he indicates that this distinction will not enable the reader to avoid telling bad jokes, nor will it ensure that every good joke the reader tells will be successful, for "no art can be taught to the inartistic." Most people have the impression that humor is more easily mastered than it is. This is because most humor books are illustrated with hardened old jokes and classic witticisms, jerked out of their context, and "tacked up for inspection like a dried fish on a boathouse door." But in fact, jokes are not so "cut and dried." Humor is fluid and transitory. This is a textbook not only in the science of generating or analyzing humor but in the art of enjoying it as well. That is why it contains so many samples. But the book is not just an anthology either, for the samples all illustrate the arguments under discussion.

1287. Harmon, William. "'Anti-Fiction' in American Humor." <u>The Comic Imagination in American Literature</u>. Ed. Louis D. Rubin, Jr. New Brunswick, NJ: Rutgers Univ. Press, 1983, xii + 430 pp.

Points out that Gertrude Stein's <u>The Autobiography of Alice B. Toklas</u> is <u>not</u> the autobiography of Alice B. Toklas. Stein's work is not atypical. "Fiction--begets its own opposite in the forms of parody, self-parody, and anti-fiction. Epic provokes mock-epic and burlesque; Richardson's grand <u>Pamela</u> breeds Fielding's grand <u>Shamela</u>; the Gothic novel is answered by Jane Austen's <u>Northanger Abbey</u>." Harmon labels such pieces "Anti-Fiction" and considers Al Capp's "Li'l Abner" to be a further example. Capp himself feels that this comic strip should be read as a novel--"a very long novel, to be sure, a novel with plenty of pictures, but still a novel." The genre of "Anti-Fiction" could be extended still further--to include <u>Time</u> and <u>Newsweek</u>, for they also contain many elements of the novel--"fabrication, invention, concoction, distortion..., and stylish prose." Harmon compares <u>Li'l Abner</u>, <u>Time</u>, and <u>Newsweek</u> to J. P. Donleavy's <u>The Ginger Man</u> and <u>The Beastly Beatitudes of Balthazar B</u>, and to Joseph Heller's <u>Catch 22</u>, with its absurd contradictions of war, commerce, and politics. Finally, in Harmon's proposed genre of "Anti-Fiction," Heller's Yossarian, and Donleavy's Sebastian Dangerfield are anti-heroes.

1288. Inge, M. Thomas. "American Literary Humor: A Bibliographic
      Guide." Choice 26.10 (June 1989): 1641-1649.

    Provides a brief evaluation of the most substantial and useful
scholarly books on humor that have been published in the twentieth
century. The section on "Reference Works" treats such books as
Trachtenberg's American Humorists, 1800-1950, Sloane's American
Humor Magazines and Comic Periodicals, Ellenbogen's Directory of
Humor Magazines and Humor Organizations of America and Canada, and
Mintz's Humor in America: A Research Guide to Genres and Topics.
The "Journals" section includes Studies in American Humor, and
Humor: International Journal of Humor Research. There is also a
section on "Critical Anthologies" including works by Walter Blair,
E. B. White, Kenneth Lynn, Robert Dodge, Franklin Meine, Arthur
Hudson, David Sloane, and others; and a section on "Criticism"
including works by Constance Rourke, Jesse Bier, Neil Schmitz,
Norris Yates, Nancy Walker, Carolyn Brown, Louis Rubin, and others.
There are a total of ninety-three scholarly books dealing with
literary humor in Inge's "Works Cited."

1289. Inge, M. Thomas. "'One Priceless Universal Trait': American
      Humor." American Studies International 25.1 (April 1987): 28-
      45.

    Alludes in the title to William Faulkner's statement that, "We
have one priceless universal trait, we Americans. That trait is our
humor." Comedians and satirists play the crucial role of social,
political, and cultural critics in a democratic system. This
article investigates this role by anthologizing the scholarly works
that have evaluated the contributions of these American comedians
and satirists. There is a section on "Reference Works," one on
"Critical Anthologies," one on "History and Criticism," one on
"Humor in the Media," and one on "Future Research." Inge concludes
that the academy has tended not to take humor very seriously even
though it is central to all aspects of American civilization.
Perhaps it's time we took humor more seriously.

1290. Nilsen, Don L. F. "Contemporary Legend: The Definition of a
      Genre." Kansas English 75.1 (Fall 1989): 5-9.

    Agrees with Paul Dickson and Joseph Goulden that there are six
features common to all prototypical contemporary legends. They
contain an abundance of seemingly-supportive specific detail; the
person who retells the stories accepts their validity because of the
sources from which they come; they reflect contemporary fears; they
frequently gain momentum from repetition in the press; and there is
often a grain of truth to the stories. In There Are Alligators in
Our Sewers and Other American Credos, Dickson and Goulden add that
formal refutation does nothing to deter the popularity of the
stories. Nilsen suggests that the features Dickson and Goulden list
for contemporary legends might profitably be extended. These
legends are often "pourquoi stories" in that they offer simple
solutions to complex and enigmatic phenomena; they tend to be very
mysterious, hyperbolic, symbolic, and dramatic; they play on
stereotypes, such as a woman's intuition and a man's machismo; they
tend to be strongly ironic; and they frequently use the rhetorical
device of antithesis, whereby the ending is the opposite of what we

would expect. The ending also often involves some sort of revenge--
a kind of poetic justice.

1291. Trachtenberg, Stanley. "Humor Criticism." Dictionary of
Literary Biography, Volume 11: American Humorists, 1800-1950.
Ed. Stanley Trachtenberg. Detroit, MI: Gale, 1982, 681-82.

Lists the major works in American humorous literary criticism,
including critical works by Stephen Becker, Jesse Bier, Walter
Blair, Mody Boatright, H. W. Boynton, Sculley Bradley, Anthony J.
Chapman, V. L. O. Chittick, William M. Clemens, Sarah Blacher Cohen,
Samuel S. Cox, Bernard DeVoto, Richard M. Dorson, Max Eastman, J.
DeLancey Ferguson, Hugh C. Foote, James L. Ford, Brendan Gill,
Alfred Habegger, Ernest L. Hancock, Margaret Case Harriman, Richard
B. Hauck, Hamlin Hill, Carl Holliday, W. Stanley Hoole, Will D.
Howe, William Dean Howells, M. Thomas Inge, Dale Kramer, Henry C.
Lukens, Kenneth S. Lynn, Thomas. L. Masson, Brander Matthews,
Franklin J. Meine, William Murrell, Martin Roth, Constance Rourke,
Louis D. Rubin, Jennette Tandy, Harold W. Thompson, James Thurber,
W. P. Trent, Arlin Turner, Arthur Frank Wertheim, George Frisbie
Whicher, Napier Wilt, and Norris W. Yates.

1292. Veron, Enid, ed. Humor in America. New York: Harcourt, Brace,
Jovanovich, 1976, 350 pp.

Includes sections on "The Comic American," "The Wise Fool,"
"The Storyteller," "The Little Soul," and "Theories and Criticism."
"The Comic American" stresses the contribution made by Washington
Irving who believed that tragedy deals with the extraordinary while
comedy deals with the prosaic world of plain people. This section
discusses how the work of Woody Allen, Kurt Vonnegut, Joseph Heller,
and others express the quintessential essence of the periods in
which they wrote. "The Wise Fool" discusses the humor of Benjamin
Franklin, Seba Smith, Artemus Ward, Bill Nye, Finley Peter Dunne,
Langston Hughes, and others who felt that in a democracy the voice
of the common man must be respected and even revered. "The Story
Teller" discusses Washington Irving, Joel Chandler Harris, George
Washington Harris, Edgar Allan Poe, Mark Twain and others who knew
the art of humorous storytelling. Veron feels that oral
storytelling is a tradition that developed in the outposts and
desolate mining camps of the American frontier. "The Little Soul"
discusses Don Marquis, Robert Benchley, Ring Lardner, James Thurber,
and others who developed characters who are overwhelmed by the
rigidity of inflexible technology and/or society. In "Theories and
Criticism" additional articles investigate the parameters of humor
in American literature, both high and low.

1293. White, E. B., and Katharine S. White. A Subtreasury of
American Humor. New York: Coward-McCann, 1941, xxxii + 805 pp.

Considers only "literary" humor. They at first considered the
possibility of including "newspaper humor" but discovered that "even
the perfect newspaper story, by the most expert and gifted reporter,
dies like a snake with the setting of the sun." The humor may
remain, but when the news is gone the heart is gone as well. The
Whites left the pieces from the New Yorker's "The Talk of the Town"
in. Even though these pieces had "grown whiskers," they were more
timely than the newspaper humor because newspapers give current

events, while magazines like <u>The New Yorker</u> entertain.   In order to
explain the nature of humor, The Whites tell about a man who had
developed the art of blowing soap bubbles to a new level.   The
bubbles were too big to be beautiful, and the blower was constantly
jumping into or out of the bubbles or doing something else
disgusting.   It was not a pretty sight.   Then they concluded that
humor is a little bit like the bubble.   It can't stand much blowing
or poking and is fragile and evasive.   The Whites also compare
humorous writing to an active child playing with a hot fire.   Humor
can get very close to the hot fire of truth, and when it does, the
reader feels the heat.

Index

Don L. F. Nilsen is a professor of English linguistics at Arizona State University. He specializes in semantics and became interested in the study of humor when he and his students discovered the challenge and the fun of analyzing sentences with double and triple meanings. Between 1982 and 1987, he chaired the annual WHIM (World Humor and Irony Membership) conferences at Arizona State University and edited the proceedings, <u>Whimsy (World Humor and Irony Membership Serial Yearbook)</u> Volumes I through VI. In 1989, he was a founding member of the International Society for Humor Studies, for which he serves as Executive Secretary. He is an advisory editor for Wayne State University's <u>Humor in Life and Letters Series</u> and is a member of the advisory committee of the Workshop Library on World Humor. He also serves on the editorial boards of <u>Metaphor and Symbolic Activity</u> and <u>Humor: International Journal of Humor Research</u>, where he edits the newsletter.